# A Companion to International History 1900–2001

# BLACKWELL COMPANIONS TO HISTORY

This series provides sophisticated and authoritative overviews of the scholarship that has shaped our current understanding of the past. Defined by theme, period and/or region, each volume comprises between twenty-five and forty concise essays written by individual scholars within their area of specialization. The aim of each contribution is to synthesize the current state of scholarship from a variety of historical perspectives and to provide a statement on where the field is heading. The essays are written in a clear, provocative, and lively manner, designed for an international audience of scholars, students, and general readers.

# A Companion to International History 1900–2001

*EDITED BY GORDON MARTEL*

**WILEY-BLACKWELL**

A John Wiley & Sons, Ltd., Publication

Edition history: Blackwell Publishing Ltd (hardback, 2007)

Blackwell Publishing was acquired by John Wiley & Sons in February 2007. Blackwell's publishing program has been merged with Wiley's global Scientific, Technical, and Medical business to form Wiley-Blackwell.

*Registered Office*

John Wiley & Sons Ltd, The Atrium, Southern Gate, Chichester, West Sussex, PO19 8SQ, United Kingdom

*Editorial Offices*
350 Main Street, Malden, MA 02148-5020, USA
9600 Garsington Road, Oxford, OX4 2DQ, UK
The Atrium, Southern Gate, Chichester, West Sussex, PO19 8SQ, UK

For details of our global editorial offices, for customer services, and for information about how to apply for permission to reuse the copyright material in this book please see our website at www.wiley.com/wiley-blackwell.

The right of Gordon Martel to be identified as the author of the editorial material in this work has been asserted in accordance with the UK Copyright, Designs and Patents Act 1988.

*Library of Congress Cataloging-in-Publication Data*

A companion to international history, 1900–2001 / edited by Gordon Martel.
      p. cm.—(Blackwell companions to history)
   Includes bibliographical references and index.
   ISBN 978-1-4051-2574-1 (hard cover : alk. paper)
   ISBN 978-1-4443-3386-2 (pbk. : alk. paper)
   1. World politics—20th century.   I. Martel, Gordon.
   D443.C577 2007
   909.82—dc22

                                                    2006027488

A catalogue record for this book is available from the British Library.

Set in 9/11.5 ITC Galliard by Toppan Best-set Premedia Limited
Printed in Singapore

1   2010

# Contents

# Notes on Contributors

**Lloyd E. Ambrosius** is the Samuel Clark Waugh Distinguished Professor of International Relations and Professor of History at the University of Nebraska-Lincoln. He is the author of *Woodrow Wilson and the American Diplomatic Tradition: The Treaty Fight in Perspective* (Cambridge University Press, 1987); *Wilsonian Statecraft: Theory and Practice of Liberal Internationalism during World War I* (SR Books, 1991); and *Wilsonianism: Woodrow Wilson and His Legacy in American Foreign Relations* (Palgrave Macmillan, 2002). He was the Mary Ball Washington Professor of American History at University College, Dublin (1977–8), and twice a Fulbright Professor at the universities of Cologne (1972–3) and Heidelberg (1996).

**Jürgen Angelow** is (apl.) Professor of Modern History at the University of Potsdam. He has published books about the Dual Alliance (*Kalkül und Prestige: der Zweibund am Vorabend des Ersten Weltkrieges*) and the German Federation and its security policy (*Von Wien nach Königgrätz: die Sicherheitspolitik des Deutschen Bundes im europäischen Gleichgewicht, 1815–1866*). He has published numerous articles on various aspects of military and diplomatic history in the nineteenth and twentieth centuries.

**Michael Bauer** is Researcher at the Center for Applied Policy Research in Munich (Germany). In the Research Group on European Affairs he heads the project Europe and the Middle East. He is co-editor of *Effectively Countering Terrorism. The Challenges of Prevention, Preparedness and Response* (Sussex Academic Press, 2009), and has published a variety of papers and articles on terrorism, international security and Middle Eastern politics. He studied international politics in Munich and Aberystwyth (UK) and holds a degree in educational science from the Munich School of Philosophy.

**P. M. H. Bell** is currently Senior Research Fellow (formerly Reader) in History at the University of Liverpool. His many publications include *The Origins of the Second World War in Europe* (2nd edn, 1997; 3rd edn in preparation); *The World since 1945: An International History* (2001); and *Twentieth-Century Europe: Unity and Division* (2006).

**Ralph Blessing** studied history in Aachen, Nottingham, Paris, and Berlin. He taught European and World History at York College – the City University of New York, and Urban Planning at Hunter College – the City University of New York. He also represents a consortium of nine German universities in North America. His latest publication is *Der mögliche Frieden: Die Modernisierung der Außenpolitikund und die deutsch-französischen Beziehungen 1923–1929* (2008). He currently works as an urban planner in New York City.

**R. J. B. Bosworth** is Professor of History at the University of Western Australia and Chair of Italian History at Reading University in the UK. He is the author and editor of 18 books, most recently his prize-winning *Mussolini* (London: Arnold; New York: Oxford University Press, 2002) and his new *Mussolini's Italy: Life under the Dictatorship* (Allen Lane, 2005–6).

**Robert D. Boyce** is Senior Lecturer in International History at the London School of Economics and Political Science. He is the author of *British Capitalism at the Crossroads, 1919–1932: A Study in Politics, Economics, and International Relations* (Cambridge University Press, 1987), editor of four books including *French Foreign and Defence Policy, 1918–1940: The Decline and Fall of a Great Power* (Routledge, 1998), and with Joe Maiolo, *The Origins of World War Two: The Debate Continues* (Palgrave, June 2003), and has published forty articles on aspects of twentieth-century international history. His monograph, *The Dual Crisis: The Collapse of the International Economic and Political Systems between the Two World Wars and the Origins of Our Time*, will be published in 2007.

**Gavin D. Brockett** is Assistant Professor of Middle East and Islamic History at Wilfrid Laurier University, Canada. His research and publications have concentrated on the social history of modern Turkey and the roots of the contemporary Turkish Islamist movement. He is currently preparing a manuscript on this subject, titled "Betwixt and Between: Print Culture and the Negotiation of a Muslim National Identity in Modern Turkey."

**Andrew Crozier** teaches at New York University in London. Since 1990 he has been a Jean Monnet Chairholder and, on several occasions since 1994, Visiting Professor at Chulalongkorn University, Bangkok. He has written on Anglo-German relations in the twentieth century, British policy in Southeast Asia, and European integration. He is the author of *Appeasement and Germany's Last Bid for Colonies* (Macmillan, 1988) and *The Causes of the Second World War* (Blackwell, 1997). He is currently completing a biography of Neville Chamberlain and a history of the European Union.

**Saki Ruth Dockrill** was Professor of Contemporary History and International Security at King's College, University of London, and a former John M. Olin Fellow at Yale University. She wrote extensively on the Cold War in Europe and Asia, and authored *Britain's Policy for West German Rearmament* (Cambridge University Press, 1991), *Eisenhower's New Look National Security Policy* (Macmillan, 1996), *Britain's Retreat from East of Suez: The Choice between Europe and the World?* (Palgrave Macmillan, 2002), and most recently *The End of the Cold War Era: The Transformation of the Global Security Order* (Oxford University Press, 2005). Sadly, she died in 2009 after a long struggle with cancer.

**Justus D. Doenecke** is Professor Emeritus of History at New College of Florida, Sarasota. He has written numerous books and articles focusing on twentieth-century American history, including *Not to the Swift: The Old Isolationists in the Cold War Era* (Bucknell University Press, 1979), *When the Wicked Rise: American Opinion-Makers and the Manchurian Crisis of 1931–1933* (Bucknell, 1984), *Storm on the Horizon: The Challenge to American Intervention, 1939–1941* (Rowman & Littlefield, 2000), *The New Deal* (Krieger, 2003), with John E. Wilz, *From Isolation to War, 1931–1941* (Harlan Davidson, 3rd edn, 2003), and *Debating Franklin D. Roosevelt's Foreign Policies, 1933–1945* (with Mark A. Stoler, 2005).

**David Dutton** is Professor of Modern History at the University of Liverpool. His recent publications include *The Politics of Diplomacy: Britain and France in the Balkans in the First World War* (Tauris, 1998), *Neville Chamberlain* (Arnold, 2001), *A History of the Liberal Party in the Twentieth Century* (Palgrave, 2004) and *Liberals in Schism: A History of the National Liberal Party* (Tauris, 2008).

**Alfred E. Eckes** is Ohio Eminent Research Professor in Contemporary History at Ohio University, Athens, Ohio. He is editor of the *Global Economy Journal* and co-author of *Globalization and the American Century* (Cambridge University Press, 2003). He is a former President of the International Trade and Finance Association (2000) and Commissioner of the US International Trade Commission (1981 to 1990).

**Jeffrey A. Engel** is an Associate Professor of History and Public Policy at Texas A&M University. He is the author of *Cold War at 30,000 Feet: Anglo-American Relations and Trading with the Enemy at the Dawn of the Jet Age* (Harvard University Press, 2007), and editor of *Local Consequences of the Global Cold War* (Stanford University Press, 2008), *The China Diary of George H. W. Bush* (Princeton University Press, 2008) and *The Fall of the Berlin Wall: The Revolutionary Legacy of 1989* (Oxford University Press, 2009).

**Giuseppe Finaldi** is a Lecturer at the University of Western Australia. His research focuses on Italy's experience of empire and he is currently writing a book on Italian fascism. He has published a variety of articles and book chapters on Italian culture and Italy's relationship with Africa.

**Erik Goldstein** is Professor of International Relations and History, and Chairman of the Department of International Relations, Boston University. He was previously Professor of International History, University of Birmingham (UK). He is the founder-editor of *Diplomacy and Statecraft*. In 1992 he was elected a Fellow of the Royal Historical Society. He is the author of *The First World War's Peace Settlements: International Relations, 1918–25* (Longman, 2002).

**Alexander Hill** is Associate Professor in Military History at the University of Calgary. His *The War Behind the Eastern Front: The Soviet Partisan Movement in North-West Russia, 1941–1944* was published by Frank Cass in 2005. More recently he has published *The Great Patriotic War of the Soviet Union, 1941–1945: A Documentary Reader* (Routledge, 2009), as well as having written on the development of Soviet naval power in the far north in the 1930s and early 1940s and the significance of Lend-lease aid for the Soviet war effort.

**Matthew Hughes** is Reader in History at Brunel University and from 2008-10 held the Maj-Gen Matthew C. Horner Chair at the US Marine Corps University. From 2004 to 2008 he was the Editor of the Journal of the Society for Army Historical Research. A Fellow of the Royal Historical Society, Dr. Hughes' recent publications include the *Palgrave Advances in Modern Military History* (2006) and *Losing the Peace* (2010).

**Gaynor Johnson** is Senior Lecturer in International History at the University of Salford. She is the author of *The Berlin Embassy of Lord D'Abernon, 1920–1926* (Palgrave Macmillan, 2002) and is the editor of *Locarno Revisited: European Diplomacy 1920–1929* (Routledge, 2004) as well as a number of other books on British foreign policy in the twentieth century. She is currently writing a biography of Viscount Cecil of Chelwood.

**Saul Kelly** is Reader in International History in the Defence Studies Department, King's College, London, based at the Joint Services Command and Staff College, Shrivenham. He is the author of *The Hunt For Zerzura: The Lost Oasis and the Desert War* (John Murray, 2002); *Cold War in the Desert* (Macmillan, 2000); and, with Anthony Gorst, co-editor of *Whitehall and the Suez Crisis* (Frank Cass, 2000).

**Greg Kennedy** is a Professor of Strategic Foreign Policy in the Defence Studies Department, King's College, London, based at the Joint Services Command and Staff College in Shrivenham, and has taught at the Royal Military College of Canada, where he remains an adjunct assistant professor. He is the author of an award-winning monograph, *Anglo-American Strategic Relations and the Far East, 1933–1939* (Frank Cass, 2002). He has published internationally on strategic foreign policy issues, maritime defense, disarmament, military education, diplomacy, and intelligence. Other books include co-editing, with Keith Neilson, *Far Flung Lines: Studies in Imperial Defence in Honour of Donald Mackenzie Schurman, Incidents and International Relations: People, Personalities and Power*, and *Military Education: Past, Present, and Future*. He is also editor of *The Merchant Marine in International Affairs, 1850–1950* and *Britain's Naval Strategy East of Suez, 1900–2000: Influences and Action*, and *Imperial Defence: The Old World Order, 1856–1956*, all with Frank Cass/Taylor Francis series. His latest book, edited with Andrew Dorman is, *War and Diplomacy, From World War*

*I to the War on Terrorism* (Potomac Books, 2008).

**Warren F. Kimball** is Robert Treat Professor Emeritus of History at Rutgers University in Newark, New Jersey, and was 2002–4 Mark Clark Visiting Distinguished Professor of History at The Citadel in Charleston, South Carolina. Twice a senior Fulbright lecturer, he was also Pitt Professor of American History at Cambridge University for 1988–9, president of the Society for Historians of American Foreign Relations in 1993, a Mellon Research Fellow, and Visiting Fellow at Corpus Christi College, Cambridge, in 1997. He has written extensively about the international history of the Second World War, including: *Forged in War: Roosevelt, Churchill, and the Second World War* (1997); *Churchill and Roosevelt: The Complete Correspondence* (3 vols., 1984); *The Juggler: Franklin Roosevelt as Wartime Statesman* (1991); *America Unbound: World War II and the Making of a Superpower* (ed., 1992); and *Allies at War: The Soviet, American, and British Experience, 1939–1945* (co-ed., 1994), as well as a number of articles and essays on Anglo-American relations. He was chair of the US State Department Advisory Committee on Historical Documentation from 1991 through 1999, and remained on the committee through 2003. From 1985 through 1995 he was the American coordinator of a joint Anglo-American-Soviet project on the history of the Second World War, a project that generated two books and a dozen scholarly articles.

**Piers Ludlow** is a Reader in the Department of International History at the London School of Economics. He is a specialist on Western Europe since 1945 with a particular interest in the European integration process during the 1950s and 1960s. His two monographs to date, *Dealing With Britain: The Six and the First UK Application to the EEC* (Cambridge University Press, 1997) and *The European Community and the Crises of the 1960s: Negotiating the Gaullist Challenge* (Routledge, 2006), are attempts to analyze a number of crucial episodes in the EEC's formative decade. He is also interested in the Cold War and has edited *European Integration and*

*the Cold War: Ostpolitik/Westpolitik 1965–73* (Routledge, 2007).

**Martin McCauley** formerly taught Soviet and Russian history and politics at the School of Slavonic and East European Studies, University College, London. He has published many studies on Soviet, East European, and Chinese communism as well as on post-communist Russia. Among his publications are *Gorbachev* (Longman, 1998); *Bandits, Gangsters and the Mafia: Russia, the Baltic States and the CIS since 1992* (Longman, 2001); *Afghanistan and Central Asia* (Longman, 2002); *Russia, America and the Cold War 1949–1991* (Longman, 2004); and *The Rise and Fall of the Soviet Union* (forthcoming, 2007).

**John MacKenzie** is Professor Emeritus of Imperial History at Lancaster University. He also holds honorary professorships at the Universities of Aberdeen, St. Andrews, and Stirling, as well as an honorary fellowship of the University of Edinburgh. He has been editor of the Manchester University Press series "Studies in Imperialism" for more than twenty years and was coordinating editor of the journal *Environment and History* from 2000 to 2005. He is the author of *Propaganda and Empire* (1984), *The Empire of Nature* (1988), *Orientalism: History Theory and the Arts* (1995), *Empires of Nature and the Nature of Empires* (1997), *The Scots in South Africa: Ethnicity, Identity, Gender and Race* (2007), *Museums and Empire: Natural History, Human Cultures and Colonial Identities* (2009) and co-author of *The Railway Station: A Social History* (1986). He is is currently editing *European Empires and the People* (forthcoming, 2010) and *Scotland and the British Empire* (2011). Among his edited books are *Imperialism and Popular Culture*, *Imperialism and the Natural World*, *David Livingstone and the Victorian Encounter with Africa*, *The Victorian Vision*, and *Nations, Peoples and Cultures*. He is a Fellow of the Royal Society of Edinburgh.

**Norrie MacQueen** is Senior Lecturer in International Relations at the University of Dundee. His principal areas of research are Portuguese-speaking Africa and international peacekeeping.

His books include *The Decolonization of Portuguese Africa: Metropolitan Revolution and the Dissolution of Empire* (Longman, 1997); *United Nations Peacekeeping in Africa since 1960* (Longman, 2002); and *Peacekeeping and the International System* (Routledge, 2006).

**Gordon Martel** is Professor of History at the University of Northern British Columbia. He has been a visiting professor/research fellow at St. Antony's College, Oxford, the University of Ulster, the University of Western Australia, and Nuffield College, Oxford. He was a founding editor of *The International History Review* and is the author of *Imperial Diplomacy* (McGill-Queen's University Press, 1986), *The Origins of the First World War* (Longman, 3rd edn, 2003), and, with James Joll, *The Origins of the First World War* (Longman, 3rd edn, 2006). Among his edited works are: *A Companion to Europe, 1900–1945* (Blackwell, 2005); *The World War Two Reader* (Routledge, 2004); *The Times and Appeasement: The Journals of A. L. Kennedy* (Cambridge University Press, 2000); *The Origins of the Second World War Reconsidered: A. J. P. Taylor and the Historians* (Routledge, 2nd edn, 1999); and *Modern Germany Reconsidered* (Routledge, 1992).

**Keith Neilson** is Professor of History at the Royal Military College of Canada. He is a specialist in British strategic foreign policy, with an emphasis on Anglo-Russian/Soviet affairs. Professor Neilson is the author of a number of books, the most recent of which is *Britain, Soviet Russia and the Collapse of the Versailles Order, 1919–1939* (Cambridge University Press, 2006). In addition, he is the co-author, with Zara Steiner, of *Britain and the Origins of the First World War* (Macmillan, 2nd edn, 2003). At present he is writing a book on Anglo-American-Canadian relations in the First World War.

**Sergey Radchenko** is a Lecturer at the Division of International Studies, University of Nottingham (Ningbo campus, China). He is the author of *Two Suns in the Heavens: the Sino-Soviet Struggle for Supremacy, 1962–1967* (Woodrow Wilson Center Press & Stanford UP, 2009) and the co-author (with Campbell Craig) of *The Atomic Bomb and the Origins of the Cold War* (Yale UP, 2008).

**Kevin Ruane** is Professor of Modern History at Canterbury Christ Church University. He has written extensively on Anglo-American relations, the Cold War, and Vietnam. His books include *War and Revolution in Vietnam, 1930–75* (Routledge, 1998), *The Vietnam Wars* (Manchester University Press, 2000), and *The Rise and Fall of the European Defence Community: Anglo-American Relations and the Crisis of European Defence 1950–55* (Palgrave, 2000).

**Ian D. Thatcher** is Professor of History at the University of Ulster, Coleraine. His recent publications have focused on Lenin's funeral, the history of the Mezhraionka, and the role of a leader's personality in Soviet history.

**Andrew Webster** is European Union Centre Lecturer in Modern European History, in the School of Social Sciences and Humanities at Murdoch University, Perth, Western Australia. He has published numerous articles on the League of Nations and the international disarmament process between the world wars, most recently "From Versailles to Geneva: The Many Forms of Interwar Disarmament," *Journal of Strategic Studies* 29 (2006): 225–46. He is presently writing a history of international disarmament between 1899 and 1945.

**Samuel R. Williamson, Jr.,** is President Emeritus and Professor Emeritus of the University of the South. He has published extensively on the origins of the First World War, including *The Politics of Grand Strategy: Britain and France Prepare for War, 1904–1914* (Harvard University Press, 1969; 2nd edn, Ashfield Press, 1990), which won the George Louis Beer Prize of the American Historical Association; *Austria-Hungary and the Origins of the First World War* (Macmillan, 1991); and, with Russel Van Wyk, *July 1914: Soldiers, Statesmen, and the Coming of the First World War* (Bedford, 2003). He has taught at the US Military Academy, Harvard University, the University of North Carolina at Chapel Hill, and the University of the South.

# Preface and Acknowledgments

I wish to thank Christopher Wheeler for suggesting this project to me during his time at Blackwell Publishing; he is a most persuasive editor and I regret that we did not have the opportunity to work together on this project beyond the original conception. Once again, as in the case of *A Companion to Europe, 1900–1945*, Tessa Harvey has been responsible for seeing the project through to completion and during this process her patience and intelligence have been invaluable. Angela Cohen has once again assisted with helpful and timely guidance. I sincerely thank all three of them.

My greatest debt is to the contributors who have taken on the daunting task of compressing enormous amounts of literature and complicated historical controversies into such a small space. I trust that readers will find their essays thoughtful and informative. I sincerely thank them for their efforts and for their forbearance in putting up with an editor who remains as demanding and overbearing as ever.

# Maps

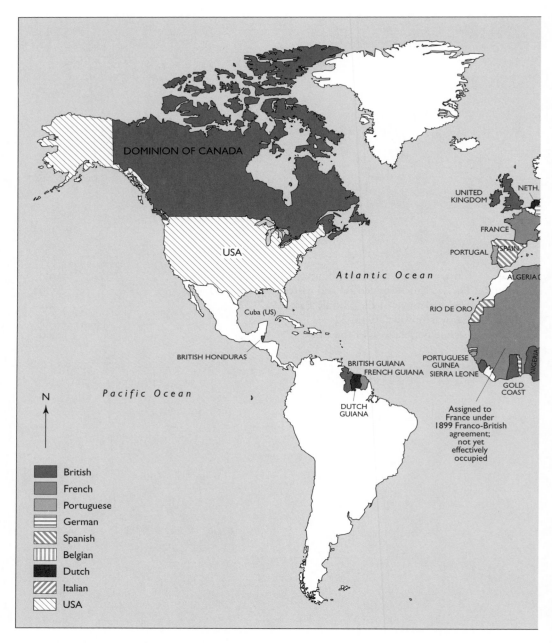

**Map 1** European and American empires, 1901.

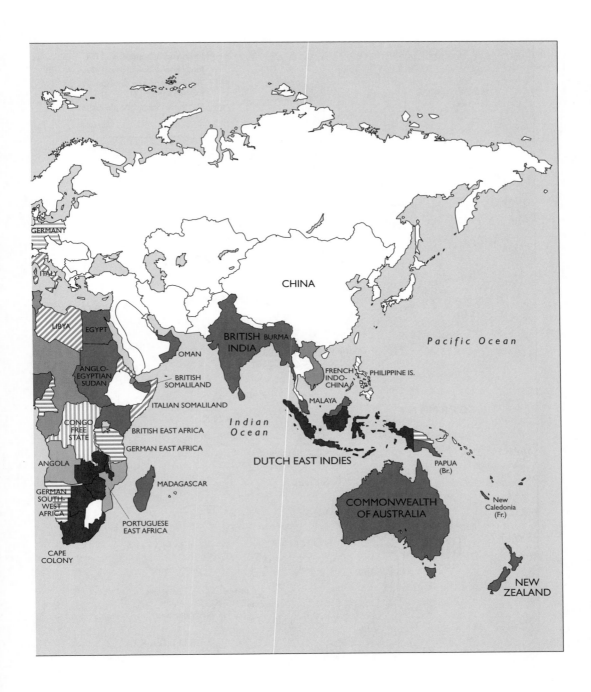

GERMANY

ITALY

LIBYA

EGYPT

ANGLO-
EGYPTIAN
SUDAN

OMAN

BRITISH
SOMALILAND

ITALIAN SOMALILAND

BRITISH EAST AFRICA

GERMAN EAST AFRICA

ANGOLA

GERMAN
SOUTH-
WEST
AFRICA

CAPE
COLONY

PORTUGUESE
EAST AFRICA

MADAGASCAR

CONGO
FREE
STATE

CHINA

Pacific Ocean

BRITISH
INDIA

BURMA

FRENCH
INDO-
CHINA

PHILIPPINE IS.

MALAYA

Indian
Ocean

DUTCH EAST INDIES

PAPUA
(Br.)

New
Caledonia
(Fr.)

COMMONWEALTH
OF AUSTRALIA

NEW
ZEALAND

**Map 2** The settlement of central and eastern Europe, 1917–22.

Legend:

········· International boundaries 1914
—·—·— International boundaries 1921
▯▯▯ Territories passing to states existing before 1914
▭ Territories subject to plebiscites

NORWAY

SWEDEN

FINLAND

• Petrograd

ESTONIA

LATVIA

• Riga

DENMARK

Meme •

LITHUANIA

• Vilna

RUSSIA

Danzig
(Free state 1921)

E. PRUSSIA

• Minsk

Berlin •

R. Bug

• Warsaw

GERMANY

POLAND

R. Vistula

SAAR

• Prague

CZECHOSLOVAKIA

R. Danube

Vienna •

SWITZ.

AUSTRIA

• Budapest

HUNGARY

ROMANIA

Trieste

• Bucarest

R. Danube

Belgrade

ITALY

YUGOSLAVIA

BULGARIA

ALBANIA

GREECE

TURKEY

N

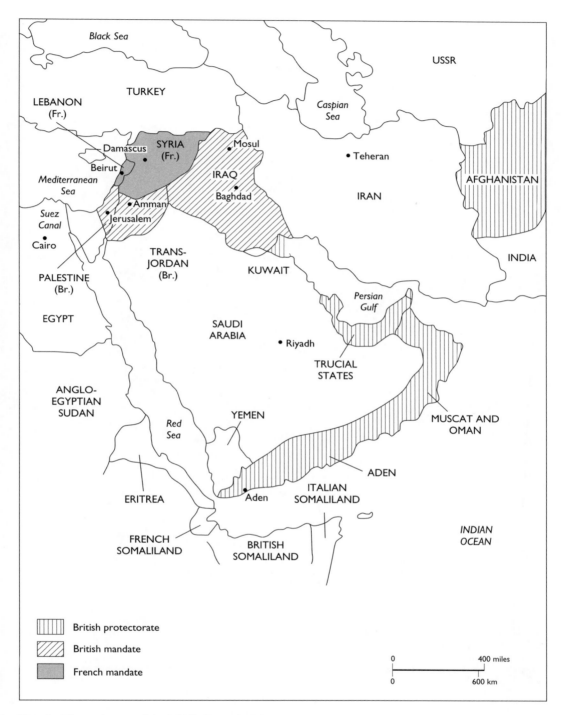

**Map 3** The settlement of the Middle East, 1917–22.
*Source*: Based on Sally Marks, *The Ebbing of European Ascendancy: An International History of the World 1914–1945* (London: Arnold, 2002).

**Map 4**  Postwar Europe, 1945–52.

*Source*: Based on Sally Marks, *The Ebbing of European Ascendancy: An International History of the World 1914–1945* (London: Arnold, 2002).

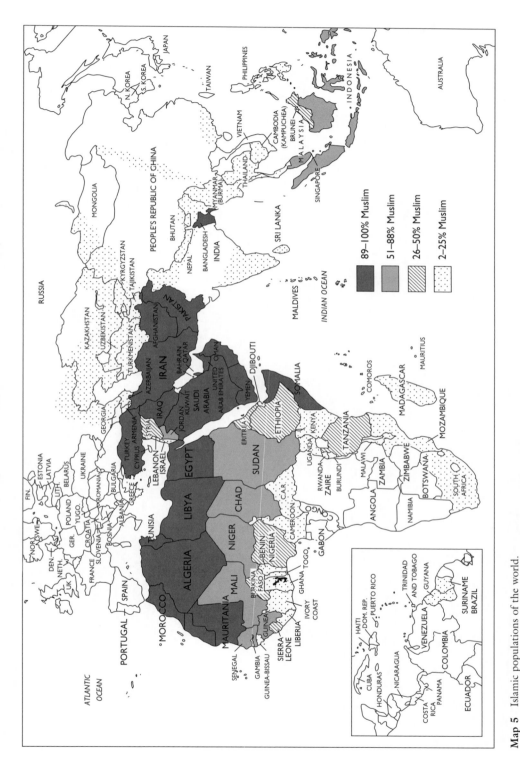

**Map 5** Islamic populations of the world.

*Source:* Based on James Lee Ray, *Global Politics*, 6th edn (Boston: Houghton Mifflin, 1995).

89–100% Muslim

51–88% Muslim

26–50% Muslim

2–25% Muslim

# Introduction

# INTRODUCTION

# Twentieth-Century International History: The Changing Face of Empire

## GORDON MARTEL

The international history of the twentieth century is best understood as one of imperial struggle in which states – usually calling themselves nations – sought to impress their own version of modernity and progress on the world. The Great Powers of the world in 1900 consisted of Britain, France, Russia, and the United States; each believed in a destiny unique to itself, and each believed that this destiny could be realized only through the assertion of power over vast tracts of territory. Germany sought to join this club by transforming itself from a European into a World Power. Japan sought to join by virtue of establishing itself as the premier power in Asia. Within Europe, Austria-Hungary clung desperately to the hope that its unique multicultural system would enable it to continue to act as if one of the great, while Italy envisioned that a revived Roman empire in North Africa and the eastern Mediterranean would give it the right to be treated as one of the great. The great and the would-be great believed that the age of small states had passed, that they were remnants of a medieval – or primeval – past.

War broke out in the summer of 1914 because everyone who mattered believed they faced a simple choice between growth and decay, between expansion and impotence. In other words, between empire and servitude. The way in which that war was fought – won and lost – produced different reactions among victors and vanquished, which in turn caused another, if different, impe-

rial conflict in the Second World War, the outcome of which produced a Cold War world in which the two antagonists proudly proclaimed their opposition to empire, while a Third World emerged to denounce them both as deceivers, hypocrites, and liars. The apparent victory of the world's only remaining "superpower" when the Cold War ended promised to usher in a New World Order, but instead has produced only a new age of chaos in which the rhetoric of empire has changed while the underlying dynamics of the imperial process has remained the same.

\* \* \*

Every Great Power before 1914 was an empire either in name or in practice. And yet, because commentators have mistakenly confused "empire" with the possession of colonies overseas, "imperialism" as a cause of war has been confused with contests outside Europe for maintaining or adding to these possessions. This attribution clearly fails the test of explaining the events of July, where none of those who mattered had their "imperial gaze" focused overseas. But the empire of the Habsburgs decided to end the imminent threat to its imperial integrity by crushing the Serb/Slav threat; the empire of the Romanovs responded by shielding its imperial satellite from destruction. The Serbs, who had precipitated the crisis by assassinating a future emperor, aimed to create an empire of their own, a "Greater Serbia," not a nation but an empire that was to include Croatians, Montenegrins, Bosnians – in fact, any Balkan peoples deemed to be devoid of "national consciousness" (deemed by the Serbs, of course). All states, great and small, chose to play the Great Game of Empire – but in Europe first, in Asia second, then in Africa and Latin America, and, finally, in the Pacific.

Before the First World War no alternative to empire was seriously considered by politicians, diplomatists, or by those who commented on their activities. The tide of history seemed visibly and irreversibly on the side of size. Small states would be reduced to satellites of the big. "The days are for great Empires and not for little States," declared Britain's colonial secretary, Joseph Chamberlain; territorial expansion was as "normal, as necessary, as inescapable and unmistakable a sign of vitality in a nation as the corresponding processes in the growing human body," asserted Herbert Asquith (British prime minister in 1914). Those already big with empire offered explanations of why this was natural and good; those who aspired to possess one explained why it was unnatural and bad that they were without one. Every existing empire and every would-be one defined "nation" in a way that subsumed it, that gave shape and structure to the distinctive future that was its destiny.

The pseudo-science of "geopolitics" was born in the age that gave rise to those other handmaidens of empire: anthropology, sociology, and eugenics. The map of the future sketched by the geopoliticians was stark in its simplicity – the future belonged to Russia and to the United States, each with its "heartland" impervious to attack, each utilizing rails of steel to connect its mineral resources to its cities, its food supply to its teeming masses. Halford Mackinder – the father of this dubious science – sought to overturn his own logic by insisting that Britain, through its empire, could overcome its geographic limitations: ships at sea could replace railways over land; the Canadian prairies, African minerals, and Indian masses could substitute for the "natural" advantages enjoyed by Russians and Americans. But where did this leave the Germans? the French? the Austro-Hungarians? – not to mention the Italians, the Japanese, the Turks, and even the

Serbs? In the language of geopolitics, on "the periphery"; in the language of eugenics, among "the decadent." So the question was, as the German chancellor, Prince Bernhard von Bülow, put it in 1904, whether twentieth-century Germany was to be "the hammer or the anvil of world politics." The Germans sought options to avoid their otherwise certain fate: Bismarck had been mistaken in his belief that a united Germany could remain a quiet and quiescent conservative force at the center of Europe. One school of thought suggested a diet of ships, coaling stations, and colonies; another a *drang nach osten*, with a railway running from Berlin to Baghdad. The kaiser refused to choose between these alternatives: the imperial center, extending south and east, would be complemented by the colonial periphery, launching pads from which to threaten or cajole the older empires in Africa, Asia – and even the Americas. In this imperial design, the alliance established with Austria-Hungary in 1879 was vital.

The Habsburgs could continue to enjoy the fruits of empire only as long as they played second fiddle to the Hohenzollerns. Wilhelm II showed what he thought of them when he thanked Franz Josef for acting as his "brilliant second" during the Moroccan crisis – a crisis that had been conjured up to show the French that their empire was mortgaged to the German army. The Habsburgs willingly accepted their role: second fiddle still left them with a vast multinational empire that produced unprecedented prosperity in Vienna and Budapest; without Berlin to support them they would be at the mercy of the discordant voices within the empire. Conversely, the French refused to accept the role assigned to them by the Germans – they had already agreed to play second fiddle to the British when they abandoned their Egyptian ambitions in the *entente cordiale* of 1904. When their prime minister wavered in the face of German threats, Sir Edward Grey conjured the British Expeditionary Force into existence in order to stiffen their resolve. Thus was the "continental commitment" made to preserve the British Empire.

The First World War did not erupt, volcano-like, as a result of "mounting tensions" bubbling below the surface or because of the "escalating arms race" or because of the "alliance system" or because of diplomatic miscalculations arising from the secretive "old diplomacy." War broke out because southeastern Europe was the one spot where the imperial fears of Austria-Hungary and Russia collided, on the one kind of issue that assured each of them of the support they needed from their allies. The apparent parallels with the Moroccan crises of 1905 and 1911, with the Bosnian annexation crisis of 1908, with the tensions arising from the Libyan and Balkan wars of 1912 and 1913 are misleading – the Great Powers never came close to war. The alliances and armaments, diplomacy and investments arose from assumptions concerning empire; they were its instruments, not its source.

The war as a contest for empire also determined the actions of the less-than-great. Italy and Romania, both apparently committed to their allies, Germany and Austria-Hungary, declared their agreements null and void and waited on the sidelines until one side or the other proved willing to meet their expansionist demands. Japan joined the Entente in order to seize German territories in the Far East; Turkey joined the Central Powers in order to realize the dreams of the Young Turks. Denouncing the cosmopolitanism of the sultan's court, rejecting Islam as the foundation of empire, and inventing a secularized Pan-Turanianism, the "modernizing" regime in Constantinople offered an imperialist ideology that would unify all Turkic-speaking peoples within the mythical entity of "turan." Turkey went to war to recover those parts of the empire that had recently been lost, to include their turkic "brothers" in Russian Azerbaijan and Persia, and, eventually, to establish an empire that would stretch from the Balkans to China.

The imperial dreams of all those involved have largely been ignored in favor of the standardized version of the war as an Anglo-German confrontation. Commonplace too is the belief that the war was a tragedy because it was really fought for nothing: this was no clash of civilizations, no ideological confrontation between different philosophical systems. It must then have been precipitated and prolonged by wicked men in high places – by militarists, the manufacturers of armaments, fat financiers, and the politicians who con-

nived with them. Almost unthinkable is the reality that most contemporaries saw the war as one on which their destiny depended – and that they were prepared to fight for empire. We can, however, believe this of the Italians; little talk of "making the world safe for democracy" or "abolishing militarism" emanated from Rome. The Italian position was relatively clear and straightforward: they held back in July 1914, and waited for the bids to come in (sealed in imperial envelopes that would include £50 million in cold, hard cash). The Italians have never been forgiven for stating their aims so starkly. Woodrow Wilson thought he could cheat them out of their ill-gotten gains when he denounced "secret agreements, secretly arrived at," but the Italians, who would suffer over 600,000 dead for the sake of the promises they had received, refused to abandon them – and when they believed themselves cheated at Paris in 1919, they turned to the fascists who proudly proclaimed their revisionist ambitions.

The Japanese were aggrieved as well, in spite of losing only 300 men in the conflict. They joined the Italians, the Germans, the Russians, and the Americans on the long list of those who looked at the new world order and decided it offered them little. The disaffected were aggrieved not for philosophical reasons but for imperial ones: they looked to the swollen empires of the British and the French and concluded that the war had been fought solely for the purpose of enlarging them. And fought successfully, too: empire had proved a source of strength, not weakness. Historians who think the Boer War highlighted the weaknesses of empire think wrong: it demonstrated precisely the opposite. And a decade later the South Africans proved themselves loyal subjects of the Crown – as did the Anzacs and Canadians, Sikhs and Gurkhas, all of whom marched proudly to war at the beat of the imperial drum. While Germany and Austria-Hungary were running out of resources and slowly being starved into submission between 1914 and 1918, empire offered the Allies the bounty of the world in men, metals, and food.

No one believed that empire was dead after the First World War, and few believed that the League of Nations – and its system of "mandates" – was anything more than camouflage to hide the fact that the Entente now ruled practically all of Africa, the Middle East, and the Pacific. Thus, the war and the peace conference that ended it were object lessons in the meaning of imperialism: the First World War taught everyone that war in the twentieth century was about empire – fought to keep it or to expand it, fought successfully by those who had it, lost by those who did not. Paradoxically, the world after the war was infused with idealism. What mattered in the world that followed the war were the competing ideals of the losers on the one hand and the winners who felt like losers on the other. The only realists left were the British and French – and they did not stand a chance in the ideologically charged world that they had themselves created. Pragmatism inspires no one. Neither the British nor the French could offer much to placate the idealistic demands emanating from within their own empires, where their policies veered from repression to indifference to retreat.

The likelihood of success on the part of the revisionists seemed remote to begin with: Russia was embroiled in civil war, Germany was in disarray, Italy on the verge of revolt, and Japan beset by rioting. Over the course of the next decade, all this would change – each of the revisionists would establish new regimes and lay idealist foundations for new empires. Each rejected its past in favor of a brave new world based on "modernist" philosophies of race and class, using "futurist" techniques of mass communication, propaganda, surveillance, and control to accomplish its radical new agendas. Among the revisionists, imperialism, far from being discredited, was strengthened, reshaped, and reconstituted into radical new designs that were bolder, more aggressive, and perhaps limitless; the response of the older empires of Britain and France lacked self-confidence. While the imperial military machine in India and Iraq, Syria and Algeria, was happy to go on quelling native revolts in the manner of the previous century, the imperial *mentalité* at home had changed.

The way that the war had been fought tore the heart out of the old imperial system. The empires of the Entente had been purchased at little cost to those "at home" in Europe. The vast expansion that occurred during the new imperialism of the

nineteenth century had been accomplished by minuscule military forces usually commanded by down-at-heel aristocrats who failed to fit the modernizing liberal/republican mercantile regimes at home. The war, the propaganda, and the peace profoundly changed perceptions of empire, particularly in Britain, but also in France and the United States. In Britain, the most popular wartime rallying cry was "Save the Empire"; propaganda portrayed the kaiser and his cohorts as conspiring to destroy it. If this were true, the cost of empire proved unimaginably high: almost a million dead and a treasury nearly bankrupt. The empire itself, which rallied round the Union Jack, began to demand a price as well: having fought for empire, they demanded less imperialism from London, more control for themselves. Granted independent representation in the League of Nations, given mandatory responsibilities in Southwest Africa and the Pacific, the "white dominions" throughout the empire seemed intent on going their own way – with the Statute of Westminster confirming that this indeed was the road to the future. In spite of the surprising loyalty of the Irish Volunteers to the empire and the war effort, demands for Irish independence grew more violent and more insistent from Easter 1916 onwards. In spite of India's efforts in the war, Gandhi launched his first non-cooperation campaign. The "new empire" established at Versailles required unprecedented policing and administration: from Palestine to Iraq, the Middle East proved a hornet's nest. By the 1930s, when the settlement of 1919 was under assault, an emotional equation had been made between the tragedy of the trenches and the persistence of empire. A generation had been sacrificed, the "best and the brightest" mowed down for the sake of what? The Irish Free State? Dominion status for India? A settlement for Zionists in Palestine? The only *raison d'être* for this "Third British Empire" was that it was to benefit "the natives" by setting them on the path to democracy. But what then was to be done when they took the rhetoric to be real and demanded, with increasing shrillness, that the imperialists leave? This was a dilemma not shared by the racial empires of Germany and Japan or the ideological ones of the USSR and the United States.

While the interwar empires of Britain and France professed to act in the interests of those they ruled, the imperial ethos that emerged in Germany and Japan differed; theirs was a racist one, claiming the right to command lesser beings by virtue of their racial superiority. The quest of social scientists to compare and contrast the "meaning" of fascism in Germany and Japan is misguided: what they shared was the racist assertion of their inherent superiority – one based on modern pseudo-science, the other on mystical mytho-history. The difference between "nation" and "race" was not at first comprehended in Germany, even among German Jews, who attempted to assert their German-ness, to prove their patriotism and their loyalty. They soon discovered that their religion was not at issue: their blood was. The Koreans were the first to learn this lesson at the hands of the Japanese in Asia. The two most ferocious theaters of the Second World War were the Pacific – where the purity of the "Yamato soul" allowed "one hundred million hearts to beat as one" – and in eastern Europe – where Nazi ideas of the enemy as *Untermenschen* were paramount. In Asia, the Japanese rejected the European science which assigned them to a place of inferiority and discovered, instead, the origins of their superiority in the divine descent of their sovereign and the racial and cultural homogeneity of the sovereign's loyal subjects. Deity, monarch, and populace were one. The Greater East Asia Co-Prosperity Sphere would benefit all Asians – engineered and administered by the *Yamato minzoku*, the race defined by an exclusivity which no outsider could hope to penetrate.

The experience of Germany and Japan during war and its aftermath had schooled them in the lessons of empire: they needed it in order to succeed in war and to prosper in peace. They could not acquire it by offering equality, self-determination, or ideological salvation. They demanded it as their destiny – a right that was theirs because of a racial supremacy that could be discerned in their culture and proved on the field of battle. In contrast, the "natural" empires that the early geopoliticians had described needed no such assertion: the United States and the USSR had simply to retain what was already theirs. American "revisionism" between the wars – so

popular and pervasive that it became the governing ethos and enshrined in "neutrality" legislation – insisted that the United States had engaged in war for the sake of empire. According to this view, the followers of Captain Mahan had combined with J. P. Morgan & Co. and led the nation into war in the belief that trade would follow the flag, that a big, two-ocean navy was an essential requirement for a "free enterprise" economy to flourish in the twentieth century. T. R. Roosevelt was the almost iconic symbol of this phenomenon: leading the cavalry charge up San Juan Hill (having resigned as assistant secretary of the navy to do so), leading the political charge to retain the Philippines after the war with Spain, explaining, in *The Winning of the West* (published precisely as the new century began), how America had accomplished the first stage of its "manifest destiny" by extending from sea to shining sea. Americans recognized that TR was an imperialist, but most were surprised when the Calvinist academic, Woodrow Wilson, turned out to be one as well. They should not have been. Wilson was convinced, now that "the West" had been "Won," a substitute had to be found for the frontier. In the twentieth century, he declared, America would have to conquer the markets of the world, and the essential instrument for this, he asserted, would be "the imperial president." So it was not Wilson and the Americans who were naïve at Paris in 1919 but the Europeans, who failed to consider the implications of the American occupation of Cuba and the Philippines, or Wilsonian "intervention" in Mexico, the Dominican Republic, and Haiti.

What Wilson promoted was imperialism in one hemisphere: he insisted that the United States would continue to intervene in the affairs of its neighbors under the Monroe Doctrine whenever necessary – "I shall teach the Latin American republics to elect good men." And his formula of self-determination for nations "struggling to be free" would have dismantled all European pretensions to empires that could compete with the American. That the Monroe Doctrine would continue to operate was enshrined in the Covenant of the League itself. This was a brilliantly designed imperial system for the twentieth century; but Americans were not ready for it until 1945.

Republicans and Midwesterners were horrified that a so-called "League of Nations" could send American boys to fight all over the world.

Wilson's greatest fear was the advent of an alternative imperial system in the form of international socialism. Instead of grounding itself in trade, nation, or race, the Bolshevik brand of empire was based on class. And class would cut through both the old European imperialism and the new American version. The creation of the Comintern, along with the proclamations of Lenin, Trotsky, Bukharin, and the other proponents of world revolution, left no doubt that they saw the expansion of their system as essential for its (and their) survival. Lenin had learned during the war that imperialism was "the highest stage of capitalism"; thus, by definition, the new Soviet state could not be imperialistic. The peace taught him a new lesson: that the western capitalists were capable of coalescing, of carving up the world by mutual agreement – which was the real purpose of the League of Nations. So the bourgeoisie might not annihilate one another after all and the alternative to this new imperialism was the Soviet model: the proletarians and peasants coming "freely" together in a new socialist federation. The Politburo, the political commissars sent out from the Kremlin and OGPU, soon showed what this meant in reality: in every region of the old tsarist empire that had not broken away during the civil war, a new centralized authority was imposed that would have been the envy of any tsarist administrator.

When confronted by a vigorous and acquisitive Nazi Germany, the USSR discovered that the League of Nations might be a legitimate international instrument and proposed a popular front against fascism. But this gambit ended with the Nazi–Soviet pact, usually defended by apologists of the regime as being imposed on the Soviets by the foot-dragging of the British and the French appeasers. In reality, Stalin was enticed by the possibility of expanding the Soviet empire in Poland, Finland, and the Baltic. And thus the Second World War: a racist empire of Nazi-German *Volk* in the center and east of Europe, aided and abetted – temporarily, at least – by a Communist-Russian regime that would extend its authority over all parts of eastern Europe not claimed by the Nazis; and then a desperate, last-ditch Anglo-French diplomatic effort to draw a line in the great Polish plain – an effort that almost destroyed them, and surely would have done without the assistance of the Soviet and American empires.

Instead of destroying Britain and France, the Second World War destroyed the short-lived empires of race established by Germany and Japan. Imperialism itself survived: even while the war was being fought, the Allies recommitted themselves to empire. Stalin and the Politburo were absolutely convinced that future Soviet security depended upon extending the territories under their control, and of exerting what imperial Britain had earlier called "paramountcy" in the states bordering on their territories. Churchill and De Gaulle were absolutely convinced that the future of both Britain and France required the retention of their empires. These convictions surprised no one at the time, but suggesting that the Second War of the Entente against the German people(s) was fought for the sake of empire seems to border on heresy. Nazi demonology has been popularized and the Holocaust memorialized to the point that most westerners today vaguely assume that the war was fought to preserve democracy and/or to rescue the Jews. The fact that the Anglo-French Entente, supported by the United States (in both world wars), would have ignored Nazi (and Japanese) authoritarianism and would have turned a blind eye to the treatment of Jews (and Koreans) had the Axis not threatened the British, French, and American empires does not make good movies and is not the stuff of which myths are woven.

But the Second World War did more than eradicate the empires of race; the face of empire began to change, first in the United States, then in "old Europe," and finally in the "Third World." In the United States the Wilsonian vision – discredited and abandoned by all but a few ideologues between the wars – was revived and realized by one of his bright young men from 1919, Franklin Roosevelt. FDR's grand design for the future was imperial from start to finish. It consisted first of abandoning altogether American isolationism: the United States must play a leading role in world politics. The Japanese attack on Pearl Harbor presented the most stunning display of the impracticability of isolation. The League of Nations would be reconstituted as the United Nations and relocated to New York, symbolizing the shift in power both from the Old World to the New and from the "neutral" ground of Geneva to the greatest metropolis of the greatest power. The League, in FDR's view, had failed because it was not "imperial" enough; he proposed that "four policemen" would uphold the new World Settlement – with the US, USSR, Britain, and China responsible for maintaining "order" within their own spheres. If this vision had been fully realized it would have been the greatest imperial scheme for the division of the world by empires in human history. It failed because of the revolution in China and because of mutual suspicions among the Allies in Europe. Instead of four great empires peacefully partitioning the globe, the world became a "bipolar" struggle for dominance between two of them.

America and Russia each denied its own imperial credentials while accusing the other of having empire as its very essence. Imperialism thus became the policy that dare not speak its name: it was a grenade to be thrown at an iron curtain, an explosive charge laid at the foundations of someone else's structure. The manipulation of politics in other states, the aid packages, the strategic support, even outright military intervention were never justified as a "right" of the stronger – as they had been in the heyday of the old imperialism – but explained away as being in the interests of others. "In your own best interests" was a phrase, as C. P. Snow pointed out, which meant some unsuspecting soul was about to get it in the neck. Saving socialism from capitalist imperialism and defending democracy from the Evil Empire turned every uncommitted place in the world into contested terrain, into a potential battlefield. It was in this context that the "Third World" was invented by those meeting at Bandung in 1955. This term, since devalued and misappropriated, was not supposed to be a synonym for "where the poor live" but rather proclaimed that some wished to avoid making a choice between which imperial colossus it would cleave to. Simultaneously, new postcolonial elites steeped in the rhetoric of anti-colonialism discovered that, if they played their

cards right, they could use the Russo-American imperial struggle for their own purposes – which seldom turned out to be for the benefit of their people as a whole. Sukarno, the leading figure at Bandung, was engaged in establishing a police state in Indonesia that would have been the envy of the most reactionary Dutch imperialist at the same time that he was denouncing colonialism.

Also present at Bandung were Gamal Abdel Nasser and Kwame Nkrumah, who conjured up alluring visions of what it would take to remain outside the orbit of the Russian and American empires. These turned out to be new, improved versions of imperial designs: "Pan-Arabism" and "Pan-Africanism" would, they suggested, enable these vast new postcolonial territories to stand tall and independent. This particular postcolonial assumption assumed that states, if too small, could not continue to exist, or if they did, that they could exist only by substituting new imperial controllers for their old ones. Their dreams died with their dreamers.

The invention of a Third World, which would change the face of postcolonial politics, is inextricably connected with the third of the sea changes that followed the Second World War – that which occurred in the "old Europe." The first to change here were not the great but the small. In the aftermath of another devastating war, the lesser states of Europe abandoned the vision of an imperial future and imagined a new past: banished from Belgium and the Netherlands were the horrors of the Congo and the Aceh War, and taking their place were the rights of small states who hoped for a future within Europe. "Benelux" – at first an apparently insignificant trading arrangement among the inconsequential – took shape and grew at the same time that events in Suez and Algeria were "ending empire" as Britain and France knew it. The process of "decolonization" did not seem swift at the time; it now appears to have been electrical. Within the space of a few short years, the colonies fell away or hacked themselves off. The French struggled against this new reality more violently than the British, but both faced a resistance that grew even from those who had earlier collaborated, while those "at home" seemed no longer to care about empire – past, present, or future. Paradoxically, while their empires of property shriveled and died, an older, mid-Victorian ideal of empire revived to take its place. The old European empires were reengineered. Why colonize and occupy, administer and police those who demanded their freedom when the metals and the oil would still make their way to Europe and pay a healthy margin to those who managed from the head office in London or Paris? Was the old colonial world not best seen from the beaches of a Club Med or from the commanding heights of the Hyatt, Hilton, or Intercontinental? Why live among "the natives" and take on all the troubles that this entailed when one could travel at one's leisure, be served all the fruits of the world, and spared the pain of attempting to "solve" its problems? One might even insist that "they" preserve their forests and jungles, their whales and the bears that Europeans would like to see, no longer having any of their own. And so as it was learned that the old empires of property were unsustainable, it was also discovered that they were unnecessary, that new ones of profit and play could happily take their place.

When the real wall of Berlin came down, and the metaphorical one of the Iron Curtain along with it, it appeared that the old story of imperial competition and conflict might come to an end as well. Some went so far as to suggest that the end of the Cold War marked the "end of history," meaning that the future would not be contested, that the world was at last one in the sense that all would soon share the principles of the free market economy, sustained by democratic political systems; the twentieth century had shown that no other system worked – not the old empires of property, nor the new ones of race or ideology. All this talk of the new world order really represented little more than American triumphalism, the belief that with the challenges of racial and ideological imperialism vanquished, the only model that made sense was the liberal one offered by the United States. The horrors of Rwanda, Kosovo, and Mogadishu seemed but echoes of a regrettable, colonialized past that would gradually, if painfully, be silenced as the new order solidified.

The attack on the World Trade Center on September 11, 2001, shattered this neo-imperial daydream. The attack not only demonstrated that the imperial metropolis was itself vulnerable to a tiny group of determined terrorists, but also the so-called "War on Terror" that followed it showed that history had not ended, that the world was not one, that the future would continue to be contested terrain. The war of words was almost as significant as the war that erupted on the ground in Afghanistan and Iraq: "Islamic Fundamentalism" emerged as a rhetorical catch-all to represent an alternative system to that of western liberalism. Proponents and detractors alike use it to sketch the outlines of a way of life fundamentally incompatible with the system that appeared only a decade before to be accepted around the globe. No one a century ago anticipated a world in which religious difference would define the shape of international politics; the fact that the world continues to be divided by competing visions of empire would have surprised few.

# Part I

# Undertones

# CHAPTER ONE

# Imperialism

## JOHN MACKENZIE

European and American empires seemed to be at their peak when the twentieth century opened. By its end, decolonization, at least in a formal sense, seemed to be complete. Imperialism, some would argue, had moved into a different phase, but it is certainly true that the world had been shaped by empires and their legacies were universally apparent. Everywhere, boundaries (often artificial) and problems of ethnicity were the product of the imperial age. Many of these, such as the crises in the Middle East, the communal tensions in Sri Lanka, Kashmir, Fiji, Somalia, and many other places, were fraught with conflict. For empires had not only distributed white people of European origin around the globe, they had also stimulated flows of Africans (not least through the slave trade) to North and South America and some parts of Asia, Indians (through indentured labor) to Indian Ocean islands, the Caribbean, and Africa, and Chinese to the Indian Ocean, the Pacific Rim, Australasia, and the Americas. In the twentieth century, these earlier population flows created many stresses and strains. Non-European territories of white settlement sought to stem such migration in the period before and after the First World War, and in the post-Second World War era, European states became the destination for many migrants from the so-called Third World. On the one hand, such population movements were vital in the filling of jobs which whites were no longer prepared to occupy, but they also sparked right-wing, quasi-racist (or openly racist)

movements which vainly sought to maintain white ethnic purity and keep such people out. Many international problems, including the legacy of the Holocaust in Israel, were rooted in these imperial phenomena. Moreover, by the end of the century a global nation-state order, represented in the extensive membership of the United Nations, had taken over. Politics generally represented the successful long march to power of an educated, more or less westernized, nationalist bourgeoisie almost everywhere.

## Empires in the Early Twentieth Century

By 1900 most of the major acts of imperial acquisition had been completed. The final decades of the nineteenth century had witnessed the partition of Africa – the almost complete carve-up of that continent – as well as a scramble for Pacific islands involving the British, the Germans, the French, and the United States. At the end of the century, the US had developed further as an overseas imperial power (the earlier expansion of the original colonies across the continent, as well as the annexation of Alaska and Hawaii, had already made it a major imperial force despite all protestations to the contrary). In the Spanish–American War of 1898, one old European imperialist power gave way to the thrusting new federal state, which acquired the Philippines and territory in the Caribbean. The tsarist empire of the Russians had consolidated its hold over its East and Central Asian possessions through the building of railway lines, including the trans-Siberian. Elsewhere, older rivalries had appeared to continue unabated. In that same year, military forces of the French and the British came face to face on the Upper Nile in the Fashoda incident, when General Kitchener, who had just reconquered the Sudan (Anglo-Egyptian forces had been defeated by those of the Mahdi in 1884–5), faced down Colonel Marchand. Another new imperial power, Italy, had received a major setback when defeated by the Abyssinians (Ethiopians) at the Battle of Adowa in 1896. In the twentieth century, a fascist Italian government was to be restless to avenge this defeat.

By the beginning of the twentieth century, the European and American empires, rapidly joined by the Japanese, had effectively carved up the world into zones of "formal" and "informal" empire. In formal empire, the imperial power directly administered territory, developing infrastructure and ports in favor of international trade. In informal empire, the imperial power exercised economic influence, but permitted the territory to be ruled, however weakly, by indigenous agents. The British also maintained the concept of the "protectorate," a territory whose boundaries were generally established by the imperial power but which maintained some semblance of traditional rule. The fiction was maintained through oversight by the Foreign Office. However, many of their protectorates were formalized into Crown Colonies in the early twentieth century, a transition which moved their control to the Colonial Office. Other diverse modes of governance were exercised in various places and the considerable complexity of imperial rule was dependent on a range of indigenous rulers, commercial collaborators, and westernized elites who normally used their training in western ideas and techniques to advance themselves within the imperial systems. It was from this essentially bourgeois group that the new nationalisms of the twentieth century were to arise.

Other zones of influence resulted from the decline of former empires, notably the Ottoman. The weakness of this empire, which had been at the peak of its power between the sixteenth and eighteenth centuries, had already produced major political changes in Greece and the Balkans in the course of the nineteenth century. Islands such as Cyprus had been lost to the west, while subsidiary rulers in North Africa had progressively asserted their independence – as with the khedives in Egypt – before falling under European influence. In the early twentieth century, the British were the nominal rulers of Egypt, although they only declared a protectorate in 1914. Algeria and Tunisia were under the formal control of France, while Morocco fell into the informal French sphere after a series of crises in which Germany attempted to assert an interest. Libya became Italian after a brief war in 1911–12.

Elsewhere in the world, it is possible to demarcate these formal and informal spheres. In the Caribbean and Central and South America, different systems coexisted: European empires had formal control of almost all the Caribbean islands, as well as territories on the northern coast of South America and the lands of Central America. American influence had been established in Panama, preparatory to the opening of the canal there in 1914. South American countries labored under a sort of dual system. The British were economically powerful, notably in Argentina, but the Americans effectively insisted that it was their zone of influence, a notion first established by the Monroe Doctrine of 1823. The British maintained formal hold over the Falkland Islands off the coast of Argentina (known to the Argentineans as the Malvinas), a situation which was to stimulate conflict in the Anglo-Argentine War of 1982. Other Atlantic islands held by the British included Ascension, Saint Helena, Tristan da Cunha, and South Georgia.

Sub-Saharan Africa was almost entirely under the control of the Portuguese, British, French, German, Italian, and Belgian empires. The Spanish had enclaves in the north and the west, while the Americans maintained informal and economic control over Liberia. Only Ethiopia was fully independent. In Asia, the British exercised authority over a vast swathe of territory from the Yemen and the Gulf, through their most important possession, India, to Ceylon (Sri Lanka) in the south and Burma (Myanmar), the Malay states, and Singapore in the east, with outriders in Sarawak and

North Borneo. Hong Kong on the coast of China was rapidly becoming a bustling commercial emporium, recently rendered viable by the cession of the New Territories from China (1898) on a ninety-nine-year lease. The Japanese had acquired Formosa (or Taiwan) in 1895 and added Korea to their empire in 1910. The French were powerful in Indo-China, in the territories of Vietnam, Cambodia, and Laos, while the Dutch possessed the extensive empire of the East Indies, Java, Sumatra, Sulawesi, and many other islands, including parts of New Guinea and Borneo. Siam (Thailand) was effectively under informal control, mainly that of Britain. In some places, the British ruled through companies. At the beginning of the twentieth century, the Royal Niger Company had only recently been wound up (1898), but the British South Africa Company (Southern and Northern Rhodesia, the future Zimbabwe and Zambia) was to continue to exercise authority until 1923. The British North Borneo Company survived until the Second World War, while Sarawak remained under the rule of supposedly independent rajahs who were British in nationality. Commercial companies were also powerful in Mozambique and elsewhere.

## The Unique Power of the British Empire

In these imperial systems, the British Empire was uniquely powerful. In many respects, there were several British empires. India was often demarcated as an empire in its own right. It too reflected the complexities of imperial rule: vast areas were under the direct rule of British authorities, but there were also many Indian princely states which supposedly ruled themselves, under the watchful eye of a British resident, while their princes offered allegiance to the monarch through the viceroy. Along the northern frontiers of the subcontinent there were a number of buffer states, like Sikkim, Bhutan, and Nepal, nominally independent, over which the British kept careful external control. It was as a result of anxieties about encroachments from competing empires like Russia and China that the British also kept a close watch upon Afghanistan and went so far as to invade Tibet in 1905.

The second British Empire was the empire of colonies of white settlement. Although Britain's greatest setback had been the loss of the thirteen North American colonies in the 1770s, the settlement colonies had remained extensive. By the early twentieth century, Canada had been progressively federated from 1867 (though Newfoundland was not to join until after the Second World War). The Australian colonies of New South Wales, Queensland, Tasmania, Victoria, South Australia, and Western Australia had formed the Commonwealth of Australia in 1901. New Zealand, the Cape, and Natal were also colonies which exercised "responsible government," full internal self-government. All still looked to Britain for foreign and defense policies. As we shall see below, seismic changes in South Africa were to produce the Union of South Africa, adding the Transvaal and the Orange Free State (or after 1902 Orange River Colony) to the Cape and Natal, in 1910. To India and the white settlement colonies we could add two more British "empires," that of islands and strategic staging posts important as commercial way-stations, as coaling or telegraphic cable places, or as naval supply points, a system which effectively spanned the globe. And finally there were the "dependent" colonies, those which were administered as colonies under the authority of the Crown or as protectorates. These multiple imperial systems were to have varied effects upon the international systems of the twentieth century.

## Loss of Equilibrium in the International Imperial Order

But the developments of the turn of the twentieth century failed to consolidate the imperial order. Major instabilities were now becoming apparent in the international system. The British, who had generally overcome challenges to their authority in the previous century, were beginning to show signs of weakness. Despite possessing what commentators described as the largest empire the world had ever known, the empire on which the sun never set, Britain was rapidly losing influence. The colonial secretary, Joseph Chamberlain, described the United Kingdom as a "weary Titan, staggering under the too great orb of its fate."

Both the US and Germany surpassed it in steel production. Its navy, the source of its nineteenth-century power, was unlikely to maintain its two-power standard (the notion that the Royal Navy had to be larger than those of the next two navies combined). Internal stresses, including the restlessness of Irish nationalists, labor and trade union problems, and other social discontents, aroused alarm. But the major threat to the international standing of the British came from the efforts of Chamberlain and the high commissioner in South Africa, Alfred Milner, to consolidate their power in the southern African subcontinent. The Anglo-Boer War, which broke out in 1899, largely provoked by the British, was designed to reestablish their authority over the Boer (or Afrikaner) republics of the Orange Free State and the Transvaal. The British government hoped to bring the major gold production of the Transvaal (or South African Republic) under its control (important from the point of view of maintaining the stability of the international currency, sterling), establish the political freedoms (what would today be called "civil rights") of European migrants within the republic, and, above all, protect the strategically important colonies of the Cape and Natal against the dangers of foreign alliance. Despite the existence of the Suez Canal, South Africa remained important strategically as a commercial route to India and to Australasia. There was also an important naval base at Simonstown.

But the war between the world's largest imperial power and republics that were relatively thinly populated by whites was no "pushover." The British experienced a series of major reversals and three important centers, Mafeking, Kimberley, and Ladysmith, were besieged by the Boers over many months. Even when the sieges were raised and the British captured the Boer capitals, the war was not over. The Afrikaners became guerrillas and used their knowledge of the terrain and their formidable bushcraft to continue to confound the British. When the Peace of Vereeniging was signed in 1902, the Boers could maintain a semblance of never having been defeated.

Far from solving problems, from the point of view of the British, the war created new ones. Many Afrikaners remained irreconcilable and, in some respects, they won the peace. Plans for a major movement of British immigrants and the Anglicization of the region never materialized. Africans, too often left out of consideration in historical assessments of the war, in fact became its major victims, ultimately losing land, any semblance of political involvement, and opportunities to advance their fortunes within the South African economy. In many respects, the foundations of the later notorious apartheid system were laid during this period. It would take the whole of the twentieth century to work these problems through.

On the international front, the British were now fully aware of their weakness. It was apparent, for example, that Britain could no longer maintain the necessary naval and military presence in the Far East. The British had been intrigued by the rise of Japan, a state made up of an archipelago of islands with a hostile continental power nearby. The parallels with Britain itself, not least because the Japanese were adopting British engineering and technological expertise, as well as modeling their rapidly expanding navy on the Royal Navy, were much discussed in the period. Moreover, the Japanese emergence as an imperial power whetted its ambitions for further acquisitions. In 1902, the British abandoned their policy of "splendid isolation" and signed a treaty with Japan. Soon the disequilibrium which the British most feared was heightened by the developing power of Germany. Recognizing the true source of British predominance, the kaiser and his ministers ordered a major naval building program which caused great alarm in the British Admiralty. It also produced a reversal in British naval policy. Whereas in the past the Royal Navy had been concerned with global authority, preferring to police the seas with a large number of relatively small vessels, the Admiralty, under the influence of Admiral Jack Fisher, set about concentrating on defense in Europe through the medium of larger battleships known as dreadnoughts, the first one being launched in 1906.

The perceived German threat caused the British to form new ententes that were to have effects upon imperial policy. The Anglo-French entente of 1904, just ahead of the resonant centenary of the Battle of Trafalgar, meant that the longstanding friction between the two empires was put to rest. This was followed by an entente with Russia which, like France, had been a traditional enemy. The British had been afraid of Russian pressure at a number of points, notably upon the Ottoman Empire in the Black Sea region, seeking to force their way into the Mediterranean through the Dardanelles (thus securing an ice-free route into the wider world). The Russian encroachment from their Central Asian possessions upon Persia (modern Iran), Afghanistan, and the Northwest frontier of British India had caused widespread alarm in British quarters for some time. The British and Russian bout of shadow-boxing on this frontier had prompted the coining of the celebrated phrase "The Great Game." Third, Russian continental power reaching out to the Far East had caused alarm with regard to the commerce and "treaty ports" of western Europeans in China. In these ports, Europeans enjoyed "extraterritoriality," the right to run their commercial enclaves according to their own laws.

But the Russian threat had been removed by the growing power of the Japanese. The Russo-Japanese War of 1904–5 had been concluded by Japanese victories, notably in the naval Battle of Tsushima in 1905, which the Japanese Admiral Togo had regarded as the equivalent of Trafalgar one hundred years earlier. The British entente with Russia helped to alleviate tension in some areas of "informal imperialism." Persia was divided into two spheres of interest, the Russians in the north, the British in the south adjacent to the Persian or Arabian Gulf, which they regarded as their commercial and strategic zone. They maintained a powerful British Resident in the Gulf, under the aegis of the Indian presidency of Bombay, with agents in Kuwait, Bahrain, Qatar, the Trucial states (now the United Arab Emirates), and Muscat. The extensive imperial shipping line, the British India Steam Navigation Company, maintained a frequent service from Bombay to many of the Gulf ports.

Indeed, the dominance of Europeans and Americans throughout the world has to be understood in terms of the advanced technologies of the day, technologies that were being increasingly adopted by non-European peoples. British shipping companies were to be found all over the world dominating trade routes in the North and South Atlantic, the Mediterranean, the Indian and Pacific Oceans, as well as the Far East. The great majority of the ships passing through the Suez Canal were British, and the British shipbuilding industry, on the rivers Clyde, Mersey, Tyne, and Wear, was by far the largest in the world. There were also major German, French, Italian, Portuguese, Dutch, American, and, increasingly, Japanese shipping concerns. Marine engines were much more efficient than they had been in the past and the latest steam turbine technology was installed in ships where speed was vital, as on the North Atlantic, and in the dreadnoughts. But it was not only the deep-sea trades that were important. Rivers such as the Euphrates, the Irrawaddy, the Nile, the Niger, the Congo, the Amazon, the St. Lawrence, and those that were navigable in India and China abounded in river steamers. So did lakes, such as the great lakes of North America and those of East Africa. The Irrawaddy Flotilla Company, to take one example, had a fleet of more than a hundred vessels. Coasting trades were also important, with services like the Straits Steamship Company, based on Malaya and the eastern islands, and Burns Philp, an Australian concern connecting Australian ports to Pacific islands and Southeast Asia. Powerful shipping companies had also emerged in Canada, New Zealand, and elsewhere. These were supplemented by more advanced rail technology, connecting much of the interior of Africa and Asia to the ports, with engines built in Europe or North America. By the beginning of the twentieth century much of the world was connected by telegraphic submarine cable and landlines. Commercial messages, as well as military and naval dispositions, could be sent almost anywhere within minutes. By the time of the First World War, this system would be supplemented by nascent radio transmission. Machine guns and other artillery, small arms, together with naval armament and firepower had become increasingly sophisticated. Theoretically, European and American technological dominance should have been complete. But increasingly, if intermittently, examples of these new technologies were beginning to reach, and be utilized by, non-European peoples.

Yet the years up to the First World War were a time of considerable apprehension and anxiety for the imperial system. Violent revolts, the Maji Maji and the Herero respectively, took place in German Tanganyika (Tanzania) and in Southwest Africa (Namibia). Both were suppressed with great brutality. The British would shortly face a revolt in Somaliland (Somalia) led by a leader they named the "Mad Mullah" (Sayyid Abdullah Hassan). Of even greater significance for the future was the fact that nationalist movements were gaining in strength, notably in India, but also in South and West Africa, where educated elites were founding parties. But it has often been argued that when the First World War broke out, it was for essentially European rather than imperial reasons. Nevertheless, as the British journalist and politician Leopold Amery pointed out, the Germans were intensely jealous of the British Empire. Despite this, on the eve of war, the Germans and the British confirmed an agreement on the division of the Portuguese Empire in Africa (first contracted at the end of the nineteenth century) if the republican government established in 1910 should decide to withdraw. But if the origins of the First World War within competing empires are obscure, the imperial results of the conflict were profound.

## Imperialism and the First World War

In Africa, there were campaigns against the Germans in Southwest Africa and in Tanganyika. South African troops, with the participation of British and Belgians in East Africa, effectively captured these colonies, while the Germans also lost Togo and Cameroon in West Africa. In the east of the continent, the German General von Lettow Vorbeck continued to mount a guerrilla campaign which continued until the end of the war. These campaigns provided the South African Jan Smuts with experience, power, and influence that led to a seat in the British Imperial War Cabinet, the rank of field marshal, and considerable influence at Versailles and over the foundation of the League of Nations. Similarly, the German Pacific possessions were captured. The Ottoman Empire, under considerable German

influence before the war – notably in the building of the Baghdad railway – took the German side, a decision which led to its ultimate destruction. The British fomented the Arab revolt, led by Colonel T. E. Lawrence and the Sharif Husayn, Emir of the Hijaz, and after initial setbacks to British and Indian forces in Mesopotamia (the modern Iraq), the Ottoman provinces fell one by one. One of the characteristics of the war was the conclusion of secret agreements among participants. When the Italians entered the war on the Allied side in 1916, they sought rewards in the enhancement of their imperial possessions. The French and the British agreed to a division of the Middle Eastern spoils as well as debating the possibility of a Jewish homeland in the region.

In 1919, at Versailles, some of these agreements bore fruit. When the League of Nations was established, it was agreed that the German and Ottoman possessions should be administered under a mandates system, whereby victorious Europeans would exercise authority under international supervision. Through these arrangements the British secured Tanganyika (with some redistribution of land to the Belgians in the Congo and Rwanda Burundi), parts of Togo and Cameroon, together with Palestine, Transjordan, and Mesopotamia. The French took some of the German territory of West Africa together with Lebanon and Syria. The startling development was that some European colonies now became imperialists in their own right: South Africa secured the mandate for Southwest Africa while Australia and New Zealand assumed authority in the German parts of New Guinea and Samoa respectively. The Italians got no more than a few crumbs from the imperialists' table, namely a rearrangement of the boundaries of Libya and Italian Somaliland. But just as the empires of Britain and France reached their widest extent, it became obvious that the postwar world was going to be highly unstable.

In India, the interwar years were to be a time of great turbulence. A brief Afghan war broke out in 1919. The Indian nationalist movement had been fractured in various ways from the years before the First World War. The Indian National Congress, founded as far back as 1885, had become divided into militant and constitutional wings. The war had invoked a certain amount of "loyalty" and the man who was to become the leading nationalist symbol, Mohandas Karamchand Gandhi, soon known as the Mahatma, even served in an ambulance corps. The British were now attempting to mix limited constitutional reform with a crackdown on dissidence, but the latter resulted in the notorious Jallianwallabagh massacre in Amritsar when troops fired upon unarmed demonstrators, killing some 400 people. Gandhi was nonetheless able to secure a degree of control over the nationalist movement through what was effectively a "third way": passive resistance, combined with constitutional talks. But another major faction was to develop its power during this period. This was the Muslim League. The original Congress had set out to bring Hindu and Muslim together, but the Muslim League was founded as a separatist Islamic movement in 1905. In 1940, under the leadership of a westernized and secular lawyer, Mohammed Ali Jinnah, it demanded a separate Muslim state.

## The Interwar Years

There is a curiously ambivalent air about European imperialisms in the interwar years. On the one hand, the strains and tensions that would ultimately lead to decolonization are unquestionably present. On the other, it seems in many ways to be something of a golden age. Imperial administrations were placed on a more systematic footing than had been the case before. In all the empires, administrators were selected and trained more carefully. Partly because of the economic problems of the period, governments were anxious to foster an imperial spirit. It was a period of intensive official propaganda in the French Empire. The last great empire exhibitions took place in this era, including those at Wembley in 1924–5, Glasgow in 1938, Paris (1925 and 1931), Liège and Brussels (1930 and 1935), as well as in many other parts of the world. In Britain, the Empire Marketing Board was founded in 1926 to encourage the purchase of empire produce. Imperial preference was finally, after many years of controversy, introduced in the Ottawa agreements of 1932. Moreover, the development of the Ameri-

can quota system and the resulting barriers to large-scale European migration that had been such a characteristic of the pre-First World War years meant that more Europeans headed for the empires. More Britons migrated to imperial territories between the wars than went to the US (though many returned). Italians and Portuguese also headed for colonies within their own imperial systems, as well as to British and South American territories. The British also created ex-servicemen's settlement schemes, partly in an effort to draw off some of the resentments generated by the fact that the mother country had not proved to be a "land fit for heroes."

The British dominions progressed further down the path of becoming fully independent states. Having been involved in Versailles, they joined the League of Nations and, in some areas, began to pursue independent foreign policies. In 1926 the "Balfour Declaration" proclaimed that, with Britain, they were "free and equal states, in no way subservient one to the other." This was given expression in the Statute of Westminster of 1931. Moreover, strains and stresses were working through both on the domestic front and in respect of the Middle East. In 1922, treaties with both Ireland (excepting the six counties in the north) and Egypt effectively restored independence to those countries. In Egypt, the imperial power retained control of defense and foreign affairs in order to protect its interests in the Suez Canal. A further treaty followed in 1936. Similar developments occurred in Mesopotamia (Iraq). In both of these countries, and in Transjordan, the British tried to develop constitutional monarchies and maintain their informal influence. They succeeded until the 1950s.

If the British imperial system was fraying around the edges, strenuous efforts were made to replace formal with informal controls. The Americans granted self-government to Cuba in 1934 and the Philippines in 1935, while maintaining their "protection" of these territories. They continued to hold Puerto Rico.

But the prime conditioning factor in imperial relations in these years was the severe cyclical depressions in the world's economic system. The first of these occurred in the early 1920s, followed by a severe downturn after 1929 which continued until some improvement occurred just before the Second World War. Only South Africa was relatively free of these economic crises because of the significance of its gold production. Elsewhere, economic problems and an accompanying downturn in wages and standards of living produced social and political discontents throughout the imperial systems. By the end of the 1930s, partly under pressure from labor troubles in the West Indies and elsewhere, the British began to produce schemes for the central funding of empire development. In the French Empire, government-sponsored propaganda and tighter economic and administrative controls were developed. This was also true of the Belgian and Dutch empires. The Portuguese Empire came to be seen as a central characteristic of the new Estado Nuovo founded in 1926, while the Italian fascists placed their empire at the center of their concerns. The capital of Eritrea was developed as a major Art Deco city, now appreciated for its extraordinary architectural and aesthetic achievements, despite its rather dubious origins. And Mussolini, under pressure from internal problems, resolved to avenge Adowa by invading Ethiopia in 1935–6. This shamelessly opportunistic action, which the western powers entirely failed to prevent, was hailed by Afro-Asian nationalists as indicative of the aggressive decadence of Europe. The one state in Africa, with a major Christian population, that had managed to resist imperial conquest was subjected to twentieth-century aggression.

The League of Nations, lacking an international armed force, was also powerless to prevent the increasingly aggressive actions of Japan in the Far East. Manchuria was invaded in 1931 and a puppet ruler was imposed upon the new colony of Manchukuo, a territory which happened to be rich in iron resources, which Japan itself lacked. This was followed by brutal incursions into the Chinese mainland. The Anglo-Japanese alliance had not been renewed after the First World War and the British now recognized that Japan constituted a major threat to its possessions in the Far East and Southeast Asia. Extensive fortifications were built in Singapore, mainly pointing out to sea, and were clearly designed to protect the extremity of the Malaysian peninsula from the potential for Japanese aggression.

## The Second World War

Whereas the imperial campaigns of the First World War largely took place in sub-Saharan Africa and involved the conquest of the German colonies, those of the Second took place primarily in Asia and the Pacific, in the war against Japan, and in North Africa. Japan and Italy, on the Allied side in the First World War, were realigned with Germany in the Second. The Japanese were able to demonstrate the extreme weakness of the European empires by rapidly overrunning all of their colonies in the Far East and Southeast Asia in 1941–2. They used their alliance with Thailand to attack Burma, bringing them within reach of British India itself (though they faced insurrection in Thailand as they did elsewhere in the territories they conquered). The Japanese also moved into the Pacific islands and began to threaten the security of Australia and New Zealand.

Elsewhere, the imperial status quo was further undermined by the fact that the allegiance of the French territories was divided into those which supported the German puppet Vichy government and those which allied themselves with the Free French. France's North African territories were ruled by the Vichy regime, as French West Africa was initially, while French Equatorial Africa supported the Free French forces of General de Gaulle. This divide was even apparent in North America where the tiny French islands of St. Pierre and Miquelon in the Gulf of St. Lawrence were loyal to the Vichy regime until captured (to the distress of the Americans) by the Free French, with Churchill's support, to remove any threat to Canada. French Vichy North Africa and Italian Libya ensured that a major campaign would be fought along the Mediterranean shore, with the British and later the Americans using Egypt as their base.

The Japanese occupation of the Asian territories of western empires helped to stimulate the emergence of communist resistance movements. These were a feature of resistance to Japan in Indochina, Malaya, and Indonesia. With the defeat of Japan after the dropping of the atomic bombs on Hiroshima and Nagasaki, the Americans became convinced that the western empires had to be removed from the region. Their very weakness might ensure the spread of communist ideology, as had happened in North Korea after the withdrawal of Japan. The Korean War and the partitioning of that country was one of the legacies of Japanese imperialism. The Dutch, much weakened by German occupation of the Netherlands, were unable to resume their colonial authority and Indonesia became independent in 1949 after an insurrection led by Sukarno. The French attempted to return to Indochina and suppress communist insurrection, but they were effectively defeated at the Battle of Dien Bien Phu in 1954. The subsequent Geneva agreements partitioned the country, though the communist north sought to reunite it in subsequent years. By 1964, the Americans had been drawn into the exceptionally violent and destructive Vietnam War, a war which the Americans lost and which caused a major rethinking of American policy.

Meanwhile in Malaya the British used a number of techniques, including the creation of fortified villages and a "hearts and minds" campaign, to defeat a communist insurgency which was mainly inspired and conducted by ethnic Chinese. The fact that the British wished to hand power to indigenous Malays who had little sympathy with the Chinese insurgency greatly helped the British in their suppression of the revolt.

## Decolonization

The postwar era, as with the interwar years, has something of a paradoxical feel to it. No one would predict that the European empires were going to be largely decolonized within a quarter of a century. Both the French and the Portuguese attempted to consolidate their colonies with the metropole more strongly than before. The French and the British embarked on major schemes of investment in their colonies, the British through their Colonial Development and Welfare Acts and the French through the Fonds d'Investissement pour le Développement Economique et Sociale. The League of Nations mandates, particularly those in Africa and the Pacific, were transferred (with the exception of Southwest Africa) to the United Nations trusteeship system. African colonies in particular seemed to be a long way from achieving independence. Yet the reality was that a vast colonial logjam was beginning to move as

it was propelled by floods within both the international system and the social and political systems of the individual territories.

The most notable act of decolonization of the period was the British departure from India. And this abandonment by Britain of its major imperial territory highlights some of the significant issues surrounding the decolonization process. India had, in effect, become increasingly ungovernable in the years leading up to and including the Second World War. The British never moved at a speed which would satisfy Indian aspirations. In 1935, the Government of India Act had devolved some domestic powers to the Indian provinces in a mixed system which was known as "dyarchy." While Indians came to control many internal matters, the British held on to the major levers of authority at the center, notably defense and foreign affairs. When the Second World War broke out, the viceroy, Lord Linlithgow, immediately declared war on behalf of India without any consultation with Indian politicians. While he was strictly within his powers in doing so, it was a highly undiplomatic move which deeply offended Indians. While India, both in the form of the nationalist movements and in the shape of the princely states, had remained loyal during the First World War, this was not to be the case in the Second. In 1941, the Quit India movement was instigated and many leading Indian politicians, including Gandhi, were imprisoned.

By this time, the Indian nationalist movement had lost all semblance of unity. The Indian National Congress had originally been founded on a nonsectarian basis, but the Muslim League had successfully developed its communal base, not least through the provincial elections which took place under the 1935 constitution. The League was able to campaign effectively during the war when the Indian National Congress was in many ways disabled. In the course of the war, the British promised that dominion status would be granted to India after its conclusion. But by this time the ambitions of Indian politicians had moved on. The dominion status which had been developed by the territories of white settlement no longer appealed and only a full independence, with republican status, would suffice. After the war, it was abundantly apparent that the British, struggling with massive debts, could not afford to maintain extensive armed forces and other personnel in India. The Labour government of Clement Attlee decided that independence had to be granted as soon as possible. Lord Mountbatten was sent to carry out the job and he soon decided, to the horror of Congress, that only partition of the subcontinent would satisfy the demands of Muslims and avoid civil strife. The date of independence was brought forward and the political arrangements as well as the "division of the spoils" took place in a helter-skelter manner. A boundary commission sought to establish the incidence of Muslim populations, with the result that a partition line was duly established which left millions of Hindus and Muslims stranded on either side of the line, causing a massive exchange of populations (ten million Hindus from Pakistan to India and seven and a half million Muslims in the other direction), with over a million people killed in communal strife. The princely states were encouraged to abandon the remnants of their sovereignty. A new state with the synthetic name of "Pakistan" (made up from the initial letters of some of its provinces) emerged and was divided into the larger West and the smaller East. This was to prove a highly unstable arrangement. Pakistani politics became notably more turbulent and less stable than those of India, and in 1971, after the Indo-Pakistan War, the ill-favored East broke away to become the independent state of Bangladesh.

The British were now in rapid retreat. Sri Lanka (the former Ceylon) and Burma became independent in 1948. In that year, the Indian government discovered a formula whereby it could remain a member of the Commonwealth despite being a republic, King George VI being recognized as titular head of the Commonwealth. The same notion was adopted by Sri Lanka, but Burma left the Commonwealth, as had the Republic of Ireland. Meanwhile, in the Middle East the British had effectively bestowed independence upon Mesopotamia (Iraq) and Transjordan (Jordan). Perhaps the most shameful British departure from the region occurred in Palestine. There the numbers of Jews arriving to escape Nazi Germany had become a flood. The British, mindful of the rights of the Arab Muslim population, attempted to stem this flow, but were put under considerable pressure by Jewish resistance, notably through the Irgun and the Stern gang, which behaved as terrorist organizations. The situation became so uncontrollable that the British decided to cut and run. Jewish settlers fought the first of their several wars against Palestinians and other Arabs, succeeding in establishing the state of Israel in 1948.

Once the communist insurrection had been suppressed, the British set about decolonizing in Southeast Asia. There, as in other parts of their empire in Africa and the Caribbean, they hoped to decolonize to larger states by instituting a federation. The Malay states, where the traditional rulers had continued to exercise some authority, had been federated since 1896. Malaya secured its independence in 1957 and, in 1963, moved into a federation with Singapore, North Borneo, and Sarawak (Brunei refused to join). The major problem with this was that the population of Singapore was predominantly Chinese and this imbalanced the delicate demographic structure of the new territory. The Singaporeans soon felt that their best interests would be served by the creation in 1965 of an independent island state.

In Africa, the post-Second World War era threw up severe economic and social strains. Many black soldiers who had served in the Second World War (the British, for example, had employed them in the Burma campaign) returned to their home colonies and agitated for more employment opportunities. Postwar reconstruction was inhibited by unstable commercial conditions and developing nationalist movements had fertile social soil in which to generate. The British began the processes of decolonization in West Africa, generally seen as more "advanced" than the eastern and central colonies, granting a degree of internal self-government in Ghana as early as 1951. Once this door was partly open, politicians and their followers pushed for further rapid constitutional advance. Ghana became independent in 1957, swiftly followed by the other British territories – Nigeria, Sierra Leone, and the Gambia. By contrast, the French tried to tie French West Africa and French Equatorial Africa (federations of colonies) more tightly into the constitutional and political arrangements of the postwar Fourth Republic. But by the 1960s these attempts at forms of integration were becoming shakier.

The 1960s turned out to be the decade of decolonization. The violent Mau Mau campaign in Kenya, coinciding with the Malay emergency and intercommunal strife in Cyprus, convinced the British government that the continuation of formal empire was impractical. Although they had hoped to maintain the power and significance of the "sterling area" as a trading partnership through a common currency, the military and financial realities were increasingly apparent. The British also decided to abolish the conscription of young men into the army and concentrate on a smaller professional force. In swift succession, the British departed from Kenya, Uganda, and Tanganyika, the latter combining with the island of Zanzibar to become Tanzania. The inauguration of the Fifth Republic and Charles de Gaulle's assumption of the presidency led to the French withdrawal from their African territories in West and Equatorial Africa in 1960. Tunisia and Morocco had secured independence in 1955–6, but Algeria was much more fraught because of the presence of so many French settlers (or pieds noirs). Against strenuous opposition amounting almost to a civil war, Algeria was granted independence in 1962. France (like Portugal later) provided an example of colonial conflict producing major political change in the metropolitan state. The Belgians also departed from their vast Congolese territory in 1960 after unrest had made their rule untenable. The Congo risked falling apart in the face of separatist movements in the Katanga, the copper-rich region in the south.

The British had attempted to stave off decolonization in Central Africa (on the grounds that the numbers of educated Africans were insufficient and that the technical, social, and political infrastructures were inadequate) by creating in 1953 the Central Africa Federation of Southern and Northern Rhodesia together with Nyasaland. It was soon apparent that this was a means of maintaining white power in the region and African nationalism was galvanized into action. A Declaration of Emergency was made in 1959 after considerable resistance and rioting in Northern Rhodesia and Nyasaland. The federation was broken up and these two countries became independent as Zambia and Malawi. Further south, Britain also gave independence to three states which had been, in economic terms, hostages to South Africa: Bechuanaland (Botswana), Basutoland (Lesotho), and Swaziland. The South African government had made attempts in the twentieth century to incorporate these territories as part of its expansionist drive, but the British had maintained control.

The zone of white power in Africa rapidly retreated, though pockets of whites set up considerable resistance. In 1965, the prime minister of Southern Rhodesia, Ian Smith, declared unilateral independence from the British. The British government failed to intervene and, despite United Nations sanctions, the territory continued under white rule until 1980, when it was decolonized as Zimbabwe. It had been able to do so only because of the support of the apartheid regime in South Africa, which had come to power in 1948. This regime seemed more or less invincible, despite extensive African resistance which, after the independence of Zimbabwe, became increasingly violent and transcended frontiers. But progressive geopolitical changes in the region, together with sanctions and increasing white, as well as black, restlessness, produced dramatic change. The Portuguese quasi-fascist government was overturned in 1974, partly as a result of the tremendous drain on resources caused by campaigns in Portuguese Guinea, Angola, and Mozambique. These territories became independent in the following year and the two in southern Africa immediately gave sanctuary to anti-South African guerrilla movements. They were also the victims of civil wars, exacerbated by South African support for insurgent groups. South Africa itself attempted a wholly spurious form of internal decolonization, pursuing a myth that every African had a "Homeland" (or Bantustan) which could become a semi-independent country. These territories never received any international diplomatic recognition except from Israel.

However, by 1994 the zone of white power in southern Africa had finally been eliminated. In a remarkable series of events, the leading nationalist Nelson Mandela and his associates were released from prison and the white government abdicated to what became known as "the great transformation." Namibia, ruled from South Africa since it had been a German colony, became independent in 1990. Moreover, from 1989 onwards, the Soviet Empire, based on that of the Romanovs and on the outcomes of the Second World War, began to fall apart. The Berlin Wall came down; Germany was reunited; the eastern European states that had been in the Soviet bloc now sought to realign with the West, including applying for membership of the European Union. Many of the former Soviet republics of Central Asia and the Black Sea region emerged as independent states.

One of the final acts of supposed decolonization of the century was the British abandonment of Hong Kong in 1997, when the lease on the New Territories ran out. Hong Kong was merely handed over by one empire, the British, to another, the Chinese (which had consolidated its hold over Tibet after the crushing of a rising in 1959). The effect of all these acts of decolonization was to enlarge the international nation-state order. Traditional indigenous authorities had, by and large, been overturned, and bourgeois nationalists, more or less educated in western styles, had come to control their political fortunes, not always in the best interests of their peoples. By the end of the twentieth century, it was apparent that Asia was going to be the continent of the twenty-first. The "tiger economies" of the Pacific Rim had already begun their period of striking growth and China was emerging as a major force. Some would argue that, with the decline of Russia as a superpower, the United States and China operate quasi-imperial functions in the world. The regulation of world trading and investment systems, formerly in the hands of the imperial powers, has been transferred to the World Bank, the International Monetary Fund, the "Group of Eight," and other modes of international economic management. The world remains divided, as in imperial times, into the powerful and the rich on the one hand, and the weak and the poor on the other. This is reflected in strikingly unequal patterns of consumption, education, and health and in the frustrated ambitions of many people to transfer into the more prosperous states.

## GUIDE TO FURTHER READING

C. M. Andrew and A. S. Kanya Forster, *France Overseas: The Great War and the Climax of French Imperial Expansion* (London: Thames & Hudson, 1981). A valuable study of French imperialism.

F. Ansprenger, *The Dissolution of the Colonial Empires* (London: Routledge, 1989). Good on the process of decolonization.

C. A. Bayly, *The Birth of the Modern World, 1780–1914* (Oxford: Blackwell, 2004). Contains an immensely stimulating discussion of imperialism and globalization in the formation of the power relationships of today.

Judith M. Brown and William Roger Louis, eds., *The Oxford History of the British Empire*, vol. 4, *The Twentieth Century* (Oxford: Oxford University Press, 1999). Valuable essays on the British Empire.

Gervase Clarence-Smith, *The Third Portuguese Empire, 1825–1975: A Study in Economic Imperialism* (Manchester: Manchester University Press, 1985). Offers a corrective to earlier interpretations of Portuguese imperialism.

John Darwin, *Britain and Decolonisation: The Retreat from Empire in the Post-War World* (Basingstoke: Penguin, 1988). Excellent on British decolonisation.

D. K. Fieldhouse, *The Colonial Empires: A Comparative Survey from the Eighteenth Century* (London: Weidenfeld & Nicolson, 1966). An older work that remains a valuable examination of all the European empires.

R. F. Holland, *European Decolonisation 1918–1981* (Basingstoke: Penguin, 1985). A useful overview of the process of decolonization.

Paul Kennedy, *The Realities behind Diplomacy: Background Influences on British External Policy, 1865–1980* (London: Allen & Unwin, 1981). An analysis which offers some insights into imperialism; also see the modern sections of his *The Rise and Fall of the Great Powers: Economic Change and Military Conflict from 1500 to 2000* (London: Unwin Hyman, 1988).

V. G. Kiernan, *European Empires from Conquest to Collapse* (Leicester: Leicester University Press, 1982). Offers comparative insights on imperialism.

M. Kuitenbrouwer, *The Netherlands and the Rise of Modern Imperialism: Colonies and Foreign Policy* (Oxford and New York: Berg, 1991). Good background on Dutch imperialism.

William L. Langer, *The Diplomacy of Imperialism 1890–1902* (New York: Knopf, 1935). An older work that continues to offer an excellent background to imperialism in the international relations of the early twentieth century.

Dominic Lieven, *Empire: The Russian Empire and its Rivals from the Sixteenth Century to the Present* (London: Pimlico, 2003). A magisterial sweep through Russian history down to modern times.

P. J. Marshall, ed., *The Cambridge Illustrated History of the British Empire* (Cambridge: Cambridge University Press, 1996). Offers useful background on various aspects of imperial culture and international relations.

Wolfgang J. Mommsen and Jurgen Osterhammel, eds., *Imperialism and After: Continuities and Disconti-nuities* (London: Allen & Unwin, 1986). Contains much useful discussion of informal empire and the role of imperialism in the dynamic balance of international relations.

Jane Samson, ed., *The British Empire* (Oxford: Oxford University Press, 2001). Readings that illumi-nate various aspects of imperialism, including the diplomatic.

Tony Smith, *The Pattern of Imperialism: The United States, Great Britain, and the Late-Industrialising World since 1815* (Cambridge: Cambridge University Press, 1981). Good on the shift in power from Britain to the United States in the late nineteenth and early twentieth centuries.

Woodruff D. Smith, *The German Colonial Empire* (Chapel Hill, NC: University of North Carolina Press, 1978). A useful study of German imperialism.

Martin Thomas, *The French Empire between the Wars* (Manchester: Manchester University Press, 2005). Good on this period of French imperialism.

Hans-Ulrich Wehler, *The German Empire, 1871–1918* (Leamington Spa: Berg, 1985). An influential study of German imperialism that emphasizes the impor-tance of social structures.

# CHAPTER TWO

# Nationalism

## R. J. B. BOSWORTH

*Fluellen*: Captain MacMorris, I think, look you, under your correction, there is not many of
your nation –
*MacMorris*: Of my nation? What ish my nation? Ish a villain and a bastard and a knave and a
rascal? What ish my nation? Who talks of my nation?

So, in 1599, William Shakespeare portrayed in
*Henry V*, a play that often reads as a paean to
English glory, a Welshman and an Irishman quar-
reling. Perhaps they do so because of their individual personalities. But they rapidly evoke their
"nations" to fuel their contest and reinforce their
identities. In telling phrases, Shakespeare suggests
the visceral power of what was then not yet called
nationalism, its potent allure and its malign, divisive, and violent character. Fluellen and MacMorris, it is implied, are men ready to "die for their
nation."

They therefore well introduce a subject that is
impossible to study without reflection on its
ability to inspire both sacrifice and murder and to
occasion both good and evil. For all the talk of
globalization, presently the nation, though in one
view challenged and in another fearfully expanded
by religious fundamentalism, lies at the heart of
our most dearly held collective identities and our
best established practices of governance. In the
twenty-first century, the great majority of human
beings own a national passport, pay taxes to a
national government, serve in a national army,
cheer a national sporting team, rejoice at a national
festival, use the adjectival form of their nation to
define themselves, or do all of the above. The
planet Earth, it often seems, is and long has been
structured into national groups.

A globe chopped up into nations is one matter,
but the difference is always itself arranged into a
hierarchy. It is not, and never has been, possible

to "belong to a nation" without some yardstick
which excludes those who do not belong, which
measures the Other and finds it wanting. Nationalism has to be exclusive. Whatever might be
thought to guarantee membership of the nation
is always shadowed by factors that demonstrate
that there are those who cannot claim this nationality. Here lie dangers since logic, passion, and
practicality suggest that the Other is malevolent
and dangerous. The establishment of a settled
hierarchy and its associated process of exclusion
may be forceful, or, not to put too fine a point on
it, bloody. For at least a century the happy idea of
belonging has been twinned with the unhappy
one of "ethnic cleansing," a quasi-medical undertaking designed to ensure that "we" are pure and
healthy, safe and victorious.[1]

The hierarchy of nations, in other words, can
never be fully cemented into place. Instead it
heaves with contest, ambition, and discontent.
Many nations, many quarrels, both external and
internal, becomes the rule. Nor is such perennial
disputation the only canker concealed below the
social cohesion of love for the nation. Perhaps
always but certainly now more than ever, identification with a nation prompts reflection on bad
times as well as good ones over an allegedly long
history. In our new millennium, national identity
often fixes on some terrible tragedy, the moment
when members of the nation were victims, and
survivors, of some past "holocaust." This memory
enhances the present and future virtue of the

nation and steels its determination to defend its cause to the uttermost. Having been a victim in history makes it easier to feel good about being tough when defending the nation in the here and now.

## Arguing about the Nation

Given that nationalism is such a ubiquitous and dominating feature of modern life, it is not surprising that theoreticians from almost every field have commented on it. Among the historians and social scientists, key figures include Ernst Gellner, Eric Hobsbawm, Benedict Anderson, and Anthony D. Smith. Their interpretations of the subject vary. Yet all agree that the nation is, in essence, an idea, with only Smith pressing the line that ethnic identity has a very long history and carries roots which penetrate deeply or "organically" (to use a favored nationalist term) into society. The others argue that nationalism is a modern matter, generated through the political, economic, social, and cultural impact of the Enlightenment and the French Revolution. The Marxist Hobsbawm is the most convinced that the nation is a fake and illusion, a "false consciousness," imposed on humankind by "inventors of tradition"[2] who, for one reason or another, saw benefit in a world of nations rather than a global collectivity, and did so for their own malevolent reasons. Benedict Anderson, whose initial work on the subject was stimulated by his experience in Asia rather than Europe, is more optimistically ready to grant a genuine popular base to what he has memorably called "imagined communities," arguing that, in its replacement of premodern familial, kinship, patron–client, owner–slave, or other loyalties and connections, the nation has brought people more joy and comfort than persecution and killing.[3]

## The Nation Defined: Nature

What factors, then, might constitute the bases of a nation? Here it is easy to make the conventional list, which scholars might query but which most nationalized citizens take as read. If planet Earth is sundered into nations, the reason is obvious. Geography divides the world. Here a river, there a

sea; here a mountain chain and its watersheds, there a plain. The placement of these natural features seems eternal, "god-given." How simple, then, it is to decide that the Pyrenees would not be where they are unless a French nation was meant to be separated from a Spanish one (Catalans, Basques, Portuguese, and immigrants may be a problem, somewhere in the fine print of this geographical story). Japan is Japan, Malta Malta, and Australia Australia because each is an island (of rather differing size). The Rhine and the Danube, as they flow to the North and Black Seas, mark out the natural borders of Germandom, roughly speaking. The plains that stretch beyond the Alleghenies explain the manifest destiny of the United States to rule the land from sea to shining sea. The "boundless" Central Asian steppe prompts the Russian imperium. Every nation hails its existing borders or justifies its pretensions to expand to new ones by appeals to "natural features." All nationalists are likely to wax lyrical about the virtues of their "native soil" and to imply that it is different from that of others. Plants or animals or a native cuisine symbolize national difference. A tulip or a chrysanthemum or a kiwi or a tiger or a plate of *spaghetti al dente* or a pint of Guinness make it my country, not yours.

This discourse about "blood and soil" was severely besmirched when it became a central plank in the philosophy and practice of Nazi Germany. Yet, as the appalling history of that regime fades from memory or is reduced to being no more than Shoah business, the vocabulary and habits of "natural" belonging have resurfaced in our contemporary world. Why did the feverishly traveling pope, John Paul II, always stoop to kiss the soil (in practice the airport tarmac) of the latest country that he was visiting except to give his Catholic blessing to the local national civic religion? Why do we grow misty-eyed at other evocations of our "native land," unless we somehow frame its soil as timeless and elemental, greater than us and, in quite a few senses, our eternal "mother"?

It does not take very long to see that most of these ideas and assumptions about geography and the natural world are delusions. Every aspect of nature is in fact in flux. The earth is constantly evolving, both on its own part and as a result of human intervention. The "soil" that once was farmed is now concreted over by the spreading streets and suburbs of Mexico City, Moscow, or Mumbai. Rivers are channeled to stop their deadly and destructive "natural" floods; lakes retreat; the sea eats into coastlines. Flora and fauna do not stay the same, with migration being but one factor of change.

Moreover, physical alteration is not the only story since what human beings understand by nature alters over time. The idea that the sea and the beach are places of leisure, sex, sun, and sport began only a century ago among the richer peoples and is still not universally accepted. European Romanticism invented much of the appeal and meaning of the mountain. Some societies see benefit in "fresh air"; others fear it. Humans do not universally agree on what constitutes cold and heat. An Icelander goes in shirtsleeves at 15°C; a Jamaican shivers. Wherever you look there is little that is natural or primordial about nature.

## The Nation Defined: Language

When advocates of soil and blood turned from extolling nature, they typically found the next proof of the nation in language. People, it is assumed, know that they belong to their nation because they speak one language, while foreigners use other tongues. When early postwar Australia was convincing itself that it could cope with non-British migrants, a social scientist implied that no good Australian wanted newcomers to use their "language" – his assumption apparently was that foreigners just spoke foreign – in "public places."[4] The French Academy zealously, if ineffectually, strives to expunge franglais from demeaning the glorious national language. The framers of the Oxford English Dictionary boasted that their sensible Englishness was reflected in their readiness to admit linguistic change (but only at the borders of the vast empire of words their dictionary hammered into place). All modern European nation-states were justified linguistically. Italians, it was argued, spoke Italian and so were Italian; Norwegians spoke Norwegian and so must leave the Swedish Crown; Latvians spoke Latvian and so should not be gobbled up by a Russian or Soviet empire.

Again, however, a moment's reflection will explode any claim that language charts the frontiers of national belonging. Nicholas Ostler asserts that there are some 6,800 languages still existing on the planet, although he complains that one dies out every fortnight.[5] Even if autonomous zones are generously assumed to be proto-nations, the present world possesses only some 230 states and the inhabitants of many speak such great imperial languages as English, Spanish, or Arabic. Language cannot assure that you are Canadian or Paraguayan or Yemeni. In any case, arithmetic demonstrates that the possession of a language does not equate with the ownership of a state. Moreover, languages, even more than nature, are perpetually affected by human manipulation. Hebrew, modern Greek, Italian, each is a way of speech that was invented after the nations of Israel, Greece, and Italy came into existence or where the linguistic invention was part of the political process of nation-building. Nor are other languages different in their trajectories. None of us speaks as once our "ancestors" did.

Any subtle mapping of linguistic behavior is still more complicated. Languages are affected certainly by class and perhaps by gender. Since human beings have always moved and, in the twenty-first century, probably the majority of humankind has some migrant experience, each language is likely to be jostled by another and in the jostling borrowing is inevitable. No doubt we live in a society where there is much pressure on us to homogenize. Nonetheless, many human beings speak more than one language and everyone uses a certain vocabulary in the office or on the factory floor, another in bed, and yet another as death approaches. It may be true that we speak and therefore we are, but speech is complex; it does not express primordial certainty.

## The Nation Defined: Culture and History

When those who sketch the lineaments of the nation are confronted with such objections, they often have recourse to the vaguer idea of a national "culture." A guide book trying to explain the mysteries of Italy to postwar tourists was sure that "the Italian type can be very easily distinguished among other ethnical [*sic*] groups of Europe" and then went on to list behavior, art, food, and physiognomy as proof.[6] The claim typically is, then, that "history," amply drawn, is what makes a nation. Common experience lies behind a common culture. A national people live in communion with those generations that preceded them, just as they are bonded to their future heirs.

This relationship between history and the nation is troubling for professional historians, just as it is often rewarding for those who comb the past for national patterns, utilizing the tools of memory or celebratory non-academic history. Hobsbawm set down as dogma that no "serious historian of nations and nationalism can be a committed political nationalist." "Nationalism requires too much belief in what is patently not so," he stated superbly.[7]

Being superb carries a tinge of arrogance. Certainly, despite the Hobsbawm doctrine, the nation and its cause are imbricated into the practice of history in every country. In Australia, nowadays you are expected to justify each research funding application by displaying the benefit your work will bring to the nation. The present may be seeing a more florid growth of such interference in the quest to comprehend the human condition, but the discipline of history has always been propelled by its relationship with the nation. History became a subject with its own academic borders, its own rights to university courses, its own professional journals and monographs at the moment when most commentators agree that nations and nationalism were born. The *English* and *American Historical Review* and the *Rivista Storica Italiana* bore their titles because they purveyed the English, American, and Italian view of the past and their most significant articles focused on their nations' histories. The *Revue Historique* and *Historische Zeitschrift* left out the words French and German but otherwise did the same for a French and German past. Peter Novick may have written movingly about the "noble dream" of the practitioners of history in science and objectivity, implying that our discipline must be a cosmopolitan undertaking,[8] yet the majority of university history courses in every country have been and remain linked to a national past.

In the nineteenth century historian-forgers of the nation could be found in every country or proto-country. Michelet thrummed the French soul; Bancroft did the same in the United States. Each used a biblical vocabulary to preach the gospel of their nation's past. Frantisek Palacky acted as a midwife to the Czech nation by writing its multivolume history. With some paradox the language he used was German. Every Balkan people found a historian ready to evoke thrilling past glory, to mourn their nation's unfair blotting out, and to advocate urgent national revival. In the twentieth century, the process became ever more complicated, especially as a post-imperial world unveiled numerous new nations in Latin America, Africa, Asia, and the Pacific. In such places, the most obvious reason of being was an artificial line drawn by an erstwhile imperial administrator, but where history now had to discern some more noble and popular derivation. No nation has ever been able to contemplate existence in the present alone. Time is the first zone to require national control. Identity is meaningless unless it conjoins future and past to what is presently occurring. History is both the primary tool of "nation-building" and, when pursued rigorously, the most trenchant critic of this process.

This wrenching into national service of a usable past should not surprise. Nations are not the only social institutions to behave that way. Families are prone to look to history for comfort and defense. With women often acting as the chroniclers of a hearth kept warm not merely for the day, the family has long sought deep roots. At the extremity of effrontery, every monarchy, whether in Europe or elsewhere, traces a heritage of the present dynasty back to the gods. Genealogists can show that the lackluster Windsors, titular heads of the surviving British Commonwealth, number Wotan among their ancestors. Roman emperors were elevated to the celestial realm at or before their deaths, with the plainspoken soldier, Vespasian, in 79 AD earning himself a place on the honor role of skeptics by remarking laughingly as he drew his last breath that he could feel himself being transmuted into a god. Less grand families did not behave differently. Contemporary researchers have traced the "imaginary genealogies" treasured by ordinary men and women in Renaissance Italy and, in the twenty-first century, the family history business is a global enterprise.

## The Nation Defined: Myth

Over the last two centuries, the term that has become most associated with this adaptation of time is "myth." Nations, it is said, have harnessed myths to win the people over and, more positively, to express the popular longing for collective identity. George Mosse, a historian with his own fascinating personal, family, and ideological path, coined the term "nationalization of the masses" to trace how the growth of the nation was underpinned by the teaching of history.[9] In the Enlightenment, he affirmed, the process to be called modernization began. Fundamental to it was the "death of God" since human beings believed that they could become the agents of their own perfection. Armed with rationality, they could classify and assess the world, and deploy science to improve human circumstance, overcoming their ancestors' subjugation to religion, belief, and magic. Politically, the French revolutionary state sparked the process through which sovereignty could no more be passed by an unseen and imponderable god to a monarch, acting as vice-regent over an earthly realm. Rather, now was the time for the triumph of the "popular will," when the rights of the people surpassed any selfish claims by dynasts and their aristocratic courts.

This sketch of the hopes and rhetoric of the revolutionary era can be shown to possess many flaws when exposed to the sobriety of historical research. The French Revolution scarcely delivered universal liberty, equality, and fraternity. Yet, the issue was neither the extent to which *anciens régimes* lingered in Europe nor the hypocrisy and cruelty of much revolutionary practice, nor yet its irrelevance to many women, peasants, and slaves. Instead what mattered, and what became universal in the twentieth century, was that, when the old god, acting as the architect of social peace and order, was put out the window, another god crept in as replacement. This deity was the god of the nation. To be more accurate, there now arrived the competing gods of the competing nations. Revolutionary rule in Paris, it was noticed, was accompanied by ceremony and symbol in a fashion that was more overbearing than it had been under the Bourbon kings. Men and women, Mosse maintained, could not live without faith. Even as they bravely harnessed science to universal benefit, they paradoxically needed new national myths and festivals to convince themselves of their own belonging.

The most durable and ubiquitous expressions of this modern faith were national flags and anthems. The French tricolor communicated the immediate gospel of the triumph of the French Revolution but its enduring message was that France was a united and powerful nation. Once the Church had paraded the images of saints and the Virgin to cheer and rally the populace. Evocations of an extraterrestrial presence shored up the rule of earthly kings, popes, archbishops, and aristocracies. Similarly, premodern religious services had been warmed spiritually by the hymns and chants of the Church. Now the Church was disestablished and the people sang national anthems, with the militant and aggressive *La Marseillaise* acting as the model for the rest. While the process of the nationalization of the masses spread across Europe and the world, so the national flag and the national anthem were made to incarnate the people. Still today such objects are often labeled "holy" symbols. Those who traduce or tear the flag, it is frequently argued, should be punished for their insult to the nation. Their behavior is blasphemous. Sporting teams and their fans arouse themselves emotionally before a match by intoning the national anthem while standing to attention, with clenched right fists placed over their hearts to emphasize their total commitment to their country's cause. Politicians ostentatiously pin onto their lapels badges of their flag, thereby apparently guaranteeing that they will back their nation to the uttermost at the current international meeting. The nation, it seems, is the fount of a civic religion that, in its mystery and power, possesses all dutiful citizens of a democratic state based on popular sovereignty at least as soulfully as once premodern and world-ranging religions held people in thrall.

In analyzing these processes, Mosse was partially motivated by his own history. His family were assimilated liberal and patriotic German Jews, from a sector of society appalled and assaulted by the rise of the Nazis. Mosse escaped this horror to find sanctuary successively in fascist Italy, liberal democratic Britain, and the United States. Much of his research was clinical in intent in wanting to expose what it was that made Germans carry the irrationalities of the nationalized masses to a frenzy in the Final Solution. Yet, with his Jewish heritage, however lay and unnational it may have originally been, Mosse lived to watch the creation of the state of Israel in 1948 and the subsequent nationalizing through myth of the Jewish or Zionist masses, the vast majority of them immigrants.

The exquisite dilemmas of a Jewish nation will be considered further below. For the moment it is necessary rather to note that, although the nationalization of the masses may have paved a dark path toward Auschwitz, it also coincided with the spread of the Industrial Revolution and what contemporaries called Progress, that is, the improvement in the economic well-being of humankind. Critics may be troubled by the "dark, satanic mills" and mines in nineteenth-century Europe and in the Third World even now. Yet it is hard to deny that men and women in the twenty-first century live longer, are taller and healthier, and have more options in their lives than was dreamed of before 1789. Those who hail the nation say, logically enough, that, if the winning political form from 1789 to 2000 was the nation, then its presence must have assisted and ensured these evident advances in overall well-being. The time of the nations, they urge with some conviction, was the happiest era in human history.

## The Nation before the Nation

Perhaps. But, before proceeding to a more detailed analysis of the history of the nations and nationalism in the twentieth century, it is worthwhile to ponder whether nations existed before the Enlightenment. Anthony Smith argues this case and plenty of historians of the early modern period in Europe or of the Chinese past automatically use the word nation to describe the societies they study. Richard Cœur de Lion,

largely absentee king of England (1189–99), his biographer states, "had come to represent the English nation, a man whose wars were demonstrations of English superiority over other nations, especially the French."[10] Before 1066, the author of a study of the "first English empire" (1093–1343) contends, Anglo-Saxon England "was becoming a powerfully imagined community, a nation-state." After the Norman conquest, the process accelerated, bolstered by an invention of tradition that bore comparison to that known much later. "In the past-oriented and past-validating societies" of the Middle Ages, "control and exploitation of the past" were "critical to credibility in the present," perhaps paradoxically so given that the nineteenth and twentieth centuries, when professional history was to flourish, were future-oriented cultures which similarly drew sustenance from their control (and understanding) of the past. All in all, it is claimed with a predictable hint of hierarchy and competition, England was "much the earliest as it was the most enduring of European nation states."[11]

Yet a contrary view of what might constitute identity can be detected in such realms. An "English" chronicler, writing in Latin, pictured a minor battle in 1138 as fought between "Normans, Germans, English, Northumbrians, Cumbrians, men of Teviotdale and Lothian, Picts (who are commonly called Galwegians) and Scots."[12] Under the conquering Henry V, three centuries later, a monk-historian, who was patriotically sure that Joseph of Arimathaea had brought Christianity to England well before St. Denis had transported it to France, proclaimed that the "English nation" used six languages – English English, Scots English, Welsh, Irish, Cornish, and Gascon – and that number proved its superiority over the French nation, which spoke only French.[13] Similarly, in the infant Paris university of 1220, students were categorized into four "nations," the Normans, Picards, "English," who embraced most of northern Europe, and the "French," who included men from the Italian peninsula.[14]

At best, then, while it may be conceded that premodern societies used the word "nation" commonly enough, the usage lacked the precision and commitment that it would acquire after 1789. In premodern societies, the framing of borders between states was scarcely as fixed as it was to become in modern times. More significantly, the gaps between classes and genders, clerical and lay, corporatized artisans and the unskilled, dwellers in town or countryside, the literate and the illiterate, and free men and slaves were huge, accepted, and, if not in every circumstance continuing, regularly passed from one generation to the next in a way that mocked later accounts of a coherent and united national community or a nation heartened by the popular will.

## The Nineteenth-Century Nation

The changes that modernity has brought in the way we consider everything are so immense and profound that it is fruitless to spend long speculating about currents of premodern nationalism. The world order was severely challenged by the conflicts of the revolutionary era from 1789 to 1815 and its decades of global war. The leading figure of the time, the eventual self-proclaimed French emperor Napoleon Bonaparte, embodied the move to modernity, given his own youthful ability in precise (or precise-seeming) mathematics and his later forceful imposition of organized, centralized, and scientific "Jacobin" rule. Napoleon's mind and personality brilliantly expressed the new desire to classify and improve the world. Since Napoleon was born in Corsica, an island which had acknowledged Bourbon rule for only a few decades (not for nothing would later Italian nationalists assert that the great conqueror was "really" Italian), and to a family whose behavior was heavily conditioned by Mediterranean familism, he can be comprehended as simultaneously carrying the future of a modern French nation and the past of a world in which national division was not clear cut.

However many opposing tendencies eddied through Napoleon's personal history, there can be little doubt that the wars of his era sparked an acceleration in the birth of nations. First, the South American territories of the Spanish and Portuguese empires broke free from metropolitan rule, as did Greece and, in the second half of the century, the other Balkan states from Ottoman charge. Moreover, the revolutionary wars shook the old regimes in the Germanic and Italian states

in a fashion that soon led to the formation of an Italian nation-state in 1861 and a German one in 1870. Each was automatically hailed as a Great Power, joining France and Britain, perhaps already nations of a kind, and Austria-Hungary and Russia, the lingering multinational royal empires (although the Romanov dynasty, before 1914, was growing alert to the advantage which might come from evoking Russian nationalism).

The creation of Italy and Germany was not the end of the process. Norway became independent in 1905, while the First World War, waged as a conflict of the nations, resulted in the "revival" of Poland and Hungary, independence from Russia for the Baltic states and Finland, the creation of Czechoslovakia, drastic border changes for other European countries, and the promise of a world of "self-determination" as delineated by the US president, historian turned politician Woodrow Wilson, at the Paris peacemaking.

After the Second World War "self-determination" extended to the rest of the globe. Decolonization entailed the end of the British, French, and other European empires, at least in the direct sense, and, with India and Pakistan in the vanguard, the whole world now became nationalized. By the end of his presidency in 1920, Woodrow Wilson may have been an embattled and politically defeated figure but, after his death, he had become the prophet of modern times, just as his nation (if that was what it was), the United States, steadily advanced to be the greatest power in the world. Wilsonian "democracy" fused capitalism, liberalism, and nationality into a formula that still underpins political thought and action. Yet, the endless bloody crises that beset interwar Europe were proof that "Versailles" had scarcely mapped a path to domestic or international peace. Perhaps Wilson was deluded. Perhaps the marriage of freedom and self-determination meant not harmony but perpetual war.

Wilson's own role in the imposition of nationality should not be exaggerated. During the two centuries of the rise of the nations, many social changes were assisting the victories of the new political form. Modern industry functioned best in nations with territories that were contiguous and bounded, and not scattered at dynastic whim as had been true of the pre-1789 states. The railway, greatest symbol of nineteenth-century science, running from one city, one grouping of factories, one port, to the next, could not function effectively if it was expected to stop at too many frontiers. The locomotive might seem to promise full-scale free trade and the victory of the liberal universalism of Adam Smith and the "market" but, in practice, the spread and efficient functioning of railways, in many societies, required investment from, and management by, the state. Every country after 1815 saw the growth of a modern bureaucracy, the key mechanism through which the collectivity assisted and marshaled economic progress and human improvement.

Those who signed up to civil services needed to be trained. Every modern nation had as a crucial area of government an education policy, designed to harness the people's talents. It was useful and important to train doctors, architects, and engineers to improve physical health, encourage efficient building, and foster manufacturing. However, the fundamental subjects to be taught to bureaucrats and politicians were language and history. A literate society was the first step toward democracy, but the literacy came with a nationalized version of the nation's history. The rule became: to be modern we must be educated, to be educated we must be modern, and modernity, knowledge, and belonging were all embodied in the nation.

The hegemony of the national idea and the view that nationalism was the most cohesive way to manage humankind did have challengers. Monarchies, aristocracies, and such world-girding institutions as the Vatican were not wiped out by the French Revolution, but instead remained influential into the twentieth century, although often themselves acquiring a national gloss. Both technology and the market pushed liberal capitalism toward globalization. Yet, for a century after 1850, the most serious of non-believers in a nationalized world were a new force. In 1848, Karl Marx and Friedrich Engels reacted to the revolutions of that year, in common view the "seed time of the nations," the trialing of the union between liberalism and nationalism, with a universal heresy. Class, not ethnicity, they proclaimed, was what characterized modern times. It alone could achieve the final utopia of liberty, equality, fraternity, and sorority. The *Communist Manifesto* urged the workers of the entire world to unite and free themselves, disdaining the idea that they might be arranged into petty and competing nations. The disciplined "science" of Marx, it seemed to many, refuted the passionate faith of Giuseppe Mazzini, greatest preacher of a gospel of a national order of what he deemed the "historic" peoples of Europe.

## The Anti-Nation: Socialism

Until 1914, in almost every country, socialist movements, owing impulse to Marxist ideas, spread and flourished. Socialist parties and trade unions talked "revolution," prompting a huge fear among the existing elites that socialism controlled the future. The Marxist theory of history replicated the track of those trains steaming the modern era into every country. Presently the world was stopped at the station of the rule of the bourgeoisie. But, sooner or later, the "locomotive of history" would move to the final destination, Marxists maintained. Then the proletariat would overthrow their present capitalist masters and all would be free at the last station on the human track.

The reality was rather different from this simple image. With the biggest and most intellectually sophisticated Marxist movement, the German Social Democratic Party (SDP), offering a telling example, pre-1914 Marxists were as vulnerable as were others to the allure of the nation. When workers acquired greater prosperity, as, contrary to the vulgar reading of Marx, they were doing, they were ready to give credit to the nation and to find their belonging there. When the First World War broke out, the SDP delegates to the Reichstag (in 1912 they had become the most numerous party represented in the lower house of the Imperial German parliament) abandoned the principle that they must engage in a general strike to block nationalist warmongers abroad and at home. Instead they unanimously voted war credit to their reactionary but national government. In great majority other European socialists similarly mustered to their national cause, giving lie to the theory of the Socialist International, a body that had been promising to bureaucratize prewar universalism.

## The Anti-Nation: Communism

The First World War, with its preaching that even truth was national (as an Italian nationalist put it, Italian truth should not be confused with German, French, or other foreign truth), struck hard at any form of universal idea. Benito Mussolini who, when a prewar socialist, had derided his nation's flag as a "rag on a dung-heap,"[15] now demanded that his nation be forcefully bound into a whole by fascist dictatorship. Yet, in 1917, Russia was driven to retire from the war after power in the country's major cities was seized by Marxists in the Bolshevik Revolution. Although the practice of the Soviet regime scarcely brought happiness to the peoples of all the Russias, thereafter the USSR, until its fall at the end of the century, offered a model of a state where the nation was in theory subordinate to the collectivity, a union of socialist republics. Soviet "new" men and women (however old in reality) sang not a Russian national anthem but instead the *Internationale*, the hymn of the universally toiling masses.

With sublime irony, Joseph Stalin, the man who incarnated the tyranny that misgoverned the USSR, was born a Georgian (his enemies would say he was "really" an Ossete) from those southern frontier sectors that had only fallen to the Russian empire in the eighteenth and nineteenth centuries.[16] When jobs were shared out in the new revolutionary government, Stalin became Commissar of Nationalities and, if without profundity or conviction, he duly wrote tracts examining the nationality "problem" under Marxist rule. Both while the Stalin personality cult dominated the USSR from 1929 to 1953 and thereafter, the Marxist regime never quite made up its mind about what to do with the numerous complex cultures that it had inherited from Romanov rule. When it was fighting its "Great Patriotic War" against the Nazi invader from 1941 to 1945, the regime opted for Russian nationalism as a patriotic glue and the shades of Ivan the Terrible, Peter the Great, the generals who had defeated Napoleon in 1812, and even of the priests of the Orthodox Church were retooled by propaganda to steel the people in battle. On other occasions, however, the regime nourished local cultures, urged the retention and spread of local languages, and talked as though the Union of Soviet Socialist Republics was a free assembly of great and small.

## The Case of the Jews

As the historian Yuri Slezkine has contended, about no people was the USSR more ambiguous than the Jews,[17] while people of Jewish heritage were equally contradictory in how they measured their own identity against the reality and hope of international revolution. For no group was the triumph of nationalism more paradoxical in its effect than it was for the Jews. By 2005 there are scores of successor states established both in Europe and in Central Asia in which peoples who were once governed by the Romanov, Habsburg, and Hohenzollern empires have created nations from some part of what was imperial territory. Only for the Jews is the situation diverse. Since 1948, they do possess a nation-state. But, for this in considerable majority European people, the state is not located in Europe but in the Middle East, on land carved from land long ruled by the Ottomans and where a native people, now called the Palestinians, resided.

Israel can be portrayed as having a history on its side. Before the sacking of Jerusalem by Vespasian and his son Titus, a "Jewish state" existed and some historians assert that, of all premodern peoples, the Jews most closely resembled a nation even then. In recent times, however, matters become more controversial. What sort of people were nineteenth-century Jews? The answer varied from one part of Europe to another but, generally speaking, the Jews were a segment of society who had benefited greatly from the Enlightenment. Before 1789, for centuries they had been the targets of social and religious persecution. Pope Pius IX (1846–78), enemy of Italian Unification, was a surviving example of an old-fashioned anti-Semite, convinced that the Jews were Christ-killers. To overwhelm such prejudice, in Italy and in other European societies, logic said that Jews should welcome the new world. They should confine what belief they maintained in the Jewish religion to the private sphere and publicly cleave to the systems and civic religion of the nation. Many did, thinking themselves assimilated to their state and to modernity. Others, with not unrelated logic, followed Marx and socialism, and did so into the USSR after 1917. As Slezkine has underlined, many Soviet chiefs were Jewish and, certainly to 1945 and even after, Jews stood as a "national" group at or near the top of crucial sectors of Soviet society.

The choice, as Isaac Deutscher, historian and biographer of Stalin, was to phrase it, to be "a non-Jewish Jew"[18] was reinforced by the rise of racism and by that atrocious ideology's own derivation from nationalism. For the theoreticians of "scientific" racism, as for Adolf Hitler, the popularizer of their ideas and the politician who would seek to put them into practice, the Jews were the most alien people of Europe. Their menace, it was said, sprang from the fact that they lacked a proper national past within Europe. They had no "natural" territory there; they were not usually peasants. They spoke no single language. For anti-Semites, these absences proved that the Jews were "eternally" malign, the plotters of the downfall of real nations. Their crypto-universalism was demonstrated in Bolshevism or in the market, which they were thought to control. All was exposed, it was falsely said, in the *Protocols of the Elders of Zion*, a pre-1914 Russian forgery which was widely believed in the aftermath of the First World War. Two decades earlier, Theodore Herzl, based in that Habsburg Vienna where the "national problem" was debated most keenly, had in reaction sketched the creation of a Zionist state in Israel, with, he suggested, German as its "national language."[19]

Racists, twisting Wilsonian self-determination in an extreme manner, added (pseudo-)science to their recipe for comprehending the world, so opening the path to the attempted extermination of the Jews at Auschwitz. "Blood," they claimed, decided history; its presence and quality could be measured with the exactitude that, since the Enlightenment, had become the aim of understanding in every discipline. When, after 1933, the Nazis ruled Germany, the most powerful of the European states, and aimed to bring all Germans under German rule, they commenced policies which tabulated the Jews of Germany, Europe,

and, potentially, the world, categorizing them as bodies who did not belong. When war, especially the profoundly ideological Nazi–Soviet war, broke out, the terrible corollary was that the Jews must be "scientifically" eliminated in the "Final Solution." The optimistic classifying of the Enlightenment, with its hope to perfect humankind, and the nationalizing of the masses transmuted into the idea of a world divided into "races," combined to create a policy of universal murder.

## The Post-1945 Nation

Nazi-fascism was defeated in 1945 through the combined, if not always happily united, efforts of the USSR and the liberal West. The results were mixed in regard to the history of nations and nationalism. In 1948, the survivors of the Holocaust (as it was not yet universally known) were permitted by the Great Powers to establish the state of Israel from what had been the mandated territory of Palestine. The USSR, recovering with difficulty and tardiness from its own Second World War, turned in on itself to become for two generations a political and cultural gerontocracy, unwilling and unable to accept change and bewildered by the national divisions its rule had in practice sponsored. The "Cold War" between it and the "West" seemed of menace but, meanwhile, the great victor of the war, the United States, and its version of liberal and national capitalism, triumphed everywhere outside the communist bloc (whether led by the USSR or by China, which soon separated itself from Russian hegemony and looked to an "Asian" or national version of communism).

With the universal organization, the United Nations, symbolically given its headquarters in New York, the US seemed to have found a formula for an unimaginably contented and ever more prosperous world. With Wilsonian self-determination now updated to embrace not just Europe but every continent, "Progress" reached out to all. By the end of the 1980s, even the USSR, once it was possessed of a leadership that had not itself fought the Great Patriotic War, admitted that shopping mattered more to its citizens than did revolution. The Berlin Wall fell and Francis Fukuyama heralded the "end of history."

Fifteen years later, in our new era of fear and terrorism, these seem in retrospect heady days. Now, in the latest adaptations of nationalization, we can discern special reasons for alarm. With the defeat of fascism and communism, the United States stands as the embodiment of globalized democracy and "freedom." It simultaneously stands as a nation. In no country has the flag been better loved, the national anthem sung more fulsomely. Yet the US was a new society; it could not match those European pretensions "really" to have existed for 3,000 years. Until its Civil War (1861–5), the United States had also been a slave society. After the abolition of slavery, its black citizens crowded the bottom ranks of every social index. Still more importantly, the US was, at one and the same time, supremely proud to be a nation, yet, through a constant immigration, on which its economic prosperity depended, perennially changing. As we have seen, the nation implied certitude and the conquest of time. Immigration meant variation, the arrival of ever more histories (and languages) onto American shores, and the perpetual likelihood that time had not been mastered. The US was riven by a national contradiction.

In practice, an effective solution was found to this dilemma. A popular culture emerged which, reflecting the newcomers' unreliable literacy in English, the language of the first immigrants and those who had forged American political institutions, was not too demanding intellectually but was very satisfying emotionally. European nationalists, like European socialists, clung to the hope that modernity meant that every man and woman could embrace high culture. In the more populist United States, demands on the people were less. Furthermore, the original arrivals to "New England" transported to the new world the religious commitment of the seventeenth century and this Christian fundamentalism became what might be called the "primary acquisition" of American identity. Whereas, in Europe, the social rallying needed to defeat Nazism in "peoples' wars" and the appalling horror the resultant campaigns directly inflicted on every participating society tended to reinforce the assumption that religion was a private matter, in the US religion retained the possibility of being public. There, for

perhaps a majority of citizens, no contradiction appeared in the intimate linking of the alleged rationality of the nation and the irrationality of Christianity and other faiths. Whereas the European states, with whatever equivocation, accepted a limitation of national sovereignty through international union, the American elites became less willing to countenance any charge that their nation and its policies did not embody virtue. "American-style democracy" – still, in reality, the Wilsonian fusion of capitalism, liberalism, and nationalism – was proclaimed the universal hope of humankind. In the Bush doctrine, all must accept that or be damned as rogue societies.

Of the participants in the Second World War, the US had suffered the least direct devastation from the conflict. Ironically, the people who were the most evident victims of Nazism, the Jews, in girding the state of Israel against its enemies, similarly moved to unite their nationalism with a revived Jewish religion. Itself another immigrant society, Israel, as Jews were drawn to settle from the Third World and from the USSR and its successor states, also became a place where premodern religious practice merged with the civic religion of the nation. Although Israel remained a country with a highly democratic press subjecting every aspirant hegemony to the severest criticism, nonetheless the construction of the Israel Wall and the continuing spread of Jewish settlements onto once Palestinian land were declared virtuous by Israelis determined to be both nationalists and believers in a Jewish religious state.

Nor was the Third World immune to similar developments where the modern religion of the nation became entangled with premodern universal religions, reframed to express the national purpose and mission. In India the JRP brought Hindu fundamentalism to national government. Most alarming were the Arab states, where modernity had arrived haltingly. There was, after all, no Arab nation; it was not clear that the linguistic group of Arab speakers constituted a nation. Egypt is a state which gives lip-service to nationalizing its masses but, when it deploys history, it is not the same past that might serve in Iran. The Muslim universal religion is fractured by heresy and division, with the clash between the Shi'ites and Sunnis being the most obvious.

Nation-building for Muslim peoples through a usable history was a taxing task, and marrying the modernity of a civic religion with traditional faith was even more explosive. The most likely result of the irresolvable conundrums seemed to be ever greater irrationality and ever more bloody fundamentalism.

This journey through the history of nationalism has come to an uncomfortable conclusion in its attempt to assess whether the evident rise and triumph of nationalism have brought benefit to humankind. The creation of a world of nations since 1789 coincided with spectacular advances in knowledge and with splendid improvements in the human condition. However, from its birth, nationalism carried an internal contradiction, which, in the new millennium, threatens to lay waste the gains of the last centuries. The nation came into being when men and women started to believe in the achievement of liberty, equality, and fraternity and in universal human perfectibility through rational means. Simultaneously, however, the nation deployed irrational techniques from past regimes to encourage a sense of belonging. Nation-states became unimaginable without faith, hierarchy, and exclusion. Such matters entailed a world in permanent battle. By the end of the twentieth century, that conflict threatened to become universal.

## NOTES

1 For its link with early fascism, see R. J. B. Bosworth, *Mussolini's Italy* (London: Allen Lane, 2005), pp. 155–8.

2 See the essays in E. Hobsbawm and T. Ranger, eds., *The Invention of Tradition* (Cambridge: Cambridge University Press, 1983).

3 B. Anderson, *Imagined Communities* (London: Verso, 1983), esp. pp. 129–31.

4 J. Wilton and R. Bosworth, *Old Worlds and New Australia* (Ringwood: Penguin, 1984), pp. 23–6, 146–7.

5 N. Ostler, *Empires of the Word* (London: HarperCollins, 2005), p. 7.

6 Touring Club Italiano, *Italy* (Paris: Hachette, 1956), p. xxv.

7 E. Hobsbawm, *Nations and Nationalism since 1780* (Cambridge: Cambridge University Press, 1990), p. 12.

8 P. Novick, *That Noble Dream* (Cambridge: Cambridge University Press, 1988).

9 G. Mosse, *The Nationalization of the Masses* (New York: Fertig, 1975). See also his memoirs, *Confronting History* (Madison: University of Wisconsin Press, 2000).

10 J. Gillingham, *Richard I* (New Haven: Yale University Press, 1999), p. 9.

11 R. R. Davies, *The First English Empire* (Oxford: Oxford University Press, 2000), pp. 41, 50, 201.

12 Ibid., p. 61.

13 C. Allmand, *Henry V* (New Haven: Yale University Press, 1992), p. 419.

14 C. Jones, *Paris* (London: Allen Lane, 2004), p. 66.

15 R. J. B. Bosworth, *Mussolini* (London: Arnold, 2002), pp. 84–6.

16 See A. J. Rieber, "Stalin, Man of the Borderlands," *American Historical Review* 106 (2001): 1651–91.

17 Y. Slezkine, *The Jewish Century* (Princeton: Princeton University Press, 2004).

18 I. Deutscher, *The Non-Jewish Jew and Other Essays* (New York: Oxford University Press, 1968).

19 For acute placement, see C. Schorske, *Fin-de-Siècle Vienna* (London: Weidenfeld & Nicolson, 1980).

## GUIDE TO FURTHER READING

B. Anderson, *Imagined Communities: Reflections on the Origin and Spread of Nationalism* (London: Verso, 1983). A fundamental text on the optimistic side.

E. Benner, *Really Existing Nationalisms: A Post-Communist View from Marx and Engels* (Oxford: Clarendon, 1995). Useful review of Marxism's coping with the nation.

J. Cocks, *Passion and Paradox: Intellectuals Confront the National Question* (Princeton: Princeton University Press, 2002). Sympathy for intellectual doubts.

F. Fukuyama, *The End of History and the Last Man* (London: Hamish Hamilton, 1992). Liberal universalist (or American nationalist) hubris after the end of communism.

P. J. Geary, *The Myth of Nations: The Medieval Origins of Europe* (Princeton: Princeton University Press, 2002). Critique of nations in the *longue durée*.

E. Gellner, *Nations and Nationalism* (New York: Cornell University Press, 1983). Fundamental text emphasizing connection with development of bureaucracy.

J. A. Hall, *The State of the Nation: Ernest Gellner and the Theory of Nationalism* (Cambridge: Cambridge University Press, 1998). Respectful appraisals of Gellner.

A. Hastings, *The Construction of Nationhood: Ethnicity, Religion and Nationalism* (Cambridge: Cambridge University Press, 1997). Emphatic about religious aspects.

E. Hobsbawm, *Nations and Nationalism since 1780: Programme, Myth, Reality* (Cambridge: Cambridge University Press, 1990). Fundamental text emphasizing manipulation involved.

E. Hobsbawm and T. Ranger, eds., *The Invention of Tradition* (Cambridge: Cambridge University Press, 1983). Fundamental and critical collection of essays.

J. Hutchinson and A. D. Smith, eds., *Nationalism* (Oxford: Oxford University Press, 1994). Usefully lengthy reader.

E. Kedourie, *Nationalism* (London: Hutchinson, 1960). Early critique seeing a division between good (western) and bad (central and eastern European) nationalisms.

P. Lawrence, *Nationalism: History and Theory* (London: Pearson, 2005). Very useful introduction to the key debates.

A. D. Smith, *Theories of Nationalism* (London: Duckworth, 1971): first exploration by important theorist; *The Ethnic Origin of Nations* (Oxford: Blackwell, 1986): fundamental statement of the long past view; and *Nations and Nationalism in a Global Era* (Cambridge: Polity Press, 1995): updating of his theoretics after the "end of history."

# CHAPTER THREE

# Internationalism

## ANDREW WEBSTER

The ideal of "internationalism" has extended across the twentieth century. At its core, it has constituted a strategy for transcending the perceived anarchy of international relations caused by the central position of sovereign states in a world lacking an effective arbiter between them.[1] In the place of competitive relationships between selfish nations each acting solely for its own benefit, it is argued, a more integrated international society in which states surrender their exclusive jurisdiction over key areas of interstate relations is vital to secure peace and to manage a world where old definitions of national identity are steadily being transcended. In this respect internationalism stands at odds with the longstanding "realist" view of international politics that stresses the difficulty or even impossibility of eliminating the dominant role of the state.[2]

"Internationalism" embraces a range of meanings, which vary according to the type of transformation of the international system that is desired and the means to be employed for achieving it. At its most general, it implies little more than an underlying belief that states have at least a moral obligation to act in a cooperative manner with other states on issues with considerations that extend beyond their own borders. This emerged as states began to participate in the various international organizations that sprang up during the nineteenth century to establish common economic and technical practices and understandings. At a more profound level, inter-

nationalism means that on matters of common international interest, and particularly those dealing with peace, security, and law, states ought to be willing to accept formal commitments that restrict their ability to act unilaterally or solely in their own national interest. This has found expression in attempts to codify international law and to impose humanitarian rules governing the conduct of warfare, as well as in the creation of institutions like the League of Nations and the United Nations with powers to resolve political crises and prevent or even intervene in armed conflicts. Finally, internationalism has involved an aspiration that the many divisions between states (economic, social, and political) should be steadily dissolved into a new mode of world organization that is not defined by national boundaries. The belief that strictly national forms of identity are increasingly irrelevant has led to ambitious conclusions about a world being transformed into a single integrated unit – whether through the spread during the first half of the century of the universalist ideology of socialism, or more recently through the expanding activities and reach of non-governmental international institutions into matters previously considered exclusively the province of the state (for instance in the field of humanitarian relief). None of these internationalist ideals has gone unchallenged, however. Indeed, the constant tension between the competing claims and powers of the nation and of the international community has served as one of the defining features of twentieth-century international history.

## Pre-1914 Forms of International Organization

The nineteenth century saw the development of a range of new forms of international organization, conceived and arranged primarily on a functional basis to supervise those aspects of the expanding spheres of global commerce and communications that crossed national frontiers. There was an obvious need to ease constraints on international transactions and these new organizations were a pragmatic response that safeguarded sovereign rights through their limited powers and narrowly drawn focus. Most prominent was the outburst of "international public unions" established to oversee the standardization of practices and a more efficient administration of international business. The range of issues dealt with by these new bodies was enormous. The Universal Postal Union, created in 1874 and formalized in the 1906 Treaty of Rome, swept away the former convoluted web of bilateral treaties that had meant "sending a letter from the United States to Australia . . . would cost 5 cents, 33 cents, 45 cents, 60 cents or $1.02 per half-ounce, according to the route it was sent."[3] In its place was created a single postal territory for the reciprocal exchange of correspondence, with a central bureau in Berne that fixed and oversaw a standardized set of transit charges. There was also the International Telecommunication Union (1865), the Intergovernmental Organization for International Carriage by Rail (1883), and the Comité Maritime International (1897). The idea of common management of certain commodities was embodied in organizations such as the Permanent Sugar Commission, created in Brussels in 1902, which operated by majority vote. Scientific and intellectual collaboration was given a systemic form in the International Bureau of Weights and Measures (1875), the Geodetic Union (1886), and the International Health Office (1907). International organs also exercised control over regional territorial issues: the European Commission for the Control of the Danube, for example, created in 1856, administered one of the continent's most important commercial waterways. The fifty-year period from 1864 to 1914 thus represented an enormous expansion in the arena of internationalism, as over 250 multilateral conventions were concluded on topics where uniformity of law and practice were desirable.

The nineteenth century also saw the advent of organizations carrying out humanitarian tasks across the globe on a non-national basis. The Comité International de Secours aux Blessés was founded in 1863, initially with the aim of providing aid to wounded on battlefields. It gave birth to a host of national societies across the globe, from Finland (1877) to Venezuela (1895). By the start of the twentieth century, Geneva was established as the home of the renamed International Committee of the Red Cross (ICRC) and the coordinating center for all Red Cross activities. The ICRC represented the beginning of a non-state presence and role in international conflicts, in the shape of an impartial institution that brought assistance to casualties, prisoners of war, and non-combatants during times of war. Yet the success of the ICRC over many years in steering through agreements on the duties owed by combatant states to victims of war, beginning with the adoption of the Geneva Convention for the Amelioration of the Condition of the Wounded in Armies in the Field in 1864, was due in large part to the committee's attention to the rights of states. From the very beginning it was clear that the work of the Red Cross societies had to be embedded within the fabric of the states in which they sought to operate. At the very first meeting in February 1863, there was an insistence on "the necessity to obtain the unanimous consent of the princes and nations of Europe; then to specify what will be the general forms of activity."[4]

What was significant about all such international bodies created before 1914 was that they attempted to limit themselves to the promotion of interests that were universal rather than national, that they contained only the most limited powers of compulsion, and that they dealt with problems that did not involve issues of national security. This was, to a large degree, the key to their success. Of course there remained stiff conflicts of national interests within the fledgling institutions, however apparently uncontroversial or beneficial their specific focus: the possibility of being outvoted and so compelled to take action against its own sovereign wishes led Britain to withdraw from the Permanent Sugar Commission in 1913. This was even more the case when attempts were made to consider areas of much more obvious sensitivity, in particular the management of interstate political disputes or negotiations for international disarmament, as governments insisted upon unqualified sovereignty in matters of security and defense.

The two Hague Peace Conferences of 1899 and 1907 represented the most significant internationalist efforts to address the dangers of the expanding armories of Europe and the possibility of total and unconstrained warfare. Called at the behest of the tsar of Russia, they were very well attended, with delegates coming from Europe, North and South America, and Asia. The increasing degree to which the nations of the world were entwined on issues of war and peace, proclaimed the president of the 1899 conference, had produced "a community of material and moral interests between nations, which is constantly increasing. The ties which bind the various branches of the great human family are ever drawing them closer to each other. If a nation wished to remain isolated, it could not. . . . It is part of a single organism."[5] The conference sadly achieved nothing in the field of actual disarmament, though there were three prohibitory declarations on the use of certain types of weaponry (expanding bullets, projectiles diffusing asphyxiating gases, and the discharge of explosives from balloons). Yet the two conferences together did signify a real advance in terms of international law. Laws of war had existed for centuries, but only in the form of custom, broad principles, national laws and codes of practice, and religious prohibitions. The 1899 Convention on the Law and Customs of War on Land represented the first general codification of land war in the form of a multilateral treaty. A set of conventions dealing with aspects of maritime war was also drawn up (one in 1899 and eight more in 1907). Overall, the Hague conferences represented a significant step forward toward an acceptance of the idea that states could owe obligations to some external authority. Yet the fundamental unwillingness of all the major states to accept binding commitments also stood out as a defining feature of the conferences, for they produced no processes for identifying violations of the laws of war or mechanisms for their enforcement.

The situation was similar in the case of schemes of international arbitration. The nineteenth century saw a steady growth in the resort to arbitration treaties as states began to come into contact with each other with greater frequency, both physically through competitive imperial expansion and across the range of new fields of commerce. There were 159 arbitrations between states between 1876 and 1900, and a further 114 between 1900 and 1914. They were primarily over problems such as boundary and territorial disputes, maritime issues, and private claims for compensation. The 1899 Hague conference created a Permanent Court of Arbitration, though it was neither permanent nor a court but rather a panel of nominated individuals from which arbitrators could be selected by the disputant parties if they chose to make use of the process. The generally insignificant disputes dealt with by the court in the years before 1914 demonstrated the limited ambitions of the states which made use of it. All attempts to extend arbitration, for instance by making it compulsory, were fiercely resisted by governments. The outbreak of the First World War seemed to give the lie to all the hopes invested in these tentative steps toward internationalism – shown most brutally in the German violation of Belgian neutrality on August 3, 1914 despite its signature to the 1907 Hague Convention V on the Rights and Duties of Neutral Powers and Persons in case of War on Land, the first article of which stated plainly that "the territory of neutral Powers is inviolable."[6]

## The League of Nations

"Today we stand on a bridge leading from the territorial state to the world community," proclaimed Christian Lange, the Norwegian secretary general of the Inter-Parliamentary Union, in the lecture accompanying his acceptance of the 1921 Nobel Peace Prize.[7] The title of Lange's lecture was "Internationalism" and the ideal he expressed was a common one in the years following the cataclysm of the First World War. The great clash of nations of 1914–18 seemed to have opened the door to a new way of organizing international relations. Nation-states had served as the central actors in international relations since the seventeenth century, but it now appeared to many that old certainties about the absolute rights of sovereign states needed to be challenged in order to ensure there could be no repeat of the conflagration that unbridled nationalism had set alight. The new system for managing conflict between states that emerged was the League of Nations, created at the Paris Peace Conference of 1919 with its Covenant included as the first part of each of the several peace treaties between the victorious Allies and the defeated Central Powers. The Covenant was surprisingly brief, but its twenty-six articles nevertheless covered a vast range of issues – from disarmament, collective security (though the term itself was not used until much later), the settlement of disputes, and the employment of sanctions, to social and economic cooperation, the trusteeship of former enemy territories (known as "Mandates"), and organizational principles.[8] The League took a tripartite physical shape with a Council, an Assembly, and a Secretariat. Most important was its executive organ, the Council, which had primary responsibility for dealing with the League's security provisions. Originally it was intended that the Council be comprised of only "great" powers, but pressure from "lesser" powers led to the inclusion of non-permanent members from among the smaller states on a rotating basis. Decisions were by unanimous vote, ensuring the major powers could retain control over the Council's judgments. All League member states were automatically members of the Assembly, each with a single vote. After some argument, it was decided that the Assembly would meet annually and over time these meetings would develop into the organization's chief public forum for the mobilization of world opinion, especially as the smaller states discovered that it offered them a platform from which they could exercise a new and disproportionate voice in world affairs. In spite of the lack of precedents, the permanent Secretariat successfully developed a role as an international civil service, presided over by a secretary general who acted as an admin-

istrator and coordinator rather than an active player in world diplomacy in his own right. Over its lifetime, some sixty-three states became members of the League, though the United States, despite the preeminent role of President Woodrow Wilson in its creation, ironically was the only major state that did not. The US would initially take an aloof and even hostile attitude toward the League, but this steadily evolved into a policy of more or less formal cooperation in a variety of the League's functional activities and participation in its major conferences (including on security-related issues such as disarmament). Of the chief postwar pariah states, Germany was admitted in 1926 (but withdrew in 1933) and the Soviet Union in 1934 (but was expelled in 1939), both having been granted permanent seats on the Council.

The core of the Covenant was its security provisions, for first and foremost the League was intended to maintain peace. War was not in fact totally outlawed, but the intention was clear that conflicts were to be prevented through the peaceful settlement of disputes and that any resort to war in violation of the terms of the Covenant would invoke a collective response from all League members. Underlying this was the notion that the normal state of international relations was one of peace, with war permitted only as an exceptional act requiring justification. Under Article 10, the League's members undertook "to respect and preserve as against external aggression the territorial integrity and existing political independence" of all other members. Through Articles 12, 13, and 15, states agreed to settle "any dispute likely to lead to a rupture" by submitting it either to arbitration, judicial settlement, or consideration by the League Council, with a pause of at least three months to be observed after any decision was rendered before a "resort to war." Article 14 called for the creation of a Permanent Court of International Justice (PCIJ), which was duly established in 1922. The Covenant's teeth for enforcement lay in Article 16, which stipulated that any state that disregarded these procedures would "be deemed to have committed an act of war against all other members of the League." The offending state was to be subjected to an immediate and obligatory economic, financial, and diplomatic boycott. No military sanctions were specified, though military operations "to protect the covenants of the League" could be recommended by the Council. For itself, the League was to have no armed forces of its own. Herein lay its essential weakness: the League was only a mechanism for the management of international relations, the success or failure of which depended upon the willingness of states to make use of it. The sovereignty of individual nation-states remained fixed and paramount; they formed the sole basis for the League's authority and power and their participation in any of its actions was entirely voluntary. One of the most consistent assertions by participants at early League meetings was the emphatic denial that the new institution possessed authority over its sovereign members. The British foreign secretary, Lord Curzon, took great pains on this point at the very first meeting of the League Council in Paris during January 1920:

> It has sometimes been said that the League of Nations implies the establishment of a super-state or a super-sovereignty. The very title "League of Nations" should be sufficient to dispel this misconception. The League does not interfere with nationality. It is upon the fact of nationhood that it rests. The League is an association of sovereign states whose purpose is to reconcile divergent interests and to promote international cooperation in questions which affect – or may affect – the world at large.[9]

The new international institutions developed by the League would thus operate in a world dominated by fiercely independent nation-states; it did not replace Great Power politics, as some hoped, but rather grew into an adjunct to them.

For all that, the League of Nations was nonetheless a radical departure in the practice of international relations; as proclaimed by its most ardent supporter, it was indeed "a great experiment" in internationalism.[10] The interwar period, and particularly the 1920s, represented a period when many issues previously considered solely matters of national concern were deemed to be now open for international discussion. As captured in the optimism of Lange's 1921 speech, it was the heyday of the internationalist ideal. There seemed some basis early on for the high hopes invested in the League's primary task of preserv-

ing the peace: the settlement of a dispute between Greece and Bulgaria in 1925 demonstrated that the League could act effectively in a crisis involving two smaller states when the Great Powers had no vital interests at stake. Efforts to strengthen the League's collective security provisions proved unsuccessful, with the 1923 draft Treaty of Mutual Assistance and the 1924 Geneva Protocol for the Pacific Settlement of International Disputes both coming to grief in the face of British resistance – demonstrating that the Great Powers still possessed the governing voice in diplomacy. On the other hand, at least such efforts were being made. The 1928 Paris Peace Pact renounced war as an instrument of national policy, apparently creating a new norm of international behavior, though it possessed no enforcement provisions and even its moral force was doubtful despite the ambitious claims of enthusiasts that it had "abolished" war. Similarly futile were all efforts at achieving substantial international disarmament, called for in Article 8 of the Covenant and the subject of enormous public expectations, but again it was significant that in the face of intense governmental reluctance the League nevertheless continued to sponsor negotiations over a disarmament process for some fifteen years.

There were myriad other ways, not all of which were anticipated, in which the fabric of internationalism expanded. Member states steadily developed the habit of making use of the League to manage a wide range of international business. There were attempts to regulate or suppress the international traffic in drugs, liquor, slaves, women and children, and armaments; controls were drafted for obscene publications and counterfeit currency; cooperation was developed on humanitarian issues such as health and the protection of minorities and refugees; conferences were held to promote economic and financial cooperation and the harmonization of practices on technical issues such as communications and transit. Much of the work on these questions took shape as a sustained effort for the development of international law, with over 120 new international instruments drawn up. Though many of these instruments failed to enter into force, the mere process of their creation was a significant step. One of the most valuable services performed by the Secretariat was its role as a central clearing-house for the vast efforts made by the League in gathering and disseminating information on social, economic, and humanitarian questions. The push toward international cooperation was real, as one commentator concluded in 1933: "To a far greater degree than even the boldest thinkers contemplated in 1919 the League has reached out into almost every field of human effort. Conceived primarily as a compact to maintain the peace, it has been used as an active agency of international cooperation in a world in which the need for such a body is growing at an ever-increasing pace."[11]

Despite these successes, it was only in the late 1930s that the League's functional work came to be regarded as its most important achievement – by which time it had suffered complete political eclipse. The early 1930s dealt a triple blow to internationalist hopes with the League's inability to check Japanese aggression in Manchuria, the failure of its efforts to promote international economic cooperation, and the humiliating collapse of the historic World Disarmament Conference of 1932–4. In the battle between the irreconcilable demands of nation and international community, it was a decade when national considerations dominated and the claims of internationalism steadily faded. The final political crisis for the League came with the inept Anglo-French handling of the 1935 Italian invasion of Ethiopia, which demonstrated conclusively the organization's impotence when the major powers were unwilling to back decisive action against transgressors of the Covenant. When Austria, a League member, was forcibly absorbed by Germany in 1938, the lack of reference to or action by the League highlighted its unhappy irrelevance.

Furthermore, only fitful efforts were made between the world wars to extend the work begun at the Hague conferences of codifying the laws of war. The most prominent achievement was the 1925 Geneva Protocol for the Prohibition of the Use in War of Asphyxiating, Poisonous or Other Gases, and of Bacteriological Methods of Warfare, yet this was not a complete ban on such weapons, for it only prohibited their use and not their study, production, or storage. Nor was the sphere of arbitration successfully expanded, despite debate in the later 1920s over ambitious schemes of conflict resolution such as the General Act for the Pacific Settlement of International Disputes and the Model Treaty to Strengthen the Means of Preventing War, neither of which was ever applied. The famous "Optional Clause" of the PCIJ's statute gave states the option of accepting its jurisdiction as compulsory and forty-five states did eventually accept this provision (though most did so with highly limiting reservations attached). Yet only eleven such cases were actually brought before the PCIJ and in only four of them was jurisdiction unchallenged – the most important case brought to decision was a Danish–Norwegian controversy over sovereignty of certain parts of eastern Greenland. Over its lifetime, the new court rendered only thirty-two judgments and twenty-seven advisory opinions on all matters (with forty-five of these taking place before 1933).

Assessments of the League's achievements must be seen in the light of both what was hoped for it and what was actually possible. In that it did not prevent the outbreak of another world war, it has since consistently been judged a failure, often in harsh and unfair terms. The flaw lay at its core, for if an international organization was to safeguard the peace it had to possess meaningful enforcement powers, yet this was (and perhaps remains) incompatible with a world where the principle of absolute national sovereignty was paramount. Yet in terms of what had gone before it, the League was a massive advance of internationalism. It would prove possible for other organizations to build upon the foundations it had established, both in terms of the extent of international cooperation that was now expected of states and in the many political, judicial, economic, social, and administrative agencies created that would serve as models for successors. As the League was wound up in 1946, it was addressed at its final session by its most tireless champion, Lord Robert Cecil, who closed with the proclamation: "The League is dead: long live the United Nations!"[12]

## The United Nations

Just as had the First World War, the turmoil of the Second World War led to the creation of an innovative international approach to maintaining the peace: the United Nations. The 111 Articles of its Charter, drawn up at the San Francisco Conference of 1945, laid out its organizational structure, principles, powers, and functions.[13] Influenced by the League, to which it was the spiritual and in some respects the legal heir (though the ties to its embarrassing elder relative have always been publicly downplayed), the United Nations adopted what was, essentially, a similar structure with a Security Council, General Assembly, Secretariat, and International Court of Justice.[14] The Security Council was given "primary responsibility for the maintenance of international peace and security" with members agreeing in advance to accept and implement its decisions. In order to harmonize the principle of the sovereign equality of member states with the perceived need to retain control of decisions in the hands of the major powers, the five major Allied victor powers of the Second World War (United States, USSR, Britain, France, and China) were made permanent members of the Security Council and possessed a veto over all its decisions, with other states serving on a rotating basis. While often criticized, the veto power of the permanent members merely registered the fact of Great Power predominance at the time; for the two new superpowers in particular, it did not create any inequality of power which did not already exist and indeed it underestimated their actual capacity to dictate terms or act independently of all international restraint. The General Assembly, meeting annually, again soon became the principal forum for public debate, though its agenda has since frequently been commandeered in the service of ideological or regional interests. The Secretariat has continued in the League's pioneering role as an international civil service, though on a vaster scale, its work complicated by the fact that in contrast to its forerunner's bilingual existence (English and French), the UN currently functions in six official languages (English, French, Russian, Chinese, Spanish, and Arabic). The UN's secretary general quickly took on a quite different role from the administrative focus of his League predecessor, acting instead "as a bold leader of international thought and action, as a genuinely international figure stimulating the member states to rise above their nationalistic dispositions."[15]

From its original membership of fifty-one states in 1945, the UN grew to 191 member states in 2005. Of the ex-enemy states from the Second World War, Italy was admitted as a member in 1955, Japan in 1956, and, after much ideologically motivated delay, West and East Germany were admitted together in 1973. None was granted a permanent seat on the Security Council. In contrast to the League's experience, none of the major powers has abstained from membership and no major government has yet sought a political or propaganda advantage through an ostentatious withdrawal from the organization. There have been some important changes, however: the Republic of China (Taiwan) was expelled and replaced in the Assembly and on the Security Council by the mainland People's Republic of China in 1971; the USSR's seat on both bodies was taken over by its designated successor state, the Russian Federation, in 1991.

The primary goal of the United Nations was again the maintenance of international peace and security. The Charter enshrined a commitment that the normal condition of international relations should be one of peace, in which any use of force would have to be justified and could take place only under certain conditions. Article 2 stated that all members should "settle their international disputes by peaceful means in such a manner that international peace and security, and justice, are not endangered." All members were additionally directed to refrain "from the threat or use of force against the territorial integrity or political independence of any state." Unlike the Covenant, which viewed war as a result of disputes running out of control and attempted to resolve clashes before they grew into armed conflicts, the Charter was aimed at stopping naked aggression. Thus, instead of measures for conciliation, arbitration, or "cooling off" periods, the UN system was designed to respond immediately to violence between states through the application of lawful military force. Article 42 allowed the Security Council to "take such action by air, sea, or land forces as may be necessary to maintain or restore international peace and security." Such police action by the UN, under the Security Council's direction, was the exclusive form (joined only by the stop-gap of self-defense) in which armed force was permitted. In the largest sense, the Charter's ban on the use of force has steadily created a widespread tacit understanding that any unilateral resort to military force by a state constitutes not a legal state of war but an unlawful act of aggression committed in peacetime.

However, in practical terms, the UN did not prove effective in its principal task: almost from the moment of its inception the Security Council became embroiled in the bipolar divisions of the Cold War. Meant to serve as a kind of Great Power directorate, it instead became merely a forum for rhetorical ideological attacks. The veto power of the permanent members consequently tended to serve as a transparently political tool, with the Soviet Union exercising it 106 times between 1946 and 1965 and the United States sixty-eight times between 1971 and 1990. The two sides sought collective security not through the UN but through their respective alliances, NATO and the Warsaw Pact. For most of the Cold War, the UN was a stalemated organization as the superpower standoff prevented the creation of any meaningful security architecture and indeed permeated all aspects of the UN system. Only once did the UN approach implementing collective security, during the Korean War (1950–3), and this was carried out in extraordinary circumstances in which the United States effectively circumvented the Soviet Union's veto and pushed through a military operation that was overwhelmingly American.

The United Nations nonetheless survived. Unlike the League, political setbacks did not lead to its complete irrelevance or demise, though its character did steadily change. As the organization expanded during the 1950s and 1960s with the admission of newly decolonized Third World states, its agenda widened and began to focus far more overtly on issues of development and economic activity rather than international security, where it seemed to be ineffective. By the 1980s, the UN was drifting toward impotence amid widespread disenchantment with its failure to resolve ongoing international conflicts. The secretary general, Javier Pérez de Cuéllar, lamented in 1982 that the world was "perilously close to a new international anarchy . . . one symptom of which is the crisis in the multilateral approach in

international affairs and the concomitant erosion of the authority and status of world and regional intergovernmental institutions."[16] Yet the decade ended with dramatic and profound changes to the international landscape, as the opportunity seemed to emerge for the UN again to attempt its intended purpose: the Charter, designed to deal with sudden acts of aggression between states, was highly relevant to the circumstances of the Iraqi invasion of Kuwait in 1990. The successful expulsion of Iraq, carried out under the aegis of UN authority, led many to believe that it could indeed function as a world policeman. The end of the Cold War also brought an expansion in the number of UN peacekeeping missions, with much success despite the high-profile failures in Yugoslavia and Rwanda. The UN may lack the credibility that goes with the possession of armed forces, it is true, but it has acquired a distinctive legitimacy over its lifetime and this gives it a real kind of authority. The American-led military intervention in Iraq in 2003 was carried out without the sanction of the UN Security Council, arguably in contravention of international law. To some commentators, this demonstrated the impotence and even irrelevance of the UN as an institution in the post-Cold War period. Yet the firestorm of criticism which raged around this disregard for the UN also represented an implicit acknowledgment of the existence of a meaningful international community in which the UN plays a central role. Assertions of the Iraq war's illegality have meaning only insofar as there is a common acceptance of norms of international law.

Perhaps the most problematic of the UN's principal organs is the International Court of Justice, the direct descendant of the League's Permanent Court of International Justice, which holds a position of great eminence but has not instilled the universal acceptance of norms of international law. In its first fifty years of existence (1946–96), the court rendered only sixty-one judgments and twenty-three advisory opinions. As was the case with its predecessor, only governments of states could be parties before the court. This does not mean that international law as a whole has failed to develop, however, in terms of both its theory and its practice. Since 1945, the unlawful use of force may provoke criminal prosecutions before an international tribunal of the individuals responsible for planning and executing aggression. The charter of the International Military Tribunal that presided over the 1946 Nuremburg trials of leading Nazis labeled this offense "crimes against the peace."[17] More recently, new formulations of international law have begun to attempt to apply its precepts to armed conflicts within states rather than solely between states. The International Criminal Tribunal for the Former Yugoslavia, created by the Security Council in 1993, noted how "Hague law" regulating armed conflict, based around state sovereignty, was being "gradually supplanted by a human-being-oriented approach."[18] In 1998, a multilateral treaty produced a statute for a new International Criminal Court, duly created in 2002, that would have jurisdiction to try individuals for the crimes of genocide, crimes against humanity, war crimes, and aggression (once an agreed definition of this had been resolved). Yet it still remained the case that this tribunal was to function as a court of last resort: it was to be "complementary to national criminal jurisdictions" and would act only if the state possessing jurisdiction was unwilling or genuinely unable to prosecute.[19]

The purposes of the UN, as laid down in Article 1 of the Charter, were from the start deliberately cast wider than those of the League: not only was the organization intended "to maintain international peace and security" but it was also charged "to achieve international cooperation in solving international problems of an economic, social, cultural, or humanitarian character." Attached to the United Nations therefore was a series of specialized agencies, intergovernmental institutions separate from the main organs of the UN established to serve different functional tasks. Each has an autonomous existence and operates in conjunction with the UN according to special agreements. They have expanded at an amazing rate, and across a vast range of business. While fewer than fifty intergovernmental organizations were created before 1914, over 200 (most but not all connected with the UN) were created between 1945 and 1985. As was the case with the League, it is here that the most impressive expansion of internationalism has taken place. Prominent spe-

cialized agencies and related organizations of the UN include the United Nations Education, Scientific, and Cultural Organization (UNESCO), the International Atomic Energy Agency, the International Civil Aviation Organization, the International Telecommunication Union, and the Food and Agriculture Organization. The UN also oversees a series of special programs, including the United Nations High Commission for Refugees and the United Nations Children's Fund (UNICEF). Some of the new UN bodies had their roots in organizations created by the League, or even earlier: the Permanent Health Organization of the League was a predecessor of the UN's World Health Organization; the International Labor Organization was created as an autonomous institution in close cooperation with the League and after 1945 became a specialized agency of the United Nations; the Universal Postal Union has existed continuously since its creation in the nineteenth century, though since modified and modernized by numerous additional treaties.

In the end, the contribution made by the United Nations to a new and lasting world order, rooted in still-evolving concepts of international law, will continue to depend upon the political will of its member states to subscribe to an internationalist ideal. It is a political organization that wrestles with the competing claims of national sovereignty and international community in exactly the same fashion as did the League of Nations. As a recent commentator has concluded: "States create the law through the United Nations, states break the law in spite of the United Nations, and states must enforce the law through the United Nations. . . . Hence, international law created through the United Nations can only be as strong as its member states – especially the great powers of the Security Council – are willing to make it be."[20] The internationalist ideal remains, as before, paradoxically dependent upon the self-denial of nation-states.

## Internationalist Ideals Beyond the State

The global revolutionary call of communism was a radically different internationalist vision to emerge out of the First World War's destruction of the nineteenth-century order of international relations. While the League of Nations supposed an international community of sovereign nation-states, meeting to solve issues which touched upon them all, socialist internationalism envisioned a world without borders in which the state itself would be transcended as the world was reorganized on the basis of an international class solidarity of the proletariat. Workingmen, in short, had no country. The short-lived First International Workingman's Association was created in 1864 (by Karl Marx, among others); it was succeeded in 1889 by the Second International, which lasted until the outbreak of war in 1914 disappointed the hopes of all those who had believed that working-class solidarity would triumph over nationalist chauvinism. The situation was altered completely by the revolution in Russia during 1917, however, when a regime emerged in one of the Great Powers of Europe dedicated to the violent overthrow of liberal, capitalist, and imperialist governments around the globe. The Communist International (known as the "Comintern" or the Third International) was born officially in Moscow in March 1919, with the task of channeling the rising socialist tide. At its seventh and final World Congress in 1935, there were seventy-six national parties represented with a total membership of over three million (though only 785,000 of these came from parties outside the Soviet Union). The Comintern was intended to be cohesive and ideologically uniform: conditions for membership by national communist parties required that they accept the binding leadership of the executive committee in Moscow. From the beginning, however, the organization served as a tool of the Soviet government, which invariably put the interests of the "first socialist state" before those of particular national parties and imposed numerous switches in policy direction right until the Comintern's dissolution in 1943. Through its agents and propaganda campaigns, the Comintern did its hapless best to stimulate revolution, but it failed everywhere except in the unusual case of Mongolia. In the years after 1945, within the context of the Cold War, communist internationalism as an alternative model of international relations

increasingly became little more than traditional imperial expansionism in a new guise. This did not bring an end to arguments insisting upon the inevitability of the worldwide spread of socialism, but they had an all-too-obviously hollow ring. As one tract from Moscow instructed in the 1970s, for the benefit of "our friends abroad": "The unity between workers of all nations and countries, the equality and friendship between the national contingents of the working class, and the socialist community of peoples incorporate the prototype of mankind's existence in the future."[21] Though the end of the Cold War and the collapse of the Soviet Union during 1989–91 did not bring a complete end to the ideal of socialist internationalism, it has been discredited by the bankruptcy of its practical realization and nothing that has since happened in enduring communist countries such as China, Cuba, or Vietnam suggests that the promised stateless, classless world of socialist societies is even distantly in sight.

In contrast to this failed vision, there has been a truly successful manifestation of internationalism during the twentieth century based on the spread of non-governmental international organizations made up not of states but of individuals, companies, advocacy or issue groups, or even national sporting bodies. They range from the International Olympic Committee (founded in 1894) to the Fédération Internationale des Échecs (1924) to Amnesty International (1961). Perhaps the single most high-profile field of activity in which such organizations work is that of humanitarian relief. Following the adoption of the 1864 Geneva Convention, the Red Cross continued to drive forward a process of codification of humanitarian law and practice that culminated in the acceptance of the landmark four Geneva conventions of 1949, which covered treatment for the wounded on land and sea, the treatment of prisoners of war, and the protection of civilians and neutrals. The special status and responsibilities designated to the ICRC in the 1864 and 1949 conventions and in the Additional Protocols of 1977 have given it a unique place within international humanitarian law and a moral authority that remains without equal. (Its founder, Henri Dunant, was the co-recipient of the first Nobel Peace Prize in 1901; the organization itself was subsequently awarded the prize in 1944 and again in 1963.) The ICRC has inspired the creation of other private international humanitarian organizations, such as the Save the Children International Union (1920) and the Oxford Committee for Famine Relief, or "Oxfam" (1942). Particularly after the Second World War, it was these non-governmental organizations that tackled what they perceived as the vacuum left by the ponderous responses of national governments to humanitarian crises. They recruited volunteers, raised funds, provided emergency medical assistance, and assembled critical supplies of clothing, shelter, fuel, and food. Yet the international humanitarian law at the basis of the ICRC's mandate was drafted to regulate armed conflicts between sovereign states, with a clear distinction between the laws of peacetime and of wartime. As wars have increasingly come to be fought within states rather than between them, often with civilians rather than soldiers as specific targets, and in a protracted fashion that blurs clear distinctions between war and peace, the reliance upon codes based upon traditional state prerogatives and practices has raised new challenges. In particular, the principle of strict neutrality observed by the ICRC – abstaining from any role in or comment on the politics of a crisis in order to secure access to individuals and sites unobtainable by national representatives – has brought substantial criticism in recent years as being naïve and morally questionable. The "new humanitarianism" practiced by groups such as Médecins Sans Frontières (1971), awarded the Nobel Peace Prize in 1999, instead rejects neutrality in favor of a role that includes an overt political outlook, deliberately assessing the long-term political impact of relief and employing humanitarian aid as a tool to achieve wider human rights and political objectives. Such organizations see themselves as actors in crises and not merely as tools to perform services that states are unable or unwilling to carry out themselves.

## Conclusion

By the end of the century, the internationalist ideal had come full circle. In his 1992 report to the General Assembly on new, interventionist approaches to peacekeeping, Boutros Boutros-Ghali, the UN secretary general, emphasized both the growing permeability of national boundaries and the irreplaceable role of the state. "The foundation stone of this work is and must remain the state. Respect for its fundamental sovereignty and integrity are crucial to any common international progress. The time of absolute and exclusive sovereignty, however, has passed. . . . It is the task of leaders of states today to understand this and to find a balance between the needs of good internal government and the requirements of an ever more interdependent world."[22] The quandary of internationalism remains that it demands a surrender of national sovereignty and this cannot easily be accomplished in a world where the state continues to serve as the central element of the international system. Yet there can be no question that the idea of an "international community" has become established to a degree unimagined a century ago. It was no accident that the United Nations Development Program's Human Development Report for 1999 referred meaningfully to "the aspirations of a global citizenry."[23] The principle of internationalism has become too deeply ingrained to be casually shrugged off, despite its many failings in practice. Perhaps only the "hyperpower" United States, at one end of the spectrum, and the "hermit state" of North Korea, at the other, could seriously contemplate ignoring all other states and taking unilateral action over any of the many issues that demand internationalist solutions, from the environment to the global economy to the management of the Internet. However diluted or challenged – most recently by American administrations over issues such as the International Criminal Court or the 1997 Kyoto Protocol on climate change – the existence of an international community creating and exercising norms of cooperative behavior on a scale beyond individual national self-interest is now too widely accepted to ever be discarded entirely. The continuing dissolution of distinctions between global and local is steadily producing interlocking networks of governments, international governmental organizations, non-governmental organizations, multinational corporations, professional associations, and other groups – in short, what might be called a global civil society. The bridge from the territorial state to the world community proclaimed by Christian Lange in 1921, however long and unwieldy it might be, may yet reach its far bank.

## NOTES

1  There has been a vast range of approaches to this question across the century, reaching widely different conclusions. For example: Alfred Zimmern, *The League of Nations and the Rule of Law, 1918–1935* (London: Macmillan, 1936); Inis L. Claude, Jr., *Swords into Plowshares: The Problems and Progress of International Organization* (New York: Random House, 1956); Robert O. Keohane and Joseph S. Nye, *Power and Interdependence: World Politics in Transition* (Boston and Toronto: Little, Brown, 1977); Kjell Goldmann, *The Logic of Internationalism: Coercion and Accommodation* (London: Routledge, 1994).

2  A classic statement of the "realist" school is Hans J. Morgenthau, *Politics Among Nations: The Struggle for Power and Peace* (New York: Alfred A. Knopf, 1948).

3  Francis Bowes Sayre, *Experiments in International Administration* (New York and London: Harper & Brothers, 1919), p. 19.

4  Jean-François Pitteloud, ed., *Procès-verbaux des Séances du Comité international de la Croix-Rouge, 17 février 1863–28 août 1914* (Geneva: Société Henri Dunant/International Committee of the Red Cross, 1999), pp. 17–18.

5  James Brown Scott, ed., *The Reports to the Hague Conferences of 1899 and 1907* (Oxford: Carnegie Endowment for International Peace, 1917), p. 9.

6  Ibid., p. 533.

7  Tyler Wasson, ed., *Nobel Prize Winners* (New York: H. W. Wilson, 1987), pp. 595–7.

8  Claude, *Swords into Plowshares*, Appendix I: The Covenant of the League of Nations.

9  League of Nations, *Official Journal*, no. 1 (February 1920), pp. 20–2.

10  Viscount Cecil, *A Great Experiment* (London: Jonathan Cape, 1941).

11  C. K. Webster, *The League of Nations in Theory and Practice* (London: George Allen & Unwin, 1933), p. 301.

12  League of Nations, *Official Journal*, special supplement no. 194 (Geneva, 1946), p. 30.

13  Claude, *Swords into Plowshares*, Appendix II: The Charter of the United Nations.

14  The other two of the UN's six principal organs are the Economic and Social Council and the Trusteeship Council.

15  Trygve Lie, *In the Cause of Peace: Seven Years with the United Nations* (New York: Macmillan, 1954), p. 41. Lie was the UN's first secretary general (1946–53).

16  David Armstrong, Lorna Lloyd, and John Redmond, *International Organization in World Politics* (Basingstoke: Palgrave Macmillan, 3rd edn, 2004), p. 73.

17  Eugene Davidson, *The Trial of the Germans* (Columbia: University of Missouri Press, 1966), p. 19. There have since been no further international prosecutions under this heading.

18  Stephen C. Neff, *War and the Law of Nations: A General History* (Cambridge: Cambridge University Press, 2005), p. 343.

19  Rome Statute of the International Criminal Court, UN Doc. A/CONF.183/9 (1998).

20  Christopher C. Joyner, "The United Nations as International Law-Giver," in C. C. Joyner, ed., *The United Nations and International Law* (Cambridge: Cambridge University Press, 1997), p. 457.

21  M. S. Junusov et al., *The Theory and Practice of Proletarian Internationalism* (Moscow: Progress Publishers, 1976), p. 39.

22  Boutros Boutros-Ghali, *An Agenda for Peace: Preventive Diplomacy, Peacemaking and Peace-keeping* (New York: United Nations, 1992), p. 9.

23  Armstrong, Lloyd, and Redmond, *International Organization*, p. 254.

## GUIDE TO FURTHER READING

David Armstrong, "From International Community to International Organization?" *Commonwealth and Comparative Politics* 39 (2001): 31–50. A good discussion of the problems facing the modern Commonwealth.

David Armstrong, Lorna Lloyd, and John Redmond, *International Organization in World Politics* (Basingstoke: Palgrave Macmillan, 3rd edn, 2004). The standard overview of the development of international organizations during the twentieth century.

Patricia Clavin, "Defining Transnationalism," *Contemporary European History* 14 (2005): 421–39. An interesting examination of an alternative mode of viewing cross-border networks.

Fiona Fox, "New Humanitarianism: Does it Provide a Moral Banner for the 21st Century?" *Disasters* 25 (2001): 275–89. On the overt political agendas of the "new humanitarian" organizations.

Michael Graham Fry, Erik Goldstein, and Richard Langhorne, eds., *Guide to International Relations and Diplomacy* (London and New York: Continuum, 2002). A valuable source for data on the development of the international system.

Michael Howard, George J. Andreopoulos, and Mark R. Shulman, eds., *The Laws of War: Constraints on Warfare in the Western World* (New Haven and London: Yale University Press, 1994). Useful essays on the evolution of a key element of international law.

Franz Knipping, Hans von Mangolt, and Volker Rittenberger, eds., *The United Nations System and Its Predecessors*, 2 vols. (Oxford: Oxford University Press, 1997). An immense and fascinating collection of documentation on twentieth-century international organizations dealing with interstate relations.

Evan Luard, *A History of the United Nations*, 2 vols. (London: Macmillan, 1982, 1989). Standard history of the UN.

Caroline Moorhead, *Dunant's Dream: War, Switzerland and the History of the Red Cross* (London: HarperCollins, 1998). Excellent recent study that devotes attention to both the ICRC and the wider Red Cross movement as a whole.

Stephen C. Neff, *War and the Law of Nations: A General History* (Cambridge: Cambridge University Press, 2005). An accessible and insightful overview.

Tim Rees and Andrew Thorpe, eds., *International Communism and the Communist International, 1919–1943* (Manchester and New York: Manchester University Press, 1998). A diverse set of essays on the heyday of the Comintern.

Adam Roberts and Benedict Kingsbury, eds., *United Nations, Divided World: The UN's Roles in International Relations* (Oxford: Oxford University Press, 2nd edn, 1993). Informative essays on the place of the UN in international society.

Zara Steiner, *The Lights that Failed: European International History, 1919–1933* (Oxford and New York: Oxford University Press, 2005). Contains excellent analysis of how the conflicting pulls of nationalism and internationalism affected international relations following the First World War.

Derek W. Urwin, *The Community of Europe: A History of European Integration since 1945* (London and New York: Longman, 2nd edn, 1995). A concise introduction to the story of federal Europe.

F. P. Walters, *A History of the League of Nations*, 2 vols. (London: Oxford University Press, 1952). While perhaps too sympathetic, this classic study by a former deputy secretary general of the organization is still the most complete account of the full range of the League's work.

# CHAPTER FOUR

# A Shrinking World

*JEFFREY A. ENGEL*

The twentieth century witnessed great strides in long-range communications, commerce, and travel, leading to a more intimate and interconnected global culture than at any previous point in history. The changes themselves were profound. By the close of the century humans on one side of the globe could (electronically, at least) speak and see each other in real time. They could travel from any one spot on the globe to another in mere hours. They could simultaneously read the same ideas, view the same images, and hear the same music. Most profound of all, while not yet universal, the majority of citizens of the developing world had access to these opportunities. So too did a growing number in underdeveloped lands. By the end of the century, the fall of communism and the end of the Cold War removed the last barriers hindering establishment of a truly global marketplace, making it possible to state that this is truly the most global age of all.

These were profound changes, yet in an important sense they were merely advances of scale and speed. The formation of a global society has been an ongoing process that well predates the modern age. The Punic Wars that pitted Rome against Carthage were in effect disputes over which might control trade and communications through the Mediterranean Sea, then the world's most highly trafficked highway. Development of a modern global capitalist marketplace, which historians trace to the fourteenth century, sped this process further.[1] Advances in global communications

(and in turn development of a global consciousness) dovetailed with improvements in trade and travel. Fifteenth-century traders connecting Europe and China for the sake of spices and exotic goods believed themselves on the vanguard of a global communications network, while explorers who brought news of a New World back to the Old during the Columbian Epoch sailed with trade and profits foremost in their minds. So too did railroad designers of later centuries conceive of themselves as the connectors of humanity and harbingers of a new golden age, even as they linked far-off lands and peoples for the sake of sales, commerce, and power.

This intermingling of trade, travel, and communications was hardly a western phenomenon. Centuries before Europe's Renaissance, Genghis Khan and his Mongol descendants forged a road and communications network connecting Europe and the Middle East with South Asia and the Pacific Rim.[2] Their horses could not keep their empire intact, but by the twentieth century it appeared newer technologies might succeed where older ones had failed, leading to a centralization of political power like none seen before. In 1904, the British geographer Halford Mackinder famously lamented that industrial production, and the railroad especially, might spawn a new global power capable of dominating Eurasia.[3] Newer technologies still, the airplane and wireless communications especially, ultimately proved Mackinder wrong, though some perceived the totalitarian threat posed by the Soviet Union as fulfillment of his dire prediction. Indeed, increased exposure to news and information from around the world seemed to spawn not massive states by the close of the century but rather (and perhaps ironically) the desire for greater local autonomy.[4] The point is not that technological improvements of the twentieth century bred empire or political devolution, but rather that this century, for the first time, featured technologies capable of making truly global political, financial, and cultural networks and structures possible. That people emboldened by access to such technology used them in unforeseen ways should come as no surprise to any serious student of history.

The very concept of a shrinking world, often termed "globalism," significantly predates the twentieth century. Humans have consistently over the millennia believed themselves more fully integrated with their neighbors than those that came before. They just as often believe, all evidence to the contrary, that greater trade and connections might lead to a more pacific age. The idea that nations linked by commerce would refuse to fight each other – the idea central to prophesiers of a new utopian age at the end of the Cold War – is provably false. Germany was France's greatest trading partner in 1914, and vice versa. Yet belief in the idea that trade and contacts lead inexorably to peace and harmony grows in strength with every technological advance capable of further forging a global cultural and political consciousness. Each invention described below – the telegraph, radio, the automobile, the airplane, or the Internet – catalyzed prophesies of a new global utopia. Each such prophesy has thus far proved premature at best. Optimism remains, however. When viewed in its totality, what the twentieth century brought in the area of communications and transports (which affected politics, business, and culture) was less something profoundly new than a pace of change to this ongoing process unlike any that came before.

## Communications

Advances in global communications have arguably outpaced those seen in other areas. The century began with a system for speedy international communications already in place, as great strides had been made in the field of electric telegraph (more commonly known as the telegraph) throughout the nineteenth century. In lay terms, this was a relatively simple technology. First installed over land, a telegraph is merely an uninsulated wire, originally copper or iron, strung from one point to another. Electric pulses initiated at one end could be perceived at the other end, and through codes or preset means of transmitting data, information could be passed at unprecedented speed across long distances. Among the most efficient and widely incorporated of these early codes was that developed in the 1830s by Samuel Morse, whose system of long and short pauses in the electrical burst corresponding to the alphabet still bears his name. Ironically, Morse turned his attention to advancing telegraphy in America only after a failed artistic career in Europe, proof of a transatlantic culture and trade that well predated rapid global communication.

By the middle decades of the nineteenth century telegraph cables connected all parts of Europe and the United States, but establishment of a truly intercontinental communications network demanded transoceanic cables. This proved a daunting problem. The cable itself required insulation if its electrical pulses were to operate in a watery environment, and in turn had to be sturdy enough to survive strong ocean currents. Engineers first laid a communications cable across the Channel separating France from England in 1850, for example, but it broke almost immediately in the tides. A stronger cable armored with iron succeeded a year later, linking Britain to Europe in a profound new way. By 1858 such a cable across the Atlantic existed as well, laid at great expense. It was immediately hailed as a breakthrough capable of fostering a new era. "Rejoice all nations," New Yorkers declared of this transatlantic "marriage," performed "in the Church of progress, at the altar of commerce, the Old to the New World. May they never be divorced!"[5] Alas, this first relationship lasted a mere three months. Without knowledge of the ocean's floor at its deepest points, engineers presumed it to be smooth, laying their cable without slack. It consequently snapped. Recognition of this problem led to the first true mapping of the ocean's floor by the United States Navy in 1853. For hardly the first or the last time, the need for greater communication between points on the planet led, out of necessity, to a greater scientific understanding of the planet itself.

Not all setbacks lead to failure, however. One historian, David Nickles, has concluded that the initial transatlantic cable's malfunction in fact helped keep the peace between Britain and the United States during the latter's Civil War. The time required to transmit information across the Atlantic by boat (upwards of two months) gave diplomats in both countries time to defuse disputes. Speedier communication would have allowed passions to flourish, making conflict more likely. For every proponent of the argument that closer communications between states reduces their likelihood for war, there is a counterexample. A new cable bridging the Atlantic was laid in 1866, and by 1900 the New and Old Worlds were truly linked by a single information network. In 1917 this network helped speed deterioration of relations between Germany and the United States, when captured German telegraph communications with Mexico (promising return of lands lost in the Mexican–American War as reward for aid in a German–American war) inflamed American passions. In the reverse of what occurred during the Civil War, this "Zimmerman Telegram" demonstrated that speedy communications (when not secure) contributed not to peace but rather to conflict.[6]

More than merely the Atlantic was in play in the effort to link the world's far-off places with a single communications network. Lofty ideals flourished, but politics and commerce drove the process. Imperial planners in Britain did the most to establish the world's most wide-ranging telegraph system, by 1865 linking London to India through a series of cables. The system worked, but was expensive and slow. Messages typically required up to six days to reach their destination, though faster transmission could be had for a price. This was far quicker than any ship or rail of the day, but a more efficient system was clearly needed (especially as British strategists feared for the safety of their cable during a crisis given the number of hostile countries it passed through).

Their solution was a fully submerged network. The ambitious project required a fortune and decades to complete. By the first decade of the twentieth century and the subsequent outbreak of the First World War, London's strategists finally had their secure "All-British" network in place, though ironically, as Daniel Headrick noted, they achieved their long-desired accomplishment just as the age of wireless communication began.[7]

Before leaving telegraphy it is vital to consider what this first global communications network, fully operational during the first decade of the twentieth century, meant for the shrinking world. The ability to transmit information at such unprecedented speed and across such wide distances further fostered creation of a global marketplace. Long-range trade predated telegraphy by millennia. But for the first time, traders could deliver goods from halfway around the globe confident of the price to expect well before they arrived. Global finance boomed accordingly, and to no small extent because of its lead in establishing the world's telegraph networks, London became embedded as banking hub of the world. Only the costs of financing two world wars in a generation would supplant it. In the meantime, American wheat and cotton were traded in London exchanges alongside Indian rice and textiles, Latin American and African coffees, and after development of refrigerated ships, even Argentinean and Australian beef. The telegraph allowed for construction of a whole series of financing, shipping, and warehousing improvements, and the sale of global commodities at a more efficient, and hence more profitable, rate than ever before. One historian has calculated that the level of raw cotton stocks held in British ports and mills was far lower following introduction of the telegraph than before, a sure sign that business used these new communications technologies in its quest for greater efficiency.[8] "Time itself is telegraphed out of existence," declared London's *Daily Telegraph*, a newspaper named to inspire confidence in the speed and accuracy of its information.[9]

The world was indeed shrinking, and so too was global life more intimate, though yet more changes were in the offing. Alexander Graham Bell patented the telephone in 1876, demonstrating that voice communications could be carried by wire. A decade later over 250,000 telephones were in use worldwide, and one in ten American homes possessed the technology. Today telephones are ubiquitous, and there are more than one billion mobile phones in use worldwide (a technology described below). Early twentieth-century traders valued pricing and shipping information transmitted across such lines, and strategists plotted their geopolitical moves with cables in mind. At the same time, gossip and theater news leapt the oceans as well, creating among the ranks of actors, athletes, and authors the first global celebrities. For many the opportunities offered by the increasingly integrated global marketplace included the promotion of cultural and political values. "With the inspiration of the thought that you are Americans and are meant to carry liberty and justice and the principles of humanity wherever you go," President Woodrow Wilson told a convention of salesmen before the First World War, "go out and sell goods that will make the world more comfortable and more happy, and convert them to the principles of America."[10]

Not every political system lent itself to such an open embrace of information and cultural expansion. Whereas phones became a central part of life in the oft-termed "free world" during the twentieth century, communist and authoritarian rulers frequently limited their use in order to better control the flow of information and knowledge throughout their countries. A homeowner or businessperson in Australia in 1970 could, with operator assistance, call to a relative or friend in Japan, America, Britain, Brazil, or any number of countries linked by satellites and underseas cables. By the 1980s that same caller could do the same without use of an operator. Similarly, in 1925 a three-minute coast-to-coast call cost nearly a full day's salary for the average American factory worker. In 1983, that same call cost less than five minutes of her salary.[11] By the last years of the Soviet Union, conversely, citizens in Moscow seeking to call a relative in Leningrad (St. Petersburg) had to journey to one of a handful of state-controlled telephone centers where their conversation was undoubtedly supervised and extremely expensive. Soviet leaders possessed

global communications technologies; they just chose not to provide them for their own citizens. Technologies require the will to use them, after all.

Wireless technology offered even greater communications opportunities throughout the century. Radio developed simultaneously in several countries during the 1890s, though Guglielmo Marconi won the technology's first official patent in 1896 and is thus generally credited as the medium's primary creator. With American investors and political backing in Britain (Lloyd's of London, the world's most influential insurer, determined in 1901 that it would only give its highest credit rating to ships equipped with his ship-to-shore system), Marconi's wireless radio quickly became the global norm. Following the first transatlantic radio message in 1901 (delivered in Morse code), his technology led to rapid improvements in the speed and efficiency of transmitting data, and to safer travel as well. Where once ships at sea were "lost" until their arrival in port, by the beginning of the twentieth century the addition of the first wireless technologies ensured not only that their arrival could be anticipated (and markets prepared accordingly), but also that disaster could, with luck, be averted. At least some of the passengers aboard the ill-fated *Titanic* were rescued following a wireless plea for help, for example.

Being transmitted in the open air and thus available to anyone with a similarly tuned receiver, radio spawned improvements in coding and mathematics as politicians and businesspeople sought new ways to safeguard their information. The military rushed to incorporate this new tool, especially during the First World War. The technology had played a significant role in the conflict's outcome. Britain's global cable network allowed London near-constant communication with its allies during the First World War. Germany's wireless network failed to offer the same sort of secure communications, with diplomatic results already described. The security (or lack thereof) of communications played an even more central role in the Second World War, when Anglo-American codebreakers intercepted and interpreted Japanese and German military and diplomatic communications (most transmitted by way of a presumably impenetrable coding machine named "Enigma"). That both Berlin and Tokyo believed their networks incapable of penetration showed, if nothing else, the impact of hubris on international affairs.[12]

A communications boom followed quickly after the Treaty of Versailles ended the First World War, and news and entertainment programs rapidly became a staple of daily life throughout the world. The flourishing use of the airwaves led governments around the globe to control their use for the public good (and to ensure public safety). The 1912 Radio Act, for example, gave American officials the right to assign particular frequencies to particular users. Government and military operations took priority alongside commercial ventures. Amateurs were left with the little that remained, in a story repeated throughout the world. Given that most news operators (newspapers and writers) had by the 1920s become wholly dependent upon large wire services for their information, and that these large wire services demanded regulation of the airwaves to ensure their profitability, political opposition to government controls was muted at best. Commercial interests were never far from the surface as this medium developed. Less than two years after Pittsburgh station KDKA offered the first publicly available radio broadcast in announcing Warren Harding's presidential election, a New York station broadcast the first paid advertisement. The intertwining of profits with progress did little to thwart the enthusiasm of radio's early pioneers, however, such as one engineer who called his product "Messenger of sympathy and love . . . consoler of the lonely . . . promoter of mutual acquaintance, of peace and good will among nations."[13] Yet again, technological improvements figured prominently in dreams of a more pacific future. Radio could not prevent conflict, however. Indeed, wartime broadcasts from the front helped spur American support for Britain during the early days of the Second World War, though Washington's codebreakers proved unable to decipher Japanese plans to attack Pearl Harbor in 1941 until mere hours after the first bombs fell.[14]

Radio's prewar golden age fell after 1945 to television, which became the entertainment medium of choice in the latter half of the century.

Scientists, by the beginning of the twentieth century, realized that visible light, being composed of electromagnetic waves shorter in length and higher in frequency than radio waves, might be transmitted in much the same way. Russian scientist Constantin Persky coined the term "television" to describe this process in a paper delivered to the 1900 World's Fair. Turning this theoretical understanding into a workable product proved difficult, however. Breakthroughs occurred in the 1920s, led by Vladymir Zworkin, a former Russian Army officer exiled to the United States, who first patented a means to project an image on a screen through use of a cathode-ray tube. Scotsman John Logie Baird headed the pack across the Atlantic when he demonstrated the ability to transmit images wirelessly in 1925. He presented his technology to a scientific society, the Royal Institution of Great Britain, but funded his work by entertaining fascinated crowds gathered before one of London's poshest stores. Further developments came rapidly. The first magazine solely devoted to the new technology, aptly named *Television*, began publication in 1927, and General Electric's Ernst Alexanderson broadcast the first televised melodrama in the fall of 1928. Legislators and futurists had already predicted such advances. The American Radio Act of 1927, for example, defined radio as any "message, signal, power, *picture* or communication" delivered wirelessly – despite the fact that there was no effective picture broadcasting at the time.[15] The future seemed in this way right around the corner.

The Great Depression of the 1930s and then the Second World War each stunted television's commercial growth, though important advances occurred during this period, most famously the broadcast of the 1936 Berlin Olympics to twenty-eight state-run television rooms located throughout Nazi Germany. Fearful lest enemy ships or pilots home in on the signals, authorities halted television broadcasts by the British Broadcasting Corporation throughout the war. Western consumers in particular made up for lost time after 1945. A mere 8,000 American households owned television sets in 1946. Fourteen years later the number totaled more than 45 million. Global use of the medium lagged behind the prosperous United States, but only barely. By 1965, when the first communications satellite intended for television use entered orbit, images could be beamed (and received) the world over. With the advent of cable television in the 1970s – which transmitted data using wires and then, increasingly, via satellites – consumers without clear access to over-the-air television broadcasts could receive increasingly specialized programming. As production costs dropped, the variety of programming boomed. In 1977 there were a mere 100 cable receiving stations capable of rebroadcasting satellite transmissions the world over. Two years later there were more than 1,500. By the close of the century, television's presence and cultural impact were ubiquitous. The proportion of households with televisions in formerly isolated (from a communications perspective) countries such as Vietnam or Poland shot up an average of 191 percent from 1989 to 2004. The average American watched over 4.7 hours of television a day at century's end, a statistic that proved a boom for programmers and advertisers, but that many critics feared contributed to the country's growing rate of obesity as well. As with all technological changes, utopian visions and clear advantages came with a Pandora's box of unexpected complications.[16]

Telephone communication also boomed during this period. In the early 1950s the first transatlantic telephonic cable more fully linked the New World with the Old (the first such transpacific line came online in 1964). The former initially carried only thirty-six simultaneous telephone calls, but its ability to transmit telegraph traffic exceeded all the world's submerged cables combined. Successors made instantaneous global communication the norm, and further embedded western (and American in particular) financial and political power. Western firms, flush with profits amidst the greatest period of sustained long-term economic growth in the modern era, increasingly looked to direct foreign investments for profits. Being able to direct business affairs half a world away allowed American firms (and, to a lesser extent, those throughout the developed world) to further regulate global trade. The global marketplace became increasingly interconnected as a consequence, with the predictable growth in the world's largest firms, and with the ensuing homogenization of easily available goods and services.

By the twentieth century's final years, these increases in communications technology once transmitted via cables and then radio waves led to a further explosion in global consciousness. Humans watched agape in 1969 when astronauts first walked on the moon. They witnessed celebratory dances along the Berlin Wall in 1989, and the terror of the Chinese government's crackdown on democracy protestors in Tiananmen Square that same year. Billions simultaneously viewed sporting events at century's end, while annual celebrations of Hollywood garnered an equally large audience. Such mass consumption of culture led not only to political opposition to these seeming vanguards of western society (American cultural hegemony, transmitted largely through broadcast media and film, receives criticism from European and Asian political leaders as well as from Islamic fundamentalists), but also to the creation of cultural icons larger and arguably more influential than religious or political leaders of earlier times. Soccer star David Beckham or basketball icon Michael Jordan were each arguably more famous throughout the world than the pope at the dawn of the twenty-first century. Fame had always crossed borders. Unlike in previous eras, however, their faces were recognizable in lands they had never visited to a degree unlike any other period in history.

These new media changed the nature of global politics. Soviet and American leaders installed a direct "hotline" telephone link following the near disaster of 1962's Cuban Missile Crisis, reasoning (as others before had done with varied results) that greater ease of communication could avert crises from truly leaping out of control. Within a few decades the hotline remained, but the opportunity it offered for leaders to communicate with ease and speed had lost its novelty. The truly powerful and those with only powerful aspirations could by century's end announce their intents with far greater ease and far fewer government restrictions than ever before. Thus, for example, both presidents Bush could speak directly to the Iraqi people during the first and second Persian Gulf Wars, while their primary antagonist, Saddam Hussein, offered competing messages and interviews broadcast far beyond Iraq's borders. So too could hostages to any number of political causes be thrust before a watching world, their ordeals and, all too frequently, their executions broadcast for public consumption and for full political effect. With the rise of personal wireless communications (cellular phones and on-the-spot email especially) totaling more than one billion in use by century's end, coupled with the rise of the Internet age, the age of global communications had arrived by the twenty-first century, as prophesied centuries before. It made good on the phrase that "all politics are local" in a new way, as events the world over could be experienced, electronically at least, throughout the globe.

## Travel

Information moved with increasing speed across the twentieth century, and so too did people and goods. Improvements in transportation and travel abounded, beginning with the automobile. Arguably no other invention did more to define modern life (with an impact equally social, economic, and environmental) than did the car. Its history begins with development of the internal combustion engine during the last decades of the nineteenth century, a propulsion device in which the controlled explosion of flammable fuel powers a drive train directly. Such engines were far more efficient (and potentially compact) than the external steam engines (for example) that frequently powered both trains and boats at the time. The internal combustion engine was simple in theory, however, yet complex to design and produce in fact. The first workable model was developed in Belgium by Etienne Lenoire in the early 1870s, but with a top power generation of two horsepower – though weighing several hundred pounds – its utility in propelling a passenger vehicle was clearly limited. German inventor Nicholas Otto's 1876 contribution is therefore generally credited as the antecedent to all modern automobile engines. His four-stroke piston design compressed fuel with air to produce a more efficient output of power, and inventors throughout Europe and the United States rushed to put his design to use. German designers took the lead, with names (Gottlieb Daimler and Karl Benz in particular) that would help define the industry throughout the twentieth century. By 1900 automobile manufacturing

thrived, based upon German models, in France and Britain as well.

American manufacturers lagged behind, but soon made up for lost time. Automobile construction in the United States was haphazard at best before 1900, driven primarily by tinkerers (bicycle mechanics especially) and thrill-seekers. Their hand-built models were impressive for the day, but hardly useful for a mass market. It took more than a year for one pioneering pair of brothers, Charles and J. Frank Duryea, to construct twelve cars based upon their initial design. Yet the industry seemed primed for growth, if its first trade journal (*Horseless Age*, initiated in 1895) was to be believed. "All signs point to the motor vehicle as the necessary sequence of methods of locomotion already established and approved," its editors wrote. "The growing needs of our civilization demand it; the public believe in it, and await with lively interest its practical application to the daily business of the world." For the 300 independent automobile manufacturers in the country at the time, what was needed was a means to make their products profitable by making them affordable, plentiful, and easy to produce. By 1910 nearly 500,000 cars were registered in the United States alone, but as one manufacturer celebrated (and in part lamented), the public was "fairly howling" for more.[17]

It was at this moment of unmet public demand that Henry Ford changed the automobile industry forever. He did not invent the car. Neither (though he claimed otherwise) did he invent the system of line production that made him both famous and wealthy beyond his wildest dreams. What he did instead was perfect the assembly-line system of manufacturing for an industrial technology that verily cried out for mass production. Ford was committed to producing low-cost cars of high quality, and by developing specialized machine tools for workers trained in their use (though often not trained in much else), he clearly satisfied the market. Workers pieced together premade parts and components on cars that were built from scratch on moving conveyor belts before them, a system that simultaneously dropped production costs and vastly increased production volume. His 1908 "Model T" generated impressive horsepower and comfort, but at a price (initially $825) even his own blue-collar workers could afford. Sales and profits soared, but never content to rest on his laurels, Ford plowed much of his earning back into increasingly efficient production lines. The time required to produce a single Model A fell between October and December 1913 from 12 hours 30 minutes to under 3 hours. "Every piece of work in the shop moves," Ford later boasted. "It may move on hooks or overhead chains . . . it may travel on a moving platform, or it may go by gravity, but the point is that there is no lifting or trucking of anything other than materials."[18] By 1916 his company sold more than 500,000 cars a year. Others copied Ford's methods, and by the 1930s other manufacturers (General Motors in particular) produced more cars. The net result of this mass production and intense competition was an American automobile industry that dwarfed all others by the onset of the Second World War.[19]

The decades after the Second World War saw automotive production in the United States rise to unparalleled heights, as American machines set the global standard for style and quality. With most European manufacturers struggling to survive lean postwar years, these were golden times for American car producers, at least for those that survived in this naturally competitive industry. Whereas dozens of firms produced cars in the 1940s, by 1968, only four companies remained: General Motors, Ford, Chrysler, and American Motors. Each would be rocked by foreign competition, environmental assault, labor disputes, and consumer safety concerns by the end of the 1960s, and increasingly by European and then Japanese competition by the 1970s. Automobiles were never merely for transportation: in developed and developing nations alike cars represented their owner's status, style, and visible prosperity. With gasoline cheap and plentiful, style and power became the driving factors behind design in the first postwar decades. Not until 1959 did any of the Big Three even offer its customers a compact model. Fuel crises of the 1970s and after, sparked largely by an oil embargo imposed by the Organization of Petroleum Exporting Countries (OPEC), when coupled with low-cost and highly efficient Japanese models in particular, led to a new emphasis on fuel efficiency in the United States. Relatively higher fuel and consumption taxes in Europe contributed to an even greater emphasis on fuel efficiency – and thus to generally lighter vehicles – though by the close of the twentieth century, despite continued pressure on oil prices worldwide (exacerbated by prosperity and industrialization in India and China especially), average car size and weight continue to creep ahead yet again. It is a coincidence neither that the richest countries in the world utilize energy at the highest per capita rates nor that these same countries see energy-producing lands as vital security interests.[20]

European and Japanese producers benefited from the turn to smaller and lighter cars during the postwar decades, and automobile use became a vital part of European culture and life during the 1950s. Whereas in 1953 only 8 percent of French workers owned a car, for example, fourteen years later half of them did. French households with autos rose from 22.5 percent to 56.8 percent over the same period.[21] Several firms and models embedded themselves in global markets accordingly. Chief among these were the Volkswagen Beetle, a fuel-efficient compact whose diminutive nature made it a natural pick for American consumers increasingly eager to snub the conventions of the 1950s. Of greater future import was the growing availability of Japanese models, including Toyota and Nissan, which appeared in America's marketplace in 1957 and 1958, respectively. Already buffeted by these imports, America's auto industry came under assault from consumer and environmental advocates as well. In 1965, attorney Ralph Nader published *Unsafe at Any Speed*, a critique of the industry's safety record with the dramatic claim that faulty vehicle design was a major factor in highway accidents. Public furor over Nader's revelations helped spawn the 1966 National Traffic and Motor Vehicle Safety Act and the Highway Safety Act, which mandated that numerous safety devices, such as seatbelts, become standard issue on every American car. As was so often the case in the Cold War (and after), governments throughout the world followed Washington's lead, many adopting American standards wholesale.[22]

Worldwide, the industry also suffered from environmental criticisms during these years, especially after scientists reported that 70 percent of Los Angeles' famous smog was produced by automobile exhausts. In London, a "killer" smog caused the death of more than 4,000 residents in 1952 when an atmospheric anomaly stilled the winds that otherwise would have removed pollutants from the city's air. Industry and energy producers were undoubtedly partly to blame, but cars were the visible culprit. More than 200 people died in a similar smog attack a year later in New York City.[23] California lowered acceptable emissions levels in 1960, and Congress later passed its own automobile emissions regulations. Such standards have been a vital part of automotive design ever since, though in the rush to improve prosperity, rapidly developing nations are frequently becoming greater per capita producers of the air pollutants produced most visibly by cars. Tokyo, Delhi, Seoul, Mexico City, and Beijing each feature skyscrapers frequently obscured by smog and residents who find masks a necessary part of their daily commutes.

The growth in automobility led throughout the world to a surge in road and highway development, and in turn to a radical reshaping of urban and rural landscapes and settings. Road construction had been a largely haphazard affair before the twentieth century (in comparison to what would come next), but cars and trucks demanded new surfaces for optimal use. Governments, both local and national, quickly helped fill this void, recognizing the economic and social benefits of easy and rapid transportation. Washington's 1956 Interstate Highway Act offers an example of this trend, with an initial plan of 42,000 miles of federally funded highways linking the country. Cold War strategists, meanwhile, saw the roads as miles and miles of uncharted landing strips useful in repelling any enemy attack. Though arguably less militaristic in tone, other governments sponsored similar highway projects in due course, and by century's end both India and China lead (by a large margin) in new road construction. The automobile had changed global society, clearly for better and for worse: it allowed cities to grow and commercial networks to expand, and highlighted the world's dependence on fossil fuels with all its ancillary geopolitical concerns. There would be no retreat from such changes.[24]

The car changed daily life for billions, and so too did the airplane radically change global society. Unlike the automobile, which like the communications revolution had its origins in the nineteenth century, the airplane's development is almost predominantly a twentieth-century story. Humans had always dreamed of flight, and though rudimentary sketches of flying machines proliferated long before the twentieth century, it was not until Orville and Wilbur Wright kept a manned aircraft aloft for 59 seconds in December 1903 that the air age truly began. Others laid claim to this "first flight" before. Balloonists in particular proliferated during the latter half of the nineteenth century, but it was the Wrights who are generally credited with the feat. As with other inventions, they were not driven purely by scientific delight or altruistic desires. On the contrary, the Wrights recognized from the first that there was money to be made in their new technology, especially from buyers eager to gain control of the ultimate high-ground of the air. "It is our intention," Orville declared, "to furnish machines for military use first, before entering the commercial field." By 1909 the Wrights had contracts with Britain, France, the United States, and Germany for their machines.[25]

Competition had been fierce to see which nascent aircraft designer would be first to fly, and once news of the Wrights' technological and commercial success spread, the ranks of aspiring aircraft designers grew exponentially. By 1911 more than a dozen American firms competed for lucrative government aviation contracts, and Glenn Curtiss had designed a dirigible capable of soaring more than a thousand feet in the air. Competition was equally fierce across the Atlantic. In 1909, France's Louis Blériot made headlines by flying across the English Channel. Crowds celebrated such achievements, but not everyone responded with enthusiasm. "The news is not that man can fly," newspaper magnate Lord Northcliffe pronounced in 1906 upon learning of a successful French flight, "but that England is no longer an island." Northcliffe recognized that manned flight dramatically changed Europe's geopolitical landscape, bringing civilian populations in cities large and small but far from frontiers within range of enemy soldiers. Protected by their ocean moats,

American commentators typically greeted similar news with their typical millennial enthusiasm. "Sail forth, winged Argonauts of trackless air," one American poet wrote in 1909, yearning for the day when nations might find commonality through aerial proximity. "On sun-blessed wings, bring harbingers of peace."[26]

Sadly, the Europeans were right. Before aviation could transform global society through its promise of increased travel and commerce, military strategists used the new technology first. Each major European capital was bombed during the First World War. London suffered assault from German airships (aircraft that flew not by moving air across their wings and fuselage, but rather by controlling a streamlined balloon containing lighter-than-air gases), and each side produced fighters and bombers by the thousands. The stimulus of wartime spending spurred the industry to new heights. Whereas American producers had manufactured and sold a total of 411 aircraft in 1916, to take one example, orders from Europe combined with Washington's own requirements ensured that by 1917 those same manufacturers produced more than 20,000 machines. By the time peace arrived, so too had the first ocean-leaping aircraft, as a British bomber flew more than 2,000 miles in 1919 in crossing the Atlantic without a stop. When Charles Lindbergh repeated the feat in 1926 – making the far longer trip from New York's Long Island to Paris in a solo machine – the commercial possibilities for the new technology appeared boundless. Lindbergh himself became an international celebrity, parlaying his fame into great wealth by contributing to the rise of one of the world's first great airlines, Pan American.[27]

Pan American was hardly unique, but its story illustrates the way airline executives used power, influence, and the lure of great profits to forge a new transportation network in the first decades after the First World War. Lead by Juan Trippe, an impeccably well-connected young New Yorker, the airline subsidized its initially unprofitable formation of seaplane routes connecting Miami with ports of call throughout Central and Latin America by transporting mail as well as passengers. Such mail contracts were lucrative and steady, and by the 1930s Trippe's airline extended throughout the western hemisphere, where it built not only a loyal clientele through its posh service and commitment to on-time performance, but also a series of weather and radio-control stations that further helped link the hemisphere's commercial networks. By 1935 Pan Am's Clippers regularly completed the 8,500-mile journey from San Francisco to Asia as well. Trippe's company embodied style and class (air travel was, at that time, predominantly available to the wealthy), and as he was fond of stating when in Washington, its success as America's "chosen instrument" ensured German, Japanese, and even British airlines would not gain similar access to strategically vital ports of call in the western hemisphere. President Franklin Roosevelt called Trippe a "gangster" for the way he peddled money and influence in his quest for commercial dominance, but at a time when European airlines were themselves competing for market share throughout the developing world, he also appreciated the way Pan Am spread American power. British European Airways, for example, offered daily service from London to Egypt by the mid-1930s, four flights a week to India, three a week to East Africa, and twice-weekly service to Australia. Such flights connected the empire and helped counter dramatic French and German aviation growth, but did little to match America's embrace of air travel. More than 475,000 Americans flew during the Great Depression year of 1932 – the country's vast geography headed by a single government made it a perfect incubator for airline development – as did an even greater number of travelers of other nationalities. By 1941 that number was four million.[28]

Much of the growth in airline productivity during the interwar period came from impressive advances in aircraft design and performance. The planes that dominated during the First World War were capable of carrying only a few passengers and crew (at best), were limited in their range, and frequently required far more hours of service on the ground than they spent in the air. Those that came next literally soared in comparison. Airships took the initial postwar lead, headed by German designs. By 1931 the *Graf Zeppelin* operated a regular transatlantic service for the wealthy and elite (and, of course, for airmail), halving the time required to cross the ocean by ship. Tragedy befell its sister-ship, the *Hindenburg*, whose fiery crash in May 1937 above New Jersey proved a death-knell for this promising, though ultimately dangerous, aerial technology.[29]

Planes ruled the day thereafter, led commercially by models such as the Douglas DC-2 and DC-3, and the Boeing 247. Designed explicitly for passenger service, each made transcontinental travel not only feasible, but profitable as well. The DC-3 required only three crew members to serve its twenty-plus passengers, and with an unparalleled safety record, it became the global standard. By 1939 more than 90 percent of airline travelers journeyed in DC-3s, a record of market dominance by a single type unmatched before or since.[30]

The war stimulated aircraft design even further, specifically in the development of four-engine machines as long-range bombers and in the nascent development of jet engine technology. Both combined soon after the war in a new breed of jet-powered airliners, the first of which, Britain's De Havilland Comet, flew commercially in 1952. Years ahead of any competitor, the plane threatened to rip market dominance away from the United States. Britain and America were the only two free world nations truly capable of producing planes for every international market immediately following the war. It cut the time required to fly from London to Johannesburg to under 20 hours, and larger models scheduled to begin flying by the mid-1950s were expected to cross the Atlantic and even the larger Pacific Ocean as well. Its jet engines offered passengers high-altitude flights above the bumpy weather patterns that made propeller-driven flights frequently akin to a roller-coaster ride. "No passenger who rides in the quiet, vibrationless cabin of a plane driven by a spinning turbine will ever again spend a shilling to ride in the most perfectly silenced plane driven by a reciprocating engine," announced jet inventor Sir Frank Whittle after his first Comet flight.[31]

These dreams went unfulfilled, however, when the Comet suffered a series of tragic – and fatal – crashes. By 1954 the fleet was grounded, leaving American planes unchallenged in their pursuit of market dominance. Firms such as Boeing, Douglas, and Lockheed produced for buyers both at home and abroad, and each made nearly immeasurable profits supplying the Pentagon's insatiable Cold War appetite for arms. Profits from such military contracts helped offset the development costs of commercial machines. Boeing's 707, for example, the first successful American jetliner, used the same fuselage and wing design as the KC-135 tanker developed only years before for the Air Force. Given that the Soviet Union proved incapable of or uninterested in plying global aircraft markets throughout the Cold War's first half, the question following the Comet was not which nation would dominate global aviation, but which firm. Not until the 1970s did challengers to American aerial hegemony arise. The supersonic Concorde, a joint Anglo-French project, set the standard for speed and service, but the planes never proved profitable and were retired from active service by century's end.[32]

A European alternative to Boeing did arise in Airbus, whose family of models challenged for market dominance both in quality and in price. The fierce Atlantic competition for market dominance drove prices down for aircraft, aided by start-up firms in Brazil, China, and India, making airline travel affordable for much of the developed world. By the beginning of the twenty-first century Airbus had test-flown a machine, the A-380, capable of carrying more than 600 passengers aloft. As the ranks of developed nations grow, so too will such machines prove capable of meeting the massive appetite for business and travel of their blossoming though once-impoverished populations. Aided by such machines, by the twenty-first century it is quite possible to be anywhere in the world within 24 hours, a fact that brings new meaning to the concept of a shrinking world. The A-380, and the Boeing 747 before it, each offers a wingspan longer than the total distance of the Wright brothers' first flight, a fact more than any other that reveals the grand technological strides in the first century of flight. As yet, such machines have not provided a new messianic age of the kind promised whenever new communications and travel technologies arose during the twentieth century. Such optimism remains, however, renewed by every new development that seems to link humanity in a tighter embrace.

The twentieth century was therefore marked, and marred, by technological achievements in communications and transportations. As with most widely used technologies, these innovations carried benefits and consequences. The airplane that helped bridge the oceans and connect global society was used, almost from the first, to deliver bombs. The television that designers believed would bring a new era of cultural discourse and education to the masses has become a key ingredient in the rise of obesity in the western world. Not all technological developments lead inexorably to unfortunate consequences, of course. The Internet is both the haven of criminal networks and the means by which political and social groups eager for positive change coordinate and develop their pleas for a new world order.

Technology, in this sense, is morally neutral. It is up to each user to employ new technologies for good or for evil as they see fit. This is not a new phenomenon for twentieth-century advances. But the changes witnessed in the twentieth century, highlighted by the tremendous explosion of human knowledge fostered by the communications media discussed above, appeared at an unprecedented pace. Most societies and generations throughout history have believed themselves to be in the vanguard of human evolution, living in the most modern of times with the most modern of problems. Global society at the start of the twenty-first century is no different. Surely those who lived at the start of the twentieth century believed their times unlike any others. But what sets the twentieth century apart from those that came before is the speed of change. As described above, globalization is a process more than a destination. The changes in communications and transportation technology witnessed over the past century make it appear that this process is moving at a faster clip than ever before. And nothing in the twenty-first century, thus far at least, would suggest a slowing of this process anytime soon.

## NOTES

1   Peter Hugill, *World Trade since 1431: Geography, Technology, and Capitalism* (Baltimore: Johns Hopkins University Press, 1995); Fernand Braudel, *Afterthoughts on Material Civilization and Capitalism* (Baltimore: Johns Hopkins University Press, 1979); Immanuel Wallerstein, *World-Systems Analysis: An Introduction* (Durham, NC: Duke University Press, 2004); Thomas McCormick, *America's Half-Century* (Baltimore: Johns Hopkins University Press, 1995).

2   Jack Weatherford, *Genghis Khan and the Making of the Modern World* (New York: Three Rivers Press, 2005).

3   H. J. Mackinder, "The Geographical Pivot in History," *Geographical Journal* 23 (1904): 421–37; Brian Blouet, ed., *Mackinder and the Defence of the West* (New York: Frank Cass, 2005).

4   Silvio Pons, ed., *Reinterpreting the End of the Cold War* (New York: Frank Cass, 2005).

5   Peter Hugill, *Global Communications since 1844* (Baltimore: Johns Hopkins University Press, 1999), p. 31.

6   David Nickles, *Under the Wire: How the Telegraph Changed Diplomacy* (Cambridge, MA: Harvard University Press, 2003).

7   Daniel R. Headrick, *The Invisible Weapon* (New York: Oxford University Press, 1991). See also Headrick, *When Information Came of Age* (New York: Oxford University Press, 2002).

8   James Foreman-Peck, *A History of the World Economy* (New York: Pearson, 1995), p. 67.

9   Peter Jay, *The Wealth of Man* (New York: Public Affairs, 2000), p. 191.

10  N. Gordon Levin, *Woodrow Wilson and World Politics* (New York: Oxford University Press, 1970), p. 18.

11  E. F. O'Neill, *A History of Engineering and Science in the Bell System* (New York: The Laboratories, 1975), p. 786.

12  F. H. Hinsley, *Codebreakers: The Unknown Story of Bletchley Park* (New York: Oxford University Press, 2001); David Kahn, *The Codebreakers: The Comprehensive History of Secret Communications from Ancient Times to the Internet* (New York: Scribner's, 1996).

13  Ruth Schwartz Cowan, *A Social History of American Technology* (New York: Oxford University Press, 1997), p. 289.

14  Tom Lewis, *Empire of the Air: The Men Who Made Radio* (New York: HarperCollins, 1991); Susan Smulyan, *Selling Radio: The Commercialization of American Broadcasting* (Washington, DC: Smithsonian Books, 1994).

15  Cowan, *Social History*, p. 290.

16  Albert Abramson, *The History of Television, 1942–2000* (Jefferson, NC: McFarland, 2003); Erik

Barnouw, *Tube of Plenty: The Evolution of American Television* (New York: Oxford University Press, 1992).

17  Cowan, *Social History*, p. 227.

18  Ibid., p. 229.

19  James Fink, *America Adopts the Automobile, 1895–1910* (Cambridge, MA: Harvard University Press, 1970); John Rae, *The American Automobile Industry* (Boston: G. K. Hall, 1984).

20  George Daniels and Mark Rose, eds., *Energy and Transport* (Beverly Hills, CA: Sage, 1982); Daniel Yergin, *The Prize: The Epic Quest for Oil, Money and Power* (New York: Simon & Schuster, 1991).

21  David Landes, *The Wealth and Poverty of Nations* (New York: W. W. Norton, 1999), p. 468.

22  Ralph Nader, *Unsafe at Any Speed* (New York: Grossman, 1965).

23  Cowan, *Social History*, p. 241.

24  Kenneth Jackson, *Crabgrass Frontier* (New York: Oxford University Press, 1985).

25  Roger Bilstein, *Flight in America: From the Wrights to the Astronauts* (Baltimore: Johns Hopkins University Press, 2001).

26  Joseph Corn, *The Winged Gospel* (New York: Oxford University Press, 1983), p. 38; Alfred Gollin, *No Longer an Island* (Palo Alto, CA: Stanford University Press, 1984); David Edgerton, *England and the Aeroplane* (London: Macmillan, 1991).

27  Michael Sherry, *The Rise of American Airpower* (New Haven, CT: Yale University Press, 1987).

28  Matthew Josephson, *Empire of the Air* (New York: Arno Press, 1972); Marylin Bender, *The Chosen Instrument* (New York: Simon & Schuster, 1982).

29  Henry Beaubois, *Airships* (New York: Two Continents, 1976).

30  Ian Gould, "The Modern Jet Airliner: The Trailblazers," in *Modern Air Transport*, ed. Philip Jarrett (London: Putnam, 2000).

31  Derek Dempster, *The Tale of the Comet* (New York: McKay, 1958), p. 85; R. G. Davies and Philip Birtles, *De Havilland Comet* (McLean, VA: Airlife Publishing, 1999).

32  Jeffrey A. Engel, *Cold War at 30,000 Feet* (Cambridge, MA: Harvard University Press, 2007).

## GUIDE TO FURTHER READING

Erik Barnouw, *Tube of Plenty: The Evolution of American Television* (New York: Oxford University Press, 1992). Offers an easily accessible one-volume introduction to a technology that changed American culture and society.

Marylin Bender, *The Chosen Instrument* (New York: Simon & Schuster, 1982). The best single volume on Pan American Airways, a trendsetter in global transportation.

Brian Blouet, ed., *Mackinder and the Defence of the West* (New York: Frank Cass, 2005). An excellent overview of one of the twentieth century's most influential geographers.

Joseph Corn, *The Winged Gospel* (New York: Oxford University Press, 1983). The single best work on America's love of aviation from the Wright brothers through to 1945 (with a new paperback edition published in 2002 from Johns Hopkins University Press).

Ruth Schwartz Cowan, *A Social History of American Technology* (New York: Oxford University Press, 1997). Offers an excellent example of the current trend in technology studies to reveal not only the inner working of products or inventors, but their social and cultural context and impact as well.

Daniel R. Headrick, *The Invisible Weapon* (New York: Oxford University Press, 1991); and *When Information Came of Age* (New York: Oxford University Press, 2002). Each is among the best works setting communications in a global strategic context.

Peter Hugill, *World Trade since 1431: Geography, Technology, and Capitalism* (Baltimore: Johns Hopkins University Press, 1995) provides a brief though frequently insightful introduction to capitalism's premodern and modern development.

Thomas McCormick, *America's Half-Century* (Baltimore: Johns Hopkins University Press, 1995) is an insightful thematic view of American foreign policy during the Cold War with an eye toward long-term global trends and world-systems analysis.

Michael Sherry, *The Rise of American Airpower* (New Haven, CT: Yale University Press, 1987). Winner of the Bancroft Prize as the best book published in American history, this is a thought-provoking study placing American aviation history in a broader strategic and cultural context. See also Sherry's *In the Shadow of War* (1997) for the author's further investigation into military and social affairs in modern American history.

Daniel Yergin, *The Prize: The Epic Quest for Oil, Money and Power* (New York: Simon & Schuster, 1991). An award-winning (and deservedly so) exploration of a crucial topic, and a text all other writers on the subject are forced to engage.

# CHAPTER FIVE

# A Changing Diplomatic World

## *RALPH BLESSING*

The twentieth century saw unprecedented change in every field of human activity. These transformations of course also had a profound impact on how governments conducted their foreign policies and the conditions under which diplomats had to work. Changing circumstances naturally also altered organizations and organizational behavior, and this chapter will examine major administrative changes in the foreign services in the past century. The analysis will focus on two basic issues. It will, firstly, address the causes for the administrative changes in the foreign services such as technological progress, changing values regarding the aims and means of national foreign policy, including the growing importance of securing peace, and the growing number of actors participating in foreign relations. Secondly, it will explain how the foreign services reacted to the new challenges and which administrative steps were taken to meet them: foreign services around the world became more professional, they expanded in size as well as in scope (which, conversely, led to increasing internal specialization), and the decision-making process increasingly became located in the central administrations rather than in the missions abroad. Finally, it will discuss which issues the diplomatic world is facing at the beginning of the twenty-first century and whether diplomacy itself is disappearing.

Since the space of this study is limited and the period of examination spans a whole century, it is impossible to even attempt a survey of all 191 member states of the United Nations and their diplomatic services. Therefore, this overview will largely focus on the reforms and changes in the French Ministère des affaires étrangères, the German Auswärtiges Amt, the British Foreign Office, and the American State Department. Although a limitation in scope of course always bears dangers, there are good arguments for focusing on these diplomatic services. First of all, diplomacy, and the way it is practiced today, is largely based on European traditions. Even the Soviet Union and its satellite states, when they existed, adopted the administrative structures of the western diplomatic services, and the same is true for the countries that were formerly colonized by European countries. Additionally, the European countries, and France in particular, initiated many of the reforms that were later adopted in other countries as well. The choice of the United States is obvious. Not only does it deserve, as the only remaining superpower, special consideration, but it was also the United States which, with President Woodrow Wilson's "14 Points" and his initiative for the creation of the League of Nations, set off a series of fundamental changes in diplomacy after the First World War.

## A Changing World

On a very abstract level, the main cause for administrative changes within the foreign ministries of almost all countries in the twentieth century was the growing complexity of international relations, which in turn reflected dramatic political, economic, and social shifts on a global scale. There are three basic reasons why international relations in the 1900s became more complex: technological changes, a new diplomatic agenda, and a larger – and still growing – number of actors in foreign relations.

The first technological development that had a major impact on diplomacy was the transportation revolution of the early nineteenth century. The invention of the steamship and the railway not only opened new territories and countries for conquest, exploitation, and economic exchange but also created the need for consular and diplomatic representation there. This also sped up the delivery of diplomatic mail and made it much more reliable. The invention of the telegraph a few decades later made information almost immediately available everywhere and therefore vastly changed how diplomats in missions abroad communicated with their ministries at home. This trend toward the "global village" increased during the twentieth century with the advent of commercial aviation, the telephone, the personal computer, television, and, most recently of course, the Internet. Technological change, however, influenced diplomacy not only directly but also indirectly. The invention of mass circulation newspapers, for example, created for the first time what is nowadays called public opinion, and the public, in turn, increasingly demanded information in order to participate in domestic as well as foreign affairs. The most important impact, however, that technological and, as a direct result, societal change had on diplomacy was how the character of war changed in the twentieth century. With the advent of increasingly deadly weapons and the invention of the first weapons of mass destruction – the introduction of chemical warfare on the battlefields of western Europe in the First World War – the character of war changed dramatically. If, in the past, war mainly affected the soldiers while the homeland, except for the actual battlefield, remained largely unscathed, the total war of the twentieth century increasingly blurred the division between the frontline and the hinterland. The economic hardships of the total mobilization of the industry for the war effort, and in particular the massive air raids of the Second World War, made virtually everyone a combatant. This, of course, also had dramatic consequences for diplomacy. While in the nineteenth century Clausewitz could still claim that war was the continuation of politics – and, one might add, diplomacy – by other means, the total war of the new century proved so abominable that it could no longer be justified by political means and became completely discredited instead.

These developments in warfare were mainly responsible for the second set of causes that changed diplomacy and its administrative conduct in the twentieth century – the new character of diplomacy. While the dominating notion of the "old diplomacy" – the term used to describe international relations before 1918 – was that diplomacy should serve the interests of one's own country, the preservation of peace and the peaceful settlement of conflicts became the paradigm of the "new diplomacy," most effectively promoted (but not invented) after 1917 by the US president, Woodrow Wilson. According to the advocates of the new diplomacy, peace was to be secured by three basic means, the first of which consisted of promoting democracy. Authoritarian states, it was believed, could not be trusted to meet their international obligations. That is why Wilson insisted that the German kaiser had to abdicate before the conclusion of a peace treaty with Germany; an autocratic and militaristic regime like the one in Berlin, the American president assumed, would not be able to guarantee durable peace. Secondly, the adherents of new diplomacy believed that free trade and economic exchange between the states would be an effective safeguard against conflict because it was supposed that nations would not dare – or even be able – to attack those countries on which their supply of raw materials depended or where they sold their products. This theory, popularized by the Englishman Norman Angell even before the outbreak of the First World War, was further supported by the assumption that international trade, according to the principles of free trade postulated by David Ricardo, would create greater wealth for all and thus reduce social conflicts which, if unresolved, could possibly lead to international tensions.

Finally, proponents of the new diplomacy wanted to create a binding system of arbitration and collective security which would lead to the peaceful resolution of international conflicts. Collective security was an advancement of the theory of "balance of power" that was the guiding principle of British foreign policy in the nineteenth century to secure peace in Europe. The premise on which the balance of power theory relied was that two power blocks of equal strength would not attack each other and thus peace would be preserved. Britain therefore constantly tried to create equilibrium on the European continent, siding with the weaker powers in order to maintain peace. The British desire for peace and quiet, however, was only partly philanthropic; realistically, they wished to exploit the spoils of their own empire undisturbed. But the idea that the balance of power would preserve the peace was obviously proven wrong by the First World War and new means for safeguarding peace had to be found. Collective security was meant to repair the flaws of the balance of power doctrine. In a system of collective security, all countries have to come to the assistance of another nation under attack. This would make war impossible because the aggressor would have to fight against all the other powers combined. Facing certain defeat, the potential aggressor would give up its plans and stick to peaceful means of conflict resolution. This of course means that no country in the system of collective security is stronger by itself than all the other nations combined; there is no room for an aggressive "superpower" in this concept. Another fundamental difference between balance of power and collective security is that the former means a constant ad hoc shifting of power in favor of the potentially inferior party, while collective security was conceived to last and be safeguarded by international organizations.

New diplomacy, however, was conceived not only as an alternative to power politics, which had been so badly discredited by the First World War, but also as a reaction of the democratic and "capitalistic" countries to socialism and communism, which had claimed that war would come to an end once the workers of all nations were liberated from the yoke of capitalism and its twin, imperialism.

But new diplomacy did not only mark a new beginning regarding the overall objective of diplomacy, the preservation of peace; new diplomacy was also remarkable because it was not concerned exclusively with the safeguarding of the political power of a nation (in which economic factors were only auxiliary means) but was involved with economic aspects (via free trade) and moral factors (via "good" democracy versus "bad" autocracy). New diplomacy, therefore, opened up genuinely new fields for diplomacy which had, before the First World War, been widely disregarded. This was particularly true for foreign economic policy and cultural diplomacy as a means to influence public opinion abroad. Later on in the twentieth century, other concerns were added to the diplomatic agenda, such as the fight against diseases like smallpox and today HIV/AIDS, or the protection of the environment – the Rio Conference and the Kyoto Protocol are examples for those endeavors. A broader diplomatic agenda in itself meant an increase in the complexity of foreign relations because the formerly neglected fields of economic and cultural diplomacy now had to be coordinated with classic diplomacy, in other words, the political interests of a country.

But new areas of diplomatic activity also led to the emergence of new actors in foreign relations, which increased the complexity of diplomacy even further and is the third fundamental factor of administrative change. New topics in foreign policy made the introduction of experts necessary, be they from other branches of the government or specialists from outside the political system, such as economic experts from private enterprises or specialists from other fields. Moreover, the democratization of foreign policy, via the inclusion of the public through the news media, created another entirely new group of actors in foreign relations, independent from diplomacy altogether – the non-governmental organizations (NGOs). The creation of new states, especially in Africa and Asia in the wake of decolonization after the Second World War and in eastern Europe and Central Asia after the collapse of communism, multiplied the number of players in international relations even more. The same is true for the emergence of new international and regional organizations such as the League of Nations, and its successor the United Nations (UN), with its affiliated organizations such as UNESCO, the European Union (EU) and its predecessors, or other regional associations such as ASEAN, the Organization of American States, and so on.

Other new actors in the field of international relations include multinational corporations that generate revenues equal not only to those of developing countries but also to those of some smaller industrialized economies. Adding to the universe of players is the news media, which, with the advent of CNN some twenty years ago and, more recently, Al-Jazeera, has reduced the role of diplomacy in gathering and distributing information. The sheer presence of a topic in the news, the fact that it is covered (or not) by one of the major news networks, has already become an important factor in international relations. Terrorism, too, exercises a growing influence on international relations, and the "War on Terror" that was declared after the events of September 11, 2001 now occupies a significant part of the international agenda. Terrorists, for example, exploit all technological means to promote their aims and influence politics. The publication of images of the execution of western hostages in Iraq on the Internet, for instance, had a great impact on public opinion in the western countries vis-à-vis the overthrow of Saddam Hussein's regime, and had possibly a more dramatic and decisive impact on public opinion in the West than hundreds of memos from diplomats on the pros and cons of an intervention in Iraq.

## The Administrative Response

Faced with the growing complexity of international relations caused by technological change, new agendas, and new actors, diplomacy had to find administrative answers in order to remain relevant. Periodically, efforts to overhaul the foreign services succeeded in adapting the existing structures to the new demands of the international system. Generally speaking, administrative reforms in the foreign services of the major European countries and the United States took place along the lines of professionalization, expansion, specialization, and centralization of the foreign services. But while the turn from "old" to "new"

diplomacy immediately after the First World War meant significant changes regarding the contents of foreign policy, administrative changes often followed a path of reform that had already been established in the nineteenth century.

This is particularly true for the professionalization of diplomacy. As early as the nineteenth century, the major European powers had begun gradually introducing entrance qualifications and, later, entrance examinations for the foreign service. Starting in Prussia in 1827, and followed by Britain in 1855 and France in 1877, applicants for the diplomatic service had to fulfill certain minimum qualifications (such as holding a university degree) and pass specific tests. In the United States, where the awarding of diplomatic posts mostly followed the spoils system introduced by President Andrew Jackson in the 1830s, it was only in 1906 that the consular service became based on a merit system. The establishment of minimum requirements, however, did not mean that privileges of birth, wealth, or political allegiance were completely replaced by merit. Despite the entrance exams, the British foreign minister had the right to nominate his own candidates for the foreign service; and in Russia, which had introduced entrance tests in 1859, Jews and peasants were excluded from the foreign ministry regardless of their qualifications. Often, diplomats were not paid at all or received only a symbolic remuneration for their services, therefore excluding poor but able candidates. France introduced only in 1905 a rule that attachés would be paid. Before this, every candidate for the foreign service had been required to work as an unpaid attaché for three years. Other European states had similar regulations. Even the United States, which regarded the aristocratic mores of many of the European countries with suspicion, introduced a sufficient salary for its diplomats only with the Rogers Act of 1924.

The professionalization of diplomacy was reflected in the creation not only of minimum requirements but also of a rank system (and therefore clear-cut hierarchies). France set the example in 1858 and Britain followed three years later by establishing a set career path. This showed another trend of diplomacy in the nineteenth century, the decline of the so-called "family embassy." At the beginning of the century, the appointed ambassador or envoy usually brought his own personnel with him to the post. With the increasing political and technical demands and the growing number of personnel in diplomatic missions abroad, this became impractical and was gradually phased out.

The second important aspect of administrative change was expansion, and the first dimension of this expansion was geographical. With the Latin American countries gaining independence from their Spanish and Portuguese motherlands in the early nineteenth century, European powers established diplomatic relations with them and the new countries established missions abroad. The First World War, with the collapse of the tsarist, Habsburg, and Ottoman empires, led to the emergence of several new countries in eastern and central Europe. This was followed by a third wave of newly founded countries after the Second World War, when, as a result of decolonization, the number of states in Africa and Asia multiplied. The collapse of the Soviet Union and Yugoslavia after the implosion of communism led to the creation of a host of new states at the beginning of the 1990s. All these new states had to build up their own diplomatic missions and the other states had to be represented there. And while it is true that not every state is represented in all other states – this is in particular true for smaller developing countries – this development led to an enormous increase in diplomatic missions, personnel, and contacts. The creation of international organizations led to a further expansion of foreign services, because often it is not the embassy of a nation in the country where the international organization has its headquarters that is responsible for relations with the international organization, but specialized and separate missions with the particular international organization. Therefore, many EU member countries that also happen to be members of NATO have not one but three missions in Brussels: the embassy in Belgium and permanent missions for the EU and NATO, respectively. The decades following the Second World War in particular saw the creation of an increasing number of new international organizations, such as the UN and its affiliated and specialized organizations, including UNESCO and

the Food and Agricultural Organization (FAO). The process of European integration also created several international organizations, the largest one undoubtedly the European Union, but also specialized institutions such as the Organization for Economic Cooperation and Development (OECD) for economic issues and the Organization for Security and Cooperation in Europe (OSCE) for security questions. Other regions of the world also created their political and economic confederations, such as the African Union and the South American Free Trade Zone (MERCOSUR). Yet even though international organizations multiplied and gained importance after the Second World War, it was the League of Nations, founded after the First World War, and its affiliates that had created the international organization as a new tool of diplomacy and a forum for multilateral consultation. Older international institutions, such as the Universal Postal Union (established in 1874) and the International Telecommunication Union (founded in 1865), the oldest international organization, were only partnerships of convenience with narrowly defined purposes.

The extent of expansion of international relations, especially after the Second World War, becomes clear when one looks at the growing numbers of personnel in the foreign services. In France, the number of diplomats more than quintupled from 477 in 1945 to 9,293 in 2004. The United States foreign service grew from 1,228 in 1900 to 15,506 in 1997, and the German foreign service expanded from ca. 350 members in 1900 to 6,550 today. Since many of the Americans employed at the missions abroad were not members of the foreign service but belonged to other government agencies, ranging from the CIA to the Department of Agriculture (by the 1960s only one-third of the staff at American missions abroad were actually in the service of the Department of State), the number of officials working in the context of international relations rose even higher than the numbers of foreign service personnel suggest.

The expansion of the foreign services resulted in specialization, and specialization, conversely, promoted expansion. Specialization was caused by the new demands that were posed by the new topics of diplomacy. Those were, at the end of the nineteenth century, mainly economic questions. Until then, the foreign services dealt almost exclusively with political questions, while foreign economic relations were covered by the consular services. While both diplomatic and consular services were under the roof of the foreign ministry, they were administratively separate, with the consular service being regarded as the lesser of the two. The first step in increasing the economic profile of foreign services was to merge the diplomatic with the consular services. As a side effect, the diplomatic services of the European countries also became socially more inclusive because, until then, the consular service had been staffed with commoners while the diplomatic service had been the domain of the aristocracy. Women, however, were still mostly excluded from the foreign service, explicitly in France until after the Second World War and implicitly elsewhere. The appointment of a female head of mission by American President Franklin D. Roosevelt before the Second World War was only a singular event and emancipation reached diplomacy only after the war.

As on so many other occasions, France was at the forefront of change and became the first country to merge its consular with its diplomatic service in 1907. The French ministry of foreign affairs, the Quai d'Orsay, gave up its functional organizational structure and was divided into geographical units in which both consular and political functions were united. In Germany and Britain, the inclusion of economic tasks took longer. Despite the criticism of Germany's economic leaders before the First World War who condemned the – in their eyes – outdated division of the Auswärtiges Amt, which they felt did not take into account the economic needs of one of the largest economies of the time, only the breakdown of Kaiser Wilhelm II's regime in 1918 led to a radical reform of the German foreign ministry. The fusion of diplomatic and consular services was one of the most important aspects of the reform, and this was done in order to secure Germany's economic interests abroad. The protagonist of the reform, veteran diplomat Edmund Schüler, even went so far as to introduce not one but two secretaries of state (i.e., the highest civil

service in a German ministry), one of them exclusively responsible for foreign economic policy. This structure, however, proved impractical and the Germans reverted to the traditional system with a single secretary of state in 1922. The reforms in Germany and France are also remarkable insofar as they created some of the basic organizational principles that still are in place today: in both countries, the foreign ministry was divided into different departments which covered certain regions of the world. In Britain, during the interwar period, the integration of economic and political aspects of foreign relations was much less advanced than in France and in Germany. For questions of foreign economic policy, the Department of Overseas Trade was created under the joint supervision of the Foreign Office and the Board of Trade – the British ministry of economic affairs – and the fusion of diplomatic and consular services was not really achieved until 1943. In the United States, too, the division between consular and diplomatic services continued to exist between the two world wars, even though, with the reform of 1909, geographic divisions had been created in the Department of State. Even after the Second World War, the American foreign service did not become unified. While the Department of State remained in charge of political questions, other departments, for example the Department of Agriculture, added specialized divisions to American missions abroad. These divisions did not become part of the foreign service but continued to be attached to their respective departments in Washington, DC. Also, new specialized agencies were created which had their role in American foreign relations. While the Department of State was coordinating the activities, many of the agencies, such as the CIA, the United States Information Agency (USIA), and the Agency for International Development (USAID), remained largely autonomous. This development, which differentiated the United States from the European countries, was to a large extent the result of resistance from within the State Department: it had been mainly the foreign service officials who had rejected the suggestions of the Hoover and Rowe commissions (1949 and 1950, respectively), which had called for the creation of a united foreign service.

Another aspect of the growing importance of economic matters was the creation of specialized departments for economic questions within the central administrations of the foreign ministries. Here, too, the continental European powers set the pace. France created a department for economic affairs (sous-direction des affaires commerciales) in 1919. The German Auswärtiges Amt followed shortly after. The creation of those two departments reflected the devastating economic effects of the First World War and the need for reconstruction. The reparations problem that existed between Germany and the victorious western powers and the problem of inter-Allied debts aggravated the economic muddle of the interwar period. In Britain and in the United States, however, those important financial questions were hardly dealt with by the foreign ministries, instead being handled by the respective treasuries and, in the United States, by the World War Foreign Debt Commission. Even though an Economic Relations Section was created within the Foreign Office in 1934, it was not until 1943, when diplomatic and consular services were finally merged, that economic questions began to play a more important role in British foreign policy. Only after the Second World War, during the early phases of the growing confrontation between East and West, when the need to rebuild war-ravaged Europe became urgent, did foreign economic policy begin to become more important in the United States. Even then, however, it was largely delegated to specialized agencies and not under the auspices of the State Department.

But economics was not the only area in which specialization took place. Another field was public relations and cultural diplomacy. Driven by a sense of civilizing mission, it was again the French who brought forward innovation. In 1883, they founded the Alliance française in order to promote the French language and civilization, and, although independent from the Quai d'Orsay, it became an important precedent for foreign cultural politics. It took, however, until 1920 before a special department for cultural affairs was created at the French foreign ministry, but this department, too, had had a smaller predecessor in the French administration, mainly responsible for French schools abroad. French interest in cultural diplomacy also became apparent in the foundation of the Institut international de coopération intellectuelle, the predecessor to UNESCO, in 1921. The institute was largely funded by the French government and had its headquarters in Paris (as does UNESCO). The Auswärtiges Amt had also been responsible for German schools abroad prior to the First World War, but in Germany, too, a real cultural department was only created after the war. Because of Germany's federal structure, in which cultural policy was – and still is – the domain of the individual states, the scope of the Auswärtiges Amt culture division was much narrower than that of its French counterpart. In interwar Germany, cultural diplomacy was mainly aimed at the German minorities in eastern Europe that emerged after the collapse of the Austro-Hungarian Empire and the cession of formerly German territories following the Versailles Treaty. Again the Anglo-Saxon powers, where the government plays a much lesser role in cultural affairs in general, were latecomers. Britain followed in 1934 with the creation of the British Council. This was a reaction to the cultural work of the French and to the increasing propaganda efforts of Italian Fascism and German National Socialism in the 1930s. In the United States, cultural diplomacy became established with the creation of the aforementioned USIA in 1953, but this institution had several predecessor organizations dating back to the counterpropaganda efforts of the First World War (the so-called Creel Committee). Only in 1999 did the USIA become incorporated into the Department of State in the course of the Foreign Affairs and Restructuring Act, which also transferred the responsibilities for arms control and development from semi-autonomous agencies directly to the State Department.

While public diplomacy addresses the public abroad, twentieth-century diplomacy was also faced with growing public interest and scrutiny at home. This was the result of democratization – in Germany, for example, foreign policy only became subjected to parliamentary control with the constitutional reforms of October 1918, when the German Reich effectively became a constitutional monarchy – and the growing importance of the news media, at first the press and later radio, television, and the Internet. President Wilson's claims for open diplomacy put even more pressure on the foreign ministries to commit to public relations. The more traditional approach toward public relations was the publication of diplomatic documents in order to convince the public of the righteousness of one's own policy. The British government started this in 1763 with the publication of its first "bluebook" (after the color of the cover), Prussia and later Germany published "whitebooks," and in 1861 France began publishing its "yellowbooks." In the same year as the French, the United States started to publish their own series of official documents, the "Papers Relating to the Foreign Relations of the US." But the publication of these documents was frequently guided by propagandistic aims and not by the desire to clarify one's policy. After the First World War, Germany tried to liberate itself from its "war guilt" by publishing an extensive account of its prewar documents under the title "Die Große Politik der Europäischen Kabinette 1871–1914," which, of course, sparked similar projects in the other belligerent countries. This publication also marked a certain shift in the publication of documents, which henceforth came to be guided increasingly by principles of historical research. Today, the major countries publish important diplomatic documents edited by teams of international historians.

The second aspect of public relations consisted in influencing the press and the media. This was done firstly by granting certain journalists privileged access to information, which made some newspapers, such as the French *Matin* in the first half of the twentieth century, the semi-official spokesperson of the Quai d'Orsay. This was even truer for the totalitarian states like Nazi Germany and the Soviet Union, where the policy expressed in the party (and all other) newspapers was the official policy. The phenomenon of the "embedded journalist" in the last Gulf War still reflects the desire, in this case of the military, to influence the press. Less honorable ways of manipulating the press in the past included bribing journalists or providing newspapers with financial support. In terms of organizational specialization of the foreign ministries, the creation of specialized press departments is of particular importance. France and Austria set up the first press divisions

in 1870, but those were largely concerned with monitoring the media at home and abroad. In the United States the Division of Information within the Department of State followed a similar logic. It was once again the First World War which set the pace for things to come. As the first "total" war, the mobilization of the entire population for the war effort became of critical importance and propaganda was to play the key role in this. In Germany, the Zentralstelle für Auslandsdienst and the Nachrichtenabteilung were founded at the Auswärtiges Amt, and in France the Maison de la Presse was the center of the Quai d'Orsay's propaganda efforts. Britain reacted in a similar manner by creating the War Propaganda Bureau, which was originally part of the Home Office but was later transferred to the Foreign Office. The aforementioned Creel Committee (the official title of which was the Committee on Public Information) in the United States was founded shortly after the US entered the war in April 1917 in order to mobilize the American public for the war effort. While the Creel Committee was dismantled shortly after the war, the propaganda efforts in Germany and France had an afterlife. In France, the Maison de la Presse became the Service de la presse et de l'information of the Quai d'Orsay. Germany created a unified press department for the government, but this division was administratively part of the foreign ministry. Today, of course, foreign ministries all around the world have specialized departments dealing with the media and public relations.

Since "new" diplomacy was more strongly concerned not only with social and economic questions, open diplomacy (and public relations), and cultural diplomacy but also with the creation of organs of collective security by establishing the League of Nations, foreign ministries also had to take the new phenomenon of "multilateral" diplomacy into account. France addressed this challenge with the creation of a specialized department, the Service français de la Société des Nations. Germany, one of the losers of the First World War, was originally excluded from the League of Nations. With the détente between the former belligerents in the middle of the 1920s, however, demands for Germany to join the League became louder and a department dealing with the League of Nations was created in the Auswärtiges Amt in 1923. In the United States, which did not ratify the Versailles Treaty and therefore did not become a member of the League of Nations, this differentiation did not take place. The same is true for Great Britain, where the attitude toward the League was more reluctant than in France, and therefore League of Nations Affairs was only a subdivision of the Western Department. After the creation of the UN in 1945 and several other international organizations, the foreign ministries of all major countries now had specialized departments dealing with multilateral questions and international organizations. In European countries, the process of European unification also led to the creation of specialized divisions for questions regarding European integration. The still-growing complexity of international relations and new challenges such as arms control and security, human rights issues, and so on led to even further administrative differentiation.

Specialization also found its expression in the deployment of attachés, officials from other ministries, to embassies and missions abroad. The driving forces were, as with many other developments, military considerations and economic necessity. Napoleon Bonaparte was the first to send military experts to assist French missions abroad in analyzing military matters, but the practice was not very common until the 1860s, when international tensions rose and the European Concert, which had been created after the Congress of Vienna, began to show alarming signs of disintegration – as became apparent in the Crimean War and the wars of German unification. Even the United States, which was hardly involved in European affairs at that time, followed the European example in 1889. The military attachés, usually attached to the ministry of war (or defense) of their country, began to play a crucial part in military intelligence. Within a military alliance such as NATO or the former Warsaw Pact, military attachés are essential for coordinating common military strategy and planning. Commercial attachés were introduced by the British in 1880, while France followed in 1908. Their main task was to advise merchants, to provide information about the regional marketplaces, and to find new economic opportunities

for the producers at home. The appearance of these attachés, who were often officials from the ministry of trade or commerce, was closely related to the growing protectionism at the end of the nineteenth century, comparable to the rise of the military attachés at the height of imperial conflicts. Other attachés – e.g., financial attachés – connected to other ministries or agencies followed. The emergence of the attachés was the result of the increasing specialization of foreign relations but also of the growing involvement of other ministries and departments with originally domestic duties in international affairs. The globalizing economy of the late nineteenth century made economic policies less and less a matter of primary national extent but had a growing international dimension as well. However, the introduction of attachés was not without problems. They often felt a stronger allegiance to their former ministries than to their new one and sometimes they bypassed established diplomatic channels and competed with the diplomats. Occasionally, attachés also judged matters from a different perspective than their consular or diplomatic colleagues, which led to uncoordinated political action. While, for example, the German embassy in Britain tried to ease naval conflicts between Berlin and London in the run-up to the First World War, the German military attaché, with the backing of his superiors in Berlin, counteracted those efforts.

As the example of the attaché illustrates, the growing diversification of foreign relations and the specialization of the diplomatic service created the need for better coordination. This was mainly achieved by growing centralization. Until the nineteenth century, ambassadors and other envoys enjoyed a fair amount of leeway. With their superiors hundreds or thousands of kilometers away and means of communications being unreliable and slow, the representatives of a country were given only broad instructions, which they had to implement and adjust according to their own judgment and the situation on the spot. The autonomy of the posts abroad was particularly strong in Britain: it was only in the 1920s that the diplomatic service (i.e., the personnel abroad) was merged with the personnel in the Foreign Office, thus enabling the interchangeability between posts in the central administration and the missions abroad. The telegraph changed this dramatically. Almost every spot in the world (at least the more important ones) could, after the 1850s, be reached by telegraph. Instructions and reports could now be delivered in the span of a few hours, compared to the days, weeks, and months it took for a letter to reach its destination before then. This allowed bureaucrats and politicians at home to exercise much closer supervision of the diplomatic posts abroad. And since more and more "domestic" departments also became involved in foreign relations, decisions were increasingly made in the capitals, where policies could be coordinated with everyone involved. The information revolution of the 1850s thus weakened the position and the influence of the ambassadors and the diplomatic personnel abroad. Since faster means of communication also increases the amount of available information and demands faster decision-making, there was also a quantitative increase of work in the foreign ministries. Therefore, it was not only specialization and new areas of international relations that led to the growth of the foreign services worldwide but also the faster pace and larger volume of available information. Between 1900 and 1914, for example, the number of telegrams sent to and from the State Department increased tenfold.

Centralization of foreign politics was also helped by faster and more convenient modes of transportation. The invention of steamships, trains, and later the airplane enabled heads of state, foreign ministers, and officials to travel more quickly and more easily to meet their colleagues in their capitals or at international conferences. The First World War in particular was important for the development of "conference diplomacy." The need for Britain and France to coordinate their common war effort against the Germans and the relative proximity of London and Paris led to frequent meetings between French and British ministers and high-level officials, who could reach important decisions much faster in a direct conference than with the help of diplomatic intermediaries. In the interwar period, the General Assembly of the League of Nations, which met every September at the League's headquarters in

Geneva, became important meeting places for European statesmen. Legendary are the Geneva "tea parties," which were attended by the foreign ministers of France (Aristide Briand), Germany (Gustav Stresemann), and Britain (Austen Chamberlain). These meetings contributed in large measure to the détente between European countries in the 1920s, but they also illustrated some of the problems of conference diplomacy. Often not fully briefed, foreign ministers made decisions that were not always feasible, and good personal relations often covered political divisions and problems which came to a head when the players in the "tea parties" changed. A logical step forward from conference diplomacy is summit diplomacy, i.e., meetings between the heads of governments or states. While this practice has been around for quite a while – French President Raymond Poincaré, for example, visited St. Petersburg in 1914, returning a visit of Tsar Nicholas II to Paris in 1896 – it became a means of politics only during the Second World War with the meetings between Roosevelt, Churchill, and Stalin in Tehran and Yalta and the meetings between American presidents and Soviet leaders during the Cold War. Today, summit meetings are often institutionalized events, for example within the context of the seven leading industrialized countries (G7 meetings) and the meetings between the G7 and Russia (G8). What is true of conference diplomacy, however, also applies to summitry: the results often seem quite meager in comparison to the public attention and enormous security measures. Another advancement of conference diplomacy is shuttle diplomacy, i.e., indirect negotiating between two parties by means of a mediator. The term was coined when United States Secretary of State Henry Kissinger shuttled back and forth between Israel in Egypt in the early 1970s in order to achieve a peace settlement between the two countries.

Centralization also became apparent in the inner structure of the foreign ministries. While the foreign offices emerged with only the minister in charge of politics and the remaining personnel concerned mainly with administrative tasks, both the qualitative and quantitative expansion of foreign policy saw the creation of the powerful "political" bureaucrat, determining to a certain degree the foreign policies in a country. In Britain, the position of permanent under-secretary, created in 1831, became the link between the minister and the bureaucracy. In France, the foreign minister at first had several departments under his control. During the First World War, the post of the *secrétaire général* emerged as the liaison between the political leadership of the ministry, consisting of the minister and his personal staff (the *cabinet du ministre*), and the bureaucratic apparatus. With the appointment of Philippe Berthelot in 1920, the position of the *secrétaire général* also became established officially. In Germany, a "real" foreign ministry only emerged with the collapse of imperial rule at the end of the First World War. In Bismarck's constitution, only the chancellor was appointed by the kaiser; the other members of the government were simply officials, subordinated to the chancellor's decisions. Only the Weimar Republic saw the emergence of a foreign ministry and, within the foreign ministry, a *Staatssekretär* (secretary of state) became the head official of the Auswärtiges Amt. In Germany, with the expansion of the foreign ministry's tasks, there are today two *Staatssekretäre*. The United States saw a similar development with the creation of the under-secretary of state in 1919. Today, there are six under-secretaries of state responsible for the major fields of United States foreign policy (political, economic, and security affairs, public diplomacy, democracy, and global affairs) and administrative matters (undersecretary for management).

Today, the foreign ministries in Europe and the United States are complex organizations, divided into functional divisions responsible for foreign economic policy and development, security policy and disarmament, international relations and public diplomacy, and public relations, geographic divisions, and administrative units responsible for recruitment, personnel accounting, and so on.

How the individual foreign services adapted to the new challenges that were imposed on them differed significantly, however. Even though there was a general pattern of quantitative expansion, specialization, and centralization, developments between Europe and the United States followed different paths. The individual European foreign

ministries largely followed a similar pattern of reform development. France and Germany in particular reacted to the challenges imposed by the "new" diplomacy that emerged after the First World War as they found themselves in the very center of the postwar convulsion. They both created specialized departments for economic affairs and for League of Nations matters and emphasized public relations and foreign cultural policy. France especially initiated many reforms that were later at least partly adopted by other countries. This is true in particular for the amalgamation of consular and diplomatic services and the creation of geographic divisions, and the new emphasis on multilateral diplomacy and foreign cultural policy and public relations. While the following decades saw, of course, the quantitative expansion and many adaptations to new developments of the foreign services in Germany and France, especially with the emergence of new countries in the processes of decolonization and the collapse of the Soviet bloc, it is remarkable that the basic administrative structures in the administration of their foreign relations date back essentially to the 1920s. The British foreign service followed the example of the continental powers only slowly and belatedly, and it was only in the 1930s and 1940s that the reforms already initiated in France and Germany became adopted in Britain as well (for example, the creation of the British Council, the fusion of the consular and diplomatic services). Even though the United States, and especially President Woodrow Wilson, was responsible for the emergence of "new" diplomacy, it did not implement the administrative measures necessary to deal with the new challenges until or even after the Second World War. The main cause for this was the fact that the Republican administrations that followed Wilson very much returned to a more traditional, isolationist foreign policy. Only the stronger involvement of the United States in Europe and other parts of the world after the Second World War and during the confrontation between East and West led to the modernization of the foreign service there. But even then, the United States – because of different administrative and political traditions and resistance within the State Department to various attempts at reform – followed a rather different path to modernization. Instead of creating specialized new departments within the State Department, semi-autonomous agencies such as the USIA were founded. It was only the Foreign Affairs and Restructuring Act of 1999 that led to a more integrated foreign service in the United States.

## The End of Diplomacy?

In the twentieth century, diplomacy was confronted with a rapidly changing set of challenges that increased the complexity of foreign relations. These challenges consisted of new technologies, a changed diplomatic agenda, and the multiplication of actors in foreign relations. Foreign ministries around the world reacted to the alterations in international affairs with expansion, professionalization, specialization, and centralization. However, now, at the beginning of the twenty-first century, diplomacy seems to be in a somewhat precarious position; in fact, diplomacy seems to be in danger of becoming irrelevant.

This decline in the importance of diplomacy is, first of all, because the foreign services, once the "eyes" and "ears" of a country, have diminished substantially in relevance as sources of information. Today, it is CNN and other media agencies that cover important political events first and, therefore, to a large extent set the international agenda. With the "Global War on Terror," diplomacy has been more or less excluded from the design of international relations and has been replaced by the secret services. This seems to have been true in particular for the preparation of the latest Gulf War. But it is not only the news media and the intelligence agencies that have limited the foreign services as sources of information on foreign countries, it is also less official organizations. Alongside official communiqués, NGOs such as Amnesty International and Greenpeace have become critical sources of information about certain aspects of international relations. This development also sheds light on other developments which have led to a decline of diplomacy. The number of actors in international relations has grown even more than the number of diplomats, thereby making the diplomat increasingly only one of many players in international rela-

tions. International news agencies, NGOs, multinational companies, and, last but not least, mass tourism have created forces that are outside the powers of diplomacy. Even on a strictly administrative and bureaucratic level, the foreign ministries are not the masters of foreign relations any more. Other ministries have come to play an important role in foreign relations as well. Examples of this are the meetings of the G8 finance ministers in which they discuss international economic problems and problems of exchange rates. Ministers of the interior and justice also assume more important roles in the fight against international terrorism and in migration problems. Also, responsibilities that in the past were part of the foreign ministries have been taken away and have become their own administrative units; one important example of this is intelligence, another is ministries or agencies for economic development. In Britain and in Germany, for instance, international development is the responsibility of specific ministries of the central government. In European countries in particular, European affairs are often dealt with in specialized departments of the foreign services with a high degree of autonomy. Both France and Britain have designated ministers for European affairs within their foreign departments. Since European integration has affected almost every aspect of government that is considered "domestic," the traditionally "domestic" ministries have created their own divisions for European affairs, with the Council of the European Union – the assembly of the responsible ministers – as the EU's most important decision-making body. The growing number of international organizations – most importantly, of course, the UN and its affiliated organizations – and their growing influence have also reduced the importance of the "classic" diplomat.

While international relations in the twentieth century did become more intense and complex than ever before, the role of the specialized branch of government that deals with foreign relations, paradoxically, seems to have declined. From a scholarly point of view, this development is neither to be regretted nor applauded but simply to be observed as a noteworthy change. This might hint at the possibility that, in the future, as the distinction between "foreign" and "domestic" becomes increasingly blurred, there simply may not be the need for an agency which exclusively deals with "foreign" affairs any more.

## GUIDE TO FURTHER READING

Jean Baillou, ed., *Les affaires étrangères et le corps diplomatique français. Histoire de l'administration française*, vol. 2, *1870–1980* (Paris: CNRS, 1984). Extensive study of the French foreign service.

William Barnes and John Heath Morgan, *The Foreign Service of the United States: Origins, Development, and Functions* (Washington, DC: Department of State, 1961). Official history of the US foreign service.

Donald G. Bishop, *The Administration of British Foreign Relations* (Syracuse, NY: Syracuse University Press, 1961). Dated, but important for the development of the Foreign Office from its beginnings.

Keith Hamilton and Richard Langhorne, *The Practice of Diplomacy: Its Evolution, Theory and Administration* (London and New York: Routledge, 2000). Concise overview of the development of diplomacy from its beginning to the 1990s.

John E. Harr, *The Professional Diplomat* (Princeton, NJ: Princeton University Press, 1969). Development of US diplomacy from the beginnings to the mid-1960s.

Paul Gordon Lauren, *Diplomats and Bureaucrats: The First Institutional Response to Twentieth-Century Diplomacy in France and Germany* (Stanford, CA: Hoover Institution Press, 1976). Important because it uses a comparative approach and deals with the crucial reforms that took place during the transition from the "old" to the "new" diplomacy after the First World War.

David Paul Nickles, *Under the Wire: How the Telegraph Changed Diplomacy* (Cambridge, MA: Harvard University Press, 2003). Examines the impact of technological advancements on diplomacy.

Heinz Sasse, *100 Jahre Auswärtiges Amt 1870–1970* (Bonn: Auswärtiges Amt, 1970). Official history of the German foreign service.

Zara Steiner, ed., *The Times Survey of Foreign Ministries of the World* (London: Times Books; Westport, CT: Meckler, 1982). Outline of the development of foreign services.

## INTERNET RESOURCES

The websites of the foreign ministries also contain some historical information. For information about the administrative history of the Auswärtiges Amt, see the short article by Ludwig Biewer, "Die Geschichte des Auswärtigen Amts. Ein Überblick" (www.auswaertiges-amt.de/www/de/infoservice/download/pdf/geschaa.pdf).

For the State Department, see "A History of the United States Department of State 1789–1996" by William Z. Slany (www.state.gov/www/about_state/history/dephis.html#conclusion).

On the website of the Foreign and Commonwealth Office are various articles that deal with different aspects of the administrative history of the British Foreign Service (www.fco.gov.uk/servlet/Front?pagename=OpenMarket/Xcelerate/ShowPage&c=Page&cid=1036517694428).

A rather short overview of the development of the French foreign service can be found at www.diplomatie.gouv.fr/fr/ministere_817/missions-organisations_823/historique_806/du-louvre-au-quai-orsay_4020.html.

# Part II

# The First World War and Its Consequences

# CHAPTER SIX

# The Triple Alliance

## JÜRGEN ANGELOW AND GORDON MARTEL

The nation-states of Germany and Italy were established by war between 1859 and 1870–1, largely at the expense of the Habsburg monarchy. One year after its defeat in the Austro-Prussian War of 1866, the Habsburg monarchy was transformed into the "Dual Monarchy," which gave the Hungarians significantly enhanced political power; technically speaking, they were to be the equals of the Austrians who had dominated the political system for centuries. The successful wars fought by Prussia against Denmark in 1864, Austria in 1866, and France in 1870–1 created a Prussian-dominated German Empire. The Italians had not succeeded in defeating the Austrians in war, but, with the military assistance of France and the diplomatic support of Britain, had nevertheless been united in a constitutional monarchy headed by the king of Sardinia. Thus, the three states that would form the "Triple Alliance" – the most enduring international alignment in Europe before the First World War – owed their political system and constitutional arrangements to events on European battlefields between 1859 and 1871. Military conflicts were, in retrospect, seen as legitimate engagements in the realization of national aspirations. The consequence of this conclusion was that each member of the Triple Alliance believed that – just as each had been constructed or reconstructed by war – it could be unmade by war. Thus, the series of agreements that constituted the Triple Alliance was signed by Berlin, Vienna, and Rome in order to prevent a war that might result in their undoing.[1] Ironically, these defensive arrangements were instrumental in establishing the system of alliances that precipitated the First World War and undid both the German Empire and the Dual Monarchy.

## The Beginnings of the Bismarckian System

The foundation of the German Reich in 1871 marked the end of the old European state system in which the existence of states was supposed to be assured by law. Henceforth, the right to exist could be assured only by military strength: the new world was a Darwinian one in which only the strongest would survive. In this new era, no European state believed that it could maintain its traditional rights and privileges without the political support of other states, and that without military might of its own such political support would be hard to find. The situation after 1871 marked the beginning of the modern era in European diplomacy.[2] Paradoxically, this new era produced a period of unprecedented peace in Europe, bringing to an end the military conflicts that had beset Europe from the beginning of the Crimean War in 1854 to the end of the Franco-Prussian War in 1871. Instead of the "survival of the fittest" establishing endemic warfare, it ushered in a period of peace which lasted until 1914, with only minor conflicts along the southeastern periphery of

Europe disturbing the peace. Accompanying this period of peace were the alliances formed by the Great Powers – alliances which were not in themselves stable, and in which the goals of the various partners changed over time along with changing circumstances – which, in the decades of crisis before the First World War, succeeded in maintaining the peace and which contributed significantly to security and stability in the immediate decades after 1871.

The European system of alliances began with the formation of the Dual Alliance between Germany and Austria-Hungary in 1879. In 1881 the system was expanded through the creation of the *Dreikaiserbund* (Three Emperors' League) that – for a time at least – attached Russia to the members of the Dual Alliance. These arrangements were completed in 1882 when Italy joined Germany and Austria-Hungary in the creation of the Triple Alliance. The Dual and Triple Alliances were surprising – shocking even – given that Germany and Austria had gone to war with one another only fourteen years before, and given that the Italians had long regarded the Austrians as their historic enemies, with the Habsburg Empire actively preventing the creation of a united Italy. What had caused these enemies to coalesce and form alliances with one another?

The history of the alliance system began at the Congress of Berlin, held in the summer of 1878. This meeting of the Great Powers, which was managed by Chancellor Otto von Bismarck of Germany, sought to mitigate (temporarily, at least) the tensions among them, while balancing their various interests in southeastern Europe and in the Mediterranean. This balancing act had been necessitated by the Russo-Turkish War, and particularly by the gains made by Russia's client, Bulgaria, in the Treaty of San Stefano. The "Big Bulgaria" created by the treaty would have given the Bulgarians a foothold on the Aegean, brought them to within 80 miles of Constantinople, and included what would become Macedonia. The Congress agreed to reduce considerably this big Bulgaria – which it was assumed would assist the accomplishment of Russian expansionist designs in the Balkans and against the Ottoman Empire. While the Congress succeeded in avoiding war among the Great Powers, the system remained

fragile. The Russians, in particular, felt cheated of the gains they had won in defeating the Turks on the field of battle – and for this they blamed Bismarck. Russia regarded itself as the guardian of the Balkan Christians and sought to control the Straits leading to the Black Sea in such a way as to enable them to prevent another seaborne invasion of Russia such as had occurred at the Crimea in 1854–5. As a result of these disappointed ambitions, the relations between Germany and Russia deteriorated rapidly after 1878. The nightmare that haunted Bismarck was a coalition between France, seeking revenge for its defeat in 1871, and Russia. Accordingly, he attempted to deflect French *revanchisme* by encouraging them to act on their ambitions in the Mediterranean by expanding their colonial territories in North Africa beyond Algeria, perhaps to include Tunisia, Morocco, and even Egypt – ambitions which would renew the old conflicts with Great Britain and probably stimulate new ones with Italy. Bismarck correctly anticipated that such Mediterranean conflicts would enhance his negotiating position vis-à-vis the British, who would be anxious for his support in any crisis with the French. During his last decade in office, Bismarck succeeded in maintaining cordial relations with Britain, although the British were never dependent upon Germany to the point that they felt compelled to join the Triple Alliance in order to counter both France and Russia.

In spite of the offense given to them at the Congress, Bismarck's aim was to draw the Russians back into a cordial relationship with Germany. As he saw it, Germany had no reason to find itself in a conflict with Russia; he had no expansionist ambitions to the east and his objective was to secure the *Kaiserreich* as established in 1871.[3] The danger was that Russian and Austrian interests would clash, particularly over the future of southeastern Europe – and in an Austro-Russian confrontation, Germany and France might well be drawn in. Bismarck explained his formula to the Russian ambassador in 1878: "Try to be *à trois* as long as the world is governed by the unstable equilibrium of five Great Powers."[4] Therefore, he sought to ameliorate Austro-Russian tensions by revitalizing the *Dreikaiserbund* of 1873. The principles he enunciated were conservative: politically, they were tied together in support of traditional monarchical regimes – in opposition to the demands of radical republicans, liberal democrats, and socialist reformers – and internationally, their interests coalesced in the preservation of the territorial status quo in eastern and southeastern Europe. Such an arrangement would isolate France and thereby diminish the threat posed by those French determined to recover the "lost provinces" of Alsace and Lorraine.

The first step in Bismarck's alliance diplomacy was the formation of the Dual Alliance between Germany and Austria-Hungary, signed on October 7, 1879, and which lasted (with some revisions) until the end of the First World War in 1918. The alliance was purely defensive, providing for mutual assistance should either of them be attacked by Russia, and providing for at least "benevolent neutrality" for one another if either were attacked by "another Power" (which, realistically, could only be France), and mutual assistance "with the whole fighting force" should the "attacking party" be supported in any way by Russia.[5] Thus, Bismarck had assured that, were his nightmare of a two-front war to be realized, Germany would at least have the support of Austria-Hungary.

But Bismarck sought simultaneously to reduce the likelihood of conflict with Russia. If the Russians recognized that an attack on Austria-Hungary would lead to war with Germany as well, they were much more likely to restrain themselves in the Balkans. With the Dual Alliance established, Bismarck sought to attach Russia to it by reviving the *Dreikaiserbund*, in which he succeeded on June 18, 1881, the pact providing mutual promises of neutrality and consultation. This pact was renewed in 1884, but disintegrated in June 1887 when another crisis over Bulgaria divided Vienna and St. Petersburg. Bismarck nevertheless succeeded in keeping Russia attached to Germany via the so-called "Reinsurance Treaty" signed on June 18, the same day that the *Dreikaiserbund* was abandoned. The Reinsurance Treaty was a secret bilateral promise of neutrality between Germany and Russia which expired in 1890, after Bismarck's departure from the political scene in Germany, and which marked a new course in

German policy, as Russia would have agreed to extend it had Germany been willing.

## The Formation of the Triple Alliance

The *Dreikaiserbund* was the highlight of Bismarck's foreign policy after 1871, but the Dual Alliance, which was extended through the creation of the Triple Alliance in 1882, proved to be more enduring. What sustained the *Triplice* (and distinguished it from the Dual Alliance) was, primarily, the conflicting ambitions of France and Italy in the Mediterranean. Since the French annexation of Tunis in the spring of 1881 and attacks against Italian workers in Marseilles in June 1881, the Italian–French relationship had deteriorated – and reminded the Italians that "unredeemed" Italy (*Italia irredenta*) applied to the territories of Nice and Savoy taken for France by Napoleon III during the years of Italian unification, as well as to those territories in the Tyrol and Trieste retained by Austria-Hungary after 1859. The "slap of Tunisia" especially incited the colonial competition between the "Latin sisters." Henceforth, the Italians sought the assistance of stronger powers in protecting them against France and assisting them in accomplishing their own expansionist designs in the Mediterranean. Since the German Reich was seen as the hereditary enemy of France, the Italians regarded it as their natural ally, once they too came to regard France as their enemy. Rome sought a binding contract with Berlin, one which would provide support in the event of confrontation with France, and one which would thereby enable it to pursue some of its territorial ambitions. But before any such arrangement could be concluded, Rome and Vienna had to come to terms over Italian claims to the south Tyrol and Trieste as well as some agreement on the "Roman question" (in which the Austrian Catholic monarchy had supported the papacy against the assertions of Italian nationalists). Bismarck told the Italian ambassador, Eduardo de Launay, in Berlin in 1882 that the key of the door to the German Reich could only be found in Vienna.[6] Already, before the Triple Alliance was formed, it was clear that the Germans regarded it more as an instrument of surveillance and pacification than as an opportunity to extend their political power: it would enable them to monitor the activities of their allies and to restrain their ambitions, thereby reducing tensions and maintaining an equilibrium in Europe.

After the visit of King Umberto I of Italy to Vienna in October 1881, the tough negotiations between Vienna and Rome started. Even though the negotiations did not remove the substantial contradictions in the interests of the two parties, and even though they did not produce a mutual guarantee of their territories, the negotiations did have a calming effect. On May 20, 1882, a secret agreement on defense and neutrality was signed by Germany, Austria-Hungary, and Italy. After its official launching, the Triple Alliance, because of its potential to act as a deterrent against war, came to be regarded as a vehicle likely to contribute to the peace of Europe and to the maintenance of the status quo. Nevertheless, an obvious fragility plagued the alliance from the beginning: Berlin had pushed Rome and Vienna into a partnership that neither truly desired – Rome and Vienna both wanted the connection with Berlin, not with one another, and it seemed unlikely that a cordial relationship would ever be established between the two reluctant allies. When the Austro-Hungarian emperor, Franz Joseph I, refused to visit Rome following the signing of the alliance, it seemed to manifest, symbolically, that Vienna was prepared to degrade its Roman ally. What, then, did the Italians believe they got out of the alliance? In the first instance, it protected them against an "unprovoked attack" from France by assuring them of the military assistance of Germany and Austria-Hungary in the case of such an attack. In return, the Italians committed themselves to assisting the Germans if France attacked them. The alliance also provided that if any of the three parties were to be attacked by two others (meaning Russia and France), this would be regarded as a *casus foederis* for each of them. Even though the Triple Alliance did not preclude the possibility that one of the parties might initiate a war in the interests of its own safety, such an eventuality would not mean that it could rely upon the assistance of its allies. In other words, the alliance was almost exclusively defensive, aiming on the one hand to deter a

Franco-Russian war against either Germany or Austria-Hungary, and on the other to restrain the ambitions and activities of Italy in the Mediterranean and Austria-Hungary in the Balkans – either of which might precipitate a general European war.

The Triple Alliance was not a combination of "nations" but one of monarchs and their cabinets: there was little popular enthusiasm to support the alliance – and in the context of 1882, none seemed necessary. The preamble to the alliance made it clear that the contracting parties wished to defend the principles of conservatism: the object of the signatories, they declared, was "to increase the guarantees of general peace, to strengthen the monarchical principle, and by that to assure the maintenance of social and political order in their respective states."[7] This indicated that the Triple Alliance was intended to work against the republican and anticlerical movements within its member states, and particularly in Italy. Neither Berlin nor Vienna regarded Rome as an equal. The Italian promise of military support for Germany in a war with France had not been the primary goal of German diplomacy, and no military agreements followed the signing of the alliance. Nevertheless, Germany did not wish to see Italy marginalized to the point that it might become the pawn of republican France. The isolation of France would benefit both Berlin and Rome, while Vienna might benefit from the promise of Italian neutrality in the case of a war between Austria-Hungary and Russia. The Italians, who had hoped that Britain might be drawn into the alliance, had to be satisfied with a declaration – named after the Italian foreign minister, Pasquale Stanislao Mancini – that the alliance was not directed against Britain and that the three powers would welcome London's accession to it. On the one hand Italy's attitude was defensive: the extensive Italian coastline could not be protected against an attack by the British Mediterranean fleet; on the other hand it was offensive, hoping that the British policy of opposing French colonial expansion might entail support for Italian colonialism as a counterpoise – something that Italy's partners in the Dual Alliance could not provide. These Italian hopes were later shattered by the German–British antagonism that grew increasingly bitter from the end of the century on, and which helps to explain Italy's decision to remain neutral in July and August 1914.

The Triple Alliance was renewed regularly, first on February 20, 1887, then on May 6, 1891, and thenceforth every six years until July 8, 1920. But on May 3, 1915, the alliance became void when Italy terminated its commitment, contrary to the terms of the contract. The Dual Alliance and Triple Alliance were not considered to be interdependent contracts, and the intentions of the two arrangements were different. Over the course of their existence, each arrangement developed differently and each was transformed as the interests and the values of the partners changed. Berlin at first regarded the Dual Alliance as the initial step on the way to revitalizing the *Dreikaiserbund* that it regarded as paramount to German security. Vienna at first regarded the guarantee of German support in the case of an unprovoked attack from Russia as useful to Austro-Hungarian security. Hence, at the beginning, both powers regarded the Triple Alliance as useful, but not as essential. Ironically perhaps, the alliance was more important to Italy, which regarded it as essential in elevating it to the status of a Great Power, as giving it opportunities for maneuver in foreign policy that it would not have otherwise, and as containing some of the radical irredentists at home. But in order to achieve the alliance, Italy had, quite obviously, to accept a subordinate position to the other two partners; according to the *Frankfurter Zeitung*, Italy had started as *Hospitant*[8] of the Dual Alliance and endeavored to gain equality within the alliance until abandoning it in 1915.

The Triple Alliance as a defensive arrangement against French aggression remained important to Italy, but it proved a completely unsuitable instrument in assisting Italian expansionism in the Mediterranean. In the first decade of its existence, Bismarck withheld any concessions from Rome on the questions of Morocco, the Red Sea, Tunis, or Egypt. Instead, he tended to support French colonial interests, especially in the early 1880s, with the hope of keeping French eyes averted from the Rhine and the recovery of Alsace-Lorraine. A similar situation characterized the Dual Alliance, in which Vienna was unable to utilize the alliance as an instrument for realizing Austro-Hungarian ambitions in the Balkans during the *Doppelkrise* of 1885–7 (see below). The value of the two alliances was also rarely measurable in trade agreements. The basic pattern stayed the same: every time one of the allies attempted to utilize the alliance in pursuit of its own expansionist and egoistic aims, its partners refused their support. This led to disillusionment in both Vienna and Rome, where it gradually came to be understood that the alliances did little more than enhance their security and perhaps add to their political weight. On the other hand, in the first decade of the existence of the Triple Alliance, it did not radiate a threat to other states.

Between 1885 and 1887 a period of crisis – the so-called *Doppelkrise* – led to the restructuring of the alliance system in general, with important ramifications for the Triple Alliance. One side of this crisis involved the antagonism between Russia and Austria-Hungary in the Balkans as a consequence of the newly established state of Bulgaria; the other side involved the risk of a war between Germany and France as a consequence of the revival of the revanchist and nationalist movement led by General Boulanger in France. As a result of these intersecting and overlapping crises, the system of alliances was rearranged by the time the crises ended in 1887. The *Dreikaiserbund* broke down over the conflict between Russian and Austro-Hungarian interests in the Balkans and led to the German–Russian Reinsurance Treaty. The promises of neutrality exchanged in this agreement did not directly contradict the commitments made by Germany in the Dual Alliance but, if it had become public, it could have been interpreted as demonstrating Berlin's disloyalty toward Vienna. Bismarck attempted to strengthen the Triple Alliance by drawing the British closer to it – which he succeeded in doing via the *Orientdreibund* (Mediterranean agreements), which promised British support to Italy and Austria-Hungary in maintaining the status quo in the Mediterranean, and which gave Austria-Hungary the hope that British support for the status quo in the Balkans might also be forthcoming.[9] Bismarck believed that he could, in this way, continue to maintain the balance of power in Europe from the sidelines.

A side effect of these developments was to upgrade Italy's inferior position. During the negotiations for the renewal of the Triple Alliance, the Italians were able to push through additional clauses, one of which obligated Germany to support Italy on North African issues, while another provided that Austria-Hungary would have to present Italy with compensation in order to assure Italian neutrality in the event of an Austro-Russian conflict, and, finally, the renegotiated agreement provided Italy with the assurance that it would receive compensation if the status quo in the Balkans were altered to the benefit of Austria-Hungary. It was Germany that had forced an unwilling Austria-Hungary to accept these changes, a diplomatic initiative that demonstrated the need Germany perceived to integrate Italy more firmly into the alliance. The formal renewal of the Triple Alliance on February 20, 1887, the visit of the Italian prime minister, Francesco Crispi, to celebrate Bismarck's birthday at Friedrichsruh in October 1887, and the beginning of military talks among the members of the alliance all served to signify the increased importance of Italy's place within it.[10] The nature of the alliance itself was also changing: the new terms were thought to signify the end of the antagonism between Italy and Austria-Hungary and to mark the isolation of France. Italy now regarded itself as a serious European power.

However, the military side of both the Dual and the Triple Alliances failed to keep pace with the changing political terms and objectives. Three years passed between the signing of the Dual Alliance and the establishment of military consultations between Berlin and Vienna which established military contacts with the passing of the Silesian *Herbstmanöver*. The possibility of a military conflict with Russia quickly became the pivotal point of all military discussions, and the chiefs of staff eventually agreed to embark on a combined offensive against Russia in the east. In spite of these arrangements, as Germany increasingly concentrated its forces in the west during the 1890s, its forces in the east were drained, making it more difficult to envision how the combined offensive with Austria-Hungary would be feasible. No meaningful operational arrangements were made between the partners of the Dual Alli-

ance after 1897, and even after direct discussions between their respective chiefs of staff were renewed in 1909, their strategic plans remained fundamentally unchanged and developed independently of one another. The military planning of the Dual Alliance was uncoordinated and characterized by wishful thinking. Germany and Austria-Hungary each pursued its own strategic objectives, which were difficult to combine – as was demonstrated when war began in August 1914: Germany focused on the offensive campaign against France on the western front and expected Austria-Hungary to lead the fight against Russia on the eastern.[11] Meanwhile, the Dual Monarchy aimed to achieve its own objectives against Serbia and assumed that Germany would cover its back against Russia. Each of the allies tried to use the other against Russia.

Within the Triple Alliance, the military discussions began during the Crispi era, after a delay of three years. The delay signified the relatively minor role assigned to Italy in the early stages of the alliance's history. Even after military discussions were initiated, they did not develop any meaningful operational plans and were conducted in an informal manner. It was agreed in 1888 that Italy would send troops to Germany in order to support its ally in the case of war against France. Similarly, a naval convention was concluded between the two allies in 1900, but this merely provided for operational zones in the Mediterranean, not for real cooperation between their combined fleets.[12] It was not until June 23, 1913, that the three allies agreed on a naval convention that was supposed to provide for uniting forces under a combined command in the Mediterranean. Even so, neither Berlin nor Vienna took the promise of Italian naval assistance seriously, and both proceeded on the assumption that, if war came, they could not rely upon Italy to assist them. In 1912, Germany began to scrutinize more carefully the military arrangements of the Triple Alliance, during the course of which Italy reaffirmed its loyalty to the alliance but would confirm only that it would mobilize its troops – and not necessarily deploy them to Germany, as previously promised.[13] Nevertheless, only a few weeks before the war began in 1914, Italy promised to dispatch three army corps and two cavalry divisions to the

Rhine. Nevertheless, there was sufficient uncertainty surrounding the military arrangements within the alliance that none of the allies could be certain how the others would behave upon the outbreak of war; the discussions of the chiefs of staff and the military negotiators notwithstanding, it was the executive authority in Germany, Austria-Hungary, and Italy who would decide whether the alliance would be an effective military instrument or not.

## The Alliance System after Bismarck

After Bismarck's resignation in 1890 important political alterations were made to both the Dual and the Triple Alliances – alterations that reflected new developments in the European situation. After the unification of Italy and Germany, European politics were stabilized in the later Bismarckian era, as the Great Powers turned their attention to overseas expansion rather than focusing on territorial disputes and national differences within Europe itself. This calm, which lasted until the first decade of the twentieth century, was also due in part to the creation of the countervailing alliance formed between France and Russia in 1891, symbolized by the visit of the French fleet to Kronstadt on July 23 that year. Their alliance, which was supplemented by a military convention in 1893, stabilized European relations and, ironically, by reducing tensions in Central Europe, made the Dual and Triple Alliances more porous and more ambiguous. This, in turn, encouraged individual members of the alliances to take initiatives in foreign affairs independently of one another.

Already during his first term in office, the Italian prime minister, Francesco Crispi, had entered into negotiations to renew the Triple Alliance, which had to be arranged by 1892. The terms of the renewed alliance, which was signed on May 6, 1891, changed little, but the alliance was extended to last another twelve years (with the possibility of revised terms being agreed upon after six), and it remained fundamentally unchanged from that time until its cancellation in 1915. Crispi's main concern was to promote Italian colonial expansion in North Africa; he had succeeded in establishing Italy at the port of

Massowa on the Red Sea in January 1885 – and he accomplished this without the support of his two allies. Although Crispi did not even consult his allies, Germany and Austria-Hungary were largely indifferent to the move, as it did not affect the alliance and was likely to increase Franco-Italian antagonism in the future. Crispi's dream of a large Italian empire along the Red Sea suffered a severe setback with the military defeat of Italy's forces at the hands of the Ethiopians at Adowa in March 1886. Nevertheless, the territories along the coast itself were united under the name of Eritrea in 1890, but much of the impetus behind Italian colonial expansion had been lost, and Italian imperialism discredited, by the disaster suffered at Adowa.

While Italy's international prestige suffered a blow as a result of its defeat in Ethiopia, the balance of power in Europe seemed at the same time to be shifting to the disadvantage of Germany, although no one was certain what the long-term effects of the change would be. After Bismarck's downfall, Berlin counted on establishing closer cooperation with London and believed that Britain would eventually be forced to join the Triple Alliance because of the challenges posed to the British Empire by French and Russian imperial aspirations.[14] Although an agreement on Heligoland and Zanzibar was reached in June 1890, Britain resisted Germany's efforts to draw it into the Triple Alliance. Moreover, Germany believed that Britain's reluctance to assist its colonial aspirations indicated a general unwillingness to cooperate; as a result, German diplomacy turned again to Russia with the hope of improving relations. The success of the Russo-German trade agreement of 1894 exaggerated Germany's hopes for a future détente with Russia – which, if it succeeded, might divide the Franco-Russian alliance and promote the formation of an anti-British "continental league" under Germany's leadership. St. Petersburg, however, refused to abandon the alliance with France or to cooperate in an anti-British alignment.

Germany's relationship with Britain declined further when, in 1897, the construction of a German high seas fleet began. Bernhard von Bülow, the secretary of state for foreign affairs, personified the imperialist *Zeitgeist* in Germany, arguing that naval expansion was essential to Germany's future as a Great Power in the twentieth century.[15] As a result of this new direction in German policy, the nature of the alliance system began to change fundamentally. Vienna reacted skeptically toward the "new course" in Berlin's international diplomacy under Bülow; Rome reconsidered its commitment to the alliance; together, they believed that Germany was attempting to exploit them as instruments of its imperial ambitions and feared that German diplomacy was unstable and unreliable. When the Mediterranean agreements with Britain expired in 1897, Austria-Hungary and Italy alike began to fear the consequences and regarded the new situation as increasingly precarious. As a result, Austria-Hungary attempted to reduce the potential of a conflict with Russia, while Italy attempted to reduce the potential of a conflict with France; both sought to reduce their dependence on a Germany that they began to regard as dominating and unpredictable.

The most important result of this attitude was an Austro-Russian rapprochement, beginning with a Russian initiative to reduce tensions in 1897 and which culminated in the Mürzsteg Convention of October 2, 1903. The convention provided for their mutual supervision of Balkan affairs and hence defused decades of antagonism between Vienna and St. Petersburg. The outbreak of the Russo-Japanese War in February 1904 precipitated an even closer arrangement: a neutrality pact was agreed on October 15, 1904, when Austria-Hungary and Russia promised benevolent neutrality toward one another in a war with a third power. Among other things, this meant that, in a conflict with Russia, Britain could not count on any support from Austria-Hungary. It also meant that, if Italy were to come into conflict with Austria-Hungary, the Austrians could count on Russia's benevolent neutrality. But it was Berlin that, potentially at least, suffered most from the arrangement; now, if Germany were to face a war on two fronts, it may no longer be able to count on the support of its partner in the Dual Alliance. Although the wording of the neutrality pact was not inconsistent with the Dual Alliance, Vienna had pushed the alliance to the breaking point.

At the same time, Italy was unable to convince Germany to abandon its increasingly anti-British attitude. Berlin refused to accept the renewal of the Mancini Declaration, which might have compensated for the abandonment of the Mediterranean entente with Britain. Germany, it seems, was losing its grip on reality, as well as its ability to exert control over its allies. Rome strove to normalize its relations with Paris, although it did not see this as a contradiction with its membership in the Triple Alliance. Italy accepted the establishment of a French protectorate over Tunis, which created the foundation for a profitable trade agreement between the two. A normalization of relations was established that replaced the previous antagonism, formalized in an exchange of notes between the Italian foreign secretary, Emilio Visconti-Venosta, and the French ambassador to Rome, Camille Barrère, which assured France that Italy would not support Britain in Morocco (in exchange for French recognition of Italian territories in North Africa), and that the terms of the Triple Alliance did not commit Italy to go to war against France. Reciprocal naval visits in 1899 and 1901 intensified the Franco-Italian rapprochement on an emotional level. The agreement of June 30, 1902, also provided for neutrality between the two in the event of war: if France were to be involved in a war that it had not provoked, Italy promised to remain neutral – and it was up to Italy to decide whether such a war had been provoked or not. Therefore, Italy was able to remain within the Triple Alliance while simultaneously improving relations with France.

## The Alliance and the Prewar Crises

At almost the same moment, the Triple Alliance was renewed on June 28, 1902, with Italy confirming that it was committed to military cooperation with Germany in the event of war with France. Italy, in attempting to balance its continental with its colonial interests, began tacking between Paris and Berlin. This became conspicuous during the first Moroccan crisis in 1905 when Germany, unaware of the secret agreement between Italy and France, assumed that it could count on Italy's support at the Algeciras conference that was to settle the crisis, but at which the

Italians remained true to their agreement to support the French position in Morocco.

The prospect of continuing Austro-Russian cooperation in the Balkans declined once the Russo-Japanese War ended. Russia's interest in Europe was reactivated as a result of the failure in the Far East and by the entente with Britain of August 31, 1907, that promised to bring an end to their antagonisms outside of Europe.[16] More and more the interests of Vienna and St. Petersburg collided – over railway affairs, for example, which were really contests to determine which was the more powerful in the Balkans. That the period of cooperation had ended became clear when Vienna annexed the Ottoman provinces of Bosnia-Herzegovina in October 1908 (which it had occupied and administered since 1878, but which had remained formally under Ottoman sovereignty). A crisis between Austria-Hungary and Russia immediately followed the annexation, during which it became clear that Vienna had succeeded in winning Berlin's support for its new, more aggressive policy in the Balkans. Germany decided that it was in its interests that Austria-Hungary should be enabled to consolidate its position there, and therefore supported the expansionist initiative.[17] Thus, the purely defensive nature of the Dual Alliance began to change in favor of a more offensive approach in the Balkans. Italy, however, indicated its lack of support for such a policy when it proposed that the crisis be solved by holding a conference – a suggestion that Austria-Hungary did not welcome. In the end, the solidarity of the Dual Alliance in the crisis left Russia with no choice but to submit to the annexation. But the crisis left a legacy of distrust and disorder in the Balkans, while simultaneously increasing the tendency of each of the partners in the Triple Alliance to assert its own interests and to exploit the others.

This latter development was emphasized by the second Moroccan crisis between Germany and France in 1911, which Italy seized as the opportunity to realize its own expansionist goals. During the Italian conquest of Libya in the war with the Ottoman Empire in 1911–12, it became obvious that Italy had little support from its partners in the Triple Alliance. In fact, Austria-Hungary regarded its interests in the Balkans as

threatened by its Italian ally and, accordingly, it was neither France nor Russia nor Great Britain that kept Italy on a short leash, but Austria-Hungary. Both the first and the second Balkan wars of 1912–13 led to the ordeal of the Triple Alliance: Austria-Hungary and Italy began to clash over the future of Albania, and the military strategists in Vienna began to consider carefully strategies for a preventive war against Italy. Even though the plans were not put into effect, information about Vienna's intentions leaked to Rome and occurred at the worst possible moment.

After the end of the Balkan wars the European situation appeared calm. Although the potential for a major conflict seemed to have been eliminated, the situation remained unpredictable – as was shown in the discordant reactions of the Great Powers to the delegation of a military mission to Constantinople under the command of a German, General Otto Liman von Sanders, in 1913.[18] Although a major crisis was averted, Europe more and more seemed to resemble a powder keg, simply waiting for the fuse to be lit. When the archduke of Austria and the heir of the throne of Austria-Hungary, Franz Ferdinand, was murdered by Serb nationalists, Vienna almost immediately decided to use the assassination as a pretext to "solve" the threat that Serbia was perceived to present to the integrity of the Dual Monarchy. But from the beginning of the July crisis, the localized war that Vienna envisioned threatened to escalate into a general European one. Nevertheless, Berlin and Vienna were prepared to accept the risk because they believed that in the long term the balance of power in Europe was shifting against them. During the last days of July and first days of August in 1914, Berlin decided that it was prepared to run the risk of war with Russia and France. Germany's awareness of the fragility of the Dual Alliance convinced the decision-makers in Berlin that it was essential for them to support the Habsburg monarchy, that failure to do so might well end in the isolation of Germany in Europe. Simultaneously, Vienna felt the need to maintain its fading status as a European Great Power by taking action against Serbia – action that would also demonstrate its power to act as a useful (if not equal) partner in the Dual Alliance.[19] Although Germany and

Austria-Hungary made their decisions on the basis of their own perceptions of self-interest, part of the picture they considered was the effect that action – or inaction – would have on their partnership within the alliance.

Italy chose to stand aside and was kept aside by its partners in the alliance. The perception on the part of Germany and Austria-Hungary that Italy was not to be relied on led them to ignore the requirement to consult their ally, which, in the opinion of Italy, rendered void its commitment via the terms and spirit of the Triple Alliance to join them in going to war. So the Italian government decided to stay neutral, even though it could have interpreted the terms of the alliance differently and chosen to go to war if it had decided that it was in its interests to do so. On the one hand, Rome felt it was unable to influence the decisions of the two preponderant powers in the alliance and that it was a virtual hostage of the expansionist policies of Berlin and Vienna. On the other hand, Berlin and Vienna refused to take the Italians into their confidence because they did not believe they would behave loyally to the alliance. When the Italians insisted that they be promised compensation for entering the war on behalf of the alliance (to which they were entitled), Berlin and Vienna tried to circumvent such claims. Here the essential differences between the Dual and the Triple Alliances become evident: the Austro-German connection via the Dual Alliance almost inevitably moved them in the direction of war; their suspicions of Italian disloyalty to the Triple Alliance moved them to ignore Italy's position during the July crisis – which, in part, became a self-fulfilling prophecy as Italy regarded the absence of proper consultation as an inclination on the part of its partners to ignore its interests.

After the declarations of war in August 1914, Italy negotiated its neutrality or support with both in order to gain something for itself.[20] Its demands for compensation from Austria-Hungary, which became more and more extensive, were undiplomatically refused to begin with until, under pressure from Germany, the Austrians offered some German-speaking territories to Italy as compensation. In the end, however, the Entente offered a more attractive set of inducements and, on May 3, 1915, Italy terminated its membership

in the Triple Alliance (which was supposed to continue until July 8, 1920). The moment of truth for the alliance had arrived: cooperation turned into bitter antagonism, and, on May 23, 1915, Italy declared war on Austria-Hungary. The Austrians responded immediately with a manifesto by the emperor, Franz Josef, which was filled with hatred, accusing the Italians of a defection unprecedented in history (*"dessengleichen die Geschichte nicht kennt"*) and glorifying Austria's great victories against Italy in 1848 and 1866. The German chancellor, Theobald von Bethmann Hollweg, used almost as vitriolic words in his speech in the Reichstag a few days later. It is impossible to determine whether Italy's entry into the war had a decisive impact on its outcome. Nevertheless, it is certain that Italy's declaration of neutrality in August 1914 redirected resources of the Central Powers, resources that they regarded as vital for them in achieving the quick victories that were essential if they were to win the war. Moreover, Italy's entry into the war on the side of the Entente restored the balance of power in 1915 that was being threatened by the victories of the Central Powers against Russia.[21] The failure of the Triple Alliance proved to be a vital factor in the undoing of both the Hohenzollern and the Habsburg empires.

## Conclusion

The Triple Alliance had not been designed for positive purposes; it had not been constructed to enable the three partners to pursue expansionist goals or to facilitate triumphs over their enemies. Rather, the alliance consisted of a system of reassurances to one another that each would assist the other in maintaining its sovereignty and territorial integrity against potential enemies, and as an instrument of surveillance against the pursuit of irredentist or revanchist ambitions. The Dual Alliance was not dissimilar: it too was primarily defensive, as Germany and Austria promised one another support in the event of war with Russia. More subtly, the Dual Alliance prevented the formation of a coalition of Russia, France, and Austria-Hungary against Germany (two of whom had recently been defeated on the battlefield by Prussia-Germany) and enabled Bismarck to perform the role of "honest broker" in disputes between Russia and Austria-Hungary in eastern Europe – disputes that Bismarck regarded as the most likely cause of a European war that could not (in his opinion) serve German interests. The creation of the new German Empire in 1871 had, according to Bismarck, transformed Germany into a conservative power whose primary goal was to maintain the new status quo in Europe. The alliances that he constructed reflected this purpose.

Bismarck's alliance system ultimately encouraged Russia and France to form their own corresponding alliance and – perhaps ironically given the role of the alliances in the July crisis of 1914 – actually decreased tensions within Europe throughout the 1890s and, arguably, continued to do so until the years immediately prior to the outbreak of the First World War. Following Bismarck's departure, when Germany embarked on the "new course" in foreign policy in which the aim was to become a world power, the alliances became looser and more porous, with each of the partners in the Triple Alliance pursuing its own agenda.[22] Germany lost its position of leadership in the alliance as Austria-Hungary pursued its own rapprochement with Russia and Italy pursued its own agenda with France. When Germany decided to construct a high seas fleet, its partners in the alliance worried that this might lead to conflict with Britain – a prospect neither of them welcomed, nor had anticipated when the alliance was originally formed. The growing estrangement between Germany and Britain pushed Rome and Vienna farther from a straightforward commitment to Germany (and to one another) and persuaded them to settle problems on their own, independent of German wishes.

The "re-Europeanization" of Great Power politics in the first decade of the twentieth century had contrasting effects on the Dual and Triple Alliances. Whereas the weakness of Russia in the aftermath of the war with Japan and the refocusing of its attention from the Far East to Europe led to the Bosnian annexation crisis in which Austria-Hungary scored a decisive political victory, it also led to a revaluation of the Dual Alliance in which both partners concluded that they had no alternative but to remain loyal to the other – a conclusion that proved decisive in July

1914. In the case of the Triple Alliance, the refocusing of attention on the Balkans, along with the growing cooperation of the Triple Entente in the Mediterranean, led Italy to reconsider whether the alliance was in its own best interests; here the litmus test of July 1914 indicated to Italy that it was not, that the risks involved in fighting a war with the Entente powers were something that it was not prepared to undergo – particularly when its alliance partners were unwilling to offer any substantial support for either its irredentist claims in Europe or its expansionist dreams in Africa. Although there were moments when the aims of the partners in the *Triplice* converged in the decade before 1914, and although there were ongoing military discussions among them until the war broke out, these were insufficient to stem the gradual erosion of the alliance.

Did the erosion of the Triple Alliance contribute to the outbreak of war in 1914? Given that the original aim of the alliance was to prevent war, this seems a plausible conclusion. The alliance did contribute to the maintenance of peace in Europe for three decades: it restrained Italy from launching an irredentist war against Austria-Hungary, and restrained Austria-Hungary from launching a preventive war against Italy; more importantly, when it spawned the countervailing Franco-Russian alliance, it led all the European Great Powers to conclude that a war among any two of them would lead to a general war – a conclusion that led to a policy of restraint until the period immediately preceding the outbreak of war. Nevertheless, although the alliance purported to be about the maintenance of peace, each of the powers came to define its interests in the era before 1914 as not necessarily being peaceful. Germany believed that it could survive as a Great Power only as long as it – in combination with Austria-Hungary – was as powerful as a Franco-Russian combination, and that the advantage was steadily moving to the side of Russia and France; thus a "preventive" war now was preferable to a gradual decline. The Dual Monarchy believed that it could survive only by quashing the nationalist and irredentist claims of the "nationalities" in southern and southeastern Europe – and that it could do so as long as it enjoyed the support of Germany.[23] Thus, the Dual Alliance remained effective by redefining "defense" as "offense." Italy disengaged from its partners in the Triple Alliance when it calculated that remaining loyal to them would result in being attacked by both Britain and France – an attack against which it was almost defenseless, and in return for which it was offered too little. Thus, the Dual and Triple Alliances, apparently instruments designed to maintain the peace, never aimed to remove the sources of competition or friction; as such they were unlikely to foster a structured and organized system for keeping the peace.

## NOTES

1   The text of both the Dual and the Triple Alliances as well as the supplemental and collateral agreements may be found in Alfred F. Pribram, *The Secret Treaties of Austria-Hungary 1879–1914*, 2 vols. (Cambridge, MA: Harvard University Press, 1920–1).

2   Klaus Hildebrand, *Das vergangene Reich. Deutsche Außenpolitik von Bismarck bis Hitler* (Stuttgart: Deutsche Verlags-Anstalt, 1995), p. 53.

3   Bascom Barry Hayes, *Bismarck and Mitteleuropa* (Rutherford, NJ: Farleigh Dickinson University Press, 1994).

4   Quoted in James Joll and Gordon Martel, *The Origins of the First World War* (London: Longman, 3rd edn, 2006), p. 54.

5   Michael Hurst, ed., *Key Treaties for the Great Powers 1814–1914*, vol. 2, *1871–1914* (London: David & Charles, 1974), p. 590.

6   Bismarck's notes of a conversation with the Italian ambassador, Count de Launay, Berlin, January 31, 1882. In *Die Große Politik der Europäischen Kabinette*, vol. 3 (Berlin: Der Arbeitsausschuss, 1927), pp. 205–8, doc. 545.

7   Quoted in A. J. P. Taylor, *The Struggle for Mastery in Europe, 1848–1916* (Oxford: Oxford University Press, 1954), p. 275.

8   Quoted in Holger Afflerbach, *Der Dreibund* (Vienna: Böhlau, 2002), p. 95.

9   Cedric J. Lowe, *Salisbury and the Mediterranean* (London: Routledge & Kegan Paul, 1965).

10  See Christopher Duggan, "Francesco Crispi and Italy's Pursuit of War against France, 1887–9," *Australian Journal of Politics and History* 50 (2004): 315–29.

11  On Germany's war plans, see Arden Bucholz, *Moltke, Schlieffen, and Prussian War Planning* (New York: Berg, 1991); Annika Mombauer, *Helmuth von Moltke and the Origins of the First World War* (New York: Cambridge University Press, 2001); and Norman Stone, "Moltke–Conrad: Relations between the Austro-Hungarian and German General Staffs, 1909–14," *Historical Journal* 9 (1966): 201–28.

12  Paul Halpern, *The Mediterranean Naval Situation, 1908–14* (Cambridge, MA: Harvard University Press, 1971).

13  Michael Palumbo, "Italian–Austro–Hungarian Military Relations before World War I," in *Essays on World War I: Origins and Prisoners of War*, ed. Samuel R. Williamson and Peter Pastor (New York: Brooklyn College Press, 1983), pp. 37–53.

14  See Gordon Martel, "The Limits of Commitment: Rosebery and the Definition of the Anglo-German Understanding," *Historical Journal* 26 (1983): 387–404; and H. W. Koch, "The Anglo-German Alliance Negotiations, Missed Opportunity or Myth?" *History* 54 (1969): 378–98.

15  On German naval policy and its relationship to "world power" see: Holger Herwig, *"Luxury" Fleet: The Imperial German Navy 1888–1918* (London: Ashfield, rev. edn, 1987); Ivo N. Lambi, *The Navy and German Power Politics, 1862–1914* (Boston: Allen & Unwin, 1984); and Jonathan Steinberg, *Yesterday's Deterrent: Tirpitz and the Birth of the German Battle Fleet* (London: Macdonald, 1965).

16  Andrew Rossos, *Russia and the Balkans: Inter-Balkan Rivalries and Russian Foreign Policy, 1908–1914* (Toronto: Toronto University Press, 1981).

17  See R. J. Crampton, *The Hollow Detente: Anglo-German Relations in the Balkans 1911–1914* (London: George Prior, 1979).

18  See Ulrich Trumpener, "Liman von Sanders and the German Ottoman Alliance," *Journal of Contemporary History* 1 (1966): 179–92.

19  John Leslie, "The Antecedents of Austria-Hungary's War Aims," *Wiener Beiträge zur Geschichte der Neuzeit* 20 (1993): 307–94.

20  See William A. Renzi, *In the Shadow of the Sword: Italy's Neutrality and Entrance into the Great War, 1914–1915* (New York: Peter Lang, 1987).

21  John Gooch, "Italy before 1915: The Quandary of the Vulnerable," in *Knowing One's Enemies: Intelligence Assessment Before the Two World Wars*, ed. Ernest R. May (Princeton, NJ: Princeton University Press, 1984), pp. 205–33.

22  Ludwig Dehio, *Germany and World Politics in the Twentieth Century*. Eng. trans. (London, 1959).

23  This view of events led one historian to argue that it was the fundamental cause of war in 1914: Lau-

rence Lafore, *The Long Fuse: An Interpretation of the Origins of World War I* (London: Weidenfeld & Nicolson, 1966).

## GUIDE TO FURTHER READING

Holger Afflerbach, *Der Dreibund. Europäische Grossmacht- und Allianzpolitik vor dem Ersten Weltkrieg* (Vienna: Böhlau, 2002). The most detailed account of the Triple Alliance from its origins to the First World War.

Jürgen Angelow, *Kalkül und Prestige. Der Zweibund am Vorabend des Ersten Weltkrieges* (Cologne: Böhlau, 2000). Detailed analysis of the Dual Alliance up to the eve of the First World War.

Volker R. Berghahn, *Germany and the Approach of War in 1914* (Basingstoke and New York: Macmillan, 2nd edn, 1993). A comprehensive view of German foreign policy.

Richard J. B. Bosworth, *Italy and the Approach of the First World War* (London: Macmillan, 1983). A useful synthesis of Italy's role in the international system.

Francis Roy Bridge, *From Sadowa to Sarajevo: The Foreign Policy of Austria-Hungary, 1866–1914* (Boston: Routledge & Kegan Paul, 1972). Well-researched and thorough synopsis of Austro-Hungarian foreign policy and diplomacy.

Jost Dülffer, Martin Kröger, and Rolf-Harald Wippich, *Vermiedene Kriege. Deeskalation von Konflikten der Grossmächte zwischen Krimkrieg und Erstem Weltkrieg (1856–1914)* (Munich: Oldenbourg, 1997). Excellent essays on prewar crises and how they were handled, conceived as a synthesis.

Fritz Fellner, *Der Dreibund. Europäische Diplomatie vor dem Ersten Weltkrieg* (Munich: Oldenbourg, 1960). Persuasive and ground-breaking analysis of a complicated relationship.

Paul M. Kennedy, ed., *The War Plans of the Great Powers 1880–1914* (Boston: Allen & Unwin, 1985). Military-historical analysis of the operational planning of the European Great Powers.

Wolfgang J. Mommsen, *Grossmachtstellung und Weltpolitik. Die Aussenpolitik des deutschen Reiches 1870–1914* (Frankfurt am Main: Propyläen, 1993). An important study of German foreign policy that emphasizes the significance of domestic political and social influences.

Graydon A. Tunstall, *Planning for War against Russia and Serbia: Austro-Hungarian and German Military Strategies, 1871–1914* (Boulder, CO: Social Science Monographs, 1993). Analysis of the diverging military plans within the Dual Alliance.

Samuel R. Williamson, Jr., *Austria-Hungary and the Origins of the First World War* (London: Macmillan, 1994). The best account of Austrian policies and problems.

# CHAPTER SEVEN

# The Ententes, 1894–1914

## KEITH NEILSON

For most of the nineteenth century European politics were dominated by the need to isolate France in order to prevent a recrudescence of the Napoleonic attempt to establish French hegemony on the continent. This was largely successful. From 1815 to 1854, France wriggled in vain to escape the straitjacket imposed at the Congress of Vienna. During the Crimean War France had at last found allies, but this freedom did not continue after 1856 and, by the late 1860s, Paris was again isolated, this time because of the machinations of the Prussian prime minister, Otto von Bismarck, who was determined that France would have no allies in a war with Prussia. Following the Franco-Prussian War, as chancellor of the new German Empire, he maintained the policy of isolating France in order to discourage any thoughts the French might have of seeking *revanche* by creating an anti-German coalition.

However, this seeming verity of the European international scene did not long survive Bismarck's dismissal from office in 1890. In 1894, a Franco-Russian alliance was signed, ensuring that the rapidly growing power of Imperial Germany would face a two-front war should it attempt to expand its boundaries by force. This "encirclement" (as the Germans called it) flew in the face of barriers to its creation that were thought insurmountable. Republican France and autocratic Russia lay at the opposite ends of the political and ideological spectrums. The two countries were separated not just by governmental norms (Russia

had no elected parliament until the creation of the Duma in 1905), but also by sharply differing beliefs about human rights and the relationship between state and citizens generally. Moreover, there were strong elements in Russia that favored closer relations with Germany, contending that the two countries had a certain natural sympathy for each other based on their similar governmental and social structures.[1]

However, there were equally strong forces drawing the two states together.[2] France was in a demographic trough; its population was growing only slowly compared with that of Germany, with all that this implied militarily in an age of conscripted armies. Russia, on the other hand, was in the midst of a population boom, with numbers increasing by about two-thirds between 1861 and 1914. However, while Russia was also experiencing strong economic growth, the country was dependent on foreign capital to finance this expansion. France, on the other hand, had a surplus of capital. These complementary national strengths, combined with a growing perception in both countries that Germany constituted a threat to Europe, were the forces that drew the two countries together in 1894.

Thus, after 1894, there were two blocs in Europe: the Triple Alliance of Germany, Austria-Hungary, and Italy and the Franco-Russian alliance. However, these blocs had not solidified and there was always the chance that the differences in national aspirations – for example, between

Italy and Austria-Hungary in the Balkans – might lead to their demise. And, of course, there was another Power – Great Britain – that remained outside either grouping. London's ability, the result of its geographical position and the strength of the Royal Navy, to remain uncommitted was the great unknown in European power politics.

Of course, another unknown was the nature and intent of the Franco-Russian alliance. While the threat of Germany had provided the impetus for the creation of the alliance, it was not clear that Berlin was necessarily the target of the rapprochement between Paris and St. Petersburg. Given that republican France and tsarist Russia were both traditional enemies of Britain, policy-makers in London were concerned that the new alliance would operate against them, particularly with respect to naval matters. This apprehension was underlined by the fact that the exact terms of the treaties binding France and Russia together were secret. Thus, on the eve of the Russo-Japanese War, British decision-makers were in the dark as to whether any British actions against a possible Russian naval blockade also might entangle London in a war against France.

Nor did the new Franco-Russian grouping particularly concern the Germans, for those on the Wilhemstrasse believed that Britain and Germany were destined to be allies. This assumption was based on a number of things. First, there was the historical reality that Britain and Prussia had been allies against France since the eighteenth century and Britain had favored the unification of Germany in 1871. Second, British and French interests were thought to be both inimical to one another and irreconcilable. This hostile state of affairs was even more marked between Britain and Russia. The empires of those two countries clashed everywhere: in the Middle East, in the Far East, and, most manifestly, in Central Asia, where Russia's advances threatened the Northwest Frontier of India. Finally, tsarist Russia and liberal Britain were separated by an ideological gap that seemed to preclude any idea of a warming of relations between them.

In addition to this, it was widely believed that Britain and Germany had much in common. Some of these factors were concrete: both nations were Protestant and the monarchical ties between

them were strong. Each was a strong industrial nation and the other's best trading partner. Even the "made in Germany" scare of the 1890s was insufficient to overshadow the strong economic links between the two countries. Other factors were more abstract. In both Britain and Germany there were elements who believed in social Darwinism and felt that Anglo-Saxons and Germans were linked by some mystic bond – a bond that neither the Latin French nor the Russian Slavs could hope to share. The fact that the British did not see the inevitability of a London–Berlin axis was one of the driving factors behind the German decision in 1898 to create a navy – the so-called "risk fleet" – powerful enough to threaten the Royal Navy. The Germans believed that, when the British realized that their naval supremacy would be undermined unless they joined with Germany, even John Bull would be perspicacious enough to see on which side his bread was buttered and abandon his non-aligned status.

Although British policy is often described as one of "isolation" or even "splendid isolation," this is not really accurate.[3] Where clear British interests were involved, in limited geographic locales and for limited periods of time, London had always been agreeable to joining with other European powers, as the Mediterranean agreements of 1887 had demonstrated. Nonetheless, in the 1890s, first under Lord Rosebery and then under Lord Salisbury, successive British governments were unwilling to commit themselves to either of the two major groupings.[4] Since the two blocs were roughly equal in strength, neither side seemed likely to be able either to defeat or to overawe the other. The result of this happy equipoise was that Britain retained a freedom of maneuver denied to the other powers. It would not be obligated to take action as a result of alliances, and, even when its own direct interests were affected, it could choose how, when, and whether to intervene. Thus, London could concentrate on maintaining its empire free from continental distractions.

Notwithstanding this, it was overseas rather than European matters that ended this happy idyll. In 1894, the Sino-Japanese War began. Japan's rapid and decisive victory was an assertion of its claim to be East Asia's most dominant power. However, the extent of Japan's gains, as contained in the Treaty of Shimenoseki of 1895, led to the so-called "Triple Intervention" of France, Germany, and Russia. These three countries, each having its own designs in the region, preferred the existence of a weak China to the establishment of a stronger Japan. They thus wished to limit Tokyo's expansion by forcing the Japanese to revise the terms of settlement with China. Britain refused to join in this coercion, believing that its own interests were better served by not opposing Japan than they were by aiding in the establishment of other European powers in the region.

However, the instability in the Far East caused by the Sino-Japanese War – Germany and Russia each obtained a warm-water port (Tsingtao and Port Arthur, respectively) from China – indicated to the British that questions of empire could no longer be isolated from European affairs. This conclusion was driven home by a series of quarrels with Russia and Germany over railway concessions in China.[5] This new circumstance was doubly underlined in 1898, when Britain and France nearly came to blows over their conflicting claims to Fashoda, a town on the Upper Nile whose real significance was that it symbolized the French effort to undermine Britain's imperial position in Egypt. Both of these events fueled debate among the British as to whether they could continue to pursue a policy of isolation, or whether they would have to join one or the other of the two European power blocs.

By 1900, this debate was in full swing.[6] The outbreak of the Boer War in 1899 had demonstrated further the difficulties of isolation. While any attempt to change the status quo in Europe inevitably led all the other powers either to prevent it or to ensure that its results did not disturb the balance of power, the British found that their war in South Africa merely strained their own resources and, as a corollary, lessened their influence in Europe. While London was able, in 1900, to make common cause with the other European powers and Japan to suppress the Boxer rebellion in China, it was clear from the myriad crises of the preceding five years that the British policy of responding to each new disruption as it occurred needed reconsideration.

This was evident to many in the British cabinet, where a younger element that preferred a proactive policy, the "Edwardians," began a challenge to the preference of the older leaders, the "Victorians," for a reactive policy.[7] The difficult question was which country to ally with and what price each potential partner would charge. Tentative negotiations with Russia in 1898–9 over China had led to an agreement over railway concessions. However, Russia's continuing threat to India and her far-reaching ambitions in China – symbolized by her refusal to withdraw her troops from Manchuria after the joint European intervention during the Boxer rebellion – resulted in British enquiries being ignored in St. Petersburg. The British turned next to Germany, a move favored both by such influential politicians as Joseph Chamberlain, the colonial secretary, and the fact that Germany and Britain had many cultural similarities.[8] But here, too, the British found the asking price too high. The Germans wanted a British commitment to defend Berlin's long eastern frontier against Russia in exchange for any colonial agreements. This seemed excessive and, after desultory negotiations, the talks collapsed.

If a general alliance with one of the European Great Powers was not able to be reached in 1901, this did not mean that London had ceased to look for a way to eliminate potential points of friction and, not incidentally, to lessen the financial burden that these entailed. Instead, the British foreign secretary, Lord Lansdowne, looked to conclude an alliance with Japan. Often seen as marking the end of British isolation, the Anglo-Japanese alliance was not conceived as such by Lansdowne.[9] Rather, he saw it as a regional pact, one that would safeguard British interests in East Asia by sharing the burden of defending them with Japan. Thus, the kind of paralysis that was affecting British diplomacy because of its ongoing extra-European imbroglio – the Boer War – could be avoided in future. The result was the Anglo-Japanese alliance, signed on January 29, 1902.

However, not all the initiatives in European politics were launched by the British. In France, the Fashoda crisis had led to a reconsideration of French policy. The French foreign minister, Théophile Delcassé, had come to the conclusion that France could no longer pursue its historic policy of enmity with Britain simultaneously with maintaining a hostile posture toward Germany.[10] As France's grievance with and threat from Germany were much greater than its corresponding problems with Britain, Delcassé decided to pursue a policy of rapprochement with London. The focus of these talks was the elimination of the sort of colonial irritations that had led to Fashoda. A resolution of the points of imperial contention – over Southeast Asia, Egypt, and Newfoundland – lay at the heart of the Anglo-French *entente cordiale* that was signed in April 1904.

It is important to remember that this agreement, often wrongly portrayed as the first step in dividing Europe into the two power blocs that formed the opposing sides in the First World War, was in no way a military alliance. Instead, by eliminating the extra-European frictions that had ensured Anglo-French antagonism, the *entente cordiale* only changed the European diplomatic landscape and was widely hailed, particularly in Britain, as a step toward ensuring the maintenance of peace rather than as a means to fight a war. However, the timing of the negotiation and signing of the Anglo-French agreement soon gave the event a greater significance than its terms warranted. This was again the result of extra-European activities.

The Russian refusal to evacuate their troops from Manchuria ensured that Russo-Japanese relations remained tense. By 1903, there were indications that this tension might lead to war. This had possible dangerous ramifications for both Britain and France, now deeply enmeshed in the negotiations for an entente. Each was concerned that a war between Tokyo and St. Petersburg would result in Anglo-French complications – even war – as a result of the Anglo-Japanese and the Franco-Russian alliances. When the Russo-Japanese War broke out in February 1904, both London and Paris were relieved that they were able to avoid a clash that might have derived from their commitments to the warring parties; in fact, the hostilities in the Far East in no way impinged on the ongoing negotiations between Britain and France. However, the war in Manchuria did prompt other countries to attempt to change the diplomatic constellations in Europe.

At the turn of the century, Germany had seemed in an enviable position. The Triple Alliance guaranteed its European position, and it was being courted by the British, something that seemingly provided Berlin with a "free hand" in diplomacy. However, in the circumstances of the Russo-Japanese War, Germany attempted to convert this "free hand" into having the upper hand by driving a wedge between Paris and St. Petersburg, taking advantage of Russia's military preoccupations. This took two forms. The first was an attempt to wean Russia away from France by offering the Russian emperor German support against Japan. This came to nothing. The second was more serious, and took the shape of a challenge to the French position in Morocco in 1905.[11] By the end of the year, a crisis had emerged, one which forced the British to give full consideration to the nature of their entente with France.

This occurred at a particularly awkward time, for Britain was in the midst of a general election that brought Sir Edward Grey to office as the foreign secretary in a new Liberal government. The Liberals were divided with respect to foreign policy. The bulk of the party hewed to the "Little Englander" traditions of the nineteenth century and opposed any expansion (some favored elimination) of empire. Others were opposed to any foreign entanglements, instead preferring arbitration and arms control as a means of maintaining international order. Grey, however, was a member of a small but politically significant cadre – the "Liberal Imperialists" – who favored continuity in foreign policy. While Grey wished to prevent Britain's empire from involving it in any international quarrels and had no desire to increase Britain's overseas possessions, he was not willing to have any portion of them wrested from London's control. And, while Grey was willing (and indeed eager) to attempt to find a compromise between France and Germany, he was not willing to have France bullied.

Grey's preferred solution was to have Russia "re-established in the councils of Europe," so as to reinstate the balance of power that Russia's involvement in the Russo-Japanese War had temporarily put in abeyance.[12] But this would take time. In the short term, Grey was forced to authorize military and naval talks with the French, in order both to strengthen their resolve and to demonstrate the value of the entente. Grey was, however, careful to make it clear to Paris that the talks were exploratory only and not binding. And, while he initially informed only a small fraction of his cabinet colleagues (the election was still ongoing, the cabinet itself was not formed in its entirety), there is no truth to the later allegations that the cabinet was kept in the dark about any possible ramifications of the military conversations.[13] The result of Grey's firmness was that Germany decided not to press the issue of Morocco with France and the matter was decided at a conference held at Algeciras.

Thus, by the beginning of 1906, Britain was not committed to either of the two power groupings in Europe, but it had made it clear that it was not a disinterested bystander. While Britain would not commit its forces to aid France in advance of any particular European quarrel, neither would it stand by in the face of German aggression. In these circumstances, in the course of the next few years, Grey pursued simultaneously a number of policies. The first was a general attempt, in line with the general tenor of the Liberal party's position with respect to such matters, to work for arms limitation and the rule of law in warfare at the Second Hague Peace Conference in 1907.[14] This effort foundered on German intransigence. The latter was linked to another aspect of Grey's policy: his attempt to find a *modus vivendi* with Berlin.

Here, Grey found himself stymied by German policy generally. Still convinced that Britain could be persuaded to abandon the entente with France and that they had a "free hand" in European diplomacy, the Germans did not learn the lesson that the Russo-Japanese War should have taught. Just as Berlin had attempted to coerce first St. Petersburg and then Paris into abandoning their alliance, so, too, did the Germans attempt to threaten London after 1905 into joining an expanded Triple Alliance. The means to do this was the so-called German "risk fleet." The "risk fleet" was the brainchild of Admiral Tirpitz, the German minister of the marine. Tirpitz realized that Germany was unable to build a fleet sufficient in itself to wrest command of the seas away from the Royal Navy, but he believed that, if Germany built a fleet sufficiently strong that any clash between it and the Royal Navy would fatally weaken the latter against other opponents, the British would decide that an Anglo-German rapprochement on Berlin's terms was a better alternative to a naval war.[15] This was a mistaken judgment. Instead, the British initiated a naval building race with the launching of the first modern battleship, *HMS Dreadnought*. The result was an increase in Anglo-German tensions until the naval race lost steam in 1912.

The third strand of Grey's diplomacy, and one that underlined the continuity in British foreign policy, was his attempt to improve Anglo-Russian relations. This had two aspects. The first was general. Grey hoped that an Anglo-Russian rapprochement would help Russia overcome the effects of the Russo-Japanese War (much of Russia's fleet had been damaged, its finances had been weakened, mutinies had racked the army, and there had been revolution domestically) so that the European balance of power might be restored. The second was more parochial. Grey believed that resolving the outstanding colonial issues between the two countries would permit Britain to isolate its empire from any European connections and so restore to London the freedom of maneuver that it had possessed in European diplomacy in the mid-1890s.

The result of Grey's initiative was long and hard bargaining with St. Petersburg. On August 31, 1907, the Anglo-Russian Convention was signed. Its terms were purely colonial in scope. Britain and Russia agreed that each would have a sphere of influence in Persia, Russia would not treat with Afghanistan except through Britain, and that neither country would attempt to impose its will on Tibet. The reason for the success of this negotiation was entirely Russian. The Russian foreign minister, Alexander Izvolsky, realized that Russia was too weak in the aftermath of the Russo-Japanese War both to continue to play a major role in European politics and to pursue colonial enmities with Britain. Judging the former to be more important than the latter, Izvolsky was willing to listen to British blandishments – something that his French allies supported enthusiastically.

Thus, by the end of 1907, Europe seemed divided into two groupings: the Triple Alliance and the new Triple Entente of Britain, France, and Russia (sometimes even construed as a Quadruple Entente by adding Japan to the mixture[16]). However, it is important to remember that this division was more apparent than real. Unlike the Triple Alliance, which was a full-blown military alliance, the "Triple Entente" had no such features. Neither the Anglo-French *entente cordiale* nor the Anglo-Russian Convention committed either side to giving the other military assistance. Nor were the two agreements linked in any way to each other. The Franco-Russian alliance existed independently of either of the other two arrangements, and Grey was always careful to inform both St. Petersburg and Paris that British support in any continental war would not be guaranteed and would certainly not be automatic. Instead, British policy would be contingent upon events.

There was a whiff of sophistry about this position. While Grey was sincere in his arguments and technically correct about the lack of any formal agreement binding Britain, it was equally clear that he did not see Britain as willing to stand aside in the case of a continental conflict – this had been shown in the Moroccan crisis. So, just what was Grey's position, and what did this mean for the European balance? Grey's policy resulted from several things. The first was personal. As a good nineteenth-century liberal, he believed that reasonable men could find reasonable ways to resolve their differences, short of violence. This applied equally well to countries. And Grey's personal beliefs in this regard were entirely consonant with the ethos of his own party. Thus, he was constrained by party politics as much as by personal belief from entering into any formal, binding agreements.

However, there were countervailing factors that needed to be considered. First, Grey was a practical man and not devoid of experience in international affairs. He thus realized that the lion was not always willing to lie down with the lamb (except, perhaps, in order to find a more comfortable position in which to ingest it), and that force and the threat of force underpinned European politics. Second, Grey required cross-bench support in order to pursue practical policies, since there were extremist elements in his own party (the Radicals) who opposed participation in any alliance and denounced the concept of the balance of power.[17]

As a result, Grey was forced to pursue a careful balancing act. On the one hand, he would not give unequivocal support to France and Russia. This was both for political reasons and because he felt that to do so would encourage France and Russia to adopt a more truculent attitude toward the Triple Alliance. Further, he believed that, if Britain were to stay outside the continental power blocs, this would allow London to act as a moderator in all crises, allowing for the possibility of a negotiated settlement rather than the certainty of war that formal adherence to a functioning Triple Entente would ensure. The weakness of this position, as 1914 would demonstrate, was that it was an effective policy only when neither side was determined to push things to the point of hostilities.

The difficulties of such a balancing act even short of war were clear in the period after 1907. After the Russo-Japanese War, Russia had undergone a number of changes as a result of its defeat. Domestically, the tsar reluctantly had granted a measure of responsible government with the creation of the Duma and military and financial reforms had been initiated to repair the damages caused by the Far Eastern defeat. Foreign policy initiatives had also been used to shore up Russia's weakened position. In addition to eliminating all outstanding issues with Japan by signing a fisheries treaty, St. Petersburg had negotiated several neutrality treaties ensuring its Baltic position. Most importantly, Izvolsky had agreed to the Anglo-Russian Convention. These actions had the effect of returning Russia's attention to Europe and particularly to the Balkans, which became St. Peterburg's first priority. The result was the major crisis that erupted over the Austro-Hungarian annexation of Bosnia in 1908.[18] The crisis demonstrated how limited were the bonds that held together the Triple Entente. Russia was annoyed by the annexation, for Izvolsky felt that he had reached an agreement with the Austro-Hungarian foreign minister that Russia would receive Constantinople as compensation for Austria-Hungary's taking of Bosnia. Izvolsky called for a conference to adjudicate matters. Both France and Britain were willing to support him in this, but neither was prepared to go to war over the issue. This left Russia, despite its having "alliance" partners, to bargain alone. When, in early 1909, Germany made it clear that Austria-Hungary had its full support, St. Petersburg was forced to capitulate. A similar episode happened to France. At the same time as the Bosnian crisis occurred, Germany attempted to put pressure on France over Casablanca, again relying on Russian weakness and the British unwillingness to resort to arms to ensure that Paris would buckle.[19] Clearly, the Triple Entente was, at best, a grouping that would cooperate diplomatically, not a fully fledged alliance.

And even the solidity of the Entente could not be taken for granted. During the Bosnian and Casablancan crises, Germany attempted to lure Britain into abandoning France and Russia. In mid-1909, the Germans offered the British a comprehensive settlement of both their colonial quarrels – primarily concerning differences about railway concessions in the Middle East – and the Anglo-German naval rivalry. However, the German price – British neutrality in any European war – was thought excessive and indicative of Germany's seemingly unlimited ambitions. In addition, such a bilateral settlement would offend Russia, which also had interests in the region. Thus, Grey suggested that both St. Petersburg and Paris should be invited to participate in a general settlement in the Middle East, something that the Germans rejected. The rejection seemingly confirmed Grey's suspicions of German motives.

The solidarity of the Triple Entente was threatened not just by German offers to Britain. In the aftermath of the Bosnian crisis, Izvolsky was replaced as Russian foreign minister by Sergei Sazonov. The latter felt that Russia's relations with Germany had to be improved, at least until Russia could make the necessary repairs to its armed forces, in order to avoid further humiliations. The result was the Potsdam conversations of late 1910. Despite the threat that these seemingly posed to the Entente, Grey favored them, providing that they did not result in any diminution of the Anglo-Russian Convention. In fact, Grey even proposed a naval arms control understanding to Berlin early in 1911.

By that date, the fluid nature of the Entente still was evident. Franco-Russian relations had cooled after Paris had offered only limited support during the Bosnian crisis, something that the Potsdam conversations had emphasized, and British support remained contingent on events.[20] A further test came in the summer of 1911, again over German actions in Morocco. This, the so-called Agadir crisis, both severely tested the bonds holding the Triple Entente together and clearly outlined its limitations.[21] Russia's support for France mirrored that offered by Paris to St. Petersburg during the Bosnian crisis. It was not until mid-September, after the likelihood of war had decreased, that the Russians offered anything more than lukewarm support to their ally. It was in London, however, where the crises caused a thorough examination of policy.

Grey continued to attempt to walk his tightrope. His first inclination was to call for a conference, but this was rejected by Germany. As had been the case in the first Moroccan crisis, Grey was unwilling to see the French bullied by Germany. However, he was equally unwilling to give them unconditional support, lest this encourage the French to adopt a provocative and uncompromising stance. On August 23, the Committee of Imperial Defence (CID), the British body that brought together the fighting services, the Foreign Office, and leading politicians to discuss policy, met. At this meeting, various plans were discussed with respect to what support the British could give France should the Moroccan crisis lead to war. While many historians have seen this as marking an end to Grey's even-handed policy and as a time when it was definitely decided to commit British troops to the continent, this is not the case.[22] Instead, what occurred was that the primacy of civilian control was reaffirmed. While it was agreed that a British Expeditionary Force (BEF) should be sent to France's aid, the decision whether to send it remained entirely in the hands of British politicians. The Triple Entente remained just a figure of speech, not a definite military alliance.

And it was by no means certain that this grouping would remain intact. The Anglo-Russian Convention was, in particular, a difficult pillar to maintain. Many Liberals – in particular the

Radical wing of the party – had always opposed any agreement with tsarist Russia, seeing the latter as too reactionary to be suitable for a partnership, even of a limited nature, with Britain. Russian actions in Persia were particularly repugnant. They, along with the belief of the Radicals that Grey had nearly committed Britain to war at the August 23 meeting of the CID, led to a cabinet revolt in the autumn of 1911. Grey was able to prevail over his critics, but only at the price of having to emphasize again the conditional nature of Britain's commitment to the Triple Entente. In addition, the cabinet insisted that a further effort be made in 1912 to eliminate any friction with Germany. The result of this was the sending of a mission to Germany under the secretary of state for war, Lord Haldane, in 1912 to discuss naval issues. This was not annoying to Grey: he favored any measure that would reduce tensions among the Great Powers. However, the result – a German reiteration that the price for any agreement with Germany was a British declaration of neutrality in any European war – meant that the Haldane mission failed. So, too, did attempts at finding an Anglo-German colonial compromise.

However, these setbacks did not mean that the Triple Entente was strengthened. Grey also rejected a French proposal that Britain join in a Franco-Russian naval agreement. And Russian actions in Persia continued to be a thorn in his side.[23] Equally, when the First Balkan War broke out in the autumn of 1912, Grey chose to cooperate with Germany, not with France and Russia, in an attempt both to end the conflict and to prevent it from spreading. However, his attempt to work with Berlin foundered over the latter's pledge of support to Austria-Hungary should the war become generalized. Here, Grey was firm. He told the Germans that Russia would not back down, and, through Haldane, intimated to Berlin that Britain would not stand aside in a continental war. This latter warning was not repeated to either Paris or St. Petersburg in order not to encourage bellicose elements in either capital. Despite German rancor at what was construed as a veiled British threat, Grey had his way, and a conference of ambassadors was convened in London in December 1912 to find a solution to the Balkan struggle.

In fact, by the middle of 1913, Grey's delicate balancing policy seemed to make the need for the Triple Entente, in any form, superfluous. Russia's rapid recovery from the effects of the Russo-Japanese War made this more likely for two reasons. The first was that Russia's burgeoning strength meant that the balance of power between the Triple Alliance and the Franco-Russian alliance was closer to equal than it had been at any time since 1904. This opened up the pleasant vista that Britain could revert to the policy that it had followed prior to 1895, intervening only when its own direct interests were threatened. The second was less pleasant. Russia's recovery had led to a more aggressive policy by the tsarist state in Persia. By 1914, it was clear that the Anglo-Russian Convention needed revision, and unclear whether any arrangement between the two states was possible at all.

Grey's policy during the July crisis leading to the First World War made manifest the fact that the Triple Entente was no piece of well-oiled machinery leading its members to war.[24] Initially, he attempted to work with the Germans to convene a conference. When it became clear both that Berlin had given Austria-Hungary unequivocal support and that the latter had no intention of stopping short of war unless its demands were fully met, Grey's policy came crashing down. The fact that British participation in the war was by no means a foregone conclusion is shown by the consternation in Paris and St. Petersburg. The French withdrew their forces from the frontiers in order to avoid any incidents that would allow the Germans to play on British susceptibilities by claiming that a war had broken out because of French provocations. The Russians sent entreating messages, calling on what they knew was uncertain British support. All hinged on events and politics. What converted the uncertain Triple Entente of 1907 into the firm Anglo-Franco-Russian alliance of the First World War was Germany's launching of military action against France and Russia. British options were grim. A victory by either side with Britain remaining neutral would be disadvantageous to London, since the winning side would be in a position either – in the case of the Central Powers – to dominate the continent or – in the case of France

and Russia – to threaten Britain's imperial interests. With the European balance shattered, Britain
would be unable to pursue, even tentatively, the
balancing act that had served it well in the past.
Going to war seemed to be the lesser of two
evils.

The history of the Entente in the generation
before 1914 makes evident the complicated nature
of European politics in this era. While Triple Alliance faced Triple Entente when the guns of
August began to fire, this was not a foregone
conclusion. At various points, even France and
Russia, the two members of the Entente most
directly threatened by Germany's aggression,
either contemplated switching sides or giving less
than wholehearted support to their alliance partners. Such ambiguity was even greater for Britain.
That country refused to commit itself to the
Franco-Russian combination, instead satisfying
itself with the elimination of colonial frictions
with the pairing. At the same time, Britain repeatedly offered an olive branch to Germany, but was
unwilling to pay the price of neutrality in a continental war that Berlin continued to make the
essential element for any Anglo-German agreement. Thus, Britain's alignment with and commitment to France and Russia remained tentative
and contingent on events and domestic politics.
The Triple Entente of the history books emerged
only once the war began.

## NOTES

1   Dominic Lieven, "Pro-Germans and Russian
    Foreign Policy 1890–1914," *International History
    Review* 2 (1980): 34–54.
2   For the formation of the alliance, see George F.
    Kennan, *The Fateful Alliance: France, Russia and
    the Coming of the First World War* (Princeton, NJ:
    Princeton University Press, 1979).
3   C. H. D. Howard, *Splendid Isolation* (London:
    Macmillan, 1967).
4   For Rosebery's policies see Gordon Martel, *Impe-
    rial Diplomacy: Rosebery and the Failure of Foreign
    Policy* (Montreal and Kingston: McGill-Queen's
    University Press, 1986).
5   T. G. Otte, "Great Britain, Germany and the Far-
    Eastern Crisis of 1897–8," *English Historical
    Review* 90 (1995): 1157–79.

6   G. W. Monger, *The End of Isolation: British Foreign
    Policy, 1900–1907* (London: Nelson, 1963).
7   Keith Neilson, *Britain and the Last Tsar: British
    Policy and Russia, 1894–1917* (Oxford: Oxford
    University Press, 1995), pp. 48–50; T. G. Otte,
    "'Heaven Knows where we shall finally drift': Lord
    Salisbury, the Cabinet, Isolation and the Boxer
    Rebellion," in *Incidents in International Rela-
    tions*, ed. G. Kennedy and K. Neilson (Westport,
    CT: Greenwood, 2002), pp. 25–46.
8   Paul Kennedy, *The Rise of the Anglo-German
    Antagonism, 1860–1914* (London: Allen & Unwin,
    1980).
9   Ian Nish, *The Anglo-Japanese Alliance: The Diplo-
    macy of Two Island Empires, 1894–1907* (London:
    Athlone Press, 1966); Keith Neilson, "The Anglo-
    Japanese Alliance and British Strategic Foreign
    Policy 1902–1914," in *The Anglo-Japanese Alli-
    ance*, ed. P. P. O'Brien (London and New York:
    Routledge, 2004), pp. 48–63.
10  For this, see Christopher Andrew, *Théophile Del-
    cassé and the Making of the Entente Cordiale, 1898–
    1905* (London: Macmillan, 1968).
11  F. V. Parsons, *The Origins of the Morocco Question
    1880–1900* (London: Duckworth, 1976); E. N.
    Anderson, *The First Moroccan Crisis, 1904–1906*
    (Chicago: University of Chicago Press, 1930);
    Keith Hamilton, *Bertie of Thame: Edwardian
    Ambassador* (Woodbridge: Royal Historical
    Society, 1990), pp. 69–124.
12  Grey to Sir Cecil Spring Rice, December 22, 1905,
    as quoted in Keith Neilson, "'Control the Whirl-
    wind': Sir Edward Grey as Foreign Secretary,
    1905–1916," in *The Makers of British Foreign
    Policy*, ed. Thomas Otte (Basingstoke: Palgrave,
    2002), p. 130.
13  J. W. and P. F. Coogan, "The British Cabinet and
    the Anglo-French Staff Talks, 1905–1914: Who
    Knew What and When Did He Know It?" *Journal
    of British Studies* 24 (1985): 110–31.
14  A. J. A. Morris, *Radicalism Against War 1906–
    1914: The Advocacy of Peace and Retrenchment*
    (Totowa, NJ: Rowman & Littlefield, 1972), pp.
    97–121; Calvin Davis, *The United States and the
    Second Hague Peace Conference: American Diplo-
    macy and International Organization, 1899–1914*
    (Durham, NC: Duke University Press, 1975); and
    J. W. Coogan, *The End of Neutrality: The United
    States, Britain and Maritime Rights, 1899–1915*
    (Ithaca, NY: Cornell University Press, 1981).
15  Kennedy, *Anglo-German Antagonism*, pp. 413–31;
    D. W. Sweet, "Great Britain and Germany, 1905–
    1911," in *British Foreign Policy under Sir Edward*

*Grey*, ed. F. H. Hinsley (Cambridge: Cambridge University Press, 1977), pp. 216–35.

16  John Albert White, *Transition to Global Rivalry: Alliance Diplomacy and the Quadruple Entente, 1895–1907* (Cambridge: Cambridge University Press, 1995).

17  Rhodri Williams, *Defending the Empire: The Conservative Party and British Defence Policy 1899–1915* (New Haven and London: Yale University Press, 1991).

18  F. R. Bridge, "Izvolsky, Aehrenthal, and the End of the Austro-Russian Entente, 1906–8," *Mitteilungen des Österreichischen Staatsarchives* 29 (1976): 315–62; F. R. Bridge, *Great Britain and Austria-Hungary 1906–14* (London: Weidenfeld & Nicolson, 1972), pp. 80–91.

19  G. E. Silberstein, "Germany, France and the Casablanca Incident 1908–9: An Investigation of a Forgotten Crisis," *Canadian Journal of History* 11 (1976): 331–4; E. W. Edwards, "The Franco-German Agreement in Morocco," *English Historical Review* 78 (1963): 483–513.

20  J. F. V. Keiger, *France and the Origins of the First World War* (London: Macmillan, 1983), pp. 42, 88–9; D. C. B. Lieven, *Russia and the Origins of the First World War* (London: Macmillan, 1983), p. 38.

21  On the Agadir crisis and British policy, see J.-C. Alain, *Agadir 1911: Une crise impérialiste en Europe pour la conquête de Maroc* (Paris: Université de Paris, 1972); Hamilton, *Bertie of Thame*, pp. 214–47.

22  Samuel R. Williamson, *The Politics of Grand Strategy: Britain and France Prepare for War, 1904–1914* (London and Atlantic Highlands, NJ: Ashfield Press, 1990), pp. 167–204, is typical. For a convincing revisionist approach, see Hew Strachan, "The British Army, its General Staff and the Continental Commitment," in *The British General Staff: Reform and Innovation, 1890–1939*, ed. David French and Brian Holden Reid (London and Portland, OR: Frank Cass, 2002), pp. 9–25.

23  Jennifer Siegel, *Endgame: Britain, Russia and the Final Struggle for Central Asia* (London and New York: I. B. Tauris, 2002).

24  Zara Steiner and Keith Neilson, *Britain and the Origins of the First World War* (Basingstoke and New York: Macmillan, rev. edn, 2003), pp. 229–57; Stephen J. Valone, "'There Must Be Some Misunderstanding': Sir Edward Grey's Diplomacy of August 1, 1914," *Journal of British Studies* 27 (1988): 405–24; Keith Wilson, "Britain," in *Decisions for War, 1914*, ed. Keith Wilson (New York: St. Martin's, 1995), pp. 195–208.

## GUIDE TO FURTHER READING

V. R. Berghahn, *Germany and the Approach of War in 1914* (Basingstoke and New York: Macmillan, 2nd edn, 1993). The standard account of Germany's responsibility for the outbreak of the First World War.

R. J. Crampton, *The Hollow Detente: Anglo-German Relations in the Balkans 1911–1914* (London: George Prior, 1979). A detailed analysis that shows how Germany's actions in the Balkans soured Anglo-German relations.

Nicholas d'Ombrain, *War Machinery and High Policy: Defence Administration in Peacetime Britain 1902–1914* (Oxford: Oxford University Press, 1973). A useful account of the creation of the Committee of Imperial Defence and how this affected the formulation of British defense policy.

E. W. Edwards, *British Diplomacy and Finance in China 1895–1914* (Oxford: Oxford University Press, 1987). Shows how British diplomacy utilized British economic and financial resources as a tool to maintain British interests in China.

David French, *British Economic and Strategic Planning 1905–1915* (London: Allen & Unwin, 1982). The best description of British economic planning for a European war, which illustrates how British thinking had to change once war broke out.

Peter Gatrell, *Government, Industry and Rearmament in Russia, 1900–1914: The Last Argument of Tsarism* (Cambridge: Cambridge University Press, 1994). A definitive and detailed account of Russia's economic preparations for war before 1914. Essential reading for an understanding of Russia's war effort.

J. A. S. Grenville, *Lord Salisbury and Foreign Policy: The Close of the Nineteenth Century* (London: Athlone Press, 1964). The classic account of Salisbury's foreign policy, which still retains much value after forty years.

David G. Herrmann, *The Arming of Europe and the Making of the First World War* (Princeton, NJ: Princeton University Press, 1996). A valuable account of the pre-1914 arms races, which adds some extra-European dimensions not dealt with by Stevenson's magisterial study.

Nicholas A. Lambert, *Sir John Fisher's Naval Revolution* (Columbia, SC: University of South Carolina Press, 1999). A revisionist approach to British naval policy before 1914, which effectively replaces the classic study of Arthur Marder.

David M. McDonald, *United Government and Foreign Policy in Russia, 1900–1914* (Cambridge, MA: Harvard University Press, 1992). The best available study of Russian foreign policy before 1914, which emphasizes the domestic political context.

Annika Mombauer, *Helmuth von Moltke and the Origins of the First World War* (Cambridge: Cambridge University Press, 2001). An important book which makes clear the aggressive nature of the German General Staff before 1914.

A. J. A. Morris, *The Scaremongers: The Advocacy of War and Rearmament 1896–1914* (London: Routledge & Kegan Paul, 1984). A good study of those publicists who trumpeted the need for Britain to maintain its military strength before 1914.

Keith Neilson, "'Control the Whirlwind': Sir Edward Grey as Foreign Secretary, 1905–1916," in *The Makers of British Foreign Policy*, ed. T. G. Otte (London: Palgrave, 2002), pp. 128–50. The best recent overview of Grey's foreign policy which emphasizes his efforts to keep European and Imperial affairs separate from one another; "'Greatly Exaggerated': The Myth of the Decline of Great Britain before 1914," *International History Review* 13 (1991): 695–725, a revisionist study that demonstrates that Britain was not in a period of decline before 1914; "'My Beloved Russians': Sir Arthur Nicolson and Russia, 1906–1916," *International History Review* 9 (1987): 521–54, a useful examination of the impact of an individual on British policy toward Russia; "Watching the 'Steamroller': British Observers and the Russian Army before 1914," *Journal of Strategic Studies* 8 (1985): 199–217, a valuable case study of the pre-1914 balance of power, which should be read in conjunction with Stevenson.

Ian Nish, *Alliance in Decline* (London: Athlone Press, 1972). The classic study of Anglo-Japanese relations after 1907. Essential reading to understand the Far Eastern aspects of British policy.

T. G. Otte, "The Elusive Balance: British Foreign Policy and the French Entente before the First World War," in *Anglo-French Relations in the Twentieth Century: Rivalry and Cooperation*, ed. Alan Sharp and Glyn Stone (London and New York: Routledge, 2000), pp. 11–35. Outlines the British desire to maintain a balance of power before 1914.

Zara Steiner, *The Foreign Office and Foreign Policy, 1898–1914* (Cambridge: Cambridge University Press, 1969). An essential and pathbreaking study of the impact of civil servants on the creation of British foreign policy. It stands as the basis of all modern studies of British foreign policy.

David Stevenson, *Armaments and the Coming of War: Europe 1904–1914* (Oxford: Oxford University Press, 1996). The best account of pre-1914 European arms races. Illustrates how the arms races between the smaller states affected those of the Great Powers.

Samuel R. Williamson, *The Politics of Grand Strategy: Britain and France Prepare for War, 1904–1914* (Cambridge, MA: Harvard University Press, 1969). A classic account that retains much value, although more recent work has put greater emphasis on the contingent nature of British support for France.

Keith Wilson, ed., *Decisions for War, 1914* (New York: St. Martin's, 1995). A valuable collection which includes chapters on such lesser-studied states as Serbia and the Ottoman Empire; *The Policy of the Entente: Essays on the Determinants of British Foreign Policy, 1904–1914* (Cambridge: Cambridge University Press, 1985), a contentious study that argues that the British "invented" the German threat in order to defend its empire.

# CHAPTER EIGHT

# The July Crisis

## SAMUEL R. WILLIAMSON, JR.

At his desk in his summer hunting lodge at Bad Ischl, in the peaceful serenity of the Salzkammergut, Emperor Franz Joseph on July 28, 1914 signed – without enthusiasm – a declaration of war against the neighboring kingdom of Serbia. With that act, the Habsburg monarchy of more than fifty million persons launched a war against 4.4 million Serbs living in Serbia. This declaration came exactly one month after the assassination in Sarajevo, Bosnia, by a Bosnian Serb student of the monarch's nephew and heir, Archduke Franz Ferdinand, and his wife Sophie. Spurred by the Balkan Wars and then by Serbia's incitement of South Slavs inside the Habsburg realm against the monarchy, Franz Joseph's signature brought to an end almost two years of continuous diplomatic tension between Vienna and Belgrade. Within ten days of his decision, all of Europe's Great Powers (save Italy) would be at war. Four years later four empires had disappeared, more than nine million combatants had died, and Europe's place in the world irrevocably reduced. In the summer of 1914, a series of decisions and trends converged to create a perfect storm. In that summer a group of experienced, senior statesmen took their countries to war with disastrous results, none more so than for the Habsburg monarchy led by the 83-year-old emperor.[1]

## I

On July 1, 1911, the German government sent a gunboat into the Moroccan port of Agadir in a blatant attempt to thwart the French seizure of all of Morocco. Germany's aggressive response triggered a crisis that preoccupied Europe for the next four months. When it ended, the French had gotten all of Morocco and the disappointed Germans a part of the French Congo. But Agadir's ramifications were just beginning to unfold.

First, the French government considered itself victorious, and so did French opinion. In the midst of the crisis the government of Joseph Caillaux appointed General Joseph Joffre as chief of the French General Staff with enhanced powers. Joffre immediately began to develop an offensive war plan against Germany. Within months Raymond Poincaré, whose Lorraine homeland had been seized by the Germans in 1871, became first the French premier and then, in 1913, president of France. In the months before July 1914, Poincaré and his colleagues strengthened their alliance with Russia, made the entente relationship with Britain more explicit, and expanded the size of the French standing army with the three-year-service law.[2]

France's southern neighbor, Italy, utilized the tensions over Morocco to launch an invasion of Libya and wrest it from the Ottoman Empire. This September–October 1911 military adventure did not go well for the Italians: a substantial part of the Italian army was still there in July 1914. But the Italian campaign revealed the extreme vulnerability of the Ottoman holdings,

not least in the Balkan territory known as Macedonia and in Albania, which the Turks still controlled. With this almost irresistible temptation
before them, the covetous Balkan states, encouraged by an increasingly confident Russian foreign
minister, Sergei Sazonov, negotiated a secret
Balkan League in the spring of 1912. At some
point the group would attack the Ottoman
Empire. With this step, the Russian government
embarked on a foreign policy that became increasingly assertive over the next two years.

For its part the German government also drew
lessons from the Moroccan debacle, chiefly the
belief that the German army required an immediate increase in troops to offset the perceived
dangers posed by the Franco-Russian alliance.
Berlin would slow down, though not end, its provocative naval race with Great Britain. But now
its main attention centered on the army, as
Germany added 136,000 troops over the next
two years, an increase that nearly matched the
entire size of the British army. Not surprisingly,
the French and the Russians moved to counter
the increase and thus escalated the armaments
race even further.[3]

In Vienna the Habsburg leadership also pressed
for an increase in military manpower. In the
summer of 1912, for the first time since 1889, the
number of recruits coming into the Habsburg
army actually increased. At the same time,
Habsburg Foreign Minister Count Leopold Berchtold learned of the Balkan League among
Serbia, Greece, Montenegro, and Bulgaria, an
alignment he recognized as certain to challenge
the Ottoman possession of Macedonia and
Albania. He was not wrong.

On October 8, 1912, tiny Montenegro
launched an attack on Turkish positions in Kosovo;
its allies soon joined the fighting. To the surprise
of all, the League won a series of rapid-fire victories over the Turks and by early December had
nearly pushed the Ottoman Empire out of Europe.
At this point, the warring parties, pressured by
the Great Powers, reluctantly agreed to a ceasefire
and diplomatic talks in London.

The sudden Serb victories confronted Berchtold with a set of dangerous challenges. He wished
to limit Serbian expansion, especially to prevent
Serbia's direct access to the Adriatic Sea where it

might pose an additional strategic threat to
Habsburg holdings. But he also had an unprecedented strategic calculation to consider, for Russia
had retained an extra 220,000 troops on active
duty along the northern edge of the Habsburg
territories. Any military confrontation with Serbia
would almost certainly trigger an Austro-Russian
war. Still, Berchtold could not ignore the threat
posed by a Serbia bent on its own expansion. To
thwart this possibility he managed to get the
European powers to agree to the creation of the
new state of Albania, thus blocking Serbia from
the sea.[4]

Even with this diplomatic victory Vienna
worried about Serbia. In December 1912, the
senior Habsburg leadership, goaded by General
Conrad von Hötzendorf, chief of Austro-
Hungarian General Staff, seriously considered
war with Serbia. But Franz Joseph, Berchtold, and
Franz Ferdinand rebuffed the idea, as did their
German ally. In late February 1913, the Russian
and Habsburg diplomats negotiated a mutual
reduction in troop strength along their common
frontiers. A crisis had passed, or so it seemed.

In late April, however, Vienna nearly went to
war again, this time with tiny Montenegro over
its failure to respect Albania's new borders.
Indeed, the senior decision-makers in Vienna,
including Franz Joseph but not the heir apparent
Franz Ferdinand, were prepared to attack Montenegro. But King Nikita, the wily monarch of
this isolated kingdom, took a bribe and evacuated
Albanian territory. Another crisis had been
averted.

Then came the Second Balkan War of June–
July 1913. The fighting saw the former Balkan
League allies, joined by Romania, turn and rapidly
defeat their rapacious former ally, Bulgaria. Once
more Serbian prestige soared. This victory
emboldened Belgrade to attempt anew in October
1913 to infringe on Albania's borders. Once more
Vienna responded, this time with a seven-day
ultimatum to Belgrade to vacate the territory
assigned to Albania or face military consequences.
Serbia complied and the fourth Habsburg war–
peace crisis in a year eased. From the perspective
of Vienna, militant diplomacy worked.

But Vienna's leadership also faced internal
issues. The German–Austrian/Magyar domi-

nance of the multiethnic monarchy faced serious domestic challenges, not least from the Czechs in Bohemia, the Romanians in Transylvania, and the South Slavs in Bosnia-Herzegovina. These domestic issues had international dimensions, whether with Italy, Russia, Romania, or Serbia. Coupled with the emperor's age and a possibly climatic showdown for political primacy between Archduke Franz Ferdinand and the Hungarians when he ascended to the throne, these ethnic challenges left the monarchy's future an open question.

To complicate matters further, Vienna's alliance with Germany and Italy, and silent partner Romania, also showed signs of disarray. New friction flared with Italy over who would dominate Albania, despite efforts at a high-level summit between Berchtold and Italian Foreign Minister Antonino di San Giuliani in April 1914 to calm it. Still more ominously, St. Petersburg became increasingly successful in wooing Bucharest away from its secret commitment to the Triple Alliance. Not only did Romania's possible defection create a new strategic threat to Austria-Hungary, it meant also that the Romanian government had little interest in continuing to see three million Romanians live in Transylvania under the Magyars. The Magyar elite, led by Premier István Tisza, faced a serious domestic challenge.

Vienna's closest ally, Germany, faced its own problems. With a new focus on land armaments after 1912, the Anglo-German naval race eased somewhat. Moreover, in 1914 London and Berlin negotiated a "vulture-like" agreement over the possible future division of Portuguese territory in Angola. But if Berlin's relations with London improved, those with Russia deteriorated sharply during late 1913 and the opening months of 1914. In the fall of 1913, St. Petersburg objected to German General Liman von Sanders's appointment as adviser to the Ottoman military forces, an assignment that gave him effective command of Turkish troops. Eventually Berlin yielded to Russian pressure, only to see the military journalists in both countries begin a heated set of exchanges. The verbal volleys centered in part on German anxiety about Russia's proposed military expansion, in part from fear that the Russian military might actually become more effective, and in part because enhanced Franco-Russian

military cooperation sharply increased Germany's vulnerability in any two-front war. For his part, General Helmuth von Moltke, chief of Prussian General Staff, began to talk of a preemptive war and German Kaiser Wilhelm II echoed these views from time to time.[5]

Nor could Berlin be comfortable with intelligence reports that suggested, correctly, that the Anglo-French military and naval conversations continued despite Sir Edward Grey's public denials. More worrisome still, in the spring of 1914 the British government agreed to naval talks with St. Petersburg, talks that Grey denied in the House of Commons but which German Chancellor Theobald von Bethmann Hollweg knew from secret intelligence sources to be true. In Berlin there was mounting frustration, even pessimism, about Germany's long-term international position, a growing anxiety that Germany was in fact being "encircled."

Within the Triple Entente of Britain, France, and Russia there were indeed efforts to strengthen the military and naval cooperation among the partners. Poincaré and Joffre for the French, Grey, General Henry Wilson, and Winston Churchill for the British, and Sazonov and his military colleagues for the Russians did seek to make their entente relationship less ambiguous. These efforts translated not surprisingly into a more confident stance vis-à-vis Germany and Austria-Hungary, one that could only be seen as threatening by Vienna and Berlin.

But the Triple Entente members had their own domestic problems. In the spring and summer of 1914 the Irish question flared so sharply in Britain that civil war seemed a real possibility. A veritable army mutiny in March followed by gunrunning and increasingly vitriolic domestic rhetoric made Britain appear an uncertain entente colleague. In France the May elections saw the socialists win more seats and influence the shape of the new government headed by René Viviani, a former socialist. Support for the three-year-service law appeared in jeopardy. In the east, increasing labor unrest and strikes plagued the Russians, with consequent new tensions within the Russian political system. Europe on the eve of Sarajevo was far less tranquil than subsequent memories of the glorious summer suggest.

If the great powers had domestic problems in May–June 1914, the counterpart problems in Serbia were far more potentially lethal and, ultimately for Europe, more consequential. For in Belgrade the Balkan War victories prompted the emergence of new clashes between military and civilian authorities, this time over who would administer the lands of new Serbia, almost equal in size and population to old Serbia. The government of Nikola Pašić wanted to control the territory; the military disagreed. Among those who disagreed was Colonel Dragutin Dimitrijević (nicknamed Apis), the head of Serbian military intelligence. A key founder of the Crna Ruka (the secret terrorist organization, the Black Hand, dedicated to the creation of a Greater Serbia by any means) and one of the chief conspirators behind the 1903 murders of King Alexander and his mistress/queen, Apis had become by 1914 a veritable government within the government.

In the midst of this tension Apis got an unexpected opportunity to challenge his own government and to push the case against Habsburg rule in Bosnia-Herzegovina when three Bosnian Serb students in Belgrade indicated that they wanted to kill Archduke Franz Ferdinand when he visited Sarajevo in late June. Apis did not hesitate. He had Gavrilo Princip, Trifko Grabez, and Nedeljko Cabrinović trained with Browning revolvers, equipped with money and bombs (as well as cyanide), and smuggled back into Bosnia in late May through his Black Hand network. The assassins then made their way to Sarajevo, where they gained additional recruits.

In early June information about the conspirators reached the civilian authorities in Belgrade. An alarmed minister of the interior, Stefan Protić, asked Premier Pašić if he had known of this group and warned that their activities could lead to very dangerous consequences for Serbia. While it is not absolutely certain that Pašić shared this information with the entire Serbian cabinet, he certainly discussed it with some ministers. Moreover, he authorized Protić to stop any further movement and demanded an explanation from the army, and thus Apis, about the matter. When the colonel responded, Apis objected to any interference with his intelligence operations and lied about the movement of the conspirators. Nevertheless, on the very eve of Sarajevo, some senior officials in the Serbian government were aware of the plot. Whether the Russian military attaché, Victor A. Artamonov, a close confidant of Apis, knew is less certain. Nor is there any hard evidence that Serbia formally tried to warn Vienna about a possible attack on the archduke. In any event, a compromised Serbian government had to be uncomfortable with the situation when the archduke and his wife embarked on the trip to Bosnia-Herzegovina, with Franz Ferdinand scheduled first to participate in the summer army maneuvers, then make an official state visit to Sarajevo.[6]

The army exercises went off without incident. And on Saturday, June 27, the royal couple happily visited the markets in Sarajevo, making a series of purchases for their young children. That evening at dinner at a nearby resort, there was some talk about the risks of a journey to the town center the next day, but the archduke brushed this aside. No one in the group disagreed enough to force a reconsideration, though a more imaginative group might have remembered that the Serbs commemorated their 1389 defeat in Kosovo by the Turks on June 28 in St. Vitus Day celebrations. That historic day was about to be eclipsed.

The royal couple traveled in an open touring car along the long Apel Quai that paralleled the River Miljaćka on one side with stores and buildings on the other. At mid-point one of the conspirators threw a bomb, which hit the royal car but bounced off and exploded, with minor injuries to two of the archduke's accompanying military officers. The entourage proceeded to the City Hall, the Konak, for an awkward reception. For security reasons, and because Franz Ferdinand wanted to check on the wounded officers, the officials agreed to avoid the planned route through many of Sarajevo's narrowest streets. New orders were given to the drivers of the cars in the procession. But General Oskar Potiorek, the governor general of Sarajevo and the official host, forgot to tell the driver of the car in which he and the royal couple were traveling. Thus, when their driver turned to follow the original route, the general told him to stop, reverse, and go back down the Quai. As he did, Gavrilo Princip stepped forward, and at very close range fired two shots into Franz Ferdinand and Sophie. They were dead within minutes. Because of their deaths, a war would come that eventually claimed 9.5 million more combatants' lives. A simple command failure brought disaster.

## II

As the July crisis unfolded over the next five weeks, there was a series of successive, distinct stages. Although some overlapped, each had its own special character. The first phase went from the murders on June 28 through July 7 with Vienna's decision to punish Serbia for the attack. The second phase began on July 8 and continued until July 18, ten days in which Vienna and Berlin attempted to lull Europe into complacency though with only limited success. The next, short phase, four days long, ran from July 19 to July 23, culminating with the delivery of the ultimatum. During this period there was renewed public speculation about possible Habsburg action, even as the long-planned French state visit to Russia proceeded. The presentation of the ultimatum on July 23 opened the penultimate phase, one that continued until Vienna's declaration of war on July 28 and the exchange of gunfire that evening near Belgrade. The final stage to a general European war began on July 28–9 and moved relentlessly to August 4 and British entry into the expanding conflagration.

By late afternoon, Sunday, June 28, news of the Sarajevo assassinations had swept across Europe. Shock, dismay, fear characterized some reactions, though not in Italy, Hungary, or Serbia where Franz Ferdinand was unloved and there was public rejoicing. The murders, of course, immediately put the Serbian government at risk, for Pašić realized that Serbia would be blamed. He offered condolences, put the Serbian flag at half-mast, even visited the Habsburg legation. But he made no effort to investigate the plot's connection to Belgrade. Nor, despite official efforts, could he muzzle the Serbian press that praised Princip, delighted in the disappearance of Franz Ferdinand, and called for unity among all South Slavs, including those in the Habsburg lands. And if Pašić could not control the Serbian press, he could not ignore the fact that the authorities in Sarajevo had rounded up not only Princip but also almost all of the other conspirators, some of whom had recently been in Belgrade. The question soon became: what would they say that could implicate Serbia? "Official Serbia" now became vulnerable.[7]

The reaction to Sarajevo among the senior Habsburg leaders ranged from anger and sadness to an almost uniform desire to punish Serbia for the deed. But first Vienna had to deal with grief. The aged emperor, Franz Joseph, whose relations with his nephew were always formal to the point of coolness, signaled that he wanted the funeral low key and subdued. Vienna informed Berlin that it would be better if Kaiser Wilhelm II refrained from coming, in part because they feared another attack, in part because some worried that he would be too effusive about the archduke whom he had visited just two weeks earlier. In short, Vienna treated the tragic event in a very modest fashion.

But behind the scenes the Habsburg decision-makers had by July 3 agreed that Serbia must be held accountable. For Generals Conrad and War Minister Alexander Krobatin, Austrian Premier Karl Stürgkh, and Finance Minister Leon Bilinski, this meant a military confrontation; for Hungarian Premier Tisza, this meant a diplomatic victory; and for Franz Joseph and Berchtold it meant the willingness to go beyond militant diplomacy to demands that could lead to a local war. Vienna reached this conclusion, it must be stressed, without any explicit pressure from Berlin and the Habsburg leadership never wavered from this view in the coming weeks. On the other hand, Vienna had to be sure that Germany, unlike its vacillation during the four earlier war–peace crises, would commit in advance to support a Habsburg decision. Berchtold clung to his hope that Berlin could deter Russian involvement in any local war. But this time he would seek German agreement before he moved forward, rather than later.

On July 4 Vienna notified Berlin that a special envoy, Count Alexander Hoyos, the *chef de cabinet* of the foreign ministry, would travel to Germany with a communication for Kaiser Wilhelm II. Hoyos arrived in the German capital on Sunday morning, July 5, with a handwritten letter from Franz Joseph to Wilhelm that left little doubt that

Vienna wanted to settle with Serbia. He also brought a late June memorandum from the foreign ministry that outlined a new, aggressive Habsburg diplomatic policy in the Balkans, one designed to isolate Serbia. Duly briefed by Hoyos, Habsburg Ambassador Ladislaus Szögyény went to nearby Potsdam to see the German kaiser.

Wilhelm II's reception could only have pleased the Habsburg envoy. Wilhelm pledged support – the infamous "blank check" – and urged Vienna to move quickly. But he also said that he had to consult Bethmann Hollweg, the civilian head of the government, and he promised to do that later in the afternoon.

Historians have endlessly debated the kaiser's promise. Some see it as German pressure on Vienna, some see it as Germany finally agreeing to help an ally, and some see it as a pretext for a larger German effort to launch a preventive war. Almost certainly Wilhelm and Bethmann had discussed, before July 5, what Germany might do, even without knowing the details of any Habsburg request. But there is no evidence to suggest that they knew, in advance, exactly what Vienna might propose. However judged, the kaiser had made a monumental, fateful decision for Germany and for Europe, and he had left future decisions almost entirely in the hands of his Habsburg ally.

Later in the afternoon of July 5, the German monarch, his chancellor, his war minister, and senior aides again discussed the ruler's pledge of support. They agreed with Wilhelm's assurances, which Bethmann repeated again the next day to both Szögyény and Hoyos, who then telegraphed news of German support to Vienna even before Hoyos returned. Vienna could now move ahead to a showdown with Serbia. At the same time, however, War Minister Falkenhayn and others in Berlin had serious doubts that anything would happen. The German military and naval authorities checked the status of their war plans but took no further action; indeed, many of the senior German officials, including the foreign minister and the army chief of staff, remained on holiday.

On Hoyos's return to Vienna, he briefed the senior ministers who now had to make a decision. They did so in a very long session of the Common Ministerial Council on July 7, a meeting that saw a thorough examination of the pros and cons of a military showdown with Serbia. Among those present only Tisza resisted war, calling instead for a diplomatic confrontation first, with war a second possibility. While the group assumed that Franz Joseph favored war, the ministers also knew that he would do so only if they were united.

Despite's Tisza's resistance, the group heard General Conrad give a synopsis of his war plans and repeat his mantra that only war would resolve the monarchy's internal problems. Though his own memoranda were less confident, he assured his political colleagues that Austria-Hungary could handle Serbia – on the assumption that Berlin kept Russia out and thus the rest of Europe. At the meeting he almost certainly informed the ministers that no military action could start before July 21–2, since Habsburg troops were scattered across the monarchy on "harvest leave," a policy that Conrad had himself instituted to help farm families. This policy, ironically, now prevented quick military action, one that might have won more favor with the rest of Europe.[8]

This institutional delay gave Berchtold additional time to convince Tisza and Franz Joseph of the need for action. It also allowed Habsburg investigators more time to find direct evidence linking Belgrade to the murders, a task in which they were only partly successful. But the delay also meant that the French state visit to Russia would take place just when Vienna wanted to present its demands to Serbia, a situation that worried Berchtold and his associates. The delay further worried the Germans, who thought that Vienna ought to move to exploit European anger over the deaths before it was too late. A third consequence flowed from these two concerns: the two allies had to engage in a concerted effort to lull Europe about Vienna's eventual intentions. It is those efforts, only partly successful during the second stage of the crisis, that demand consideration, for their failure put the Russians, the Italians, and the Serbs on alert much earlier than Vienna desired.

The deliberate effort to lull Europe worked, at least at first. President Poincaré and Premier René Viviani departed by sea on their long scheduled visit to Russia, arriving in St. Petersburg on July 20. Businesses and investors appeared calmed as the Vienna stock market, after some wild gyrations, settled down, thanks to assurances from the foreign ministry. Franz Joseph remained at Bad Ischl, with Berchtold traveling to and fro, along with senior aides. Conrad conspicuously went on a hiking trip in the Tyrol. The ministers also sought to restrain the tone of the Vienna newspapers. Elsewhere Europe turned to other, apparently more pressing concerns. The French public awaited the trial of Madame Henriette Caillaux, wife of the former premier, for the murder of a newspaper editor. In Britain the threat of civil war over Ireland increased to the point that King George V desperately summoned a conference at Buckingham Palace to calm the situation. The German kaiser, for his part, continued his annual North Sea voyage, though he did not go as far north as usual.

But there were cracks in the edifice of calm. The German Foreign Office on July 11 cabled its ambassador to Italy, Hans von Flotow, with the gist of Vienna's plans for a confrontation with Serbia. Flotow, on vacation at the same spa with Italian Foreign Minister San Giuliano, informed him of the plans – with or without instructions from Berlin. The Italian leader wasted no time (July 14 and July 16) in sending two dispatches to his senior envoys abroad, including St. Petersburg, Berlin, Belgrade, and one to Vienna that contained a general picture of Habsburg plans. The codebreakers in Vienna, who easily broke the second telegram, in turn informed Berchtold by July 18 of the indiscretion. In the remaining days before the ultimatum was delivered, Berchtold shared very little with Berlin for fear of further leaks. For their part the Russians and Serbs knew well before July 23 about a possible ultimatum and were prepared for it, a point that Tisza's own indelicate speech on July 15 to the Hungarian parliament certainly reinforced. And Serbian Prime Minister Pašić, in dispatches to his envoys on July 18–19, stated that he would never accept any infringement of Serbian sovereignty, not least (though unstated) because such a step would reveal his own complicity in the Sarajevo events and put him at personal risk with the dangerous Apis.[9]

The third stage of the crisis started on July 19. By then, thanks to Flotow, Tisza, and loose talk in Vienna, even by Berchtold, the European polit-

ical circles were aware of hints of a pending Habsburg action. In Berlin the *North German Gazette* on July 19 stated that it was not unreasonable to expect Vienna to make demands on Belgrade, suggesting that any ensuing tension should remain localized. In St. Petersburg a sharp exchange between Poincaré and Friedrich Szápáry, the Habsburg ambassador, at a diplomatic reception on July 21 reflected French knowledge of a possible move. In London, British Foreign Secretary Sir Edward Grey finally had a meeting with Habsburg Ambassador Count Albert Mensdorff on July 23, his first session with the envoy since early July. In their discussion Grey pointedly cautioned against hasty Habsburg action. No one was lulled into complacency any longer.

In Vienna, meanwhile, on July 19 the Common Ministerial Council met again, this time secretly at the private residence of Count Berchtold where they agreed on the final terms of the ultimatum. They also accepted Tisza's demand that there be only minor territorial adjustments after the war, a step taken to assure that no additional Slavs were added to the ethnically divided monarchy. After the meeting, Conrad contemptuously dismissed this self-limiting demand, noting that before the Balkan Wars there had been talk of no territorial changes and afterwards there had been plenty.

On July 20 the 48-hour Habsburg ultimatum was sent to Belgrade for transmittal to the Serbian government at 6 p.m. on July 23. Vienna had deliberately set the date and time to ensure that the French president had actually sailed from St. Petersburg on his way to Sweden. Slightly more than three weeks after Sarajevo, Vienna finally made its demands on Belgrade. These demands were framed to be rejected because Vienna wanted a military confrontation with Serbia.

Many historians now consider the next stage of the crisis, July 23–8, as the pivotal period, when the chances for peace essentially disappeared. The reasons for this perspective will soon become evident. When Austrian Minister Wladimir Giesl delivered the ultimatum, Pašić was away from Belgrade on an election campaign. He soon returned. Over the next 30 hours he and his colleagues drafted a reply at once gracious and conciliatory, at once forthcoming and evasive, and on the central point – the demand for a joint investigation into the murders – completely unyielding. Without any Russian pressure to resist, indeed St. Petersburg sent confusing signals to the Serbian government, Belgrade refused to concede on the key point. When Giesl received the reply at 6 p.m. on July 25, he promptly declared it unacceptable, broke diplomatic relations, and fled the capital to Habsburg territory at Zemun just across the Danube–Sava Rivers. The Serbs moved to mobilize their army.

Confirmation of news of the ultimatum reached St. Petersburg during the night of July 23–4. When informed, Foreign Minister Sazonov immediately called for a meeting of the Council of Ministers that afternoon, while spending the morning exploring possible military options with the senior military leaders. From the start Sazonov determined to support Serbia, including a limited mobilization, a step that the other ministers accepted without knowing the military had no such plan. Nevertheless, at 4 p.m. that afternoon, as new documentation reveals, the military command center telegraphed four key military districts – Odessa, Moscow, Kiev, and Kazan – to take steps to recall troops. These measures did not long escape the notice of German intelligence.

The next day, July 25, the tsar joined the discussions. Once more the ministers agreed to support Serbia, to order further preparatory steps for a partial mobilization, and to press the British to declare their support for the Triple Entente. Meanwhile, public demonstrations of support for Serbia swept the Russian capital. The Russian military, while ordering additional steps, also moved to demand a full, not partial, mobilization. Not only was this easier, it also reflected their desire to help France by putting the Germans under pressure from the earliest possible moment. In that sense, alliance obligations clearly propelled the crisis forward. However judged, the Russians thus became the first Great Power, even before Vienna, to take military measures, measures which the German intelligence network quickly discerned.

In Berlin, reaction to the ultimatum's delivery at first changed little. The kaiser continued his cruise, though now more anxious; Moltke remained away; and Bethmann Hollweg stayed at his country estate. But by July 26 the German

leaders were returning, worried in part by intelligence reports about the Russian measures, worried about British intentions, and worried (for some) that the Habsburgs might flinch. On July 27 the kaiser returned, which meant all of the key leaders were in Berlin before Vienna's declaration of war.[10] By the next day the German military leaders had become increasingly anxious about the Russian steps, while Bethmann could not be comforted by the ambiguity with which Sir Edward Grey continued to respond to the situation. Nor could Berlin ignore the precautionary measures taken by the British navy to remain assembled after the annual fleet exercises had ended, a step that Churchill and Grey hoped would be noticed by the Germans. It was noticed but without the desired consequences.

In London, the Irish question continued to dominate all political considerations, whether the cabinet, the parliament, or the press. To be sure, news of the ultimatum had jolted the cabinet but not enough to displace Ireland. And Grey, while trying to broker some kind of mediation agreement in the Balkans, did not press ahead with much urgency. Indeed, his cautious approach has drawn critical comment from historians ever since.

Across the Channel, in Paris, the Caillaux murder trial still mesmerized the French public (she would be acquitted). With their leaders still en route home and essentially out of touch, the caretaker French regime took some precautionary military steps and awaited news, often much delayed, from St. Petersburg. The increasing militancy of the Russian actions did not prompt any cautions from Paris or the French ambassador to Russia, Maurice Paléologue, who strongly supported the Russian alliance. Indeed his failure to urge restraint on the Russians has also drawn much subsequent criticism.

In Vienna decisions were taken that deliberately escalated the crisis. On July 25 the emperor agreed to mobilize against Serbia with the understanding that a full mobilization would follow if Russia backed the Serbs. For the moment, Vienna continued to hope for a local war against Serbia. Yet Berchtold also had to weigh information coming from Berlin, information that suggested by July 26–7 that the German leaders were growing apprehensive about the turn of events and wished for more caution, perhaps even a commitment to halt in Belgrade once the fighting started. To confuse the situation further, even as the German foreign ministry talked of caution, Moltke pressed Conrad to move ahead with his plans. At one point this ambiguity prompted Berchtold to remark: "How odd! Who runs the government: Moltke or Bethmann?"[11] For his part, Berchtold pressed for the war with Serbia, getting Conrad to agree to a war declaration on July 28, days before he had thought it necessary. That action effectively foreclosed the remaining chances for peace, though this would not be apparent immediately.

Then an incident on the night of July 28–9 irrevocably altered the situation. That evening Habsburg and Serb forces exchanged gunfire near Belgrade. Initial Serbian press reports denounced the Habsburgs for their attack, while wildly exaggerating the extent of the damage. Those reports, which reached St. Petersburg on July 29, galvanized Sazonov and the Russian generals to demand general mobilization. From that point the already dwindling chances to localize the crisis essentially vanished.

With the declaration of war and the shelling near Belgrade, the July crisis moved to its final stage, July 29–August 4. During these days the carefully developed war plans of the Great Powers became juxtaposed with desperate diplomatic efforts to slow the confrontation. For its part Austria-Hungary continued to act as if a local war remained possible. Conrad had carefully developed Plans B and R for war situations; now he moved to put Plan B (the Balkan plan) into effect even as intelligence reports indicated that he might also face Russia. Thus, on July 30, ahead of schedule, he began implementing Plan B, sending a key part of his offensive contingent southward. This key strategic mistake has never been adequately explained, for within days he had to cancel those orders and implement Plan R. For their part, the troops already on board trains had to continue southward, then detrain, and reboard for a tortuous trip to their locations along the Russian frontier. His initial decisions had given the monarchy the worst possible chances of eventual success.

In St. Petersburg news of the Belgrade shelling pushed Sazonov and the generals to seek the tsar's approval for mobilization, strongly preferring a general order to a partial one. Nevertheless, Tsar Nicholas II decided on July 29 to sign two mobilization orders – one partial, one general. Before either could be put into effect, he rescinded the orders after he received telegrams from his cousin, Kaiser Wilhelm II, pleading for mutual action to restrain the situation. But the next day, July 30, Sazonov and the military again pleaded with the tsar, insisting that the situation required general mobilization. This time the tsar yielded to Sazonov and signed the order at 4 p.m. With this order the Russians became the first Great Power to move to general mobilization, ahead of both the Habsburgs and the Germans. In doing so, the Russian decision created a crisis for the German high command, caught between the Franco-Russian allies, with the need to respond immediately, a step that guaranteed a European war once the German order went into effect. In that sense, the Russian general mobilization of July 30 not only culminated the aggressive Russian steps taken since July 24, it directly contributed to the escalation to general war.[12]

In Berlin, meanwhile, the intelligence reports about Russian military measures had multiplied since July 26. An increasingly worried Moltke and War Minister Falkenhayn wanted the chancellor to agree to a German military response. But Bethmann, now convinced that Britain would enter the war on the side of the Triple Entente, hesitated. Above all, he now wanted to portray the Russians as the aggressors, in the hope that this might sway London or at least ensure domestic support inside Germany. Thus the chancellor rebuffed the military demands, awaiting confirmation that Russia had actually ordered general mobilization, a confirmation that came on July 31. With that news, Berlin sent ultimatums to France and Russia that demanded that they cease their military preparations or face the consequences. The allies did not stop, and Germany's mobilization and war plans went into effect on August 1.

The much-analyzed Schlieffen–Moltke war plan, a product of years of careful and detailed staff planning, sought to overcome Germany's

strategic vulnerability. Caught between two powerful allies, the German planners concluded that
only a flanking attack through neutral Belgium
would enable them to defeat the French, perhaps
allowing them to reach Paris, and above all bringing a quick end to the war in the west. Once this
had been achieved, they could turn and defeat the
slower-moving Russian forces in the east. To
achieve the prompt annihilation of the French
forces required the immediate seizure of Liège,
Belgium; there could be no delays once mobilization began.[13] Even under the most optimistic calculations, the German plan demanded rigorous,
perfect execution to succeed. No delays, no hesita-
tion, no qualms could intrude. Because Russia
had accelerated its mobilization schedules in early
1914, word of which reached both Berlin and
Vienna that spring, there was an additional
emphasis on speed. It was this war plan, carefully
planned and based on excessive confidence in the
fighting ability of the German soldier and studied
disdain for their opponents, that became operational on the morning of August 2.

On July 29 the French public welcomed the
belated return of Poincaré and Viviani. By the
time of their arrival in Paris, the options for
France and peace were severely limited. Russia was
on the verge of declaring general mobilization, a
step that Poincaré and others had hoped to delay
or prevent but to no avail. The French leaders
knew the Germans would respond. For them,
ensuring British involvement in the war and
domestic support for a war on behalf of Russia
became their primary considerations. To achieve
these twin goals French President Poincaré,
usurping the role of the prime minister, ordered
that no French troops approach within 10 kilometers of the German frontier. Despite Joffre's
strong protests, this self-imposed restriction
remained in effect until late Sunday, August 2. By
then the news from London had become more
favorable and the surge of French public support
for the government reassuring. Poincaré had
achieved his minimal goals of British assistance
and public unity.

In London the debate within the British
cabinet about the European situation had finally
begun in earnest on July 29. Until that point the
Irish issue had dominated. In the initial cabinet

discussions, Grey, thoroughly committed to the
Triple Entente and especially France, had been
unable to get the cabinet to agree to any statement, either for France or for neutrality. On the
other hand, the cabinet did not neglect purely
British interests. They approved, after the fact,
Churchill's actions to hold the British navy
together. During the night of July 29–30, the
British battle fleet had sailed, without lights,
through the Channel to its North Sea stations,
making it the first fleet to be ready for action.
Also, the British army had by July 29 begun preparations for mobilization, though no orders were
given until August 3. Throughout the mounting
tension the French ambassador, Paul Cambon,
repeatedly urged Grey to commit Britain to
France and to allow the nearly decade-old secret
military and naval arrangements between the two
entente partners to come into effect. But Grey
refused to make a public commitment, despite his
own intention to resign if the cabinet finally
deserted France.

Then on Saturday–Sunday, August 1–2, the
momentum in the cabinet shifted. As the European armies moved to mobilize, the cabinet could
no longer ignore the potential threat to British
security interests. Prime Minister Henry Asquith,
Grey, Lord Haldane, and Churchill favored
action, while David Lloyd George, the chancellor
of the exchequer, remained uncommitted, and the
majority of the cabinet remained opposed to
intervention. But the question of Belgian neutrality, which the German government had injected
into the debate on July 29 when Berlin asked Grey
to allow Germany to violate it, became paramount
in the cabinet's deliberations. So also did pressure
from the Conservative leaders who sent Asquith
a letter on Sunday, August 2, declaring their
support for France. The letter left no doubt that
if the Asquith government fell over the issue of
the Triple Entente, a new Conservative one would
support France. These twin considerations –
Belgium and Tory pressure – created the context
for the two long cabinet meetings on Sunday,
August 2.

By the end of the meetings, the cabinet agreed
that Germany could not be allowed to operate
against France's north coasts, an implicit recognition that secret naval conversations had created a

strategic obligation in which France protected British naval interests in the Mediterranean and Britain those of France in the English Channel and the Atlantic. Second, the cabinet agreed that Britain would intervene to defend the neutrality of Belgium if there were a "substantial" violation of its neutrality. In the discussions Lloyd George had made Belgium the key issue. In this he was helped by the prospect of a Conservative government if the cabinet collapsed. In the final analysis, only two ministers quit over the question of war, a testimony both to the impact of the Belgian argument and to the prospect of losing power to a party that would certainly wreck any agreement over Ireland. In the final analysis, Belgium became the glue that ensured British participation in the spreading war.

Yet even on Monday, August 3, Grey, in speaking to the House of Commons, strongly suggested that Britain's main role in the war would be naval, an assurance he almost certainly knew to be false. In any event, the Germans substantially violated Belgian neutrality that day and rejected the British demand that they stop. By the time Britain officially declared war at 11 p.m. on August 4, plans were well under way to move the British Expeditionary Force, or most of it, to France in accordance with the long developed secret conversations with the French General Staff. Ultimately, the British Expeditionary Force of four infantry and one cavalry divisions would confront the might of two German armies when they clashed along the Franco-Belgian border.[14]

On Sunday, August 2, Italy declared its neutrality in the war. Although a member of the Triple Alliance since 1882, Italy's relations with Austria-Hungary had always been problematic. The Italian declaration came as no great surprise. During July the Italian foreign minister, San Giuliano, had relentlessly tried to exploit the situation by demanding that Vienna surrender Trentino in return for Italian participation in the war. In spite of German pressure, Berchtold refused to pay, offering only Valona in Albania to Rome. Indeed, given the attitude of Italian public opinion against Vienna, it is not clear that even the concession of Trentino could have gotten Italy into the fray. Thus by mid-August 1914, the Triple Alliance had become reduced to the Central

Powers of Germany and Austria-Hungary. In April 1915 Italy did enter the war, since the Triple Entente powers were perfectly prepared to pledge Trentino and more to Rome for its decision. That commitment brought Italy's entrance into the war; it did not much change the strategic calculations. But it ensured the dismantling of Austria-Hungary should the entente win.

### III

The peace treaties of 1919–20 blamed Germany and Austria-Hungary for the origins of the First World War. Almost immediately the German government and German historians challenged this verdict as one-sided and began to publish, selectively, German diplomatic records before 1914 to buttress their claims. This step in turn forced the other governments, including the Soviets but not Serbia, to publish collections of diplomatic documents. This new and unprecedented documentation allowed historians to study the July crisis in detail. Over the next eighty years it has become one of the most studied events in all of history.[15]

Those historians, prominent in the United States and Germany, who suggested that the July crisis involved more than just German and Austrian responsibility were often called "revisionists." Those who backed the Versailles verdict became the orthodox defenders, prominent in France, Britain, and a few in the United States. Later the prominent Italian journalist turned historian, Luigi Albertini, joined the group who supported the main thrust of the Versailles verdict while offering many nuanced interpretations of the events leading to the war. On the other hand, some writers, most notably Lloyd George, asserted that Europe had slithered into war and that no one government alone had been responsible. For those writers the First World War had been inadvertent. Still other historians suggested that profound, underlying forces, including the alliance/entente structures, imperialism, nationalism, social Darwinism, unspoken assumptions, militarism, and the arms races, had created conditions which made a war inevitable, a context that no decision-maker and no government could single-handedly overcome.

In the 1960s the debate on the origins of the war abruptly shifted, or seemed to shift, when the German historian Fritz Fischer broke ranks and became the first prominent German historian to assert that Germany had indeed caused the war. In fact, he even argued that it had been a preventive war, one possibly planned as early as December 1912, and that the conflict had grown out of Germany's increasingly tense domestic situation. In the decades since historians have considered and often rejected many of Fischer's assertions, while accepting his key point about the centrality of Germany's role. More recent studies make clear that each government in its own way helped to contribute to the eventual escalation. In this evaluation the German and Austro-Hungarian governments remain paramount for provoking the dynamics behind the crisis, but Serbia, Russia, and even France and Britain made decisions (or failed to make them) that reduced the chances for peace.

Historians have also come to accept that the contextual situation of the alliances and unspoken assumptions were important, as was the dialectic between domestic and international considerations country by country. More recently some writers have begun to study anew the individual decision-makers, suggesting that the monarchs, generals, admirals, or statesmen in positions of power were responsible for the decisions that led to war, not some autonomous forces.[16] Historians now accept that the war was advertent, with the leaders in Vienna and Berlin and even St. Petersburg prepared to risk a land war rather than lose face in the crisis. Some have even asserted that the concept of "honor" came to dominate the thoughts of the leaders who could not bring themselves to renege on their earlier assurances, however horrible the consequences might be for their governments and for those who would fight.[17] Historians also argue that individual leaders made decisions that could have been different, that each leader made his separate personal, professional, and political calculations and reached his own conclusions. As in the case of the United States in the spring of 2003, a small group of men concluded that war represented an acceptable policy option. In 1914 those separate conclusions converged to cause the First World War; the world has not yet seen the end of the consequences of that perfect storm.

## NOTES

1  On the crisis, see Hew Strachan, *The Outbreak of the First World War* (Oxford: Oxford University Press, 2004); Samuel R. Williamson, Jr., and Russel Van Wyk, *July 1914: Soldiers, Statesmen, and the Coming of the Great War: A Brief Documentary History* (Boston: Bedford/St. Martin's, 2003).

2  J. F. V. Keiger, *Raymond Poincaré* (Cambridge: Cambridge University Press, 1997), pp. 130–92.

3  David Stevenson, *Armaments and the Coming of the War: Europe, 1904–1914* (Oxford: Oxford University Press, 1996), pp. 231–328.

4  Samuel R. Williamson, Jr., *Austria-Hungary and the Origins of the First World War* (New York: Palgrave Macmillan, 1991), pp. 121–42.

5  Fritz Fischer, *War of Illusions: German Policies from 1911 to 1914*, trans. Marian Jackson (New York: W. W. Norton, 1975), pp. 330–88.

6  On the conspiracy, see David MacKenzie, *Apis: The Congenial Conspirator. The Life of Dragutin T. Dimitrijević* (New York: Columbia University Press, 1989), pp. 105–37.

7  Mark Cornwall, "Serbia," in *Decisions for War, 1914*, ed. Keith Wilson (New York: St. Martin's, 1995), p. 67.

8  Williamson, *Austria-Hungary*, pp. 199–200.

9  Copies of these dispatches are in Williamson and Van Wyk, *July 1914*, pp. 34–5, 160–1.

10  For contrasting views of the German reactions, see Annika Mombauer, *Helmuth von Moltke and the Origins of the First World War* (Cambridge: Cambridge University Press, 2001), pp. 196–226; and Mark Hewitson, *Germany and the Causes of the First World War* (Oxford: Berg, 2004), pp. 203–16.

11  Luigi Albertini, *The Origins of the War of 1914*, trans. and ed. Isabella M. Massey (London: Oxford University Press, 3 vols., 1952–7), vol. 2, p. 674.

12  On the Russian decision, see Strachan, *Outbreak of the First World War*, pp. 101–7, and Stevenson, *Coming of the War*, pp. 379–87.

13  On the concept of annihilation as a feature of the plans, see Isabel V. Hull, *Absolute Destruction: Military Culture and the Practices of War in Imperial Germany* (Ithaca, NY: Cornell University Press, 2005), pp. 165–78; on the plans themselves, see the provocative study by Terence Zuber,

*Inventing the Schlieffen Plan: German War Planning, 1871–1914* (Oxford: Oxford University Press, 2003), pp. 220–304.

14 Zara S. Steiner and Keith Neilson, *Britain and the Origins of the First World War* (New York: Palgrave Macmillan, 2nd edn, 2003), pp. 245–57.

15 For two surveys of the controversy, see Annika Mombauer, *The Origins of the First World War: Controversies and Consensus* (London: Longman, 2002); and John W. Langdon, *July 1914: The Long Debate, 1918–1990* (New York: Berg, 1991).

16 For instance, Richard F. Hamilton and Holger H. Herwig, eds., *The Origins of World War I* (Cambridge: Cambridge University Press, 2003).

17 Avner Offer, "Going to War in 1914: A Matter of Honor?" *Politics and Society* 23 (1995): 213–41.

## GUIDE TO FURTHER READING

Luigi Albertini, *The Origins of the War of 1914*, trans. and ed. Isabella M. Massey (London: Oxford University Press, 3 vols., 1952–7), reprinted by Enigma Books (New York, 2005). Though dated, Albertini remains the most detailed assessment of the origins of the war.

Volker Berghahn, *Germany and the Approach of War in 1914* (London, 1971), 2nd edn (New York: Palgrave Macmillan, 1993). Provides a good introduction.

Niall Ferguson, *The Pity of War* (New York: Basic Books, 1999). Provocatively argues that Britain should not have intervened in the Great War.

Fritz Fischer, *War of Illusions: German Policies from 1911 to 1914*, trans. Marian Jackson (New York: W. W. Norton, 1975). Contends that Germany sought the war, not least to escape from domestic tensions.

Richard F. Hamilton and Holger H. Herwig, eds., *The Origins of World War I* (Cambridge: Cambridge University Press, 2003). Excellent essays on the July crisis.

David Herrmann, *The Arming of Europe and the Making of the First World War* (Princeton, NJ: Princeton University Press, 1996). Chronicles the arms races.

Mark Hewitson, *Germany and the Causes of the First World War* (Oxford: Berg, 2004). Insists that Germany's decisions in 1914 reflected confidence about its situation, not fear.

James Joll and Gordon Martel, *The Origins of the First World War* (London and New York: Longman, 3rd

edn, 2006). Remains a succinct treatment of the background to the July crisis and of its decision-making.

John F. V. Keiger, *France and the Origins of the First World War* (London: Palgrave Macmillan, 1983). A crisp assessment of France's dilemma.

D. C. B. Lieven, *Russia and the Origins of the First World War* (London: Palgrave Macmillan, 1983). Insights into the Russian calculations.

Annika Mombauer, *Helmuth von Moltke and the Origins of the First World War* (Cambridge: Cambridge University Press, 2001). Utilizes the German army archives returned from the old Soviet Union to reassess Moltke's role; *The Origins of the First World War: Controversies and Consensus* (London: Longman, 2002), surveys almost a century of writing about the July crisis.

Zara S. Steiner and Keith Neilson, *Britain and the Origins of the First World War* (New York: Palgrave Macmillan, 2nd edn, 2003). The most integrated examination of British policy.

David Stevenson, *Armaments and the Coming of the War: Europe, 1904–1914* (Oxford: Oxford University Press, 1996). One of the most important books written on the road to war and on the military role in the decisions of 1914.

David Stevenson, *Cataclysm: The First World War as Political Tragedy* (New York: Basic Books, 2004). A comparative analysis of 1914.

Hew Strachan, *The Outbreak of the First World War* (Oxford: Oxford University Press, 2004). Contains the opening chapters of his *The First World War*, subtitled *To Arms* (Oxford: Oxford University Press, 2001); currently the single best introduction to the crisis.

Samuel R. Williamson, Jr., *Austria-Hungary and the Origins of the First World War* (New York: Palgrave Macmillan, 1991). Exploited the Austrian archives.

Samuel R. Williamson, Jr., and Russel Van Wyk, *July 1914: Soldiers, Statesmen, and the Coming of the Great War: A Brief Documentary History* (Boston: Bedford/St. Martin's, 2003). Explores the crisis from the point of view of civil–military relations.

Keith Wilson, ed., *Decisions for War, 1914* (New York: St. Martin's, 1995). Has valuable essays, especially on Serbia.

Terence Zuber, *Inventing the Schlieffen Plan: German War Planning, 1871–1914* (Oxford: Oxford University Press, 2003). A controversial but useful study.

# CHAPTER NINE

# Wartime Promises and Postwar Europe

## DAVID DUTTON

For many years diplomatic history was the poor relation of the historiography of the First World War. Attention focused primarily on the conflict's military history, with writers striving to make sense of the enormous sacrifice of life and resources involved or else trying to show that no rationale actually existed and that the whole affair had been a tragic waste of manpower and wealth. Considerable diplomatic interest did exist, but it was concentrated on the conflict's causes rather than its course. This bias was easily explained. Almost from the outbreak of hostilities in August 1914, and certainly from the signing of the Treaty of Versailles nearly five years later, the war's causation became a matter of intense political as well as historical debate. To the desire to make sense of an apparently senseless decision to resort to armed conflict was added the political imperative to justify or to undermine, according to national perspective, the settlement imposed upon the defeated powers, particularly Germany. The settlement's moral justification lay in the premise that the vanquished powers bore responsibility for the war's outbreak. During the 1920s and 1930s research on the origins of the war became a veritable industry, fueled by the provision of a mass of documentation. Driven by the need to confirm or confound the verdict of German guilt embodied in the notorious Clause 231 of the Treaty, the belligerent governments strove to put their prewar diplomatic archives, or at least purposefully edited selections from them, into the public domain.

The aim was generally to present each individual government's activities in the best possible light, although the purpose of the Bolsheviks in the Soviet Union was in part to discredit their tsarist predecessors. But the coverage of most of these batches of diplomatic archives ended abruptly with the coming of war in 1914. Only the Soviets attempted to provide a diplomatic narrative of the war itself. It was as if diplomacy had come to an end with the outbreak of hostilities. To the extent that formal relations between countries which now opposed one another on the battlefield were wound up, there was some truth in this proposition. But war diplomacy is conducted as much in relation to allies as it is against enemies. Nevertheless, it remained the case that there was no corpus of documentation open to would-be historians of wartime diplomacy comparable to that available to students of the conflict's origins. It would thus be left to a later generation of historians to explore the often revealing links between what countries did between 1914 and 1918 and their prewar intentions and ambitions.

Furthermore, the most common conclusion about the war's causation derived from the vast series of published documents was that it was all a tragic and avoidable accident. Though several historians, working in the interwar years, reached different, and in some cases more accurate, explanations, the most usual was that expressed by David Lloyd George in his immensely influential war memoirs published between 1933 and 1936.

According to the former British prime minister, the Great Powers "slithered over the brink into the boiling cauldron of war" without obvious intention and without really knowing what they were doing.[1] After "reading most of the literature explaining why the nations went to war, and who was responsible," Lloyd George was left with an impression of "utter chaos, confusion, feebleness and futility."[2] Such an analysis soon permeated academic circles. In 1950 a group of leading French and German historians reached the then politically convenient conclusion that "the documents do not allow one to ascribe in 1914 to any one government or people the conscious desire for a European war."[3] And, if this were so, it seemed unlikely that any attempt to make sense of wartime diplomacy would prove particularly profitable. The diplomatic history of the war seemed to fit into a wider pattern, in which the conflict as a whole "had no history, in the sense of a story expressing the meaning of events, but was anti-historical, apocalyptic, an incoherence, a gap in time."[4] Even if some underlying purpose did exist, there was always the knowledge that events in the war's latter stages had cut across, if not destroyed, the diplomatic pattern of its early years. The configuration of power politics in 1914 had been transformed by the time of the armistice. As the American president, Woodrow Wilson, noted in July 1917, "England and France have not the same views with regard to peace that we have by any means. When the war is over we can force them to our way of thinking because by that time they will . . . be financially in our hands."[5] The intervention of the United States in April 1917 followed by the November Revolution in Russia and the emergence of the Bolshevik regime created the climate from which sprang a very different sort of diplomacy in the 1920s and 1930s. The doings of the Great Powers of 1914 had surely been superseded by the rise of a "new diplomacy," the creation of a League of Nations and the unfolding of an era of ideological division in international relations.

As a result, serious study of the diplomatic history of the war had to await the opening of government archives which began with those of Great Britain in the 1960s. Even then, the material available was compromised in the cases of

Germany and the Soviet Union by the restrictions of the Cold War and in that of France by the extensive destruction of documentation. By the 1970s, however, the war's diplomatic history finally emerged as a significant subdiscipline, while remaining overshadowed in Britain at least by an ever more acrimonious debate about its military conduct. What was revealed was that the political leaders of the war years did indeed know what they were doing and that, at least to their own satisfaction, their diplomacy made sense. The war was, as Clausewitz had anticipated, the continuation of politics by other means. At the same time, what was revealed was an important new dimension of the overall historiography of the First World War which, because of its intimate connection with its military history, offers new understanding to the conflict as a whole. The war's military and diplomatic histories emerge as indissolubly intertwined. Neither makes full sense in isolation.

## Britain

Britain was the most innocent belligerent power in the sense that it entered the war with no strong desire to change the European status quo or, for that matter, to extend its already vast overseas empire. Its aims were essentially defensive, to preserve its naval supremacy, to eliminate Germany's challenge to Britain's world power, and to restore a balance to the continent which would not require a permanent British presence to maintain. Yet this did not stop Britain becoming involved as the conflict progressed in a series of promises and commitments to change the frontiers of Europe. Recent writing on Britain's wartime diplomacy has emphasized two key related factors about the country's situation.

The first is Britain's position as a member of the Triple Entente. This was always a double-edged sword. On the one hand France and Russia were indispensable to prospects of ultimate victory. Even though hopes that a Russian "steam-roller" of inexhaustible and irresistible manpower would be the basis of an early Allied victory soon faded, Russia's presence in the war remained vital. It ensured that Germany had to fight on two fronts while giving the Allies an overall superiority in armed forces. Almost until the end of 1917 the Germans had to maintain an army of around 100 divisions on the Eastern Front. "The war cannot possibly be conclusive in our favour," wrote the former prime minister, Arthur Balfour, in December 1914, "unless the Western Allies have Russia wholeheartedly on their side till the end."[6] France's contribution was scarcely less crucial. The prospect of trying to sustain the Western Front alone was not one that British strategists cared to contemplate and the possibility of a French government emerging, ready to sue for a compromise peace, was a matter of ongoing concern almost to the end of the conflict.

At the same time, Britain's leaders had not forgotten that their partnerships with France and Russia were of recent creation. These countries had been the nation's traditional enemies and the issues which had set them at odds with Britain had not entirely disappeared. "In the minds of many members of the policy-making elite," writes David French, "the rise of the Anglo-German antagonism had only overlaid, but had not abolished, Britain's quarrels with France and Russia."[7] The possibility existed that the two countries would reemerge, particularly in the wake of a German defeat, as significant challengers to British interests. Britain had no wish to fight the war against Germany to a victorious conclusion only to find itself confronted by an even graver threat from an enhanced France and Russia at some point in the medium-term future. Thus, part of the recent rehabilitation of the reputation of Field Marshal Lord Kitchener, secretary for war until his death in June 1916, has been based upon an appreciation of his strategic thinking, not only in relation to Germany but toward France and Russia as well. It was Kitchener's aim to conserve as much as possible of Britain's resources in the early stages of the war, leaving the continental powers to fight themselves to a standstill, so that his New Armies could secure victory some time in 1917 with Britain then in a position to dictate the terms of peace to victor and vanquished alike.[8]

The second factor has been an appreciation of Britain's relative weakness within the Triple Entente, at least during the war's first two years. Its naval and economic strength were long-term assets whose immediate impact was less apparent than its comparative military weakness vis-à-vis the mass conscript armies of continental Europe. Much that Britain did between 1914 and 1918 was therefore determined not so much by what its leaders believed to be in the country's own intrinsic interests as by the insistent demands of its two main allies or by the requests of other countries whose support Britain courted to strengthen the Allied cause. Thus, as the permanent undersecretary at the Foreign Office admitted, Britain "purchased" Italy's entry into the war in April 1915, even at the cost of complicating and compromising its diplomacy elsewhere in Europe. Similarly, when, two years later, it looked as if Russia, Romania, and Italy might all be forced to leave the conflict, a War Office official suggested that this would be no great disadvantage since it would free Britain from obligations "contracted for no reasons of policy other than that of getting as many allies as possible on any terms that might be asked."[9] Some of the anxiety about a French or Russian defection was removed when, in an exchange of notes on September 5, 1914, the three members of the Triple Entente agreed not to conclude a separate peace with the Central Powers. But the price paid for this reassurance was that the claims of France and Russia to the territory of the Central Powers became to an extent British claims also.

For the first half of the war the British government proved extremely reluctant to make public statements about its war aims. In part this reflected a nervous realization that the aims of the various allies, once disclosed, might prove incompatible; in part it resulted from an inherent uncertainty about what was theoretically desirable and a lack of conviction that the sort of victory could ever be secured which would make the realization of extensive war aims possible. Behind everything, however, was a reluctance to engage in detailed consideration of such issues prompted by the sheer enormity of the task at hand. Britain's own aims might be strictly limited, but it was scarcely likely that the other Allied powers would be satisfied with a return to the situation existing in 1914. As Sir Arthur Nicolson of the Foreign Office put it, it was "appalling to think of the difficulties which will arise when the moment comes for the discussion of peace terms . . . It will practically amount to a remodelling of the map of Europe."[10]

Only on two issues were the British steadfast and fully confident of their purpose in being at war. One was to restore the independence and territorial integrity of Belgium, violated by the German advance of August 1914. The other was the need to root out "Prussian militarism" – an ill-defined notion which implied depriving Germany of its future capacity to wage aggressive war. These two goals formed the kernel of a speech by Prime Minister Asquith at the Guildhall on November 9, 1914, and were not significantly expanded upon in public governmental declarations for the next two years. About other issues the British government remained purposefully vague. In the first half of the conflict it made no formal commitment to restore Alsace and Lorraine to France or to create an independent Polish state. At face value neither the restoration of Belgium nor the extirpation of Prussian militarism seemed to imply any change to European frontiers. But, as the war progressed, it became clear that Britain's ally France might have plans for Belgium which went beyond the simple restoration of the prewar status quo, while rooting out Prussian militarism, if it had any tangible meaning, might necessitate some change to Germany's territorial integrity or even the country's partition.

Much of Britain's early wartime diplomacy was focused on securing new recruits to the Allied cause. As most of the uncommitted nations of continental Europe were located in the Balkans, efforts were concentrated in this area. The belief was that the uncertain territorial settlement resulting from the two Balkan Wars of 1912 and 1913 provided scope for further frontier readjustments which could even lead to the emergence of a Balkan bloc united under the Entente's banner. Such hopes were largely frustrated. Indeed, it soon became apparent that Turkey had been lost to the Central Powers and Britain had no alternative but to declare war on the Ottoman Empire on November 4, 1914. The chances of an active Balkan bloc were not helped by Romania's receipt of a Russian guarantee of Transylvania and a promise to divide Bukovina along ethnic lines between Romania and Russia merely in return for

Romania remaining neutral. But Britain was in no position to challenge Russia over such matters. Indeed, British policy had to be developed in ways that would keep Russia firmly committed to the Entente, at least until Britain had had the time to raise and equip massive armies of its own.

Such thinking determined the British foreign secretary, Edward Grey, to encourage Russia to lay claim to Constantinople. This would have the added advantage of deflecting its ambitions away from German and Austrian territory, thereby protecting a European balance of power for the postwar world. As early as October 20, 1914, Asquith advised King George V that Britain was ready to abandon the once sacred formula of maintaining the integrity of the Ottoman Empire, and on November 12 Grey gave an assurance to his Russian opposite number that Constantinople would be settled in accordance with Russia's wishes, once the war had been fought to a successful conclusion. Such a statement would, it was hoped, remove any remaining Russian doubts of the need to commit itself without equivocation to the Allied camp. The agreement was formalized the following March. By this time the Russians had clarified their ambitions and Sazonov now demanded Russian annexation not only of Constantinople, but also of the European shore of the Straits and the Asiatic coast of the Bosphorus. The British had no alternative but to agree. As Grey noted, "it was very important to avoid . . . a breach with Russia, or any action which would incite Russia to make a separate peace."[11]

It is difficult to exaggerate the enormous importance of the Straits Agreement of March 1915. The Liberal cabinet regarded it as such a departure from existing policy as to justify taking the opposition Conservative leadership into its confidence. Though Britain had long since transferred the strategic pivot of its Near Eastern defenses from Constantinople to Suez, the promise to transfer the ancient city to Russia marked a dramatic reversal of the priorities of Britain's nineteenth-century diplomacy. Not only would Russia now emerge as a Mediterranean naval power, but the dismemberment of at least one – albeit the weakest – of the Great Powers of the prewar era was clearly envisaged. Britain and France now had to give thought to their own claims within the Ottoman Empire. The genie of partition was out of its bottle and there could be no going back. There followed, as discussed in the next chapter, a series of competing and sometimes contradictory claims and commitments that would transform the map of the Near and Middle East in ways which profoundly affect the course of international relations to the present day.

At the same time, the remaining undeclared Balkan states were left to flaunt their wares to the highest bidder. Bulgaria eventually opted to join the Central Powers in September 1915, seduced by the promise of the so-called "contested" and "uncontested" zones of Macedonia, lost as a result of the Second Balkan War. At one point it looked as if Romania might follow suit, tempted by the offer of Bukovina from Austria and of Bessarabia at Russia's expense. In the event, however, the Allies managed to trump this and, under the Treaty of Bucharest of August 1916, Romania could look forward to the eventual doubling of its territory and population as a result of incorporating Transylvania, the Banat of Temesvar, and Bukovina. Finally, and only after the forces of Britain and France had deposed its supposedly Germanophile king, Greece also joined the Allied cause in late June 1917, though Smyrna, offered by Grey as a bait for Greek intervention in January 1915, was no longer on the table.

The military contribution of Romania and Greece to the Allied cause proved to be marginal. But the prospect of securing Italian intervention seemed, at least on the surface, to be a more attractive proposition and much Allied diplomatic activity was devoted to securing this end. "It will be the turning point of the war," suggested Grey, "and will very greatly hasten a successful conclusion."[12] Finally, under the terms of the Secret Treaty of London of April 26, 1915, Italy was persuaded to renounce its theoretical commitment to the Triple Alliance and declare war on Austria-Hungary. In return Italy would receive the Trentino, the South Tyrol, and Istria, together with the Northern Dalmatian coastline. According to Asquith, "the importance of bringing in Italy without delay appeared to be so great that it was agreed to give a general consent to what she asks and to press on Russia to do the same."[13] The treaty marked a subtle but significant develop-

ment in British war aims. Whereas the commitment to Russia over Constantinople had been dependent upon the war being fought to a successful conclusion, the Treaty of London bound Britain to continue the war to secure the territorial ambitions of its new ally. "Italy's war aims had become Britain's war aims."[14] Later, under the St. Jean-de-Maurienne agreement of April 1917, Italian prospects were further extended with a promise to make the whole of southern Asia Minor an Italian dependency. But the St. Jean terms were denounced by the British and French in November 1918 on the grounds that they had not, as was required, been ratified by the Russian government.

British interest in central and eastern Europe had always been limited. Most obviously, the area was outside the range of influence of the Royal Navy. So, for example, in the late eighteenth century Poland had been partitioned three times by the continental Great Powers before finally disappearing altogether, without significant British involvement. As the First World War progressed, however, it became increasingly open to question whether the prewar map of central and eastern Europe, dominated by the great empires of Russia, Germany, and Austria-Hungary, would survive unscathed. Might not one or more follow the course already envisaged for the Ottoman Empire? Long before it became the leitmotiv of Woodrow Wilson's foreign policy, the question of self-determination for the subject peoples of eastern Europe had entered the diplomatic equation. But for Britain the determining factor was always strategic necessity rather than abstract political principle. While it was well understood that unsatisfied national aspirations had added to European instability and played a part in bringing the war about, responding to such aspirations would always take second place to the essential goal of defeating Germany. Furthermore, changing perceptions and understanding of the military outlook served to militate against any consistent British line on the question of national ambitions.

Over the course of the conflict the British government came into contact with émigré Polish, Czech, and Yugoslav national movements which did their best to persuade Britain to sign up to their cause. Between 1914 and 1916, the British tended to see advantages in supporting these movements. In August 1916, a Foreign Office committee under William Tyrrell and Ralph Paget recommended that the Habsburg Empire should be broken up in accordance with the principle of nationality. Some individuals went further. Arthur Balfour, then First Lord of the Admiralty, advised the cabinet in January 1916 that "if the map of Europe was brought by the present war into close harmony with the distribution of nationalities, one perennial cause of international disturbance would be mitigated."[15] But the government's position remained flexible. When, therefore, in 1917, against a background of continuing military stalemate and mounting official pessimism about ultimate victory, attention turned to the possibility of removing Austria-Hungary from the war by negotiating a separate peace, the emphasis was necessarily changed. The more Britain appeared to be linked to the cause of the subject peoples, the harder would be the negotiations with Vienna. The pragmatic nature of the British stance was emphasized when, in May 1918, the government finally decided to give all possible support to the subject nationalities. This way, either Austria would be forced out of desperation to conclude a separate peace or else the empire itself would be destroyed. Either outcome would be of benefit to Britain's war effort.

The proposals of Tyrrell and Paget about the future of the Habsburg Empire were part of a wider discussion of war aims and peace objectives within the British government in the second half of 1916. At the end of August, Asquith invited members of the War Committee to submit papers on the question of peace terms. It was a time of optimism about the military situation with promises of a significant breakthrough resulting from the Somme offensive and exaggerated expectations about the impact of Romania's entry into the war. "Robertson told me only yesterday," noted Lord Hardinge, the newly installed permanent under-secretary at the Foreign Office, "that complete victory is only a matter of time, the superiority in everything having passed into our hands."[16] The mood did not last, and France and Russia declined to get involved in an inter-Allied discussion of the question, but the last months of

Asquith's premiership still witnessed a more thorough and systematic consideration of what Britain hoped to achieve from victory than had yet been seen.

It was striking that, as part of the Foreign Office's contribution to this debate, in which the War Office and Admiralty also participated, Tyrrell and Paget proposed that, while Germany should be weakened in the west by the loss of territory to France and Denmark, it should be correspondingly strengthened by the acquisition of German-speaking Austria following the dismemberment of the Habsburg Empire. The traditional British concern for a European balance, which could only be maintained if Germany remained a strong continental power, had not been forgotten. In like vein, the chief of the Imperial General Staff suggested that a reduced Austria-Hungary closely associated with Germany and having a port at Fiume "might not altogether [be] to our disadvantage on land as limiting the power of Russia and the Slav States, and on sea as preventing the Mediterranean from becoming a French and Italian lake." At the same time Tyrrell and Paget questioned the wisdom of the promises already made to Italy as "a very distinct violation of the principle of nationalities, and there is consequently no doubt that it involves the risk of producing the usual results, namely irredentism, and lack of stability and peace."[17] It fell to the secretary to the War Committee to draw together the elements of consensus upon which ministers and officials appeared to be agreed. These were the restoration of Belgium; the evacuation of the occupied areas of France and the cession to it of the French-speaking parts of Alsace and Lorraine; a Polish settlement acceptable to Russia; the acquisition of Constantinople by Russia; the fulfillment of the obligations already made to Italy and Romania; and the restoration of Serbia. As 1916 drew toward a close, however, it became clear that the precondition upon which all this depended – the military defeat of Germany – was less imminent than had been imagined. Moreover, the fall of Asquith's government in December meant that securing victory and whatever territorial changes this would entail now became the responsibility of the new prime minister, Lloyd George.

The new administration had the task of responding to peace notes issued by the German government and the American president at the end of 1916. In a speech on December 12 the German chancellor, Bethmann Hollweg, professed his willingness to consider peace. Then, on December 18, Wilson, whose earlier efforts at mediation had been rebuffed, invited both sides to state their war aims to see whether any basis for a compromise settlement existed. Only the desire not to alienate American opinion and thus lose out in the ongoing propaganda battle compelled the Allies to treat the two initiatives with a measure of circumspection. Replies were drawn up at an Anglo-French conference in London on December 26–8. That to Germany specified the need to restore Belgium but otherwise dismissed the enemy's initiative as fundamentally fraudulent. That to the United States was more forthcoming. Delivered on January 10, 1917, it called for the restoration of Belgium and Serbia, together with the evacuation of occupied territory in France, Russia, and Romania. There was a reference to the principle of nationality, but statements about the future of the Austrian and Turkish empires were in general vague, and coy in relation to the secret agreements already entered into. The chief British objective of not being outmaneuvered by the enemy was at least achieved. British vagueness was not, however, just for American consumption. Even when, in April 1917, the Imperial War Cabinet established a subcommittee under Lord Curzon to consider the territorial terms of peace, its report was largely confined to generalities, proving, as Harold Nelson has written, that "Woodrow Wilson had no monopoly on resounding phrases which hid disagreements and incompatibilities."[18] Even this report was accepted merely as an "indication" of the "relative importance" of objectives which might be sought at the peace conference and would in any case need to be "correlated with those of the allies."[19]

## France

French war aims bore a superficial similarity to those of Great Britain. Like Britain, and indeed in common with all the belligerents, the French government saw obvious advantages in presenting their country's involvement in the war of 1914 in defensive terms. Nor, in the case of France at least, was this entirely inaccurate. In the simplest terms, France went to war because it had been attacked. In the first instance, therefore, and in common with Britain, France sought to reverse the German military advances of August 1914 – some of its most important provinces had been rapidly overrun – and to remove the threat of further German aggression in the future. But, unlike Britain, France nurtured fundamental grievances about the map of Europe as it existed at the outbreak of hostilities. In particular, it cherished the hope of recovering the provinces of Alsace and Lorraine, lost following defeat in the Franco-Prussian War of 1870. This ambition would not of itself have been sufficient to persuade France to launch a war for their recovery. But the fact of being at war opened up possibilities of territorial readjustments which few French politicians were prepared to ignore. Indeed, the French made known to their allies their claim to the lost provinces within hours of the outbreak of hostilities.

But, fearful of fracturing the domestic political truce to which the coming of war had given birth and fully aware that, with thousands of German troops ensconced on its soil, its bargaining hand was far from strong, the French government was slow to define its objectives in public. Indeed, with German guns within earshot of Paris, the French could have been forgiven if their aspirations had not extended beyond the goal of national survival. Yet there was something slightly disingenuous about the statement of the senior Quai d'Orsay official, Pierre de Margerie, that "our time being absolutely devoured by pressing and immediate business, nobody, except for professors and idealistic theoreticians, has the leisure to study these [postwar] questions."[20] Premier René Viviani's statement to the Chamber of Deputies in December 1914 echoed Asquith's Guildhall speech of the previous month. He spoke of the restoration of Belgian independence, indemnities for regions devastated by the German advance, breaking Prussian militarism, and recovering Alsace and Lorraine. Behind the scenes, however, it became clear that this was only the minimum of French desires. Most strikingly, in return for agreeing to the Straits Convention with Russia,

Foreign Minister Théophile Delcassé secured the inclusion of a quid pro quo for France in terms of compensation within the Ottoman Empire itself "and elsewhere." Both the French and the Russians understood that this vague phrase was meant to indicate the Rhineland. As the Russian tsar told the French ambassador in St. Petersburg, it meant "everything that your Government may desire. Take the left bank of the Rhine; take Mainz; take Coblence; go even farther if you see fit."[21]

Very quickly, influential circles in France began to question whether the mere return of Alsace and Lorraine with their pre-1870 frontiers would be sufficient to meet future French security needs. It would ensure French control of the majority of the Lorraine–Luxembourg iron ore field, but would create only a partial Rhine frontier while excluding the Saar and thus leaving France uncomfortably dependent on imported coal. By as early as February 1915, the pages of the *Echo de Paris* began to carry a series of articles by Maurice Barrès exploring the possibility of France acquiring the whole of the left bank of the Rhine or, alternatively, of the creation of autonomous Rhineland buffer states removed from German control. The Barrès articles were characteristic of a French trend for which there was no comparable British equivalent. Much of the discussion of war aims and of possible changes to the map of Europe was conducted at the level of unofficial pressure groups, often commanding significant support within the French parliament. The historian faces a not always straightforward task in deciding which ideas permeated the government's policy-making processes and which remained confined to the wish-lists of these non-governmental agencies.

The Straits Agreement of March 1915 was of considerable importance in prompting France to rethink its ambitions in the eastern Mediterranean. Delcassé had hoped that, if Anglo-French forces had taken Constantinople as a result of a successful Dardanelles campaign, this would have been compatible with the maintenance of the Ottoman Empire, which was necessary "to safeguard France's political and economic interests."[22] Now, however, French diplomacy had to prepare itself for the dismemberment of the sultan's realm.

President Raymond Poincaré was clear that "everything is inevitably linked. We can only support Russia's claims in proportion to the satisfaction we ourselves receive."[23] In addition to prompting a flurry of claims-staking in the Middle East, the diplomatic revolution of March 1915 helps explain French enthusiasm for the campaign launched at the Greek port of Salonika in October, at a time when logic suggested that all available military resources should be concentrated on the Western Front. The Salonika *Armée d'Orient* became the expression of France's postwar aspirations in the eastern Mediterranean with the scarcely concealed goal of carving out a new French sphere of influence. This would redress the imbalance created by the attribution of Constantinople to Russia. Correspondingly, the British found themselves obliged to support the campaign, against the better judgment of their military advisers, out of a desire to preserve the Entente and to reinforce France's commitment to the overall war effort.[24]

By the summer of 1916 the French government, buoyed up by the illusory expectation of an imminent breakthrough on the Western Front, began a more systematic consideration than hitherto of the sort of territorial changes which might be necessary to guarantee future French security. Now the War Office General Staff began to contemplate the attachment of Belgium to France in a permanent alliance, cemented by a full military and customs union. By October it had been decided to demand a free hand to settle the future of the left bank of the Rhine. This was incorporated in the so-called Cambon letter of January 1917 which called for a preponderant French voice in settling the matter. German sovereignty over the left bank would be ended while Alsace and Lorraine would be returned to France with the frontiers of 1790, a provision which allowed for the incorporation of much of the Saar. This development of French demands inevitably threatened the stability of the Anglo-French alliance. In the words of Harold Nelson, "how far could and should the British government go in supporting the detachment of more and undisputed German territory and peoples without either tipping the balance too far in France's favor or defeating, by the creation of an uncontrollable German desire for revenge, the aim of political stabilization in western Europe?"[25] Though the Cambon letter was not shown to the British until July 1917, by which time it had largely been overtaken by the course of events, it was used as a starting point by Colonial Minister Gaston Doumergue in discussions with the Russians in February. Doumergue secured agreement from the Imperial government that France could regard the entire Saarland as the very least of its entitlement, while the left bank should be split up into nominally independent buffer states, effectively controlled by France. In return, the Russians would secure complete freedom to fix their own western frontiers. Though the Doumergue negotiations were soon aborted by the fall of the tsar's government, they cast a revealing light on the development of French ambitions, ambitions which would be carried forward to the peace conference. In June 1917, by which time the Provisional Government was in power in Russia and the United States had entered the conflict, French Prime Minister Alexandre Ribot confirmed to a secret session of the French Senate that his country still looked to annex the Alsace-Lorraine of 1790 and to create a buffer state between France and Germany. This "cannot be considered a conquest," he insisted. "It is a protective measure."[26]

## Russia

Russia was the least reticent of the Allies when it came to defining its objectives for territorial change in Europe. These objectives, like those of France, reflected a determination to end the war in a way that would improve Russian security against future German aggression. In this respect Poland was the key. The Russians looked for a buffer state under their effective control. A proclamation of August 1914 called for Poland to be united "under the scepter of the Russian Emperor." This implied expansion at the expense of both Germany and Austria-Hungary, but precisely what was entailed was not spelt out. More revealing was the "Thirteen Points" program drawn up by Foreign Minister Sazonov for presentation to Britain and France in mid-September and a statement of aims delivered by the tsar to the French ambassador, Paléologue, two months later. From these it was clear that Russian aims

matched those of Germany in ambition and extent. Both the tsar and his foreign minister placed the destruction of German military power at the heart of their goals. To this end Germany would be deprived of territory on both its eastern and western frontiers. Sazonov claimed the lower Niemen basin from Germany and eastern Galicia from Austria-Hungary. Poland would receive eastern Posen and southern Silesia from Germany and western Galicia from the Habsburg Empire. The break-up of that empire was implied, though the Russians trod warily, conscious that the application of the principle of national self-determination could have serious implications for the future of their own empire, while affording Germany the possibility of union with German Austria.

As discussed above, Turkey's entry into the war gave the Russians scope to pursue their traditional goal of occupying Constantinople and thereby transforming their potential as a Mediterranean naval power. Rejecting all approaches for a separate peace, the tsarist government remained faithful both to its allies and to this expansionist program until it was toppled in March 1917. Following military setbacks in 1916, it is true that doubts grew as to whether such a program could ever be realized. At the end of the year the tsar admitted to the British ambassador that Russia would probably have to settle for its frontiers of 1914. But the official position remained unchanged as Russia's rejection of the German peace note of December 1916 and participation in the Doumergue agreement three months later revealed.

## The Central Powers

Germany's position within the Central Powers was unlike that enjoyed by any member of the Triple Entente. Though Britain, France, and Russia were in varying ways and at various times indispensable to one another's war efforts, none ever secured a position of direction, let alone domination, over its partners. Indeed, Russia's geographical separation encouraged the perception that it was in some senses fighting a different war, even if the main enemy was the same. Within the Central Powers, on the other hand, there was never any doubt about who was in charge and, while Austria-Hungary, Turkey, and Bulgaria had their own ambitions for the peace settlement, it was the aims of Germany which predominated. As a result, war aims were in some ways a more straightforward matter on the side of the Central Powers than was the case with the Allies and the issue of assuming war aims "by proxy" scarcely arose. That said, more controversy surrounds the ambitions of Germany in the First World War than those of any other belligerent, and in no case was the opening of the diplomatic archives of greater significance.

The conventional view of Germany's participation in the First World War, carefully fostered by German historians who traditionally maintained an unhealthily close relationship with the apparatus of the state, was that only the perception of threatening encirclement by the powers of the Triple Entente forced it into military action in 1914. Thus Germany's involvement was "defensive" in much the same sense that the term could be applied to its opponents. This view, convenient for Germans as they struggled to shoulder the largely unquestioned and unquestionable responsibility for launching a second and indubitably aggressive world war in 1939, was forcefully challenged by the Hamburg historian Fritz Fischer in his *Germany's Aims in the First World War*, first published in German in 1961. Fischer suggested that, far from being the innocent victim of encirclement, Germany had willfully launched war in 1914 and had done so in order to secure a long list of carefully thought-out expansionist war aims. Presenting painstakingly documented evidence not only in *Germany's Aims* but also in his second book, *War of Illusions*, Fischer's thesis provoked a lively debate which extended far beyond the realms of academic scholarship. Much of this debate lies outside the scope of this essay. In particular, we may leave aside questions as to whether Fischer fully succeeded in linking into a seamless progression the aims Germany pursued after the outbreak of war with its prewar activities, and the whole issue of the implied similarity between the ambitions of Wilhelmine Germany and those of the Third Reich. But Fischer's description of Germany's wartime aims has been more generally accepted, not least because it is difficult to refute the documentary evidence upon which it was based.

Fischer's crucial documentary discovery was the so-called September Memorandum, approved by the German chancellor, Bethmann Hollweg, just over a month into the war. This document, argued Fischer, formed a solid basis for the discussion of the country's war aims for the rest of the conflict. Almost unbelievably, Germany's political and military leaders continued to hold a series of war aims meetings in 1918, by which time the chance of turning such ambitions into reality had all but disappeared. The memorandum's celebrated opening paragraph, containing what was described as "the general aim of war," has often been quoted but bears repetition:

> Security for the German Reich in west and east for all imaginable time. For this purpose France must be so weakened as to make her revival as a great power impossible for all time. Russia must be thrust back as far as possible from Germany's eastern frontier and her domination over the non-Russian vassal peoples broken.[27]

Apart from being disarmed and deprived of most of its colonies, France would lose the economically significant region of Longwy–Briey and the western Vosges. Belgium would be turned into a vassal state, dependent in military, economic, and political terms upon Germany and deprived of the fortress of Liège and possibly the port of Antwerp. Luxembourg was to be incorporated into the Reich, while a looser form of association awaited the Netherlands. Overall, the emphasis was less on annexation than on economic control, and to secure this Germany envisaged the creation of a massive customs union – *Mitteleuropa* – dominating the continent and subject to German control. It would combine western Europe, Poland, Scandinavia, and the Central Powers.

Fischer emphasized two key points. The first was that Bethmann envisaged this far-reaching program as one of moderation in contrast to the more extreme ambitions of the military and the royal court. In the second place, the September program enjoyed the support of the vast majority of Germany's influential political, commercial, industrial, and intellectual opinion throughout the war. But historians now tend to emphasize, more than did Fischer, the military background against which the September Memorandum was drawn up. After initial sweeping successes, an outright German victory seemed a distinct possibility. Within a matter of weeks, however, it was clear that the Schlieffen Plan, designed to put France out of the war and preempt British participation, would not bear its promised fruits. With the Battle of the Marne the French stabilized the military situation and the war soon settled into a largely static pattern of long-term attrition. As a result, Germany was confronted by the reality of a two-front war and of enemies enjoying an overall superiority of manpower. In such a situation the German government had to be more flexible than Fischer implied and, as feelers toward Russia in 1915 revealed, be ready to seek a compromise settlement with at least one member of the Triple Entente on terms considerably short of the September program.

Conversely, as Russia declined to rise to the German bait and as the kaiser's armies achieved considerable success on the Eastern Front, there was a tendency for Germany's eastern ambitions to harden. A key element in the eastern equation was inevitably Poland. The countries which had once contrived to keep Poland partitioned now found themselves competing for Polish nationalist support to bolster their respective war efforts. To begin with Bethmann seemed content to allow Russian Poland to be incorporated into the Habsburg Empire, and, in August 1915, the Austrians proposed uniting Galicia and Russian Poland in an autonomous kingdom under Habsburg sovereignty. But German minds changed, not least because a series of Austro-Hungarian military reverses in 1916 posed question marks over the stability of any "Austrian solution" to the Polish question. By the autumn the influence of the new German military commanders, Hindenburg and Ludendorff, was paramount and it prompted Bethmann to issue a joint proclamation with Austria on November 5, 1916, promising to set up a nominally independent Polish Kingdom, under German occupation and tied to Germany economically. The hope – largely unfulfilled – was that this gesture would lead to an influx of Polish volunteers into the German army. This reversal in German policy over Poland was indicative of the fundamental subordination of Austro-Hungarian wishes within the Central Powers. Elsewhere Austria-Hungary hoped to achieve minor frontier changes at Italy's expense and more substantial gains in the Balkans from Serbia and Montenegro. But any hope of securing such goals remained dependent upon German acquiescence and, of course, upon a German military victory.

The German peace note of December 1916 was more of a move in the propaganda battle than a serious attempt to bring the war to a close and did not go far in defining the specific terms upon which the fighting might cease. Behind the scenes, however, the German stance was hardening, not least because of repeated public declarations that there was no possibility of concluding peace on the basis of the status quo of 1914. German leaders believed that the successful implementation of a victorious peace with tangible gains was their best guarantee of preserving domestic harmony in support of the existing autocratic government. Internal discussions in November 1916 showed that Bethmann was being obliged, under the influence of the army high command, to adopt an even more explicitly annexationist program than that contained in the September Memorandum. Indeed, we have the evidence of the Treaty of Brest-Litovsk of March 1918, by which Germany imposed its victory over Russia, of the sort of territorial changes which Germany would have demanded had it been successful in the war as a whole. Under the terms of the treaty Russia lost 90 percent of its coal mines, 50 percent of its industry, and 30 percent of its population. Russia was forced to give up the Ukraine, Finland, and the Baltic states, while Poland would await partition between Germany and Austria.

## Conclusion

Such, then, was the pattern of conflicting aims and ambitions, of promises, half-promises, and commitments which existed before the events of 1917 transformed the nature and later course of the First World War. The entry of the United States into the conflict brought into play a government which was uncommitted to any of the war aims of the countries with which it was now "associated" – the United States declined to become a full member of the "Allies" – and suspicious of their intentions. But America was a force which Britain and France could not ignore. Indeed, as the war progressed, it seemed that the United States would advance "towards the status of a dominant partner" in the Allied camp.[28] On the other hand, what Balfour described as the "rapidly moving cinematography of Russian politics" forced a reassessment of the situation in the east.[29] The Revolution of 1917 weakened the overall position of the Entente, made Britain and France conscious that the achievement of their war aims might now be even more difficult than before, and gave rise to a clamor for a peace settlement which would avoid annexations and be based upon the principle of self-determination. At the same time, Russia's withdrawal from the war by the end of 1917 and the resulting Treaty of Brest-Litovsk of March 1918 witnessed the implementation – albeit temporary – of Germany's war aims in the east.

What, though, should we make of the position which existed before these dramatic events took place? The diplomatic history of the war adds to a growing consensus, to which military historians have made the greatest contribution, that the conflict did indeed make sense. The statesmen of the various capitals understood what they were doing and believed that the stakes were sufficiently high to justify the military effort their armies were making and the sacrifices it entailed. More than that, the diplomatic narrative forms an essential backcloth to the military history of the war against which the latter can be more easily understood. But the aims and ambitions of the major belligerents also reveal why it proved so difficult to bring the war to a compromise conclusion. While some of the aims, promises, and commitments were always going to be provisional and subject to modification in the light of the changing progress of the conflict, each of the powers was sufficiently committed to some of its goals to make the reconciliation of military opponents almost impossible. Each of the major belligerent powers found itself pursuing major ambitions for territorial change in Europe which were totally unacceptable to one or more of its leading adversaries. In such circumstances, the war was doomed to follow its

bloody course. Outright victory was perhaps the only answer.

## NOTES

1   D. Lloyd George, *War Memoirs* (London: Odhams Press, 1938), vol. 1, p. 32.
2   Ibid., p. 34.
3   H. W. Koch, ed., *The Origins of the First World War* (London: Macmillan, 1972), p. 6.
4   S. Hynes, *A War Imagined: The First World War and English Culture* (London: Bodley Head, 1990), p. 455.
5   S. Tillman, *Anglo-American Relations at the Peace Conference* (Princeton, NJ: Princeton University Press, 1961), p. 16.
6   National Archives, FO800/376, Nicolson MSS, Balfour to Nicolson, Dec. 28, 1914.
7   D. French, *British Strategy and War Aims 1914–1916* (London: Allen & Unwin, 1986), p. xii.
8   K. Neilson, "Kitchener: A Reputation Refurbished?" *Canadian Journal of History* 15 (1980): 207–27.
9   "Addendum to General Staff Memorandum of 31 August 1916," March 28, 1917, cited in *War Aims and Strategic Policy in the Great War 1914–1918*, ed. B. Hunt and A. Preston (London: Croom Helm, 1977), p. 34.
10  Cited in ibid., pp. 26–7.
11  National Archives, CAB 42/2/3, War Council minutes March 3, 1915.
12  K. Calder, *Britain and the Origins of the New Europe 1914–1918* (Cambridge: Cambridge University Press, 1976), p. 34.
13  Ibid.
14  French, *British Strategy*, p. 86.
15  Calder, *Britain and Origins*, pp. 98–9.
16  Hardinge to Chelmsford, July 27, 1916, cited in V. H. Rothwell, *British War Aims and Peace Diplomacy 1914–1918* (Oxford: Clarendon Press, 1971), p. 40.
17  E. Goldstein, *Winning the Peace: British Diplomatic Strategy, Peace Planning, and the Paris Peace Conference, 1916–1920* (Oxford: Clarendon Press, 1991), p. 12.
18  H. Nelson, *Land and Power: British and Allied Policy on Germany's Frontiers, 1916–19* (Newton Abbot: David & Charles, 1971), p. 21.
19  Rothwell, *British War Aims*, p. 71.
20  D. Stevenson, *French War Aims against Germany 1914–1919* (Oxford: Clarendon Press, 1982), p. 21.
21  Ibid., p. 27.
22  Château de Vincennes, Archives de Guerre 7N1344, Delcassé to Millerand, April 28, 1915.

23  Institut de France, Pichon MSS 4397, Poincaré to
    Paléologue, March 9, 1915.
24  D. Dutton, *The Politics of Diplomacy: Britain and
    France in the Balkans in the First World War*
    (London: I. B. Tauris, 1998), passim.
25  Nelson, *Land and Power*, p. 28.
26  Stevenson, *French War Aims*, p. 70.
27  F. Fischer, *Germany's Aims in the First World War*
    (New York: W. W. Norton, 1967), p. 103.
28  Stevenson, *French War Aims*, p. 76.
29  Nelson, *Land and Power*, p. 17.

## GUIDE TO FURTHER READING

Kenneth Calder, *Britain and the Origins of the
New Europe 1914–1918* (Cambridge: Cambridge
University Press, 1976). Early study of British atti-
tudes toward the future of central and eastern
Europe.

David Dutton, *The Politics of Diplomacy: Britain and
France in the Balkans in the First World War* (London:
I. B. Tauris, 1998). Explores French ambitions in the
Balkans and the eastern Mediterranean and British
reactions to them.

Fritz Fischer, *Germany's Aims in the First World War*
(New York: W. W. Norton, 1967). Controversial
work which definitively changed perceptions of
Germany's role in the war.

David French, *British Economic and Strategic Planning
1905–1915* (London: Allen & Unwin, 1982); *British
Strategy and War Aims 1914–1916* (London: Allen &
Unwin, 1986); *The Strategy of the Lloyd George Coalition* (Oxford: Clarendon Press, 1995). An indispensable trio of works which make sense of Britain's
strategic thinking.

Erik Goldstein, *Winning the Peace: British Diplomatic
Strategy, Peace Planning, and the Paris Peace Conference, 1916–1920* (Oxford: Clarendon Press, 1991).
Links Britain's wartime diplomacy with the final
peace settlement.

Barry Hunt and Adrian Preston, eds., *War Aims and
Strategic Policy in the Great War 1914–1918* (London:
Croom Helm, 1977). An early collection of essays on
the theme of war aims.

Keith Neilson, *Strategy and Supply: The Anglo-Russian
Alliance 1914–17* (London: Allen & Unwin, 1984).
Successfully places Russia at the center of the Entente's
war strategy.

Harold Nelson, *Land and Power: British and Allied
Policy on Germany's Frontiers, 1916–19* (London:
Routledge & Kegan Paul, 1963). Largely focuses on
the peace settlement, but with some material on the
war years.

V. H. Rothwell, *British War Aims and Peace Diplomacy
1914–1918* (Oxford: Clarendon Press, 1971). A pioneering work thoroughly grounded in the relevant
British archives.

David Stevenson, *French War Aims against Germany
1914–1919* (Oxford: Clarendon Press, 1982). An
authoritative study of the subject; *The First World
War and International Politics* (Oxford: Oxford University Press, 1988), lucid and wide-ranging; *1914–
1918: The History of the First World War* (London:
Allen Lane, 2004), the best single volume survey of
the war containing important chapters on war aims
and diplomacy.

A. J. P. Taylor, "The War Aims of the Allies in the First
World War," in *Essays Presented to Sir Lewis Namier*,
ed. A. J. P. Taylor and R. Pares (London: Macmillan,
1956). A pioneering study written without access to
the archives.

# CHAPTER TEN

# Wartime Promises and the Postwar Empires

## MATTHEW HUGHES

During the First World War, British-led forces attacked the Ottoman Empire in the Middle East and, by 1918, Britain had occupied all of what would become, after the war, the newly formed states of Palestine, Transjordan (later Jordan), Syria, Lebanon, and Iraq (previously Mesopotamia).[1] What remained of the Turkish rump of the Ottoman Empire became the modern republic of Turkey in 1923. In Africa, British, South African, Belgian, French, and, from 1916, Portuguese forces invaded and occupied the German colonies of Southwest Africa (later Namibia), Togoland, Cameroons, and German East Africa (later Tanganyika/Tanzania).[2] Finally, in the Far East, Japanese, Indian, New Zealand, and Australian forces took German territory in China at Kiaochow[3] and in the Pacific (the Mariana and Caroline islands, northern Papua New Guinea, Nauru, the Solomon islands, and Samoa). Before, during, and after these conquests, the attacking powers – notably the British and French, but also local powers such as Australia, Japan, New Zealand, and South Africa – made a series of arrangements, commitments, and promises, both amongst themselves and with local peoples, regarding the future status of captured enemy territory that shaped the international history of the twentieth century.

## The Middle East

British or British Empire troops did most of the fighting in the Middle East during the First World War; in some Middle Eastern campaigns, British or Empire troops did all of the fighting. The imperial troops came from Australia, India, or New Zealand, but included small contingents from Canada, Rarotonga, South Africa, the West Indies, Hong Kong, and Singapore. In Mesopotamia, Britain completely dominated the fighting, while in Palestine small token French and Italian units fought alongside the British.[4] On the Gallipoli peninsula, France contributed about 12 percent of overall troop strength, with many of France's troops also coming from its empire.[5] The only exception to this was the Caucasian front, one of the least-studied theaters of war of the First World War, where Russian forces drove back the Ottomans before themselves collapsing in 1917 following the Russian Revolution (after which Ottoman forces invaded the Russian Caucasus area and took the city of Baku in September 1918).[6]

As the major military power in the Middle East, Britain dominated political events in the region during and after the war. Power on the ground meant power at the negotiating table. Britain restricted French and Italian military contributions and made sure that the British army controlled the region by the war's end, thus greatly helping Britain's politicians and diplomats negotiating at the 1919 Paris Peace Conference for the future status of captured enemy territory.

Before 1914, British policy had been, broadly speaking, to support the weak Muslim Ottoman Empire, mainly as it acted as a bulwark against

Russian expansion into the Middle East, a move that Britain was keen to check as it threatened its all-important route to India. This in some measure explains why Britain fought in the Crimean War in the 1850s on the side of the Ottomans against the Russians. However, once the Ottomans decided, in late October 1914, to join Germany and the Central Alliance, Britain reevaluated its policy toward what was now an enemy power. As part of this reassessment, on November 2, 1914, Britain formally gave up its commitment to the territorial integrity of the Ottoman Empire.

At the same time, and in a ground-breaking move, the British and French informed the Russian foreign minister, S. D. Sazonov, that the matter of the Straits region (the area along the littoral of the Dardanelles, the Sea of Marmara, and the Bosphorus around Constantinople/Istanbul) would be settled in the manner desired by Russia. Russia was keen to gain access to the Straits as it would give it an ice-free port for its navy. Sazonov, who would have been satisfied to have obtained free passage for Russian warships, was delighted with the news that Russia was to be given control over the Straits.[7] It would seem that the British and French still hoped for some form of internationalization of the Straits rather than outright Russian control. Certainly, France did not want to concede the Straits but was obliged to go along with the more generous British offer.[8] Then, in early 1915, with British and French naval forces gathering for an attack on Constantinople by way of the Dardanelles, Russia moved to firm up the offer made in November 1914. This led to an exchange of notes known as the Constantinople Agreement (in March 1915) in which Russia received a definite promise of the Straits on successful conclusion of the war. Having said this, under the Constantinople Agreement, Istanbul would have been made into a free port and the right of passage for all shipping guaranteed.

Why did Britain agree to this change in policy? Britain saw Russia as a key ally in the fight against Germany and was determined that it should not make a separate peace that would leave Germany free to concentrate all its military resources on the Western Front. Britain saw the offer of the Straits as a suitable carrot to keep Russia in the war – the "richest prize of the whole war" as it was later

described.[9] The Constantinople Agreement raises another issue that is worth bearing in mind throughout this chapter: the countries fighting the First World War thought that the conflict would end with some form of negotiated settlement in which all promises and agreements would be discussed and revised at any peace conference.[10] Promises made during the war were not necessarily seen as binding agreements by those involved at the time; rather, they were there as war measures to help ensure victory. Until the war's end, the British assumed that the Ottomans, with German support, would dominate the Middle East.[11] Thus, offering the Russians control over territory that would be up for discussion at the war's end was not a bad strategy, especially if such an offer kept Russia in the war as any separate peace it might sign with the Germans–Ottomans during the war would mean giving up its demand for the Straits region promised in March 1915. These diplomatic moves also meant that Britain and France looked for their spoils of war in the Middle East.

After the Constantinople Agreement, the French approached the British to arrange their respective claims (or desiderata) in Asia Minor (what is now Turkey) and the Middle East at the expense of the Ottoman Empire. In response, on April 8, 1915, the British appointed Sir Maurice de Bunsen to chair a committee to look into this and report on different options for the future of the Ottoman Empire. What the de Bunsen Committee aimed for was not a rapacious carve-up of the Middle East but the establishment of a new British policy in the region now that the Ottoman Empire was an enemy power. The initial British claims were modest. Sir Mark Sykes, a British "eastern" expert, suggested to the committee that Iraq (Mesopotamia) was the focus of interest for the British administration in India, and that there should be a connection to the west at the port of Haifa (in what would become Palestine after the war) to provide some linkage for Britain across the region. (Sykes, someone who played an important part in British policy development in the region, died in the influenza epidemic of 1919.) The mention of Haifa raised the possibility of a British interest in Palestine and suggested a division – or partition – of the Middle East into three zones of influence: Russia in the north, France in the center, and Britain in the south.

However, in the end, the de Bunsen Committee suggested in its conclusions, delivered in May–June 1915, a set of four options: firstly, partitioning the empire among the Entente powers; secondly, establishing Entente zones of influence in a nominally independent empire but one that would be under effective European control; thirdly, leaving the empire largely intact but subject to some small but significant territorial adjustments; finally, decentralizing the empire along federal lines, but subject to some territorial losses. The preference of the committee was for the last scheme or, if this were not possible, option two (dividing the empire into zones of influence). While the committee had discussed partition, this was not the preferred choice. The rather modest conclusions of de Bunsen might suggest that Britain was uninterested in partition. But even the federal scheme would have done much to weaken the Ottoman Empire and establish Britain in the Middle East. De Bunsen's general conclusions formed the basis for British policymaking through the rest of the war. The de Bunsen Committee pointed to a new British policy toward the Ottoman Empire and raised the possibility of the partition of its territory across the Middle East.

Fighting against Ottoman forces in the Middle East, the British looked for new allies in the region. An obvious choice was Emir (or King) Husayn, a local Hashemite Arab leader who was nominally an Ottoman subject and whose territory in the Hijaz area of northwest Arabia included the Muslim holy cities of Mecca and Medina. Husayn came from the Quraysh tribe, the Prophet Muhammad's tribe, and as ruler of Mecca and Medina controlled the two foremost religious sites for Muslims, an important consideration for the British Empire that ruled many Muslims, especially in India. Militarily, an Arab uprising in the Hijaz would, the British hoped, tie down and distract the Ottoman army fighting against the British in Palestine; politically, it would support Britain's war effort among the British Empire's large Muslim population. (In the 1920s, Ibn Saud defeated and removed the Hashemites from the Hijaz and established the modern Kingdom of Saudi Arabia.)

The correspondence that started on July 14, 1915, and continued until January 30, 1916, between the British high commissioner in Cairo, Sir Henry McMahon (also with Sir Ronald Storrs), and Husayn that led to the Hashemites entering the war in June 1916 has aroused much interest and controversy, not least as it seemed to contradict other agreements that Britain made in the region. The British authorities in Cairo opened talks with the Hashemites in the summer of 1915, the aim being to work out what the Hashemites wanted in return for joining Britain in the war against the Turks. Then, suddenly, on July 14, 1915, one of Husayn's sons, Abdullah, asked for British recognition of an Arab caliphate (the caliph being the chief Sunni Muslim ruler, regarded as the successor of the Prophet Muhammad) in addition to Arab independence across the Middle East. It is not known why the Hashemites made this extensive demand.[12] The British response, which came through the high commissioner in Cairo, was ambivalent: they would concede the caliphate but thought it too early to talk about frontiers for an independent Arab state. Husayn then sent a letter that detailed how he was asking for the territory in the name of the entire Arab people. Under pressure, the British then caved in and, on October 24, 1915, McMahon wrote to Husayn and largely agreed with the latter's demands for an Arab state across the Middle East.[13]

In the letter of October 24, McMahon wrote that Britain was "prepared to recognize and uphold the independence of the Arabs in all the regions lying within the frontiers proposed by the Sharif of Mecca [Husayn]."[14] As Husayn's territorial demand in his letter to McMahon of July 14, 1915 (and to which McMahon was referring) had been for the whole of the Arabian peninsula up to what is now southern Turkey, with the sole exception of Aden in the far southwest of Arabia, it would seem that Britain was giving the whole of what is now Israel/Palestine, Jordan, Lebanon, Syria, Iraq, Kuwait, Saudi Arabia, the Gulf States, Oman, and Yemen to an independent Arab state. But McMahon also specified exclusions that would later cause much debate: (1) territory that France had a claim to in the region, (2) Mersin and Alexandretta (now called Iskenderun), and

(3) "portions of Syria lying to the west of the districts of Damascus, Homs, Hama and Aleppo" that McMahon claimed were not purely Arab. McMahon also pointed out that Britain would supply special advisers to the Arabs, especially in Iraq.

The issue of whether Britain later betrayed the Arabs by not sticking to this agreement will be discussed shortly. At this stage, we need to ask the question: why did Britain agree to such an extensive claim by a relatively weak local Arab leader? Scholars have presented three main reasons for the decision. Firstly, a deserter from the Ottoman army, Lieutenant Muhammad Sharif al-Faruqi, brought to Cairo a story concerning the existence of a vast secret society to which 90 percent of Arab officers in the Ottoman army were said to belong. These Arabs, the deserter told the British, would throw in their lot with Britain and the Entente powers if the Arabs were promised independence. Although there were question marks surrounding the deserter's tale, he still made a big impression on the British, the more so as his story appeared to confirm Husayn's extravagant claims. Secondly, at this stage of the war (1915), the British campaign on the Gallipoli peninsula was close to defeat and Britain feared that any withdrawal from Gallipoli would dent British imperial prestige. An Arab revolt would ease this situation. Finally, the feeling amongst British decision-makers was that Britain could still control any "independent" Arab state that would be forced into a patron–client relationship with Britain. Indeed, a pro-British Arab client state would also help in excluding unwelcome French claims to the region during and after the war.

French officials on the ground in the Middle East – such as the former French diplomat in Lebanon, François Georges Picot – were keen on partition of the region and, in February–March 1915, the French staked their claim to Syria and Lebanon, an area with which they had a long-standing connection. While most French people were little interested in the Middle East, at least while the war raged on the Western Front, a strong colonial party within France bolstered the demand for territorial spoils.

In November 1915, Britain began negotiations with France on the future status of the Middle East, with Sykes negotiating for Britain and Picot for France. France was suspicious of Britain's alliance with the Hashemites and was worried that it was going to be excluded from those parts of the Middle East in which it had a traditional interest. Thus, France was keen to pin Britain down on postwar territorial arrangements. In their talks, the more diplomatically adept Picot secured Lebanon and Syria, leaving Sykes with what would become Iraq (less the town of Mosul in the north, which went to France). The status of Palestine was left in limbo, it being internationalized, although Britain received the ports of Haifa and Acre. In May 1916, Britain and France signed what became known as the Sykes–Picot Agreement (properly the Asia Minor Agreement), to which Russia became a signatory (receiving territory in eastern Asia Minor).[15] Finally, Italy, which had joined the war in 1915, demanded its share of territory in southern Asia Minor around Adalia. The Italian zone was fixed in the agreement of St. Jean-de-Maurienne in August 1917 – when Italy's sphere was increased to include the towns of Smyrna (now Izmir) and Konya – although Russia never ratified this.

The Sykes–Picot and St. Jean-de-Maurienne agreements divided the Arab Middle East and large parts of what would become Turkey after the war into five zones: British, French, international, Italian, and Russian. Each of the British and French zones was further divided into territory that would be directly controlled by the colonial power (blue for France and red for British areas) and semi-autonomous territory (zones A for France and B for Britain). Britain and France planned to control all of their respective areas, including the semi-autonomous zones in which the colonial power would supply advisers, finance, and so on. The international zone – excluding a British enclave at Haifa/Acre – covered the Holy Land of Palestine, in which all the major Christian powers felt that they had an interest.

The Sykes–Picot Agreement caused much furor later as it seemed to clash with the Husayn–McMahon correspondence and subsequent promises made by the British and French to the Arabs and others. Malcolm Yapp argues that the Sykes–Picot Agreement was broadly compatible with what Husayn and McMahon had agreed. Only in three areas were there serious differences.[16] Firstly, Sykes–Picot had placed Iraq in the British red zone, notwithstanding the fact that McMahon had promised it to the Arabs. As, after the war, Britain helped establish a Hashemite state in Iraq, this was something of an academic dispute. Secondly, McMahon only made brief mention of Britain giving advice and assistance to the Arabs – otherwise, he promised Husayn full independence in the Arab areas. Yet, under Sykes–Picot, Britain and France would supply much of the Arab territory (zones A and B) with British and French advisers and finance, giving the strong impression that these, too, would be run effectively as British and French colonies. Many see this is as duplicitous; others argue that this was a practicable arrangement that reflected the realities of international relations at this time in history. They also point to the fact that the Hashemites simply did not have the capacity to run such large areas and would have required support anyway. Finally, there was the question of Palestine, the issue that caused the most trouble throughout the remainder of the twentieth century.

McMahon made no mention of British control of Haifa and Acre, something that Sykes and Picot agreed to. This is part of the wider debate on Palestine. McMahon said nothing about Palestine so it was presumably to pass to Arab control. Yet, Sykes and Picot internationalized Palestine and gave Haifa and Acre to Britain. Surely the Arabs were betrayed if McMahon said one thing, and Sykes–Picot another? This whole question of who promised what to whom has generated considerable scholarship, exemplified in Elie Kedourie's *In the Anglo-Arab Labyrinth: The McMahon–Husayn Correspondence and its Interpretations, 1914–1939* (1976).

Various explanations have been put forward to explain the contradictory statements made. One debate involves the translation of the word "vilayet" into "district" in McMahon's exclusion in his 1915 letter to Husayn detailing those "portions of Syria lying to the west of the districts of Damascus, Homs, Hama and Aleppo" (the argument revolving around whether "vilayet" applied to a town or to a bigger Ottoman administrative district). Another debate focuses on the fact that McMahon said he could not speak for those areas

in which France had a claim (such as Palestine). None of these arguments is very convincing. What Kedourie is good at showing in his book is the muddle and haste surrounding Britain's decision-making at this time (and also Britain's subsequent understanding of what was and was not promised), and he makes the valid point that the Husayn–McMahon letters were not necessarily binding documents. They were seen by both sides as the basis for future negotiations to be resumed in the postwar peace settlement. Husayn saw the letters as a provisional wartime understanding between two unequal partners laying down declarations of intent that would inevitably be contingent on changing circumstances.

Before the war's end, Britain made one more statement of policy: the Balfour Declaration of November 2, 1917, from the foreign secretary, A. J. Balfour, to Lord Rothschild, a leading Jewish banker and Zionist (a Jewish nationalist seeking a state for the Jews in Palestine).[17] The Balfour Declaration, published in *The Times* on November 9, 1917, is in the form of a short letter, the key section of which reads:

His Majesty's Government view with favour the establishment in Palestine of a national home for the Jewish people, and will use their best endeavours to facilitate the achievement of this object, it being clearly understood that nothing shall be done which may prejudice the civil and religious rights of existing non-Jewish communities in Palestine, or the rights and political status enjoyed by Jews in any other country.

The Balfour Declaration has achieved some notoriety, not least as it seemed to lay down the bedrock of the later Arab–Israeli conflict and proved that Britain was supporting Zionism. The situation is not this simple. Britain made the declaration partly as a genuine expression of support for Jewish nationalism but also because it was hoped that Jewish support would help the war effort. The Balfour Declaration also helped Britain evade its promise to internationalize Palestine (embodied in the Sykes–Picot Agreement), as the Zionists could be used as British agents in Palestine, thus helping to exclude annoying French demands that Palestine be ruled by an international administration. Moreover, the declaration is carefully phrased, offering very little in concrete terms (what is a "national home"? what does "view with favour" mean? what are "best endeavours"?). What is harder to explain is Britain's commitment after the war to help Jewish immigration to Palestine, as laid down in the League of Nations mandate document that Britain agreed for Palestine, when the British were not fighting a war and when they knew full well that the local Palestinian Arab population was firmly opposed to any Jewish immigration. Jewish immigration to Palestine after the war, supported by Britain until 1939, would set Palestine on the road to the current Arab–Israeli conflict.

At the end of the war, Britain was in a commanding position: Russia had collapsed and British or British-led armies had conquered and occupied Palestine, Lebanon, Transjordan, Syria, and Iraq. France had been marginalized. This meant that at the Paris peace talks in 1919, the British extended their zone of control to include all of Palestine and Mosul in northern Iraq (promised to France under Sykes–Picot), the latter being important because of its potential oil deposits. After some considerable diplomatic fighting, France eventually got Britain to agree to its having Lebanon and Syria, a decision that forced Britain to end its support for the Hashemite regime led by Prince Faysal (another of Husayn's sons) that Britain had helped install in Damascus in 1918. Eventually, in 1922–3, the League of Nations formally agreed that Britain should get Palestine, Transjordan, and Iraq as "Class A" mandates, while France would get Syria and Lebanon, also as Class A mandates. Class A mandates were deemed to have reached a stage of development where their independence could be provisionally recognized subject to administrative advice and assistance by the mandatory power. What of the Arabs? Britain established and sponsored Hashemite regimes in Transjordan and Iraq led by, respectively, Husayn's sons Abdullah and Faysal. (While a revolution in 1958 toppled the Hashemite regime in Iraq, Jordan is still ruled by a Hashemite king.) Palestine was ruled directly by a British high commissioner. The status of Class A mandates meant that these territories should have got independence fairly quickly, something that did not happen fully until after the Second

World War (although Iraq received nominal independence in 1932).

At this stage, it is worth making some remarks about the League of Nations mandate system, as it would affect the future status of captured territory in the Middle East, Africa, and the Far East. European powers such as Britain and France wanted to establish traditional colonies in captured territory and were not keen on the mandate system, not least as the League of Nations supervision element to the mandates threatened their desire for imperial expansion at the expense of the German and Ottoman empires. In order to reduce the degree of international control, Britain proposed that colonies be graded by their stage of development into A, B, and C mandates: "C Mandates were to be administered as integral parts of the territories of the mandatory, which meant League surveillance over arms, slavery and fortifications but not over immigration and trade. B Mandates differed little in practice, beyond League supervision to ensure open door trade practices. . . . A Mandates suggested eventual independence and were applied to the Middle East."[18] The Mandates were empire in all but name. States such as Britain and France wanted to reduce the degree of international League of Nations control on the Mandates and aimed for (and achieved) *de facto* if not *de jure* imperial rule after the war.

## Africa

Africa was dragged into the First World War because it was almost completely controlled by European powers. While militarily Africa was a sideshow, there was fighting there as Entente armies conquered Germany's African colonies. Moreover, both sides mobilized Africa's resources and manpower, thus touching the lives of vast numbers of Africans and proving the value of empire as a strategic resource. Because of appalling communications, the major military difficulty was not defeating the enemy but reaching him. The war in Africa involved company-size columns operating with little artillery support, the machine gun being the heaviest weapon used in most engagements.

Troops from Britain, France, Belgium, and (from 1916) Portugal assaulted Germany's African colonies in Togoland (Togo), Cameroons (Kamerun), Southwest Africa (Namibia), and East Africa (Tanganyika/Tanzania). When Portugal joined the war in 1916, her troops defended Portugese-held Mozambique. Locally recruited soldiers and porters played a vital part in these campaigns. In Togoland on August 12, 1914, a sergeant major of the West African Frontier Force fired the first shot of the war; on November 25, 1918, two weeks after the war had ended in Europe, the last German-led forces in East Africa surrendered at Abercorn in Northern Rhodesia. Germany's colonies were weakly defended and Togoland fell quickly. As the Germans had based their most powerful wireless station in Togoland, its loss restricted communications with Berlin. Bounded by British and French colonies, German forces in the Cameroons, short of munitions, held out in the northern highlands until 1916, after the bulk of the force had escaped to Spanish-controlled Muni. Britain and France then divided Togoland and the Cameroons, thus expanding their African empires.

Meanwhile, South African forces attacked German Southwest Africa. A revolt of pro-German white Afrikaners in South Africa (September–October 1914), led by a South African officer, S. G. Maritz, delayed the invasion. Eventually, loyal South African forces quelled the revolt, after which they invaded Southwest Africa by land and sea across the Orange River, from Lüderitz and from Walvis Bay. The last German forces surrendered at Tsumeb in July 1915. Casualties were low: more South Africans died in Maritz's revolt than in fighting the Germans. South Africa's conquest of Southwest Africa was an example of local empire-building, and in this case it was successful: South Africa remained in charge in the country until 1990.

The major campaign of the war in Africa was in German East Africa against German-led askaris – local black troops commanded by Germans. Under the overall command of Paul von Lettow-Vorbeck, 218 Europeans and 2,542 askaris were divided into some twenty-one companies, each with 150–200 askaris and 16–20 German officers and NCOs. A small police force plus the guns and crew of the wrecked German light cruiser *Königsberg* augmented Lettow-Vorbeck's force. The Germans repulsed a bungled British-led Indian Expeditionary Force landing at Tanga. Thereafter, Lettow-Vorbeck kept his force in being until the war's end, tying down Entente troops needed elsewhere. He avoided major battles, instead invading at different times Mozambique, Northern Rhodesia (Zambia), and Nyasaland (Malawi). While Lettow-Vorbeck kept fighting until after the war was over, his command in East Africa is not as impressive as it might seem. His sustained defense of the colony lasted only from March 1916 to November 1917 – comparable in length to the German defense of the Cameroons – and he had no theory of guerrilla war, preferring classic German theories of envelopment and the decisive battle.

Two million Africans served in the war as a whole, as either soldiers or laborers, and some 200,000 died or were killed in action. Africa was used as a vast pool of manpower by the Entente, with hundreds of thousands of men from Belgian, British, French, German, and Portuguese Africa employed as porters and soldiers against Germany's colonies, many dying from disease, especially malaria (as did many white troops). While the war certainly dented European racial superiority in Africa, too little is known about black Africans' experience of the war.

Echoing the famous "Scramble for Africa" of the late nineteenth century, after the First World War there was a second "partition of Africa" that took little or no account of ideas of Wilsonian self-determination, not least as black Africans were deemed to be unable to rule themselves.[19] Britain took the lion's share of conquered territory: German East Africa and slices of Togoland and Cameroons. France received the rest of Togoland and Cameroons, while Belgium got the heavily populated northwestern part of German East Africa that would become Rwanda and Burundi. South Africa took charge of Southwest Africa. Finally, Portugal and Italy received some minor territorial gains: Kionga, a coastal strip of East Africa, added to Portuguese Mozambique; the Juba Valley in East Africa and some minor adjustments along the Algeria–Libya border for Italy.

Unlike the Middle East, these new colonies were not deemed to be advanced enough to become Class A mandates so they all became Class B mandates, except Southwest Africa, which was made a Class C mandate. This meant that independence was a long way off. European powers in charge of Class B mandates were responsible for the administration of the territory under conditions that would guarantee freedom of conscience and religion. For Southwest Africa, the League of Nations mandate empowered South Africa to administer the territory as if it were an integral portion of South Africa itself (something South Africa did until it finally withdrew in 1990). In the 1960s, the other former German colonies finally gained their independence: Togo (1960), Cameroon (1960), Tanzania (1964), and Rwanda/Burundi (1962).

## The Far East

While Germany was no danger to Japan, the latter – allied to Britain in 1902 – wanted the German-controlled territory of Kiaochow (and its main port of Tsingtao) on the Chinese coast and had designs on Germany's extensive island colonies in the Pacific. Britain was keen for Japan to join the war, assuming that Japan's armed forces, especially the navy, would help in the fight against Germany in the Far East. Thus, the Entente promised support for Japan's claims to Kiaochow and to Germany's Pacific islands so as to get Japan into the war.[20] As long as Japan remained neutral and Britain concentrated on the war in Europe, Germany stood a reasonable chance of defending Tsingtao. Once Japan entered the war on August 23, 1914, it was only a matter of time. Without naval support, the German governor of Tsingtao, Clemens Friedrich Meyer-Waldeck, drew in men and matériel for a siege against 60,000 Japanese troops plus a small Anglo-Indian contingent. First contact was on September 18, 1914, the main advance beginning on September 25 against a German garrison of 184 officers and 4,390 men. The Japanese employed a gradual siege warfare approach – also the innovative use of airpower for bombing – and, running out of ammunition, Meyer-Waldeck sought an armistice on November 7.

Japan, Australia, and New Zealand also attacked and occupied Germany's island colonies in Micronesia and New Guinea. Japan occupied the Micronesian islands in October 1914; to the south, New Zealand took German possessions to the east of longitude 170°, while Australia got those to the west. This meant that, by late November 1914, New Zealand had Samoa, while Australia had Germany's New Guinea possessions. In the Pacific, the equator became the effective dividing line between Japanese-controlled German islands to the north and Australian/New Zealand ones to the south. While the collapse of Germany's empire in the Pacific freed up British and Entente forces for the war in Europe, it also represented the rise of Japan as a major regional power whose aim was to expand its empire across the Pacific and into China. As with South Africa's conquest of Southwest Africa, Australia and New Zealand were also proving that they, too, had regional ambitions.

Japan's rise to become a great power started in 1868 with the Meiji restoration that brought to a close feudalism in Japan and pushed the country down the road to becoming a modern state. In 1894–5 and in 1904–5, Japan fought wars against China and Russia, emerging victorious from both and in charge of conquered enemy territory. In July 1907, two years after the war with Russia, Japan signed an agreement with Russia that ostensibly pledged both states to the maintenance of the status quo in the Far East and proclaimed recognition of each other's territorial integrity. But the agreement also contained secret clauses (not revealed until the Bolsheviks made them public in the First World War) whereby Japan and Russia divided up the Chinese region of Manchuria into spheres of influence. Japan obviously had designs on the Chinese mainland.[21]

The First World War was an opportunity for Japan to realize these expansionist foreign policy aims. Firstly, Japan set about fortifying the recently conquered German possessions in the Pacific (which it was not supposed to do). This was something that happened in the 1920s and 1930s. Secondly, and more immediately, in 1915, she presented China with a series of demands (known as the Twenty-One Demands) that tried to extend further Japanese influence over China. The Twenty-One Demands comprised five sections. These five sections demanded the following: (1) that Japan assume Germany's position in

Kiaochow; (2) that Manchuria and Mongolia be reserved to Japan for exploitation and colonization; (3) that Japan control the main coal deposits of China; (4) that the other powers be excluded from further territorial concessions; and (5) that Japan guide China's military, commercial, and financial affairs. The demands for control of Chinese affairs were dropped, partly at the insistence of the United States. After the Japanese threatened to attack China, Chinese President Yüan accepted the remainder of the demands. As a symbol of Japanese intent, Japan made (and presented to the Chinese) the Twenty-One Demands on paper watermarked with dreadnought warships and machine guns. Put simply, the Twenty-One Demands, if fully implemented, "would have virtually turned China into a Japanese protectorate."[22]

The Twenty-One Demands, setting a pattern for Japanese domination, were forced on China, but the treaties were not ratified by the Chinese legislature. The Japanese reinforced their claims in 1917 and forced a second agreement from the Chinese in 1918. At the Versailles Conference, Japan was awarded the German possessions in Kiaochow despite strong Chinese protest. China refused to sign the Versailles Treaty, and this event led directly to widespread anti-Japanese demonstrations across China known as the May 4, 1919, movement. At the Washington Conference (1921–2), Japan agreed to restore full sovereignty to China but this was only a stopgap measure as, in the 1930s, Japan renewed its aggression against China by occupying Manchuria and then launching an all-out invasion in 1937 that led to a Sino-Japanese war that lasted until 1945.

When the victors discussed the future status of captured German Far Eastern territory at the Paris Peace Conference in 1919, Australia, New Zealand, and Japan all united in their opposition to international control of the conquered territory.[23] Britain supported the Australian and New Zealand claims. As with captured lands in Africa and the Middle East, the colonial powers (and Japan) had to deal with US President Wilson's self-determination ideals and, after 1917, the Russian revolutionaries' demands for peace without annexation. For Britain, the aim was to keep intact the substance of imperial rule while pretending to domestic and foreign opinion that its intentions toward these colonies were purely altruistic.[24] President Wilson, keen to establish a new course in world affairs with his anti-imperial ideas of plebiscites and self-determination, battled against the imperial ambitions of the European colonial powers (including the semi-autonomous "white" parts of empire such as Australia, New Zealand, and South Africa). The Australians were not alone in wondering how the "head-hunters" of New Guinea would react to a plebiscite concerning their future.

Japan got drawn into this debate as it insisted on securing Germany's Chinese and Pacific lands without even a formal reference to League procedures. Notwithstanding concerns from New Zealand, Australia, and, to a lesser extent, Canada, in February 1917, in return for the provision of additional Japanese cruisers for war duties in the South Atlantic, Britain had agreed to support Japan's retention of the German islands north of the equator and of Kiaochow. In doing this, Britain was making a virtue out of necessity since nothing short of force would have induced Japan to give up its territorial gains. This diplomatic move threatened to involve Britain in an embarrassing confrontation with President Wilson, who refused to accept these private arrangements.[25]

At the Paris talks in January 1919, the leaders of Australia, New Zealand, and South Africa tried to convince Wilson that the Pacific islands (south of the equator) and Southwest Africa were so essential to the security of the British Empire that the mandates system should not be applied to them. At the same time, Japan demanded the outright annexation of the northern Pacific islands and recognition of its acquisition of Germany's former rights in Kiaochow.[26] On January 27, 1919, Wilson agreed to the establishment of mandates but rejected South African, Australasian, and Japanese annexationist demands. Representing British imperial feeling, the Australian prime minister, William Hughes, led the opposition to Wilson. He was only won over after Lloyd George and the South Africa statesman Jan Smuts pressured and convinced him that the mandates were annexation in all but name. The mandate system was then accepted by the British Empire.[27]

Annoyed at Hughes's opposition, Wilson delayed making a decision on mandates until May 1919 when the territory that Australia, Japan, and New Zealand had conquered was given to them as mandates (with the exception of Kiaochow). At the same time, the African mandates were agreed.

One of Wilson's objections to a colonial carve-up of the Far East was his fear of Japanese ambitions in the region. Japan's decision to send troops to the Russian Far East (via the Russian port of Vladivostok) in 1918 during the Russian Civil War strengthened America's fears, and prompted the US to send troops to the Russian Far East to keep an eye on the Japanese. While Britain was also fearful of Japan, it could not protest too much considering its own claims for new colonies in Africa and Asia. Indeed, when negotiations with the Japanese began in earnest in April 1919, Lloyd George insisted that Britain was bound to support Japan's claims under the 1917 treaty. Clemenceau stated that France would follow suit. Thus, Wilson was isolated. Japan refused to agree to the mandate system being extended to cover Kiaochow and Lloyd George tried in vain to persuade the Japanese to accept a C mandate for Kiaochow.[28] Japan threatened to walk out of the Paris talks and so a face-saving gesture was arranged whereby Japan promised that sovereignty of Kiaochow would eventually revert to China. But no time limit was imposed on this transaction. China was furious and so refused to sign the Treaty of Versailles in June 1919. Without support from France and Britain, Wilson had been forced to accede to Japanese demands and when the mandates were finally divided in May 1919, Japan got everything it wanted.[29]

So it was that thousands of tiny atolls and reefs stretching across the expanse of the Pacific, whose peoples had passed the centuries in peaceful obscurity, were drawn into the imperial orbit: "the spread of modern technology and the growth of modern navies had made them valuable properties for outsiders, first the Germans and now the Japanese."[30] Japan was behaving like the European powers in its attitude to empire. On January 27, 1919, the Japanese read out a statement to the Paris Peace Conference pointing out that the local Pacific islanders "were a primitive people who

could only benefit from Japan's protection and benevolence."[31]

In all of this, the Japanese were playing the European imperial game, in the face of considerable hostility and racism from European powers and America. In the US before 1914, Japanese immigrants had faced considerable discrimination, including segregation of their children. As Japan prepared to take its place at the Peace Conference, Japanese newspapers were full of exhortations. "Now is the time," said one editorial, "to fight against international racial discrimination."[32] At the peace talks, Australia was not alone in opposing a Racial Equality Clause that Japan put forward for ratification, and the failure to have this ratified (in April 1919) infuriated the Japanese, who felt they had earned the right to be treated as equals. In the interwar years the Japanese did exactly what the US feared: they established themselves on their Pacific island conquests and eventually fortified many of these former German islands. From the 1920s onwards, foreigners found it hard to visit these islands as Japanese military forces and settlers moved to them. Indeed, from the 1920s onwards, foreigners found it hard to visit these islands as Japanese military forces, settlers, and military contractors moved in. When Japanese militarism emerged in the 1930s, Japan was set on the road to war with first China (1937) and then America (1941). In the subsequent Pacific War with the US, Japan's island fortresses would witness some of the bloodiest battles of the Second World War as the US checked Japanese expansion before counterattacking, defeating, and then occupying Japan.

## Conclusion

In the Middle East, the First World War saw the end of the Ottoman Empire and the rise of the modern Middle East boundary system based on the mandate boundaries. Thus, the war established the basic political framework that has endured to this day, notwithstanding subsequent revolutions and coups in the 1950s and 1960s. In this sense, the war was significant. In Africa, there were some minor boundary adjustments after the war but the main change for Africa was the transfer of colonial power from one European power to another (or to South Africa in the case of German Southwest Africa). It was not until the 1950s and 1960s that Africa moved to throw off colonial rule. It was in the Pacific that the First World War had the biggest immediate impact as it signaled the continuing rise of Japanese power that would reach its apogee in the long war Japan fought in China and then with the United States from 1937 to 1945.

## NOTES

1   In this chapter, the terms Turkey and Ottoman will be used interchangeably. This is, strictly speaking, incorrect inasmuch as the modern republic of Turkey was not formed until 1922–3 when the Ottoman Empire finally disappeared.

2   For the fighting in Africa and Asia, see Hew Strachan, *The First World War* (Oxford: Oxford University Press, 2001), vol. 1; Strachan, *The First World War in Africa* (Oxford: Oxford University Press, 2004); and Ross Anderson, *The Forgotten Front: The East African Campaign, 1914–1918* (Stroud: Tempus, 2004).

3   Kiaochow (Jiaozhou) was the German territory of some 200 square miles (520 square kilometers) along the southern coast of Shantung (Shandong) province. Its administrative center was the city of Tsingtao (Qingdao). Chinese place-names are Giles–Wade spellings; those in parentheses are Pinyin spelling.

4   For the Palestine campaign, see Matthew Hughes, *Allenby and British Strategy in the Middle East, 1917–19* (London: Frank Cass, 1999), and E. Erickson, *Ottoman Army Effectiveness in World War I: A Comparative Study* (London: Routledge, 2007). For Mesopotamia, see A. J. Barker, *The Neglected War: Mesopotamia, 1914–1918* (London: Faber & Faber, 1967); Nikolas Gardner, "Sepoys and the Siege of Kut-al-Amara, December 1915– April 1916," *War in History* 11 (2004): 307–26; and Edward Erickson, *Ordered to Die: A History of the Ottoman Army in the First World War* (Westport, CT: Greenwood, 2001).

5   Matthew Hughes, "The French Army at Gallipoli," *Journal of the Royal United Services Institute* 150 (2005): 64–7.

6   For the Caucasus, see W. E. D. Allen and Paul Muratoff, *Caucasian Battlefields: A History of the War on the Turco-Caucasian Border, 1828–* 1921 (Cambridge: Cambridge University Press, 1953).

7   Malcolm E. Yapp, *The Making of the Modern Near East, 1792–1923* (Harlow: Pearson, 1987), p. 275.

8   Ibid.

9   Quoted in ibid.

10   Ibid.

11   See the British policy documents in the National Archives (London), CAB 29/1 (P17 "Notes on Possible Terms of Peace" dated April 11, 1917), CAB 25/43 ("The Turkish and South Russian Problem" dated January 4, 1918), CAB 25/73 ("The Political Aspects of the Campaign of 1919" dated March 21, 1918), and CAB 25/87 ("War Aims and Military Policy" dated June 15, 1918).

12   Yapp, *The Making of the Modern Near East*, p. 279.

13   Ibid., pp. 279–80.

14   G. Antonius, *The Arab Awakening* (London: Hamish Hamilton, 1938), p. 419.

15   Yapp, *The Making of the Modern Near East*, pp. 277–8.

16   Ibid., pp. 281ff.

17   The classic work on the Balfour Declaration is L. Stein's *The Balfour Declaration* (London: Vallentine, 1961).

18   Michael J. Dockrill and J. Douglas Goold, *Peace Without Promise: Britain and the Paris Peace Conference, 1919–23* (London: Batsford, 1981), p. 66.

19   David Killingray, "The War in Africa," in *The Oxford Illustrated History of the First World War*, ed. Hew Strachan (Oxford: Oxford University Press, 1998), p. 102.

20   David Stevenson, "War Aims and Peace Negotiations," in *Oxford Illustrated History of the First World War*, p. 208.

21   E. W. Edwards, "The Far Eastern Agreements 1907," *Journal of Modern History* 26 (1954): 350.

22   Margaret Macmillan, *Peacemakers: The Paris Peace Conference of 1919 and its Attempt to End War* (London: John Murray, 2001), p. 337.

23   Dockrill and Douglas Goold, *Peace Without Promise*, p. 64.

24   Ibid.

25   Ibid., p. 65.

26   Ibid., p. 66.

27   Ibid.

28   Ibid., p. 68.

29   Macmillan, *Peacemakers*, p. 325.

30   Ibid., p. 322.

31   Ibid., p. 325.

32   Ibid., p. 326.

## GUIDE TO FURTHER READING

George Antonius, *The Arab Awakening: The Story of the Arab National Movement* (London: Hamish Hamilton, 1938). While dated, this is the classic text written by an Arab scholar detailing the rise of Arab nationalism and how the British betrayed the Arabs during the First World War.

Ian Beckett, *The Great War, 1914–1918* (Harlow: Pearson, 2001). This is a well-written survey of the war by a leading military historian that, as well as touching upon the war in Africa and Asia, also provides good contextual background.

Michael Crowder, "The First World War and its Consequences," in *General History of Africa*, vol. 7, *Africa Under Colonial Domination 1880–1935*, ed. A. Adu Boahen (London: Heinemann, 1985). A very useful chapter in a general history of Africa. Too little has been written on Africa's experience in the war.

Michael J. Dockrill and J. Douglas Goold, *Peace Without Promise: Britain and the Paris Peace Conference, 1919–23* (London: Batsford, 1981). One of the classic texts on the Paris Peace Conference. The coverage of the talks on the Middle East is especially useful; it has less to say on Africa and the Far East.

E. W. Edwards, "The Far Eastern Agreements 1907," *Journal of Modern History* 26 (1954): 340–55. A good article on the 1907 agreement that details the secret partition clauses.

David Fromkin, *A Peace To End All Peace: Creating the Modern Middle East 1914–1922* (London: Penguin, 1989). A more recent readable history of the Paris Peace Conference; only deals with the Middle East.

P. Helmreich, *From Paris to Sèvres: The Partition of the Ottoman Empire and the Paris Peace Conference 1919* (Columbus, OH: Ohio State University Press, 1974). Another classic academic text on the division of the Middle East at the Paris Peace Conference.

Elie Kedourie, *In the Anglo-Arab Labyrinth: The McMahon–Husayn Correspondence and its Interpretations, 1914–1939* (Cambridge: Cambridge University Press, 1976). This is a specialist text that examines the Husayn–McMahon correspondence and how the British subsequently understood the correspondence. It also makes more general points about British attitudes to Arab nationalism.

Margaret Macmillan, *Peacemakers: The Paris Peace Conference of 1919 and its Attempt to End War* (London: John Murray, 2001). An up-to-date account of the Paris talks in 1919, well received by the critics. This is a lucid account of the peace talks that covers all geographical areas.

John Moses and Christopher Pugsley, eds., *The German Empire and Britain's Pacific Dominions: Essays on the Role of Australia and New Zealand in World Politics in the Age of Imperialism* (Claremont, CA: Regina, 2000). This extensive set of essays by a range of authors examines the oft-neglected subject of the rise of Australia and New Zealand as regional imperial powers.

Harold Nicolson, *Peacemaking* (London: Constable, 1933). A personal account of the Paris talks from one of the British diplomats involved.

Melvin Page, ed., *Africa and the First World War* (London: Macmillan, 1987). A general account of Africa in the war.

Andrew Roberts, *A Cambridge History of Africa*, vol. 7, *1905–1940* (Cambridge: Cambridge University Press, 1986). This general history in an acclaimed series provides both specifics and general context on Africa in the war.

Zara Steiner, "The Peace Settlements," in *The Oxford Illustrated History of the First World War*, ed. Hew Strachan (Oxford: Oxford University Press, 1998). A brief but effective chapter on the Paris Peace Conference from a leading scholar of diplomatic history.

David Stevenson, *1914–1918: The History of the First World War* (London: Allen Lane, 2004). The latest history of the First World War that provides a readable and scholarly account.

Hew Strachan, *The First World War*, vol. 1, *To Arms* (Oxford: Oxford University Press, 2001). While only dealing with the period up to the end of 1914, this account of the war has well-written specific chapters on the war in the Pacific and Africa in 1914 based on a wide range of sources.

Bruce Vandervort, "New Light on the East African Theater of the Great War: A Review Essay of English-Language Sources," in *Soldiers and Settlers in Africa, 1850–1918*, ed. S. Miller (Leiden: Brill, 2009).

Xu Guoqi, *China and the Great War: China's Pursuit of a New National Identity and Internationalism* (Cambridge: Cambridge University Press, 2005). This is a volume that examines China's role in the war, and how growing ideas of national identity struggled with Japanese aggression and international diplomacy.

Malcolm E. Yapp, *The Making of the Modern Near East, 1792–1923* (Harlow: Pearson, 1987). This book provides a scholarly examination not just of the Middle East during and after the war but also of the vicissitudes of key diplomatic events such as the Husayn–McMahon correspondence, Sykes–Picot Agreement, and the Balfour Declaration.

# CHAPTER ELEVEN

# Envisioning a New World Order

## IAN D. THATCHER

The First World War was a significant turning point in the international history of the twentieth century. Three emperors – Nicholas II, Wilhelm II, and Franz Joseph – were toppled from power, their empires in ruins. The destruction of the former imperial powers of Central–East Europe also opened opportunities for the creation of a new world order. Competing visions of international affairs were quickly advanced by what would become the superpowers, Soviet Russia and America. To a certain extent the ideological aspect of what has been called the "First" Cold War had a personal dimension. The president of the United States, Woodrow Wilson, had a clear idea of how international affairs should be conducted in the interests of order, justice, and peace. The chair of the Council of People's Commissars and head of the Bolshevik movement in Russia, Vladimir Lenin, was equally convinced of the correctness of a very different view of the world. Both men felt themselves to be at the dawn of a new era in world affairs, each representing progress. This chapter will examine these competing visions, the motives behind them, and the degree of public support that they enjoyed.

## Wilson and the New World Order

The desire to construct a new world order issued from a critique of the way in which international affairs had been conducted. Wilson and Lenin were united, if only in a surface sense, by their distaste for the imperialism of the major European powers. It was the imperialist order, with its alliances, arms races, and rapacious battle for control over colonies, that was responsible for the First World War. Imperialism corroded both domestic and international peace. It had to be overcome. Their condemnation of imperialism was, however, rooted in profoundly different analyses of its nature and, consequently, they offered competing visions of a post-imperial world order.

After the outbreak of war in 1914, Wilson, unlike Lenin, did not undertake a profound analysis of its causes, nor did he propose to alter US policy. He wanted America to be absolutely neutral in the conflict, maintaining "impartiality and fairness and friendliness to all concerned."[1] He was convinced that each of the European powers who were spilling blood and spending resources were doing so out of their convictions that right was on their side, that the war was being fought for ideals. While it remained unclear which side would prevail, the United States should be understanding of all, a role for which its history made it ideally suited. The United States, according to Wilson, was composed of a blend of different European traditions. Since America was in a state of kinship with European peoples, and did not desire to make any territorial or other gains, it was singularly placed to be neutral and to uphold the cause of peace and justice. When Europe was ready to settle its battles, it could rely on Washington to act as a disinterested and sympathetic mediator whose vision was that of humanity and moral force.

When it was far more likely that America would itself intervene in the conflict, Wilson became more outspoken and very judgmental about what had caused the First World War. At a general level, he condemned the "old world order" and its obsession with a "balance of power." In this system nations pursued their interests in a zero-sum game of "your loss is my gain." A country's security was tied to alliances made on the basis of overlapping but not necessarily mutual self-interest. One could not be certain that even one's allies would keep to promises that could become inconvenient. As well as making and remaking alliances, nations in a "balance of power" system sought also to make their armed forces and military might as powerful as possible. The outcome of this very savage balance of power system was not respect, peace, and the cultivation of open and honest diplomacy, but the very opposite. Statesmen were encouraged to tell lies and engage in deception; the military awaited the opportunity to test its mettle in warfare, a most likely outcome given the pursuit of naked self-interest.

In a system that was likely to produce a war, it was nevertheless Germany and the Central Powers that were the most rapacious and under the sway of sinister interest. It was in the closed elite circles of Berlin and Vienna that the plots were made that led to the First World War. Wilson drew a stark distinction between the German people and their rulers. He painted a bleak moral picture of the kaiser and his immediate entourage. They had used their countries' material and intellectual resources to base ends, without seeking the prior approval of the people. The intention was nothing short of global domination and the elimination of democracy and freedom.

It was because Germany and its allies had revealed their wicked and evil spirit in unlimited submarine warfare that displayed no regard for any sense of fair play that the United States had decided to throw its decisive material and moral weight behind the Entente. Especially following the demise of Romanov rule in Russia, the war was clearly a battle between democracy and dictatorship.

While he committed American forces to battle, Wilson made it plain that the United States was not fighting for imperial conquest. It was an established tenet of liberal philosophy, evident, for example, in John Stuart Mill's writings on representative government, that the greatest danger to democracy lay in the sway and domination of sectional interest over the common good. Wilson applied this principle to international relations. The greatest danger to world peace and order came, as in the case of Germany, from the pursuit of an autocratic sectional interest opposed to the general democratic interest. Wilson believed that there was a body of principles common to humanity, around which a just world order could be created. It was vital that the old diplomacy be replaced by a new world order in which "nations must in the future be governed by the same high code of honor that we demand of individuals."[2] The leading example of moral behavior was the United States.

Wilson's certainty of purpose and vision was based upon a particular conception of the American people and their values. The purity of American diplomacy was rooted, for Wilson, in its people's love of freedom. Migrants to the American continent sought refuge from sin and oppression. America had a moral vision that came from a Christian code of conduct. It is hard to overestimate the importance in Wilson's outlook of a belief in God and that diplomacy should be conducted according to holy scripture. For him, America's rulers, democratically elected, embodied the spirit of a people that respected high principles like no other. It was not accidental, therefore, that Wilson had a very benign view of US diplomacy: despite the occasional lapse in succumbing to self-interest, its record was generally positive. The Monroe Doctrine embodied American ideals: it proclaimed the determination to preserve the western hemisphere from interference from Europe – and it aimed to do so without dominating Mexico and Cuba. As the world's greatest power, America would continue its traditions of restraint and abhorrence of any attempt to force a people to bow to external pressure. The United States would be first in line to subordinate naked self-interest to the common international good. Even after the horrors of the First World War, and despite Wilson's preference for democracy of the American type, the United States would not insist that every country should adopt its notion of freedom and democratic governance. Peoples should have not only the right to territorial independence but also the freedom of choice to resolve their own system of government. However regrettable the demise of democracy in Russia, for instance, the United States would wait passively until Russians returned to the democratic fold.

Wilson requested that international statesmen follow the American example and make a moral leap from an old world order governed by a naked battle of self-interest to a new world network of interconnected nation-states that agreed to abide by the rule of law and mutual respect, and to uphold common human values to which all peoples and nations could subscribe. Wilson was certain that there existed "eternal principles of right and justice" that represented the interests of all of humanity. In his speeches and his writings he frequently referred to "mankind" and its "moral force." His most famous enunciation of new world order based upon principles of justice and the interests of all was the "Fourteen Points" speech of January 1918.

First and foremost no people should live under external rule. Each nation, large and small, should have the right to national self-determination. Only domestic populations, not external governments, should resolve issues of internal sovereignty. Furthermore, each independent country should be viable and stable, having sufficient natural and human resources to sustain it. For postwar Europe this would mean a peace that did not expose the vanquished to extreme exploitation and humiliation: there would be no victor's peace but one to which both winners and losers could subscribe. Most importantly, a defeated Germany must not be left with such an overwhelming sense of unfair treatment that it would place as its immediate priority rearmament to win back its lost pride and potential. After all, it was Germany's elite, not its people, that was to blame for the war – and ordinary citizens should not be punished for the sins of their leaders. At the same time, however, a renewed Germany should accept and support a new Central European order. There should be an independent Poland, a free Belgium and France, the establishment of autonomous

states in the former Austro-Hungarian Empire and in the Balkans, and the removal of all foreign armies from Russia. As well as redrawing the European map according to national self-determination, the colonial world should also benefit from the application of this principle. European nations should negotiate with their colonies with the intention of encouraging self-government in the interests of the indigenous peoples. Wilson placed such importance upon the construction of free, agreed, and viable states because only in democratic, open, and settled nations are people able to hold their governments to account and insist upon honest diplomacy.

Once each country had established its boundaries and system of government in a free and open spirit, there should be an equal opportunity to engage in world trade. Markets should be open and fair, access to the seas should be available for all. The spirit of open competition should not, however, be allowed to ride roughshod over the rights of workers. Workers across the world should have equal rights to labor protection. Markets had to be equitable to workers as well as to capitalists.

Finally, the acceptance of a common interest in sovereignty and trade should allow the international community to place its security in a common bond of trust. The guarantee of a just, fair, and equal world order would be a voluntary League of Nations, composed initially of the United States and other great democracies but also open to nations that had proved their commitment to its values and practices. The League of Nations would replace the sinister "balance of power" with an honorable code of practice. Nations would submit any disputes to the League for settlement without recourse to war. Nations would thus be more secure, freed from the threat of armed conflict and the demands to waste resources on military expenditure. The arms race that had contributed to the outbreak of the First World War would be replaced by a policy of the reduction of arms stocks to the bare minimum required to guarantee domestic safety. The culture of the barracks would be reduced to an insignificant role in democracies concerned above all with peace. Governments could be democratic and diplomacy open and honest. With a system of common

security and mutual respect and trust, governments, like people, could observe the demands of
a moral way of life while enjoying greater prosperity. If nothing else, pure national self-interest
should guarantee that future diplomats would
abide by Wilson's recommendations. And in the
more unlikely event that any nation should break
the norms of a just international order, it would
face the wrath and the penalties, from an economic boycott to military intervention, of a united
League of Nations.

Wilson felt that there were very good reasons
why such a moral community of nations was a real
possibility. For him the League of Nations was
not a utopian dream but an accurate reflection of
an interconnected world of nation-states. The
destruction wrought by the First World War had
surely taught statesmen that conflict of this type
was so dysfunctional to the internal and international order that disagreements were better solved
by peaceful arbitration. The security of each was
tied to the security of all. No nation could sit in
isolation. It was in the interest of all to respect
and guarantee the independence of each nation-
state. Economies would be more prosperous as
they benefited from open world markets. Citizens
would be happier as they enjoyed new labor rights
that set humane limits to their exploitation.
Second, there was a growing consensus in world
opinion that demanded a permanent peace. For
Wilson, the surest guarantee of the new world
order was world opinion. People were aware of the
promise of a new world order and would not be
content unless statesmen turned demands into
reality. This, in turn, rested upon an acceptance
of equality of opportunity and respect for all
nation-states. Third, the disruption experienced
by non-combatant nations to their trade and prospects had revealed that there was no issue faced
by one or several countries that was not a matter
of concern to the rest of the world. For humanity
to achieve its common interests, it would support
Wilson's program for a new world order. Indeed,
given the various advantages of belonging to the
democratic association of free and rich nations,
any non-democratic orders would have every
encouragement to democratize on a voluntary
basis. A world union of democracies was the best
of all possible outcomes for democracies were less

likely to spy on one another, to try to undermine
other democracies from within, or to declare war
on one another. Wilson's vision for a new world
order was complex and daring, but once established was meant to be self-reinforcing, appealing,
and for the long-term realization of humanity's
common values.

## Lenin and the New World Order

While many would applaud Wilson for the coherence and appeal of his vision, such applause was
not forthcoming from Lenin. Wilson's program
for world order and diplomacy was based on a
liberal democratic capitalist philosophy linked, in
Wilson's case, to western Christianity. Lenin
belonged to a very different tradition. The conceptual tools central to Lenin's outlook – class,
dictatorship of the proletariat, monopoly capitalism – were completely absent from Wilson's discourse. Although there are themes common to
Wilson and Lenin, the right of nations to self-
determination, for example, their understanding
of these terms and how they would be achieved
were absolutely opposed.

Lenin's appraisal of international affairs and its
potential for change issued from an analysis of
contemporary imperialism. For Lenin, if one did
not comprehend the economic essence of the
modern form of imperialism, one would be lost
in the fog, unable to understand national and
world politics. The contemporary form of imperialism that had resulted in the horrors of the First
World War was, for Lenin, that of monopoly
capitalism, the peculiarities of which explained
the causes of international conflict while providing the prerequisites for a future world order in
the form of a worldwide federation of socialist
states.

Lenin did not distinguish between the warring
countries. Each was equally bound to a system of
world monopoly capitalism. It was therefore nonsense to identify "good" and "bad" nations, even
at the level of governments. For Lenin, all sides
could be nothing other than annexationist and
predatory, for this was written into the very nature
of contemporary capitalism. According to Lenin,
a key feature of capitalism was its uneven pace of
development. Even within an overall period of

expansion, there would be wide variations of growth. Nations were caught in a constant battle for favor and influence. Tensions and conflict surrounding the struggle for economic resources had become acute in the recent period as a result of the nature of monopoly capitalism. In this system the opportunities for free trade and open competition were drastically reduced. Ownership of the means of production and sources of investment had become more and more concentrated into fewer and fewer hands through the establishment of cartels and trusts (monopolies) and through the merger of bank and industrial capital into finance capital. The replacement of free competition by monopolies in the economic sphere was mirrored in international relations by the division of the globe amongst the leading capitalist states, chiefly Britain, America, France, and Germany. Just as a handful of capitalists could decide the fate of millions, so the maneuvers of a few leading nations could determine the fate of the globe.

The central role enjoyed by several nations or individuals would not produce any stability in the international economy or international relations. For Lenin, "monopoly" capitalism was its "highest" stage – and the last. It would be characterized by crisis, decay, and further wars. Again and again Lenin defines imperialism as predatory, precisely because the national economies and foreign policies were trapped in a struggle for hegemony and scarce resources. In one quote from many, Lenin insists: "The more capitalism is developed, the more strongly the shortage of raw materials is felt, the more intense the competition and the hunt for the sources of raw materials throughout the whole world, the more desperate the struggle for the acquisition of colonies."[3] It was therefore a utopian dream for Wilson to think that international affairs could be governed by a voluntary association of capitalist democracies committed to policies such as free trade. The system of free trade itself was being replaced by monopolies caught in a life-and-death fight for survival and domination. Stability is impossible because monopoly capitalism increases unevenness and contradictions in the world economy. Whatever the political form of rule in the imperialist nations, from autocracy and monarchy to democracy, the foreign policy of these

countries would be rapacious and predatory, bringing wars between temporary periods of "peace." There could be no hope that intracapitalist cooperation and peaceful negotiation would replace intracapitalist rivalry and war.

Imperialism in the period of monopoly capitalism and finance capital was not only a system full of contradictions and conflict. It was also, according to Lenin, a transitional form of economy representing the final stage of capitalism into the first stages of socialism. Although monopolies represented the socialization of the means of production, they held back progress because of private ownership. Socialized production under private ownership would decay, partly as a consequence of the disincentive to innovation brought on by monopoly, and partly because monopolies led the richest nations to accumulate capital rather than exporting goods. Only world socialism could guarantee the future development of the forces of production that had become socialized and international.

Lenin's analysis of the world economy thus revealed two conflicting tendencies. One was linked to the old world order, the other presaged the emergence of a new world order. The former was an imperialist imperative to hegemony and domination in an era of monopoly capitalism. Hence, the First World War was a war fought for economic gain by each of the warring powers. The latter was the growth of global forces of production that would decay under monopoly capitalism and demanded socialist management for their further development. Lenin's theory of imperialism was therefore in a real sense his theory of socialism, for only socialism would resolve the contradictions of monopoly capitalism. But how would humanity make the leap from monopoly capitalism to international socialism? Certainly not from above through Wilsonian diplomacy; it could only be achieved by an international revolution from below. For Lenin, "the period of imperialism is the eve of the social revolution of the proletariat."[4]

From the outbreak of the war onwards, Lenin outlined the strategy that socialists should adopt in order to bring about a revolution. Above all, revolutionary socialists should refute and rebuff any form of patriotic ideology amongst the working class. It was essential for Lenin that rev-olution should break out and be victorious in the heart of the leading capitalist nations. It was pre-cisely here, however, that the profits made from imperialist conquest had been used to bribe the upper strata of the working class. It was for this reason, for example, that British workers were susceptible to bourgeois ideology, to the notion that Britain was fighting a "war of defense" against Germany rather than a war between "two rival imperialisms, two monopolies, two groups of finance capital."[5] Social patriotism, a form of socialism that backed the national campaigns of the imperialist powers, had to be exposed as a treachery and a betrayal of the workers' genuine interests. Lenin therefore engaged in angry polemics against former comrades such as the German thinker and activist Karl Kautsky. Kautsky argued that capitalism could learn that war was inimical to its true interests and that there could be a peaceful form of "ultra-imperialism" charac-terized by international arbitration and disarma-ment. Lenin rejected Kautsky's "petty-bourgeois" suggestions in numerous articles aimed to protect the workers from such opportunism.

The tactics that a genuine revolutionary move-ment should pursue at a time of capitalism's ulti-mate crisis would be to turn the imperialist war into a civil war. Rather than die on the battlefields for the bourgeoisie, the proletariat should turn their weapons onto the ruling classes. The inten-tion would be to smash the machinery of the bourgeois state and to usher in the dictatorship of the proletariat. Given the unevenness of capi-talist development, it would be likely that the socialist revolution would occur in one or several countries taken separately. However, the coming period of history would be defined by the battle between nascent socialist states and the rest of the world. Either a world socialist federation would be born, or humanity would remain in the period of monopoly capitalism with its repression and war. In order to encourage the triumph of a world socialist federation, socialists would have to remain true to revolutionary Marxism at home and forge new international ties. For Lenin, the failure of the parties of the Second International to prevent the outbreak of war in 1914 signaled its collapse. The organization that was created to

conduct a Marxist strategy in international affairs had become fatally imbued with opportunism and must be abandoned. Revolutionary Marxists had to regroup into a new International.

The road to the Third International was long and tortuous. Its modest beginnings can be traced to meetings of the "internationalist left" in Zim-merwald and Kienthal in 1915 and 1916. The small gatherings were noted as much for their disputes as agreements. Nevertheless, they did keep an internationalist flame blazing during the imperialist slaughter. The founding congress of the Third International in Moscow in 1919 could at least celebrate one victorious revolution, and champion what was thought to be the irresistible movement of the world toward socialism, evident in the declaration of soviet forms of government in Bavaria and Hungary. The tactics of the Third International were intent on the spread of the world revolution. The formation of revolutionary communist parties was to be encouraged and sup-ported across the globe. That the international revolution would take national forms and peculi-arities was recognized, but the Communist Inter-national and its central bodies and publications were on hand to offer advice and share experience. Above all, communists everywhere should expose the lies and failings of bourgeois diplomats and their lackeys in the working-class movement and elsewhere. The Third International placed an either/or choice at the center of its program: either the international revolution and a new world order of a world socialist federation, or the failure of the revolutions to date in Russia and elsewhere and movement back to the horrors of imperialist monopoly capitalism.

The exact nature of a world socialist federation and how it would operate was not expounded in any great detail. There was no discussion of how international trade would be organized, let alone of how territorial disputes and war would be over-come. Presumably the latter would simply cease to exist. The emphasis in Lenin's vision remained on promoting revolution. The world socialist fed-eration was at best a vague phrase, used primarily for propaganda purposes. No doubt the assump-tion was that issues of detail could be sorted out amicably enough once the major task of over-throwing world capitalism had been achieved.

In any event it was perceived to be crucial that the Russian Revolution should extend beyond its national boundaries. It was hoped that the center of the international communist movement would leap from Moscow to Berlin. This points to another crucial difference between Wilson and Lenin. Wilson thought that American democracy could survive, even if other nations had non-democratic governments. Despite his belief in an interconnected world of nation-states, Wilson believed that the nation-state was secure enough to preserve its preferred form of government in isolation. Lenin, on the other hand, argued that Soviet Russia could not survive in isolation. The Russian Revolution would become secure only if it could link itself to the creation of the dictatorship of the proletariat on a world scale. It was in the vital interest of the Soviet regime to support similar revolutions in all non-socialist regimes or it would founder: it could not survive on its own, in Russia, because it would be unable to stand up to the combined opposition of the capitalist states who would be determined to crush it. Lenin's vision of a new world order was as courageous and daring as Wilson's. If anything, he aimed for a far greater – and far more radical – transformation of international affairs.

The competing visions of a new world order offered by Wilson and Lenin are sometimes seen as complementary. A recent biography of Lenin, for example, mentions that "Lenin's ideas on self-determination even supposedly affect[ed] US President Woodrow Wilson's Fourteen Points for ending the war."[6] In an autobiography of the late 1920s, Leon Trotsky points to the overlap between his booklet *War and the International* of 1914 and Wilson's "Fourteen Points." Trotsky claims that the American president made a special request for advance proofs of a current translation of Trotsky's work and was amazed to find in it the very principles that he wished to espouse.[7]

Reference to similarities in the outlooks of Wilson and Lenin and other Bolsheviks, especially on the point of national self-determination, are at best surface and shallow. Yes, both leaders talked of the desirability of national self-determination. But for Wilson this was achieved through an exercise in democracy, in which imperial and colonial countries could reach an appropriate settlement and agreement. For Lenin, national self-determination under capitalism would result not in freedom but a different, if temporarily preferable, form of oppression. For Lenin, an "independent" Poland under capitalism would be neither independent nor free, but it would be preferable to one ruled by tsarist Russia. Wilson was proud of the creation of an independent Czechoslovakia. Lenin rejected this as an invention of the imperialist "peace" conference, bearing no relation to history or to current national aspirations. What for Wilson was more or less an end in itself was for Lenin a step in the struggle to weaken imperialism and establish socialism. Lenin's conception and resolution of the issue of self-determination was thus very different than Wilson's.

The references to Wilson contained in Lenin's writings are not surprisingly biting. At the Second Congress of the Third International, for example, Lenin argues that the "'roots' of Wilson's policy lay in sanctimonious piffle, petty-bourgeois phrase-mongering, and an utter inability to understand the class struggle."[8] After identifying himself as a precursor to Wilson's "Fourteen Points," even Trotsky then turns on Wilson, referring to the American president subsequently in his autobiography as a dreamer of "anemic professorial utopias."[9] Wilson was also dismissive of Bolshevism, seeing it as a great tragedy for Russia. He was not prepared to contemplate offering official recognition to the Soviet regime, even if he did try to arrange a conference on Russia to which the Bolsheviks would be invited. Soviet historiography would remember Wilson as a man divided between words and deeds. Wilson may have talked about peace and respect, but he was an imperialist who sent American troops into Russia's civil war, ordered American forces into the regimes of Central and South America, and signed up to the rapacious peace at the conclusion of the First World War.

## Competing Visions, Public Reactions

The profound gulf between the new world orders envisioned by Wilson and Lenin was also reflected in their campaigns to promote their visions. Each set about his task in his own way, appealing to separate audiences, employing different strategies couched in discourses as wide apart as their authors' visions. Of course their strategies were also conditioned by circumstance.

Wilson was head of state of the most powerful democracy in the world. He was therefore guaranteed a hearing amongst the world press and international opinion. It was natural for Wilson to take his message to the people as in an electoral campaign, seeking approval above all at the ballot box. In this Wilson was aided by the fact that his vision did enjoy some prior support in society. Indeed, it has been argued that Wilson was not original in his vision of a new world order. The American president merely developed a synthesis from various liberal and socialist pressure groups, both at home and abroad. The most prominent peace organizations that influenced Wilson in America included the Woman's Peace Party and the Socialist Party of America. There was also a host of other peace bodies, from the League to Enforce Peace to the Christian Federal Council of Churches of Christ of America, that advocated a League of Nations. As chief spokesman for a progressive internationalism, Wilson's idealism struck a broad chord with societies suffering from the consequences of the most brutal war in history. Labor and liberal bodies across the globe welcomed Wilson's keynote addresses on the new world order. The British Labour and the French Socialist parties, for example, applauded Wilson's "Peace without Victory" speech of January 1917 to the US Senate. The League of Nations Society in Britain expanded after Wilson's enunciation of the Fourteen Points. Following Germany's eventual surrender, Wilson was greeted across Europe with massive outpourings of popular acclaim in Paris, London, Rome, and Milan. The force of "world opinion" undoubtedly gave Wilson a moral standing unequaled amongst the diplomats and heads of state of the day. It added to a sense of urgency and momentum that enabled Wilson to achieve much in establishing agreement on the need for a League of Nations.

Wilson was unable, however, to turn the popular approval and appeal of the broad outlines of his new world order into a detailed plan of action around which all nations could agree. This was evident above all in the United States. The presidential election of 1916 and the congressional elections of 1918 reflect the high and low points of Wilson's fortunes at the ballot box. Neither election was won or lost on foreign policy issues or the grand vision of a new world order. Nevertheless, the former has been interpreted as a triumph for the liberal–socialist coalition's new world outlook. The latter witnessed, if not the triumph of a Republican "American nationalism," then at least the rejection of Wilson's plea to the American electorate to endorse his Fourteen Points as the foundation of US foreign policy. Wilsonian principles then became so tarnished in the hard bargaining at the Paris Peace Conference that even some Democrats were unwilling to vote for the treaty when it was brought before the US Senate. The Senate's failure to ratify the treaty meant that Wilson's belief that America would freely enter into a League of Nations was confounded. The turn of popular opinion against Wilson seemed to be confirmed by a crushing Democratic defeat in the 1920 presidential elections, before which Wilson had successfully sought to write the League of Nations into the Democratic program.

Other than as an opportunity for propaganda, Lenin largely disregarded the process of bourgeois democracy. For him, the battle for world socialism would be won not in an electoral college but through the triumph of the proletarian revolution. The fundamental question here was, who has power over whom? Who is at the right end of a gun? The chief aim was to win over the masses to a genuine, revolutionary Marxist outlook. One of Lenin's key tasks was to distinguish parties of revolutionary social democracy from reformist socialism across the globe. This would take time, especially as numerous countries had as yet no separate communist movement. Indeed, the conditions of entry to the Third International were established only at the Second Congress in 1920. It was subsequently that, for example, a Communist Party of Great Britain was formed. One could not have a Bolshevik revolution without a Bolshevized party.

Lenin was thus involved in a politics profoundly removed from that of Wilson. As the head of a revolutionary pariah state, Lenin could not enjoy Wilson's access to the world's media and public opinion, not to mention heads of government. It was not possible for Lenin to be greeted by the millions in the major cities and capitals of Europe. It was next to impossible for delegates to make their way to Russia for the founding congress of the Communist International in 1919 that had to be composed of foreign communists already in Russia. The politics of international communism continued, in a real sense, to be the politics of the underground.

Despite his isolation, Lenin did enjoy some public relations success outside Russia. Progressive forces in western Europe, even if they did not share Lenin's vision of communism, were appalled by Allied intervention in Russia's civil war. Wilson's commitment of US troops to Russia, however half-hearted, undoubtedly helped to fragment the liberal–socialist coalition that had contributed to Wilson's triumph in the 1916 presidential elections. American involvement in the Russian civil war also confirmed the conviction of some US radicals that Wilson was also, in essentials, an imperialist. Had he not, for example, intervened extensively in Central America? There was much anti-Wilson, pro-Lenin sentiment amongst American workers who accepted the extreme left view of the League of Nations as another "imperialist club." The American Socialist Party abandoned the reformist Second International for the revolutionary Third. Sympathy from below for Bolshevism is also evident in campaigns such as the "Hands off Russia" movement in Britain. This helped to guarantee that plans for a more extensive assault on Bolshevism came to nothing. What Lenin did not achieve in his lifetime was a significant movement of popular support away from reformist socialist parties to the new communist parties. The revolts in Hungary and Bavaria that were greeted in Moscow as the outbreak of a worldwide socialist revolution were soon extinguished. In this sense the forces of bourgeois nationalism were still too strong for Lenin, as they had proved for Wilson.

## Conclusion

Lenin and Wilson had a mutual contempt for the international disorder that had produced a most destructive war. They abhorred the drive for territorial expansion and aggrandizement typical of the European empires. They championed the rights to national self-determination, the triumph of democracy, open and honest diplomacy, and the rule of a universal peace. Both wanted to establish a new world order that would protect humanity from senseless conflict and wars, a state of international affairs governed by transparency and justice in the interests of all. They differed fundamentally on the question of what a just system of international affairs would consist of and how it could be achieved.

Wilson championed a world order of liberal democratic states, united by commitments to free trade and mutual respect for the rights of others. Wilson's vision was rooted in a sense of America's special role in the world, as a model of freedom, prosperity, and a moral Christian outlook. The extension of this model was in no sense seen by Wilson to be an imperialist mission. The adoption of American-style democracy around the globe was simply in humanity's best interests, for no other society was as successful and as open as the United States. Indeed, America would not force any other country to accept American values. The best means to encourage non-democratic countries to join the progressive march of history and become a democracy was to show democracy's superiority through fair and honest competition. The means by which the world's democracies would ensure that fair and just norms and practices were upheld would be through a voluntary association, a League of Nations.

Lenin was equally convinced that the liberal democratic world order promoted by Wilson would reap only further oppression and wars. It was simply in the nature of capitalism in the imperialist epoch to seek a solution to its internal contradictions through armed conflict. There was no appeal to God from Lenin, just the application of a rigorous Marxist logic. The Bolsheviks could not rest with their victory in Russia. Not only was the building of communism in one state impossible without communism's establishment across the globe, the security of a nation seeking to build socialism could not be guaranteed if it was surrounded by capitalist states. Only the establishment of a world socialist federation could attain a just and peaceful international order. If Wilson maintained that the United States could not establish democracy in non-democratic states in the absence of a desire from within a country for democracy, Lenin insisted that it was the prime business and concern of Soviet Bolsheviks to encourage and support the development of communist revolutions in other states. Moscow thus became the home of the Third International, through which communist parties would unite to seek the best means to overthrow each and every non-socialist government.

The subsequent history of the twentieth century was to a significant extent a battle between Wilson's and Lenin's conflicting resolutions to the problem of world conflict. Given the scope and ambition of their visions, it is not surprising that in their own time each experienced disappointment and defeat. Wilson's conviction that the United States would be a willing and leading participant of a League of Nations was rejected in America. Despite Wilson's insistence that, in an interdependent world, no state could isolate itself from security issues that had to be of general concern, the United States' refusal to join the League of Nations fatally weakened this grand project. Lenin's belief that militant communism would spread across Europe did not result in a single triumphant revolution. Despite the Third International's efforts, Soviet Russia remained an anomaly in the global system for several decades. Lenin's successor would trumpet "socialism in one country," seeking to isolate the USSR from a hostile international capitalism. That their visions were not realized should not obscure the fact that Wilson and Lenin were in a fundamental sense correct. The dangers of a new global catastrophe were already apparent as the last shots of the First World War were being fired. The failure to make a new world order left the international environment easy prey to even worse disorder.

## NOTES

1  August Heckscher, ed., *The Politics of Woodrow Wilson: Selections from His Speeches and Writings* (New York: Harper, 1956), p. 248.

2  Ibid., p. 259.
3  V. I. Lenin, *Collected Works* (London: Lawrence & Wishart, 1974), vol. 22, p. 260.
4  Ibid., p. 194.
5  Ibid., p. 290.
6  Christopher Read, *Lenin* (London: Routledge, 2005), p. 115.
7  Leon Trotsky, *My Life* (Harmondsworth: Penguin, 1984), p. 249.
8  Lenin, *Collected Works*, vol. 31, p. 223.
9  Trotsky, *My Life*, p. 375.

## GUIDE TO FURTHER READING

H. W. Brands, "Woodrow Wilson and the Irony of Fate," *Diplomatic History* 28 (2004): 503–12. Offers an explanation of the failure of Wilson's vision for a new world order.

Donald E. Davis and Eugene P. Trani, *The First Cold War: The Legacy of Woodrow Wilson in US–Soviet Relations* (Columbia, MO: University of Missouri Press, 2002). A close examination of US–Soviet relations under Wilson.

Robert H. Ferrell, *Woodrow Wilson and World War I, 1917–1921* (New York: Harper & Row, 1985). Offers a useful overview of Wilson, the war, and its aftermath.

Neil Harding, *Lenin's Political Thought* (London: Macmillan, 2 vols., 1977, 1981). A detailed examination of Lenin's thinking, including on foreign policy.

August Heckscher, ed., *The Politics of Woodrow Wilson: Selections from His Speeches and Writings* (New York: Harper, 1956). Wilson in his own words.

Thomas J. Knock, *To End All Wars: Woodrow Wilson and the Quest for a New World Order* (Princeton, NJ: Princeton University Press, 1992). Focuses upon Wilson's vision for a new world order.

N. Gordon Levin, Jr., *Woodrow Wilson and World Politics: America's Response to War and Revolution* (New York: Oxford University Press, 1968). Covers the ideological dispute between Wilsonianism and Bolshevism in some detail.

Arthur S. Link, *Woodrow Wilson: Revolution, War, and Peace* (Wheeling, IL: Harlan Davidson, 1979). A compressed and lucid introduction to the main aspects of Wilson's foreign policy.

Elizabeth McKillen, "Ethnicity, Class, and Wilsonian Internationalism Reconsidered: The Mexican-American and Irish-American Immigrant Left and US Foreign Relations, 1914–1922," *Diplomatic History*

25 (2001): 553–87. Focuses upon radical opposition to Wilson's foreign policy.

Robert Service, *Lenin: A Political Life* (London: Macmillan, 3 vols., 1985, 1991, 1995). A thorough investigation of Lenin's politics, including international affairs.

James D. White, "Theories of Imperialism in Russian Socialist Thought from the First World War to the Stalin Era," *Coexistence* 30 (1993): 87–109. Contains a brilliant exposition of the broader context in which Lenin developed his theory of imperialism.

# CHAPTER TWELVE

# The Versailles System

## ERIK GOLDSTEIN

In the wake of the most destructive war in history, the victorious powers sought to construct a system that would help ensure future stability in Europe and in particular that would prevent future wars. One young British diplomat who attended the postwar Paris Peace Conference, Harold Nicolson, commented that, "We were preparing not Peace only, but Eternal Peace."[1] Germany, and the inherent power of Germany, was viewed as the primary factor in the outbreak of the First World War. The treaty of peace signed at Versailles was more than a closure on the war, it envisaged a new international order. It has been observed that "No treaty in history has produced so much comment, has been so freely criticized, and possibly so little read and understood as the treaty of peace signed at Versailles."[2] The Versailles system, as envisioned in the treaty's 440 clauses, was an elaborate web of provisions intended to constrain Germany's power in the future. The German economy would be kept hobbled by a high level of reparations payments spread over decades, German military power would be limited by strict arms control provisions and international inspections. In addition, the postwar Germany lost territory to its neighbors, some territory was placed under international administration, and any effort to unite with its kinsmen in Austria was prohibited. Also embedded in the treaty were provisions for new international organizations that would facilitate cooperation and, hopefully, reduce tensions.

In constructing this system there was certainly a high degree of intent to punish Germany for the war. This in particular was the policy of France, which sought to further enhance its security by seeing Germany weakened and even partly crippled through harsh financial impositions and partial military occupation. Britain in the first phase of the drafting of the peace treaty followed this policy to some extent, but not as harshly as did France. Part way through the process, though, Britain shifted tack, with the British government discerning that if too harsh a regime was established, there was the possibility of political instability. A poor, weak Germany would not be able to once again become a major market for British goods. The British prime minister, David Lloyd George, articulated this new policy in his Fontainebleau Memorandum, which called for a reworking of the treaty to be less harsh, and in many ways more constructive. In this approach he came more in line with the American president, Woodrow Wilson.

Wilson had been the architect of the terms on which the war had ended through the principles he had enunciated in January 1918 in his "Fourteen Points" speech, together with subsequent elaborations. Wilson's ideas were part of a general evolution of thinking on the conduct of international relations. He was himself very much a follower of the British Liberal prime minister, William Gladstone. In Europe there were groups with similar ideas, such as the New Europe group, which envisaged a political geography of Europe based more closely on national identity and the protection of minorities. Wilson in particular, but also many others involved in the drafting of the Versailles Treaty, wanted to take this opportunity to reform international and European relations. The treaty is generally seen, in retrospect, as a bad treaty, a contributory factor to the rise of Hitler and the Nazis and to the outbreak of the Second World War through imposing a Carthaginian settlement upon Germany. What often is omitted, however, is that in part what was being attempted in the treaty and subsequent technical adjustments to it, however imperfectly, was to create the fundamentals of a new international and European system. Innovations included the concepts of demilitarized zones, arms control, and verification through inspection. The need to deal with large transfer payments led to new international financial mechanisms and institutions which remain an important part of international financial relations. The concept of war crimes and their punishment through international tribunals emerges through the treaty, as does the protection of minorities, thereby initiating the protection of human rights through international agreements.

The final treaty certainly made Germany, in effect, a pariah state. With the defeat of the treaty in the US Senate, the United States withdrew in part from the system, though as events would show it remained active at key junctures in efforts to make it work. With the withdrawal of American participation France was able to push its hardline policies, which would result in a series of major crises. Germany, shunned by other countries, inevitably found a relationship with Europe's other pariah state, Soviet Russia. This, together with the failure of France's policy, led to efforts to reintegrate Germany into the international system. This effort culminated in the Locarno Pact.

The Locarno Pact of 1925 was the result of the convergence of several factors occurring simultaneously from late 1924 through early 1925. First was a renewed German attempt at international rehabilitation through an offer, initially to Britain, of a guarantee of the western European territorial status quo; second was the desire of France to reinsure its security vis-à-vis

Germany through a security pact with Britain; and third was the decision of the new Conservative government in Britain to refuse to ratify the Geneva Protocol. The latter was an effort by the League of Nations to prevent conflict through the Permanent Court of International Justice or arbitration. Failure to do so would be taken as an act of aggression by other League members. The architects of this diplomatic breakthrough were the British foreign secretary, Austen Chamberlain, the French foreign minister, Aristide Briand, and the German chancellor, Gustav Stresemann. The latter saw that the only way forward for Germany was to pursue a policy of "fulfillment," of meeting all its obligations under the Versailles Treaty. This would demonstrate that Germany was not a threat to European stability, which would in turn allow Germany to resume its place in international affairs.

At Locarno, Germany confirmed that it accepted the frontiers with France and Belgium as determined by the peace treaty. While the Versailles Treaty had, in effect, been imposed on a defeated Germany, this voluntary act helped to change the diplomatic atmosphere. Britain and Italy became guarantors of the borders, in effect protecting France and Germany from attack by each other. People at the time spoke of "the Spirit of Locarno." Stresemann in presenting the Locarno Pact to the German people observed that "Locarno may be interpreted as signifying that the States of Europe at last realize that they cannot go on making war upon each other without being involved in common ruin."[3] For their efforts Chamberlain, Briand, and Stresemann were subsequently awarded the Nobel Prize for Peace.

As a consequence of Locarno, Germany in 1926 entered the League of Nations, with a permanent seat on the Council; arms inspection teams were soon thereafter withdrawn, and the financial burden placed upon Germany by the Versailles Treaty was renegotiated. Locarno marked the rehabilitation of Germany as a full member of the international community, and marked a move to begin the amelioration of the harsher aspects of Versailles.

In 1943 President Franklin Roosevelt ordered an annotated copy of the Versailles Treaty, with the annotations meant to analyze the outcome of each of its provisions. The final document was just over one thousand pages. In assessing this complex treaty, it is possible to discern the following key components: the question of reparations, responsibility for war crimes, attempts at arms control, territorial alterations, and general innovations. In each of these areas there are developments that can still be clearly observed in the workings of the contemporary international system.

## Reparations

Unable to agree a reparations amount to be assessed on Germany, the Versailles Treaty left the sum to be determined by a Reparations Commission, which was to report on May 1, 1921. In the interval Germany was required to pay $5 billion, mostly to cover the expenses of the army of occupation. Germany claimed in January 1921 that it had made the requisite payments, and therefore was halting further payments until the final sum was decided. The Allies claimed that only $2 billion had been received and that Germany was in default, and occupied three German cities (Düsseldorf, Duisberg, and Ruhrort) and took over the collection of customs duties on the western borders of Germany. This was meant to indicate that the Allies were firm in their intention to hold Germany to the terms of the treaty.

On May 1, the Reparations Commission announced that the sum owed by Germany was $33 billion, together with a further $1.4 billion to cover the Belgian war debt. Germany was called upon to pay $250 million within twenty-five days and then $500 million annually, plus 26 percent of the value of all German exports. Germany was to issue bonds immediately to cover the $33 billion debt, at 5 percent interest, and establish a sinking fund of 1 percent. Only $12.5 million of the bonds would go into circulation immediately until additional funds became available to meet the interest and sinking fund payments.

Implementing this system almost immediately caused a crisis. Germany's industrial infrastructure was in poor repair, there was little demand for its products abroad, other than for some natural resources. As Germany began to try to meet its payments, its currency, the mark, began

to fall. By the end of 1921, the mark was worth a mere 2 percent of its prewar value. Meeting at the Cannes Conference in January 1922, the Allies allowed Germany a partial moratorium, but this only postponed the crisis.

Britain wanted to see the German economy stabilized, in part to restore it as a market for British goods, which before the war had accounted for 25 percent of British exports. The French, led by Premier Raymond Poincaré, however, sought to keep Germany weak, in part through keeping its economy weak. Over British objections France succeeded in convincing a majority of the Reparation Commission states, on December 26, 1922, to declare Germany in default. The following month, again over British and American objections, France and Belgium occupied the Ruhr, the industrial heart of Germany, with the intention of taking over the coal mines to ensure payment. The impact on the German economy was disastrous, with the government simply printing more money as the currency began to collapse in value. "In the last months before the collapse more than 30 paper mills worked at top speed and capacity to deliver notepaper to the Reichsbank, and 150 printing firms had 2,000 presses running day and night to print the Reichsbank notes."[4] In 1913, 1 mark equaled 23.8 US cents. In late November 1923, 1 US dollar equaled 4,200,000,000,000 marks. It proved to be one of the greatest inflations in history.

The Germans tried to defy the French through passive resistance, leading one American to observe: "only two people have ever been able to bring about German unity, Bismarck and Poincaré."[5] The French reacted with draconian force, deporting 140,000–150,000 Germans, imposing heavy fines and prison sentences, and confiscating property. There was also violence which left seventy Germans and twenty Allied soldiers dead. Germany was now a country with a valueless currency and with its most productive area occupied. Under these circumstances, the German government capitulated. Under a new chancellor, Gustav Stresemann, Germany ended passive resistance and sought talks with France.

The Ruhr crisis had many consequences that would ultimately lead to the weakening of the Versailles system. Anger at the French actions unleashed extremist forces, one example being an abortive attempt by the wartime hero General Ludendorff and a heretofore unknown figure, Adolf Hitler, to overthrow the Bavarian and ultimately the German government in what became known as the Beer Hall Putsch. The inflation wiped out the savings of the middle classes, helping fuel the radicalization of German politics which in turn would become a factor in the rise of the Nazis to power in 1933. In France the cost of the occupation caused inflation, weakening an already weak economy, with long-term consequences. A way out for France was provided by the United States.

The United States became concerned that the reparations system was unworkable. The Americans proposed an international committee of experts to examine the true capacity of Germany to pay. In the context of the Ruhr mess, the parties agreed to such a commission, chaired by the American Charles Dawes. The result was the Dawes Plan, which arranged for Germany to start with annual payments of $250 million a year, increasing over four years to a regular payment of $625 million, adjustable for current rates of prosperity. To help Germany get back on its feet, it would receive a loan of $200 million. At the same time, the evacuation of the Ruhr was agreed. The German currency was also stabilized at around this time by the introduction of a new currency, the rentenmark (or gold mark). Although in reality it had little to back it up, a new sense of confidence allowed it to succeed, leading economic historians to refer to it as the "miracle of the rentenmark."

The Dawes Plan did not determine the finite amount Germany would pay, given that it had still to pay the $33 billion in reparation, the Belgian debt, interest, and the cost of the armies of occupation. This led to a second commission of experts, chaired by an American businessman, Owen Young. In 1929 they produced the Young Plan, which scheduled German payments over the next thirty-seven years, with average annual payments of $512,500,000, to be followed by somewhat lower payments over the following twenty-two years. German payments therefore would cease in 1988. The final amount owed by Germany would be about one-third of that initially assessed. Payments would be made through a new International Bank of Settlement, located in Basle, Switzerland. This bank still exists as the oldest international financial institution and the primary mechanism for cooperation between central banks.

With the onset of the Great Depression in 1929, the ability of Germany to pay reparations became increasingly unlikely. The recipients of those payments in turn became unable to repay their war debts owed to the United States. In 1931 President Hoover proposed a one-year moratorium on payments of both reparations and debt repayment to the United States, a policy opposed by France, which still insisted upon the principles of the Versailles settlement. The following year at the Lausanne Conference an agreement was reached which in effect terminated German payment of reparations. Officially, Germany was not to resume repayments until it was in a position to do so. Technically, the agreement required the United States to cancel the Allied war debt, which the president felt politically unable to do. With the assumption of power by the Nazis in 1933, the debt was simply repudiated by Germany.

## War Crimes

A new concept was introduced by the Allies into the Versailles Treaty, that of war crimes. The moral right to demand full reparation for all the costs caused by the war was to be based on what came to be called the War Guilt clause, Article 231 of the treaty, in which Germany accepted responsibility for the war. Article 232 went on to acknowledge that Germany did not have adequate resources to make complete reparation, but stated that Germany would have to pay for all damage done to civilians and their property. The concept of war guilt also led the framers of the treaty to consider who were the war criminals.

By Article 227 the victors publicly charged the exiled German emperor, Wilhelm II, "for a supreme offence against international morality and the sanctity of treaties." It called for him to be tried before a court composed of judges from each of the five great Allied powers: the United States, Great Britain, France, Italy, and Japan. Article 228 provided for the trial before military tribunals of "persons accused of having committed acts in violation of the laws and customs of war." This was a dramatic development in international governance, whereby the leader of a country was named as a potential war criminal to be tried for his indicted offenses by the international community.

The German government at first refused to accept these clauses, but proposed that an international tribunal of neutrals be established to consider offenses against the laws and customs of wars by all the signatories of the treaty. While this was rejected by the Allies, the German counterproposal indicates the general acceptance of the principle of an international competence in this area. The ex-kaiser had, in any case, fled just before the end of the war to neutral Netherlands, which consistently refused efforts to extradite him to stand trial on the basis of the country's traditional protection of refugees. Interestingly, while the Dutch government refused to recognize the jurisdiction of the Allies, it did indicate that it would participate if the League of Nations in the future were to establish a mechanism to judge war crimes, which would have been defined by international agreements.

As for other individuals considered by the Allies as war criminals, Germany was provided with a list of over 900 names for extradition and trial. Germany refused to hand over these individuals. A compromise was eventually reached whereby suspects would be tried by the German Supreme Court. Eventually, forty-six test cases were presented to Germany of which only twelve resulted in prosecution and, of these, only six in convictions with light sentences.

While the effort to hold those responsible for what were considered war crimes ultimately produced a meager result, the legacy of this aspect of the Versailles system can be seen in the Nuremberg and Tokyo war crimes tribunals after the Second World War, the various United Nations war crimes tribunals, and the International Criminal Court.

## Arms Control Regimes

In the Treaty of Versailles Germany's armed forces were to be strictly limited: its army was not to exceed 100,000 soldiers, its navy was limited to six battleships, and its air force was to be abolished. The idea of limiting the number of soldiers a state could have was not new: in 1808 France had imposed upon Prussia a limit of 42,000 soldiers, while in the following year a limit of 150,000 soldiers was imposed upon Austria.[6]

No conscription was to be allowed, in order to prevent the creation of large numbers of men with military training who could then be mobilized in the event of a future conflict. Large quantities of existing munitions, arms, and war matériel were to be destroyed. An International Military Control Commission (IMCC) was established to monitor Germany's destruction of existing stockpiles of weapons and to provide ongoing inspections that established limits were not exceeded and that prohibited weapons from being manufactured. The German General Staff, which had been at the summit of German military capabilities, was abolished. All fortifications in the west were to be demolished, while those on other borders were spared in consideration of the uncertain political situation in those regions.

In addition, the left (west) bank of the Rhine was to be occupied by Allied forces, with a phased withdrawal over fifteen years at five-year intervals. It was intended that the Rhineland would ultimately be entirely and permanently demilitarized, over an area encompassing the entire left side of the Rhine plus an area extending 50 kilometers to the east. No German forces could enter this zone, nor could Germany build any fortifications in the defined area. This was intended to provide France with a security buffer against any future German threat. During the occupation, the Rhineland would be under the authority of an Inter-Allied Rhineland High Commission (IARHC).

The Treaty of Versailles was a landmark in disarmament negotiations, being the first time technical advisers assisted in the negotiations, and their imprint is to be found in the treaty's detailed limitations on all dimensions of the future German military establishment. One historian has observed that "every essential problem connected with military power and armaments was covered in detail, including the question of conscription, the size of armies and navies, the problems of communication and blockade, the use of new instrumentalities of war, such as airplanes, wireless telegraph, poison gases, and submarines, as well as the principles of executing arms limitation."[7]

Verification of the Versailles obligations was to be accomplished through Inter-Allied Control Commissions supervising the military, naval, and air clauses. By Article 213 of the Versailles Treaty Germany undertook "to give every facility for any investigation which the Council of the League of Nations, acting if need be by a majority vote, may consider necessary." The League of Nations body for dealing with such matters was its Permanent Advisory Committee for Military, Naval, and Air Questions. By a resolution on March 14, 1925, commissions of investigation, which were always to be made up of experts of three different nationalities, were given extensive rights of entry and search and full diplomatic immunity and privileges.[8] This, however, was the apogee of attempting a rigorous verification regime.[9]

Germany, under both Weimar and Nazi regimes, sought to escape the restrictions imposed upon it.[10] Verification proved to be difficult to implement. The IMCC inspectors faced continual lack of cooperation and frequent popular hostility and in 1924 some inspectors were even attacked by a mob. The inspectors' report sent to the Allied governments in February 1925 provided a list of breaches of Germany's obligations, including the militarization of the police, arms works which had not been converted to other uses, the effective reestablishment of a general staff, and military equipment retained in excess of permitted limits. This showed the difficulty "of preventing evasion of disarmament provisions, even when a Commission of Control was permanently resident in the country concerned."[11] Simultaneously with the Control Commission's investigations Germany, under the guidance of Gustav Stresemann, had adopted a policy of cooperation in foreign policy, a conciliatory approach that resulted in its rehabilitation and admittance to the League of Nations in the Locarno Pact of 1925.

In addition Germany was able to outsource some of its weapons production and development to holding companies in countries such as Turkey, Finland, and Spain. The great German armaments firm of Krupps made arrangements to develop tanks and guns in Sweden. In 1922 Germany also concluded the Treaty of Rapallo with Soviet Russia. Besides being the first country to recognize the Soviet Union diplomatically, one of the German motivations for the treaty is that it would allow training of pilots and tank crews as well as the production of armaments inside Russia and out of sight of the inspectors.

The diplomatic rapprochement of the western European powers that culminated in the Locarno Pact of 1925 saw the effective winding up of the remaining Control Commission activity. Despite the IMCC's report, there is no trace of concern in British official circles. There was a firm belief that Stresemann's, and Germany's, intentions were good. In return for Germany's willing reaffirmation of its acceptance of the borders of western Europe, the IMCC was withdrawn from Germany. In December 1926 Germany successfully negotiated the termination of the IMCC with effect from January 31, 1927, despite the fact that in the week preceding the agreement the British newspaper *The Guardian* had published an exposé of German violations.[12] In its final report, the IMCC states that "Germany had never disarmed, had never had the intention of disarming, and for seven years had done everything in her power to deceive and 'counter-control' the Commission appointed to control her disarmament."[13] Although, theoretically, the right of investigation remained, nothing further was done.

During the negotiations for the Versailles Treaty Anglo-American pressure had forced a reluctant France to agree to a statement that the arms limitations placed upon Germany were intended as the beginning of a process of arms reduction, through negotiation, across Europe. This indeed became one of the major efforts of the League of Nations. Article VIII of the Covenant of the League of Nations recognized that "the maintenance of peace requires the reduction of national armaments to the lowest point consistent with national safety," and the Council was charged to "formulate plans for such reduction." Efforts at general arms control agreements, done for the most part through the League of Nations, enjoyed some success. One example was the 1925 Geneva Protocol, which prohibited the use of poison gas and bacteriological weapons. The chief effort of the League, though, was what is commonly known as the Geneva Disarmament Conference, though its official title was the Conference for the Reduction and Limitation of Armaments. This conference was preceded by a Preparatory Commission to lay the groundwork, which first met in 1926 and completed its work in 1930. The conference itself held its first meeting in 1932, and adjourned without a result. It then spent half of 1932 trying to reconcile differences, met again for the first half of 1933, but was then adjourned for the World Economic Conference. Its last session met in October 1933 and it finally adjourned on June 11, 1934, without result. One subcommittee of the conference reportedly "used 3,750,000 sheets of typescript, 'enough to enable the Polish or Swedish delegation to walk home on a path made of League paper.'"[14]

Lord Stanhope, one of the British delegates, reported to the prime minister, Stanley Baldwin, in 1932 of progress in the disarmament talks at Geneva:

> I always thought that I was rather a master at wasting time, but I have learned that I was a mere tyro. Our committee on guns spent 2 hours in discussing whether we were justified in discussing a subject they had been talking about for 2 days, but even this was beaten by another committee who required a definition of the word "definition." The chemical warfare committee is going quite well, as the scientists forget that they are French or German or whatnot, & so discuss things on reasonable lines. I think that they will produce a unanimous report. The Air Committee still up in the air & likely to remain there. The Naval people are drafting their report which I gather will be a wishy-washy document. The Budgetary people & the "Effectives" are both deep in figures & will be old men before they produce anything at present rate of progress. The Land Committee is marvelous. There are some 55 nations, most of whom attend, & most of them bring 3 or 4 delegates. We sit under the Presidency of a Uruguayan who, as a matter of fact, is quite a good little fellow. On *every* question they divide into 3 or 4 groups or, perhaps I ought to say 4 – the Soviet for abolishing everything – their Delegate is a nasty-looking piece of work. . . . Then comes the German-Austrian-Hungarian group (with Italy) for abolishing everything they themselves are not allowed, and at the other end the French & their group who wish to abolish nothing & make constant allusions to a League Army. We & the Yanks come between the last 2 big groups. The result is 4 separate recommendations to the General Commission.[15]

Alfred Zimmern, an active and perceptive analyst of international affairs in this period, observed of the final failure of the conference that: "To expect to arrive at a Disarmament Treaty between fifty States, or between the Great Powers alone, upon a competitive basis of this kind was to expect to succeed in squaring the circle."[16]

Hitler's rise to power in Germany in 1933 was a clear threat to the Versailles system, of which he was an outspoken opponent. His actions were intended to destroy it step by step, and in the process remove what he saw as fetters to Germany's future domination of Europe. His tactic was to probe continually the willingness of the Allies to enforce Versailles. When they resisted, he would pull back, when they did not he would gain another step forward in his policy objectives. On March 8, 1936, Hitler announced the reestablishment of a German air force, which had been created in secret over a long period, many of the pilots being trained under the guise of membership of flying clubs. There being little response from the Allies a week later, on March 16, he announced that Germany would no longer be bound by the arms limitation provisions of the Versailles Treaty and announced plans to expand the 100,000-man army mandated by Versailles to 550,000. Hitler usually made these announcements at the weekend, in what became known as "Hitler's weekend surprises," catching foreign governments unprepared when officials were away from the office.

This double surprise did finally act as a catalyst for the key Allied states to meet. On April 11, at Stresa, Italy, a meeting was held between representatives of France, Great Britain, and Italy. There in fact was little appetite for confrontation with Germany. Economic problems at home, and for Italy a growing engagement with the Horn of Africa which would soon lead to its invasion of Ethiopia, prevented any real action. Instead they issued a strong denunciation of Hitler's actions and indicated that any further violations of the

Versailles system would be firmly dealt with. The Versailles system was in fact crumbling rapidly. Hitler moved to diffuse the tension by making a series of promises to uphold the concept of the Versailles system, such as it now was. He promised to respect the demilitarization of the Rhineland, Austrian independence, and the Locarno Pact. Over the next three years he would break all three pledges, but in the context of an anxious world in 1936 his promises provided false reassurance.

## Territorial Issues

The peace settlement was confronted by a number of territorial issues. President Wilson had called for frontiers to be aligned as closely as was practical with the wishes of the inhabitants. In attempting to draw new frontiers the issue of regions with a mixed population had to be confronted. Wilson insisted that the inhabitants be consulted, for which a variety of mechanisms were utilized. This was a departure from previous practice. On the German-Belgian border in two small disputed districts, special registers were set up for anyone to object to the transfer to Belgium, though few did so. On the German-Danish border, the contentious area of Schleswig was divided into two zones and the inhabitants' views obtained by a plebiscite. As a result, north Schleswig returned to Denmark and south Schleswig remained with Germany. On the German-Polish border plebiscites were held in Allenstein and Marienwerder, and Upper Silesia. As a result the former opted to remain in Germany, while Upper Silesia was partitioned. Such divisions were not without their difficulties, and there were instances of the border demarcation causing workers to be separated from their factories and miners from their mines.

By the Versailles Treaty the Saar was placed under a League of Nations commission, with a proviso that after fifteen years a plebiscite would be held to determine if the inhabitants of the Saar wished to continue the existing arrangement or to have union with either France or Germany. As compensation for the destruction of its coal mines France was given the coal mines of the Saar basin. During the period of League administration the Saar was, in effect, economically integrated with

France. During the latter part of 1934 Hitler's focus was on the run-up to the plebiscite, and in January 1935 the inhabitants of the Saar voted overwhelmingly to rejoin Germany. The Allies had to accept the result and did not interfere. This marked a turning point in Hitler's approach to foreign policy, bolstered his legitimacy as a leader, and led to him taking a more assertive line.

One of the innovations of the Versailles Treaty had been the demilitarization of the Rhineland. Most of the Rhineland had been under Allied military occupation since the end of the war. These troops were meant to remain until the Allies were fully assured of Germany's compliance with the disarmament clauses of the treaty. The area was placed under the Inter-Allied Rhine Commission, a civilian body located at Coblenz, the capital of western Prussia. After the United States rejected the Versailles Treaty it continued to send an observer to the commission until American troops were withdrawn, on the eve of the Ruhr crisis. In the aftermath of the Locarno Pact, with the "spirit of Locarno" now animating international relations, a partial evacuation of these forces began. Full evacuation was, however, not completed until 1930 when, for the first time, the Rhineland was truly demilitarized, with no military forces of any country present, and with the police force limited to 10,000.

The issue of the demilitarization of the Rhineland was one that a series of German politicians used to garner domestic support. In 1930 the British Foreign Office observed: "We have recently been struck by the sudden . . . unexpected emergence of a demand in Germany for the abolition of the demilitarisation restrictions in the Rhineland."[17] With Hitler's accession to power, the interest in remilitarizing the Rhineland escalated. Hitler made no secret of his wishes. In March 1936 German forces entered the Rhineland in direct contravention of the Versailles Treaty. Hitler, as usual, balanced this aggressive gesture with a conciliatory one. In this instance he proposed a mutual demilitarized zone on both sides of the border, and offered to sign non-aggression pacts with France and Belgium. He was aware that this offer would be impossible for France to accept, having spent heavily on the Maginot Line fortifications on its German border. To agree to

Hitler's proposal would mean having to destroy the recently completed defenses. The British government was reluctant to support France in any military action, and on the advice of the military the French government decided not to take the risk of acting alone. As a result this aspect of the Versailles Treaty's efforts at minimizing the risk of future war through a demilitarized zone failed.

By Article 80 of the Treaty of Versailles Germany was forbidden to seek a union (*Anschluss*) with Austria, except with the approval of the Council of the League of Nations. The intention of the Allies here was not to allow any increase in German strength through such a merger. At the end of the war there had been a popular move in favor of this in both countries, and the new Austrian republic at first referred to itself as German Austria while the new German constitution openly spoke of a union. The prohibition of union was reiterated in the 1922 Geneva Protocol, which provided for the economic rehabilitation of Austria. The issue was revived in the dark economic climate of 1931 when a customs union was proposed, as a way around the block of formal union. France and Czechoslovakia in particular opposed the idea, seeing it as the first step to union and therefore as a potential security threat to them. The whole matter was referred to the Permanent Court of International Justice, which ruled against the scheme, 8–7.

The interest in an Austrian–German *Anschluss* was revived when the Austrian-born Adolf Hitler came to power in Germany. One of the very first external efforts made by the new regime was to help organize an attempted Nazi takeover of the Austrian government, which would then lead to union. On July 24, 1934, the conspirators struck, seizing the Vienna radio station and broadcasting to the country, leading to revolts in several areas by organized Nazi gangs. In Vienna they had also seized the chancellor, Engelbert Dolfuss, who was shot during the takeover and slowly bled to death over the next two and a half hours. Having reached this stage in their attempted takeover but not getting any further, the conspirators telephoned Berlin for further instructions. In the end the Austrian government reasserted its authority and quashed the revolt. Italy was concerned that a German–Austrian union would seek to recover the South Tyrol, which it had gained in the peace settlement in spite of the predominance of ethnic Germans there. Mussolini now concentrated Italian forces on the border, with the implicit threat that Italy would intervene if any move toward union occurred. Hitler ordered the Austrian Nazis to stop their efforts. It was this Italian opposition to *Anschluss* that led Hitler to improve German–Italian relations, so that a way could be found to make *Anschluss* acceptable to Italy.

Hitler and Mussolini did indeed form a working relationship in many areas, the first of which concerned Austria. In October 1936 a German–Italian agreement was reached over Austria, which proved to be the beginning of the Rome–Berlin Axis. By 1938 Hitler was ready to move, provoking a crisis with Austria in March which led to the German army entering the country and its annexation to Germany. This increased Germany's population by seven million and placed Czechoslovakia in a geostrategic pincer. France failed to react, in part due to a cabinet crisis. In Britain, Prime Minister Neville Chamberlain observed in parliament that the only way to have prevented the *Anschluss* was through war, with the implication that he would continue to pursue his preferred policy of appeasement. With the *Anschluss* it was clear that the Versailles system had entirely collapsed.

The solution to the problem of the important port city of Danzig showed some of the inventiveness of the Versailles system. The city and its environs were almost entirely German, but it was also the obvious major port of the new Polish state, which otherwise would be without a usable access to the sea. The solution was to make it the Free City of Danzig, under the protection of the League of Nations. The League was represented by a high commissioner and a local parliament was established. In the event of an irresolvable dispute between the high commissioner and the Danzig government, appeal could be made to the Council of the League. In 1933 the local Nazi party took office, winning the local elections, and began agitating for annexation to Germany. It was the issue of Danzig and its relations to Poland that provided the immediate cause for the outbreak of the Second World War.

## General Innovations

The frontiers of Europe had been redrawn, so far as was practical, on grounds of ethnic national identity. It was thought that this would provide greater stability in the future by removing possible areas of friction. Given the complexity of the ethnic geography of Europe, the peace settlement inevitably left some ethnic minorities in countries dominated by other groups. To protect the rights of minorities in fourteen countries, these states were required to sign minority protection treaties. Rather than leave the protection of minorities to the domestic law of states, the peace settlement internationalized the protection by making it a treaty obligation. The treaties contained a general statement of underlying principles and specifics on the granting of citizenship, aimed at preventing discrimination against the minorities. To provide for enforcement of these commitments, members of minorities could appeal to the League of Nations, which established a special Minorities Commission. In the event of differences of opinion the newly created Permanent Court of International Justice could make a binding ruling. In their actual application during the interwar period the effectiveness of these minority protection agreements varied from state to state, but it was a significant step forward in the recognition of human rights.

A key part of the Versailles system was the League of Nations, the Covenant of which formed the first part of the peace treaty. The League was embedded at the heart of the Versailles system and was intended to provide the mechanisms that would be available to adjust aspects of the system as time passed and circumstances altered. When Hitler walked out of the League in 1934, he made clear his intention to dismantle the Versailles system. Other institutions were also established by the peace treaty, such as the Permanent Court of International Justice and the International Labor Organization, the former after the Second World War becoming the International Court of Justice.

The Versailles system also witnessed an effort to extend the concept of internationalizing Europe's main rivers used for transnational shipping. The Rhine had been made an international-ized waterway at the Congress of Vienna in 1815, and its administration placed under a Central Commission for Navigation on the Rhine. It is the oldest European organization still functioning, and in many ways laid a foundation for later European integration. The Versailles Treaty set new rules for the commission. The Netherlands, having been neutral during the war, was not directly involved with the drafting of the Versailles Treaty, but agreed to adhere to the clauses of the treaty that pertained to the Rhine. The commission set rules relating to safety, what could be transported, and issued boat masters' licenses. The Versailles Treaty now internationalized the other great European waterways, the Elbe, Oder, Nieman, and Danube, placing them under individual international commissions. Hitler repudiated the authority of the Oder commission in 1936.

A further area of innovation that was a byproduct of the peace settlement was the first effort at establishing a system for international civil aviation. The war had taught the Allies of the need for cooperation in matters relating to the new field of aviation, which had seen significant development because of the war. Building on their wartime experiences, one of the many commissions of the peace conference was an Aeronautical Commission. This in turn led to the creation of an International Commission for Air Navigation, with a secretariat in Paris. This institution was able to facilitate such things as procedures for overflight of other countries by civil aircraft. After the Second World War this body was superseded by the International Civil Aviation Organization.

## Conclusion

The Versailles Treaty and the system that evolved from it were unquestionably complex. Significant aspects were certainly meant to be punitive in regard to Germany, though many of those aspects were later ameliorated. There were also many positive developments that were envisaged through the new attention given to areas of international cooperation. While many aspects of the Versailles system failed under the extraordinary economic and political developments arising from the onset of the Great Depression in 1929 and Hitler's rise to power in 1933, many aspects of the system survived and lessons were learned that were applied to the rebuilding of the international system after 1945.

It is often argued that after the United States Senate rejected the Treaty of Versailles in 1919, the United States then pursued a policy of isolation. Though the United States opted not to participate in the League of Nations, it did not become isolationist but remained active in international affairs, as witnessed by its facilitating solutions to the reparations problem by providing the leadership of the Dawes and Young committees. It also joined the Permanent Court of International Justice in 1935, and a string of distinguished American jurists sat on its bench from 1922. The absence of the United States from the reparation commission undoubtedly contributed to the harshness of its final recommendations, and the subsequent crises caused by it, but the United States then fully engaged in helping to find solutions.

As the United States State Department later observed of the Versailles settlement, "The treaty touched in one way or another almost every question that had come on to the international scene in the period before the war which it ended, and it attempted to deal with many phases of questions newly recognized to be important."[18] The complexity of the task confronting the peacemakers in 1919 was immense. There was a need to settle the immediate issues of the war and the opportunity was simultaneously taken to address wider issues at what was the largest diplomatic gathering ever convened. The object of the system created was to bring a greater degree of governance to international relations. The system had many flaws and was perhaps a faltering step toward greater international stability, but it was an important step on the road to that goal.

## NOTES

1   Harold Nicolson, *Peacemaking 1919* (Boston: Houghton Mifflin, 1933), p. 32.

2   Department of State, *The Treaty of Versailles and After: Annotations on the Text of the Treaty* (Washington, DC: Government Printing Office, 1947), pp. iii–iv.

3   Gustav Stresemann, *Essays and Speeches on Various Subjects* (London: Butterworth, 1930), p. 238.

4   Gustav Stolper et al., *German Economy, 1870 to the Present* (New York: Harcourt, Brace, & World, 1967), p. 154.

5   Quoted in Lord d'Abernon, *An Ambassador of Peace: Lord d'Abernon's Diary* (London: Hodder & Stoughton, 1929), vol. 2, p. 167.

6   Treaty of Paris between France and Prussia, September 8, 1808; Treaty of Vienna between France and Austria, October 27, 1809.

7   Gerda Richards Crosby, *Disarmament and Peace in British Politics, 1914–1919* (Cambridge, MA: Harvard University Press, 1957), p. 104.

8   Ibid., p. 363.

9   The Aeronautical Control Commission was withdrawn in March 1922 (although an Aeronautical Committee of Guarantee functioned until August 9, 1926), the Naval Control Commission on September 30, 1924, and the Military Control Commission on January 31, 1927.

10   J. H. Morgan, *Assize of Arms: The Disarmament of Germany and Her Rearmament, 1919–1939* (New York: Oxford University Press, 1946); John Wheeler-Bennett, *The Nemesis of Power: The German Army in Politics, 1918–1945* (London: Macmillan, 1964).

11   C. A. Macartney et al., eds., *Survey of International Affairs, 1925* (Oxford: Oxford University Press, 1928), vol. 2, p. 17n.

12   The *Guardian* reports were published on December 6, 1926.

13   Hans Gatzke, *Stresemann and the Rearmament of Germany* (Baltimore: Johns Hopkins University Press, 1954), p. 51.

14   Alfred Zimmern, *The League of Nations and the Rule of Law, 1918–1935* (London: Macmillan, 2nd edn, 1939), p. 338.

15   Stanhope to Baldwin, May 25, 1932, Baldwin 118, Baldwin of Bewdley Papers, University Library, Cambridge.

16   Zimmern, *League of Nations*, p. 338.

17   *Documents on British Foreign Policy, 1919–1939* (London: HMSO, 1947), 2nd ser., vol. 1, p. 517.

18   Department of State, *Treaty of Versailles and After*, p. iv.

## GUIDE TO FURTHER READING

J. Barros, *Office Without Power: Secretary-General Sir Eric Drummond, 1919–1923* (Oxford: Oxford University Press, 1979). Good on the frustrations facing those actually charged with running the League.

R. Henig, ed., *The League of Nations* (Edinburgh: Oliver & Boyd, 1973). Useful brief history of the League and commentary on the text of the Covenant.

L. Jaffe, *The Decision to Disarm Germany: British Policy towards Post-War German Disarmament, 1914–1919* (London: Allen & Unwin, 1985). A detailed treatment of the disarmament issue.

B. Kent, *The Spoils of War: The Politics, Economics and Diplomacy of Reparations, 1918–1932* (Oxford: Clarendon Press, 1989). Another well-argued account of the politics of reparations.

L. Lloyd, *Peace Through Law: Britain and the International Court in the 1920s* (London: Royal Historical Society, 1997). Provides a good account of the early years of the new court.

W. MacDougall, *France's Rhineland Diplomacy, 1914–1924: The Last Bid for a Balance of Power in Europe* (Princeton, NJ: Princeton University Press, 1978). An account of France's attempts to structure the European system.

S. Schuker, *The End of French Predominance in Europe: The Financial Crisis of 1924 and the Adoption of the Dawes Plan* (Chapel Hill, NC: University of North Carolina Press, 1976). A compelling account of the interplay of economics and foreign policy.

M. Trachtenberg, *Reparation in World Politics: France and European Economic Diplomacy, 1916–1923* (New York: Columbia University Press, 1980). A comprehensive account of the first phase of reparations.

J. Willis, *Prologue to Nuremberg: The Politics and Diplomacy of Punishing War Criminals of the First World War* (Westport, CT: Greenwood, 1982). The best account of the origins of international war crimes tribunals.

# CHAPTER THIRTEEN

# The Legacy of the First World War

## GAYNOR JOHNSON

One of the most significant features of the peace treaties that ended the First World War was that they contained within them the rules of membership – the Covenant – of a new international organization that was intended to unite the world in a quest for permanent peace – the League of Nations. However, the failure of the League to prevent the outbreak of the Second World War led the organization to gain a negative reputation among most contemporary politicians and statesmen, a view that has influenced the opinions of subsequent generations of historians. It has been variously described as an unworkable idealist's vision and as a toothless tiger.[1] The Russians, never fans of the League, were more scathing. Lenin described it as a "band of robber nations." More tellingly, in the mid-1920s, his foreign minister's assessment was that the League was "a poorly screened coalition of victor-Powers created in order to secure their acquisitions and conquests."[2] In explaining why the League did not fulfill its potential, historians tend to fall into two camps. In different ways, both are concerned with the issue of timing and with the way in which diplomacy was conducted during the early 1920s when the apparatus of the League was first put to the test. On the one hand there are those who attribute the League's failure to an essential paradox. It was an organization that, while epitomizing the postwar vogue for diplomacy by conference, was created by statesmen whose knowledge of diplomacy was inevitably rooted in the political

order that had resulted in the outbreak of the most destructive war the world had ever known in 1914.[3] The League failed therefore because those who conceived it, shaped it, and ran it were, in terms of post-First World War diplomacy, anachronisms.[4] They were prisoners of their diplomatic heritage.

The second argument that can be made and linked to the above is that the League's architects and those charged with implementing its Covenant simply did not understand enough about how the new diplomatic order after the First World War was to work to enable them to make the League operate effectively. This argument offers a more negative spin on the same point made by historians in the last fifteen years on the wider issue of peacemaking at the end of the First World War. Alan Sharp and, more recently, Margaret Macmillan have been anxious to emphasize the enormity of the task facing the prime ministers of Britain and France, Lloyd George and Georges Clemenceau, the American president, Woodrow Wilson, and the other statesmen who gathered in Paris between January and June 1919.[5] The diplomatic map of Europe and the Middle East was so irredeemably complicated that when the guns fell silent in November 1918, constructing a lasting settlement that satisfied all of the powers involved was an impossibly difficult task. On the issue of peacemaking therefore, we are encouraged to forgive the peacemakers their trespasses. They did the best that they could under the circumstances. Unfortunately, by 1939, that had long since proved to be inadequate. But could anyone else have done better? Probably not. Yet on the question of using the League to its greatest effect – an organization which symbolized the long-term peacemaking process more than any other institution or agreement – we are still encouraged to view the peacemakers as misguided, even naïve, in hoping that it would make a difference to the way in which states would resolve disputes. But the League was actually an innovation, a genuine break with the past. That it should experience problems was consequently inevitable. Likewise, it was also likely that those charged with giving it a meaningful and effective role in postwar diplomacy would take hesitant rather than confident steps in achieving this goal. The creation of the League also had major implications for the statecraft of international diplomacy. Who was to run it? How far could League resolutions coexist alongside foreign policy decisions taken by individual member states?

## A New Approach to Diplomacy?

Another point relating to the setting of precedents is that the League epitomized a completely new and, importantly, untried approach to the conduct of diplomacy. Those charged with establishing it and asserting its authority insisted that it was through the pursuit of peace and not through recourse to war that disputes between states should be resolved. Not only did this fly in the face of more than two thousand years of recorded history when it had been accepted that humankind could take military action to assert political authority, stake claims to land, inheritance, and so on. It was also contrary to the social Darwinian view that war was part of the natural order in which the mighty would inevitably prevail over the weak. Furthermore, the "League experiment" took place during a time of unprecedented social and political upheaval. The pre-1914 map of Europe had been radically transformed by the peace treaties signed in Paris in 1919 and 1920. The old imperial power blocs of Russia, Germany, and Austria-Hungary had disappeared, while the Ottoman Empire teetered on the brink of collapse. Economically, both the victors and the vanquished searched for a way to recover from the most costly, damaging, and widespread war in human history. As other chapters in this volume illustrate, the task of reconstruction was enormous and the peace treaties, particularly the one between the Allies and Germany, were also shrouded in controversy. The imperfections of the peace settlements, whether avoidable or not, helped to provide agendas for those individuals in the 1930s, primarily on the political right, who wished to destroy all that the treaties stood for. By this time, the League, with its ethos of peace first, had little chance of survival. The remainder of this chapter charts the first steps taken by the League to find a role for itself during the 1920s.

The League was central to the peacemaking process at the end of the First World War. As already suggested, the Covenant made up the first twenty-six articles of the treaties of Versailles, Trianon, Neuilly, and Sèvres, taking their names from the Parisian suburbs where they were signed, and collectively forming the peace settlement between the Allies and the Central Powers. The connection between the conditions of membership of an organization that was intended to represent the interests of all nations and a peace settlement that was intended to foreground the priorities of a few enhanced the imprecise and often uneasy relationship the British and French governments in particular had with the League. The peace treaties were also intended to be more than the sum of their parts. The Treaty of Versailles gave the League a specific role in overseeing plebiscites (referenda) in the newly created Free City of Danzig and in the coalfields in the Saar and in Upper Silesia. In 1920, the League also oversaw a plebiscite that saw the return of Malmédy and Eupen to Belgium. In the Saar, the governing body of the League, the Council, created a governing commission which, by the time of the Franco-Belgian occupation of the Ruhr in 1923, had brought the Saarlanders into open dispute with the League and the deployment of French troops to break up strikes in the coalfields. An American diplomat was also brought in to replace the much more controversial French chair of the Saar commission, thus preventing the outbreak of violence. A similar situation arose in Danzig, with German clashes with the Polish minority persuading the Council to appoint a commissioner to draw up a constitution that would be guaranteed by the League. Within the first ten years of its existence, the Council intervened in seventeen disputes that were deemed likely to result in armed conflict and on half a dozen occasions intervened to bring hostilities to an end. Thus, during the early years of peace, the League was conceived as an arbitrator in international disputes, but, as has already been suggested, the French and British domination of the organization meant that that arbitration was far from being objective or entirely effective. What the League also failed to find was a substitute for the reliance that states had placed in the past on concluding treaties of mutual assistance. If adhered to the letter, the League should have rendered such agreements obsolete, but the British and French governments were in the vanguard of taking out diplomatic insurance measures in the form of bilateral and small-scale multilateral agreements with neighboring powers. The French, obsessed by the fear of yet another German invasion, signed a series of bilateral agreements with the successor states sandwiched between Germany and the Soviet Union, in particular Poland and Czechoslovakia. The British government was more interested in formalizing a much more imprecise and complex relationship – with France. Lloyd George and Clemenceau conducted a series of negotiations in 1919 and 1920 aimed at an Anglo-French entente, but to no avail.[6] Reaching agreement between the victorious powers thus proved to be as difficult to achieve, if not more so, as rapprochement with the defeated powers. This central, unresolved tension about how best to preserve peace thus came to be at the heart of the work of the League. It also resulted in the League failing to improve its rate of success in arbitrating disputes. But it is also true to say that the Covenant was not seriously challenged in this period to the extent to which it was in the decade that followed. For example, it was when the League considered the deployment of one of the few diplomatic weapons at its disposal, economic sanctions, in response to Mussolini's invasion of Abyssinia in 1935 that the deepest fissures within the Council became apparent. The debate about the establishment of the League was at the heart

of the uneasy relationship between the principal Allied powers during the First World War, Britain, France, and the United States.[7] However, it was given more concrete expression not by a European statesman but by one of the most liberal-minded American presidents of the twentieth century, Woodrow Wilson, in his famous "Fourteen Points." The last of these recommended that: "a general association of nations must be formed under specific covenants for the purpose of affording mutual guarantees of political independence and territorial integrity to great and small states." However, Wilson's willingness to create a leading role for the United States in the peacemaking process in 1919 was curtailed by an American Congress concerned about the financial consequences of such a policy. Wilson, a former professor and university president at Johns Hopkins and Princeton, has never lost his reputation as an idealist in international diplomacy. Even his most recent biographers view his opinions about the League as a temporary error of judgment given the shrewdness with which he judged to perfection the right moment to enter the war in April 1917. That this situation continues provides a good example of the way in which historical reputations prove difficult to change. In fact, many American businessmen shared Wilson's vision of a central role for the recovery of Europe after the First World War. Wilson's detractors should remember that the United States pursued a lucrative central role in the recovery of Europe between 1922 and 1929, albeit while remaining outside the League.

## The League and Anglo-French Relations

Throughout the 1920s, therefore, the League, despite having a membership drawn from all of the world's continents, was essentially an Anglo-French construct – or at least, a construct that was intended to place the interests of both powers at the heart of the decision-making process. It was the foreign policy considerations of the British and French governments, as the most powerful members of the Council, that influenced the way in which the League evolved and responded to international crises. The British government looked to the League to assist in the interpretation and execution of the peace settlements. The imprecise nature of British policy on both of these issues on the one hand gave the British delegation more room to maneuver than its French counterpart but also conveyed a vagueness that at different times was to frustrate the members of the British delegation and the mandarins in Whitehall. French requirements, however, were more straightforward: the League would oversee the implementation of the peace treaties, especially the Treaty of Versailles. The League was less of a debating chamber and more an organ for the enforcement of international law. It is also important to remember that the idea for an executive body – a Council – to direct League policy came from General Smuts, a former member of the War Cabinet, but also the prime minister of one of Britain's colonies, South Africa. His League Council was conceived on lines that were intended to reaffirm the authority of the European imperial powers as well as to include the world's other great powers, especially Japan and the United States, as permanent members. It was to be the Belgian government, representing a country that had been ravaged by the First World War but which lacked the same degree of influence in British circles as the French, that made the case for the inclusion of "minor" powers as non-permanent members of the Council on a rotating basis. The suggestion in this chapter will be that while British and French opinion was divided about whether the rules of membership of the League – the Covenant – were really workable, membership of the Council afforded Britain and France opportunities to influence world events in a quasi-imperialist fashion. This was an attractive proposition as both countries had suffered a demotion of status in international affairs during the First World War, which had seen the United States emerge as the world's foremost economic power. The continued absence of the United States from the League also helped to reconfirm the importance of Europe as one of the major diplomatic power bases of the world. This was a major boost to the morale of the countries of that continent for it was they that had borne the brunt of the wartime devastation and loss of life, not the United States. It was not surprising, therefore,

that the League was to be more active and more vigorously engaged in disputes that concerned the interests of the European powers, especially Britain and France, than with those that did not.

But as to the actual division of the spoils, the priority was the pivotal relationship between Britain and France. The French received the former German colonies of Togoland and Cameroon. When the Ottoman Empire was partitioned, France also took over mandates in Syria and Lebanon, territories they had been promised as early as 1916 under the Sykes–Picot Agreement. Britain's principal mandates were Palestine and Iraq.[8] The distribution of these territories was made in the style of prewar imperialism: Sykes and Picot had done little more than apply red crayon to a map. The arbitrary nature in which the territorial boundaries were drawn reflected the short-term thinking that characterized British and French policy toward their mandates. Neither government had any intention of establishing a permanent presence in their respective territories. Both were willing to defer to the Permanent Mandates Commission (PMC), a body consisting of bureaucrats expert in colonial affairs, to administer the day-to-day government of the mandates, confirming their role as status symbols to the Great Powers.[9]

Yet while the League afforded an opportunity to the British and French governments of the period to dominate the agenda in European diplomacy, they failed to define clear objectives for the organization. Wilson's description in his Fourteen Points contained only a few sentences. Apart from a broad consensus on a role to prevent war, the squabbles that ensued about the meaning of various articles of the Covenant also mirrored the inability of the peacemakers in 1919 to separate the major issues from those that were less pressing. The result was a Covenant and four peace treaties that dealt with the present but contained little real understanding of their long-term implications for postwar diplomacy. Likewise, when problems and challenges arose, the drafters of the Covenant were as reluctant to modify its contents to suit the needs of the time as they were willing to consider revisions to the peace treaties. In fact, more progress on giving precise shape to the work of the League was made by the leaders of powers closely associated with Britain and France rather than by the British and French governments themselves. Once again, Smuts's influence is important here. It was he who took the work of the PMC of the League and devised a way of categorizing, and therefore of administering, the various territories and colonies of the former Central Powers that came under Allied administration after the First World War. The priority of the British government had been the dismantlement of the Turkish and German empires and of honoring annexationist demands made by South Africa, Australia, and New Zealand. To expedite the process, Smuts's plan consisted of placing all mandates into one of three categories, depending on their level of development and the likely degree of assistance required from the supervising power. Mandates in category A were the most developed, those in C the least. In addition, the League would undertake to monitor human rights issues, especially relating to the abolition of slavery in mandates in categories B and C, as well as ensure that they agreed to disarm to a level consistent with their status and resources. Smuts's plan was used by the League to monitor the status of mandates throughout the interwar period, although the PMC did not possess the power to coerce a mandatory power to conform to what the Great Powers regarded as "acceptable" behavior. The annual reports that were produced for consideration of the PMC, chaired for much of the 1920s by the Marquis Theodoli, created a basis for dialogue between the mandatory power and local populations. It was from this basis that in the early 1920s the French were forced to adopt a less authoritarian policy in the territories ceded to them under the terms of the Sykes–Picot Agreement. Similar pressure was brought to bear on the British in Iraq and Palestine. Contrast is frequently drawn between the so-called imperialist agenda of the British and French and that of the United States. Wilson, it has been claimed, was more interested in sociological and ethnic issues than with the acquisition of mandate territories.[10] As important to the diplomatic work of the League and its role to provide "models of good practice" for mandate states to aspire to was the need for League members to be tolerant of issues of color and creed. Legislation against persecution and discrimination of religious, political, or ethnic minorities would be enshrined in the Covenant. But was it true that Wilson's agenda was more liberal than his wartime allies who were apparently more interested in politics and in engaging in the traditional practice at the end of most wars, of distributing the spoils? Firstly, American responses to upholding these values as expressed in the League Covenant went untried as the United States did not join the League or sign the peace settlements of 1919–20. Secondly, Wilson's reluctance to give concrete assurances that the United States would oversee mandate states is consistent with his more usual isolationist stance on foreign policy issues. The administration of mandates would have involved an indefinite commitment in one or more continents overseas. Wilson's nervousness can also be seen in his recognition that in order to persuade the American Senate to countenance ratification of the peace settlements and the League Covenant, some reference would have to be contained within them to the Monroe Doctrine.[11] Consequently, the United States behaved like an imperial power of the prewar era in much the same way as the British and French continued to do so. Wilson's position was further constrained by Lloyd George's desire to conclude an agreement with the United States concerning naval building. At the heart of the *raison d'être* of both Britain's and the United States' status as world powers were the size and capability of their navies. This subject was to have resonance again in 1921–2 during the Washington Naval Conference.[12]

## The German Question

Greater consensus among the Allies was reached over the involvement of Germany in the work of the League.[13] Both Clemenceau and Wilson were opposed to the immediate admission of Germany. Lloyd George was less hostile but was also less pro-League than his French and American opposite numbers. What is interesting here, however, was the response of the German government, led by Philipp Scheidemann, when it discovered that Germany was not to be one of the founder members of the League. Critical of the paradox that a body dedicated to diplomatic inclusiveness should be willing to exclude states from its membership, Scheidemann looked beyond the jealousies and resentments that dominated inter-Allied relations and Allied relations with the former Central Powers, to fix his mind on a wider picture. Like Wilson in 1917, in the spring of 1919 Scheidemann focused on the common denominator that bound rather than divided the Great Powers – their commitment to democracy. He put forward proposals for a League of Nations that was intended to demonstrate that Germany had cut the ties with its authoritarian past forever. At its heart, it contained a role for Germany that was equal to that of Britain and France. The Scheidemann proposal gained currency among those who argued that the Allies should adopt a policy of reconciliation toward Germany, that German dissatisfaction with the terms of the Treaty of Versailles could result in a rejection of democracy and an embracing of communism. Nevertheless, the plan proved to be something of a false dawn in the early 1920s as the Allies became more interested in dividing up the reparations spoils and in ensuring that it was the Anglo-French agenda that dominated the work of the League. The failure of the left to make a significant impact in Weimar politics also convinced the Allies that the likelihood of Germany drifting toward communism was not great. One of the principal issues concerning the Allies during the early 1920s was the economic regeneration of Europe after the war. The League played an important but not always consistent role in this task. As already indicated, a major concern was to shore up the embryonic democratic powers that had emerged after the collapse of the German and Austro-Hungarian empires against the peril of communist infiltration. It is tempting to view the "German Question" as being at the top of the British and French agenda, but during this period these powers were more anxious to use the League to help underpin weak currencies in such diverse places as Bulgaria, Greece, and Estonia and to organize regeneration loans to Austria (in 1922) and to Hungary (in 1924). Long-term financial assistance came to Germany in the same year as the Hungarian loan, but it was American in origin, not from the League. The Austrian and Hungarian loans were

both constructed and administered by a team led by Montagu Norman, the governor of the Bank of England, who passionately believed that a country's economic and political woes should be examined and addressed separately under the auspices of the League. The Austrian loan of 650 million gold crowns was guaranteed by a British, French, Italian, and Czech cartel on condition that the Austrian government undertook a program of fiscal reform administered by the League's Financial Committee. The arrangement remained in place until 1926. The Hungarian loan was administered in the same way. Here, the British Treasury provided more than half of the £14,200,000 loan. From his part in the creation of the Austrian and Hungarian loans, Norman hoped to establish the basis for an international banking organization that would mirror the political and diplomatic work of the League. But his efforts proved unsuccessful, primarily because the weakness of the French economy prevented France from participating fully in Norman's scheme. Subsequent critics have accused Norman of using the League as a means of promoting British economic and commercial interests.[14] By the mid-1920s, British businesses and the British government were underwriting 49.1 percent of over eighty million pounds worth of loans to eastern Europe, with the United States providing less than half that amount. That ratio changed gradually as the decade progressed. By the end of 1927, both the American and French governments were playing a much larger role, the latter reflecting not only the renewed strength of the franc but the growing diplomatic interests of France in eastern Europe through the creation of the Little Entente.

Yet despite the shaky commitment made to the League by the most powerful states of the period, its work was dominated by a number of dedicated and single-minded officials whose influence was to be felt throughout the interwar period. Indeed, when reading the official records of the debating chamber of the League, the Assembly, and of the Council, there is often a mismatch between the confused and half-hearted official policy of the governments the officials served and their own passion for the cause. What the delegations to the League seemed incapable of doing was convincing their political masters of the justness of their cause. Consequently, two parallel diplomatic universes emerged. One existed in Geneva where the League made its headquarters after 1922, where supporters of the League continued to preach to the converted, and another in the foreign ministries of the member states. At Geneva, the likes of Lord Robert Cecil, for many years head of the British delegation to the League, and Giuseppi Motta, his Swiss opposite number, who presided over the admission of Germany to the League in 1926, were revered by their peers not merely as representatives of their governments but as statesmen in their own right. In the case of Robert Cecil, it came as something of a shock when it became apparent that the British government did not view him in such a favorable light. Equally, foreign ministers who were more accustomed to discussing foreign policy within the confines of government and parliament frequently felt ill at ease when faced with the prospect of addressing the League. Both Austen Chamberlain and Aristide Briand experienced this phenomenon during the negotiations of the Treaty of Locarno in 1924–5. Others managed to bridge the gap between the work of the League and that of foreign ministries more smoothly, a gift that appears to have been in inverse proportion to the degree of influence the power wished to exert in Geneva and on whether they were permanent or non-permanent members of the Council. Notables in this category include Edvard Beneš of Czechoslovakia, Joseph Bech of Luxembourg, and Paul Hymans of Belgium, all leaders of non-permanent members of the Council.

The importance of the League as an organ of the new diplomacy was also established by men other than career politicians and diplomats. The most important was the Norwegian high commissioner for refugees, Fridtjof Nansen. A famous polar explorer before the war, Nansen epitomized the postwar *Zeitgeist* with its emphasis on utilizing the talents of all of the leading figures of the generation, irrespective of background, for the promotion of the universal quest for international peace. The most destructive war in history had created a refugee problem on an unparalleled scale, with the crisis being inevitably worse in the states that emerged from the collapsed empires of the Central Powers. A charismatic national hero, Nansen was high commissioner for refugees in Russia, a country that had been in a state of civil war since the revolutions of 1917. It was he who had persuaded the League Council of the need for such a post, which, as the decade progressed, he also combined with co-coordinator of League famine relief to the Soviet Union. Swamped by the enormity of the task, Nansen persuaded the League to set up a special commission to examine the plight of refugees in Europe. One of its innovations was the creation of the so-called "Nansen Passport" in 1922. Originally designed to ensure safe passage for Russian refugees fleeing the civil war, it was extended to include most refugee groups. By the late 1920s, the work of the refugee commission had become so extensive that it was briefly transferred to the auspices of the International Labor Organization. However, this arrangement proved unsatisfactory and by the end of the decade the refugee commission had been reconfigured in its original form.

## Minorities

Another consequence of the collapse of the great empires in eastern and central Europe at the end of the First World War and the creation of the successor states was the emergence of minority populations within these new states. In an era of unprecedented political and diplomatic upheaval, the League found a role in overseeing the preservation of the interests of these groups. The Minorities Committee was a natural bedfellow of its opposite number that dealt with the plight of refugees. Its role was to protect minority populations from persecution and other forms of discrimination, especially along the lines of race, religion, cultural background, and language. The Minorities Committee did so by persuading League members to grant official status to the minority groups living within their borders. By the middle of the 1920s, thirteen states, among them Austria, Bulgaria, Czechoslovakia, Hungary, Greece, Poland, and Turkey, had granted their minority populations protection under law against discrimination. The list continued to grow until 1932, when the British mandate of Iraq was added to the list. The work of the Minorities Committee was important because it provided one of the clearest examples of the liberal idealism of the peacemakers in 1919 and gives an indication of the enormously complex ethnic, racial, and cultural map of Europe. It demonstrated that despite all the good intentions, the new states were, in geographical terms, political compromises. And as with all compromises, they did not necessarily give complete satisfaction to any of the parties concerned. Another issue worthy of note is the type of state that was encouraged to sign minority agreements. All of them were the successor states. None was a prewar democracy, it being assumed that because they had longer liberal traditions, they did not need to be told to recognize the minority populations within their borders by anything so formal as a treaty. In the absence of the United States from the peacemaking process, the principal powers that fell into this category were, once again, Britain and France. Ironically, the failure of these powers to deal effectively with the minorities in their midst – for example, the British government's troubles with Irish nationalism as the century wore on – suggested that such faith was misplaced. Indeed, within as little as ten years of the inception of the Minorities Committee, the entire ethos of promoting the assimilation of minorities into the majority culture was challenged and overturned by a force more willing to defend its ideals than supporters of the League – National Socialism.[15] Stalin also had little compunction about subserving the needs of the individual nationalist groups that had once made up the Russian Empire to the greater good of "socialism in one country."

The work of the Minorities Committee was dependent on the good will of the majority population groups within the successor states for the effectiveness of its work. This, it seldom secured. Fiercely nationalistic, the first governments in newly created Lithuania and Turkey, for example, regarded League efforts to protect the interests of minorities as unwarranted external interference in the politics of a sovereign state. Thus we have an example of a problem alluded to earlier that was to dog the League and which continues to affect the work of its successor, the United Nations. How far should the government of a member of such organizations be able to exercise its will

domestically without external interference? Under what circumstances can it be said that intervention is justified by the international community? In order to police itself in ways other than through the use of sanctions and the threat of other forms of ostracism, the only way that the League could enforce its will brought it into direct contravention of its own Covenant. The new internationalism that the League epitomized in the 1920s required the psychological, if not the political, surrender of some form of national sovereignty in order to work effectively. That is, the member states had to be willing to allow themselves to be policed by their peers. In an era of rampant nationalism, this was unlikely to be achieved with ease.

## Early Challenges

The effectiveness of the League in the 1920s was directly linked to the strength or otherwise of the Anglo-French relationship, particularly where British and French strategic interests were at stake. The first dispute successfully resolved by the League was between Finland and Sweden in 1920 over the fate of the Åland Islands, an archipelago in the Gulf of Bothnia, an issue that was resolved through recourse to a plebiscite which went in the Swedes' favor.[16] A much less straightforward test came in the same year when the League was asked to intervene when Polish troops occupied the port of Vilna prior to a Council decision that was to determine whether the city was to remain part of Lithuania or be ceded to Poland. The issue dragged on for a further three years, during which the League failed to organize a plebiscite that produced a decisive outcome, and which compelled the Polish government to seek arbitration from the Conference of Ambassadors.[17] It was to be a further four years before the Council was able to exact a final settlement that was acceptable to the Poles and the Lithuanians, although the agreement did not raise the diplomatic temperature between the two countries significantly. Resentments and hostility continued into the late 1930s, with the League Council being asked to arbitrate. This ability of the League to paper over diplomatic cracks rather than to resolve the deeper underlying issues also contributed to its reputation as lightweight and ineffectual when considering the major issues of the day. The dispute between Poland and Lithuania over Vilna was also symptomatic of another issue that the League and few foreign ministries failed to grasp. This was the strength of nationalism in the successor states and its impact on foreign policy. Geography is as much a part of what gives a state a distinctive identity as its history, language, and culture. Disputes that in the corridors of the Quai d'Orsay and the Foreign Office may have seemed inconsequential were about much weightier issues than most of the Council members realized. This partly accounts for the failure of the League to take on such issues with greater conviction.

The issue over the future of the port of Memel on the Baltic Sea illustrated the difference in approach when the British and French did decide to intervene effectively. The dispute between the Poles and the Lithuanians erupted into violence in 1919, delaying the port's transfer to Poland as determined under the terms of the Treaty of Versailles. The French offered their support to the Polish cause, and moved that the League Council should declare Memel a Free City. When the future of Memel was finally placed before the Council in 1923, the secretary-general of the League, the British diplomat Sir Eric Drummond, conferred not with his French colleagues in the first instance but with the head of the British delegation, Cecil.[18] He, in turn, was given instructions to consult with his French and Italian opposite numbers, that is, representatives of the permanent members of the Council representing European powers. Having received assurances of French and Italian cooperation, Cecil reported back to Drummond, who authorized the creation of a special Council commission of enquiry into the future status of Memel. The result was a compromise with which neither side was completely satisfied: Poland and Lithuania were both given access to the port. The commission, chaired by the American diplomat Norman Davis, also aimed to protect the rights of the local German population. Its failure to do so was later to be used by Hitler as justification for the German Memellanders to rebel against what he saw to be a foreign occupation. The Memel dispute provides an example of cooperation between the permanent members of the League Council and of the British and French governments working in tandem. However, the willingness of the French to offer open support to the Poles illustrates the willingness of key members of the League to put their own foreign policy priorities ahead of those of the League. On this occasion there was no conflict of interests. But the Anglo-French response to the crisis over the future of Upper Silesia demonstrated the consequences when such a conflict occurred. Under the terms of the Treaty of Versailles, the future of the vast coalfield that straddled the German–Polish border in Upper Silesia was to be decided by plebiscite. The resources offered by the territory meant that its retention by Germany or its acquisition by Poland was of vital importance to the economic regeneration of both countries. The dispute over the future of Upper Silesia came to a head in 1922 after it had effectively divided the League Council. As with the dispute over Memel, the French supported the Poles, while the British and Italian governments favored Germany retaining the region. Given the diplomatic impasse within the Council, a compromise was the only course of action open to the League. In an elaborate document drawn up by the League in May 1922, two-thirds of Upper Silesia was awarded to Germany, with the remaining territory, containing the most productive mines, being ceded to Poland. The document provoked a major diplomatic row between the foreign ministries of Britain and France, which once again indicated the fragile entente between the two. Once again, the Great Powers in the League Council gave greater priority to their own diplomatic agendas instead of trying to adopt a more objective stance. On this occasion the British were just as guilty as the French as they continued to pursue their controversial policy of reconciliation with Germany – a policy that would increasingly bring them into conflict with both the French and the League. The centrality of the complex relationship between Britain and France to the effective operation of the League can be further seen in the League's handling of the Corfu incident in 1923, when Mussolini seized the island when embroiled in a dispute with Greece over Albania. The crisis that followed is important for a number of reasons. Firstly, it was the first occasion that the League had had to respond to an act of aggression instigated by a permanent member of the Council. Secondly, the crisis proved how easy it was for the mechanism of the League to be ignored or circumvented if it was in the interests of one of the permanent Council members to do so. In this case, when the Assembly decided to support the Greek position against the Italians, Mussolini's response was to insist that the dispute be settled by the Conference of Ambassadors, and not by the League. Part of the rationale for this was that the Council was stymied because the British and French could not agree on how to act.[19] The British government favored using the mechanisms of the League but shied away from making a demonstration of naval power to Mussolini, one of the possible sanctions that the Council had suggested. The French, on the other hand, embroiled in the Ruhr crisis and the run on the franc that resulted, were inclined to support Mussolini. A sticking point was the interpretation of Article 16 of the Covenant that pledged that in the event of the outbreak of hostilities, League members would go to the assistance of the victim of aggression. On this occasion it was considered inappropriate, as the dispute was not an all-out war. The willingness of key members of the Council to move the legal goal posts in this way also undermined the effectiveness of the organization in resolving international disputes. The Covenant left too much room for debate. The Corfu crisis was ultimately resolved, as the Italians had wished, by a meeting of the Council of Ambassadors in the autumn of 1923. Always more mindful of the threat of war than the British, after the crisis had been resolved the French suggested means of giving greater teeth in the use of sanctions. However, the British government, contemplating the conclusion of a multilateral security pact that would include France and Italy as well as Germany, was reluctant to enter into the debate. Consequently, the status of sanctions – the only effective redress the League had to members that did not comply with the Covenant – remained vague and imprecise. It was also consistent with the entire British approach to the conduct of relations with Europe that that should be the case. One of the central planks of British foreign policy since the days of Palmerston had

been to keep commitments to continental allies to a minimum. When commitments were deemed necessary, the British were determined to keep them as vague as possible in order to keep open the opportunity for negotiation – or to abandon them altogether if the consequence of keeping them appeared not to be in the British interest.

The problem was that during the 1920s, as has already been suggested, the British and French seldom viewed European or world diplomacy in exactly the same way. This was one reason for the deliberate vagueness of British policy toward Europe. But on the rare occasions when the British and French were in agreement, the League was able to operate to optimum effect. The key was the special rapport between the British foreign secretary, Austen Chamberlain, and his French opposite number, Aristide Briand. This was the era of the so-called "spirit of Locarno," when the British and French worked together to achieve the most significant diplomatic breakthrough in British–French–German relations since the end of the First World War, when the Treaty of Locarno was concluded in October 1925. In the same month, the League, driven by initiatives by Chamberlain and Briand, brought about a swift resolution of the conflict that had been instigated when a militarily weak Bulgaria appealed to the League for assistance after Greek troops had crossed the Bulgarian frontier in the autumn of 1925.[20] Drummond summoned a special meeting of the League Council in the French capital. Briand, then president of the Council, obtained British and Italian support for a demand that the Greeks withdraw from Bulgarian territory within a period of 60 hours. The Greeks agreed to the conditions and withdrew their forces. A special committee, chaired by Chamberlain, oversaw the ceasefire arrangements, which included the payment by the Greeks of a sum of £45,000 in reparations to the Bulgarians. This test of League resolve was viewed by contemporaries as an important example of the success the Council could achieve in resolving disputes, and of the centrality of British and French participation in the work of the League.

The League of Nations was one of the most important influences that shaped the course of 1920s diplomacy. However, like the United

Nations that was to succeed it, the League was to fall victim to the power politics of its most influential members.[21] This meant disagreement as much as agreement about the most pressing diplomatic questions of the era. The erratic and complex relationship between Britain and France was not only at the heart of understanding the strengths and weaknesses of the League but also provided a central dynamic to what eventually became an aspect of the origins of the Second World War. The League undoubtedly had weaknesses. There was a naïve optimism that a shared revulsion at the horror of war would provide sufficient impetus to hold the international community together under the terms of the Covenant. Yet, at the same time, the desire for lasting peace was a natural product of the most destructive war in history. It was inevitable that an imperfect League would emerge from what was an equally imperfect peace settlement and that, because the League represented a new approach to diplomatic problem-solving, its first efforts would prove to be less than successful. The League failed to provide the answers to the challenges posed to European stability by the fascist dictators of the 1930s, but then so did the foreign ministries of all of the democratic powers. But those who would condemn the League outright should examine the work of its successor, the United Nations. The events surrounding the start of the Second Gulf War in 2003 proved that some of the old problems relating to persuading a reluctant state to comply with international law remained. But the more successful work of the United Nations, especially in the realms of humanitarian relief and peacekeeping in the last sixty years, have shown that what the League stood for in 1919 still has relevance to international diplomacy today.

## NOTES

1   See, for example, R. Dell, *The Geneva Racket 1920–1939* (London: Robert Hale, 1941).

2   Both quotations cited in Z. Steiner, *The Lights that Failed: European International History 1919–1933* (Oxford: Oxford University Press, 2005), p. 353.

3   R. Henig, ed., *The League of Nations* (Edinburgh: Oliver & Boyd, 1973); R. Henig, "New Diplomacy and Old: Reassessment of British Conceptions of a League of Nations, 1918–1920," in *The Paris Peace Conference, 1919: Peace Without Victory?*, ed. M. Dockrill & J. Fisher (Basingstoke: Palgrave Macmillan, 2001), pp. 157–74.

4   F. S. Northedge, *The League of Nations: Its Life and Times, 1920–1946* (Leicester: Leicester University Press, 1988).

5   A. Sharp, *The Versailles Settlement: Peacemaking in Paris, 1919* (Basingstoke: Macmillan, 1991); M. Macmillan, *Peacemakers: The Paris Conference of 1919 and Its Attempt to End War* (London: John Murray, 2001).

6   A. Lentin, "*Une Aberration inexplicable*'? Clemenceau and the Abortive Anglo-French Guarantee Treaty of 1919," *Diplomacy and Statecraft* 8/2 (1997): 31–49.

7   G. W. Egerton, *Great Britain and the Creation of the League of Nations: Strategy, Politics and International Organization, 1914–1919* (Chapel Hill, NC: University of North Carolina Press, 1978).

8   The consequences of Anglo-French policy in the Middle East after the First World War are discussed in J. Fisher, *Curzon and British Imperialism in the Middle East 1916–1919* (London: Frank Cass, 1999).

9   Steiner, *Lights that Failed*, p. 105.

10  A. S. Link, *Woodrow Wilson: Revolution, War and Peace* (Arlington Heights, IL: AHM Publication Corporation, 1979).

11  The declaration made in 1823 that was intended to create an impenetrable barrier against foreign intervention in the interests of American foreign policy.

12  E. Goldstein and J. Maurer, eds., *The Washington Naval Conference, 1921–1922: Naval Rivalry, East Asian Stability and the Road to Pearl Harbor* (London: Frank Cass, 1994).

13  C. M. Kimmich, *Germany and the League of Nations* (Chicago: University of Chicago Press, 1976).

14  Steiner, *Lights that Failed*, p. 281.

15  C. Fink, "Defender of Minorities: Germany and the League of Nations, 1926–1933," *Central European History* 5/4 (1972): 330–57.

16  J. Barros, *The Aaland Islands Question: Its Settlement by the League of Nations* (New Haven, CT: Yale University Press, 1968).

17  For a comparison between the work of the League of Nations and that of the Conference of Ambassadors, see J. Heideking, "Oberster Rat – Botschafterkonferenz – Völkerbund: Drei Formen multilateraler Diplomatie nach dem Ersten Weltkrieg," *Historische Zeitschrift* 91/3 (1980): 589–630.

18 J. Barros, *Office Without Power: Secretary-General Sir Eric Drummond, 1919–1923* (Oxford: Oxford University Press, 1979).

19 P. J. Yearwood, "'Consistency with Honour': Great Britain, the League of Nations and the Corfu Crisis of 1923," *Journal of Contemporary History* 21/3 (1986): 559–71.

20 J. Barros, *The League of Nations and the Great Powers: The Greek–Bulgarian Incident, 1925* (Oxford: Oxford University Press, 1970).

21 D. Armstrong, *The Rise of the International Organization: A Short History* (New York: St. Martin's, 1982).

## GUIDE TO FURTHER READING

J. Barros, *Office Without Power: Secretary-General Sir Eric Drummond, 1919–1923* (Oxford: Oxford University Press, 1979). Good on the frustrations facing those actually charged with running the League.

R. Henig, ed., *The League of Nations* (Edinburgh: Oliver & Boyd, 1973). Useful brief history of the League and commentary on the text of the Covenant.

M. Macmillan, *Peacemakers: The Paris Conference of 1919 and Its Attempt to End War* (London: John Murray, 2001). Excellent on the diplomatic maelstrom in Paris in 1919 and the pressures facing the peacemakers and creators of the League.

F. S. Northedge, *The League of Nations: Its Life and Times, 1920–1946* (Leicester: Leicester University Press, 1988). Succinct account and good on the diplomatic heritage of the League.

A. Sharp, *The Versailles Settlement: Peacemaking in Paris, 1919* (Basingstoke: Macmillan, 1991). The clearest account of the complexities of the peace treaties and the wider issue of peacemaking after the First World War.

Z. Steiner, *The Lights that Failed: European International History 1919–1933* (Oxford: Oxford University Press, 2005). The definitive general history of the 1920s and strong on the League's role in European affairs in this period.

# Part III

## The Coming of the Second World War

# CHAPTER FOURTEEN

# Why International Finance Mattered: 1919–1939

## ROBERT D. BOYCE

The role of international finance and financiers in the events leading to the Second World War has been the subject of myths only somewhat less colorful than the myths surrounding their role before the First World War. "[T]he history of French foreign lending," Herbert Feis wrote of the pre-1914 years, was "almost equivalent to writing the history of French political sympathies, rapprochements, vague dreams of influence, alliances in arms."[1] Germany, it was said, went to war in August 1914 when French loans to Russia for the construction of strategic railways and army expansion threatened to alter the balance of power, closing Germany's window of opportunity to secure its place as a world power. Similarly, many people in America came to believe that their country went to war in 1917 to ensure repayment of the billions of dollars that its financiers had lent to the Allied powers. As for the Second World War, scarcely anyone claims that it was actually caused by international finance. Nevertheless, historians still generally accept the contemporary claim that in the 1920s and early 1930s France deliberately used its enormous financial resources to contain Germany while extending French influence elsewhere in Europe.[2] They also widely accept that during the 1920s the Republican administrations of Harding, Coolidge, and Hoover in Washington worked hand in glove with the financiers of New York, relying upon the latter's command of loanable funds to bring foreign countries into line with their foreign policy objectives, in particular the pacification of Europe and the reintegration of Germany into the world order.[3] Unfortunately, it is argued, their work remained unfinished in October 1929 when Gustav Stresemann, the German chancellor, died, and it was swiftly undone when the Wall Street crash occurred a few weeks later, bringing US foreign lending to a virtual halt. Thus, according to this version of history, international finance played little part in shaping international relations in the years immediately before Second World War, but exercised a crucial influence before that in promoting or obstructing efforts to consolidate the peace.

In a very general sense, as will be seen, the last-mentioned claim is correct. It is, however, fanciful to imagine that the major powers wielded finance as an instrument of diplomacy. The three countries in the 1920s that possessed large bank-lending capacity, namely Britain, the United States, and France, had liberal states that for the most part abstained from interfering in the activities of commercial banks or other firms and resisted the temptation to lean on their central banks for political purposes. The liberal internationalism they successfully promoted in the 1920s left the bankers largely unaccountable. The bankers in turn encouraged the spread of liberal internationalism and took advantage of the opportunities it created to increase their foreign lending and investment. The bankers of the City of London and Wall Street poured huge amounts of credit and capital into central Europe after 1923, when the main sources of instability in the region were removed. The result was new forms of dependency, implicating both the creditor and the lending countries. This situation, which the statesmen had not deliberately created and eventually found impossible to control, contributed directly to the great crisis of 1929–33, which in turn decisively shaped subsequent politics and international relations. To be sure, the Second World War could scarcely have occurred without the decision of the fascist and militarist powers to embark upon aggression. But without the coincidental breakdown of the international political system and the international economic system in 1929–33, for which international finance was largely responsible, fascism and militarism would scarcely have gained ascendancy in Europe or East Asia.

## The British-Led Revival of Liberal Internationalism

Before the Armistice had even been signed in November 1918 spokesmen for international finance from the City of London had gained the upper hand in setting Britain's postwar economic priorities.[4] Britain, the chancellor of the exchequer announced in December 1919, would return to the gold standard at the first opportunity. Officials of the Treasury and the Board of Trade, along with the governor of the Bank of England and other spokesmen for the City, meanwhile took the lead in promoting liberal internationalism or globalization as it is now commonly known. They were responsible for the creation of the League of Nations Financial Committee, the most important agency for the reestablishment of fixed exchange rates based on gold, and for the League Economic Committee, the principal agency for reversing the recent trend toward protectionism. They also played a prominent role at the Brussels conference in 1920, the Genoa conference in 1922, and the almost uninterrupted series of international conferences devoted to economic stabilization and reconstruction. The Bank of England actively encouraged cooperation among the central banks of the developed world. The City actively supported the British government's policy of pressuring France to abandon or

reduce its reparation demands on Germany. For most of Britain's statesmen and bankers, the sooner reparations were removed from Germany and its political rights were restored, the sooner tensions in Europe would be reduced and economic recovery could begin. From their standpoint, globalization and appeasement were two sides of the same coin. Since both seemed vital to Britain's prosperity, they regarded them as essential components of British foreign policy.

By April 1925 the City's strategy appeared to have been successful. Admittedly, the decision to favor an early return to the gold standard had imposed an extra burden on British industry, which slowed recovery, increased unemployment, and aggravated industrial relations. But from the City's standpoint this was a tolerable price to pay for the restoration of sterling to the gold standard. Of all the major European countries, Britain alone managed not only to return to the gold standard but also to do so at the prewar exchange rate (parity). This added to sterling's prestige, which in turn enhanced the reputation of the City of London as the world's greatest concentration of international markets. Foreign deposits were attracted to City banks, which relent them abroad. On the strength of these resources, the City took the lead over the next three years in assisting other countries to stabilize their currencies on the gold standard.

Because of the shortage of gold available for rebuilding currency reserves, the Bank of England, with the support of the League Financial Committee, encouraged other central banks to adopt a gold exchange standard, at least as a temporary expedient. On this basis, all currencies were formally defined in terms of a fixed quantity of gold, but only the major currencies such as the pound sterling and the dollar were actually backed by metallic reserves: the minor currencies were expected to rely upon sterling or dollar deposits to underpin their international exchange value. Between 1925 and 1928 central bankers from Belgium, Italy, Poland, and other countries turned first to the League Financial Committee for advice on the reforms necessary to restore their currencies to the gold standard. The main condition set by the committee was the commitment to place the operation of the gold standard in the hands of an independent central bank free from political interference. Once they were accepted, the applicant country called on the bankers of London and New York for a stabilization loan. This should have placed no strain on London since the recipient country was expected to leave much of the loan on deposit with the issuing banks in the City. The increased use of sterling was also in theory expected to favor British industry, which stood to gain export orders from the countries back on gold. Before the end of 1928 a broad area of currency stability had been created, including Britain and the empire, the United States, and nearly all of western Europe, which together were responsible for over 80 percent of the world's trade.

Meanwhile the City contributed to pressure on France to appease Germany. In 1921 Britain had joined France in occupying several towns of the Ruhr area, when Germany failed to meet its reparation payments. But in January 1923 Britain broke with France over its decision to occupy the Ruhr after Germany again defaulted on its payments. Reparations were a heavy burden on Germany, both as a financial charge that had to be covered by taxes and as a charge on Germany's balance of payments because reparations had to be paid across the foreign exchanges to France, Britain, Belgium, Italy, and other smaller creditors.[5] Germany claimed it could not afford to pay reparations because of its international payments deficit, and accused France of driving it to destruction. But in fact Germany had made little effort to pay reparations. It refused to levy the necessary taxes, and far from accumulating the foreign exchange required for their payment by collecting some of the overseas earnings of German exporters, it allowed them to leave their earnings abroad. The British government, despite its interest in reparations and appeals from France, refused to cooperate in identifying and sequestering German foreign earnings. The City, the principal beneficiary of this deliberate negligence, supported the government. Largely because of this leakage of foreign earnings, Germany's balance of payments remained weak, domestic inflation accelerated, and the mark lost most of its value before French troops had even entered the Ruhr. Nevertheless when France, frustrated by Germany's – and Britain's – non-cooperation, sent troops into the

Ruhr, City bankers joined the government in condemning French action. Repeating the highly tendentious German claim that Germany could not possibly meet its reparation obligations, they warned that France's attempt to extract reparations at the point of a bayonet was forcing Germany to print money, which was leading to hyperinflation. If France continued its occupation, it would destroy the German economy and bring down the whole of Europe with it. In the words of Montagu Norman, governor of the Bank of England, France's policy was "madness."[6]

By the winter of 1923 British statesmen found themselves in a strong position. The German government's support of passive resistance to the French occupation had accelerated the printing of money and the collapse of confidence in the mark. Exhausted, it abandoned passive resistance in September and indicated its readiness to honor its commitment to pay reparations. Payments, however, were impossible until confidence in the German currency was restored. Since this required a large hard currency loan, which only the City of London and New York could provide, the cooperation of British and American bankers was essential. The terms they set for their support ensured that France could not again impose sanctions on Germany for the non-payment of reparations without British and American approval.

The diplomatic conference in London in 1924, which ended the Ruhr occupation, decisively affected the course of interwar history. Since much of the war had been fought on French soil, France faced a much larger bill for reconstruction than Germany. It therefore regarded reparations as a crucial means of equalizing the cost of the war. Without reparation payments, French industry would face much higher tax burdens than German industry, which would gain a competitive advantage. As a result of the London conference, however, France lost its grip on reparations. Hitherto the reparations commission took its decisions by majority vote, with France able to count on Belgium and Italy joining in opposition to Britain; henceforth each member wielded a veto, and moreover its membership now included an American with close links to the banking interest. The lesson from the Ruhr crisis for France was in any case that Britain and the United States would not support direct action against Germany, if the latter again defaulted on its obligations. This encouraged Germany to pursue revision of the Versailles Treaty, which seemed likely to find favor among the English-speaking powers and leave France further isolated. Naturally this played into the hands of German nationalists.

British statesmen nevertheless persuaded themselves that their influence upon European relations was benign. Largely through their efforts, with the backing of British capital, inflation in central Europe was tamed. This in turn facilitated the provision of large-scale American loans and credits. In the immediate aftermath of the war, American financial interests concentrated their activity on Canada and Latin America while the situation in Europe remained obscure, but they returned on a large scale once the prospect emerged of a settlement of the Ruhr crisis. This helped to sustain Europe's economic recovery. Unemployment fell to tolerable levels in central Europe and vanished altogether in France. With the return of financial stability and economic prosperity, political extremism also declined. Whereas violent upheavals had occurred in Italy after the war, in Germany periodically until 1923, and in France in the first half of 1926, the next four years in Europe and most of the world were comparatively quiet.

Once the major trading currencies were reestablished on the gold standard, proponents of liberal internationalism turned toward trade liberalization. At the end of the war many countries had introduced quantitative trade controls, such as import and export quotas, embargoes, and licensing schemes, as a means of protecting their meager gold and foreign exchange reserves. Regarded by most economists as excessively rigid and arbitrary restraints on trade, they now became the object of a sustained campaign for their suppression. Meanwhile, at the first League of Nations-sponsored world economic conference, held in Geneva in May 1927, efforts got under way to reverse tariff protectionism, which had intensified after the war as well as becoming more extensive with the creation of seven additional countries in Europe and 12,500 miles of frontiers. By 1929 most countries had abandoned quantitative trade controls. Nearly all countries had also returned to

the most-favored-nation principle in its unconditional form, while the upward trend in tariff levels had been halted and modestly reduced.[7] Here, too, liberal internationalism or globalization appeared successful. As a result, the English-language press tended to treat the leading central bankers like supermen and reported the activities of international bankers in respectful terms.

## Liberal Internationalism: A Source of Global Instability

But as at least some observers appreciated, liberal internationalism, while contributing to economic recovery since the war, had exposed the world to increasing risks of crisis and breakdown. The Bank of England had encouraged the general adoption of the gold exchange standard, which no doubt had hastened the stabilization of currencies and expansion of international commerce. But Britain had overreached itself in returning to gold at sterling's prewar parity of $4.86. As a result, its gold reserves were inadequate to underpin sterling, let alone the other currencies backed by sterling deposits. The smaller countries, jealous of their independence, were in any case reluctant to hold their currency reserves in sterling. Choosing to forgo the interest earned on balances held in London or other centers, they took the earliest opportunity to dispose of their sterling and dollars in order to acquire gold backing for their currency. This added to the precariousness of sterling in 1928–9, just when other sources of pressure appeared. The Bank of England was forced to raise its discount rate to levels hitherto practically unknown in peacetime. It also reintroduced informal restrictions on capital exports, much to the frustration of the City, where it had been assumed that the return to gold would make all such restrictions unnecessary.

The decline in Britain's staple export industries, such as shipbuilding, heavy engineering, and cotton and woolen textiles, together with an overvalued exchange rate, had worsened the country's balance of international payments, leaving barely half as much as before the war for relending abroad. While City bankers tended to blame the trade unions and employers for industry's loss of competitiveness, trade unionists and manufacturers grew increasingly impatient with the City's emphasis upon overseas lending and apparent indifference to the domestic economy. No longer were they prepared to endure dear and tight money as the price of the City's international leadership. In some sectors of industry such as steelmaking, light engineering, woolen textiles, and farming, demands for an end to free trade mounted. The Conservative government led by Stanley Baldwin drew back from further support for international trade liberalization. While too divided to introduce a radical change of commercial policy, it was not prepared to antagonize its Midlands, northern, and rural supporters by siding with the City on free trade.[8]

Even more disturbing was the incapacity of America's international bankers to follow through on their policy. By 1929 they had issued $3.05 billion in loans and credits to Europe, up nearly 80 percent since 1923. Total American portfolio lending by the end of the decade reached $7,340 million, or over 60 percent of the world's total; and of this total, 42 percent was to Europe. American commitments in Germany alone exceeded $1 billion.[9] But outside the eastern seaboard, Americans continued to regard Wall Street with suspicion. They tended to regard it as a sophisticated, cosmopolitan place that wielded excessive power over the lives of ordinary Americans, a place too closely linked to Europe and too remote from the small-town values that underpinned the rest of the country.[10] Despite the crucial role that New York played in financing the recent war, or perhaps because of it, this view became stronger in the 1920s, when the Republican party regained control of both the White House and Congress. Warren G. Harding, the former newspaper publisher from rural Ohio who succeeded Woodrow Wilson to the White House in March 1921, broadly shared it. His successor in 1923, Calvin Coolidge from rural Vermont, made almost no reference to international banking or finance. But he expressed open indifference to international affairs and remained content to yield to the isolationist mood in Congress. Under their leadership, US economic policy was shaped by the outlook of small-town America and took almost no account of the country's new status as an international creditor power.

With a huge international balance of payments surplus, the appropriate policy for the United States would have been to open its markets to foreign imports, to reduce or forgive claims on its wartime debtors, to work closely with Wall Street, and to promote the development of international institutions so as to facilitate the adjustment of international payments. It did none of these things. Instead, it demanded full repayment of war debts, offering concessions only on the interest payments. Under Harding, it introduced the Fordney-McCumber tariff, turning the clock back almost to the record levels of protectionism of the nineteenth century when America was still a net debtor to the rest of the world. Once Herbert Hoover entered the White House in March 1929, relations between Washington and Wall Street became distinctly strained. Hoover's aggressive nationalism, demonstrated in his role as secretary of commerce from 1921, and his intense isolationism had already become a source of concern to New York bankers before he took office. J. P. Morgan, Jr., the most powerful figure on Wall Street, had sought to block Hoover's nomination as the Republican presidential candidate in 1928.[11] In 1929, George Harrison of the New York Fed found himself unwelcome at the White House.[12] Hoover dismissed Harrison's predecessor, Benjamin Strong, as "a mental annex to Europe."[13] So suspicious was he of Europe that he refused to allow the Fed to have any contact with the Bank for International Settlements when it was created in 1929–30. After the world depression began, he turned for help to bankers from the interior of the country, as he put it, "the solid men, not the Wall Street crowd."[14]

Thus by the late 1920s a dangerous situation had arisen. The United States now occupied the center of the world's trade and payments system, earning a huge surplus from merchandise trade and financial services which it offset through the accumulation of claims on foreign countries in the form of short-term bank credits and direct as well as portfolio investments. This was not sustainable since the foreign countries could not bear the steadily increasing liability involved. But how long it continued depended largely upon the ease with which the rest of the world obtained dollars to cover its increasing American claims. Leading

New York bankers grew aware of the predicament as early as 1927. In June of that year, Strong of the New York Fed hosted a conference of leading central bankers to address the problem of financial imbalances and means of easing the pressure on the Bank of England, which was most exposed to its consequences. Briefly, Strong encouraged the hope that US monetary and financial policy would take account of the requirements of the international payments system. But when the effect of his discount rate reduction appeared to be a shift in American bank lending from productive industry toward speculation on the stock markets of New York, the regional bankers on the Federal Reserve Board sitting in Washington demanded a tighter credit policy. Ironically, the introduction of tight money did nothing to halt the stock market speculation, but it severely affected construction activity in America, followed by other sectors of industry.

European central bankers warned Harrison in New York when the bull market raging in the stock markets in 1928 reversed the growth in US foreign lending and drew in large amounts of short-term funds from overseas. But there was now little he could do, since the Coolidge administration in Washington remained indifferent to the international consequences. So far from assisting foreign countries to meet their dollar obligations, it left Hoover to continue his aggressive promotion of US exports and jealously defend America's most-favored-nation rights abroad. Despite the European powers' decision in 1928 to revise reparation demands on Germany, the administration made no move to reduce or abandon US war debt claims. Nor was it prepared to lower the American tariff. Indeed, from the moment Hoover won the presidential election in November 1928, increased tariff protection became a near certainty.

During the election campaign, Hoover had repeatedly promised to defend "the American system of rugged individualism" against the "European philosophy of diametrically opposed doctrines – doctrines of paternalism and state socialism," through greater protection and the avoidance of European entanglements. In April 1929 he convened a special session of Congress, which, as expected, proceeded to draft a tariff bill

with substantially higher duties on agricultural and manufactured imports. The bill cleared all the legislative hurdles only in March 1930 when Hoover finally signed it into law. But the outcome of the process was already clear by late May 1929, if not well before. Foreign trading nations, already facing an acute shortage of dollars, therefore did not wait to react until the tariff was adopted. With the sole exception of Britain, they protested formally to Washington in the summer of 1929. When this brought no result, they took steps to raise their own protective barriers. Before the war, commercial treaties of ten to twelve years were not uncommon. But in the uncertain conditions after the First World War, all but 27 of 180 treaties adopted were terminable within one year. Foreign reactions to American tariff revision were therefore swift, wide-ranging, and severely damaging to international trade. By the spring of 1930, the disruption of international credit and capital flows together with the sudden and massive upward lurch in protectionism had turned a normal cyclical economic downturn into a severe depression, bringing mass unemployment, social distress, and an upsurge in political extremism in Germany, Japan, and elsewhere. The bankers' liberal internationalism, without the backing of their governments, had resulted in cataclysmic disaster.

## International Finance and the Undermining of French Security Interests

Before the First World War, French banks had engaged in large-scale foreign lending to Russia and other allies. But heavy losses on defaulted loans discouraged the banks from reentering the market after the war. France in any case was in no condition at this time to export capital. However, the economy recovered swiftly, and once Raymond Poincaré took charge of the government and restored confidence in the franc in July 1926, capital that had previously fled the country returned, augmenting the surpluses on current account that were available for lending. Over the next few years, French commercial banks cautiously resumed foreign lending. But while the French government talked of transforming Paris into an international financial center that rivaled the City of London, and the Bank of France took responsibility for creating an acceptance market in 1929, actual French financial activity was marked by caution. Commercial lending was modest, and the Ministry of Finance, whose authority was required to list foreign bonds and stocks on the Paris Bourse, frequently refused listings in order to maintain domestic liquidity to facilitate the financing of domestic projects.[15]

In London, however, France once more acquired the reputation of exploiting its financial power for aggressive, imperialist ends. From December 1926 the Bank of France had rapidly accumulated balances of sterling and other foreign exchange in an effort to hold the franc at a new competitive rate of Ff.124 = £1, amidst persistent rumors that it might eventually be restored to its former gold parity of Ff.25.22 = £1. This led to intense friction with the Bank of England, when the Bank of France sought to discourage speculation in the franc by demanding payment in gold for £20 million of its sterling balances. Though the Bank of France agreed to a compromise, its possession of massive sterling balances left British bankers nervous and suspicious of French goodwill.

The impression of French financial power was soon reinforced when the Bank of France signaled its determination to play a prominent role in the stabilization of the Polish zloty and take charge of the international credit operations required for the stabilization of the Romanian and Yugoslav currencies. British merchant banks, actively supported by the Bank of England, had planned to supply the latter countries with large reconstruction loans, some of which were earmarked for military procurement and infrastructure projects, and promised to yield valuable commissions. The transfer of control to Paris fueled resentment in London and added to France's image as an illiberal state that mixed politics, foreign affairs, and finance. In this case, there was some truth in the accusations. But from Paris, the Bank of France seemed merely to be limiting the damage already caused by the country's postwar difficulties. As French observers saw it, the cost of reconstructing the vast swathe of their territory mauled by the battles of the recent war, which France bore alone in the absence of large-scale reparation payments,

had forced the country to stand aside while British and American bankers drew one European country after another into their control. Now that the franc was strong again, France insisted upon a leading role in the currency stabilizations for Poland, Romania, and Yugoslavia because these countries formed a part of its network of defensive alliances. Far from an expansion of influence, it amounted to a means of limiting France's losses. Nevertheless, from this time onwards, the British press was full of stories of French financial imperialism and downright aggression.

With cracks appearing in the international payments system in the latter half of 1927, France came under pressure from British and American bankers working through the reparations committee to enter negotiations for a final settlement of German reparations. France agreed, hoping that a definitive payments schedule might form the security for a large international loan, enabling France to receive a lump sum payment of its claims. Given France's limited grip on reparations, advanced payment of even a reduced total seemed attractive to Paris. By the spring of 1929, experts reached agreement on a new, supposedly definitive, schedule of reparation payments, and a diplomatic conference was scheduled for The Hague in August 1929 to approve the arrangements. But, in the meantime, the British general election on June 1 returned the Labour party to office. Shortly afterwards, Labour leaders announced their intention of withdrawing British troops, if necessary unilaterally, from the last of the three occupation zones in the Rhineland before the end of the year. The French government, anxious for Germany's cooperation on reparations, had little choice but to join in this new concession.

At almost the same moment, sterling fell below gold export point vis-à-vis the franc, causing gold to leave the Bank of England for Paris. This prompted angry accusations in the British press that French authorities were using their financial power to force Britain into political concessions in advance of the Hague conference.[16] Officials in the Treasury harbored similar suspicions.[17] The accusations were wholly unfounded. In fact, sterling was weak against not only the French franc but other currencies as well, including the Dutch florin, the Swiss franc, and the US dollar. The pressure derived from the speculative bubble on the New York stock exchanges, which was drawing short-term funds from Europe, including London. French officials at this time were hopeful of a successful outcome at The Hague and saw no reason to pressure their British counterparts. Deep-seated prejudice in Britain and anxiety over the fate of sterling, however, revived the specter of French financial power, which was to reappear regularly over the next few years.

The Wall Street crash, which began on "Black Thursday," October 24, 1929, is commonly assumed to have triggered the events that brought on the world depression. Ironically, bursting the bubble of securities inflation was almost certainly beneficial for the world economy. The decline in share values reduced the nominal wealth of the roughly half-million substantial American investors or speculators and the ten million small investors affected by perhaps $30 billion (£6.2 billion).[18] But over the winter of 1929–30 the New York Stock Exchange, the largest of the markets, declined only by a third, down to the level it had been in April 1928, leaving all the previous gains since the start of the bull market in August 1921. At the same time the crash reversed the inflow of short-term funds from Europe, which saved the gold standard from almost certain collapse and enabled central banks in London and elsewhere to reduce interest rates from the penal levels they had reached before October 1929. The great dislocation had been caused not by the crash but by the vast, unchecked boom in stock market values that preceded it. The funds it attracted and the efforts to contain it had already disrupted capital flows and caused a marked slowdown in economic activity in the United States as well as Germany, which had remained acutely dependent upon foreign capital ever since the hyperinflation of 1923 had destroyed the capital base of its banking system. It was the fragile and unregulated international trade and payments system that then transformed this dislocation into a major slump.

Bankers in the major financial centers were little more than spectators to this unfolding catastrophe. British observers nevertheless largely blamed it upon France. When gold flowed almost daily from London to Paris in the summer and autumn of 1930, politicians and journalists accused the French authorities of a nefarious plot to suborn Britain to their continental ambitions.[19] In the spring of 1931 they were sure that France attempted to weaken Germany by deliberately withdrawing short-term loans. Neither charge bore scrutiny. French statesmen knew that Germany had substantially increased its military spending since 1924, and were deeply cynical about all German politicians. Yet in the aftermath of the September 1930 German election, in which the Communists and Nazis made large gains, the Bank of France, at the request of the Quai d'Orsay, actually discouraged French banks from withdrawing short-term funds and early in 1931 it urged them to participate in an issue of Reichsbahn preference shares.[20] It is not clear that government exhortations had any effect on the bankers, but French commercial acceptance credits and deposits in German banks, never large, declined only slightly by the spring of 1931 and were still approximately Ff.2,000 million (£16.3 million) as late as June of that year.[21] As for the gold movements from London to Paris, French political leaders were acutely embarrassed by them. Almost certainly at their instigation, Clément Moret, the governor of the Bank of France, volunteered to assist Norman with a loan or other means. In January 1931, Aristide Briand, the foreign minister, pressured Moret into a reduction in French interest rates. Presently, Briand also saw to it that the Paris Bourse listed several additional British shares for trading.[22] Meanwhile informal conversations on monetary and financial policy took place between British and French Treasury experts. Although the results were negligible, they confirmed that differences between them were essentially technical and not politically inspired. Nonetheless, misapprehensions about finance increased Britain's reluctance to side with France in its efforts to maintain the European status quo.

## The Ineffectualness of Financial Diplomacy

In the spring of 1931 several occasions arose when France did in fact seek to use its massive financial resources to reinforce aspects of its foreign policy. The first such occasion occurred in late May, following the revelation of plans for an Austro-German customs union two months earlier, which French statesmen correctly assumed to be the first step toward a political *Anschluss*. Since *Anschluss* had been made illegal under the Treaty of Saint-Germain and other international treaties, French authorities also regarded the customs union scheme as illegal and were determined to block it. They therefore withheld approval of a commercial credit to the Austrian National Bank when it faced a serious run on the schilling, insisting that the Austrian government should first give a public undertaking to abandon the customs union scheme and a private undertaking to take no further steps to abandon national sovereignty. British statesmen, fearing that the collapse of the Austrian schilling might bring down the whole of central Europe, were furious that France should attach political demands to its offer of help, and Norman of the Bank of England hastily extended a short-term credit to the Austrian National Bank rather than see it succumb to French "blackmail."[23] But from the French standpoint, it was the Austrians who had damaged confidence in the schilling by their decision to embark upon secret negotiations for an illegal project with Germany. In the circumstances, their own conditions for financial support were a necessary basis for the restoration of confidence.

The second and third occasions for exercising influence through finance came in June 1931, when the flight of hot money shifted from Austria to Germany and threatened to drive the mark off the gold standard. Leading central bankers responded to an appeal for help from Hans Luther, governor of the Reichsbank, by organizing a large credit to enable him to meet the speculative attacks. Moret, with the approval of the French government, provided $25 million of the $100 million credit to demonstrate France's desire to collaborate with the English-speaking powers as much as its goodwill toward Germany. A fortnight later, Pierre Laval, the president of the council, and Pierre-Etienne Flandin, the minister of finance, affirmed their willingness to contribute to a large long-term loan to Germany, in return for Germany's commitment to adhere to the postwar

political settlement. But neither the British Labour government nor the Hoover administration was prepared to contemplate support for such a loan. In their view, the spreading financial crisis demanded concessions from France to appease Germany: the interests of the international financial markets came before France's security interests. Convinced that Germany was the victim and France the oppressor, they obstructed French efforts at bilateral negotiations with Germany in order to protect it from French financial pressure. Yet the only solution they could offer was the suspension of reparations.

The fourth occasion arose in late July, when the financial contagion spread to the City of London, threatening to drive sterling off the gold standard. Moret immediately responded to a request for help from the Bank of England by organizing a credit with the leading banks in Paris and putting up Ff.3,100 million ($121,520,000) himself. A month later he organized a second credit of Ff.5,000 million ($196 million) for the account of the British Treasury. Moret, who had repeatedly urged Bank of England officials during the summer to raise a large long-term loan in Paris, renewed his offer of help when the latter credit ran down. French political leaders, so far from undercutting sterling by financial manipulation, hoped to use the Bank of France's financial resources to strengthen the entente.[24]

Unfortunately for France, none of its initiatives helped in the least to strengthen its security or improve its strategic position. In Germany, the central bank credit held off a financial collapse, but did nothing to dampen demands for treaty revision, which was supported by all the political forces from Brüning's Catholic Centrist party to Hitler's National Socialists. Signs of division between France and Britain over the customs union scheme and the treatment of Austria almost inevitably lent further encouragement to the revisionists.

President Hoover's proposal for a comprehensive one-year intergovernmental debt moratorium added to France's isolation. Announced without warning on 20 June, French officials regarded it cynically as a means of protecting the approximately £250 million in short-term funds that British and American bankers had tied up in

Germany and elsewhere in central Europe at their expense, since France was entitled to 52 percent of reparations and would bear the main cost and risks of the moratorium. Nevertheless, the French were prepared to accept it, so long as the final reparation settlement, adopted at the Hague conference, was not abandoned. This seemed essential to avoid an opening for German demands for further revision. They therefore insisted that the so-called unconditional element of German reparations was paid into a blocked account at the BIS, as provided for in the settlement. A bitter row ensued with British and American leaders, who accused France of being selfish and irresponsible, before a settlement was reached. But the seventeen-day delay occasioned by the additional negotiations brought accusations from Britain and the United States that France had dissipated the tonic effect of Hoover's proposal.[25]

Nor did the French credits to Britain earn France any goodwill from its former ally. The view that France was responsible for sterling's weakness was expressed by Sir Clive Wigram, private secretary to the king, who observed: "Attempts to embarrass us and destroy confidence in our stability as the financial centre of the world, and in the London Bill, were unworthy of a nation whom we pulled out of the fire such a short time ago."[26] Indeed, so common was this view that a British cabinet minister traveled on his own to Paris to interview Laval and Flandin in order to discover the truth.[27] Albeit completely unfounded, the suspicions caused British bankers and statesmen to hesitate before accepting French offers of financial help. They proceeded only after ensuring that matching credits would be raised in New York. They immediately called in the commercial part of the French credit out of suspicion that the participating French banks would exploit their knowledge of how quickly it was being used up. Several weeks later, after exhausting most of the Treasury credit in a vain attempt to prop up the pound, British authorities disregarded Moret's offer of a further loan and on September 21 abandoned the gold standard, leaving sterling to depreciate by over 30 percent before the end of the year.

The collapse of sterling was due to several factors: suspicions about the vulnerability of the City on account of its huge short-term liabilities

in central Europe, much of which had become frozen in the summer; hot money movements, which favored London during the financial crisis in central Europe, then abandoned London when doubts about sterling surfaced; and the grave deterioration of Britain's balance of payments where the perennial deficit in commodity trade was no longer covered by a healthy surplus in services. French monetary and financial policy played almost no part in these problems. Yet when sterling left the gold standard, British observers expressed their dismay and humiliation by lashing out at France.[28] The Bank of France lost no less than Ff.12.2 billion (£21.6 million) on its credits to Britain and its large sterling deposits when the pound was allowed to depreciate. This was greater than its total paid-up capital, thus technically bankrupting the Bank and obliging the French government to secure parliamentary approval to compensate it for its losses. As Moret pointed out to Bank of England officials, the Bank of France's hands had been tied since, as the Bank of England's agent in Paris, it could not properly have sold sterling in the midst of the crisis. The British officials reluctantly apologized for his embarrassment, but would not even consider compensation.

Between 1924 and 1932 French commercial banks arranged loans totaling approximately Ff.17.6 billion (£206 million) for the countries of central and east central Europe, excluding Germany.[29] Some of them, including participation in the £7 million loan to Hungary in July 1931, were undertaken at the request of the French government.[30] British observers regarded such loans as a form of French imperialism. But the French themselves looked upon them as serving the opposite purpose, namely enabling the recipient countries to resist the pull of German markets and political influence. The pacifist character of France's policy appears evident in its economic and financial relations with Germany. In September 1931 Laval and Briand visited Berlin, where they formally inaugurated a joint committee for economic cooperation. Their hopes of developing a constructive dialogue and a mutual interest in peace were met by cynicism and hostility from the German side. Nevertheless, they demonstrated      their      commitment      to      good relations by continuing to authorize the renewal of the central bank credit to the Reichsbank until two months after Hitler took power. These were scarcely the actions of an aggressive, imperialist power bent on Germany's destruction.

## International Finance and the Collapse of Allied Solidarity

In January 1932 Chancellor Brüning announced that Germany would not resume reparation payments when the Hoover moratorium ended. French authorities were angered by his statement, which was tantamount to repudiation of Germany's treaty commitment, and threatened to have the Bank of France withdraw from the central bank credit to the Reichsbank. They agreed nevertheless to attend a conference in Lausanne in July, where they came under strong pressure from British ministers to accept the complete suppression of reparations. Edouard Herriot, the French president of the council, regarded Franz von Papen, the nationalist who had recently replaced Brüning as German chancellor, as thoroughly untrustworthy. Familiar with Germany and aware of the strength of revisionist sentiment there, he warned British colleagues to expect another war in a few years time. But for the same reason he believed France must do everything possible to strengthen the entente with Britain and keep in with the United States. Against his better judgment, therefore, he agreed to the cancelation of reparations after a further token payment of 3 billion marks (£150 million). But he made it conditional upon the cancelation of further war debt payments, and on the understanding that Britain would join France in seeking to persuade the United States to fall in with their plans.

Immediately after the conference, the British government rejected a joint approach to Washington, when the Hoover administration warned against a common front in Europe and indicated that Britain would receive a more favorable hearing if it dissociated itself from France. In December, with another installment of war debts due and neither Hoover nor Franklin Roosevelt, the winner in the recent presidential election, prepared to take responsibility for suspending it, the British government decided to pay up rather than

embarrass Roosevelt and make it harder for him to offer concessions after taking office. Despite Herriot's strenuous appeal to do likewise, the French Chamber of Deputies decisively rejected a further payment. The deputies were influenced by the specter of heavier fiscal burdens, now that reparations were all but gone, but they were moved chiefly by a sense of injustice. They found it intolerable that the United States should enrich itself on war debt repayments from France, now that Germany was free of payments. Herriot's appeal to avoid isolating France thus fell on deaf ears. Despite the almost derisory sum involved – Ff.481 million ($19.3 million) – the deputies preferred isolation to injustice. France thus pulled away from the United States and Britain, on the very eve of Hitler's accession to power in Berlin.

But it could equally be said that the United States and Britain had pulled away from France. Hoover, discredited by his failure to address the economic slump, directed his frustration at Wall Street by inviting Congress to launch an enquiry into its activities. Initially, it was the bankers involved in pushing up share prices who were the target of the Congressional hearings. But in 1933 the enquiry turned to the international bankers, such as J. P. Morgan, Jr., who had been responsible for arranging many of the foreign loans during the First World War. The chairman's aggressive cross-examination created the impression of rich men engaged in improper activities, who had dangerously implicated America in unstable Europe. This had the effect of turning the United States even further from cooperation in international economic or security arrangements.

The effect of the slump and financial crisis upon Britain was in several respects similar. Shaken by the collapse of sterling, which seemed briefly to threaten hyperinflation and the collapse of savings as in Germany eight years earlier, the British public placed the blame on France and welcomed the decision of the National government, formed after the general election on October 27, 1931, to turn away from continental Europe toward closer relations with the Commonwealth. Too much was at stake for Britain completely to isolate itself from the continent. But, as in the United States, albeit in a less extreme way, international bankers such as Montagu

Norman, who had acquired an aura of mystery and magic in the 1920s, declined in public esteem. With the standing of sterling, the Bank of England, and the City diminished, the government and the public more readily accepted the abandonment of liberal internationalism and the introduction of trade protection and preferential arrangements with the countries of the empire.

In France as in the United States and to a lesser extent Britain, the world slump and the onset of mass unemployment prompted politically inspired attacks on bankers. The two hundred families who owned the bulk of shares in the Bank of France came to symbolize corruption in public and private affairs. Even now, an aura of power and arcane skills surrounds international finance in the interwar period. All the evidence, however, points to the conclusion that deliberate action by bankers and financiers played a negligible role in shaping the course of events that led to the Second World War. But this is not to say that finance and financiers were unimportant: far from it. Their real significance is that they were instrumental after the First World War in the sustained push for a liberal, globalized world. In pursuing this goal, they exposed the world to a dangerously unstable currency and payments system, and displayed scant regard for its effect upon the global security framework. Indeed, they actively weakened the Versailles settlement in their vain attempts to shore up the currency and payments system. They thus contributed to a doubly fragile situation. The consequence was an unprecedented crisis between 1929 and 1933, when both the international economic system and the international security system simultaneously broke down. With the leading democratic powers driven apart by the crisis and liberal governments everywhere discredited by their inability to deal with the economic problem, the way was open for authoritarian regimes in Japan, Italy, Germany, and elsewhere to embark on aggressive policies.

## NOTES

1  Herbert Feis, *Europe: The World's Banker, 1870–1914* (New Haven, CT: Yale University Press, 1930), p. 50.

2  See, for instance, Judith Kooker, "French Financial Diplomacy: The Interwar Years," in *Balance of Power or Hegemony: The Interwar Monetary System*, ed. Benjamin M. Rowland (New York: New York University Press, 1976), pp. 83–145; René Girault, "Economie et politique internationale: diplomatie et banque pendant l'entre-deux-guerres," *Relations internationales* 21 (1980): 7–22.

3  This is the basic assumption of Melvin P. Leffler, *The Elusive Quest: America's Pursuit of European Stability and French Security, 1919–1933* (Chapel Hill, NC: University of North Carolina Press, 1979); and Frank Costigliola, *Awkward Dominion, 1919–1933* (Ithaca, NY: Cornell University Press, 1984). See also John Kenneth Galbraith, *The Great Crash, 1929* (Harmondsworth: Penguin, 1963), p. 173; and Miles Kahler and Werner Link, *Europe and America: A Return to History* (New York: Council on Foreign Relations, 1996), Introduction.

4  R. Boyce, "Creating the Myth of Consensus: Public Opinion and Britain's Return to the Gold Standard in 1925," in *Money and Power: Essays in Honour of L. S. Pressnell*, ed. P. L. Cottrell and D. E. Moggridge (London: Macmillan, 1987), pp. 173–98.

5  Marc Trachtenberg, *Reparation in World Politics: France and European Economic Diplomacy, 1916–1923* (New York: Columbia University Press, 1980), pp. 67–8, estimates the reparation demand on Germany in the later 1920s to be equivalent to 7 percent of its gross national product.

6  Andrew Boyle, *Montagu Norman: A Biography* (London: Cassell, 1967), p. 155.

7  League of Nations, *Report of the Economic Consultative Committee, 1929*, p. 13. On other aspects of trade liberalization, see *Commercial Policy in the Interwar Period: International Proposals and National Policies* (Geneva: League of Nations, 1942).

8  R. Boyce, *British Capitalism at the Crossroads, 1919–1932: A Study in Politics, Economics and International Relations* (Cambridge: Cambridge University Press, 1987), pp. 174–6.

9  Cleona Lewis, *America's Stake in International Investments* (Washington, DC: Brookings Institution, 1938), pp. 652–3, 654–5.

10  R. Boyce, "Wall Street and the Spectre of the 'Money Power' in Small-Town America before and after the Crash of 1929," in *Etats de New York*, ed. Philippe Romanski (Rouen: Publications de l'Université de Rouen, 2000), pp. 19–31.

11  Hoover Library, William Castle Papers, Box 5, Castle to Mrs. Parker Maddux, February 10, 1928.

12  Hoover Library, Presidential Papers, Box 151, Subject File: Financial Matters: NYSE, Correspondence, 1929 September–October, George Akerson, Secretary to the President, to Christian A. Herter, April 2, 1929.

13  Herbert Hoover, *The Memoirs of Herbert Hoover: The Great Depression, 1929–1941* (New York: Macmillan, 1952), p. 10.

14  Hoover Library, Presidential Papers, Box 1009, Foreign Affairs, Financial, Correspondence 1931 July 18, "Telephone conversation with Secretary Stimson – 7.00 pm," July 18, 1931.

15  Léon Chavenon, "Les valeurs étrangères et le marché français," *L'Information*, February 28, 1931, p. 1.

16  "City Notes," *The Times*, July 30, 1929; *The Statist*, August 10, 1929, pp. 204, 219; *The Economist*, August 31, 1929, p. 391; *Manchester Guardian Commercial*, October 3, 1929, p. 384.

17  France, Ministère des Finances (MF), B12612, de Chalendar to Chéron, no. 53, 788, October 3, 1929.

18  Estimates of the number of shareholders vary widely, but see Steve Fraser, *Wall Street: A Cultural History* (London: Faber & Faber, 2005), pp. 347, 425; Galbraith, *Great Crash*, p. 102. On the fall in share value, Lester V. Chandler, *American Monetary Policy, 1928–1941* (New York: Harper & Row, 1971), p. 77, Table 7-12.

19  *Daily Herald*, May 20, 1930, p. 7, and July 21, 1930, p. 10; George Glasgow, "Foreign Affairs," *Contemporary Review*, June 1930, p. 783, and August 1930, p. 241; *The Observer*, July 20, 1930, p. 2; Paul Einzig, "Co-operation and the International Bank," *The Banker*, June 1930, pp. 272–5.

20  Harold James, *The Reichsbank and Public Finance in Germany, 1924–1933: A Study of the Politics of Economics in the Great Depression* (Frankfurt am Main: F. Knapp, 1985), pp. 124, 129.

21  BNF, Papiers Flandin, 51, "Evaluation des crédits d'acceptations sur l'Allemagne," n.d. (ca. June 15, 1931).

22  NA, T160/430, F12317/2, Leith Ross to Bizot, January 23, 1931; ibid., Bizot to Leith Ross, February 2, 1931.

23  BoE, OV28/69, memorandum by Francis Rennell Rodd, June 20, 1931.

24  BdF, Délibérations du Conseil Général, 18, July 23, September 22, 1931.

25  NA, 30/69/8/1, MacDonald diary, June 25, July 5 and 11, 1931; Yale University Library, Stimson diary, June 25, 1931.

26  Royal Archives, GV, M1329/10, Wigram to Sir Horace Rumbold, August 3, 1931.

27  British Library of Political and Economic Science, Dalton diaries, July 16–17, 19, 1931; Tom Johnston, *Financiers and the Nation* (London: Methuen, 1939), p. 198.

28  France, MAE, Europe 1918–1940, Grande-Bretagne 288, De Fleuriau to Briand, no. 581, November 18, 1931; NA, FO, Phipps papers, I, 2/21, Mendl to Phipps (Vienna), November 20, 1931.

29  France, MF, B32307, "Note sur l'abandon de la politique tendant à maintenir au régime de l'étalon d'or les pays de l'Europe centrale et orientale," February 15, 1932.

30  BNF, Papiers Flandin, 51, Briand to Flandin, no. 2015, July 15, 1931.

## GUIDE TO FURTHER READING

Jacques Bariety, *Les Relations franco-allemandes après la première guerre mondiale 10 novembre 1918–10 janvier 1925, de l'exécution à la négociation* (Paris: Publications de la Sorbonne, 1977). A magisterial study of Franco-German relations, highlighting their struggle for control over the economic bases of power.

Edward W. Bennett, *Germany and the Diplomacy of the Financial Crisis, 1931* (Cambridge, MA: Harvard University Press, 1962). Emphasizes the pursuit of national ambitions by German statesmen.

R. W. D. Boyce, *British Capitalism at the Crossroads, 1919–1932: A Study in Politics, Economics and International Relations* (Cambridge: Cambridge University Press, 1987). Despite the title, extensively covers the decline in relations between the main victor powers.

Eric Bussière, *La France, la Belgique et l'organisation économique de l'Europe 1918–1935* (Paris: Comité pour l'histoire économique et financière, Ministère des Finances, 1992). Surveys the ambiguous relationship between France and Belgium.

Frank Costigliola, *Awkward Dominion: American Political, Economic and Cultural Relations with Europe, 1919–1933* (Ithaca, NY: Cornell University Press, 1984). Argues that American statesmen and bankers worked hand in glove in dealings with Europe.

Harold James, *The German Slump: Politics and Economics, 1924–1936* (Oxford: Clarendon Press, 1986). Detailed account of economic policy decisions in Germany before and during the slump.

David E. Kaiser, *Economic Diplomacy and the Origins of the Second World War: Germany, France, and*

*Eastern Europe, 1930–1939* (Princeton, NJ: Princeton University Press, 1980). Surveys the commercial aspects of European relations as Germany recovered influence, but touches on financial aspects as well.

Edward P. Keeton, *Briand's Locarno Policy: French Economics, Politics and Diplomacy, 1925–1929* (New York: Garland, 1987). Emphasizes the decline in France's influence over the European balance of power, despite financial stability and prosperity.

Bruce Kent, *The Spoils of War: The Politics, Economics, and Diplomacy of Reparations, 1918–1932* (Oxford: Clarendon Press, 1989). Places reparations at the center of the growing crisis in international relations.

Charles P. Kindleberger, *The World in Depression, 1929–1939* (London: Penguin, 1973). An account by an economic historian with a political economy approach.

Franz Knipping, *Deutschland, Frankreich und das Ende der Locarno-Ëra: Studien zur internationalen Politik in der Anfangsphase der Weltwirtschaftskrise* (Munich: R. Oldenbourg, 1987). Well-integrated study of the Franco-German relationship during the slump.

Melvin P. Leffler, *The Elusive Quest: America's Pursuit of European Stability and French Security, 1919–1933* (Chapel Hill, NC: University of North Carolina Press, 1979). Presents a benign view of American policy toward Europe.

Walter A. McDougall, *France's Rhineland Diplomacy, 1914–1924: The Last Bid for a Balance of Power in Europe* (Princeton, NJ: Princeton University Press, 1978). Wide-ranging account of events leading to France's early defeats over reparations and security.

Kenneth Mouré, *The Gold Standard Illusion: France, the Bank of France, and the International Gold Standard, 1914–1939* (Oxford: Oxford University Press, 2002). Describes the paradox of a strong currency that weakens the economy and state.

Scott Newton, *Profits of Peace: The Political Economy of Anglo-German Appeasement* (Oxford: Clarendon Press, 1996). Provocative account, linking British appeasement to the priorities of the City of London.

Sir Frederick Leith Ross, *Money Talks: Fifty Years of International Finance* (London: Hutchinson, 1969). Useful survey of international economic diplomacy by a British participant.

Benjamin M. Rowland, ed., *Balance of Power or Hegemony: The Interwar Monetary System* (New York: New York University, 1976). Stimulating if now somewhat dated essays on the politics of international money.

Gustav Schmidt, ed., *Konstellationen internationaler Politik 1924–1932: politische und wirtschaftliche Faktoren in den Beziehungen zwischen Westeuropa und den Vereinigten Staaten: Referate und Diskussionsbeiträge eines Dortmunder Symposions, 18–21 September 1981* (Bochum: N. Brockmeyer, 1983). Useful collection of essays on US–West European relations before and during the slump.

Stephen A. Schuker, *The End of French Predominance in Europe: The Financial Crisis of 1924 and the Adoption of the Dawes Plan* (Chapel Hill, NC: University of North Carolina Press, 1976). Detailed account emphasizing the financial weakness that contributed to France's defeat over the Ruhr.

Marc Trachtenberg, *Reparation in World Politics: France and European Economic Diplomacy, 1916–1923* (New York: Columbia University Press, 1980). Argues that French reparation policy was more moderate than hitherto claimed.

# CHAPTER FIFTEEN

# The Far Eastern Crisis and the Balance of Power, 1920–1941

## GREG KENNEDY

When historians speak of the Far Eastern crisis there is a natural tendency to ask, "Crisis? What crisis?" Throughout the early interwar years, members of what is known as the strategic foreign policymaking elite in many western and Asian nations would not have considered the region either to be in crisis or to be the object of any crisis in international relations. In the immediate post-First World War world, Japan's reward for upholding the Anglo-Japanese alliance was rightly acknowledged by its continued acceptance as an equal with regard to the division of China and the determination of the future shape of the balance of power in the Far East.[1] Although a junior partner, Japan was a full partner with the other Great Powers that had interests in the region. The most important of these other powers were Great Britain, the United States, and Russia. While France, Italy, Germany, Holland, as well as the White Dominions (Australia, New Zealand, and Canada) all had interests in the development of China's economy and trade, their influence was minimal and sporadic.[2] China was the bone that the victorious Great Powers of the First World War would gnaw at their leisure, and as long as they were in agreement there would be no cause for dispute. That agreement, however, would prove continually harder and harder to achieve in the changing international dynamics of the late 1920s and 1930s. At that time, Japanese expansionism and militarism ran counter to Soviet protectionism and British and American status quo imperialism.

China's future was to be guaranteed by a combination of post-1918 institutions and agreements. The first of these was the newly formed League of Nations. As the international overseer of the rights of all nations to self-determination and the right to exist without fear of military aggression, the League's collective security approach was based on a combination of potential economic sanctions, military force, and international moral suasion. Japan, as a member of the League of Nations, was obliged to conduct its actions in China in accordance with League ideals, as were all other members of the Nine Power Treaty. That treaty, signed in 1922, formed the basis of the other pillar of security in the Far East in the 1920s: the Washington Treaty system. This system involved an arms limitation agreement, with the nine main powers involved in the division of China into spheres of influence agreeing to abide by a set of rules of conduct. Signatories to this agreement were to accept an agreed definition of China's sovereignty, independence, administrative and territorial rights, and to maintain the concept of "the Open Door." This last ideal was based on the principle that all nations would have equal access to commercial and industrial markets and supplies in China. In other words, the Washington Treaty system was a formalized set of guidelines constructed for the orderly exploitation of China's potential in order to ensure that a "scramble for China" did not end in conflict. It was supposed to ensure the maintenance of the status quo among the Great Powers in the region.[3]

Linked to this Nine Power Treaty was the Four Power Treaty which limited Japan, Great Britain, the United States, and France to where and what fortifications they could build in support of their various fleets. Great Britain could finish the base at Singapore but could increase the fortifications of no other base east of it. The United States could develop its facilities at Pearl Harbor and maintain its installations in the Philippines, but could not build any new naval bases west of Hawaii. France was allowed to keep what minimal facilities it had, but was to build no more. Japan was, therefore, given effective regional dominance, as it was the nation whose main naval bases were closest to the area. It, too, was limited as to how much further west it could build future naval facilities, but, given its natural proximity, this restriction was unimportant. What was more important for the naval balance of power was the Five Power Naval Treaty, which was at the core of the Washington system.[4]

The Five Power agreement saw Britain, the United States, and Japan agree to a capital ship ratio of 5 : 5 : 3 (France and Italy were the other signatories to this agreement, with a ratio of 1.75 each). This agreement, based on the main naval weapon of the period, the battleship, ensured that none of the nations would have to build those most expensive of naval weapons. At the same time, it allowed for security in terms of planning and anticipation, with each nation knowing exactly how many and what sort of battleships each would build. What was not resolved was the size and capabilities of the rest of the naval forces. These would be dealt with over the next decade. But Japan believed that its allotted ratio was a denial of its rightful status in the world's international structure. To compound Tokyo's irritation, the creation of this Washington system called for the demise of the longstanding Anglo-Japanese alliance. This perceived combination of inferior naval status, a feeling of rejection by Great Britain, and the newly realized American strength in world affairs sowed the seeds of discontent between Japan and the two English-speaking nations over the Far East.[5] However, there was another player intimately tied to the development of the strategic situation in the Far East: the Soviet Union.[6]

Like the League of Nations, the Washington Treaty system was missing a key international player. The Soviet Union was not seen as a great naval power in the postwar system and thus was not considered in any of the naval aspects of the Pacific. It was, however, a nation with a great deal of interest in the future economic and strategic development of the region, seeing its own territorial and economic security as being linked to a sustainable base at Vladivostok and a strong military presence in its eastern provinces. These military assets were essential to protect Soviet strategic railway rights and privileges. Those interests also involved any future development of China as a market, and served to deter any attempts by Japan to gain a greater continental foothold through the use of force. Therefore, Japanese desires to expand their empire further on the mainland were a serious source of tension and potential conflict with the Soviet Union throughout the interwar decades.[7]

Throughout the 1920s the Washington Treaty system appeared to keep the balance of power stable in the Far East. Issues of trade competition, immigration, and the continual build-up of a strong military presence on the Chinese mainland created disputes and tension between Japan, China, the US, and Britain, but for the most part relations were viewed as amicable and normal, "for China." The United States Navy, as well as the Royal Navy, based many of their peacetime war games on a scenario that involved a hostile Japan, but these were often seen as worst-case planning exercises, with, as yet, little real political basis. It was the rise of Chinese nationalism in the 1920s that created the areas of tension which eroded the status quo among the Great Powers that the Washington system had created.

In 1928 Chiang Kai-shek achieved his goal of creating a united, national state with his Kuomintang government based in Nanking. His ousting of the Bolshevik-supported elements of the Chinese political landscape in 1928 was a critical factor in his success. That success eventually led to an attempt to further his position through the seizure of the Russian-controlled Chinese Eastern Railway in 1929. Chiang

Kai-shek underestimated the Soviets' resolve to defend this imperial possession and his forces suffered a resounding defeat at the hands of Soviet forces in the Far East. The Soviets' expansion of their military forces in the region, and their demonstration of a resolve to use military force, heightened the tensions in Soviet–Japanese relations. Japan viewed this Soviet determination to remain in East Asia as a possible threat to its own plans for the domination of Manchuria. By 1931, the Japanese had substantially increased the power of the Kwantung Army in China, a force which was now responsible for defending Japan's border areas in Manchuria against both Soviet and Chinese incursions. Totaling only around 10,000 men at that time, it was nevertheless a well-equipped and efficient fighting force which posed a credible deterrent and threat to Japanese rivals on the mainland.[8]

These tensions, combined with ongoing struggles between Chinese Nationalist forces and Great Britain, as well as protracted tariff disputes with Britain, saw China laboring under the weight of external forces to rid itself of foreign impediments to its future development. In late 1926, Great Britain made clear its determination to abolish its extraterritorial rights in China if judicial reforms, tariff autonomy, and foreign control of Chinese revenues could be satisfactorily worked out by the two nations. As well, control of British concessions in China was to be handed over to the Chinese. Japan and the United States were not impressed with the new British line. The failure of the Chinese to put an effective national government in place because of the civil war and regional differences meant that there was insufficient stability to allow such a development to occur in an appropriate fashion. Nonetheless, China was to be protected by the League of Nations from outside forces of aggression while it struggled to put its domestic affairs in order.[9]

For Japan, the problem posed by Chinese nationalism was how to decouple its interests in Manchuria from its interests in China as a whole. That disentanglement proved to be most difficult to achieve. Soviet inroads into Manchuria along the Chinese Eastern Railway caused great concern in Tokyo, as it created the possibility that Bolshevism would spread among the Chinese people.

Such a shift in ideology was seen as potentially disastrous to Japan's exports to China, as well as posing a challenge to the regional controls exerted by the Kwantung Army. Although Japan had stated in 1924 that it would follow a policy of absolute non-interference in the internal affairs of China, the lack of a stable government increased the attraction of communism among the Chinese people, and the inability of Chinese authorities to provide security for Japanese nationals and their interests in China meant that there was increasing pressure on the Japanese to take military action in order to safeguard their national interests. Added to these factors was the unstable nature of the Japanese political system itself. Assassinations and a musical-chairs system of ministerial appointments, particularly in the foreign ministry, meant that there was a lack of continuity and oversight in Japan's foreign policy decision-making process. Increased pressures from the Japanese military with regard to the appointment of ministers meant that military solutions and conflict became a more viable approach to Japan's international problems than might have normally been the case. By 1930, Japan's use of military force to protect its Chinese interests, as well as the continued influence of the military on Japanese politics, had combined to create the perception in the Soviet Union and the West that Japan was an aggressive, militaristic power bent on creating a greater empire on the mainland of Asia at all costs.[10]

Throughout the 1920s, the relationship of the United States with Japan was driven primarily by domestic American issues. Tensions between the two increased in 1924 when America limited Japanese immigration to the United States. As well, tensions increased as Japan pushed into South American markets, fueling fears that America would lose market share to cheaper Japanese goods in this expanding economic zone. American missionaries in China waged a successful propaganda campaign in the United States against Japan, painting a picture of military oppression and violence that threatened to prevent China's finding solutions of its own making to its national crisis. Japanese pressures on China with regard to trade and tariffs added to the view from Washington that Japan was an imperial power bent on the subjugation of large tracts of

China. Such action was, however, a direct violation of the hallowed Wilsonian principle of self-
determination.[11] Without any serious or consistent
effort on the part of either nation to understand
or deal with the other's domestic needs with
regard to the Far East, there was little hope of a
better international relationship between the two.
As economic pressures built in each nation after
1929, driven by the global depression which
began that year, the ability of either to accommodate the other in terms of trade, expansion,
protectionism, or the use of military power to
safeguard interests grew smaller and smaller.

From 1929 to 1931, all the industrialized
nations of the world suffered a global economic
depression. Most importantly for the balance of
power system at work in the Far East, this depression meant that in each of those nations which
supported the League of Nations and had used
their fiscal and industrial power to create military
power to support their diplomacy, the desire for
domestic recovery would override any needs in
foreign policy. Faced with falling commodity
prices, rising unemployment, decreasing purchasing power, and falling industrial production, the
United States, Great Britain, Japan, and the Soviet
Union all looked to protectionist measures to try
to limit the damage to their economies. This
antagonistic economic environment eroded the
desire, particularly in the United States and Great
Britain, to fund increased armaments, especially
expensive navies. The needs of their own farmers,
workers, and businessmen were more important
to governments than any international action
required to maintain the economic or military
measures necessary to ensure global security. By
1931 France and Britain were the only two nations
still on the gold standard, and their protectionism
guaranteed that the postwar ideal of a cooperative, international economic order was in ruins. It
was within this global context that a group of
Kwantung Army officers, led by Ishiwara Kanji
and Itagaki Seishiro, decided that a bold move
was required if Japan were to retain its dominant
position in China.[12]

These officers believed that the time had come
for Japan to cease cooperating with western
powers in China. Unilateral action would secure
Japan's interests in Manchuria and prevent a weak

Japanese government from continuing to betray
that nation's right to dominate international
affairs in the region. On September 18, 1931,
units of the Kwantung Army attacked Chinese
units guarding the Mukden section of the South
Manchuria Railway. This attack was the first act
in what turned out to be an escalating war waged
between the Japanese military in Manchuria and
Chinese National forces. But, more importantly,
it was the first challenge by Japan to the
Washington system and the ideals of the Open
Door and the maintenance of the status quo that
had been in place for the last decade.[13] China
appealed to the other members of the Washington
system, and the League of Nations, to assist it in
its war against an aggressor. Weakened by the
Depression, without significant military forces in
the area and reluctant to act in a manner which
might antagonize the Japanese to a point where
their own possessions and interest in China might
be threatened directly, neither America nor Great
Britain rushed to China's aid.

By 1932, as Chinese and Japanese forces waged
war in the international city of Shanghai, endan-
gering the lives of British, American, and
European nationals, to say nothing of the extensive financial houses based in the city, the League
of Nations had proven itself to be unwilling to
take any military action against Japanese aggression. Considering Great Britain to be the nation
with the most at stake, and therefore the one most
naturally placed to take the lead in any solution
regarding the Manchurian crisis, other members
of the League, as well as the United States, took
a "wait and see" stance. From January to March
1932, Great Britain and the United States engaged
in a diplomatic dance, each trying to get the other
to take the lead in finding a solution to the
Japanese use of naked force. Neither was willing
to do so. Indeed, the ensuing negotiations
between the two western powers actually alienated one from the other to an extent not seen
since the end of the First World War. The realization of the unhappy truth of not being the dominant military powers in the region became a stark
reality to both western nations. Both Britain and
the US instead evoked the Japanese obligation to
the Kellogg–Briand agreement of 1928 not to use
force for its own gain, as well as its participation

in the Washington system and its requirement to allow the concept of the Open Door to exist. They were unwilling to do more than quote articles from various treaties and make declarations of outrage and disappointment at the Japanese acts. When hostilities in Shanghai drew to a close, the world waited to see what declaration the Lytton Commission, a body directed by the League of Nations to go to the Far East and investigate the 1931 attack by Japan, would make. Would it support the Japanese claims of the need to protect its position or would it declare Japan an outlaw in the international system?[14]

The Commission arrived in Japan on February 29, 1932. By December of that year it laid its findings before the League, blaming Chinese nationalism and the disorder allowed by the National government as much as Japanese militarism for the state of affairs in China. It did not, however, accept that Japan was justified in the use of force to further its aims in China, and declared the Japanese puppet regime not to be a legitimate government. The report accepted that Japanese rights needed protection but also demanded the restoration of territorial and administrative integrity in China. Japan refused to accept the report's findings and in March 1933 left the League of Nations.

Japan's leaving the League coincided with the change of the American administration and Franklin Delano Roosevelt becoming president of the United States. Roosevelt's main objective was to repair the battered American economy. As far as the crisis in China was concerned, he and his secretary of state, Cordell Hull, were willing to continue the twin tracks of the Stimson doctrine, declaring a non-recognition of the Japanese government in Manchukuo and warning that any violation of the Nine Power Treaty would result in the United States no longer being bound by the naval limits set out in the Five Power Treaty. As evidence grew that Japan was increasing its military power and violating the pledge that it had made at the Washington conference that it would not fortify its mandates in the Pacific islands, Washington grew more receptive to the idea that Japan was a rogue state that would not stop its use of military force to achieve its strategic goals. Roosevelt announced his intention to build up

the United States Navy to the strength permitted under the treaty arrangement and to send economic and military assistance to China to help it in its fight against Japan. In early 1934 Japan responded to these actions with the Amau Declaration that Japan would oppose any actions taken by China to use foreign assistance in its struggle with Japan.[15]

Great Britain was caught in a difficult middle ground. Torn between a desire to support the League of Nations to deter Japan and the realization that public opinion and a weak military presence in the Far East limited its ability to coerce Japan into a more "civilized" position, British policy was a combination of appeasement and tough talking (or bluff). To some in London, Russia's growing fear of Japanese intentions in Manchuria was a beacon of hope at a time when British imperial defense planning in the region called out for the need to find a counterweight to the growing Japanese menace. At the end of January 1932, the Sino-Japanese conflict had spread to the key British interest of Shanghai.

By March 1932, many officials in the British Foreign Office, such as Sir Robert Vansittart, the permanent under-secretary, were exasperated by the Japanese attitude toward foreign powers in China, fearful of further, bolder attacks on British interests by either Chinese or Japanese forces and desperate to find some leverage or ally that might deter any further Japanese invasion of China. In this balance-of-power dynamic, the British were skeptical about the usefulness of the new American president and his administration. The United States, like Great Britain, did not have the same military power in the region as the Soviet Union, and, also like Britain, the US was forced to try to find leverage through international agreements and trade in its attempts to deter Japan.[16] Throughout 1934 and 1935, both the United States and Great Britain viewed the chance of a clash between the Soviet Union and Japan as being highly probable. Such a clash could work to both London's and Washington's advantage by weakening each of the two potentially dangerous powers while leaving British and American interests relatively unharmed. When no such war occurred, however, it was left to both western nations to once more attempt to limit

Japanese naval power in the hope that some stability could still be achieved.[17]

In 1935 a new round of naval arms limitation talks, the London Naval Conference, was scheduled to begin. For both the United States and Great Britain the issue was now whether they would present a united front to the Japanese request for increased naval power and risk alienating them further, or instead drift further apart over the question of Japan's status within the balance-of-power structure in the Far East. Continued instability in the Japanese government, manifest in ministerial assassinations and the growing dominance of the military, worried both western nations. The question was: was there any liberal, international spirit left in the Japanese government that, with encouragement from the West, could bring Japan back into the international community? Japanese moderation at the 1935 naval talks would be an encouraging sign that there was still hope that such was the case.

Such hopes were dashed in the preparatory talks for the conference. Throughout late 1935 and early 1936, Japan's continued insistence on parity in capital ships and cruisers threatened to destroy the naval balance of power in the Far East. British and American strategic foreign policy-makers grew closer together in the face of continued Japanese demands, but refused to create any formal or obvious Anglo-American axis that could be perceived by the Japanese as a coordinated effort to deter them. Japan left the talks in the spring of 1936 and the United States, with France and Italy, agreed to a new set of terms governing their future naval construction. Both English-speaking nations recognized, however, that a new era in the naval balance of power had dawned. With Japan no longer restrained in its naval building, it could only be deterred if Britain and the United States increased their own naval power in the Far East.[18]

Japan's intentions in this period were manifold and an interpretation of its motives depends largely on the area studied. Japan's relationship with other nations at a commercial level leads researchers to the conclusion that Japan's intention in China was the use of armed force to secure markets and secure control over essential strategic raw materials. This idea of securing greater trade

and market share translates into other regions as well, although without the use of force being applicable. In South America, for instance, Japan's aggressive trade stance worried British and American businessmen, but not in a political sense. Links between Japanese bankers and businessmen remained good throughout the period from 1932 to 1939. But all interpretations of Japanese trade and fiscal policy were translated through the lens of actions in China, which undermined any credibility of the business or political systems in Japan. As well, the growing inability of the business, banking, and political elites in Japan to control the military raised serious questions about the motives of any Japanese actions, anywhere. Therefore, the actions of the Japanese military in China, particularly in subverting normal business and banking actions in Manchukuo and other parts of northern China, made any actions on the part of the other elites within the Japanese decision-making process less credible and thus less likely to achieve any successful negotiation of Japan's legitimate place in the international order.

Japan's leaving the naval armaments limitation system was not the only signal the other Powers had of Japan's unwillingness to be treated as a second-class citizen in international affairs. From 1932 to 1935 Britain, the Soviet Union, and the United States all kept a wary eye on Japan's growing economic and industrial power. The United States and Great Britain were both concerned at the increasing penetration in South American markets by Japanese goods. By 1935 British industry, such as the Lancashire cotton magnates, had become resigned to the fact that Japanese competition in the Far East was insurmountable. Indian cotton could compete with Japanese because of India's vast and cheap labor pool, but British companies in China, such as Jardine Matheson (for centuries seen as a beacon of British fiscal and economic dominance in China), were by 1935–6 seriously contemplating abandoning all but their financial interests in the region.[19] British coastal shipping companies were hard pressed to compete with cheaper Japanese lines as well, a situation that threatened to leave the vital provision of commercial sea communications in Japanese hands. American goods, such as light bulbs, dry goods, and textiles, were also being hard pressed in the Monroe Doctrine zone by an ever-increasing volume of cheap Japanese products of good quality.[20] The Soviet Union too was concerned that Japanese control of vital railways in mainland Asia would allow the latter to gain access to growing Chinese markets. The Soviet Union's poor quality goods could not compete with Japan's growing industrial and technical proficiency, especially if the latter was willing to ensure market share through the threat and use of force. Japan's growth as an industrial and commercial competitor added to the perception, particularly in capitalist nations, of it as a potentially dominant force in the Far East. By the summer of 1937 this combination of military, economic, and territorial expansion by Japan had made the three other Great Powers in the region wary of their future relations with it. The Japanese invasion of China in the summer of 1937, in the aftermath of various promises of restraint and moderation by Japanese government officials, signaled the beginning of the end for Japan and its relationship with those nations.[21]

Japan's air attacks on Chinese military and civilian targets pushed its aggressive action into the realm of international terrorism. Seen by western observers, especially newspapers and the general public, as an atrocity of the same sort as those perpetrated by the German Condor Legion in Spain, the reaction to the "unfair and inhumane" use of such weapons of war, especially against defenseless civilian populations, was absolute. Those in Britain, the US, and the USSR who believed that moderate forces in Japan could control and restrain the Japanese military were now in the minority. All three began the planning for increased military and naval capabilities in the region and saw the need to prepare for war with Japan in the near-to-medium future. Construction of key naval bases at Singapore, Pearl Harbor, and Vladivostok all received a greater infusion of funding and their already high priority was made even greater. The same held true for the naval forces which would operate from those bases. And, as to American, British, and Soviet interests in the Far East, China was now seen as their proxy defender. All three began to provide fiscal, economic, and military support to Chiang Kai-shek's war efforts. The Soviet Union and the United States in particular provided military advisers and equipment, especially aircraft, for the hard-pressed Chinese military. Britain accelerated its efforts to build and expand its Burma Road in order to ensure that, even if Japanese air and naval power closed China's eastern ports, an overland route would allow the Chinese to fight on. Without adequate political will at home or military forces of their own, Britain and the US were forced to take on China more and more as a client state. The Soviet Union, however, possessing a large and capable military force of its own in the region, was in the midst of military purges in the fall of 1937. While the Far Eastern Army of the Soviet Union was the least disrupted of all its forces by the purges, the internal turmoil produced by the purges prevented Russia from being able to create the political will to take any direct action against Japan. Finally, the inability of the League of Nations to prevent Japan's use of military force to change the international situation signaled the end of that already-weakened institution as a viable force in international affairs. The failure of the League in China marked the end of the co-operative, collective security experiment by the international community. Following Italy's and Germany's defiance of the League's authority, Japan's actions set in motion even closer Anglo-American cooperation in international affairs and security issues, and added momentum and vitality to Soviet Russia's rearmament program. Japan's participation in the Anti-Comintern Pact on November 6, 1937 (agreement among Italy, Germany, and Japan to oppose Soviet influence around the world), was seen by many British, American, and Soviet observers as being the final act that pointed out clearly the path of militarism and violence that Japan was now on. Britain in particular saw Japan's union with the two European dictatorships as being aimed not only at Bolshevism but also at the British Empire. These beliefs shaped British and American perceptions of Japanese actions from 1939 to 1941.[22]

China's war against Japan, while not endowed with many great military victories, grand offensives, or even progress, proved itself to be the quagmire that external observers had predicted it would be. China's resolve to resist the Japanese aggression, a cessation of Communist and

Nationalist hostilities to meet the threat of a common foe, an enormous pool of manpower, and considerable external assistance in the form of arms and money all combined to create a force which Japanese military power could not defeat. By the spring of 1939, the Soviet Union, the United States, and Great Britain were in the midst of massive rearmament programs that promised to give them the military power necessary to protect their respective security interests in any region of the world. Therefore, the preparation for, and outbreak of, a general war in Europe changed the global environment in which the growing Far Eastern crisis existed.[23]

The first problem for the Japanese was one of resources. With a full-scale war now a reality in Europe, American, British, and Soviet rearmament went into a level of production that Japan, with limited fiscal, economic, and natural resources, could never hope to match. The race was now on for Japanese strategic decision-makers: would the nation use its military power or risk losing its regional advantage to resurgent British and American naval power? The indications of continued Japanese dominance were not good. In the summer of 1939 a "border incident" in the Mongolian area of Nomonhan had produced a war-like condition between the Soviet Union and Japan. From mid-July 1939 until the end of September, army divisions and air groups clashed along the Soviet–Manchukuo border. By the end of the summer, Soviet forces had beaten the Japanese military decisively, revealing the weaknesses in mechanization, logistics, and firepower that marked the inferiority of the Japanese army on a European-like battlefield. To make matters worse for Japan, in preparation for its assault on Poland, Germany had negotiated a pact with the Soviet Union. On August 23, Joachim von Ribbentrop, the German foreign secretary, signed an agreement with Stalin's Soviet Russia, securing Germany's eastern flank and eliminating any threat of a two-front war interfering with Hitler's designs on Poland. This Nazi–Soviet Pact was a severe blow to Germany's Far Eastern ally. Japan's military leadership was flabbergasted by this turn of events, which saw Japan's most important ally now in an alliance with the power that represented the greatest military threat to it in the region.

As the war in Europe unfolded, the war in China remained a brutal stalemate. Even though there were groups of Japanese military, business, financial, and political leaders who desired a negotiated end to the war, the fear of how the other Great Powers would interpret this reversal of policy prevented Japan's leadership from agreeing to this conciliatory course of action. Instead, as the war in Europe revealed the military weakness of the western, imperial powers, Japan's new premier, Hiranuma, saw the opportunity to push the war in China through to a conclusion. In the face of even larger loans and more military aid from the western nations and the Soviet Union for China, Japan exerted greater financial and military pressure on Chiang Kai-shek, in the hope of forcing him to the bargaining table. This continued attack on the Chinese, in conjunction with the seizure of French and Dutch possessions in the region throughout 1940, and the signing of the Axis Tripartite Pact between Germany, Italy, and Japan in September of that year, only reinforced the belief in the United States and Great Britain that reasoning with Japan was a fruitless proposition. By the end of the year, both nations were viewing war with the Empire of the Rising Sun as almost inevitable.[24]

Along with the continued loans and military aid to China, the United States and Great Britain took other actions against Japan in a further attempt to deter it in 1940. Despite agreement that the war in Europe had the highest priority, both nations made extensive war plans for a conflict in the Far East, the Rainbow and Dog plans, to augment already existing plans such as the United States Navy's War Plan Orange. As well, informal but detailed talks between Chinese, Dutch, British, and American military staffs took place in order to coordinate any war effort in the Far East. Eventually the ABDA (Australian, British, Dutch, and American) coalition was formed in 1941 as a formal military organization to show their commitment to stopping any further Japanese advances in the region.

These were necessary, as British attempts to appease Japan through the closure of the Burma Road in 1940 had not produced any results. More and more it was becoming apparent that such meager gestures were not enough. With the fall of France, the entry of Italy into the war against Britain, and the heavy losses in warships being sustained by the Royal Navy in the North Sea, Atlantic, and Mediterranean, British resources were overstretched. American public opinion, especially in the election year of 1940, kept that nation from making a formal commitment to any military intervention in the Far East. While British strategic planners relied on the Americans to hold the ring in the Far East in the event of Japanese aggression, no alliance had yet been openly declared. Without an open declaration of Anglo-American unity, the Japanese were forced to continue to guess at the eventual consequences of any attack on Dutch and British possessions. Their conclusion was that an attack on Britain would indeed precipitate a response from the United States. From that first principle, Japanese war planning in 1941 began to swing away from a China-oriented strategy to a southern/naval one, with the United States Navy being the most important military force with which to reckon.[25]

The invasion of the Soviet Union by Germany in June 1941 enabled such a Southern Advance plan to move ahead with even greater rapidity and hope for success. With its greatest land-power rival now fighting for its life in the west, Japan's army and navy could concentrate on dealing with the western maritime powers in the south.[26] The freezing of Japan's financial assets globally and the oil and scrap steel embargoes placed on it by the United States and Great Britain in the summer of 1941 placed Japan on notice: the sinews of modern warfare would be denied unless it changed its approach to international relations in the region. Faced with such a stark choice – to use the military power at its immediate disposal and the strategic advantage provided by the war in Europe or to negotiate a peace agreement while the militarily weak western nations transformed themselves into military superpowers that Japan could never hope to emulate – Japan's leadership chose war. On December 7, 1941, Japan attempted to secure through the force of arms the necessary raw materials to ensure its future as the dominant military power in the region. Hopes that the western nations would prove too weak-willed to fight a long, tortuous war in the Pacific were allowed to override the knowledge that Japan's

war effort would be matched against industrial, financial, economic, and demographic superiority. Those hopes proved unfounded.

The crisis in the Far East was the result of three coincident trends: the illogical belief in western democracies that the use of military force in international relations would be abandoned; in fact, that the maintenance of modern arms and the investment in a powerful military would in itself cause war, not prevent it; and finally, that nations would act in a responsible, rational fashion in changing any international status quo. This series of assumptions was proven wrong in the period of the Versailles system, particularly in the Far East. The Washington Treaty system, which was designed to provide security in that region, could not do so if Japan remained unsatisfied with the terms of that system. As a result, that nation remained a revisionist, militarist, expansionist power throughout the period. After 1930 Japan leaned more and more on military power to achieve its ends than on any other form of power, and, as a result, continued to isolate itself from the international community throughout the 1930s. That isolation eventually saw Tokyo aligned with the only other nations that shared such behavior: the European dictatorships. The crisis in the Far East was a struggle between a nation which desired a greater role as a regional power but which could only do so at the expense of other nations unwilling to be forced to surrender peacefully those rights and privileges. Thus, only through war, or "politics by other means," did Japan believe that it could achieve the change it desired. Its attempt was a cataclysmic failure that ended in its destruction.

## NOTES

1   On the nature of the Anglo-Japanese alliance in the post-First World War period see Keith Neilson, "Unbroken Thread: Japan and Britain and Imperial Defence, 1920–1932," in *British Naval Strategy East of Suez, 1900–2000: Influences and Actions*, ed. Greg Kennedy (London: Taylor & Francis, 2005), pp. 62–89.

2   The best general survey of the international situation in the Far East in the period from 1919 to 1933 is provided in the relevant chapters of Zara

Steiner, *The Lights that Failed: European International History, 1919–1933* (Oxford: Oxford University Press, 2005).

3  Walter LaFeber, *The Clash: US–Japanese Relations throughout History* (London and New York: W. W. Norton, 1997).

4  Arthur Marder, *Old Friends, New Enemies: The Royal Navy and the Imperial Japanese Navy* (Oxford: Oxford University Press, 1981).

5  Chris Bell, *The Royal Navy, Seapower and Strategy Between the Wars* (London: Palgrave Macmillan, 2000).

6  The best overall discussion of the Soviet Union's place in the Far East during the interwar period is found in Keith Neilson, *Britain, Soviet Russia and the Collapse of the Versailles Order, 1919–1939* (Cambridge: Cambridge University Press, 2005).

7  Ian Nish, *Japanese Foreign Policy in the Interwar Period* (Westport, CT: Praeger, 2002).

8  Bruce A. Elleman, "The Soviet Union's Secret Diplomacy Concerning the Chinese Eastern Railway, 1924–1925," *Journal of Asian Studies* 53 (1994): 459–86.

9  P. Duus, R. H. Myers, and M. R. Peattie, eds., *The Japanese Informal Empire in China, 1895–1937* (Princeton, NJ: Princeton University Press, 1991).

10  Michael A. Barnhart, *Japan Prepares for Total War: The Search for Economic Security, 1919–1941* (Ithaca, NY: Cornell University Press, 1987).

11  Robert H. Ferrell, *American Diplomacy in the Great Depression: Hoover–Stimson Foreign Policy, 1929–1933* (New Haven, CT: Yale University Press, 1957).

12  M. D. Kennedy, *Estrangement of Great Britain and Japan, 1917–1935* (Manchester: Manchester University Press, 1969).

13  Akira Iriye, *The Origins of the Second World War in Asia and the Pacific* (London and New York: Longman, 1987).

14  Warren I. Cohen, ed., *Pacific Passage: The Study of American–East Asian Relations on the Eve of the Twenty-First Century* (New York: Columbia University Press, 1996).

15  R. Dallek, *Franklin D. Roosevelt and American Foreign Policy* (New York: Oxford University Press, 1979).

16  On the intricate relationship between the United States and Great Britain, and their attempts to deter Japan between 1932 and 1939, see Greg Kennedy, *Anglo-American Strategic Relations and the Far East, 1933–1939* (London: Frank Cass, 2002).

17  Ong Chit Chung, *Operation Matador: Britain's War Plans against the Japanese, 1918–1941* (Singapore: Times Academic Press, 1997).

18  Greg Kennedy, "1935: A Snapshot of British Imperial Defence in the Far East," in *Far Flung Lines: Studies in Imperial Defence in Honour of Donald Mackenzie Schurman*, ed. Greg Kennedy and Keith Neilson (Portland, OR, and London: Frank Cass, 1997), pp. 190–216.

19  Howard Cox, Huang Biao, and Stuart Metcalfe, "Compradors, Firm Architecture and the 'Reinvention' of British Trading Companies: John Swire & Sons' Operations in Early Twentieth-Century China," *Business History* 45 (2003): 15–34.

20  J. E. Hunter and S. Sugiyama, eds., *The History of Anglo-Japanese Relations, 1600–2000*, vol. 4, *Economic and Business Relations* (Basingstoke and New York: Palgrave Macmillan, 2000).

21  Anthony Best, *Britain, Japan and Pearl Harbor: Avoiding War in East Asia, 1936–1941* (London and New York: Palgrave Macmillan, 1995).

22  Paul Haggie, *Britannia at Bay: The Defence of the British Empire against Japan, 1931–1941* (Oxford: Oxford University Press, 1981).

23  Dorothy Borg and Okamoto Shumpei, eds., *Pearl Harbor as History, 1931–1941* (New York: Columbia University Press, 1973).

24  Andrew Field, *Royal Navy Strategy in the Far East, 1919–1939* (London: Routledge, 2004); E. S. Millar, *War Plan Orange: The US Strategy to Defeat Japan, 1897–1945* (Annapolis, MD: Naval Institute Press, 1991).

25  D. C. Evans and M. R. Peattie, *Kaigun: Strategy, Tactics and Technology in the Imperial Japanese Navy, 1887–1941* (Annapolis, MD: Naval Institute Press, 1997).

26  J. W. M. Chapman, "Imperial Japanese Navy and the North–South Dilemma," in *Barbarossa*, ed. John Erickson and David N. Dilks (Edinburgh: Edinburgh University Press, 1984).

## GUIDE TO FURTHER READING

Richard Aldrich, *The Key to the South: Britain, the United States and Thailand during the Approach of the Pacific War* (Oxford: Oxford University Press, 1993). An authoritative survey of Anglo-American perceptions of Japanese strategic intentions and the use of intelligence in assessing Japanese intentions in the decade leading up to the war in the Far East.

W. G. Beasley, *Japanese Imperialism, 1894–1945* (Oxford: Oxford University Press, 1987). Still one of the best monographs on the Japanese model of imperialism and the strategic intent of that policy.

Anthony Best, *British Intelligence and the Japanese Challenge in Asia, 1914–1941* (Basingstoke and New York: Palgrave Macmillan, 2002). The best overall look at Britain's intelligence services and the attempt to gather and assess strategic intelligence on the Far East and Japanese strategic intentions in the interwar period.

Dorothy Borg, *The United States and the Far Eastern Crisis of 1933–1938: From the Manchurian Incident through the Initial Stage of the Undeclared Sino-Japanese War* (Cambridge, MA: Harvard University Press, 1964). Still a must read in the field, but badly in need of modernization and new interpretations. Dated in terms of its methodological utility as it is entirely based on US sources.

Robert Boyce and Joseph A. Maiolo, *The Origins of World War II: The Debate Continues* (Basingstoke and New York: Routledge, 2003). A useful overview of various nations and their strategic international position in the interwar period. Last section on themes and ideologies is very useful.

Alan Cassels, *Ideology and International Relations in the Modern World* (London and New York: Routledge, 1996). One of the best works which explains the way in which ideology plays a vital part in the making of any nation's strategic foreign policy and the need for observers of any nation to be aware of the role of ideology in foreign policymaking.

Patricia Clavin, *The Failure of Economic Diplomacy: Britain, Germany, France and the United States, 1931–1936* (London: Palgrave Macmillan, 1996). Best monograph on interwar fiscal competition and the role of economics in Great Power diplomacy.

Sir Hugh Cortazzi and Gordon Daniels, eds., *Britain and Japan, 1859–1991: Themes and Personalities* (London and New York: Routledge, 1991). A very handy and useful collection of snapshot biographies of key British and Japanese policymakers.

R. P. T. Davenport-Hines and Geoffrey Jones, *British Business in Asia since 1860* (Cambridge: Cambridge University Press, 1989). Still a model for anyone interested in understanding British business and that elite's culture in the Far East. Very useful for any graduate students interested in business history and foreign policy as a starting point for topics on the links between business and foreign policy formulation aimed at Far Eastern issues.

Roberta A. Dayer, *Bankers and Diplomats in China, 1917–1925* (London and Portland, OR: Frank Cass, 1981). A solid study of the role of bankers and their relations with British diplomats in attempting to protect British strategic interests in the Far East through economic and fiscal means.

Brian Farrell and Sandy Hunter, eds., *Sixty Years On: The Fall of Singapore Revisited* (Singapore: Times Academic Press, 2002). Best collection of papers by international historians to look at why Singapore happened, its overall impact on war, and the legacy of the fall of Singapore on the British Empire. Includes very good chapters on Japanese military actions during campaign against Singapore.

John P. Fox, *Germany and the Far Eastern Crisis 1931–1938: A Study in Diplomacy and Ideology* (Oxford: Clarendon Press, 1982). One of the few scholarly works based on sound archival research that looks at the Far East from the German perspective. Good for showing where strategic connections of military and foreign policy were, or were not, between the two regions.

Erik Goldstein and J. Maurer, eds., *Washington Conference, 1921–1922* (London: Frank Cass, 1994). Collection of essays on the maritime and diplomatic aspects of the Washington Naval Conference negotiations. Good starting place on the issue of interwar naval disarmament.

Jonathan Haslam, *The Soviet Union and the Threat from the East, 1933–1941* (London: Palgrave Macmillan, 1992). Standard work on the Soviet Union's view of the Japanese threat to its interests in the Far East and the policies developed to contain Japanese expansionism.

J. E. Hoare, ed., *Britain and Japan: Biographical Portraits*, vol. 3 (London: Routledge/Curzon, 1999). Useful collection of brief descriptions of key British and Japanese policymakers in the first half of the twentieth century.

Gordon Martel, *The Times and Appeasement: The Journals of A. L. Kennedy* (Cambridge: Cambridge University Press, 2000). This book is an edited and annotated version of the journals kept by A. L. Kennedy of *The Times* who was responsible for writing most of the editorials on European affairs between 1932 and 1939. They provide details of his meetings with Mussolini, Hitler, and others, explain the relationship between *The Times*, the British government, and the Foreign Office, and provide an illuminating insight into the support for "appeasement" and the origins of the Second World War.

Ian Nish, *Japan's Struggle with Internationalism: Japan, China and the League of Nations, 1931–1933* (London and New York: Kegan Paul, 1993); *Japanese Foreign Policy, 1869–1942* (London: Routledge, 1977). Nish is the leading scholar on Japan's foreign and military policy formulation in the last half of the nineteenth and the first half of the twentieth centuries. In all his works he provides a well-structured survey of Japan's struggle for its own national and international identity from 1850 through 1945 as it emerged as one of the great powers in Asia and the world.

Ritchie Ovendale, *"Appeasement" and the English-Speaking World: Britain, the United States, the Dominions and the Policy of Appeasement, 1937–1939* (Cardiff: University of Wales Press, 1975). An examination of the attitude of the Dominions and the United States toward Neville Chamberlain's policy for the appeasement of Europe. From an examination of cabinet, Dominion, and Foreign Office documents, the work also reveals some attitudes of the British policymaking elite toward Far Eastern issues.

Aaron Shai, *Origins of the War in the East: Britain, China and Japan, 1937–1939* (London: Croom Helm, 1976). A now somewhat dated study of the diplomatic relations between these three nations, but still a good introduction to the key chronological aspects of the deterioration of relations between these nations over this two-year period.

G. R. Storry, *Japan and the Decline of the West in Asia, 1894–1943* (London: Macmillan, 1979). Still used as a text on many courses on Japanese imperialism and economic aspects of its expansion. Looks at how western nations lost ground to Japanese penetration of markets in the Far East for both business/productivity/competitiveness reasons and because of the failure of western nations to recognize Japan's willingness to used armed force in its quest for a larger place in the region.

Christopher Thorne, *The Limits of Foreign Policy: The West, the League and the Far Eastern Crisis of 1931–1933* (London: Putnam, 1972); *Allies of a Kind: The United States, Britain, and the War against Japan, 1941–1945* (Oxford: Oxford University Press, 1978). These works analyze the various strategic relationships between the British and American strategic policymaking elites, the first in the period of the League of Nations and the latter during the realities of having to fight the war against Japan that the League could not prevent.

Ann Trotter, *Britain and East Asia, 1933–1937* (Cambridge: Cambridge University Press, 1975). A narrow look at British economic and business interests in East Asia. It attempts to tie these economic topics to bigger British foreign policy issues but due to a lack of archival range it does not do so as convincingly as more modern works. Still, a good place to find the basic sequence of key events and people in British and Japanese economic circles for this period.

David Wolff, *To the Harbin Station: The Liberal Alternative in Russian Manchuria, 1898–1914* (Stanford, CA: Stanford University Press, 1999). In 1898, near the projected intersection of the Chinese Eastern Railroad and China's Sungari River, Russian engineers founded the city of Harbin. Drawing on the archives, both central and local, of seven countries, this history of Harbin presents multiple perspectives on Imperial Russia's only colony and illustrates the complex nature of Russian–Japanese–Chinese relations in the Far East at that time.

# CHAPTER SIXTEEN

# The Challenge to Empire in the Middle East and Asia

## GAVIN D. BROCKETT

To nationalist elites in the Middle East and Asia, the Paris Peace Conference following the conclusion of the First World War offered the possibility of independence from European empire. No matter how ill-defined United States President Woodrow Wilson's idea of national self-determination may have been, his vision of a new world order organized around a League of Nations, coming as it did in the context of Bolshevik repudiation of colonialism in the Russian Revolution of 1917, fueled optimism that the greatest imperial powers, Britain and France, might relinquish their grip on Africa, Asia, and the Middle East. As negotiations unfolded throughout 1919, however, it became apparent that nothing could be further from the case. Wilson lacked both the commitment and the means to impose his will on fellow statesmen, while French and British imperialists saw a unique opportunity to profit from the defeat of Germany and the Ottoman Empire by absorbing new territory and expanding their own empires to their greatest geographic extents. Ignoring persistent petitions from Middle Eastern and Asian nationalists who flocked to Paris in the hopes of receiving an audience, the British and French delegations instead set about legitimating this imperial expansion through a system of mandates under the League of Nations. In theory, as mandatory powers, they were to prepare new but not sufficiently "advanced" nations for independence; but in practice, the mandates were little more than colonialism dressed up in poor disguise. By the

conclusion of the peace conference in 1920, therefore, European empire appeared even more robust and healthy than before. Few would have predicted that in less than twenty years an even greater war would erupt, bringing with it a truly new world order and the demise of European colonialism.

In retrospect, we know that European empire rapidly unraveled in the decades following the Second World War, and consequently the interwar years appear as a period of transition from empire to nation-state in the Middle East and Asia. The historical narrative typically renders this a coherent process in terms of the "rise of nationalism" whereby "growing numbers of people" beyond Europe found themselves increasingly influenced by "the idea of self-determination of nations" such that "nationalism developed into a powerful political force."[1] However appealing this paradigm may be, it is problematic and not simply because it implies a degree of inevitability that did not exist. To be sure, Middle Eastern and Asian elites did articulate nationalist ideologies with more clarity after the First World War, but the paradigm invests too much power in the ability of western ideas to mobilize people throughout the world and thus to change the course of history. Nationalism did not pose a serious challenge to empire between the world wars; moreover, it remained a predominantly elite ideology. A new generation of "westernized" intellectuals did emerge fluent in the language of nationalism as it had come to be spoken in Europe, and their rhetoric contained the appropriate idioms and symbols as they proclaimed their pursuit of national independence. Yet with few exceptions, the social and political elite in the Middle East and Asia preferred ideas to action, either because they saw little prospect for success in challenging empire, or because they themselves were entangled in complicated relationships with imperial powers that in fact served their own personal interests.

If empire did face a challenge after the First World War, then it was primarily in the form of popular protest and unrest giving voice to what were legitimate grievances experienced by the majority of people throughout the Middle East and Asia. Correctly or not, they perceived the imperial power – and sometimes their own elite – to be responsible for their suffering. Protest in this context could be widespread but it was usually short-lived and uncoordinated; at times intense colonial repression transformed protest into full-scale armed rebellion over which imperial and national historiographies have since imposed a distinctly nationalist gloss. Ultimately each movement was brutally crushed by vastly superior colonial forces at comparatively little cost to the imperial power. Moreover, despite relatively superficial reforms aimed at preserving colonial control behind the pretense of granting greater freedoms, protest and rebellion had only minimal impact on imperial policy and certainly did not lead to national independence. Nevertheless, in those countries where popular protest was most potent in the interwar period – in India, Egypt, Syria, Iraq, and Indochina – it contributed significantly to the processes by which new nations were formed and therefore has been subsumed in the prevailing narrative of nationalism.

The paradigm which posits "the rise of nationalism" beyond Europe between the two world wars had its genesis in Europe at that time, and it served the important purpose of explaining opposition to colonialism in the Middle East and Asia in terms palatable to Europeans who were used to justifying imperialism in terms of a *mission civilisatrice*. To admit that colonial rule was oppressive, exploitive, and frequently brutal – quite the opposite of the "liberal principles that animated their own systems of government"[2] –

required far too much honesty; it was preferable to believe that non-European peoples were simply progressing through a necessary stage of "development." Rejection of "the West," therefore, became imitation of the West even if the final product turned out to be a poor representation of the original. Perhaps the most influential proponent of this paradigm was Hans Kohn. In his words, the "Orient" had been mired in "timeless immobility" and the rise of nationalism was the result of spreading western influence: "Western ideas concerning manners and customs, the principles of statecraft, religion, democracy and industry began slowly to penetrate the East . . . It spread rapidly downwards, embracing wider and wider sections of the population, and outwards, so that soon no province of Asia or Northern Africa was left unaffected."[3] Kohn's thesis retains a remarkable currency in western historiography even today, but not only because its emphasis on western cultural superiority is appealing. Significantly, it finds full expression in the prevailing historical narratives initially authored by Middle Eastern and Asian political elites who themselves promoted nationalist ideologies: for they revered western intellectual traditions and political forms, and were eager to promote themselves not only as the articulate opponents of colonialism but also as a benevolent elite committed to rescuing their "nation," mired as it was in stagnation and burdened by tradition.[4] Thus they justified the usually undemocratic – even dictatorial – programs of modernization in which they engaged at the expense of the broader population once Britain and France had granted their countries independence following the Second World War.

By far the most penetrating and influential criticism of the "rise of nationalism" paradigm emerged among South Asian scholars conscious of the hegemonic influence of western notions of power on narratives concerning non-European history. If the Subaltern Studies collective – as this broad group of scholars is known – was inspired in part by Edward Said's profound criticism of western misrepresentations of "the Orient" in literature and scholarship,[5] their own contribution was to reject elite national historiographies and to address the historical experiences of the broader populace in the process of nation formation.[6] Rather than create coherent historical narratives along the lines of western historiographic tradition, instead they have focused on the contested, untidy nature of events. Thus, their focus has been on popular opposition to colonialism, and because of the immense power possessed by colonial governments, history, as Subaltern Studies scholars present it, is as much about failure as it is about success. Nonetheless, by shifting the focus onto the "subaltern" as protagonist, they have illuminated popular influences on nationalism rather than the other way round.[7] It is in this vein that the present essay explores the challenge to empire in the Middle East and Asia, both in terms of emergent nationalist ideologies and of popular protest and resistance.

## Nationalism and Non-Cooperation in South Asia

Nationalism and popular protest in India not only posed the greatest challenge to European empire in Asia during the interwar period, it also constituted by far the most distinctive, even innovative, form of opposition to colonial domination. India differed from most other colonial possessions in the Middle East and Asia in that European commercial interests and influence in South Asia dated back to 1600; however, it was only in 1857, following a widespread rebellion, that Britain formally incorporated India as a colony, in recognition of its enormous importance to the imperial economy. Thus began almost a century of collaboration, conflict, and negotiation between the British government, India's elite, and the tremendously diverse population throughout South Asia. The very size of the area and the diversity of its population placed significant limits on the ability of the British to exercise effective control, and the British government in India – the Raj – depended heavily on a combination of collaboration with willing regional elites and the forceful repression of its opponents. The origins of nationalism among India's elite are typically associated with the establishment of the Indian National Congress (INC) in 1885, but for the first two decades its members operated with complete deference to the Raj. It was only in the context of mass opposition to British plans to partition the province of

Bengal between 1905 and 1908 that the INC became more outspoken and found itself representing popular interests. Thereafter, the INC struggled to contain two very different visions of India as a nation: one secular and elitist, but culturally inclusive; the other popular and exclusive, with an emphasis on Hindu identity. At the same time, the transition to a more popular nationalism witnessed the emergence of the Muslim League (1906); an advocate for the interests of some of India's large Muslim population, the Muslim League nonetheless remained committed to Indian national unity throughout the interwar period.

Whereas nationalists throughout the Middle East and Asia saw the Paris Peace Conference as an opportunity to achieve national independence, with no decisions concerning Indian territory pending, Indian nationalists had little reason to hope that traveling to Paris in 1919 would benefit their own struggle. Indeed, in 1917 Lord Montagu, British minister responsible for India, had been careful to declare his preference for "responsible government" rather than self-determination in India, and the subsequent Government of India Act (1919) did devolve certain powers to elected provincial assemblies, but preserved the most important powers dealing with revenue as well as with law and order within the purview of the viceroy. This led to considerable disappointment and frustration on the part of the nationalist elite, but other circumstances also contributed to country-wide dissatisfaction after 1918. The passage at this time of emergency legislation, known as the Rowlatt Acts, to legitimate further draconian measures to repress popular opposition ("sedition") added insult to injury. Indian nationalists generally had supported the British government during the war in the hopes that their reward would be constitutional reform leading to self-government, while the people as a whole had contributed both extensive tax revenue and materials to say nothing of over a million soldiers to the British army. Whereas some Indian entrepreneurs had benefited financially from the war effort, most Indians had suffered from inflation and a shortage of resources. After the war many Indian laborers lost their jobs and demobilized soldiers joined the ranks of the unemployed.

Deteriorating economic conditions throughout the country led to strikes, food riots, and even violence toward wealthy creditors and landowners. A final factor that spawned popular dissatisfaction was concern among India's Muslims with Britain's policy toward the Ottoman sultan-caliph and British control of the holy cities of Mecca and Medina following the war: it was in response to this that the India-wide Khilafat movement emerged.

On April 13, 1919, the massacre by British soldiers of 379 unarmed, peaceful Indian demonstrators in the Punjabi city of Amritsar, and the subsequent effort by the government to justify such brutality, symbolized the injustice Indians associated with the Raj. It was in this context that Mohandas Gandhi emerged as one of the most prominent opponents of European colonialism during the interwar period. By 1920 Gandhi had assumed effective leadership of the INC, and his concern to reach out to the overwhelmingly poor Indian populace, yet to maintain strong ties with wealthy supporters and to work with the country's Muslims, resulted in a truly unique moment of popular national opposition to the Raj between 1919 and 1922. Gandhi was an enigmatic character: opposed to industrial civilization, rejecting socialism and notions of class struggle which appealed to other Indian nationalists, and embodying popular Hindu beliefs and practices, he possessed an almost millenarian appeal.[8] Previously Indians had either resorted to violence against or negotiated with the Raj, but Gandhi now introduced the concept of *satyagraha*, or peaceful non-cooperation, aimed at challenging the very moral authority and legality of the Raj. Utilizing the style of protest that he had developed previously in South Africa, Gandhi led Indians in peaceful demonstrations, public strikes (*hartals*), and in courting arrest by flaunting specific, unjust laws. Gandhi promised Indians that support for *satyagraha* would lead to *swaraj* (self-rule) within a year; however, just what self-rule entailed was unclear, and despite considerable support, Gandhi discovered that a large portion of the Indian people remained unwilling to sacrifice itself or lacked the discipline to confront the Raj through non-cooperation. Instead, considerable unrest and violence occurred throughout the provinces,

each case relating more to specific local issues rather than to a call to unite behind the "nation."[9] Having failed to establish peaceful non-cooperation as the norm or to bring about independence as he had promised, Gandhi declared an end to his campaign in February 1922.

Gandhi returned to non-cooperation in 1930, but under very different circumstances. The intervening years had been characterized by considerable unrest, between Muslims and Hindus, but also among the massive numbers of poor who resented heavy taxation and landownership laws, while their own dire circumstances were exacerbated by continued economic recession and then depression. British intransigence and failure to meet growing expectations in terms of constitutional reform, to say nothing of their brutal repression of all forms of popular opposition, continued to fuel public anger. Yet at the same time, national unity remained elusive: increasingly the INC was maturing as a mass political organization, but at the same time it faced challenges from Muslims, members of the Untouchable caste, and even from Hindus who felt that their interests were not represented. Gandhi's campaign of civil disobedience between 1930 and 1935 – symbolized by his public challenge to the Salt Tax in 1930 – proved far more widespread, disciplined, and successful than that of a decade earlier. Indians based in both rural and urban areas participated, and women were visible participants. To a considerable degree Gandhi even found himself responding to pressure from the populace to intensify and continue the campaign.

However, the British response – the Government of India Act of 1935 – revealed again how little influence nationalism and popular protest had on imperial government. To be sure, Gandhi had forced the Raj to respond to his campaign for independence, but the Act reflected more debates within the British parliament than negotiations with Indians. While certain powers were granted to the provincial electorate, the central government retained tremendous power: a federal system had not been introduced and there was no indication that this might occur in the near future.[10] The British were well aware of the divisions within Indian society and capitalized on them throughout its rule. When India finally received its independence – as much due to shifting British priorities as to nationalism – the differences between Muslims and Hindus had reached such a point that Gandhi's vision of a united, independent India was shattered. In 1947 South Asia split into the states of India and Pakistan, and to this day India remains a diverse and divided nation.

## European Empire and Nationalism in the Middle East

The challenge – both popular and nationalist – to European imperialism in the Middle East in the interwar period occurred in the context of opposition to nineteenth-century British and French colonization of much of North Africa, as well as resentment at their use of the newly created League of Nations to ratify wartime decisions and claim the Arab provinces of the Ottoman Empire as their own. In 1830 the French had begun the conquest of Algeria; in 1881 they had occupied Tunisia; and in 1912 Morocco had been declared a French Protectorate. Consequently, French imperialists were concerned not only to protect their economic interests and the well-being of Christian minorities in the Levant, but also to complete their Mediterranean empire and to prevent Arab nationalism from spreading to their North African colonies. Britain too had economic interests throughout the eastern Mediterranean and claimed the right to protect Christian minorities under Ottoman rule, but its primary concern was to ensure its claim to India. Thus the British had a particular interest in the Suez Canal: originally financed by both French and British investors, it opened in 1869 and provided a cheap and fast means to reach India. Concerned to protect the canal, the British occupied first Cyprus in 1878 and then Egypt in 1882.

The secret negotiations undertaken by the British and French during the First World War reflect these preoccupations: in the Sykes–Picot Accord (1916), the British laid claim to a large swathe of land from the Mediterranean to the Persian Gulf, and the French claimed Greater Syria and much of southeastern Anatolia. At the same time, the British had entered into contradictory agreements with Sharif Husayn of Mecca to

promise him an Arab state in much of Syria in return for his efforts to lead an Arab revolt against the Ottoman Empire. Following the war, it was only after intense negotiations at the San Remo Conference (1920) that the British and French resolved their differences and formalized their claims to the Arab provinces through the Treaty of Sèvres. In 1922 the League of Nations granted Britain mandates in Iraq, Palestine, and Transjordan, while France received the mandate in Greater Syria.

By 1922, however, the British and the French had already suffered the greatest challenge to their imperial dominance during the interwar period. The Treaty of Sèvres had also legitimated plans to divide up Anatolia, the largely Turkish heartland of the Ottoman Empire. To the surprise of the French and British, the Turkish elite did not simply "do as they were told" and acquiesce;[11] rather, they successfully mobilized the war-weary Anatolian populace to undertake a struggle that would become known as the Turkish War of Independence (1919–22). Led by the Mustafa Kemal Atatürk, the Turks succeeded in driving out of Anatolia armies from Britain, France, Italy, Greece, and Armenia, and then, in Lausanne (1923), in effectively nullifying the Treaty of Sèvres with regard to Anatolia. Not only had the British and French found themselves publicly humiliated – and nationalist elites throughout the Middle East and Asia were well aware of the Turkish victory thanks to newspapers – they also suspected that Turkish nationalists were covertly supporting the revolts in Syria and Iraq in 1920. Turkey was the only country to achieve complete independence between the wars, and so it was to constitute an important inspiration for anticolonial movements in subsequent decades.

There were distinct differences between the territories that did remain under British and French colonial control in the Middle East after 1919. Egypt had a well-defined geography, concentrated as it was along the Nile river valley. Prior to British occupation it had been a largely autonomous province in the Ottoman Empire, and nineteenth-century modernization had contributed significantly to the development of the institutions necessary to an independent state. Yet despite this, through the end of the First World

War the majority of Egyptian intellectuals, while conscious of a distinct Egyptian identity, remained committed to the Islamic Ottoman Empire.[12] The situation was very different in the new states of Greater Syria and Iraq, which represented classic examples of European statesmen redrawing the map of the Middle East to suit imperial interests. Both had been formed from an amalgamation of former provinces over which the Ottoman Empire had exercised considerable control in the late nineteenth century. Moreover, the French were particularly concerned about the recurrent power of prewar Arab nationalism, which appeared to manifest itself in the short-lived independent state of Syria proclaimed by the Amir Faysal (son of Sharif Husayn of Mecca) in March 1920. Consequently, no sooner had the French assumed the mandate and defeated Faysal's army in July 1920 than they dissected Greater Syria, establishing the state of Greater Lebanon and separating Syria into four distinct units partly on the basis of religious identification. This policy of divide and rule, based on French colonialism in Morocco, proved to have a longlasting and detrimental impact on future Syrian political and social unity.[13] In Iraq, by contrast, the British struggled to incorporate an already disparate population divided along the lines of religion (Sunni–Shi'a), ethnicity (Arab–Kurdish–Persian), and social organization (tribal–urban). Ottoman provincial administration had allowed for these differences, and recent events have demonstrated that ongoing attempts to impose unity on the peoples of Iraq since the British first tried have failed to forge a coherent nation.

Arab nationalism, although feared by the French, was in fact of minimal importance as a political ideology in the Middle East in the interwar period. Despite the fact that the peoples of Egypt, Palestine, Lebanon, Syria, Iraq, Transjordan, and Saudi Arabia were almost entirely Arabic-speaking and predominantly Muslim (there were significant Christian and Jewish minorities), the emphasis that some intellectuals placed upon a common Arab and Muslim identity failed to overcome the immediate needs among the Arab elite to ensure their influence in newly established states. With the possible exception of Iraq, where the government did support Arab nationalism to

a degree, Arab elites in the 1920s developed a revised version of the "politics of the notables" by which they had preserved a significant degree of autonomy in the Ottoman Empire.[14] Concerned first and foremost with protecting their own economic and social interests, they cooperated with the colonial power and acted as an intermediary between it and the populace. At the same time, as these politics unfolded in the representative assemblies established by the mandatory powers in each country, it became clear that competition within each national elite was intense and divisive. Neither the French nor the British, therefore, faced united nationalist opposition to their rule in Egypt, Syria, or Iraq, while Arab unity across the newly created international borders was of even less consequence.

It was only subsequent to the Great Revolt in Palestine (1936–9) – itself a popular movement of protest and rebellion best understood in the context of the Israeli–Palestinian conflict – that Arab nationalism was to dominate Arab politics in the 1950s and 1960s.[15]

## Popular Resistance to European Colonialism in the Arab Middle East

The challenge to British and French colonialism in the Middle East that did emerge between the wars came in the form of popular protest and rebellion. The First World War had devastated the Arab population: Syria and Iraq had been the site of considerable conflict, while in Egypt the British had seized local resources and conscripted peasants as laborers. After the war, droughts combined with economic policies structured to favor imperial interests over those of the local population led to further shortages, inflation, and widespread frustration.

The First World War had confirmed the strategic importance of Egypt to the British Empire in terms of both the Suez Canal and human and material resources. Consequently, the British had little inclination to grant demands for Egyptian independence in 1918. No sooner had the war ended than an elitist delegation of nationalists led by Sa'd Zaghlul approached the high commissioner seeking independence on the basis of the Wilsonian principle of self-determination; they later requested permission to travel to Paris to make their case at the peace conference. Upon rejection of these demands, Zaghlul and the Wafd (as his party came to be known) launched a public campaign to convince the British that indeed they represented the Egyptian populace as a whole. Zaghlul's rural background and his education in the great Islamic institution al-Azhar facilitated his identification with the people, and the campaign was very successful: public rallies attracted thousands of supporters, petitions were signed in support of the Wafd, and newspapers joined in challenging British colonialism.

To defuse the crisis, the British then exiled Zaghlul and some of the Wafd leadership. Much to the surprise of the British, who had refused to acknowledge legitimate grounds for popular discontent, this decision ignited what is known as the Egyptian "revolution" of March 1919. For months afterwards, Egypt was shaken by widespread protests to which the British responded with characteristically heavy-handed repression, relying on aerial bombing and armored cars to kill more than 800 Egyptians. Scholars have identified various reasons for this anticolonial rebellion, and although it did occur in the context of ongoing elitist efforts to secure Egyptian independence, country-wide unrest clearly was not in response to Wafd efforts to coordinate a mass movement. Indeed, at times even the nationalist elite was shocked by its extent, and struggled to harness popular sentiment for fear that its own interests were at risk. Significantly, participants included the urban elite – lawyers, government workers, and students – conscious that complete integration of Egypt into the British colonial system threatened their status, and peasants aggrieved by the devastating impact of wartime policies on their lives. Moreover, unrest in Egypt in 1919 is noteworthy for the participation of women in urban demonstrations, and for the role played by members of ethnic and religious minorities. Finally, it is important to note that Egyptians did not engage in the sort of violent rebellion that was to occur in either Syria or Iraq. Disturbances continued throughout the rest of the year and Egyptians boycotted the subsequent Milner Commission sent to evaluate the situation, but the actions of protestors reflected the limits within which they consciously acted: apart from public demonstrations, workers withdrew services and staged strikes, while telegraph and rail lines were severed. Violence toward British soldiers and subjects, however, was limited, and care was taken not to destroy the infrastructure central to the country's economy and hence to the well-being of Egyptians themselves.[16]

The Egyptian revolution of 1919 did not lead to Egyptian independence, but it did prompt the British government to modify its approach to ruling Egypt in order to protect its strategic interests, while limiting the costs to itself. Unable to reach agreement with the Wafd, in 1922 the British government unilaterally declared Egypt "independent," elevated its ruler to the status of monarch, and later supported the establishment of a constitution and parliament. Concurrently, the British government took care to enshrine its right to protect imperial communications in Egypt, to oversee Egypt's foreign affairs, and to protect minorities in the country. Thereafter, for the remainder of the interwar period, anticolonial nationalism was depleted of much of its force; Sa'd Zaghlul died in 1927 and with no charismatic leader to replace him, Egyptian politics devolved into an elite power struggle between the Wafd and the monarch, exacerbated by ongoing British interference. A treaty in 1936 failed to negate British influence in Egypt, and it was only after a military coup overthrew the monarch in 1952 that the British agreed to leave Egypt.

Unlike Egypt, where British forces had been well entrenched since 1882, it was only with the onset of the First World War that Britain began to extend its control over Iraq, first Basra in 1914 and finally Baghdad in March 1917. The British Foreign Office and India Office (which held primary responsibility for Iraq) disagreed on how they were to govern a country that was important because of its reserves of oil, its proximity to the Persian Gulf, and the significance of its airfields to imperial communications. Occupation of Iraq during the war in no way meant complete control or pacification of the diverse population, and prior to the outbreak of violent rebellion there was evidence of considerable unrest. Shi'a ulama publicly condemned the possibility that Britain might assume mandatory power, and in 1918 two secret Islamic societies were established in the Shi'a holy cities of Karbala and Najaf, each to mobilize resistance to foreign occupation. In February 1919 a more broadly based organization under the name "The Guardians of Independence" emerged not only in Karbala and Najaf, but also in Baghdad and Kut. Significantly, it represented a coalition of many of Iraq's diverse social groups: Shi'a and Sunni Arabs, civil servants, members of the ulama, and former Ottoman military officers. At the same time, localized unrest occurred across the country, including a Kurdish revolt in the northern district of Sulaymaniyyah.[17]

By May 1920 popular opposition to British rule was increasingly evident. During the month of Ramadan the rapprochement between Sunnis and Shi'as was unmistakable as they joined together in Baghdad's mosques to celebrate religious ceremonies important to both traditions. At these commemorations appeals were made for all to join in opposition to British rule based on their common Arab and Muslim identity. A delegation was even sent to Sharif Husayn of Mecca seeking one of his sons – Abdullah – as the king of Iraq. The British high commissioner to Iraq, however, was intent on directly administering the country with as little Iraqi input as possible, and so rejected a proposal for an elected national assembly.

The British high commissioner remained confident that despite clear popular opposition to British rule, divisions among Iraqis would prevent united action. He turned out to be wrong and on this one occasion many Iraqis overcame longstanding differences to unite in a widespread yet uncoordinated rebellion against British plans. The immediate cause appears to have been the arrest of a tribal leader for failure to pay taxes and the decision by members of his tribe to free him from prison in late June 1920. For the next five months the British army and air force engaged in fierce battles with Iraqi tribes in the mid-Euphrates region where Iraqis established their own provisional government. In Karbala and other cities violence erupted in response to British efforts to suppress public demonstrations. Much of the rebellion, however, involved tribes beyond the direct influence of the urban elite who had played such an important role in fomenting unrest

to begin with. The widespread nature of the rebellion reflected the various interests of Iraqis and the shifting alliances among those who participated: members of the ulama (Shi'a and Sunni) wanted an independent Islamic government; tribesmen resented British efforts to collect taxes and conscript them for public works projects; former Ottoman soldiers and bureaucrats had no prospect of employment and income; and nationalists were intent on an independent nation-state.

It was only in November that the rebellion came to an end, as much because Iraqi forces were running low on arms and supplies as because of the ability of the British to defeat them through intense aerial bombing. Iraqi casualties numbered in the thousands, while the British themselves suffered unusually high casualties with 400 dead. The rebellion did witness unprecedented unity among Iraqis, but in the end the people had not united in opposition to colonialism, and many Iraqis had chosen to support the mandate for their own reasons. The rebellion had failed on all fronts for, although the British did modify their approach to governing Iraq, their strategy of installing the Amir Faysal as king of Iraq and granting his government a measure of autonomy through a negotiated treaty was carefully structured to preserve British influence by means of indirect rule, as in Egypt. In another treaty negotiated in 1930 the British promised to bring the mandate to an end; when this occurred in 1932, British influence diminished but did not end, and politics in Iraq became a battle between those concerned to accommodate British interests and a new generation committed to complete Iraqi independence and even Arab nationalism. Eventually this new generation was to lead a revolution to overthrow the monarchy in 1958.

In Syria, the Great Revolt of 1925–7 occurred some five years after the defeat of the Amir Faysal's Arab army and France's assumption of the mandate. Subsequently urban and rural resistance did occur, but it was neither coordinated nor strong enough to hinder severely the French efforts to occupy all of Syria. The Great Revolt itself began in July 1925 in a region south of Damascus known as the Jabal Hawran. The primary cause appears to have been deep grievances with the unjust and arbitrary nature of French rule in the area: the conscription of peasants and even tribal leaders for public works projects, and the excessive punishment of those opposed to the French presence. The instigation of the uprising was a French effort to arrest tribal leaders suspected of plotting resistance. In response Druze leaders mobilized villagers in the Jabal Hawran to fight in defense of an independent Syria, leading what amounted to a coordinated rebellion. Numbering in the thousands, very quickly Druze forces staged dramatic defeats of colonial soldiers. Significantly, the Jabal Hawran was the primary grain-producing area for Damascus and consequently the Druze had longstanding economic ties with grain merchants in the capital. This relationship proved critical to the subsequent development of the rebellion, for the Damascene nationalist elite found themselves forced to declare their allegiance, either to the revolt or to the French. The most militant nationalists from Damascus did join in the Great Revolt, but the majority of the urban elite proved unable or unwilling to translate their nationalist rhetoric into determined action, preferring instead to protect their relationship with the French mandatory government.

By October, rebellions had broken out in Syria's major urban centers, although not coordinated by the Druze. In Hama, a separate and carefully orchestrated insurrection briefly led to the retreat of French forces, while in Damascus the infiltration of the old city by bands of rebels terrified French officials. Their response was an overwhelming demonstration of force in the form of intense bombing of the old city and the dispatch of armored vehicles through its streets. The destruction of significant parts of the city led to the death of at least 1,500 Syrians. Clearly in no position to lead a revolt itself, the Damascene elite negotiated an end to the siege; thereafter the rebellion continued, but primarily in rural regions around Damascus. Remarkably, despite French military power, it was not until April 1927 that the Great Revolt was finally crushed and the Druze leaders either killed or driven into exile.

As was the case with rebellion elsewhere against empire, the Great Revolt in Syria failed to dislodge the French and to establish any meaningful form of independence. It was as a result of the Great Revolt that the Damascene elite formed the National Bloc in 1928 with the explicit purpose of promoting independence while working with the French at the same time. "Honorable cooperation," as this policy was known, proved to be a delicate balancing act dependent on a shift in French policy after the revolt toward negotiating and working with the elite rather than simply resorting to force. Following international outrage at the bombing of Damascus, the French government had little choice but to modify its policy in Syria along these lines, and so to some degree the Great Revolt did effect change, if only minimally.

The rebellion clearly had been anticolonial in nature, fought in the name of Syrian independence as well as of Arab and Muslim unity: clearly these represented different notions to different participants. Yet as the revolt demonstrated, unity among the Syrian population was an illusion: the nationalist elite in Damascus turned out to be seriously divided and the French astutely seized on this to limit the rebellion. It has been pointed out that the Great Revolt demonstrated that at some level urban and rural Syrians could cooperate, that social divisions could be overcome in common opposition to colonial government.[18] Nevertheless, just what those fighting for "Syria" imagined Syria to constitute varied considerably: clearly, commitment to the nation competed with other more deeply rooted loyalties, and these stood in the way of the concerted action necessary to challenge French control of Syria. Moreover, the French continued their policy of divide and rule with considerable success until they were forced to give up control of Syria under international pressure in 1946. Soon thereafter – in March 1949 – the first of many military coups occurred in Syria and the elite who had collaborated with the French were replaced by a new generation of Syrian Arab nationalists.

## Nationalism, Communism, and Rebellion in French Indochina

On the eve of the First World War, the French governor general in Indochina reported his concern that Vietnamese nationalists were part of

a much larger revolutionary, nationalist movement. "Liberal" colonial policies pursued by the
French and the British had failed to placate
nationalists throughout East and Southeast Asia,
and in the case of Indochina it was essential to
grant concessions in response to popular concerns
so as to minimize support for the concept of self-
government.[19] Indochina, however, was a relatively new colony and the French government
preferred to rule by force rather than placate the
people. Following on more than a century of
trade and missions in the region, the French had
begun their conquest of Indochina in the mid-
nineteenth century, and in 1887 it had declared
the Government General of Indochina, which
included the three provinces traditionally associated with Vietnam (Cochinchina, Annam,
and Tonkin) and Cambodia. By 1907 French
Indochina had gained its final form, which
included Laos. Neighboring Siam (later known as
Thailand) remained nominally independent, if
under British influence. The French moved quickly
to integrate the various regions of Indochina
under a central administration, instituting formal
taxation of the peasant population. At the same
time they incorporated Indochina within the
larger imperial economy to which it was subservient: French investment aimed at making this possible through the construction of canals, roads,
railroads, and ports. Indochina quickly became a
major world exporter of rubber and rice; the
massive peasant workforce exploited for these
industries worked under miserable circumstances
and only a tiny, wealthy segment of the population benefited from imperial programs aimed at
economic "development." The Great Depression
of the 1930s only exacerbated an already bad
situation.

Nationalism in Indochina took shape under
circumstances very different from those in either
the Middle East or India. Significantly, nationalist ideologies were not prominent in either Cambodia or Laos in the interwar period: here the
French political and cultural presence was more
moderate, while the elite were well aware that
French imperialism precluded the possibility of
either Siamese or Vietnamese expansion into their
territories as had occurred in previous centuries.
At times Vietnam itself had been a regional dynas-

tic power with a limited identity as a result of
opposition to Chinese imperial expansion. Vietnamese culture was heavily oriented toward
Chinese Confucianism; it was influenced far less
by Buddhism than were the cultures of Siam and
Burma. The earliest nationalist elite in Vietnam
drew inspiration from both Confucian and French
thought, and the Japanese defeat of the Russian
Empire in 1905 and then the Chinese Revolution
of 1911 encouraged the revolutionary fervor that
concerned the governor general in 1913. After the
First World War, nationalism in Vietnam under-
went a transformation as a new generation of
intellectuals emerged, no less radical, but more
secular in orientation and fascinated with Marxist-
Leninist thought. The 1920s marked the establishment of numerous revolutionary organizations
dedicated to defeating the French, the most
important of these being the Vietnamese Revolutionary Youth Association in 1925, and the Vietnamese Nationalist Party in 1927 (VNQDD).

Conscious of the threat posed by these organizations, the colonial government monitored
them closely and in 1929 attempted to eliminate
the VNQDD and its leadership. In desperation,
the VNQDD then launched a mutiny among
Vietnamese soldiers stationed at Yen Bay in
Tonkin, as well as an attack on a military base
nearby in Hung Hoa. The French response was
uncompromising: the rebels were quickly crushed
and the remaining VNQDD leaders publicly executed. Its leader, Nguyen Thai Hoc, went to his
death proclaiming his loyalty to "Vietnam." The
Yen Bay mutiny had been a hasty yet premeditated
attempt to generate a popular rebellion; the
mutiny failed, but its consequences were of profound importance to Vietnamese history: the
decimation of Vietnamese nationalists by the
French left a void that was soon to be filled by
Vietnamese communists committed to infusing
the nationalist struggle with a new ideology.

The Vietnamese Revolutionary Youth Association had been founded by Nguyen Ai Quoc (later
to claim the name Ho Chi Minh or "he who
enlightens") and initially was one of three separate communist organizations operating in Indochina. In 1930 the three united as the Indochinese
Communist Party (ICP): it operated in each of
the Vietnamese provinces, and in accordance with

Comintern policies pronounced in Moscow it concentrated its efforts on organizing the urban proletariat. Following on the Yen Bay mutiny in 1930, there was widespread labor unrest among workers: at a rubber plantation in Cochinchina, a match factory in Annam, and at a cotton factory in Tonkin. By May Day unrest had spread to Hanoi and Haiphong, but at this point peasants began to join the demonstrations and to initiate their own, far more extensive and longlasting movements. In Cochinchina peasant protest became widespread, but it was only following violent French repression that these developed into rebellious movements that involved small but highly effective attacks on symbols of French colonialism. By far the largest protests occurred in the northern province of Nghe An, where thousands of peasants and factory workers presented the French Resident with a list of grievances and attacked a plantation. Subsequently Nghe An and Ha Tinh provinces were engulfed in rebellion and the French government temporarily lost control. Throughout the summer and autumn the French air force struggled to defeat the effective hit-and-run peasant tactics in both provinces; ultimately it was the fear of starvation that led the peasants to submit, but only after suffering at least 3,000 deaths while inflicting relatively minimal casualties on the French.

The French government assumed that the unrest and rebellion of 1930–1 constituted a successful effort on the part of communists to exploit and mobilize a naïve populace; and in subsequent years Vietnamese communists were to claim credit for the uprisings. Scholars debate the issue: while peasants did adopt communist slogans, and "soviets" were established after the violence had begun, the Indochinese Communist Party not only failed to mobilize peasants in other provinces but also tried, unsuccessfully, to moderate the course of events at times.[20] The most convincing conclusion is that peasant rebellion was largely spontaneous in nature; it did not need communist organization and it persisted in the face of intense French repression because it was in response to legitimate and deeply rooted grievances among the peasants related to the taxes imposed on them, issues of landownership, and working conditions in factories. Moreover, the Indochinese

Communist Party had only just begun to organize: it was in no way prepared for protest on such a wide scale by the peasants rather than the urban proletariat. Communism in fact played only a minimal role in the uprisings, just as nationalism as an ideology was of limited significance. Nevertheless, Vietnamese communists learned important lessons from these events that were to be applied in the subsequent struggle for independence. However, so convinced were the French of the centrality of communist agitation to popular protest in Indochina that repression of communism after 1931 was severe and effective. Vietnamese communists were not to have the opportunity to apply the lessons they had learned until after the Second World War when Ho Chi Minh and communist ideology did indeed become central to Vietnamese nationalism and anticolonialism.

## Nationalism, Popular Protest, and European Empire

The years following the Second World War may have witnessed rapid decolonization throughout Africa, Asia, and the Middle East; however, contrary to the paradigm that presents this as the result of the spread of popular nationalism between 1918 and 1939, the challenges faced by European empires in the form either of an elite articulation of nationalism or of popular protest and rebellion simply were not all that great. The interwar period did not constitute a moment in the seamless transition from empire to nation-state in the Middle East and Asia. Rather, nationalism remained an ideology articulated by elites, but one that was also compromised by them as they placed their own interests before those of the nation. At the same time, the "nation" was not the primary locus of popular identity, and when people chose to protest and even rebel against a colonial power, it was more as an expression of very real and immediate grievances in the form of anticolonialism than it was an indication of commitment to a shared national identity. Indeed, these very acts of protest and rebellion themselves played an important part in the processes by which national identities took shape: not only did people find themselves united against a common enemy, in subsequent years these movements would be mythologized as critical to the emergence of independent nations. In fact, at the time they appeared to be movements that had resulted only in greater suffering before ending in defeat. Nevertheless, those who participated first in protest and then, at times, in rebellion did so consciously and intentionally: they were neither irrational nor manipulated by elitist ideologies. It is this history – of emergent yet weak nationalist ideologies, of popular but failed protest, and of changing yet resilient European empire – that characterizes the Middle East and Asia in the interwar years.

## NOTES

1   Jerry H. Bentley and Herbert F. Ziegler, *Traditions and Encounters: A Global Perspective on the Past*, vol. 2, *From 1500 to the Present* (Toronto: McGraw-Hill, 2000), p. 932.

2   Rashid Khalidi, *Resurrecting Empire: Western Footprints and America's Perilous Path in the Middle East* (Boston: Beacon Press, 2004), p. 16.

3   Hans Kohn, *A History of Nationalism in the East* (New York: Harcourt, Brace, and Company, 1929), p. 5.

4   But one example is Jawaharlal Nehru, *The Discovery of India*, ed. Robert I. Crane (New York: Anchor Books, 1960).

5   Edward Said, *Orientalism* (New York: Random House, 1978).

6   For an overview of Subaltern Studies see Gyan Prakash, "*AHR* Forum: Subaltern Studies as Postcolonial Criticism," *American Historical Review* 99 (1994): 1475–515.

7   With regard to nationalism see Partha Chatterjee, *Nationalist Thought and the Colonial World: A Derivative Discourse?* (London: Zed Books, 1986); and *The Nation and Its Fragments: Colonial and Postcolonial Histories* (Princeton, NJ: Princeton University Press, 1993).

8   For an example of Subaltern Studies scholarship concerning Gandhi see Shahid Amin, "Gandhi as Mahatma: Gorakhpur District, Eastern UP, 1921–2," in *Subaltern Studies III*, ed. Ranajit Guha, (Oxford: Oxford University Press, 1984), pp. 1–61.

9   Sumit Sarkar, *Modern India 1885–1947* (New York: St. Martin's, 1989), p. 210.

10  Burton Stein, *A History of India* (Oxford: Blackwell, 1998), p. 336.

11  Margaret Macmillan, *Paris 1919: Six Months that Changed the World* (New York: Random House, 2002), p. 380.

12  On Egyptian nationalism see Israel Gershoni and James P. Jankowski, *Egypt, Islam and the Arabs: The Search for Egyptian Nationhood, 1900–1930* (Oxford: Oxford University Press, 1986).

13  The best work on Syria is Philip Khoury, *Syria and the French Mandate: The Politics of Arab Nationalism, 1920–1945* (Princeton, NJ: Princeton University Press, 1987).

14  Albert Hourani, "Ottoman Reform and the Politics of the Notables," in *The Emergence of the Modern Middle East*, ed. Albert Hourani (London: Macmillan, 1981), pp. 36–66. On Iraq and Arab nationalism see Phebe Marr, "The Development of a Nationalist Ideology in Iraq, 1920–1941," *Muslim World* 75 (1985): 85–101.

15  On the Great Revolt see Ted Swedenburg, *Memories of Revolt: The 1936–1939 Rebellion and the Palestinian National Past* (Minneapolis, MN: University of Minnesota Press, 1995).

16  On the Egyptian revolution see Ellis Goldberg, "Peasants in Revolt – Egypt 1919," *International Journal of Middle East Studies* 24 (1992): 261–80.

17  On the 1920 rebellion in Iraq see Amal Vinogradov, "The 1920 Revolt in Iraq Reconsidered: The Role of Tribes in National Politics," *International Journal of Middle East Studies* 3 (1972): 123–39; and Sami Zubaida, "The Fragments Imagine the Nation: The Case of Iraq," *International Journal of Middle East Studies* 34 (2002): 205–15.

18  On the Great Revolt in Syria see Michael Provence, *The Great Syrian Revolt and the Rise of Arab Nationalism* (Austin, TX: University of Texas Press, 2005).

19  J. Kim Munholland, "The French Response to the Vietnamese Nationalist Movement, 1905–14," *Journal of Modern History* 47 (1975): 655–75.

20  David G. Marr, *Vietnamese Tradition on Trial, 1920–1945* (Los Angeles: University of California Press, 1981), pp. 378–87.

## GUIDE TO FURTHER READING

Hans Antlöv and Stein Tonnesson, eds., *Imperial Policy and Southeast Asian Nationalism 1930–1957* (Richmond: Curzon Press, 1995). Essays addressing Indochina and all of Southeast Asia.

Judith Brown and Wm. Roger Louis, eds., *The Oxford History of the British Empire*, vol. 4, *The Twentieth Century* (Oxford: Oxford University Press, 1999).

Essays addressing all aspects of British imperialism; one of five volumes.

Briton Cooper Busch, *Britain, India and the Arabs, 1914–1921* (Los Angeles: University of California Press, 1971). Early history of Iraq from the British perspective.

John Darwin, *Britain, Egypt and the Middle East* (New York: St. Martin's, 1981). Details processes by which Britain defined its role in the postwar Middle East.

Arthur J. Dommen, *The Indochinese Experience of the French and the Americans* (Bloomington, IN: Indiana University Press, 2001). Unusually thorough study of nationalism and communism in Indochina.

James Jankowski and Israel Gershoni, eds., *Rethinking Arab Nationalism in the Arab Middle East* (New York: Columbia University Press, 1997). Essays reflecting the latest scholarship on this much-debated subject.

Nadine Méouchy and Peter Sluglett, eds., *The British and French Mandates in Comparative Perspectives* (Leiden: Brill, 2004). Wide selection of essays dealing with Syria, Palestine, and Iraq.

Reeva Spector Simon and Eleanor H. Tejirian, eds., *The Creation of Iraq 1914–1921* (New York: Columbia University Press, 2004). Brief but useful overview of developments in Iraq during and just after the war.

Nicholas Tarling, ed., *The Cambridge History of Southeast Asia*, vol. 2, *The Nineteenth and Twentieth Centuries* (Cambridge: Cambridge University Press, 1992). Excellent overview of Southeast Asian history; one of two volumes.

Martin Thomas, *The French Empire between the Wars* (Manchester: Manchester University Press, 2005). Detailed comparative study of the French Empire with useful chapters on nationalism and popular protest.

# CHAPTER SEVENTEEN

# Mussolini's War in Ethiopia

## GIUSEPPE FINALDI

Thus because a few askaris [Italian colonial troops] had died by brackish water-holes in an African waste, was taken the first step to the second German holocaust. The pretext was more trivial than the murder of Franz Ferdinand.

(Sir Robert Vansittart, head of the British Foreign Office, 1930–8)[1]

## The Significance of the Italo-Ethiopian War: An Overview

On July 28, 1935, a Florentine weekly carried a particularly grotesque caricature of the emperor of Ethiopia, Haile Selassie. In it he is being told by the League of Nations doorman that he should take his grievances not to the League but to the next building along the Geneva street, the headquarters of the "Society for the Protection of Animals."[2] Crude and racist jokes such as this one abounded in Italy during the Ethiopian war, although they reflected attitudes that were certainly not confined to Italians or fascists. That Ethiopia was a member of the League of Nations was by no means universally accepted, even among Europe's liberals. In the 1930s Ethiopia was an anomaly in the international arena and it had been one ever since it rebuffed Italy's first attempt at making it a protectorate in 1896. The "survival of Ethiopian independence" (to mention the title of one important book[3] on the subject) is on the face of it a historical abnormality of the greatest importance. It was inspirational for the development of anticolonialism in Africa, and more generally it was a sign to black populations throughout the world that it was possible that they would one day stand up without the tutelage of white masters. In the 1920s the black activist Marcus Garvey took the Ethiopian experience as living proof that blacks could make it alone. Some

African Americans traveled to Ethiopia before 1935 and assigned to that kingdom the mythical capacity of liberating blacks and reuniting them after the long and bitter Diaspora imposed by whites.[4] Rastafarianism originated out of a sacralization of the figure of the Ethiopian emperor, biblical exegesis, and the desire for political and personal freedom among blacks in Jamaica.[5] Even in Britain, Sylvia Pankhurst's passage from suffragettism to socialist feminism and eventually to being the most vociferous supporter of Ethiopia's right to exist speaks volumes about the struggle for liberation of subordinate groups through the twentieth century.

In some ways the long-term consequences of the Italian invasion and eventual conquest of Ethiopia and the international uproar surrounding it tell us as much about the origins of the Second World War as they do about what shape the world would take at that conflict's end. By 1974, when Haile Selassie was removed from power by a younger generation of army officers, Ethiopia was just one independent African country among many. In 1936 he had stood up in front of the fifty-two representatives of the League of Nations and proclaimed the rights of an independent black African country to exist. That colonialism became rapidly unjustifiable after 1945 was, among other things, because of the vicissitudes of Ethiopian history in the nineteenth and twentieth centuries, and in particular the Italian conquest of 1935–6. If Italy had been wrong, and the League of Nations said that it had, then why were France and Britain right just because their empires had a somewhat longer history?

The Ethiopian war has in general been granted a place of importance in international history because it skewed the European balance of power at a very delicate moment. Hitler had been in control for two years but Germany was still too weak to pose a serious challenge to the order established at Versailles. He needed allies to forestall an early French or British nipping of Nazism in the bud, and that Italy ended up on the German side was only partly because of congruencies in fascist and Nazi ideology. Rather, it was the Ethiopian war that confirmed Mussolini's decision (always one fraught with danger for a country with thousands of miles of coastline in British-dominated waters) to ally with Germany and to tie Italy's fate to that of the Third Reich. In retrospect and on the basis of Italy's performance in the Second World War, this was not as beneficial to Germany as might have been expected, but in 1935–6 it was critical. Although the effective strength of fascist Italy was still to be proven, many had been taken in by the Duce's bluster and believed that Italy would be a crucial player in any future European conflict.

The upholders of Versailles and the guarantors of the League of Nations, Britain and France, ended up having to ditch the possibility of keeping Mussolini's friendship (for a variety of reasons that will be looked at below), and all for the sake of an African country that was strategically, economically, and politically of no consequence in Europe. In the eyes of many contemporaries, and then many historians, there is something as tragic in this as there is in poor Chamberlain's guarantee of "peace in our time" after Munich. The events of 1940–1 (when Italy quickly lost Ethiopia, Somalia, and Eritrea to the British) showed that Italy's hold on East Africa depended on free access through the Suez Canal and a Mediterranean fleet that remained unchallenged by the British: this was the case throughout the 1935–6 war.

In Italy itself, though, the conquest of Ethiopia boosted the fascist regime and strengthened Mussolini's position vis-à-vis the monarchy, the army, and the Italian people in general. Challenging the Versailles settlement and making war paid

dividends, and it appeared that fascism's promise to transform Italy and Italians was finally being fulfilled. An empire of magnitude had been created at last and appeared to confirm the superiority of the fascist over the liberal way of doing things. Adowa, where liberal Italy had been defeated in Ethiopia in 1896, had hung over Italian self-esteem like a nightmare, was no more, or so it was proclaimed up and down the country, and the massive collective effort that had warded off sanctions imposed by the League of Nations suggested that never before had the Duce and his people acted in such unequivocal harmony. In 1936, fascism appeared to be working nicely and its pledges were being honored.

The implications throughout Europe were great. For those who did not want, as so many did in these years, to see the Soviet Union as a "new civilization"[6] in a period where the latter appeared to be the only alternative to a capitalism that was failing to deliver (the 1930s depression was reaching its peak when Mussolini invaded Ethiopia), fascism seemed to have the answers. The audacity with which, for example, Franco, soon to be dictator of Spain, decided to plunge his country into civil war rather than accept a government of the left was connected to the aura of victory that clung to Mussolini after the Ethiopian campaign. For many on the European right, the time for action, whatever it entailed, had arrived.

In one recent overview the 1930s have, echoing Churchill, been referred to as the "Dark Valley." "The depression cast its pall over the world," writes Piers Brendon, "it was the worst peacetime crisis to affect humanity since the Black Death . . . It was a time of systematic obfuscation, of darkness at noon."[7] This valley of shadow was a place from which the world emerged only in 1945. It was the decade when the seed sown in 1914–18 began to give forth its bitter harvest. Auschwitz, the Gulag, the horrors of the Nazi war against Poland and the Soviet Union and the massive aerial bombings of the Allies, the war crimes of Japan in China, and so much more were all in one way or another the product of the political developments of the 1930s. In 1937 the destruction of Guernica in Spain by German bombers foreshadowed the greater horror to come. Yet notwithstanding the fact that it was soon to be beggared by a Dresden or a Hiroshima, the name of the Basque town has remained a supreme symbol of the unacceptable. The use of nerve gas by Italy in Ethiopia, however, presaged Guernica itself and set the scene for the barbarism that was to be one of the most appalling characteristics of the following decade. In Ethiopia victory was to be had at any cost, and the erasing of any distinction between military and civilian targets (and, notwithstanding the enormous casualties of the First World War, this had not occurred in that conflict) was well and truly under way. That this was justified in Italy by the fact that it brought death only to those deemed racially inferior foreshadowed the horrors of the Second World War.

The origins of Nazi violence are a hotly debated issue but their relationship with what was unquestioningly normal practice in Europe's colonies needs restating. Haile Selassie standing up in Geneva and denouncing Mussolini's gas bombings in Africa suddenly brought these two universes together in one place. The era of clean wars that involved uniformed armies battling it out in Europe and dirty ones pitting machine guns (or bombers) against civilians in the colonies was over. Normal Europeans were about to experience the contempt with which their lives were held in a way that was all too familiar to the indigenous populations of their colonies.

## The Survival of Ethiopian Independence

As has been suggested, the fact that Ethiopia remained an independent kingdom in the era of the European colonization of Africa is remarkable. There have been many attempts at explaining this fact: to some contemporaries it was the peculiarity of Ethiopia being Christian that made the difference; others rested their case on racial grounds, suggesting that the Ethiopians were biologically separate from other African blacks and had enough Semitic or even Portuguese blood to make them something of a cut above their sub-Saharan neighbors. To others, such as the Rastafarians, it was divine intervention that made Ethiopian history unique.

In reality the failure of Europe to colonize Ethiopia before 1935 was because the Ethiopians could field a large and powerful army in the critical years of the "Scramble for Africa." If the Impis of South Africa were considered to be superlative warriors and the British had been pressed to the limit to deal with them, the number of troops Ethiopia could deploy was on a scale that the Zulu could only have dreamt about.

The Ethiopian kingdom was organized much like a feudal state of the European Middle Ages. A Christian aristocratic class held land as a fiefdom from the emperor and in exchange provided troops conscripted from the peasantry. Often (as in feudal Europe) the aristocrats were powers unto themselves and loyalty to the emperor was only nominal, but there were occasions, particularly when Ethiopia was assailed from the outside, that the military feudal kingdom worked very effectively. The Christianity of the ruling class and of a large proportion of the peasantry in a sea of Islam provided a cohesion that can be almost equated to national identity. Amharic, the language of Church and state, had developed its own alphabet and a political and religious literature had come into being particularly through the work of monks in the monasteries dotted through the Ethiopian highlands. Court officials were literate and formed a rudimentary, but real, bureaucracy. Although divided among different princedoms and linguistic ethnic groups, this was material enough on which to construct a plausible "imagined community."

Hence, any attempt at reducing Ethiopia to a colony necessitated surmounting a series of powerful resisting factors that were absent in most other areas of sub-Saharan Africa. In 1868, it is true, the British had deposed the then emperor Tewodros and had successfully brought a (mostly Indian) army deep into the heart of the African highland kingdom. But the easy success of the British on this occasion did not entail the transformation of Ethiopia into a colony. The expedition had been sent in order to uphold British prestige after the Ethiopian emperor had imprisoned a British legate. Because Tewodros's barons abandoned him at the last minute, Sir Robert Napier's expedition was able to fulfill its mission and return almost unmolested to the coast. But 1868 had hardly been a real test of Ethiopian power, as unified resistance never materialized behind the emperor. Tewodros had alienated most of his Rases (Ethiopian nobles) and effectively had no army to pit against the British; if the latter had been intent on staying, things would probably have been very different.

It took the establishment of permanent Italian power in the area (as well as Islamic incursions through the Sudan), instead of the ineffectual and distant suzerainty of the languid Ottomans, to mold Ethiopia into a formidable military machine. The emperor Menelik, who had acceded to the throne in 1889, was fully conscious of the fact that he needed a loyal aristocracy at home and as many European weapons as he could lay his hands on if his empire was not to fall prey, like the rest of Africa, to Europe's lust for territory. He was a master at playing one European country off against the other and maintained Italian, British, Russian, and French delegations at his court.

It eventually became clearer that the main enemy was likely to be Italy. When the conflict came to a head in 1896, Menelik secured the allegiance of the Rases and the people at large, and, with the blessing of the Coptic Church, was able to put to good use the arms accumulated via French and Italian dealers over the last decade. At Adowa his army of more than 100,000 routed Italy's 20,000. Crispi, the Italian prime minister, fell from power and tumults greeted the news in Italy's piazzas. It would have been difficult to mount yet another expedition to the Horn. Menelik, unlike Tewodros and Crispi, conserved the loyalty of his people. As Sven Rubenson put it: "Though it might have been difficult for European statesmen to think in those terms, it was Crispi's power base that was narrow and shaky, not Menelik's. Italy was overextending herself in Africa, rather than [the Ethiopian emperor]."[8]

Adowa was not just unique because of its scale (almost 2,000 Italians were taken to Addis Ababa as POWs and held there for more than a year) but because the defeated European power came to terms almost immediately and accepted a treaty guaranteeing the integrity of Ethiopia. The implications were not immediately apparent (although some felt that after Adowa the world would never be the same again), but it was to prove a turning point in history. That Ethiopia remained inde-pendent and an anomaly in the world system of states between the Scramble for Africa and the eve of the Second World War – precisely when the internecine conflict between the upholders of that system became most acute – was to transform conceptions of both Africa's and the world's long-term future.

Although at Menelik's death in 1913 Ethiopia descended once more into civil warfare between rival claimants to the throne, by the 1920s Ras Tafari Maconnen (who would become Emperor Haile Selassie) had triumphed over all competition. Throughout the 1920s he was effectively ruling from behind Empress Zawditu's throne and there was little doubt that he would take over at her death.

His coronation in 1930 marked very much the triumph of the progressives and modernizers amongst the Ethiopian nobility. Haile Selassie had traveled extensively in Europe and his aim had always been to seek full recognition for his country at the international level. No matter that no Europeans had yet vanquished the country, Ethiopia remained an anomaly that fitted uncomfortably in the international system of European states and empires. Its independence was always on the verge of being undermined in a whimsical plan of aggrandizement of one European power or another. For example, to the chagrin of the winners of Adowa, in 1906 an agreement was reached among Italy, France, and Britain not to tread on each other's toes in assigned "spheres of influence" marked out for each of them in Ethiopia. Emperor Menelik was not consulted and naturally felt humiliated, but he could do little in a diplomatic world where there was no platform other than for Europeans, who considered only each other as peers. It was the First World War in Europe that transformed this situation. The enormity of what had happened by 1918, the feeling that there had been no real winners, the alternative on offer in Russia and the arrival in Europe of American power meant that there was a widespread determination that the old pre-1914 world dominated by a handful of European Great Powers had breathed its last. Small nations were to be granted a full right to exist, the traditional secret treaties of the Great Powers paying each other off with territory that they did not own was now illicit, the world was to be made safe for democracy and war abolished.

Ras Tafari knew that it was only through the international diplomatic recognition of Ethiopian independence that the unique African non-colony would survive without the constant need of defensive war or the risk of falling under the unwanted tutelage of a European power. Like Cavour, the maker of Italian unity who had sent Piedmontese troops to fight in the Crimea in order to get his small country noticed and listened to by France and Britain in the 1850s, during the First World War Tafari had planned to send Ethiopian troops to fight in the trenches of Europe so that Ethiopia would be present at the peace treaty. This idea came to nothing but it was in the creation of the League of Nations immediately after the conflict that he saw his (and his country's) chance. The prolonged negotiations with the League took place through 1922 and 1923 and the discussion centered on the appropriateness of admitting a country that, according to many of its members (including Britain, Australia, and Switzerland), had not yet reached an acceptable grade of civilization. Article 22 of the League of Nations Covenant stated that not all peoples of the world were ready to be given the status of "nation," and colonialism, which seemed most obviously to contradict what the League stood for, could proceed. Ras Tafari understood fully that Ethiopia might be considered one of those areas, as Article 22 stated, "inhabited by peoples not yet able to stand by themselves under the strenuous conditions of the modern world," and would be barred from entry. Ethiopia's independence still hung in the balance. In Britain, for example, it was considered that Ethiopia would benefit from a period of tutelage under a League mandate and be made essentially a protectorate of a European power, voiding therefore Menelik's life work. It was the unique and anomalous situation of Ethiopia that meant, notwithstanding everything, that its independence was permanently open to debate.

However, hard negotiations, the support of France and later Italy, as well as promises to abolish slavery and the slave trade at home, led eventually to the acceptance of Ethiopia's application to become a member of the League. On September 28, 1923, Ras Tafari's plan came to a happy conclusion. Ethiopia was recognized by the international community to be a fully independent national state and the specter of succumbing to colonialism appeared to have vanished for good. In Addis Ababa (the then dethroned emperor recollected much later), "there was great joy. The rejoicing was for no reason other than that we thought that the Covenant of the League would protect us from the sort of attack which Italy has now launched against us." Still, this was a problem for the future and in the summer of 1924 Ras Tafari (as regent of his country) embarked on a triumphant tour of Europe. He was feted in all its capitals and partook in the general optimism of the moment. Europe was a magnanimous continent in the 1920s that sought to impress this mysterious but colorful monarch from the heart of Africa with the grandeur of its achievements. There, apart from seeing the "wonders of European civilization . . . about which I had read in books," Ras Tafari wrote, "when returning to my country after my visit, I thought it would be possible to initiate some aspects of civilization I had observed with my own eyes."[9] This was a Europe as it should have been, a patchwork of discrete and fraternal nations, each with its own special qualities to show off and a serene consciousness that there were many benefits to be bestowed on a receptive African ruler. The League convention made sense, it seemed a new dawn, and Ras Tafari was bathed in its splendor. His second trip to Europe, however, in 1936 was to be altogether different.

## The Dynamics of Fascist Colonialism

From the Italian point of view Ethiopian independence represented an anomaly that besmirched the nation's military reputation and seemed to suggest that its achievements since unification (which had only happened in the 1860s) were very circumscribed. To the majority this may not have been all that important, but to some it mattered very much indeed. By 1914 Italy had three small colonies (Eritrea, Somalia, and Libya) plus a scattering of not very vital islands in the Mediterranean. Somalia had so far attracted fewer than a few hundred settlers, Eritrea had one of the hottest and most arid climates in the world, and Libya too was famous for being unimaginably torrid (in 1922 Italians measured the highest ever recorded temperature on earth, 58°C at Al' Aziziyah, just south of Tripoli). The Italian dependencies had low populations and few easily accessible resources. They were not of great strategic importance and lacked the means to make them economically viable without investments which Italy could not afford. No minerals of note were ever found during Italy's occupation and, even in Libya, oil was only discovered after the Italians left. The new Roman Empire would have to be composed of the scraps left over after the real imperial powers had gorged themselves with the choice pickings.

But even the securing of this meager loot had required of Italy a considerable investment of men and resources that often pushed it to the verge of financial collapse. In the 1880s and 1890s Eritrea was all that Italy kept after mounting one of the largest and most expensive colonial campaigns during the Scramble for Africa. As has been said, having picked a fight with Ethiopia goes a long way to explaining Italy's woeful record, but in Libya too once the cities of the north had been taken, resistance was so widespread that, during the First World War, Italy had almost had to give up the colony altogether.

Many Italians considered Adowa to be a humiliation that it was absolutely vital should be put right. Immediately after the battle, Italy's prime minister had warned the king that suing Menelik for peace would mean "the death in us of all heroism and virtue and you would have under your command flocks of sheep, beasts that let themselves be slaughtered and not legions of soldiers. Our external enemies, who do not want a strong and respected Italy, would profit from our inaction and so too would internal enemies who would like to see the end of the Monarchy."[10] Rekindling the war with Ethiopia meant, according to Crispi, a saving of Italy's military reputation, a stabilization of the Italian nation-state under authoritarian auspices, and a powerful message to the Great Powers of Europe that Italy would never accept a military setback as final and was no international lightweight. A more virile colonial policy was an agenda that remained

attractive to many liberals but also to nationalists, futurists, and a whole host of patriotic organizations and pressure groups throughout the early twentieth century. Also much had been added, in particular the idea that Italy had a right to colonies because of its excess population. Millions of Italians departed for the New World and northern Europe to find a livelihood, and it was hard not to dream that they would be better employed in the opening up of Italian territory instead of American or Brazilian or Argentinean. If Italy lacked capital, it did not lack labor, and it should rise up as the "proletarian nation" and go it alone. Fascism absorbed and developed many of these views from its inception.

Overall Italy's decision to attack Ethiopia once again after a gap of forty years can be put down to a picking up where Crispi had left off. But very significant factors had emerged since 1918 that made 1935 something different than merely a belated event in a prolonged Scramble for Africa. Most obviously one was fascism, and another was the fact that Ethiopia belonged to the League of Nations and had had half a century of independence since the Scramble got under way. But many other things had changed too: the gap between European weaponry and what a state such as Ethiopia had access to had broadened considerably (airplanes, for example, were completely beyond Haile Selassie's realm in the 1930s in a way that machine guns had not been in the 1880s); Italy had undergone its first industrial revolution and, in firms such as Fiat and Ansaldo, now vaunted its own heavy industry; it had a fairly efficient schooling system, which had only been in its infancy in the late nineteenth century; literacy was at a completely different level and cinema and radio were in the process of transforming the dispatch of information. The list could go on, but it is sufficient to say that since the turn of the century Italy had been undergoing relatively rapid economic development.

Also there had been a regime change in both Ethiopia and Italy, which transformed the relationship between the organization of the state and the people of the two countries. In Ethiopia the army was undergoing radical reorganization. Effectively it was moving from the feudal militia of Menelik's day to a modern army commanded by an officer class, trained in the European manner. When the Italians attacked in 1935 it was still neither one thing nor the other. For example, its generals tended to be the old Rases and military grades were dished out to the feudal barons of the past, but a permanent national officer corps had yet to materialize and conscription had significantly changed since the old calls to arms played on the massive Negarit war drum that would boom through the Ethiopian mountains calling the peasantry to the aid of their lords. Militarily, Ethiopia suffered the disadvantages of the old system having been undermined by Haile Selassie without a new one yet being in place. In fact, at home, on the strength of the foreign policy successes described above, the emperor was attempting to implement a wide-ranging set of reforms aimed at consolidating his power vis-à-vis that of the traditional feudal nobility. The conflicts that had ensued were very far from being resolved, and as Bahru Zewde cogently puts it: "Menelik's Ethiopia had the blessing of feudal harmony. Haile Selassie's Ethiopia was in the throes of nascent absolutism. Expressed in another way, Menelik led a more united Ethiopia than Haile Selassie."[11]

The regime change in Italy also transformed relationships between institutions, the people, and the state. Most importantly, by 1935 Mussolini had benefited from a decade of political experimentation. Opposition, which had plagued Crispi during his colonial campaigns, had been outlawed in the 1920s and control of the means of communication, from newspapers to school textbooks to cinema and radio, was firmly under the direction of the state. Clearly, a Mussolini at the height of his power and popularity was in a much different situation than that of the 1890s, when Crispi had enjoyed only limited support.

This is not a point that is made lightly. When one historian of fascism, Renzo De Felice, called the Ethiopian war Mussolini's "masterpiece"[12] and argued that it marked the zenith of the regime's support, he ignited a debate that has yet to be settled. It is, however, now generally agreed that the Ethiopian war fired the imagination of the Italian people and stilled – temporarily, at least – Italy's many social, political, and cultural

upheavals in a way that nothing (including being on the winning side of the First World War) had been able to do before. It may have been a brief moment of collective happiness, chipped away by difficulties over Italian involvement in Spain, and completely destroyed by the catastrophe of the Second World War, but it was a genuine one. On the other hand, as Nicola Labanca has suggested, it may well be "inappropriate to talk about consensus in a dictatorship,"[13] and we might also add that it was only the massive propaganda invested by the regime in and around the conquest of empire[14] that is being mistaken for genuine enthusiasm among the Italian people. Did Italians agree with Mussolini when he said that "the new Italian, an abyss from the stereotypes of the past, would be born on the African frontier, the gymnasium of boldness, sacrifice and discipline"?[15] The point is that in order to fight the war, and then to win it, the Italian people had to be mobilized and the resources of the country channeled accordingly. In constructing the machinery of conquest there is little doubt that Mussolini was extraordinarily successful. Del Boca, certainly no apologist of fascism, admits as much: "in Italy the African undertaking was met with an enthusiasm that one can define as virtually total."[16]

The invasion of Ethiopia was a colonial war of unprecedented magnitude. More than half a million troops were sent to the Horn and the campaign's cost was so huge that Italian finances had still to recover when the Second World War broke out. But draining the country's resources was less important than the fact that right in the middle of the Great Depression, when enthusiasm for fascism may have been waning due to the regime's loss of impetus, Mussolini was suddenly able to lift its prestige into the stratosphere. The dividends paid by the Ethiopian victory were high. Del Boca lists them succinctly: "Italians were satisfied. Satisfied in having won a war more easily than was expected. Satisfied that it had only cost the lives of a few thousand men. Satisfied for the acquisition of new territory that the Regime's propaganda machine continued to portray as having enormous potential and wealth . . . Satisfied in having resisted economic sanctions. Satisfied in occupying a new and different place in the world order. Satisfied in having placed their destiny in the hands of a man who had been victorious on all fronts, challenging and defying the whole world in a way that no Italian had been able to do for hundreds of years."[17]

Mussolini's determination after the Ethiopian war to drag Italy into a partnership with the Third Reich was none other than the fruit of this impregnable position of prestige at home. The shift from what can be termed the traditional Italian foreign policy of friendship with Britain (and holding the menace of a strong Germanic predator just over the Alps as axiomatic) to one that saw Britain as the main constraint on Italian aspirations was very much the result of Mussolini's self-confidence after 1936. It had now become possible for the Duce to do as he wanted, even to act against the wishes of the armed forces, the monarchy, the Church, in other words the Italian establishment, which had always been wary of fascism's vociferous calls to revise the international order. As has been said, challenging Britain meant that Italy might be subjected to the hostility of the Royal Navy (and Air Force) that controlled Gibraltar, Suez, and Malta and, as fascist propaganda now began to lament, effectively contained Italy within the Mediterranean. But raising Britannia's wrath was not as vital to Mussolini as keeping the momentum, ensuring his regime stayed on the boil. The great difference between fascist Italy and the liberal state it replaced was that the legitimizing pillars of democracy, of political plurality, and of the international appropriateness of being one more "liberal" country in western Europe were no longer available. The regime had to justify itself by other, more radical means. By 1936 Mussolini had the choice of becoming like Franco after the success of his side in the Spanish Civil War, a dictator who rocked no boats in the international system (and who lingered into the 1970s), but whose rule stagnated with compromise and tradition. Mussolini was not, like Franco, an army general, nor was he Catholic. Like most fascists who came to prominence between 1922 and 1943, he was a parvenu who based his right to power on the revolutionary credentials of his regime. Without them he was entirely replaceable. Thus it was likely that he would eventually choose the side that offered the most potential for change and it is in the dynamics of their relationship to the established order in their countries that the fates of Hitler and Mussolini became intertwined. Being on the side of the status quo (that is, the world order of Versailles, the League, of Britain and France) would have made Mussolini expendable.

Martin Kitchen expresses surprise at this great Italian policy shift: "Mussolini's change of sides in 1936," he says, "is still something of a mystery . . . Once the war was over . . . Abyssinia [Ethiopia] need not have caused a fundamental realignment of Italian foreign policy. It would seem therefore that Mussolini acted largely out of pique."[18] A sulky and snubbed Duce emerging from the distasteful League experience was not what brought the "fascist" dictators together, as the reconstitution of a Great Power just over the Brenner pass – effectively the reemergence of the enemy that Italy had defeated at such a tremendous cost in 1918 – was not an easy pill to swallow. Hitler was fully aware of the magnitude of what he was asking Mussolini to accept. Immediately before the *Anschluss*, on receiving Mussolini's go-ahead, the Führer therefore prostrated himself with gratitude: "I will never forget him for it," he is reported to have said, "never, never, come what may. If he should ever need any help or be in any danger, he can be sure that do or die I shall stick by him . . . even if the whole world rises against him."[19] However he may have regarded the Italian people, Hitler fulfilled this promise to the letter. The two dictators were now bound up in a personal relationship of reciprocal gratitude: Hitler had made Mussolini's triumph in Ethiopia possible, and Mussolini was to reply by condoning the annexation of Austria. They had leaned on each other to the point that two parvenus from the provinces flattened Versailles and completely transformed the balance of power in Europe.

## The Reaction of the Status Quo

The dynamics at work in the Italian fascist state were of no particular concern to Britain and France. What has been called Mussolini's "period of good behavior" through the 1920s earned him the respect of many across the Alps who felt, like Churchill did, that he had saved Italy from red revolution. Mussolini and Italy became more important, and potentially worrying, after Hitler's seizure of power in January 1933. The rationale behind British and French strategy toward Italy and Ethiopia in the 1930s was really all about Germany. For a while alarm on the part of Mussolini with the raucous pronouncements of Hitler concerning Austria (which was very much under Italy's protection) kept the western liberal states and Italy on the same side. The assassination of the Austrian chancellor Dollfuss in Vienna in July 1934 (just when Mrs. Mussolini was entertaining his family in the Italian seaside resort of Riccione) and an attempted Nazi coup there prompted Italian troop deployments in the Alps. Hitler, who still lacked a substantial army, had over-reached himself on this occasion, and hastily backtracked. The Stresa agreements in April 1935 were the high point of Mussolini's stance as defender of the Versailles status quo. In this pretty setting on the Italian Alpine lakes, Britain, France, and Italy agreed never to allow Austria to fall into the hands of Germany and to work together should Germany rearm to the point of being a threat (in March 1935 Germany had officially denounced its adherence to the disarmament clauses of Versailles). Until the Ethiopian crisis Italy was a reliable member of the League and apart from some distaste for Mussolinian posturing, France and Britain had not been averse to doing business with a man who had, after all, come to power through castor oil and the cosh. There was no principled anti-fascism in French and British policy toward Italy.

On Italy's part, the creation of an empire that Italians could be proud of was implicit in fascism from the start, but realistic planning for it only began after the onset of the depression, the consolidation of the regime, and the "pacification" of the colonies that Italy already possessed. Italy's support of Ethiopia's joining of the League of Nations in 1923 needs to be seen in this light. Mussolini had been Italy's prime minister (rather than its dictator) for a year and his initial concern was to allay the fears of those in Italy who had entrusted him with the rudder of the nation. If at first there was some vacillation toward Ethiopia's entry, once it became clear that all the Great Powers were in favor, in order to preserve Italian influence there, Italy also reluctantly agreed.

Italian ambitions for the East African country were put to one side for the rest of the 1920s and, in 1928, they signed a "treaty of friendship" with Ethiopia.

But the catastrophe of the depression and Hitler's rise to power made Mussolini a freer agent than he had been. His friendship was now more valuable, to France in particular, and the possibility of a more forward policy in Africa (even if it was against another League member) was not an occasion to be missed. Mussolini's original idea (in between the lines at Stresa) was that he would support the status quo in Europe and in return be granted a free hand in Africa. On the face of it, such a deal was not unreasonable. As has been said, Ethiopia was not of much significance to Britain and France and without mentioning the problem out loud, which would have embarrassed the proceedings of the League, assent looked like it could easily be had. France was quickly won over: French Prime Minister Pierre Laval consented in January 1935 and an accord was reached with Mussolini, although here too not much was stated explicitly. Britain was prepared to accept Italian economic hegemony in Ethiopia, and even Italian territorial concessions there, but stopped short at total annexation (and this remained policy throughout the Ethiopian crisis) because the swallowing of one League member by another would have had an adverse effect on the League's prestige as Ethiopia had appealed to it for arbitration after the Wal Wal incident in December 1934. In June 1935 Anthony Eden traveled to Rome and said as much, and even when the war had already begun (Italian troops entered Ethiopian territory in October 1935), the Hoare–Laval proposals of December that year offered more or less the same terms. What intervened to stop agreement between Italy and Britain in particular was another factor: public opinion.

In fascist Italy and liberal Britain public opinion was hardly the same thing but the mechanisms at work in both were similar. Mussolini needed Ethiopia to be a triumph for the regime (which he symbolized) and an agreement that conceded rights, hegemony, or bits of territory without actually giving Italy Haile Selassie's crown would pay only limited dividends. The British, on the other hand, were quite happy for

Italy effectively to rule Ethiopia but Haile Selassie had to remain at his post. Perhaps the event that best summed up the two positions unfolded in September 1935. Earlier a committee had been set up by the League (that included Britain and France) which attempted to find a solution to the dispute between Italy and Ethiopia before war broke out. Ethiopia was to be administered by the League, and Italy would hold the predominant position in whatever organization was set up to carry out this task. In the future, Mussolini was informed privately, there would be nothing in the way of transforming this nominal League mandate into a formal colony, but to do so in 1935 would have weakened the League in the face of a resurgent Germany. When this proposal reached the Italian foreign office from a happy Italian delegate at Geneva, the response of a fascist who understood the situation more keenly was: "Yes the frame is right but there is no picture of the man inside." The surprised Genevan delegate responded with, "we are in Geneva to look after the interests of Italy not to collect family pictures."[20] The latter's misjudgment of what the Ethiopian campaign was about rightly cost him his job. A slow and piecemeal diplomatic takeover of Ethiopia by Italy was not what Mussolini was after. The British hoped precisely that Ethiopia could be handed over without having to look at a load of irksome family pictures parading a triumphant Mussolini. For both Italy and Britain the whole affair was prestige politics where the media and public opinion were paramount.

In Britain and to a lesser extent in France (where things were mitigated by a greater concern over German rearmament), what could be offered to Mussolini was severely hampered by a sudden upswing in what the League had come to mean. The "peace ballot" held in Britain in the first half of 1935 was only the most obvious symbol of the groundswell of opinion that placed its trust in the League to maintain the order established at Versailles and to ensure that the calamity of 1914 would not happen again. Eleven million people filled in the ballot distributed by the League of Nations Union, stating that they would be in favor of the members of the League using force in order to stop one member's aggression on another. The majority were in favor of both mili-

tary intervention and economic sanctions. But the "peace ballot" was only the tip of an iceberg in the debate sparked by Hitler's coming to power and German rearmament that had been raging for months. The results of the ballot, however, were announced in June 1935 – precisely at the moment when negotiations with Mussolini were most tense.

There was little any British policymaker could do in these circumstances except to try and keep Mussolini as happy as possible and the British public satisfied that the League was fulfilling its obligations against an aggressor. When the League voted that Italy was in the wrong (on October 7, 1935) it was decided that economic sanctions would be imposed on it. How serious the consequences for Italy such sanctions should be caused friction between France and Britain. The former wanted them to be purely symbolic but Britain would, on the prompting of popular feeling, have liked them to hurt more. An oil embargo (Italy had no oil of its own) could have hampered Mussolini's war effort very significantly but as the United States (under no obligation to the League) happily cashed in on Italy's increased demands it would probably have made no difference. Mussolini himself had threatened war with France and Britain over the issue. In any case France would not have tolerated an oil embargo or pushed the matter to the point of a complete falling-out with Italy – and Britain's attempt to institute the embargo came to nothing. The disagreement damaged Anglo-French relations. Even the Hoare–Laval proposal of December, which saw Mussolini relatively open to compromise as the war in Africa was not going particularly well, foundered on the upsurge of opinion in Britain that would not tolerate the "rewarding of aggression."

In France the whole thing seemed mad. One influential newspaper article put it thus: "What are one hundred thousand Italians threatening Ethiopia next to ten million soldiers who are being drilled between the Rhine and the Niemen, and to what end? To defend themselves? Who is threatening them?"[21] Why were the British so worked up about Ethiopia when they did not seem to care about Hitler? In June 1935 an Anglo-German naval treaty had been signed that completely bypassed France!

In the end sanctions were applied half-heartedly. The British fleet moved into the Mediterranean but did little except watch the Italians send hundreds of thousands of troops through the Suez Canal – which the British had left open. But, in the newspapers, the League was portrayed applying sanctions rigidly, making them real and effective. Italy, as a result, appeared to be suffering agonizingly.

Both the British and the fascist regime in Italy milked the issue for all it was worth. Symbolic of what sanctions came to mean in Italy was a kind of popular answer to the British "peace ballot." The wedding ring ceremonies in the winter of 1935 marked a call by the regime for women to donate their gold wedding rings to the war effort in response to the League's sanctions. It was a remarkably successful campaign in which tens of thousands of women pledged themselves to the regime with, in theory at least – and certainly in the eyes of Italian men – the donation of their most treasured possession. However ambiguous this marriage to the regime may have been,[22] it nevertheless attested to the way in which sanctions did little to weaken Italy's war effort but rather had the effect of creating a kind of Italian "finest hour." A war of aggression was transformed into a defensive struggle in which Italy stood alone against the world. Germany continued to trade with Italy and Hitler made sure the provenance of German goods crossing the Alps was clearly labeled (indeed, by 1938 Germany was by far Italy's best trading partner). Italy fought and won the war unhindered; fascism was strengthened immeasurably. The face of the Italian dictator grinned firmly out of a collection of family photographs that Hitler, if not the British and the French, must have been very happy indeed to pore over. Stresa (and Versailles) were dead and the way was now open for the total remilitarization of Germany, for the *Anschluss* and the Axis. Like Japan and Germany before, Italy departed from the League of Nations, although was still present in time to heckle Haile Selassie when he came personally to Geneva to appeal for help. The mountain kingdom of Ethiopia benefited not a jot from all the talk, the alliances, and the fulminations in Europe except that a platform, on which the world's attention was focused,

made the League's promises (arbitration, the elimination of war through reason and discussion, and the rest) all the more hollow.

There was no consensus for the status quo. The US observed from a distance, the Soviet Union did not fit in, Japan threatened, Germany schemed, and Italy took its opportunities. Even France and Britain who, if one looked at a map of the world in the 1930s, appeared to have the most reason to be satisfied, regarded each other with some circumspection. As for Ethiopia, the survival of its independence in a world in which there was no room for the anomaly that it represented had been due solely to its own efforts. In 1935–6 these were no longer enough. By 1938 Italy's possession was quietly recognized by Britain and France and Haile Selassie was mothballed in Bath. What sums up the whole story most eloquently is Baldwin, British prime minister, who, on seeing the (ex) Ethiopian emperor enter the same venue at which he too was dining, rather than confront him, hid under the table.

## Conclusion

To what extent Italy's war against Ethiopia was the real starting point of the Second World War is a matter of debate. Certainly Vansittart, who was deeply involved, seemed to think so, as does, for example, the Ethiopian historian Zaude Hailemariam.[23] Haile Selassie at his appeal to the League in June 1936 pointed out that what had happened was not just about Ethiopia. A harrowing description of Italian gas attacks on Ethiopian villages, on defenseless women and children, was a sign of things to come: "It is my duty," the emperor asserted, "to inform the Governments assembled at Geneva, responsible as they are for the lives of millions of men, women and children, of the deadly peril which threatens them by describing to them the fate which has been suffered by Ethiopia. It is not only upon warriors that the Italian Government has made war. It has above all attacked populations far removed from hostilities in order to terrorize and exterminate them." After a lengthy description of Italian "refinement in barbarism," he came to the most salient parts of his address: "I assert that the problem submitted to the Assembly today is a much wider one. It is not merely a question of the settlement of Italian aggression. It is collective security: it is the very existence of the League of Nations . . . it is the principle of the equality of states on the one hand, or otherwise the obligation laid upon small powers to accept the bonds of vassalship. In a word it is international morality that is at stake . . . Apart from the Kingdom of the Lord there is not on earth any nation that is superior to any other."[24] These words were prophetic and agonizingly true. The world was now turned upside down: the ruler of a black African nation was lecturing Europeans on the meaning of barbarism and teaching them what the respect of international law entailed.

Vansittart saw the war in Ethiopia as the "trivial pretext" for another "German holocaust," but such a view is a gross oversimplification. The forces at work in the invasion, the reaction of the different parties involved, the way in which politicians manipulated but kowtowed to misconceived notions of what public opinion represented, the skewed moral postures adopted by all, the all-embracing fear and distrust, and the overarching arrogance of Europe vis-à-vis a nation that had mistakenly placed its hopes in what it had to offer were all signs of deep-seated crisis that was coming to a head.

## NOTES

1  Quoted in F. Hardie, *The Abyssinian Crisis* (London: Batsford, 1974), p. 3.
2  This vignette is reproduced in Centro Furio Jesi, *La menzogna della razza* (Bologna: Grafis, 1994), p. 155.
3  Sven Rubenson, *The Survival of Ethiopian Independence* (London: Heinemann, 1976).
4  See for example Alberto Sbacchi, "Marcus Garvey, the United Negro Improvement Association and Ethiopia, 1920–1940," in *Legacy of Bitterness, Ethiopia and Fascist Italy*, ed. Alberto Sbacchi (Asmara: Red Sea Press, 1997), pp. 1–34.
5  B. Chevannes, *Rastafari: Roots and Ideology* (Syracuse, NY: Syracuse University Press, 1994).
6  The first edition (1935) of Beatrice and Sidney Webb's *Soviet Communism: A New Civilization?* dropped the question mark in its 1937 edition. For this reference see Peter Clarke, *Hope and Glory: Britain 1900–1990* (London: Penguin, 1996), p. 172.

7  Piers Brendon, *The Dark Valley, a Panorama of the 1930s* (New York: Knopf, 2000), p. 690.
8  Rubenson, *Ethiopian Independence*, p. 404.
9  Haile Selassie I, *My Life and Ethiopia's Progress 1892–1937* (Oxford: Oxford University Press, 1976), pp. 77, 85.
10  Quoted in Emilio Bellavita, *La battaglia di Adua* (Genoa: Flli. Melita, 1988), pp. 404–5.
11  Bahru Zewde, *A History of Modern Ethiopia* (London: James Currey, 1991), p. 159.
12  Renzo De Felice, *Mussolini il Duce: I. Gli anni del consenso 1929–1936* (Turin: Einaudi, 1974).
13  Nicola Labanca, *Il colonialismo italiano* (Milan: Fenice 2000, 1994), p. 58.
14  For the truly huge scale of this enterprise see Adolfo Mignemi, ed., *Immagine coordinata per un impero Etiopia 1935–1936* (Turin: Forma, 1984).
15  Angelo Del Boca, "L'impero," in *I luoghi della memoria, simboli e miti dell'Italia unita*, ed. Mario Isnenghi (Rome: Laterza, 1996), pp. 421–2.
16  Angelo Del Boca, *Gli italiani in Africa orientale, II. La conquista dell'Impero* (Milan: Mondadori, 1992), p. 334.
17  Ibid., p. 714.
18  Martin Kitchen, *Europe Between the Wars* (London: Longman, 1988), p. 287.
19  Quoted in Ian Kershaw, *Hitler, 1936–1945: Nemesis* (London: Penguin, 2000), p. 78.
20  See Richard Lamb, *Mussolini and the British* (London: John Murray, 1997), p. 128.
21  Quoted in ibid., p. 130.
22  See Victoria De Grazia, *How Fascism Ruled Women, Italy 1922–1945* (Berkeley, CA: University of California Press, 1992), pp. 77–9.
23  Zaude Hailemariam, "La vera data d'inizio della seconda Guerra mondiale," in *Le guerre coloniali del fascismo*, ed. Angelo Del Boca (Rome: Laterza, 1991), pp. 288–313.
24  This version of the speech is taken from www.mtholyoke.edu/acad/intrel/selassie.htm but it can also be found in Haile Selassie I, *My Life and Ethiopia's Progress*, pp. 299–312.

## GUIDE TO FURTHER READING

Richard Bosworth, *Mussolini* (London: Arnold, 2002). An essential biography that demonstrates a profound knowledge of the literature and the historiography of fascist Italy.
Robert Boyce and Joseph A. Maiolo, eds., *The Origins of World War Two: The Debate Continues* (Basingstoke:

Palgrave, 2003). All-round historiography and history of the collapse of Versailles and the coming of war.

Piers Brendon, *The Dark Valley, a Panorama of the 1930s* (New York: Knopf, 2000). Poses some interesting juxtapositions between the cataclysmic events of the 1930s. A minefield of revealing anecdotes.

Angelo Del Boca, *Gli italiani in Africa orientale, II. La conquista dell'Impero* (Milan: Mondadori, 1992). No complete history of Italian colonialism is available in English. Del Boca's Italian works, of which this is one volume, are however the starting point for anybody interested in the subject.

Angelo Del Boca, ed., *Le guerre coloniali del fascismo* (Rome: Laterza, 1991). A collection of essays of fundamental importance.

F. Hardie, *The Abyssinian Crisis* (London: Batsford, 1974). Aging but still very good international history of the crisis.

Martin Kitchen, *Europe Between the Wars* (London: Longman, 1988). Excellent short total history of this period in Europe.

Richard Lamb, *Mussolini and the British* (London: John Murray, 1997). Mostly about diplomatic contacts between Britain and Italy, on which it is excellent, rather than being a full-scale study of British opinion as the title seems to promise.

Robert Mallett, *Mussolini and the Origins of the Second World War, 1933–1940* (Basingstoke: Palgrave, 2003). Excellent on historical controversies and Italian foreign policy.

A. Mockler, *Haile Selassie's War* (London: Grafton, 1987). Good on the vicissitudes of the Italian conquest and Britain's policies during the Second World War.

Sven Rubenson, *The Survival of Ethiopian Independence* (London: Heinemann, 1976). A magisterial explanation of the Ethiopian anomaly.

Alberto Sbacchi, *Fascism and the Colonial Experience* (London: Zed Books, 1985). Good history of Italian run-up to and actual occupation of Ethiopia.

Ludwig Schaefer, ed., *The Ethiopian Crisis: Touchstone of Appeasement?* (Boston: D. C. Heath, 1961). Old but really useful collection of views of people for whom the 1935–6 war was not just a matter of historical controversy but often a personal political experience. Contains excerpts from the writings of Churchill, Toynbee, Salvemini, etc.

William R. Scott, *The Sons of Sheba's Race: African-Americans and the Italo-Ethiopian War, 1935–1941* (Bloomington, IN: Indiana University Press, 1993). On what Ethiopian events meant for African-Americans.

Bahru Zewde, *A History of Modern Ethiopia* (London: James Currey, 1991). A brief but incisive introduction to many aspects of modern Ethiopian history.

# CHAPTER EIGHTEEN

# The Challenge in Europe, 1935–1941

## P. M. H. BELL

The title of this chapter prompts two questions: who was making the challenge, and who and what was being challenged? As to the challengers, there was no doubt that the foremost was Germany, which held the initiative in Europe in the whole of this period, making a series of bold and increasingly violent moves to which other countries were compelled to respond. Second in the scale was Italy, less powerful than Germany but still capable of dramatic and aggressive actions. Third, in various parts of eastern Europe there were countries or peoples with ambitions to be attained or grievances to be redressed, so that there were few states that were not under internal threat and few frontiers that were not disputed in one way or another.

As for who and what was being challenged, the short answer was the whole European order established by the peace treaties of 1919–20, which themselves resulted from the Allied military victories (and the defeat of the Central Powers) in 1918. A longer answer pointed to France and Britain as the two main powers in western Europe with an obvious stake in the status quo and strong motives to maintain it. In eastern Europe, the Baltic states, Poland, Czechoslovakia, and Yugoslavia all owed their very existence to the peace settlements, while Romania had benefited by doubling its prewar area and population. All these countries were threatened with loss of territory, internal disruption, or even destruction if the status quo was overthrown.

Further east, the Soviet Union was in an ambiguous position. It was in principle a revolutionary state, dedicated to the destruction of the whole capitalist order. Moscow was the headquarters of the Communist International (Comintern), whose purpose was to foster revolution abroad. Other governments were acutely, and sometimes excessively, sensitive to the Bolshevik danger, which in the 1930s influenced the response of Britain and France to the German threat – Neville Chamberlain in particular distrusted the Soviet Union profoundly. Moreover, the Soviet Union was also revisionist in the more practical sense of having lost territory (to the Baltic states, Poland, and Romania) which it hoped to recover at some stage. On the other hand, the Comintern failed to foment revolutions abroad, and at home the Soviet Union was struggling to build socialism in one country and undergoing enormous social and economic upheavals; and so in practice the Soviet government became, almost perforce, a status quo power, at any rate for a time. Thus the Soviet Union was in part revolutionary and revisionist, and in part cautious and on the side of stability. In 1939, as we shall see, Stalin was to resolve this contradiction and come down against the status quo, with decisive results.

Let us look at these two groups of countries: the challengers (often called the revisionist states, though in fact their aims sometimes went well beyond mere revision), and those being challenged (the states with a stake in the status quo).

## The Challenge from Germany

The challenge from Germany took two forms: first the comparatively limited objective of overthrowing the Versailles Treaty of 1919; and second the virtually unlimited ambitions envisaged in Hitler's ideology, which aimed at nothing less than the domination of Europe and perhaps the world.

The undermining and eventual elimination of the Versailles Treaty was a purpose shared by a large majority of German politicians and public opinion. Behind it lay the widespread conviction that Germany had not *really* been defeated in 1918, but had been stabbed in the back, so that an unbeaten army in the field had been betrayed by revolution at home. In consequence, the intense national enthusiasm and solidarity which had been so strong in 1914 had been diminished but not entirely obliterated by four years of war, so that the sentiment of "never again" – no more war – which was so fervent in France and Britain in the 1920s was less powerful in Germany.[1] In these circumstances, there was little dispute that the Versailles settlement had to be done away with. The loss of territory to Poland in the east aroused strong and widespread resentment, and in the 1920s all significant political parties, from the nationalists and Nazis on the right to the communists on the left, aimed at the recovery of these lands. The next most obvious target was the disarmament imposed on Germany, by which the army was restricted to 100,000 men, the navy was limited in the size of warships and was to have no submarines, and there was to be no military air force at all. These restrictions were a humiliating infringement of German sovereignty, and a slight on a long military tradition; and in practical terms they left the country weaker than France, or even Poland. The treaty also required Germany to pay reparations to its former enemies, and to accept responsibility for the loss and damage suffered "as a consequence of the war imposed on them by the aggression of Germany and her allies."[2] The Germans denounced this provision as "the war guilt clause," though the word guilt was not actually used; and they found the very idea of responsibility for starting the war unacceptable. In the event, Germany never paid much by way of reparations. As Sally Marks has put it, the whole thirteen-year struggle over payment "generated a mountain of paper but only 21.5 milliard gold marks"; but this cut no ice with the Germans, who thought any payments at all were unjust, and complained that the amount they did pay was ruinous.[3]

In short, most Germans rejected the Treaty of Versailles because it seemed to them harsh and unjust, and in the background because it registered their defeat in a war which for four years they had appeared to be winning, and which many of them believed they had not really lost. All German governments, even before Hitler became chancellor in January 1933, set themselves to evade or dismantle the treaty. Even before 1935, when our examination starts, they had achieved considerable success. Reparations payments had ended in 1932. The disarmament clauses had been secretly evaded. In the 1920s, under the Weimar Republic, the military authorities had prepared plans to treble the size of the army, which began to be activated in 1932; so that by the beginning of 1935 the army already comprised twenty-one infantry divisions instead of seven. The Germans also began to avoid the ban on military aviation with the aid of the Soviet Union, where Germany set up an aircraft factory and a training base in the 1920s. It was true that by 1932 the air force was still very small, and was backed up by a tiny aircraft industry; but a nucleus was ready for later expansion.

In these ways the terms of the Treaty of Versailles had been chipped away by the beginning of 1935, but much still remained in place. The treaty restrictions on the German armed forces still imposed a large measure of concealment, which inhibited the speed and scale of rearmament. The Rhineland was still a demilitarized zone, unfortified and without garrisons, which infringed Germany's control of its own territory, and left the country unprotected against a French attack – which of course was why demilitarization had been imposed in the first place. The territorial terms of the treaty were still intact, so that a union between Germany and Austria (the *Anschluss*) was forbidden, and Poland still held the lost territories in the east.

We have described the determination to overthrow the Versailles settlement as a limited objective, but it still involved a substantial challenge to the status quo. To remove all the Versailles restrictions would mean that Germany would emerge with most of its territory of 1914, plus Austria, thus becoming larger than any other country in western and central Europe. The country would be on the road to full rearmament, with no restrictions on its military capacity. This was a formidable program, and it is only in comparison with the virtually *unlimited* objectives of Hitler's Germany that it seems moderate.

Hitler became chancellor of Germany in January 1933, and became head of state as well as of government on the death of President Hindenburg in 1934. He had gained wide popular support in the early 1930s, and the Nazi Party polled 13.74 million votes in the Reichstag elections of July 1932, though its vote fell back somewhat in another election in November.[4] The advent of the new regime was accompanied by economic recovery and a fall in unemployment, which had been under way before Hitler came to power but for which he received the credit – and which he managed to continue. He also secured a wide measure of personal loyalty from the armed forces. All the officers of the new army established after 1933, with the exception of some 3,200 who were commissioned before that time, were recruited under the Nazi regime and owed their advancement to that regime and Hitler.[5] On August 2, 1934, all the officers and men of the German army took an unconditional oath of allegiance to the Führer, Adolf Hitler, which was repeated by all their successors until 1945, and which weighed heavily on their sense of loyalty. Hitler was also ruthless in eliminating opposition. All political parties except the Nazi Party were suppressed, and all trade unions were absorbed into the Nazi Labor Front. Ernst Roehm, the head of the SA and the leader of a radical faction within the Nazi Party that might have threatened Hitler's position, was murdered along with many of his associates in the Night of the Long Knives on June 30, 1934. Other enemies of the regime were sent to concentration camps.

The man who was the object of this loyalty and exercised this dictatorial power was a remarkable figure. Hitler had served four years on the Western Front, being wounded and gassed, but not rising above the rank of corporal. He had known poverty at different times of his life, and looked down on professional civil servants and generals who had not come through "the school of hard knocks" as he had done.[6] He was thus an outsider on the political scene, and difficult for more orthodox politicians to understand. He had a magnetic personality and remarkable powers of oratory and theatrical presentation. But there was much more to Hitler than his personality, however powerful and remarkable. He professed an ideology, and sustained in his mind a "world picture" with its own "systematic and inherent coherence," whose main outlines were made up of anti-Semitism, the belief that race held the key to history, the overriding need for living-space (*Lebensraum*) for the German people, and the idea of life as a perpetual struggle – the survival of the fittest transferred to relations between states.[7]

For a long time it was not clear, especially to those outside Germany, how far this world picture would actually influence Hitler's policy. The main source for understanding his ideas was *Mein Kampf*, a book which he dictated in prison and published as early as 1925–6, and it was natural for European politicians (especially the British, who were not given to ideology) to assume that when Hitler became chancellor he would put away his immature opinions and behave as a responsible statesman. And even later on, in 1939, what were British or French ministers to do when their intelligence sources told them that German policy was in the hands of "a visionary, fanatic and megalomaniac," or that Hitler's aim was nothing less than the domination of Europe and the world?[8] These were not normal or rational bases for foreign policy. Even in retrospect, some historians have seen Hitler as an opportunist, not an ideologue. Others have placed him in a line of continuity with earlier German foreign policy, especially during the 1914–18 war, when the Treaty of Brest-Litovsk (March 1918) had imposed German domination on eastern Europe and Ukraine, which was surely a form of *Lebensraum*.[9]

These controversies on the importance of Hitler's ideology have merged with another debate, on the nature of his dictatorship. One school of thought (often called "intentionalist") maintained that Hitler exercised supreme power in

Nazi Germany, and that domestic and foreign policy was the fulfillment of his intentions. The other (the "structuralist") argued that German policy was heavily influenced by structural constraints, and that Hitler's actions were restrained by semi-independent bodies within the state and by the near-chaotic nature of the state itself, in which different individuals and groups struggled for power. This debate, as Alan Cassels has written, has now largely run its course, leaving intentionalism as the prevailing orthodoxy and sustaining Ian Kershaw's conclusion that "Hitler's power was indeed real, not a phantasm."[10]

What did Hitler set out to do with that power in his foreign and military policy? On January 18, 1939, in a speech to 3,600 newly promoted officers in the German army, Hitler demanded of his audience a commitment to "the unconditional belief that our Germany, our German Reich, will one day be the dominant power in Europe."[11] This had long been Hitler's theme, and he meant what he said. Within 18 months of that speech, by the middle of 1940, he had achieved his aim, and Germany *was* the dominant power in Europe. But that was not the end. There remained Hitler's "ultimate and most far-reaching objective, the conquest of *Lebensraum* in the East."[12] Hitler's greatest war, which he consciously pursued out of ideological conviction, was that against the Soviet Union, which began on June 22, 1941. Perhaps even that would not have been the end. Klaus Hildebrand has argued that beyond the conquest of Europe and the Soviet Union lay the prospect of a conflict with the United States, in a struggle of Europe against America for world supremacy, which would be secured through the racial superiority of the German people.[13]

There was another dimension to all this. The domination of Europe and war against the Soviet Union demanded large-scale rearmament, which in turn made heavy demands on the German economy, requiring vast quantities of raw materials and oil, and large reserves of manpower. Of the key raw materials required for armaments, Germany possessed little iron ore, and that of poor quality; no bauxite as a source of aluminum, which was vital for aircraft production; and no oil. Moreover, a large army and industrial labor force needed food, some of which had to be imported.

In 1936 Hitler defined his military-economic program in a Four-Year Plan, under which the armed forces were to be operational, and the economy ready for war, within four years. The demands on the economy were enormous. By the end of 1936 the requirement of aircraft manufacturers for aluminum was 4,500 tons per month, of which only half was available. In 1937 the three armed forces together asked for 750,000 tons of steel per month, but received only 300,000. If Germany was to reduce its dependence on imported oil by the manufacture of synthetic oil at home, this demanded yet more steel for construction purposes.[14] To meet the demands of rearmament, Germany thus faced a cumulative problem of providing raw materials, food, and foreign exchange to pay for imports. One way of resolving that problem was territorial expansion to secure resources, and another was to put pressure on nearby countries which could supply oil (Romania) or iron ore (Sweden). Thus the demands of the German economy added another impulse to Germany's challenge to the European order.

To sum up, even the limited German aim of dismantling the Versailles settlement meant serious disruption of the status quo in Europe. The far-reaching program of *Lebensraum* and European domination meant its complete destruction. Either way, the challenge from Germany was of formidable proportions.

## The Challenge from Italy

Italy had been on the winning side at the end of the First World War, but Italian nationalists were aggrieved that the peace settlement denied their country some of the gains promised by the Allies during the war. Italy was therefore from an early date a revisionist power, in the sense of seeking to revise the settlement of 1919–20 in its own favor. But Italy also wanted more far-reaching changes in the status quo. Italian nationalists – for example, Mazzini in the mid-nineteenth century – had long aimed at great power status for Italy. In the late nineteenth and early twentieth centuries, Italian governments had tried to establish an empire in Africa and to secure spheres of influence in the Balkans and the eastern Mediterranean.

When Mussolini took power in 1922 he took up the same aims, and added elements of his own to them, making Italy a much more vigorous and ambitious power than before.

The role of Mussolini and fascism in Italian foreign policy has been the subject of intense historical debate, in which three main schools of thought have emerged. The first is that Mussolini's activities in foreign policy were mainly a matter of bluster, posturing, and propaganda, with more show than substance and more improvisation than consistency. Second, there is the view that Mussolini was essentially a realist, concerned with national interests and maintaining the continuity of Italian foreign policy, though in a bolder and more forceful way than his predecessors. The third line of thought is that Mussolini introduced a genuine fascist dimension into foreign policy. He believed that war forged the true destiny of a nation, so that the Italian people must be hardened in conflict. He was much influenced by geopolitics, arguing that Italy was a prisoner in the Mediterranean, and must break out by force to the Atlantic and Indian Oceans. He sought to fuse foreign and domestic policy, using adventures abroad to strengthen his prestige at home, and hoping to use a victorious war in 1940 to restrict the authority of the monarchy, or perhaps even to do away with it altogether.[15]

Of these interpretations, the last two now hold the field, with MacGregor Knox's arguments on the importance of ideology carrying much weight. It was of course true that Mussolini enjoyed posturing, and he sometimes improvised and changed his mind; but the underlying consistencies in his policy cannot be disregarded. As early as March 1925 Mussolini referred to Gibraltar, Malta, Cyprus, and Suez as a chain that imprisoned Italy in the Mediterranean, and to break that chain was still his objective when he went to war against France and Britain in June 1940. From the late 1920s onwards he aimed at control of the Adriatic, contemplating a war against Yugoslavia, occupying Albania in 1939, and launching a war on Greece in October 1940. In Africa, he restored Italian control in Libya, and conquered Ethiopia in 1935–6, showing that fascist Italy could succeed where its predecessor had failed.

Among these various objectives, Mediterranean policy was the most important, and indeed included much of the rest. It also had the most far-reaching implications. If Italy was to break out from its captivity in the Mediterranean, this would mean confrontation, and almost certainly war, with the two principal Mediterranean powers of the time, Britain and France. This was beyond Italy's strength acting alone, and demanded an alliance with a Great Power, which could only be Germany. Mussolini contemplated this alliance in the late 1920s, before Hitler came to power. When it finally came about, with the proclamation of the Rome–Berlin Axis in November 1936 and the conclusion of the Pact of Steel in May 1939, the two countries were ideological as well as diplomatic partners. The novel and high-sounding names in themselves set out to show that the agreements amounted to more than an old-fashioned alliance.

Italy, in its population, economic resources, and military strength, was a less formidable power than Germany. But from its geographical position in the middle of the Mediterranean, and through its ability to influence great issues by the application of comparatively limited diplomatic pressure or military force, the Italian challenge to the European status quo was something to be reckoned with. For example, Italy was weaker than either France or Britain separately, and much weaker than both together, but could still offer a dangerous threat to these countries *as Mediterranean powers*, because the French and British were also European and world powers, and had to disperse their strength over wide areas. The challenge from Italy was a serious matter.

## The Challenge in Eastern Europe

The territorial settlements in eastern Europe in 1919–21, partly laid down by the peace treaties among the Allies and partly decided on the spot, usually by force, left a number of dissatisfied states. The most aggrieved, and the most intent on changing the settlement, was Hungary. The Treaty of Trianon (June 1920) imposed on Hungary the loss of about two-thirds of its former territory before 1914, and left nearly three million Hungarians living outside its borders: about

1,600,000 in Romania, 720,000 in Czechoslovakia, and 500,000 in Yugoslavia. These losses were deeply resented, and the revision of the treaty became, for two decades, the principal – indeed almost the sole – objective of Hungarian foreign policy.

Elsewhere, Poland was a country with an overwhelming interest in maintaining the peace settlements which had restored its independent existence; and yet in one case even Poland was revisionist. In 1920 the Allied powers had partitioned the district of Teschen, which was in dispute between Poland and Czechoslovakia, allotting the town of Teschen to Poland, but other areas, including a valuable coalfield, to the Czechs. Neither side was satisfied, and the Poles maintained their claim, which they eventually imposed in October 1938, exploiting Czech weakness after the Munich agreement. Lithuania also maintained a revisionist claim, this time against Poland, over the city and district of Vilna (a neutral nomenclature – Wilno to the Poles, Vilnius to the Lithuanians), which after a period of dispute was incorporated into Poland in 1922. Britain and France, along with other countries, recognized this annexation, but Lithuania did not, maintaining that a state of war with Poland still existed until 1927, and refusing to open diplomatic relations until 1938. In the background to all these matters loomed the potential danger of the Soviet Union, with its revolutionary doctrines and territorial claims on all its western neighbors.

These challenges to the status quo in eastern Europe varied widely in character and importance, but they all mattered intensely to those involved, and cumulatively endangered the whole East European settlement.

## The Status Quo Powers

Let us turn to the countries with a stake in maintaining the status quo, and which might have been expected to defend it.

In western Europe, the country with the greatest interest in the 1919 settlement was France. The French were acutely aware that their victory over Germany had been gained at the heavy price of 1.3 million dead, and also at the less obvious cost of a sharp fall in numbers of births during the war, amounting to an estimated deficit against "normal" totals of about 1.4 million.[16] This gap in the population was certain to move inexorably up the age structure, until in 1936 and for three years to follow – the "hollow years" – the contingent of men reaching military age would be only about half its normal size. Moreover, victory had only been achieved with the massive assistance of the British Empire and the United States, which might not be forthcoming again, or might come too late. In these circumstances, France depended heavily upon the restrictions on German power imposed by the Treaty of Versailles, and particularly on disarmament, which secured for France a numerical superiority over the German army, and on the demilitarization of the Rhineland, which left the French with an open door to invade Germany in case of need. Reparations provided another means of restricting German strength, and in 1923 France actually used its military superiority to occupy the Ruhr to enforce payment. This move was a partial success, in that the Germans were compelled to resume payments, but the price was high. On the ground, French troops found themselves in a difficult situation among a hostile population. Politically, the occupation separated France from Britain, which opposed the use of force and was anxious to reach a negotiated settlement of the reparations question. In the event, the occupation of the Ruhr in 1923 proved to be the last time that France tried to enforce the Treaty of Versailles by military means. The French stake in the status quo was as great as ever, but they were no longer sure how to secure it, and in time they lost the will to do so.

For a long time, the British were much less committed to the European status quo than the French. Britain's island position still offered a sense of security. Britain, to a much greater extent than France, was a great imperial power, with worldwide interests, to which Europe could appear secondary. British losses in the 1914–18 war, at about 750,000 dead, were far fewer than the French, but they came as a profound shock, and the British people were deeply reluctant to repeat the experience. If that was the price of a continental commitment to maintain the

European status quo, the British had no wish to pay it. In any case, the German menace which had brought about such a commitment in 1914–18 no longer existed. The German fleet had been scuttled and lay at the bottom of the harbor in Scapa Flow. The German colonies had been conquered and shared out among the victors. Moreover, a revulsion of opinion against the Treaty of Versailles set in almost as soon as the treaty was concluded. Keynes's denunciation of reparations in his book *The Economic Consequences of the Peace*, published in 1919, had a widespread impact. Historical debate on the origins of the war moved strongly against the thesis that Germany bore sole responsibility for the catastrophe. Political opinion came to regard the Treaty of Versailles as excessively harsh, and France came to be seen as a militarist and aggressive power. This meant that from as early as 1921, British governments came to regard their objective not as the enforcement of the treaty but its gradual revision to achieve a general reconciliation in western Europe. All this made sense up to a point. But in the long run, it remained true that British security, and even imperial security, began at home and in Europe. London could not be defended in Ottawa or Canberra or New Delhi, and eventually the revival of a German menace reminded Britain forcibly that it was a status quo power in Europe. The trouble was that this realization came very late, when large parts of the status quo had already been overthrown.

In eastern Europe, most countries were, or should have been, almost by definition supporters of the status quo. No fewer than six states (Estonia, Latvia, Lithuania, Poland, Czechoslovakia, and Yugoslavia) had come into being or been revived at the end of the First World War, and their boundaries and even their very existence were bound up with the peace settlement. Czechoslovakia and Poland were the plainest examples. In Czechoslovakia in 1930, the total population of 14.7 million included 7.4 million Czechs, 3.2 million Germans (i.e., German-speakers), 2.3 million Slovaks, 720,000 Hungarians, and 569,000 Ruthenes.[17] When the state first came into existence, there was much discussion of setting up a Swiss-style system with autonomous cantons for the different nationalities, but this

seemed too dangerous to the unity of the state and was not attempted. Nevertheless, the population of Czechoslovakia was so disparate, and the balance between the different peoples so precarious, that the whole country was likely to collapse if any part of it was disturbed either internally or from outside – which was in fact what happened in 1938–9. In Poland, a population of 32 million included some six million Ukrainians and Belorussians, and 800,000 Germans. On Poland's western frontier, Germany loomed as a constant threat. In the east, military victories over the Bolsheviks in 1920–1 had allowed Poland to establish a frontier well beyond the so-called Curzon Line of 1920, which had proposed a border based roughly on ethnic divisions. Polish territory was thus bound up with the postwar settlement, and it was doubtful whether Poland's very existence could survive the recovery of strength by her two great neighbors, Germany and the Soviet Union. In the event, in 1939 Poland was wiped from the map, partitioned by these two powers.

This brings us to the ambiguous position of the Soviet Union. In the 1930s the Soviet Union was, almost perforce, a status quo power. It suffered the self-inflicted wounds of forced collectivization of agriculture. Its Five-Year Plans produced a strong industrial state, but at heavy cost. Stalin set in motion a wave of purges which swept through the country from 1936 onwards, and (among many other consequences) wrecked the Soviet high command and removed something like half of the officer corps. The Soviet Union was so preoccupied with its own affairs, and for a time so weakened militarily, that it seemed to have little option except to maintain the status quo. And yet it was also a revisionist power, hoping at some time to regain its lost territories in the Baltic states, Poland, and Bessarabia. For much of the 1930s the Soviet Union worked to defend the status quo, joining the League of Nations, making an alliance with France, and promoting Popular Fronts against Fascism. Then in 1939 Stalin suddenly changed sides, making an agreement with Nazi Germany to partition Poland and bring the three Baltic republics under Soviet military occupation. Further advances followed in 1940, when the Baltic states were formally annexed, and

Bessarabia was taken over from Romania. Once Stalin moved into action, he set about demolishing the status quo with a vengeance.

## The Challenges Succeed

In the period between 1935 and 1941 the contrast between the challengers and the challenged was striking. Hitler knew what he wanted, and was bold and ruthless in setting out to get it. Mussolini wielded less power, but was still capable of causing much disruption. On the other side, the French recognized the German menace but were losing the will to oppose it, while the British continued to believe for a long time that Germany could be conciliated and were slow to accept that there was a danger. In eastern Europe, Poland and Czechoslovakia had everything to lose if the status quo was disrupted, but failed to cooperate to maintain it. The Soviet Union suddenly threw its massive weight on the side of change. All in all, it was an unequal contest, and it is not surprising that the period from 1935 to 1941 was one of almost unbroken success for the revisionist powers.

The story of German victories, diplomatic and military, may be familiar, but still bears repetition in order to bring home the pace and magnitude of events. In March 1935 Hitler announced the introduction of conscription for the armed forces, and declared openly that Germany already possessed an air force, thus sweeping away the disarmament clauses of Versailles. The French and British limited themselves to protesting. A year later, in March 1936, German troops marched into the demilitarized zone of the Rhineland, in small numbers but with every intention of fighting rather than simply withdrawing if they were attacked. The French government confined itself to moving some units to the frontier; French public opinion was overwhelmingly against war; the British government chose to treat the German move not as a threat but as a diplomatic opportunity. The Germans thus pulled off a great success, and embarked at once on the fortification of their frontier with France. Two years later, in March 1938, Hitler annexed Austria, thus achieving the *Anschluss* which had been forbidden by the peace treaties. France and Britain again limited

themselves to protesting; and in any case a significant element in British opinion still believed that the enforced separation of Germany and Austria had been one of the errors of the Treaty of Versailles.

By that stage, most of the major burdens and restrictions placed on Germany by the peace settlements – reparations, disarmament, the demilitarized zone in the Rhineland, separation from Austria – had been removed. The greater part of Germany's limited program had been achieved, with little bloodshed and without the open use of force.

There followed a series of moves that went beyond the overthrow of Versailles and began the wider challenge for European domination. After the Munich Conference of September 28–9, 1938, Germany annexed the Sudeten areas of Czechoslovakia, and then in March 1939 took over the rest of the country, thus destroying another part of the Versailles settlement and also establishing German control over central Europe. By September 1939 Versailles was no longer an issue. The German assault on Poland was not directed at recovering territory or shifting the German–Polish border from one line to another but at destroying the Polish state. This attack finally brought Britain and France to declare war on Germany, though it was a war that remained phony until spring 1940. Then in April–May 1940 Germany launched a Scandinavian campaign against Denmark and Norway. On May 10 it opened an offensive in the west which crushed the Netherlands in a week, Belgium in three weeks, and France in six. In the same campaign the British Expeditionary Force was driven from France in disarray. It was an astonishing victory, achieving in a few weeks what Wilhelmine Germany had failed to attain in four long years between 1914 and 1918. By the end of June 1940, Germany controlled most of Europe. After a pause, Germany invaded Yugoslavia and Greece in April–May 1941 before finally launching Operation BARBAROSSA, the attack on the Soviet Union, on June 22, 1941.

Even the bare recital of this chain of political and military successes, achieved in little more than six years, remains amazing. It was not so much a challenge as an act of utter destruction. By comparison the Italian role in overthrowing the status quo was secondary, but by no means negligible. During the Spanish Civil War (1936–9) Mussolini intervened on a large scale to help to secure the victory of Franco and the Nationalists. Italy invaded Albania in April 1939, provoking a potential crisis in the Balkans. On June 10, 1940, Mussolini declared war on France and Britain, extending the existing European war to the Mediterranean, and in October 1940 he attacked Greece. On all these occasions, Italy contributed much to the destabilization of Europe.

In southeastern Europe, Hungary secured most of its revisionist claims between 1938 and 1940, through the intervention of Nazi Germany. In October 1938, in the aftermath of the Munich Agreement, Hungary annexed a long strip of territory on the southern frontier of Czechoslovakia. In March 1939, when Czechoslovakia was broken up, Germany handed the province of Ruthenia to the Hungarians. On August 30, 1940, Hitler announced the transfer of most of Transylvania from Romania to Hungary, thus virtually completing the return of the Hungarian populations separated from their country in 1920. In a wider arena, we have already seen how the Nazi–Soviet Pact of August 23, 1939, led to the complete transformation of the situation in eastern Europe.

Taken together, these events marked the overwhelming success of the various challenges to the European settlement of 1919–20, and a corresponding defeat for those powers with a stake in the status quo. The reasons for this extraordinary run of success lay in a combination of strength and boldness among the revisionist states and weakness and indecision among the status quo powers, especially Britain and France. Of these two sides of the coin, Britain and France will be examined in the next chapter. On the side of the challengers, the key lay with Germany, whose success was only partly a matter of military strength. In numerical terms, that strength was not overwhelming until a very late stage. In 1938 it was the terror struck by the *danger* of German air attack rather than the actual numbers of German bombers (greatly exaggerated by Allied intelligence sources) which rendered the British and French so anxious to avoid war during the Czechoslovakian crisis. Even in the campaign in the Low Countries and France in 1940, when the Germans won so rapid and complete a victory, the actual numbers of divisions, tanks, and aircraft available to the two sides were evenly matched; but the Germans used their forces better and moved with a speed which left their opponents bewildered and sometimes unnerved.[18] Military strength, and the fears that it inspired, counted for something in the German successes; but the daring, ruthlessness, and sheer dynamism of German actions mattered more. Hitler, by the force of his personality, his unorthodox methods, and the ideological drive behind his policies, left his opponents bewildered and unable to cope, until they realized (almost too late) the extent of the challenge he posed.

## NOTES

I am most grateful to David Dutton for reading a draft of this chapter with his usual care, and making invaluable comments, at a time when he was hard pressed by other duties.

1   See MacGregor Knox, *Common Destiny: Dictatorship, Foreign Policy and War in Fascist Italy and Nazi Germany* (Cambridge: Cambridge University Press, 2000), p. 27, for a persuasive exposition of this point.

2   H. W. V. Temperley, ed., *A History of the Peace Conference of Paris* (London: Hodder & Stoughton, 1920), vol. 3, pp. 187, 214.

3   Sally Marks, "Smoke and Mirrors," in *The Treaty of Versailles: A Reassessment after 75 Years*, ed. M. F. Boemeke, G. D. Feldman, and E. Glaser (Cambridge: Cambridge University Press, 1998), p. 367; cf. Margaret Macmillan, *The Peacemakers: The Paris Conference of 1919 and Its Attempt to End War* (London: John Murray, 2001), pp. 490–1.

4   Election figures in Chris Cook and John Paxton, *European Political Facts, 1900–1996* (Basingstoke: Macmillan, 4th edn, 1998), p. 207.

5   Knox, *Common Destiny*, p. 209.

6   Ernest R. May, *Strange Victory: Hitler's Conquest of France* (London: Hill & Wang, 2000), pp. 96–7.

7   Eberhard Jäckel, *Hitler's Weltanschauung: A Blueprint for Power* (Middletown, CT: Wesleyan University Press, 1972), passim; the quotation is on pp. 23–4.

8   Richard Overy, "Strategic Intelligence and the Outbreak of the Second World War," *War in History* 5 (1998): 465, quoting reports from British military intelligence and the French Air Force 2ᵉ *Bureau*.

9   A. J. P. Taylor, *The Origins of the Second World War* (London: Hamish Hamilton, 1961), put the case for opportunism; his arguments are reviewed in Gordon Martel, ed., *The Origins of the Second World War Reconsidered: A. J. P. Taylor and the Historians* (London: Routledge, 1999). The continuities in German foreign policy were made particularly clear in Fritz Fischer, *Germany's Aims in the First World War* (London: Chatto & Windus, 1967).

10  Alan Cassels, "Ideology," in *The Origins of World War Two: The Debate Continues*, ed. Robert Boyce and Joseph Maiolo (Basingstoke: Palgrave Macmillan, 2003), p. 234; Ian Kershaw, *Hitler* (London: Longman, 1991), passim – the quotation is on p. 8. Cf. Manfred Messerschmidt, in *Germany and the Second World War*, vol. 1, *The Build-up of German Aggression* (Oxford: Clarendon Press, 1990), p. 4, for a similar conclusion.

11  Quoted in Ian Kershaw, *Hitler*, vol. 2, *1936–45: Nemesis* (London: Allen Lane, 2000), p. 167.

12  Christian Leitz, "Nazi Germany," in Boyce and Maiolo, p. 28.

13  Klaus Hildebrand, *The Foreign Policy of the Third Reich* (London: Batsford, 1973), especially pp. 21–3.

14  Matthew Cooper, *The German Air Force, 1933–1945* (London: Jane's, 1981), pp. 62–3; Philippe Marguerat, *Le IIIᵉ Reich et le pétrole roumain, 1938–1940* (Leiden: Sijthoff, 1977), pp. 96–8; David E. Kaiser, *Economic Diplomacy and the Origins of the Second World War* (Princeton, NJ: Princeton University Press, 1980), p. 268.

15  These schools of thought may be exemplified by: (1) Denis Mack Smith, *Mussolini* (London: Weidenfeld & Nicolson, 1981); (2) Richard Lamb, *Mussolini and the British* (London: Murray, 1997); (3) MacGregor Knox, *Mussolini Unleashed, 1939–1941* (Cambridge: Cambridge University Press, 1982), and *Common Destiny*.

16  Philippe Bernard, *La Fin d'un monde, 1914–1929* (Paris: Editions du Seuil, 1975), pp. 108–9.

17  Royal Institute of International Affairs, *Bulletin of International News*, vol. 13, p. 747, citing figures from the census of 1930.

18  For this reinterpretation of the German victories, and the Allied defeats, in 1940, see May, *Strange Victory*, and especially the tables on pp. 467–8.

## GUIDE TO FURTHER READING

P. M. H. Bell, *The Origins of the Second World War in Europe* (London: Longman, 2nd edn, 1997). An overview and analysis.

R. J. B. Bosworth, *Mussolini* (London: Arnold, 2002). A first-rate biographical study.

Robert Boyce and Joseph A. Maiolo, eds., *The Origins of World War Two: The Debate Continues* (Basingstoke: Palgrave, 2003). A valuable collection of essays.

Talbot Imlay, *Facing the Second World War: Strategy, Politics and Economics in Britain and France, 1938–1940* (Oxford: Oxford University Press, 2003). Solid and illuminating in approach.

Peter Jackson, *France and the Nazi Menace: Intelligence and Policy Making, 1933–39* (Oxford: Oxford University Press, 2000). Model example of the use of intelligence sources.

Ian Kershaw, *Hitler*, vol. 1, *1889–1936: Hubris*; vol. 2, *1936–1945: Nemesis* (London: Allen Lane, 1998, 2000). The definitive biography.

MacGregor Knox, *Common Destiny: Dictatorship, Foreign Policy and War in Fascist Italy and Nazi Germany* (Cambridge: Cambridge University Press, 2000). An incisive and authoritative comparative study.

Sally Marks, *The Ebbing of European Ascendancy: An International History of the World, 1914–1945* (London: Arnold, 2002). A lucid and vigorous survey.

Gordon Martel, ed., *The Origins of the Second World War Reconsidered: A. J. P. Taylor and the Historians* (London: Routledge, 1999). Essays by leading scholars concerning a controversial interpretation.

Ernest R. May, *Strange Victory: Hitler's Conquest of France* (New York: Hill & Wang, 2000). A powerful and convincing argument; the other side of the coin to Marc Bloch's *Strange Defeat*.

Militärgeschichtliches Forschungsamt, *Germany and the Second World War*, vol. 1, *The Build-up of German Aggression*; vol. 2, *Germany's Initial Conquests in Europe*; vol. 3, *The Mediterranean, South-East Europe and North Africa, 1939–1941*; vol. 4, *The Attack on the Soviet Union* (Oxford: Clarendon Press, 1990, 1991, 1995, 1998). Massive, detailed, and indispensable.

Richard Overy, *The Dictators: Hitler's Germany, Stalin's Russia* (London: Allen Lane, 2004). A large-scale and illuminating comparison.

Anita Prazmowska, *Eastern Europe and the Origins of the Second World War* (Basingstoke: Palgrave, 2000). A clear analysis of a difficult subject.

# CHAPTER NINETEEN

# Appeasement

## ANDREW CROZIER

On October 6, 1939, Adolf Hitler, having conquered Poland, endeavored to bring about the cessation of the war with Britain and France. In a speech to the Reichstag, he suggested the possibility of a conference and added: "I still believe . . . that there can only be real appeasement in Europe and in the world if Germany and Britain come to an understanding."[1] The usage of the word "appeasement" here is interesting because it shows quite clearly that to contemporaries it meant something quite different from the meaning it has since acquired. For contemporaries it meant "pacification," "relaxation of tension," "peace." From the British point of view it might, therefore, more properly be conceived as the state of international relations to which foreign policy aspired rather than the daily functioning of that policy. Given this reality, it may well be questioned whether the word "appeasement" today is any longer an adequate conceptual tool for examining the foreign policy of the British government in the 1930s. This chapter will, therefore, avoid the use of the term as it analyzes the response of the British government to the challenges posed to the existing world order in the 1930s by Germany, Italy, and Japan.

## The Foundations of British Foreign Policy during the Interwar Years

The peace of 1919 and in particular the Treaty of Versailles should have provided much comfort to Britain. Germany had been eliminated as a naval power, as a colonial power, and it had embraced democracy and representative government. Britain was, therefore, protected in its home waters, it had eliminated an imperial competitor, and the institution of democracy in Germany would ensure that militarism was curbed. The problem, however, for the future peace of Europe was that neither the Treaty of Versailles nor the Weimar Republic possessed legitimacy in the eyes of the German political classes or the German public at large.

By the end of the 1920s it was clear that Germany was beginning to lapse into political extremism, despite the revision of the peace settlement that had been accomplished during that decade. With the onset of the world economic recession in 1929 the situation in Germany became more critical, and the British economy suffered grievously too. The problem that had to be addressed was a twofold one of achieving long-term security and restoring economic confidence. It was addressed by two Foreign Office officials, Orme Sargent and Frank Ashton-Gwatkin, in a cabinet paper of November 1931.

It was argued in the paper that the severity of French policy toward Germany since the conclusion of the Treaty of Versailles, as exhibited in the occupation of the Ruhr, had only served to make matters worse in Europe. Although it was recognized that French harshness stemmed from anxieties regarding security against Germany, it was felt by Sargent and Ashton-Gwatkin that such a situation could not be left unchecked. They therefore suggested the conclusion of an international agreement involving all European states, including Britain, which would further the cause of international confidence and security. They wrote: "World recovery . . . depends on European recovery; European recovery on German recovery; German recovery on France's consent; France's consent on security . . . against attack." In effect, the two officials recommended what was tantamount to a general revision of the peace settlement: an "'all-in' settlement" that would embrace a very substantial reduction in reparations, disarmament, guarantees of security, and the rectification of frontiers.[2] These suggestions were not acted upon immediately by the government, but the fundamental theses of the memorandum were later to underpin what has come to be known to history as the policy of appeasement. They amounted to proposals for a very substantial revision of the Versailles system.

Meanwhile, events in the Far East indicated that the peace of the 1920s was under threat. In 1931 Britain was still the major world power with interests in all parts of the globe. There were particularly substantial interests in China, mostly located in the Shanghai area, where Britain continued to be an influential force. British investments clearly began to come under threat when the Japanese Kwantung Army decided to occupy the whole of Manchuria following a Japanese-manufactured incident in September 1931. This inevitably led to a conflict with China, and the fighting extended to Shanghai in January 1932. The response of the British government was to abandon the Ten-Year Rule according to which defense estimates were based upon the premise that no war was to be anticipated for ten years. Although the Far Eastern crisis was temporarily halted by the Tangku Truce of May 1933, the appointment of Adolf Hitler as chancellor in Germany in January of that year made the future of Europe and the world more uncertain than at any time since 1919.

## The Reaction to Hitler

Inevitably, the assumption of the German chancellorship by Adolf Hitler created an atmosphere of tension in Europe. The objective of the new German government was unquestionably at least the overthrow of the Versailles system, which had governed the relationships of the European powers since the end of the First World War. In a memorandum of January 1932, Sir Robert Vansittart, the most senior official in the Foreign Office, argued that if Britain counted the achievement of stability on the continent of Europe as Britain's primary aim, then the solution lay very much in its hands. It would, however, mean Britain taking upon itself the leadership of Europe and the acceptance of the principle of further treaty revision.

The need for Britain to assume such a position was implicit in the French reaction to the continuing German problem. In 1928 the French began construction of a line of fortifications along the Franco-German border that came to be known as the Maginot Line, indicating that they would adopt a defensive strategy both militarily and diplomatically. From the beginning of the 1930s, therefore, only Britain was in a position to take the diplomatic initiative with Germany and engage constructively with the Germans, assuming, of course, that constructive engagement was an option.

Nevertheless, while British ministers were conscious of the dangerous and uncertain dimension that Hitler's assumption of power added to the European situation, this did not predict an abrupt and immediate transformation in the style and content of British foreign policy. Under the direction of the foreign secretary, Sir John Simon, the strategy of cautious involvement in Europe and cautious concession to Germany was logically and prosaically continued and was "pragmatically decided on a case-by-case basis."[3] The main focus of British foreign policy was to rescue something from the disarmament conference that was clearly failing. The British government, however, did not wish to be seen as responsible for its failure, which to some extent accounts for the British disarmament plan of March 1933, which would have allowed some German rearmament. For one historian it was a stopgap, "designed not to achieve disarmament but to prop up a conference which everyone knew to be disintegrating."[4]

The disarmament negotiations did not survive Germany's simultaneous withdrawal from both the League of Nations and the disarmament conference in October 1933. Still, Sir John Simon endeavored to turn the changed circumstances to advantage by advocating recognition of German rearmament in exchange for Germany's return to Geneva for disarmament negotiations and general League purposes. He justified his view thus: "Germany would prefer, it appears, to be 'made an honest woman'; but if she is left too long to indulge in illegitimate practices and to find by experience that she does not suffer for it, this laudable ambition may wear off."[5] It was quickly decided to enlist French endorsement of these proposals and French ministers were invited to London to discuss them in the New Year. This set a trend that recurred in the triangular Anglo-French-German relationship throughout the 1930s. The policy of France would invariably follow the British lead. Meanwhile, the precipitate action of Germany in leaving the League of Nations stimulated the first steps toward British rearmament. The Defence Requirements Sub-Committee (DRC) was now constituted to review defense deficiencies. Neville Chamberlain, the chancellor of the exchequer, for reasons of economy could not allow the full costs of the DRC's report and determined that the bulk of the resources available should be spent on aerial rearmament. This accorded with the universally held view during the 1930s that there was no adequate defense against the bomber which, in the words of Stanley Baldwin in the House of Commons in November 1932, "will always get through."[6] Naval construction was inevitably trimmed and plans for a continental army shelved. The DRC also now established that Germany, rather than Japan, was the ultimate potential enemy. Neville Chamberlain endorsed this view. In a defense white paper of March 1935, the British government named Germany as the source of tension in Europe and the cause of British rearmament.

The consequence of Anglo-French ministerial meetings of January to February 1935 was an agreement that a general settlement of somewhat limited scope should be proposed to Germany. Accordingly, Sir John Simon, accompanied by Anthony Eden, visited Berlin the following March – despite the fact that during the same month Hitler had unilaterally denounced the disarmament provisions of the Treaty of Versailles and announced the fact of German rearmament and the existence of the German air force. Hitler's action had effectively preempted the British policy of offering the legalization of German rearmament in exchange for concessions to the Anglo-French point of view. The Anglo-German talks, therefore, proved very negative. Hitler positively responded only to the proposals for a multilateral Air Pact, aimed at deterring surprise aerial bombardment, and a bilateral naval agreement between Germany and Britain. Accordingly an Anglo-German Naval Agreement was reached on June 18, 1935, under which Germany agreed to limit its surface tonnage to 35 percent of that of the Royal Navy, while submarine parity was conceded.

## A General European Settlement

By the autumn of 1935 it was clear from German evasiveness that further progress on the basis of the March talks was unlikely. Furthermore, Mussolini's Italy invaded Abyssinia in October 1935. Britain was bound to oppose this with the likely consequence that Italy would be driven toward Germany. By 1935 it was also becoming clear that in any future conflict with Germany it might not be possible to rely upon the United States financially, for the Johnson Act of 1934 forbade the extension of credit to any state that had failed to meet its obligations to American creditors. This included Britain. Sir Robert Vansittart spelled out what this meant in January 1936: "In any crisis of life and death . . . this might well mean our 'death.'"[7]

It was in these circumstances that the two Foreign Office officials, Orme Sargent and Frank Ashton-Gwatkin, who had composed the 1931 memorandum, now collaborated with another colleague, Ralph Wigram, in another far-reaching review of British foreign policy entitled *Britain, France and Germany*. In essence this represented a return to the scheme for an "all-in" settlement that had been advocated in the earlier memorandum. They believed that the British policy of coming to terms with Germany, by removing "untenable and indefensible" parts of the Treaty of Versailles, ought to receive renewed impetus. Unless Germany was brought into an agreement soon, the possibilities of ever succeeding in this aim would rapidly diminish. The officials felt that an Anglo-French colonial offer might secure German participation in an Air Pact and continued observance of the demilitarized zone. The authors of this memorandum felt that Britain should take the lead in negotiations with Germany and determine its attitude "without loss of time."[8] Fresh impetus was given to these suggestions by the failure of Simon's successor, Sir Samuel Hoare, to settle the Abyssinian crisis in a manner that would not damage Anglo-Italian relations. The leak of the Hoare–Laval Plan, which effectively would have stripped Abyssinia of two-thirds of its territory, resulted in an uproar and Hoare was compelled to resign. Inevitably, Italy drifted toward Germany.

Hoare's successor, Anthony Eden, now urged the cabinet to consider a broad strategy for dealing with Germany. He identified European hegemony as the basic aim of German policy and concluded that Britain should not only rearm rapidly, but also make every effort to arrive at a modus vivendi with Germany that might reduce European tension. This view was emphatically supported by Sir Robert Vansittart, who urged the government to treat the German problem on a European level. The object of policy should not be an Anglo-German agreement but a comprehensive, European settlement. Germany would require an inducement in the form of some sort of territorial concession and a sympathetic consideration of Germany's colonial claims might be the solution. Eden argued:

> On balance . . . I am in favour of making some attempt to come to terms with Germany, but upon one indispensable condition: that we offer no sops to Germany. There must be no concession merely to keep Germany quiet, for that process only stimulates the appetite it is intended to satisfy.[9]

The type of agreement Eden had in mind was a replacement of the Locarno Treaty by an Air Pact, in which France and Germany would, in addition to guaranteeing one another, guarantee Britain as well. Furthermore, the demilitarized Rhineland zone would disappear, there would be an arms limitation agreement, Britain and France would recognize Germany's preponderant interest in central and eastern Europe (provided its aims there were peacefully accomplished), and Britain would do what it could to facilitate the expansion of Germany's export trade.[10] The decision to end the demilitarized zone was a clear lure. Cabinet approval of these proposals was rapid. They were to form the basis of British policy over the next three years.

It was difficult to make immediate progress. On March 7, 1936, in flagrant violation of the Treaty of Versailles and the Locarno pacts (Treaty of Mutual Guarantee), Hitler remilitarized the Rhineland. Prior to the event the British had decided there was little they could do and for their part the French would not "proceed to any isolated action."[11] This once again ensured that French policy would be co-coordinated with that of Britain. The demilitarization of the Rhineland deprived the British government of its most critical bargaining counter in the putative negotiations for a general settlement. Eden, nevertheless, endeavored to advance matters by asking for more information concerning German memoranda of March 7 and 31 that accompanied the remilitarization of the Rhineland. He never received a reply. Meanwhile, the British government began an investigation of Germany's colonial claims, which had been raised in a vague manner in the German memoranda of March 1936. It was subsequently announced in the House of Commons at the end of July 1936 that while the British government would not refuse to discuss the aspect of the colonial question relating to access to raw materials, there were obstacles of a moral, political, and legal nature in the way of an actual transfer of mandated territories.[12]

During the winter of 1936–7, the British government presided over desultory efforts to convene a Five Power Conference that would both regulate the Rhineland situation and act as a prelude to a general settlement. The negotiations, however, revealed a disquieting growing intimacy between Germany and Italy, with both states arguing the case of a free hand for Germany in eastern Europe. Further evidence of this trend was Italo-German collaboration in the recently begun Spanish Civil War and the announcement of the Rome–Berlin Axis in November 1936. By March 1937, British policy in relation to Germany not only was at an impasse, but Germany's diplomatic isolation appeared to be over.

## Neville Chamberlain and British Foreign Policy

The consequence was an attempt to begin negotiations on the basis of approaches that Hjalmar Schacht, the German economics minister, had made in Paris in August 1936. He had suggested that failure to provide Germany with a colonial outlet would lead to an explosion. This had not impressed the Foreign Office, but there was alarm amongst senior Treasury officials that an opportunity was being lost. Their political chief, Neville Chamberlain, who shared their opinion, prevailed upon Anthony Eden, the foreign secretary, to explore Schacht's proposals further. He informed one of his sisters: "I have got a little scheme on hand for establishing contact with Schacht" which he thought might serve to restrain Hitler.[13]

In February 1937, Leith-Ross saw Schacht at Badenweiler. The following month Eden circulated to the Cabinet Committee on Foreign Policy a record of these conversations ostensibly because he wanted to consult the committee with regard to the nature of the reply that should be sent. Interestingly, the subsequent discussions and contacts with the French government were later referred to in a Foreign Office memorandum as *The Contemplated General Settlement of 1937.*[14] During April and May the whole issue of a general settlement was thrashed out involving treaties of non-aggression to replace Locarno, the reassurance of the states of eastern and central Europe, Germany's return to the League, and an international arms limitation agreement. In return for German compliance in these areas the British government would assist in the stabilization of Germany's economic and financial system and the outlines of a putative colonial settlement were determined. Before proceeding with these proposals it was decided once again to liaise with the French government. The French, however, were reluctant to follow the British lead on this occasion and disinclined to accept the disproportionate colonial sacrifice they would be asked to make. The attempt to reach a general settlement had for the moment perforce to be abandoned.[15]

It was in May 1937 that Chamberlain became prime minister. By this time his role in the formation of foreign policy was already formidable. Both he and Eden had played prominent parts in the formulation of the policy of trying to achieve a general European settlement: in essence, a policy that aimed at substantial renegotiation of the Versailles system. Chamberlain was to continue the effort to secure a general settlement, but he doubted the willingness of the Foreign Office to play its part. He informed his sister that "the double policy of rearmament and better relations with Germany and Italy will carry us through if only the F.O. will play up."[16] These views were widespread within the Treasury where there was a strong conviction that a fresh start would have to be made.

Chamberlain, therefore, wished to reinvigorate the policy of reaching a general settlement with Germany by himself taking a more active role in foreign policy. This was not at first resented by Anthony Eden. Chamberlain, however, wished also to repair the British relationship with Italy that had been damaged by the fallout from the Abyssinian crisis. In this way Italy might be detached from Germany's orbit, thus making the latter more amenable to a general settlement. The third part of the new prime minister's strategy was to continue with the rearmament program, although within the necessary financial restraints. The defense white papers of 1936 and 1937, of which Chamberlain was the main author, limited British defense spending over the next five years to £1,500 million, although by 1937 expenditure by the three armed services was already exceeding these limitations. The problem for the British government was to achieve military security while avoiding economic instability. As Sir Thomas Inskip put it in a memorandum of December 15, 1937: "Seen in its true perspective, the maintenance of our economic stability would more accurately be described as an essential element in our defensive strength: one which can properly be regarded as a fourth arm in defence, alongside the three services without which purely military effort would be of no avail."[17]

By the summer of 1937 the Anti-Comintern Pact had been concluded between Germany and Japan and in July 1937 the Sino-Japanese War resumed in the Far East. The nightmare of British policy was unfolding: that of being threatened simultaneously in Europe, the Mediterranean, and the Far East. A Chiefs of Staff memorandum warned:

> The intervention of Italy against us would at once impose conflicting demands on our fleet. Our policy must be governed by the principle that no anxieties or risks connected with our interests in the Mediterranean can be allowed to interfere with the despatch of a fleet to the Far East.[18]

A central difficulty for British policy, as Anthony Eden emphasized, was that from the first Hitler had seized the initiative. If the British government was to succeed in achieving a general settlement, it would have to secure the initiative and set the pace. Convinced that it was urgent to reach agreement with the dictators and, if possible, divide them, Chamberlain was determined to use every opportunity that might bring about that result.

## Chamberlain, Eden, and the Proposed General Settlement of March 1938

While Eden had welcomed Chamberlain's assumption of the premiership, their relationship had considerably deteriorated by November 1937. The reason for this lay in differences over policy toward Italy. Undoubtedly, a letter sent by Chamberlain to Mussolini on July 27, 1937, was the initial catalyst in promoting ill-feeling on the part of Eden toward the prime minister. The idea of approaching Mussolini in this way with a view to improving Anglo-Italian relations had been considered in Whitehall for some time and Eden had even considered sending a letter himself. In the event, however, it was Chamberlain who suggested to the Duce conversations that might remove causes of mistrust and misperception. What the Italians wanted was recognition of their Abyssinian Empire, while Chamberlain was only prepared to concede this in a wider agreement. Mussolini's response was favorable, but Eden urged caution in opening conversations. Chamberlain's response was to deplore a situation in which a chance to improve the international atmosphere might be allowed to slip back.

In the circumstances, Eden's resentments were to spill over into an initiative to attempt yet again to improve Anglo-German relations. This arose in the first instance as the consequence of Hermann Göring's invitation to Lord Halifax, a senior member of the British cabinet, to attend a hunting exhibition in Berlin. Neville Chamberlain thought that Halifax should go because it would provide an opportunity of making contact with Germany's leaders. It soon became evident that Hitler would only receive the British visitor at his south German headquarters near Berchtesgaden. With aristocratic disdain, Halifax informed Eden of Chamberlain's enthusiasm: "He was very strong that I ought to manage to see Hitler – even if it meant going to Berchtergaten [*sic*] – or whatever the place is. He truly observed that by that time the mask would be off, and that we might as well get all the contacts we could."[19] Eden, however, disagreed; he thought such a visit would seem like servility if the British minister was compelled to meet Hitler at the Berghof. Later, however, he relented and took the view that such a visit might not be a bad thing.

The talks that Halifax had with Hitler on November 19 produced the impression on the former that there could be no satisfactory rapprochement between Britain and Germany unless there was a settlement of the colonial question. Concluding his personal record of the talks, Halifax wrote:

> He [Hitler] did not give me the impression of being at all likely to want to go to war with us over colonies, but, no doubt, if he cannot be met on this issue, good relations, under which I suppose we might exert a good deal of influence . . . would remain impossible.

He urged further exploration of the possibility of a colonial settlement "with the idea of using it as a lever upon which to pursue a policy of real assurance in Europe . . . to try for the . . . bargain of a colonial settlement at the price of being a good European."[20]

There followed the inevitable consultations in London between the British and French governments. The French ministers were surprisingly complaisant and insisted that in the colonial question they were far more "progressive" than French public opinion.[21] It was agreed that both would be willing to examine the colonial question. Consequently, early in the New Year the British government decided to make a direct approach to the German government regarding a general settlement that would have a colonial dimension.

Given the fact that French foreign policy was by this time virtually determined by decisions in London, it is interesting to note that both Hitler and Ribbentrop were quite open about this tendency of French foreign policy to follow Britain's lead. In the so-called Hossbach memorandum Hitler stated: "France's attitude would certainly not be uninfluenced by that of Britain." Ribbentrop for his part argued that "in the last few years [French foreign policy] has become increasingly dependent on the [British] Foreign Office," and he referred to Britain as "the guarantor of France against Germany" with the clear implication of French secondary status.[22]

From the point of view of the British government, two developments in the latter half of 1937 made this approach urgent. First, the Sino-Japanese War had resumed in July 1937. This precipitated an immediate worsening in Anglo-Japanese relations, but the Brussels conference of November and its aftermath, which revealed the unlikelihood of American participation in sanctions against the Japanese, revealed the limitations of what could be done. Secondly, the British cabinet on December 22 determined that it was essential to adhere as far as possible to the restrictions on defense spending laid down in the white papers of 1936 and 1937. When the Cabinet Foreign Policy Committee met, therefore, on January 24, 1938, to consider policy toward Germany, there was a strong consensus in support of Chamberlain's proposals. What he suggested was that the colonial question would now be placed in the forefront, but that it could not be settled except within the framework of a general settlement. He envisaged that the colonial settlement would not take the form of a straightforward retrocession of Germany's former colonies, but would rather involve the creation of a new colonial regime in Africa south of the Sahara in which Germany would be given an interest. Only Eden offered major criticism – to the effect that the prime minister had not adequately stressed

the link between a colonial settlement and general settlement, whereas he had. What also would be involved was defined more sharply in a Foreign Office memorandum the following day, which was interestingly entitled "German Contribution Towards a General Appeasement." The suggested concessions from Germany that the British wanted were those that had been current since 1935.

On March 3, 1938, the substance of this program was put to Hitler by the British ambassador in Berlin, Sir Nevile Henderson. However, in the meantime, Anthony Eden had resigned as foreign secretary. The reason for his resignation related not to policy toward Germany but, in the first instance, to Chamberlain's decision to decline a proposal made by the American president, Franklin D. Roosevelt, to call a conference in Washington that would examine the economic causes underlying the world's discontents. Chamberlain turned down this initiative because he felt that it would cut across the initiatives that he himself had in mind for improving relations with the dictators. Eden, however, considered the president's action to be a prelude to American involvement in European affairs and, for him, the prime minister's rebuff seemed to be an issue over which he should resign – and probably would have been had the president's proposal not been confidential.

The following month Chamberlain endeavored to revive contacts with the Italians through his sister-in-law, Lady Ivy Chamberlain, and Sir Joseph Ball, director of the Conservative Research Department. This, and the prime minister's willingness to obtain an agreement with Italy by offering *de jure* recognition of Italy's conquest of Abyssinia, provided Eden with both an issue on which to disagree and an opportunity to claim that he had been bypassed and his function usurped by the prime minister. His resignation precipitated a major crisis in the government and Chamberlain exaggerated the differences between the two men. The reality, though, was otherwise. Eden did not resign over some great principle regarding the "appeasement" of Germany, as legend would have it, but on the rather minor issues of Anglo-American and Anglo-Italian relations.

Under Eden's successor, Lord Halifax, the policy of attempting to bring Germany into a general settlement, which Eden himself had done so much to develop, was continued and in due course Sir Nevile Henderson arranged to meet Hitler on March 3. This proved a catastrophic disappointment, all the more so because this was the first and last time prior to the outbreak of war in 1939 that the British attempted to deal with Germany on a broad basis that was designed to lead ultimately to the renegotiation of the entire Versailles system. Henderson told Hitler that Britain was prepared to satisfy Germany's colonial claims and he asked what Germany could contribute toward the wider interests of peace and détente in Europe. Hitler's response was scornful and acerbic. He could wait a decade for colonial satisfaction. Nevertheless, the following month seemed to bring some joy, for on April 16 an Anglo-Italian agreement was concluded, which provided for British recognition of the Italian conquest of Abyssinia and the withdrawal of Italian "volunteers" from Spain.

## The *Anschluss* and the Munich Crisis

A little over a week after Henderson's fateful interview with Hitler, the German army entered Austria unopposed and the union of Germany and Austria was announced. The *Anschluss* was a further setback for British policy. Moreover, implicit in the German absorption of Austria was a threat to Czechoslovakia, which was not a German state, although it contained a substantial German-speaking minority, most of whom desired incorporation into the Reich. It was felt by the British government that the logistical problems entailed in rendering support to Czech defenses in the event of a German act of aggression were insuperable. Accordingly, it was determined that no guarantee could be given to the Czechs and that efforts should be made to help them resolve their differences with the Germans peacefully. It followed on from this that Britain would not automatically come to the assistance of France if it were to become involved in a war with Germany as a consequence of its alliance with Czechoslovakia. Nevertheless, Chamberlain was very aware that Britain could not allow France to be subjugated by Germany. When, therefore, the prime minister listed Britain's alliance obligations in the

House of Commons on March 24, and also made public the cabinet's decisions in relation to Czechoslovakia and France, he added the following words:

> Where peace and war are concerned, legal obligations are not alone involved, and if war broke out, it would be unlikely to be confined to those who have assumed such obligations. It would be quite impossible to say where it would end and what Governments might become involved. The inexorable pressure of facts might well prove more powerful than formal pronouncements and in that event it would be well within the bounds of probability that other countries, besides those which were parties to the original dispute, would almost immediately become involved.[23]

Here was an admission that it would be almost impossible for Britain to stay out of such a war and that its logical end might be a world war. This was both a forecast and a warning that was intended as a deterrent.

In the wake of the *Anschluss* the British and French governments met at the end of April 1938 to coordinate their responses to the developing crisis in central Europe. The French were now led by a new team that had taken office some days earlier. Daladier was now the prime minister and Bonnet the foreign minister. Although the French at first struck a fighting pose, the primacy of Britain's position was revealed in the fact that it was decided to make joint representations in Prague in early May to the effect that the Czechs should make concessions to their German minority, the *Sudetendeutschen*. A British guarantee of Czechoslovakia was firmly refused by Chamberlain. There were, however, wider dimensions to British policy. The Czech question was arguably the only remaining obstacle in the way of Germany being brought into a general settlement. If it could be removed from the list of outstanding issues, the Powers could then concentrate upon the wider issues that had inspired the earlier British approach on March 3. The degree to which the French ministers had been brought into line with this policy is revealed in the fact that within days Bonnet conveyed the following to the German ambassador in Paris: "People in France and Great Britain saw in this very crisis an opportunity of reaching an understanding with Germany which would finally assure the peace of Europe. It was already hoped that conversations would be opened with [Germany] on this matter in the immediate future."[24]

Nevertheless, the Czech crisis steadily worsened. On May 20 rumors of a threat to Czechoslovakia provoked a firm response from the British and the French, which only served to stiffen Hitler's resolve to destroy Czechoslovakia. Following this May crisis the British intensified their efforts to bring about a mediated solution by sending Lord Runciman at the end of July to Czechoslovakia. In September the crisis finally came to a head when the Czech president, Beneş, conceded to the Germans almost the entirety of their demands. This finally called the bluff of the Sudeten Germans, who rejected the Czech offer. This and the riotous circumstances that ensued revealed that union with the Reich and not autonomy was their real aim. On September 12 Hitler delivered an inflammatory speech at the Nuremberg Rally and war seemed imminent. In order to avoid a catastrophe, Chamberlain decided on September 13 to fly to Germany to meet Hitler face to face, although the decision to do so if necessary had already been taken on August 30. On September 15 Chamberlain met Hitler at the Berghof where it was agreed in principle to transfer the Sudeten areas to Germany. On September 18 the French prime minister and foreign minister visited London, where they endorsed the plan. The Czechs, after a ministerial crisis, accepted it too on September 21. The following day Chamberlain flew to Godesberg where he was to convey to Hitler personally the agreement on the cession of the Sudeten areas to Germany. He was astonished by the Führer's reaction. There could be no further delay. There had to be a solution by October 1 and German forces would start to occupy the Sudeten areas on September 28. Moreover, Polish and Hungarian claims on Czech territory would have to be settled. After a second meeting Hitler agreed that the German occupation of the Sudeten areas would only begin on October 1.

Despite this depressing turn of events, Chamberlain felt bound to recommend to his colleagues, the French and the Czechs, the terms of Hitler's Godesberg memorandum. He now, however,

began to face resistance. Sir Alexander Cadogan, who had succeeded Vansittart as head of the Foreign Office the previous January, provoked Halifax into opposition. He felt in the light of Cadogan's criticisms that it would be improper to coerce the Czechs, who rejected the Godesberg terms.[25] Consequently the cabinet was divided, with Chamberlain's position supported by a minority. Furthermore, the French were now seemingly determined to stand by the Czechs. War seemed inevitable, for Britain could not stand by with equanimity, whatever the formalities of treaty commitments.

What saved the situation was a proposal by Mussolini for the convening of a conference. The British ambassador in Rome had suggested this move to Mussolini on September 27, but Italian mediation was a sham, for the Italian agenda for the conference had been drafted in the German Foreign Office. Nevertheless, a Four Power Conference met at Munich on September 29. The powers represented were Britain, France, Germany, and Italy. Czechoslovakia was excluded and so was the Soviet Union. In the early hours of September 30 agreement was finally reached. The Sudetenland was to be occupied by Germany between October 1 and 10; Polish and Hungarian claims were to be settled; an international commission was to determine the final frontier; and a four-power guarantee was to protect the territorial integrity of the Czech state.

War had been avoided, but that was not the end of the business of Munich. After breakfast on the morning of September 30, Chamberlain persuaded Hitler to sign the so-called Anglo-German Declaration. This emphasized the importance of Anglo-German relations for the future of peace, affirmed the desire of Britain and Germany never to go to war with one another again, and promised that Britain and Germany would work together to preserve peace. On returning to Heston Airport, Chamberlain waved his copy of the Anglo-German Declaration and stated: "The settlement of the Czechoslovakian problem which has now been achieved is, in my view, only the prelude to a larger settlement in which all Europe may find peace."[26] Chamberlain was, therefore, still seeking to achieve with Germany that general settlement that had proved so elusive.

Munich was in truth only an aspect of the foreign policy pursued by the British government toward Germany in the 1930s. The problem is that in retrospect it has come to represent, in the eyes of many, the totality of that policy and conferred upon the word "appeasement" the meaning it has today. It was, of course, easily interpreted as weakness. As Mussolini observed, when he heard that Chamberlain was about to fly to Berchtesgaden: "There will not be war. But this is the liquidation of British prestige."[27] More publicly, Winston Churchill on September 21, 1938, argued that the partition of Czechoslovakia would mark the capitulation of the western democracies to the threat of force and it is Churchill's estimation that has stood the test of time. Nevertheless, Churchill's view was a minority one among contemporaries. The relief that the Munich agreement brought to Britain was obvious and the prime minister's reputation was greatly enhanced. On his return from Munich it took Chamberlain's car some one and a half hours to travel from the airport to Downing Street because of the density of the crowds.

## The End of Appeasement

That the optimism generated by the Munich agreement was premature was revealed a little over a month later when the National Socialist regime carried out in November an anti-Jewish pogrom, known as the *Kristallnacht*. Nevertheless, British efforts seemed to be bearing fruit with Italy, for in November 1938 the Anglo-Italian agreement was ratified. This, however, was a short-lived success. In January 1939 Chamberlain and Halifax visited Rome with almost wholly negative results. In the months after Munich, Halifax was doubtful of the prospects for peace, while Chamberlain inclined toward optimism and still hoped to achieve a general settlement. This, though, depended upon the willingness of the Germans to renounce force. In March 1939 Hitler made it clear that such an inclination was not imminent when, taking advantage of Slovak separatism, the German government effectively bullied the Czech leaders into signing away the independence of the Czech provinces of Bohemia and Moravia. On March 15 German forces entered

Prague: Slovakia became a satellite state of the Third Reich and the Czech provinces became Reich Protectorates.

To some extent the British government had already begun to evince a degree of firmness. On February 1 the cabinet decided, following intelligence reports, that an attack on the Netherlands or Switzerland would compel British military intervention. Five days later Chamberlain publicly announced that if France were threatened by another power, Britain would come to its assistance and, by the end of the month, the decision had been taken to create a large continental army and accept the continental commitment. Although in the immediate aftermath of the Prague crisis the prime minister was rather bland in his condemnation, in his speech in Birmingham two days later on March 17, 1939, he displayed his disappointment and anger.

It is now clear that by the time Chamberlain made his Birmingham speech his perception was that British foreign policy had changed. Undoubtedly, Halifax had spoken firmly to Chamberlain and both that and Chamberlain's own perception that Hitler could not any longer be trusted caused the prime minister to embark upon a course from which he did not diverge until his death the following year. In a private letter he expressed the view that the recent events had "changed the whole situation" and shown that "settlement is impossible with the present regime in Germany," as they "cannot be relied upon to carry out any assurances they give." He thought that it would now be possible to bring Eden back into the government. As long as such a step would have been interpreted as a change in policy he had not been able to consider it. But now that Hitler had "made the policy impossible" he was obliged to reconsider the position.[28]

Clearly, Chamberlain considered that policy had changed. But this did not mean that his aspiration to achieve a general settlement in the long term had been abandoned. Rather, it meant that the British government would not actively pursue one until there had been a change of government in Germany, involving the removal of Hitler, or until there was palpable and reliable evidence that Hitler had been compelled to change his demeanor. A further letter written by Chamberlain to Lord

Francis Scott in June 1939 makes this clear. Scott, a settler in Tanganyika, had written to Chamberlain expressing the anxiety of his fellow settlers that the mandate might be returned to Germany. Chamberlain replied by stating that the achievement of peace and security in the world remained "the dominating purpose" of his political life. He continued: "Not peace at any price – and nothing that I have said would justify anyone to putting such an interpretation on my words – but peace at a price not inconsistent with honour and simple morality." The reality, though, was that such a peace was contingent upon an understanding between Britain and Germany, which would have to include a colonial settlement. As far as Nazi Germany was concerned, this would probably mean the restitution of the entire prewar colonial empire. Chamberlain observed:

> I could never consent to the satisfaction of German claims on such a basis. The recent action of Hitler in Czechoslovakia has destroyed confidence in his assurance, and it is difficult to see how, after his recent action, he could give such reliability in future as would carry conviction.
> . . . in my view it would be impossible even to discuss the Colonial question with Germany in the present atmosphere of resentment over her past actions, and over Hitler's breach of faith and of suspicion as to her intentions in the future.[29]

Coupled with Chamberlain's refusal any longer to chase after Hitler with proposals unless there was an obvious change of heart in Berlin, there was a policy of guaranteeing the states of eastern Europe against German aggression. The most important of these was the Polish guarantee that was converted into an alliance in the last days of August 1939. Furthermore, on April 26 the British government introduced proposals for peacetime conscription. Finally, desultory and ultimately abortive negotiations with France and the Soviet Union were entered into for the formation of a Triple Alliance. These terminated with the announcement of the Nazi–Soviet Non-Aggression Pact on August 23, 1939.

From March 26, 1939, when the Poles made it clear that they could not accept Germany's proposals for the resolution of German–Polish difficulties, relations between the two countries rapidly worsened and were focused upon the status of the German-speaking Free City of Danzig. Naturally, Chamberlain hoped that this crisis could be averted without war and at times he was optimistic that it could be, but this was the optimism of a logical mind that calculated that the overt determination of Britain to resist must give Hitler pause. It was not the squalid maneuvering of the craven desperate to avoid war at all costs.

In the end nothing could deflect Hitler from his self-appointed date with destiny and on September 1, 1939, Germany launched its offensive against Poland. From that time onwards Chamberlain was unflinching in his determination that the war could only end with the overthrow of Hitler. Such contacts as there were with Germany thereafter were designed to support the German opposition or resistance or to ascertain the state of the political situation in Germany. Chamberlain's adamantine refusal to deal with Hitler can be seen in the ministerial discussions regarding the nature of the reply that should be made to Hitler's peace overtures of October 6, 1939, and his following statement in the House of Commons on October 12. Any peace would have to encompass the restoration of Poland and Czech independence. In other words, terms that would have been overwhelmingly damaging to Hitler's prestige. In May 1940 when the German Wehrmacht was overwhelming Belgium, Holland, and France, and after Chamberlain had resigned in favor of Churchill, the cabinet, at the request of Halifax, considered using the mediatory services of Mussolini to effect a peace with Germany. Chamberlain, who had remained in the cabinet, was a critical voice in rejecting this possibility.[30]

In September 1939 France followed Britain into war, although the mood of resistance in France itself was strong. Under the leadership of Daladier, France, in the year before the outbreak of war, resisted British pressure for French concessions to Italy as a means of luring the latter away from Germany. Moreover, in the protracted, desultory, and ultimately abortive negotiations with the USSR in the summer of 1939, it was increasingly the French who made the running. By June 1939, 76 percent thought that France should go to war with Germany if it attempted to seize Danzig by force. Nevertheless, looking at the 1930s as a whole, it is difficult to disagree with R. J. Young's assessment that "the historian of France between the wars simply has to accept that the French sense of dependence on Britain has not been exaggerated."[31]

Paradoxically, just as Britain had determined upon a firm line with Germany, a temporary weakening set in in respect of Japan. Throughout the 1930s there had been a less accommodating attitude on the part of the British government toward Japan than there had been toward the Third Reich. To a considerable extent this was inevitable given the perceived need not to offend opinion in the United States. Thus the inclination in 1934 to resurrect the old Anglo-Japanese alliance, in substance if not in form, was quietly abandoned. Nevertheless, given the parlous state of the war in Europe by the summer of 1940, and the refusal on the part of the United States to render Britain assistance in the Far East, the Churchill government acceded to Japanese demands to close the Burma Road, through which the Chinese were being supplied. Nevertheless, the failure of the Japanese to honor their reciprocal undertaking to seek a peace with China, their participation in the Tripartite Pact with Germany and Italy in October 1940, and more encouraging noises from Washington all prompted Britain to reopen the Burma Road. Thereafter Britain's position in respect of Japan remained one of resistance, culminating in the Japanese attack upon Malaya on December 8, 1941.

## Conclusion

The policy that the British government pursued toward the Germany of the Third Reich is not one that can usefully be described as "appeasement," given the meaning that the word has acquired since 1940 when politicians such as Churchill and Eden sought to distance themselves from the prewar Conservative Party. The policy of the British National government toward the Third Reich from 1933 onwards was a carefully formulated strategy that involved some substantial modifications to the Versailles system that would bring Germany into satisfactory treaty relations with

the rest of Europe. It was not predicated on the assumption that a few one-sided concessions to Nazi Germany might pacify Hitler; indeed, reciprocity was the key to the policy of achieving a European and general settlement that would result in the appeasement of Europe. When Hitler demonstrated in the dismantlement of Czechoslovakia that reciprocity was not on offer, the policy of a general settlement, as far as Hitler was concerned, was to all intents and purposes abandoned. Nevertheless, Chamberlain continued to believe in the desirability of Anglo-German understanding and peace in the context of a wider European settlement – if Germany could be de-Nazified and regenerated.

## NOTES

1   National Archives, Kew, Prem 1/395, Reuters Report of Hitler's Speech to the Reichstag, October 6, 1939.
2   National Archives, Kew, CAB 24/225, Changing Conditions in British Foreign Policy, November 26, 1931.
3   A. Hillgruber, *Germany and the Two World Wars* (London: Harvard University Press, 1981), pp. 59–60.
4   D. Marquand, *Ramsay MacDonald* (London: Jonathan Cape, 1977), p. 754.
5   National Archives, Kew, CAB 24/251, Memorandum by Sir John Simon, 29.11.1934.
6   A. J. P. Taylor, *English History* (Oxford: Oxford University Press, 1965), p. 364.
7   D. Cameron Watt, *Succeeding John Bull: America in Britain's Place 1900–1975* (Cambridge: Cambridge University Press, 1984), p. 76.
8   National Archives, Kew, FO 371/1885/C7752/55/18, Britain, France and Germany and Annex, November 21, 1935.
9   National Archives, Kew, CAB24/260, Memorandum by Anthony Eden, February 11, 1936.
10  National Archives, Kew, FO 371/19885/C998/4/18, Memorandum by Anthony Eden, February 15, 1936.
11  National Archives, Kew, CAB 23/83, Cabinet Minutes March 5, 1936, and *Documents Diplomatiques Français* (Paris: Imprimerie Nationale, 1964), Series 2, Vol. 1, No. 283.
12  Andrew J. Crozier, *Appeasement and Germany's Last Bid for Colonies* (Basingstoke: Macmillan, 1988), pp. 134–68.

13  Neville Chamberlain Papers, University of Bir-
    mingham, 18/1/991, Neville Chamberlain to Ida
    Chamberlain, January 16, 1937.

14  National Archives, Prem 1/330, Foreign Office
    Memorandum, January 25, 1938.

15  M. Thomas, *Britain, France and Appeasement:
    Anglo-French Relations in the Popular Front Era*
    (Oxford: Berg, 1996), pp. 128–33.

16  Neville Chamberlain Papers, University of Bir-
    mingham, 18/1/1010, Neville Chamberlain to
    Hilda Chamberlain, August 1, 1937.

17  R. P. Shay, Jr., *British Rearmament in the Thirties:
    Politics and Profits* (Princeton, NJ: Princeton Uni-
    versity Press, 1977), p. 167.

18  J. Joll, "The Decline of Europe 1920–1970,"
    *International Affairs* 49 (1970): 1–18.

19  National Archives, Prem 1/330, Lord Halifax to
    Anthony Eden, October 27, 1937.

20  National Archives, CAB 27/626/F.P.(36)49,
    Account by Lord Halifax of his Visit to Germany,
    November 26, 1937.

21  National Archives, CAB 27/626/F.P.(36)40,
    Record of an Anglo-French Conversation, Novem-
    ber 29–30, 1937.

22  *Documents on German Foreign Policy* (London:
    HMSO, 1951–), Series D, Vol. 1, Nos. 19 and 93;
    and W. Michalka, *Das Dritte Reich* (Munich:
    Deutscher Taschenbuch Verlag, 1985), vol. 1, pp.
    241–2.

23  House of Commons Debates, Series V, Vol. 333,
    cols. 1405–6.

24  *Documents on German Foreign Policy*, Series D,
    Vol. 2, No. 144.

25  Peter Neville, "Sir Alexander Cadogan and Lord
    Halifax's 'Damascus Road' Conversion over the
    Godesberg Terms 1938," *Diplomacy and State-
    craft* 11 (2000): 81–90.

26  R. A. C. Parker, *Chamberlain and Appeasement:
    British Policy and the Coming of the Second World
    War* (Basingstoke: Macmillan, 1993), pp. 180–1.

27  Count Ciano, *Ciano's Diary, 1937–1938* (London,
    1952), entry for September 14, 1938.

28  National Archives, Prem 5/207, Neville Chamber-
    lain to Sir Walter Runciman, March 17, 1939.

29  National Archives, Prem 1/304, Neville Chamber-
    lain to Lord Francis Scott, June 12, 1939.

30  John Lukacs, *Five Days in London: May 1940* (New
    Haven, CT: Yale University Press, 1999), p. 120.

31  R. J. Young, "The Problem of France," in *The
    Origins of the Second World War Reconsidered: The
    A. J. P. Taylor Debate after Twenty-Five Years*, ed.
    G. Martel (London: Allen & Unwin, 1986), pp.
    106–7.

## GUIDE TO FURTHER READING

Anthony Adamthwaite, *France and the Coming of the
Second World War* (London: Cass, 1977) and *Gran-
deur and Misery: France's Bid for Power in Europe*
(London: Arnold, 1995). Both books argue that the
French leadership deliberately opted for a policy of
"appeasement" and abandoned opposition to the
Third Reich.

Antony Best, *Britain, Japan and Pearl Harbor: Avoiding War in East Asia, 1936–1941* (London: Routledge,
1995). Shows that the idea of Japanese guilt is hard
to apply and argues that there was a failure on the
part of Britain to bring about managed change in the
Far East.

Robert Boyce and Joseph A. Maiolo, eds., *The Origins
of World War Two: The Debate Continues* (Basingstoke: Palgrave Macmillan, 2003). The chapter on
Britain by Williamson Murray, pp. 111–33, is mainly
a restatement of the traditional view of "appeasement," but it is worth reading.

John Charmley, *Chamberlain and the Lost Peace* (Basingstoke: Macmillan, 1989). Vitiates the case for
Chamberlain by suggesting that Britain should not
have gone to war with Germany.

Maurice Cowling, *The Impact of Hitler* (Cambridge:
Cambridge University Press, 1975). Argues that
British politics in the 1930s revolved around the issue
of Hitler and Germany, but is also notable for containing a number of reassessments.

Andrew J. Crozier, *The Causes of the Second World
War* (Oxford: Blackwell, 1997). Contains a substantial historiographical section on British foreign
policy in the 1930s; *Appeasement and Germany's
Last Bid for Colonies* (Basingstoke: Macmillan,
1988), demonstrates that the foreign policy pursued
by Neville Chamberlain had steadily developed
between 1933 and 1937 and that both the Foreign Office and Anthony Eden were complicit
in it.

Richard Davis, *Anglo-French Relations before the Second
World War: Appeasement and Crisis* (Basingstoke:
Palgrave, 2001). Suggests that the inherent failure
of the *entente cordiale* lay in the two countries'
inability to overcome deep-rooted suspicion and
mistrust.

Martin Gilbert, *The Roots of Appeasement* (London:
Weidenfeld & Nicolson, 1966). Demonstrates that
British foreign policy in the 1930s had a history
extending back to the Versailles settlement.

Martin Gilbert and Richard Gott, *The Appeasers*
(London: Weidenfeld and Nicolson, 1964). The
classic anti-appeaser statement.

Peter Lowe, *Great Britain and the Origins of the Pacific War, 1937–1941* (Oxford: Oxford University Press, 1977). A reliable and perceptive survey.

Peter Neville, *Appeasing Hitler: The Diplomacy of Sir Nevile Henderson* (Basingstoke: Palgrave Macmillan, 2000). A belated but justified rehabilitation of Britain's ambassador to Berlin in the crucial years 1937 to 1939.

R. A. C. Parker, *Chamberlain and Appeasement: British Policy and the Coming of the Second World War* (Basingstoke: Macmillan, 1993). Argues that the alternative to "appeasement" was the construction of an encircling alliance system, but recognizes Chamberlain's strengths.

Keith Robbins, *Munich 1938* (London: Cassell, 1968). The first account of the Munich crisis written by an author born after the event which sought to put it in the context of fifty years of Anglo-German relations; *Appeasement* (Oxford: Blackwell, 1988), a good historiographical analysis.

M. Thomas, *Britain, France and Appeasement: Anglo-French Relations in the Popular Front Era* (Oxford: Berg, 1996). Asserts that French policymakers influenced the course of British policy in the period 1935–7, but that during 1938 Britain was increasingly able to impose its will on the Daladier government.

Neville Thompson, *The Anti-Appeasers* (Oxford: Oxford University Press, 1971). Argues that the appeaser/resister concept is misleading and that more united the two groups than divided them.

D. Cameron Watt, "Appeasement: The Rise of a Revisionist School," *Political Quarterly* 36 (1965): 191–213. Argued that the standard narrative relating to "appeasement" and Neville Chamberlain had serious flaws.

R. J. Young, *France and the Origins of the Second World War* (Basingstoke: Macmillan, 1996). Suggests that the French drift to war was the consequence of both too much and too little self-confidence.

# CHAPTER TWENTY

# Stalin and the West

## ALEXANDER HILL

The Bolshevik-led Soviet Russian republic was born into a hostile international environment. In late 1917 the Bolsheviks had to deal with the German threat which had played a crucial role in bringing down both the tsarist regime and the weakening of the provisional government. Peace with Germany at the Treaty of Brest-Litovsk in March 1918 came at the temporary price of vast swathes of Russian imperial territory, including the Ukraine, and marked the longer-term separation of the Baltic republics and Finland from the former empire. The peace also brought the Bolsheviks into direct confrontation with the Entente, determined to preserve an eastern front in the war against the Central Powers. British and French input into the civil war undoubtedly prolonged the fighting, and would not be forgotten quickly by Soviet leaders.

While by 1921 the Bolsheviks found themselves nominal masters of much of the former Russian Empire, they faced a population and particularly a peasantry weary of the excesses of the politics of "war communism" and the bloodshed of war, prompting the Bolsheviks under Lenin's leadership to take a step back from propelling the fledgling republic toward communism, a key dimension of which, for many within the party, was "forced," or at least intensified, industrialization. War communism was replaced by the semi-capitalist New Economic Policy (NEP).

There was an uneasy peace not only in Soviet society and within the Communist Party, but also between the Soviet Union and the capitalist world. While both sought to normalize relations (particularly in trade), the Soviet Union was aware of the latent hostility toward the regime, while the capitalist world was convinced that the international revolutionary project had merely been placed on hold by the Bolsheviks. Under Lenin's leadership the development of the Soviet military power required to spread "revolution" by force – as attempted in Poland in 1920 – was increasingly of secondary importance to stability, both internally and in relations with other powers. This situation was to remain under the collective leadership following Lenin's death in January 1924.[1] With the rise of Stalin, however, the pursuit of military power for use against an abstract capitalist threat would become a key justification for the ending of NEP and the associated projects of forced collectivization and industrialization from 1928 onwards, Stalin's "revolution from above."

## International Relations and the "Revolution from Above"

For the Soviet Union eventual conflict with the capitalist world was always inevitable, even if, in the short term, undesirable. The capitalist threat to the Soviet Union was, however, at least in Soviet eyes, to become more significant with the apparently increasing prospects of revolution in capitalist countries associated with depression in the 1920s, reaching an early peak with the "war scare" of the summer of 1927. Fearing revolution, capitalist powers were portrayed as likely to seek to destroy the Soviet beacon for communism across Europe in order to forestall revolution, although there is little or no evidence of concrete preparations. The "war scare" of 1927 stemmed from a series of apparently unrelated events and, in particular, the Arcos crisis with Britain, during which the London offices of the Soviet trade delegation and the joint-stock trading company Arcos were raided by the Metropolitan Police and Special Branch on the suspicion that they were being used as the base for subversive activities against Great Britain. The crisis was sufficiently serious to result in a British break in diplomatic relations with the Soviet Union.[2] The Soviet response was both to strengthen the Soviet economy and defense sector and to make certain that the Soviet heartland in a future "war" against the capitalist world would be secure.[3]

While the Soviet Union would officially continue to seek to foster revolution in the capitalist world through the Communist International (or Comintern), given its military weakness this activity could not be allowed to provoke the capitalist powers into military action. Almost as importantly, such activity could not be sufficiently threatening to the West to hinder trade and the Soviet Union's acquisition of western technology necessary for industrialization and the defense sector. Diplomatic relations with Britain, severed in 1927 as a result of the Arcos crisis, were reestablished in 1929 when a Labour minority government came to power, even if the resulting "thaw" was short-lived. However, in addition to Soviet subversion, or at least fears of it, tsarist debt continued to be a stumbling block in both British and French relations with the Soviet Union, or perhaps an excuse for preventing improved relations to be applied by the anti-communist right when Soviet attempts to settle the issue did not meet expectations. The Soviet Union, which needed the West more than the West needed it, continued to pursue improved ties behind the scenes, while the intensity of anti-western rhetoric increased within the Soviet Union. Nonetheless, that continued references to "capitalist encirclement" were principally intended

for domestic consumption is illustrated by the fact that during the show trials of the late 1920s and early 1930s, the Soviet Union was careful not to sentence foreign nationals accused of orchestrating the wrecking of Soviet industry as severely as its own. For instance, the Metro-Vickers trial of April 1933 involved the accusation of "espionage, bribery, and wrecking" against six British engineers of Metropolitan Vickers Electrical Company on contract to the Soviet Union, the first charge having some foundation if broadly defined. Two of the accused were sentenced to two- and three-year imprisonments respectively, although they actually only served two months as a result of subsequent diplomatic activity.[4] The Metro-Vickers affair was a serious threat to both diplomatic and economic Anglo-Soviet relations, resulting in short-term sanctions by the British, to which the Soviet Union responded. Nonetheless, Metro-Vickers understandably continued to obtain contracts with the Soviet Union given the priority accorded to the acquisition of foreign expertise and technology by the Soviet leadership.

Soviet planners believed that the capitalist military threat was still led by the British (who were largely unaware that their intentions were regarded as aggressive). A memorandum of 1930 by a planning official, N. Snitko, submitted to the chairman of the defense sector of Gosplan – the body responsible for Soviet economic planning – outlined three scenarios in which the Soviet Union might have to fight the capitalist powers of the West. The first scenario identified was "where the imperialists, having agreed some sort of temporary compromise amongst themselves, organize an attack on the USSR with the aim of deciding by force of arms the basic contradiction of the modern world order – the co-existence of two fundamentally opposed economic systems."[5] This was the situation which the Soviet Union claimed was threatening in the late 1920s and early 1930s, requiring the strengthening of Soviet armed forces as a matter of some urgency. While the British-led threat did not materialize in any tangible form, Japan was identified as a concrete threat in the Far East in the early 1930s, particularly after its invasion of Manchuria in 1931. However, the threat to Soviet security from Japan was not a major identifiable factor driving Soviet rearmament in general, although it was a factor stimulating Soviet naval development, including such major projects as the opening of the Northern Sea Route from the European north to the Far East.

Even with Adolf Hitler's coming to power in Germany in 1933, it was, according to the Russian historian O. N. Ken, not until the mid-1930s that Soviet defense planning at the highest levels was focused on a specific threat, that emerging from Nazi Germany, and to a lesser extent Japan, rather than an abstract "capitalist" threat involving many possible combinations of powers, but usually including Poland and Britain.[6] The construction of the Baltic–White Sea Canal, for which planning was under way in 1930 and construction completed in 1933, was primarily aimed at security against Britain. In military-strategic terms the canal was identified in Soviet planning as providing "the solution of a range of issues in the defense of the coastline from the Finnish border up to the coastline of Siberia accessible by sea, including the White Sea," with the British attack on the naval base at Kronstadt and occupation of Arkhangel'sk during the Russian Civil War being relatively recent events. The canal also allowed for "the defense of the fishing industry in coastal waters and coastal commerce between points along the coastline and river shipping routes into the heart of the country. This task is to be achieved in the Northern Theatre, primarily through the ability to transfer submarines and surface torpedo craft and cruisers from the Baltic to the White Sea." Fishing disputes with Britain in the far north during the 1920s and British forays down the River Dvina during the civil war were most probably at the forefront of the minds of Soviet planners. Finally, the canal would provide "the potential for our naval forces to operate on enemy lines of maritime communication . . . in the North Sea and eastern portion of the Atlantic Ocean."[7]

## National Socialism and Collective Security

During the 1920s and early 1930s the Soviet Union had to some extent been a pariah state in Europe. It did not, for instance, participate in the League of Nations and maintained closer links with other pariah powers than the "victors" of the First World War. Hence through the Rapallo Treaty of 1922 the Soviet Union and Germany cooperated not only politically and economically, but also militarily, sharing hostility to the Anglo-French alliance which had seen both stripped of territory, and hostility to Poland, the key beneficiary of their losses. The Soviet Union was also on sufficiently good terms with Mussolini's Italy to seek Italian assistance in the construction of a new generation of destroyers for Soviet naval forces in the early 1930s, developing relations in this sphere extending back to 1925, and culminating in the Italian construction of the flotilla leader *Tashkent* for Soviet naval forces, handed over incomplete to the Soviet Union in 1939, and Italian assistance in the construction of Type 7 series destroyers.[8]

The rise of National Socialism in Germany prompted a reorientation of Soviet diplomatic activity toward what appeared to be conciliation with the capitalist powers, with the Soviet Union joining the League of Nations in September 1934. At the same time the Soviet Union sought security agreements with those capitalist powers which themselves felt most threatened by the reemergent German threat, namely France and Czechoslovakia, with whom the Soviet Union signed mutual assistance pacts in 1935. Just how far these pacts were supposed to go was, however, a matter for disagreement. For the French and indeed British, such agreements were part of the post-Versailles international system, the web of agreements and pacts which were supposed to limit German ambitions much more cheaply than the rearmament required to add credibility to substantial and, hopefully, unnecessary commitments, along the lines which the Soviet Union was seeking. Differing views on the scope and purpose of such pacts, as well as the strength of anti-Soviet feeling in French conservative circles, influenced the time it took France and the Soviet Union to sign the mutual assistance pact of May 1935, without many of the add-ons such as military assistance to the Red Army, which had been discussed during negotiations. That the pact was signed at all had much to do with Hitler's words and actions making it increasingly difficult not to sign. The new French foreign minister, Pierre Laval, was certainly more interested in strengthening his hand in negotiations with Germany than in an agreement with the Soviet Union that might lead to significant rearmament, military action, and bloodshed.[9]

During the mid-1930s, while its rearmament progressed at an increasing pace, the Soviet Union has been seen by most western, Soviet, and post-Soviet Russian historians to have been genuinely seeking some sort of "collective security" from a reemergent Germany, be it as a short-term measure or otherwise. Key proponents of this line in one form or another in the West include A. J. P. Taylor, Jonathan Haslam, Geoffrey Roberts, and perhaps most vociferously, by virtue of his contrasting of genuine Soviet efforts with British ideologically motivated intransigence, Michael Carley.[10] Through "collective" efforts the further spread of fascism in Europe was to be prevented, and foreign communist parties were instructed by the Soviet-led Comintern to work with the "Social Democrats" in the European democracies in order to defeat the electoral threat from fascist parties, engaging in "popular front" politics against the right. This can be contrasted with the situation in 1933 when Hitler came to power in Germany, when German communist hostility toward the moderate socialists had been encouraged.

In the introduction to his 1995 *The Soviet Union and the Origins of the Second World War*, Geoffrey Roberts identifies a "German" school of historians in opposition to those who believe that Soviet support for "collective security" was sincere.[11] These historians, the most prominent of whom is arguably Jiri Hochman, see the eventual Soviet signing of the Nazi–Soviet Pact in 1939 as the result of a pro-German orientation, designed in part to divide the capitalist West, continuing on from Rapallo despite the rise of Hitler and behind the smokescreen of the quest for "collective security." This line is, however, very much a product of the Cold War, and receives even less support amongst academics today than it did in 1995, despite the publication in 1997 of the veteran exiled Soviet historian Alexander Nekrich's *Pariahs, Partners, Predators*, very much part of this school.[12] Although the "German" school receives little support from established historians,

it is widely accepted that – given the mutual suspicion between the Soviet Union and the capitalist powers – British, French, and Soviet leaders did not rule out some sort of "coming to terms" with Nazi Germany if it would delay or prevent war. Despite ideologues on both sides, the leanings of diplomats toward one or the other alternative need not have been because of ideological disposition or some sort of grand scheme, but a pragmatic assessment of the likelihood of peace and stability being preserved in Europe, something both the Soviet Union and the Anglo-French "bloc" were seeking, at least in the short term.

Soviet pragmatism in the pursuit of short-term security, set in the broader ideological context of the inevitable clash between capitalism and communism, is emphasized by Silvio Pons in *Stalin and the Inevitable War 1936–1941*.[13] His work represents something of a compromise between the "German" and "collective security" schools that can be termed the "realist" school, incorporating a range of compromise positions. Pons, however, emphasizes the longer-term expansionist dimension to Soviet foreign policy, a tendency motivated by a fusion of communist ideology and the Soviet Union's pre-Versailles tsarist heritage. Certainly, as John Ferris notes, to talk of a "realist" school which does not consider ideology is nonsense in most instances, given that very few statesmen are psychopaths genuinely intent on power for its own sake. As he goes on to note, the noun "realism" has to be combined with an adjective, be it "Marxist-Leninist" or indeed "Stalinist" in the case of the Soviet Union under Stalin.[14] The diplomatic confusion and misunderstanding created in negotiations with Britain and France by the pragmatic Soviet advancement of foreign policy goals informed by the heady ideological brew of the Stalinist international outlook is highlighted by Keith Neilson. Both Britain and France were committed to the post-Versailles order and had foreign policies which varied as a result of western pluralism, a very different motor to their foreign policies to that of the Soviet Union, making understanding and agreement between them and the Soviet Union difficult at best.[15]

Despite genuine Soviet efforts to promote "collective security," something not in conflict with the notion of "inevitable war" if seen as a short- to medium-term measure, with the threat of military action against a non-compliant Germany being anathema to Britain and France, the western powers were more inclined toward appeasement of German, and indeed Italian, ambitions. Many British and French conservatives were, ultimately, more fearful of Bolshevism than they were of National Socialism – with whose aims many in Britain at least sympathized. German reoccupation of the Rhineland in March 1936 passed with barely a murmur from the British, taking place behind the smokescreen of the Italian invasion of Abyssinia in October 1935, itself only provoking half-hearted sanctions from the League of Nations. After the outbreak of the Spanish Civil War in July 1936, Britain and France proved willing to tolerate flagrant German and Italian intervention on the side of Franco, for whom there was considerable sympathy on the right in Britain. Soviet unwillingness to wholeheartedly support the left in Spain was, to a significant extent, in order to prevent a rift with these powers, and particularly France, which would threaten the alliances that were designed to protect the Soviet Union from German ambitions in the east and prevent the emergence of an alliance between fascist and other capitalist powers against the Soviet Union.

The value of the Soviet Union's mutual assistance treaties would be put to the test in September 1938, when, following the *Anschluss* with Austria of March 1938, Hitler sought the Sudeten border region of Czechoslovakia at the conference table in Munich, to which the Soviet Union was not invited. The Soviet Union had also not been invited to participate fully in other key international conferences of the 1930s, for instance the London Naval Conference of December 1935– March 1936. Whether this was because the Soviet Union was not taken seriously as a major European, and particularly naval, power or because it remained a political pariah to European conservatives is, from a Soviet perspective, and in the context of the current discussion, less important than the fact that the Soviet leadership once again could claim to have been sidelined by Britain and France. The Soviet Union was understandably skeptical of the likelihood of an Anglo-French commitment to a tripartite stand against German ambitions.

## The Munich Crisis and the Nazi–Soviet Pact

British and French appeasement of Hitler at Munich led to German acquisition not only of the Sudetenland but also of the remainder of Czechoslovakia in March 1939, including its substantial arms industry. Prime Minister Neville Chamberlain's vacillation in taking action could not help maintain faltering Soviet confidence in an effective Anglo-French and Soviet alliance emerging against Hitler's ambitions. The Soviet Union could, with good reason, suspect that Hitler's attentions were being directed eastwards and toward its borders. Nonetheless, the Soviet Union was less than enthusiastic about intervention, and certainly unenthusiastic about a unilateral one. While Soviet forces in the western border regions were mobilized during the Munich crisis, there is little evidence they were being readied for offensive action of any sort. According to Zara Steiner, even if the Czechoslovaks had made a stand, significant Soviet support could not have been relied upon on the ground, with which Hugh Ragsdale agrees, although as he notes, serious preparations seem to have been made to provide air support to Czechoslovakia in late September.[16] It remains unclear what degree of western support would have been required for the Soviet Union to commit to military action, significant stumbling blocks being Soviet relations with Poland and Romania. Any attack on Germany would have had to have been through a hostile Poland or Romania, the former of which would not countenance the transit of Soviet forces through its territory lest they remain there indefinitely – the Soviet invasion of Poland of 1920 was still a recent event. Poland also had designs on Czechoslovak territory. Romania's position was less obvious, but its poor transport network made it less desirable as a transit link to Czechoslovakia anyway. The Soviet Union had not worked hard in the longer term on trying to improve relations with either the Poles or Romanians, whom its regional policy was geared to undermine, giving some credibility to Hochman's argument that the Soviet Union shares at least some responsibility for the failure of "collective security" leading up to the German occupation of Czechoslovakia.

A second issue restraining the Soviet Union from action against Germany in late 1938 or indeed early 1939 was the fact that the Red Army was in a state of turmoil, undergoing a massive enlargement after having suffered the loss of experienced cadres during the great purges of 1936–8. This was also a factor in low estimations of Soviet military capabilities by the western powers at the time of the Munich crisis, which was an additional reason (or justification) for dismissing the value of Soviet participation in any deterrent activity against Germany. The great purges were, as the Russian historian Oleg Khlevniuk argues, a product of the international situation.[17] While identification of internal opposition was nothing new, dealing with it was now more urgent with war looming, during which such elements might destabilize the Soviet rear and threaten Stalin's position.

For the Soviet Union, particularly after Munich, it was crucial to buy time to prepare for an inevitable clash with Nazi Germany. British and French guarantees to Poland in March, and then to Romania in April 1939, were understandably considered to be of little value to Soviet defense given Anglo-French inactivity over Czechoslovakia, and in part because Poland was seen as a potential German ally and hostile to the Soviet Union. At the same time, Britain and France were justifiably seen as unenthusiastic about reaching agreement with the Soviet Union on dealing with the German threat during negotiations in the spring and summer of 1939. It is in the context of diplomatic failure at the time of the Munich crisis of 1938, a centralization of control over foreign policy, and a British and French lack of enthusiasm for agreement with the Soviet Union that the removal of the pro-western commissar for foreign affairs, Maxim Litvinov, in May 1939 should be seen. His replacement by Vyacheslav Molotov might have signaled to Germany that the Soviet Union would be more receptive to new proposals from them, but it did not represent a fundamental shift in Soviet policy, nor did it rule out agreement with Britain and France.[18]

While the British had been dismissive of Soviet overtures in the spring of 1939, they became more willing to enter into negotiations as the threat of war became more serious during the summer. However, the issue of the transit of Soviet troops through Poland or indeed Romania remained, and which the British and French were reticent to sanction without Polish and Romanian agreement. At the same time it was apparent to Soviet negotiators that the British and French were still not in any hurry to reach agreement. As Taylor noted in his 1961 *The Origins of the Second World War*:

> The diplomatic exchange shows that delays came from the West and the Soviet government answered with almost breathtaking speed. The British made their first tentative suggestion on 15 April; the Soviet counter-proposal came two days later, on 17 April. The British took three weeks before designing an answer on 9 May; the Soviet delay was then five days. . . . Thereafter the pace quickened. The British tried again in five days' time; the Soviet answer came within twenty-four hours. . . . If dates mean anything, the British were spinning things out, the Russians were anxious to conclude. There is other evidence that the British treated negotiations in a casual way, more to placate public opinion than to achieve anything.[19]

At the same time Soviet negotiators noted that the British and French had no grand strategic plan for war against Germany, not surprising given that British and French intentions were to take measures to avoid war well in advance and to prevent the need for anything more than the most abstract planning for it. Both were rearming, but deterrence was the principal purpose of such efforts. The "Maginot" mentality which indeed dominated during the "phoney war" of late 1939 and early 1940 would, it apparently seemed to Soviet observers, be likely to prevent significant Anglo-French moves against Germany even in the event of war. For the Soviet Union, deemed by foreign observers to be unprepared for war, the option of coming to terms with Germany remained.

The Nazi–Soviet or Molotov–Ribbentrop Pact of August 1939 would result in the two powers dismembering Poland, the Soviet Union providing Germany with significant raw materials and even with very limited assistance in the war against Britain and France in order to shift German attentions to the west and away from the Soviet Union.[20] The second possible international scenario identified by Soviet planners in 1930 was "where the imperialists start a new world war amongst themselves," a situation Stalin was now very much encouraging.[21] At the same time as directing German attention to the west, against whom it would most probably become embroiled in a protracted war, the Soviet Union would be free to expand its borders in what was deemed by the pact, and subsequent additions, to be its sphere of influence.

The purpose of this expansion was subsequently argued by Soviet historians to be the provision of a defensive buffer zone between Germany and Soviet territory of 1939.[22] This argument was certainly consistent with Stalin's constant harking back to the civil war in discussion on contemporary defense matters.[23] It does seem that the intention of negotiations prior to the Soviet invasion of November 1939 was to prevent Finland becoming the eventual launching pad for a German invasion. The Soviet regime was fully aware of the historical precedent for this: the landing of German troops in Finland in February 1918 and the threat this posed to Petrograd had hastened the signing of the Treaty of Brest-Litovsk. The occupation of Latvia, Lithuania, and Estonia during the summer of 1940 was similarly justified by Soviet security concerns, an argument perhaps given more credibility by the success of German operations in France.

However, the Soviet Union was not beyond opportunistic expansion, an accusation appropriately applied to the Soviet acquisition of Bessarabia and northern Bukovina from Romania in June 1940. The Soviet Union had most certainly not given up on the idea of spreading "revolution" across Europe through force of arms – a task likely to be easier if the capitalist powers were fighting or had fought amongst themselves. Indeed, the third scenario identified in the planning memorandum of 1930 was for a situation where there was the prospect of the Soviet Union pursuing the never-forgotten international "revolution," from a position of relative strength, where "the

adequate development of the revolutionary movement in capitalist society, a sufficiently strong economic and political base and purely military preparation might place before us the question of a move towards a military offensive against capitalism in order to further world revolution."[24]

## The Icebreaker Controversy and Soviet Intentions in 1941

In the second half of 1940 and early 1941, with Nazi Germany at the height of its power, the Soviet Union was in the middle of the third, and the most obviously defense-oriented, Five-Year Plan, due to be completed in 1942. The immediate likelihood of the Soviet Union taking preemptive offensive action against Nazi Germany, or more broadly against capitalist Europe, was made even less likely after the poor performance of the Red Army during the Soviet invasion of eastern Poland in September 1939, and the subsequent invasion of Finland in November 1939, during which the Red Army had suffered horrendous losses against a poorly equipped, well-fortified Finnish opponent. Such dismal Soviet performance during the initial stages of its invasion of Finland, bringing the Soviet Union the diplomatic embarrassment of expulsion from the League of Nations for its aggression, encouraged the German development of plans for the invasion of the Soviet Union in the summer of 1941. While Anglo-French intervention in Finland did not materialize before the Finns had sued for peace with the Soviet Union in March 1940 and Germany had subsequently invaded Norway in April, preliminary British and French planning for such an operation was carried out, with discussions of landing either French mountain or Polish troops at Petsamo.[25] Had such an operation taken place, it would have further complicated the diplomatic and strategic situation in Europe, with the prospect of the Nazi–Soviet Pact leading to joint military activities by the Soviet Union and Germany against Britain and France!

Red Army failings in Poland and Finland came under considerable scrutiny in the Soviet Union, eventually resulting in reorganization and rearmament far from complete in the summer of 1941. Soviet performance against Japan at

Khalkin-Gol in Manchuria in August 1939 had, however, been more encouraging, which along with their commitments in China encouraged the Japanese decision to restrict their ambitions in the region, culminating in the Soviet–Japanese non-aggression treaty of April 1941.

By mid-June 1941 the Red Army was, at least on paper, an impressive force. Prior to the German attack a considerable proportion of its forces was massed on the Soviet–German border, with a second echelon moving into position – but for what purpose is not entirely clear. With the focus of Soviet military doctrine by this stage very much on the offensive, and the eastern front, ostensibly at least, a little more secure than it had been at the beginning of the year, it is easy to see how it could be suggested that the Soviet Union was massing forces for an attack, be it aimed at preempting the now-delayed German invasion of the Soviet Union or part of longer-term preparations for the third prewar scenario mentioned above.

The argument that the Soviet Union was intending to attack Germany in July 1941 was presented by a Soviet defector writing under the pseudonym "Viktor Suvorov" in the mid-1980s. This started a significant debate in Germany and Russia concerning Soviet intentions in 1941; only later did the debate receive attention in the Anglo-Saxon world. According to Suvorov, in his first article on the subject in 1985, a TASS report of June 13, 1941, with which the Soviet government sought to dispel rumors of an imminent German attack on the Soviet Union, was a desperate attempt to cover Soviet preparations for military action against Germany in July, for which Soviet forces were moving into position and which was in full accordance with the offensive thrust of Soviet military doctrine.[26] His subsequent work, most of which is available only in Russian, has, to a large extent, been geared to elaborating on this thesis.[27] Suvorov has at times presented interesting but also poorly thought-out arguments or snippets of information suggesting that the Soviet Union had been engaged in longer-term preparation for this invasion of Europe during the 1930s, culminating, in his view, in moves in the summer of 1941.

This argument had considerable appeal to revisionist historians in post-Soviet Russia, who were more than willing to adopt an argument running counter to the Soviet image of the Soviet Union desperately seeking to preserve peace. It also appealed to right-wing German historians such as Joachim Hoffmann, who could present the German invasion of the Soviet Union as a preventive strike.[28] Suvorov's argument was rapidly countered by much of the established Russian historical community, with the support of western historians such as Gabriel Gorodetsky on the diplomatic front and David Glantz on military issues. Glantz showed in *Stumbling Colossus* that the Soviet Union was actually in no position to attack Germany in June 1941, with Soviet forces lacking, for instance, the logistical capabilities for offensive operations against German forces.[29] Gorodetsky essentially reiterated the established Soviet line, with minor embellishments and additional supporting material. He argued that the Soviet Union was desperate to ensure peace in the summer of 1941 and did not intend anything more than a spoiling attack; he did not examine Soviet long-term intentions, and ignored the ideological dimension to Soviet foreign policy and the notion of spreading revolution by force.[30] Perhaps the most useful product of Suvorov's work and the response from those such as Gorodetsky has been intensification of debate over Soviet intentions during the summer of 1941 and beyond, fueled by sporadic new materials from Soviet archives, which has led to a much more nuanced picture of Soviet intentions emerging than that dominant in the mid-1980s and indeed portrayed by Gorodetsky.

Firstly, it is apparent that the Soviet Union was preparing for war against Germany, even if not in July 1941, and that such a war, in line with Soviet doctrine, would involve initial offensive operations by Soviet forces. Secondly, it became apparent that the Soviet military leadership had, understandably, considered offensive operations against Germany in the summer of 1941, and the Soviet leadership had started to intensify propaganda efforts to prepare the Soviet people for war before switching abruptly back to a line of preserving peace with Germany at all costs, presumably in the face of the absence of the necessary military preparations.

Plans for operations against German forces massed on the Soviet border dated May 15, 1941, appeared in Russian publications after the collapse of the Soviet Union, as did the text of a speech made by Stalin to graduating officers on May 5, during which he can reasonably be seen to have been preparing those present for war with Germany in the not-too-distant future.[31] Supporting this, V. A. Nevezhin has presented evidence of a planned, if abortive, shift in Soviet propaganda toward an anti-German stance – which contrasted with the placatory line taken as a result of the Nazi–Soviet Pact.[32] What is not apparent, as Evan Mawdsley discusses, is the extent to which these developments were geared toward Soviet action within weeks or months, the latter placing the May plan more in line with a gradual Soviet mobilization of forces, including the transfer of units from the Far East, taking place before and after May 15.[33]

While our picture of Soviet intelligence prior to mid-May does not suggest that the Soviet Union was convinced of the imminence of the German attack, a factor no doubt assisted by the delay in Operation Barbarossa from mid-May to June, at least some in the Soviet Union had sufficiently good intelligence from a variety of sources to be convinced, by mid-June 1941 at least, that a German attack was imminent. This was not, however, a conclusion reached by Stalin. The fact that an intensification of defensive measures did not occur, or was undertaken covertly and half-heartedly at best, was because – from Stalin's perspective – if the Soviet Union was not in a position to go on the offensive because its armed forces were simply not ready, then he would have to buy as much time as possible from the Nazi–Soviet Pact. On his insistence the Soviet Union would do all that was possible not to provoke Germany into striking first, something it was, according to the official Soviet line, not intending to do anyway.

The Nazi–Soviet Pact, in embroiling Germany in a war in the west, was no doubt intended by Stalin and the Soviet leadership to buy more time than the less than two years it had done by the summer of 1941. While France had been defeated more rapidly than expected by most observers, Britain remained in the war and was, by mid-1941, starting to receive significant US support through lend-lease. In the early summer there were British warnings of Germany's intention of invading the Soviet Union which, despite corroboration by other sources, were not taken seriously by Stalin, who ignored them as an attempt to provoke the Soviet Union into joining the war before it was ready. Stalin, it is widely assumed, sought to convince himself that Germany would not intentionally make the mistake of the First World War of fighting on two fronts. This belief was reinforced by German talk of an invasion of Britain, and despite fears of a British "coming to terms" with Germany, particularly after Hess, Hitler's second-in-command in the Nazi Party, had made his unauthorized flight to Britain in May 1941. The Soviet response to intensified insecurity was to increase the flow of resources to Germany, provided under the umbrella of the Nazi–Soviet Pact. With the war against Britain continuing, Germany was seen by the Soviet Union as desperately short of the strategic resources being provided to it, and presumably would not be so foolish as to throw away the opportunity to continue receiving them in the context of the drawbacks of a two-front war. Soviet deliveries continued to roll across the Soviet–German border right up to the invasion, for which the Soviet Union was not receiving what it had been promised in return. Up until the point on June 22, 1941, that it was clear that German operations were not mere "provocation," Stalin remained unwilling to allow subordinates to take reasonable defensive measures in case they should provoke Germany or provide justification for German attack, for which the Red Army paid a high price.

Only with both Britain and the Soviet Union embroiled in war with Germany and the Axis would the Anglo-Soviet alliance, long toyed with, actually come to fruition. Britain under Churchill, who had identified the benefits of alliance with the Soviet Union against Nazi Germany in the 1930s, gained obvious benefit from the bulk of the German army being committed in the east, and Soviet survival was therefore a high priority, particularly until the US was eventually dragged into the war. The Soviet Union found itself in an increasingly serious military and economic situation, with Axis forces threatening both Leningrad and Moscow toward the end of the summer of 1941. Not only had the Red Army suffered horrendous losses, but the Soviet regime had lost vast expanses of territory along with a significant fraction of its population, much prime agricultural land, as well as losing industrial plant destroyed or captured, with a significant proportion of the remainder in the process of evacuation to the east. British aid was, particularly during the critical months of 1941, most welcome, and realists such as Churchill, aware of the significance of the Soviet war effort for British survival, only too happy to provide it.

## NOTES

1   On the conflict between diplomatic stability and destabilization of, in this instance, Poland in the mid-1920s, see D. Stone, "The August 1924 Raid on Stolpce, Poland, and the Evolution of Soviet Active Intelligence," *Intelligence and National Security* 21 (2006): 331–41.

2   See H. Flory, "The Arcos Raid and the Rupture of Anglo-Soviet Relations, 1927," *Journal of Contemporary History* 12 (1977): 707–23.

3   See N. S. Simonov, "'Strengthen the Defence of the Land of the Soviets': The 1927 'War Alarm' and its Consequences," *Europe-Asia Studies* 48 (1996): 1355–64. See also Lennart Samuelson, *Plans for Stalin's War Machine: Tukhachevskii and Military-Economic Planning, 1925–1941* (Basingstoke: Palgrave, 2000).

4   Gordon W. Morrell, "Redefining Intelligence and Intelligence Gathering: The Industrial Intelligence Centre and the Metro-Vickers Affair, Moscow 1933," *Intelligence and National Security* 9 (1994): 520, 531 n.6.

5   Report of the Character of Future War and Tasks of the Defence [Sector], April 1930, in O. N. Ken, *Moblilizatsionnoe planirovanie i politicheskie resheniia (konets 1920–seredina 1930-x godov)* (St. Petersburg: Izdatel'stvo Evropeiskogo universiteta v Sankt-Peterburge, 2002), p. 365.

6   Ken, *Moblilizatsionnoe planirovanie*. For an English-language overview of this important work, see my review in *Journal of Strategic Studies* 28 (2005): 894–5.

7   Preparatory Materials of the Council of People's Commissars of the USSR, "Towards a justification for the construction . . . of the Baltic-White Sea Canal," no later than May 1930, in Alexander Hill, *The Great Patriotic War of the Soviet Union, 1941–1945: A Documentary Reader* (London/New York: Routledge, 2009), pp. 11–12.

8   J. Rohwer and M. S. Monakov, *Stalin's Ocean Going Fleet: Soviet Naval Strategy and Shipbuilding Programmes, 1935–1953* (London: Frank Cass, 2001), pp. 34–5, 45–6, 51–2.

9   See Peter Jackson, "France," in *The Origins of World War Two: The Debate Continues*, ed. Robert Boyce and Joseph A. Maiolo (Basingstoke: Palgrave Macmillan, 2003), pp. 94–8.

10   A. J. P. Taylor, *The Origins of the Second World War* (London: Hamish Hamilton, 1961); J. Haslam, *The Soviet Union and the Struggle for Collective Security in Europe, 1933–39* (London: Macmillan, 1984); G. Roberts, *The Soviet Union and the Origins of the Second World War: Russo-German Relations and the Road to War, 1933–1941* (London: Macmillan, 1995); M. J. Carley, "Behind Stalin's Moustache: Pragmatism in Early Soviet Foreign Policy, 1917–1941," *Diplomacy and Statecraft* 12 (2001): 159–74.

11   Roberts, *Soviet Union*, pp. 3–4.

12   J. Hochman, *The Soviet Union and the Failure of Collective Security, 1934–1938* (Ithaca, NY: Cornell University Press, 1984); A. M. Nekrich, *Pariahs, Partners, Predators: German Soviet Relations, 1922–1941* (New York: Columbia University Press, 1997).

13   Silvio Pons, *Stalin and the Inevitable War 1936–1941* (London: Frank Cass, 2002).

14   John Ferris, "Image and Accident: Intelligence and the Origins of World War II, 1933–1941," in *Intelligence and Strategy – Selected Essays*, ed. J. Ferris (Abingdon: Routledge, 2005), p. 107.

15   See Keith Neilson, *Britain, Soviet Russia and the Collapse of the Versailles Order, 1919–1939* (Cambridge: Cambridge University Press, 2006).

16   Zara Steiner, "The Soviet Commissariat of Foreign Affairs and the Czechoslovakian Crisis in 1938: New Material from the Soviet Archives," *Historical Journal* 42 (1999): 751–79; Hugh Ragsdale, *The Soviets, the Munich Crisis, and the Coming of World War II* (New York: Cambridge University Press, 2004), p. 120.

17   O. Khlevniuk, "The Objectives of the Great Terror, 1937–38," in *Stalinism: The Essential Readings*, ed. D. L. Hoffmann (Malden, MA: Blackwell, 2003); and in *Soviet History 1917–1953: Essays in Honour of R. W. Davies*, ed. J. Cooper et al. (New York: St. Martin's, 1995).

18   Albert Resis, "The Fall of Litvinov: Harbinger of the German–Soviet Non-Aggression Pact," *Europe-Asia Studies* 52 (2000): 33–56.

19 Taylor, *Origins of the Second World War*, p. 231.

20 See for instance, from a largely German perspective, T. R. Philbin III, *The Lure of Neptune: German–Soviet Naval Collaboration and Ambitions, 1919–1941* (Columbia, SC: University of South Carolina Press, 1994).

21 Ken, *Moblilizatsionnoe planirovanie*, p. 365.

22 See for instance V. Sipols, *Taini diplomaticheskie: Kanun Velikoi Otechestvennoi. 1939–1941* (Moscow: TOO "Novina," 1997), pp. 160–5.

23 For an illustration of this regarding Finland, see M. Jakobsen, *The Diplomacy of the Winter War: An Account of the Russo-Finnish War, 1939–1940* (Cambridge, MA: Harvard University Press, 1961), pp. 115–19.

24 Ken, *Moblilizatsionnoe planirovanie*, p. 366.

25 See Alexander Hill, "The Birth of the Soviet Northern Fleet 1937–1942," *Journal of Slavic Military Studies* 16 (2003): 70–1. For a broader perspective on British, German, and Soviet interests in the region, see Patrick Salmon, *Scandinavia and the Great Powers, 1890–1940* (Cambridge: Cambridge University Press, 1997).

26 V. Suvorov (pseud.), "Who was Planning to Attack Whom in June 1941, Hitler or Stalin?" *Journal of the Royal United Services Institute for Defence Studies* 130/2 (1985): 50–5.

27 Available in English is V. Suvorov, *Icebreaker: Who Started the Second World War?* (London: Hamish Hamilton, 1990). His work in this field continued in Russian with *Den'-M* (Moscow: AST, 1995).

28 J. Hoffmann, *Stalin's War of Extermination, 1941–1945: Planning, Realization, and Documentation* (Capshaw, AL: Theses and Dissertations Press, 2001). See also J. Hoffmann, "The Red Army until the Beginning of the German–Soviet War," in *Germany and the Second World War*, vol. 4, *The Attack on the Soviet Union*, ed. H. Boog et al. (Oxford: Clarendon Press, 1998), pp. 72–93.

29 D. Glantz, *Stumbling Colossus: The Red Army on the Eve of War* (Lawrence, KS: University Press of Kansas, 1998).

30 G. Gorodetsky, *Grand Delusion: Stalin and the German Invasion of Russia* (New Haven, CT: Yale University Press, 1999).

31 See Jürgen Förster and Evan Mawdsley, "Hitler and Stalin in Perspective: Secret Speeches on the Eve of Barbarossa," *War in History* 11 (2004): 61–103.

32 V. A. Nevezhin, "The Pact with Germany and the Idea of an 'Offensive War,'" *Journal of Slavic Military Studies* 8/4 (1995): 809–43. See also Nevezhin, *Sindrom nastupatel'noi voini. Sovetskaia propaganda v predverii "sviashchennikh boev,"* *1939–1941 gg.* (Moscow: AIRO-XX', 1997).

33 Evan Mawdsley, "Crossing the Rubicon: Soviet Plans for Offensive War in 1940–1941," *International History Review* 25 (2003): 837–8. See also P. N. Bobilev, "Tochku v diskussii stavit; rano. K voprosu o planirovanii v General'nom shtabe RKKA vozmozhnoi voini s Germaniei v 1940–1941 godakh," *Otechestvennaia istoriia* 1 (2000): 41–64.

## GUIDE TO FURTHER READING

M. J. Carley, "Behind Stalin's Moustache: Pragmatism in Early Soviet Foreign Policy, 1917–1941," *Diplomacy and Statecraft* 12 (2001): 159–74. Argues that the Soviet Union consistently and sincerely pursued a policy of "collective security" under Stalin.

D. Glantz, *Stumbling Colossus: The Red Army on the Eve of War* (Lawrence, KS: University Press of Kansas, 1998). Soviet military preparation for war, including military material used against the Suvorov thesis.

G. Gorodetsky, *Grand Delusion: Stalin and the German Invasion of Russia* (New Haven, CT: Yale University Press, 1999). A thorough refutation of the Suvorov thesis, even if not of more sophisticated developments of it.

J. Haslam, *The Soviet Union and the Struggle for Collective Security in Europe, 1933–39* (London: Macmillan, 1984). Pre-1991 but still valuable survey of the Soviet pursuit of "collective security" after the rise of Hitler in Germany.

J. Hochman, *The Soviet Union and the Failure of Collective Security, 1934–1938* (Ithaca, NY: Cornell University Press, 1984). Argues that the Soviet Union bore considerable responsibility for the failure of "collective security" from 1934 to 1938.

J. Hoffmann, "The Red Army until the Beginning of the German–Soviet War," in *Germany and the Second World War*, vol. 4, *The Attack on the Soviet Union*, ed. H. Boog et al. (Oxford: Clarendon Press, 1998), pp. 72–93. Incorporates a sophisticated development of the Suvorov thesis.

Evan Mawdsley, "Crossing the Rubicon: Soviet Plans for Offensive War in 1940–1941," *International History Review* 25 (2003): 818–65. A well-documented attempt to ascertain Soviet military intentions in the summer of 1941 and beyond.

Silvio Pons, *Stalin and the Inevitable War 1936–1941* (London: Frank Cass, 2002). Highlights the pragmatism of Soviet foreign policy, set in a broader ideological context.

Hugh Ragsdale, *The Soviets, the Munich Crisis, and the Coming of World War II* (New York: Cambridge University Press, 2004). Examines Soviet diplomatic and military activity at the time of the Munich crisis of September 1938.

C. Roberts, "Planning for War: The Red Army and the Catastrophe of 1941," *Europe-Asia Studies* 47 (1995): 1293–326. Examines Soviet strategy on the eve of war.

G. Roberts, *The Soviet Union and the Origins of the Second World War: Russo-German Relations and the Road to War, 1933–1941* (London: Macmillan, 1995). A good survey of Soviet foreign policy from 1933 to 1941.

Zara Steiner, "The Soviet Commissariat of Foreign Affairs and the Czechoslovakian Crisis in 1938: New Material from the Soviet Archives," *Historical Journal* 42/3 (1999): 751–79. A succinct look at new material on Soviet activity and intentions during the Munich crisis of 1938.

V. Suvorov (pseud.), "Who was Planning to Attack Whom in June 1941, Hitler or Stalin?" *Journal of the Royal United Services Institute for Defence Studies* 130/2 (1985): 50–5. Viktor Suvorov's first outline of his controversial thesis.

T. J. Uldricks, "The Icebreaker Controversy: Did Stalin Plan to Attack Hitler?" *Slavic Review* 58 (1999): 626–43. A good survey of the debate surrounding Viktor Suvorov's *Icebreaker* thesis.

# CHAPTER TWENTY-ONE

# The United States and the End of Isolation

## *JUSTUS D. DOENECKE*

If there was ever a period in history when the fate of the world itself lay in the balance, it was during the years 1939–41. Franklin Delano Roosevelt had seen his nation endure many crises throughout his life, a Great War and a Great Depression among them, but by 1940 he saw himself confronting one that overshadowed anything he had yet experienced. This was the ascendancy of the Axis powers and, in particular, the Germany of Adolf Hitler. Indeed, by 1941 the president was willing to risk war itself so as to ensure Britain's survival.

### Roosevelt's Interventionist Rationale

Roosevelt repeatedly offered his rationale. In his fireside chat of December 29, 1940, he claimed that the Nazi masters of Germany were seeking to enslave all Europe, then to use the continent's resources to dominate the rest of the world. In Nazi hands, any country in South America could serve as a jumping-off place for attacking the western hemisphere. At one point, he noted, the distance from Africa to Brazil was less than that from Washington to Denver. Besides, the flying range of bombers had so increased that one could fly round-trip between the British Isles and New England without refueling.

To FDR, this threat was not purely military. On May 27, 1941, he asserted that Germany posed grave economic challenges. A victorious Hitler could exploit slave labor in the rest of the world and thereby be able to undersell American goods everywhere. In order to withstand such economic warfare, Roosevelt said, the United States would have to regulate wages and hours, abolish trade unions, and lower living standards.

The chief executive did not neglect matters of ideology. In December 1940 FDR claimed that Hitler himself perceived an inevitable clash between Germany's political philosophy and that of the West. In September Roosevelt called Germany an enemy of all law, all liberty, all morality, all religion.[1]

Japan did not receive such public condemnation, though by September 1940 Roosevelt found it too a mortal danger. In January 1941 he wrote his ambassador to Japan, Joseph C. Grew, that the hostilities in Europe, in Africa, and in Asia were all parts of a single conflict.

### The Challenge Unfolds

Roosevelt did realize that his countrymen were averse to entering global war directly, though by April 1941 one major poll indicated that they would risk such involvement if Germany and Italy could not be defeated in any other way. Yet, until Hitler's invasion of Poland on September 1, 1939, the president himself had been most cautious. In the 1930s he had acceded to the neutrality acts, legislation that had tied his hands in such matters as arms and loans to belligerents, even if such nations were victims of outright aggression. In

January 1937, upon his recommendation, an almost unanimous Congress had levied a special arms embargo that weakened the Spanish republic in its fight against the troops of General Francisco Franco. In September 1938, on the eve of the Munich conference, Roosevelt endorsed the efforts of the British prime minister, Neville Chamberlain, to reach an accommodation with Hitler. Until the middle of 1940, the regular US army consisted of a quarter of a million men and the National Guard slightly less; Roosevelt raised no objection, though in 1939 the US ranked seventeenth among the world's armed forces.

To be sure, by 1939 the president was becoming more confrontational. When, in November 1938, the Nazis engaged in massive anti-Semitic activities in an evening forever remembered as *Kristallnacht*, FDR uttered a strong condemnation and recalled the American ambassador from Berlin. Six months later he requested that Hitler and his Italian counterpart, Benito Mussolini, pledge not to invade some thirty-one countries in Europe and the Near East. By May 1939 he futilely sought a new neutrality act, one that would permit nations to buy munitions on a cash-and-carry basis (that is, provide the shipping and pay on the spot).

Only, however, when outright conflict broke out in Europe could Roosevelt successfully gain support for supplying Britain and France. In mid-September he called upon Congress to repeal the arms embargo and institute cash-and-carry. An American ban on war credits would remain and the president would be given authority to establish war zones from which American vessels, planes, and citizens would be banned. Though Roosevelt did remind Congress that the current embargo deprived sea powers (i.e., Britain and France) of a natural advantage over land powers (i.e., Germany), he stressed gains to American industry. Expressing itself far more candidly, *Time* magazine noted that retaining the existing arms embargo practically gave Hitler the equivalent of an Atlantic fleet, for neither France nor Britain could yet receive American arms.

Opponents offered a variety of objections. FDR's proposal, they claimed, violated international law, showed partisanship between the belligerents, promoted an immoral arms traffic, and would lead to full-scale participation in the conflict just as it had in 1917.

The Senate passed the measure 63–30, the House 243–181, and FDR's proposal became law on November 4. With 62 percent of Americans polled backing the measure, one pro-New Deal editor commented aptly that the majority sought to be as unneutral as possible without entering the conflict. As noted, however, by historian Warren F. Kimball, Roosevelt assumed that the British navy would eventually win the struggle not by a cross-Channel invasion but by simply quarantining Germany through its continental blockade.[2] Repeal of the arms embargo came too late to rescue Poland, which in mid-September also experienced invasion by the Soviet Union. Roosevelt similarly sought to aid Finland, which Russia invaded in late November, but the Finns surrendered in March 1940, before even the paltry sum of $20 million could be effective.

As Hitler had not yet attacked western Europe, Roosevelt briefly toyed with the idea of mediation. In February 1940, he sent Under-Secretary of State Sumner Welles to Europe, there to meet with the leaders of France, Britain, Germany, and Italy. Although Welles's instructions focused on fact-finding, he was obviously to remain alert to possible negotiation. Historian Irwin F. Gellman finds the mission poorly conceived, planned, and prepared. Welles himself exceeded his orders by placing a naïve faith in the still-neutral Mussolini: the American diplomat erroneously believed he could personally act as mediator, an initiative Roosevelt instantly squelched.[3]

Though neither Roosevelt nor the great majority of his countrymen predicted a quick victory for the Allies, few were prepared for Hitler's sudden conquest of Norway and the Low Countries and, in particular, the surrender of France on June 22, 1940. Now, suddenly, all bets were off as the United States itself suddenly felt vulnerable. Congress did not need the president's urging to vote massive military appropriations in June, exceeding Roosevelt's own $1.5 billion request by $320 million. During the following month Congress appropriated an additional $1.7 billion, enlarged the regular army to 375,000 men, and gave the president the power to call the National Guard into active service.

In May some prominent Americans established a new emergency organization, the Committee to Defend America by Aiding the Allies (CDAAA), with Kansas publisher William Allen White serving as chairman. The committee called for the immediate shipment of 500 American planes to Britain and France. Eventually the CDAAA listed 750 local units and membership might have been as high as 750,000.

On May 22 Roosevelt ordered the sale of First World War equipment to Hitler's foes. Within two weeks FDR's legal advisers claimed his administration could legally sell surplus military supplies to private parties, who in turn could resell them to the Allies. Early in June, however, acting with the private backing of military leaders, Congress forbade the sale of additional surplus matériel unless the Chief of Naval Operations and the Chief of Staff found it unessential for American defense.

## Initial Confrontations

In June, two staunch conservatives, Senator Edward R. Burke (Dem.-Nebr.) and Representative James S. Wadsworth (Rep.-NY), introduced a bill calling for a peacetime draft. The bill would increase the regular army to 500,000, the National Guard to 400,000. Some forty million men between the ages of 21 and 45 were required to register. Though at first fearing that such a move would be unpopular in an election year, FDR told the press on August 2 that the current volunteer system could not supply the trained manpower that the new emergency needed. Other conscription advocates warned that Hitler's forces could now take European colonies in Latin America.

Even though a few prominent anti-interventionists favored a draft, the aviator Charles Lindbergh among them, many more balked. Claiming that the existing volunteer system had thus far worked well, such critics noted that so far every army quota had been filled. Moreover, to fulfill even more broadened responsibilities, the regular army needed no more than 400,000 men. The recent German campaign in France, these opponents claimed, proved that conscript armies were ineffective while demonstrating the importance of relatively small cadres of elite tank corps. They

did concede, however, that the American army needed many skilled mechanics, pilots, and technicians. Conscription, however, would simply give millions of men a year's training in peripheral tasks – military drills, manual of arms exercises, bayonet practice. Even greater dangers lay in store, for the Burke-Wadsworth program could lead to militarism and the death of civil liberties.

Moreover, argued the anti-interventionists, the United States faced little danger. Certainly, a Hitler not yet able to cross the English Channel could not traverse the Atlantic. The United States possessed the largest navy in the world, indeed, one seven times the strength of Germany's, and an air force expanding at the potential rate of 8,000 planes a week. Should Hitler capture the British fleet, he still would not possess the strength to gain naval and air bases in the western hemisphere, much less land an expeditionary force and destroy the American armed forces. By September 8, both houses of Congress, backed by public opinion polls, had passed the bill by close to a two-to-one margin.

As Congress was winding up debate over the draft, the Roosevelt administration had taken another major initiative. On September 2, 1940, Secretary of State Cordell Hull and the British ambassador, Lord Lothian, signed papers for the transfer of fifty American destroyers of First World War vintage. At the same time, the United States took out ninety-nine-year leases on British bases scattered over 4,000 miles of hemisphere coastline, including such locales as the Bahamas, Jamaica, St. Lucia, Antigua, Trinidad, and British Guiana. Sites in Bermuda and Argentia, Newfoundland, were granted outright.

The destroyers-for-bases deal had been in the offing for several months. On June 15 the British prime minister, Winston Churchill, had cabled the president that Britain's need for American destroyers was literally a matter of life and death. Roosevelt was cautious, uncertain whether Britain would survive Germany's pounding air attacks, much less a possible Wehrmacht invasion. Other prickly matters concerned the legality of any such transfer, possible American needs for the ships, the danger of their falling into the hands of a victorious Germany, and the possibility that such a move might provoke Hitler into declaring war against the US.

Fortunately for the president, by the summer of 1940 Britain's survival did not appear in question. American military chiefs reported that the US could spare fifty destroyers. The British pledged that if Germany did overrun the British Isles, the ships would not go to Hitler. Attorney General Robert Jackson assured FDR as to the move's legality. Roosevelt became increasingly confident that Hitler sought to avoid any clash and therefore would not interfere.

Though the chief of naval operations, Admiral Harold Stark, certified that the destroyers were expendable, FDR's critics remained unconvinced. Even more important, they argued, the president had acted most high-handedly by ignoring the Congress. Other objections centered on the cost of the leases and the illegality of the destroyer transfer in light of both international and US law. Alternatives included requesting Congressional permission, outright seizure of such French territories as Martinique, and cession of the British and French West Indies in return for forgiving First World War debts.

The agreement worked well for both sides. The United States found Argentia a priceless base for naval and air patrols protecting transatlantic convoys from German subs, and new American installations in Bermuda played a similar, if less crucial, role. Admittedly, the destroyers needed a radical overhaul, as problems ranged from leaking pipes to defective electrical systems. One British admiral later commented that they were the worst such craft he had ever seen.

Yet, as the ships went on to see heavy action on the Atlantic, historians Thomas A. Bailey and Paul B. Ryan could aptly claim that the deteriorating four-stackers certainly did something to provide the difference between victory and defeat for Hitler on the high seas – and hence on the land. Warren F. Kimball finds the arrangement a good deal for America in every sense of the term. Admittedly, writer Robert Shogan has argued that its secrecy has served as a destructive precedent for such surreptitious commitments as the Vietnam War and the Iran–Contra scandal. Kimball in turn responds that premature public debate would have almost certainly brought the wrong answer – as far

as FDR, Britain, history itself are all concerned. Not only has foreign policy been placed primarily with the executive branch, but Congress and public opinion – as expressed in polls, print, and radio – supported the arrangement.[4]

In the presidential election of 1940, foreign policy became the most significant issue. Republican presidential candidate Wendell Willkie, a Wall Street lawyer and utilities magnate, shared much of Roosevelt's interventionism. Seeing, however, his strength wane late in October, he accused FDR of planning to take the nation into the conflict within six months. Roosevelt responded with a pledge made at a rally in Boston: "I have said this before, but I shall say it again and again: Your boys are not going to be sent into any foreign wars."[5] The war issue was undoubtedly significant, for had it not been for the global conflict voters claimed to have preferred Willkie.

Clearly, according to Warren Kimball, Roosevelt did not take the public into his confidence during the election campaign of 1940. He avoided and evaded answering awkward questions about how the United States could be neutral and still provide naval war vessels and war supplies to one of the belligerents. At the same time, Kimball asserts that Americans sought no unpleasant choices and, in a sense, wanted to be lied to.[6]

## Lend-Lease: The Crucial Decision

Once he was safely reelected, Roosevelt became far more aggressive in aiding Britain. On December 7, 1940, Churchill cabled a clear warning to the president: unless the United States came to its rescue, Britain could well go under. The prime minister pointed to heavy losses at sea, the danger of France's Vichy government (which controlled West Africa) joining the Axis, and the possibility of a Japanese thrust toward Singapore and the Dutch East Indies. Moreover, he asserted, Britain's dollar reserves were running low, threatening its capacity to buy American arms.

Roosevelt responded in a fireside chat delivered on December 29. If Britain were defeated, he claimed, the Axis powers would control the continents of Europe, Asia, Africa, Australasia, and the high seas – and they would be in a position to bring enormous military and naval resources against the western hemisphere. Hence the British Empire was the spearhead of resistance to world conquest.[7]

Within days, Congress confronted Roosevelt's lend-lease proposal. Under the terms of the bill, the US could lease or lend articles and defense information to any country whose defense the president deemed vital to the defense of the United States. No limits were set on the quantity of weapons loaned or the sums to be appropriated. Moreover, friendly belligerents could use American ports. *Newsweek* correctly observed that FDR was being given permission to lend anything from a trench shovel to a battleship. *Time* remarked that no American had ever asked for such powers.

The ensuing debates were impassioned. Historian Charles A. Beard warned that the bill placed the nation's entire wealth – and all its people as well – at the president's disposal. Others believed it weakened the United States without appreciably adding to its defense. Still other critics feared national bankruptcy, claimed that the bill was a flagrant act of war, and pointed to the dangers of a forthcoming economic cycle of boom followed by bust. Furthermore, so opponents charged, it was impossible to ship such goods without supplying needed convoy protection, yet these very convoys would invite German submarine attack, thereby triggering the United States directly into the conflict.

It was during the debate that the America First Committee really came to the fore, taking the lead in opposing the bill. By then 648 chapters were on its books. Some anti-interventionists offered alternatives, recommending a straight loan or even an outright grant. For example, General Robert E. Wood, national chairman of America First, suggested selling spare American ships to Britain and providing long-term credits for food and war supplies. Herbert Hoover advised an outright gift of spare defense materials as well as some two or three billion dollars to buy other items.

All such options, however, lacked the full-scale US commitment the administration sought. Financial credits and grants minimized the American stake in British victory. A loan of major military items, however, gave the United States a material interest in German defeat.

Despite the intensity of the debate, the measure clearly drew the needed support. The House vote backed the legislation 317–71, the Senate 60–31; polls indicated popular approval. On March 11, 1941, Roosevelt signed the bill. Certainly, the US was now poised on the very edge of the European conflict. By assuming responsibility for Britain's long-term purchases, Roosevelt relieved the British government of a costly burden and demonstrated his faith in Britain's survival. With that irrevocable commitment, a genuine Anglo-American alliance was forged. Kimball notes that today few can quarrel with the stated purpose of the bill, though he writes that one is still disturbed and even shocked by the lack of candor displayed by the Roosevelt administration during the evolution of its legislation, particularly in regard to convoys. The president was certainly not prepared to debate the ultimate question of war or peace, nor is there any indication that he had made a choice. Although he did not envision American ground forces in Europe, he might have already considered the use of air and naval units.[8]

In challenging an existing myth, historian David Reynolds writes that lend-lease was not outstandingly novel, or notably altruistic, or even particularly important in 1941.[9] Throughout that year, lend-lease provided only 1 percent of Britain's munitions total; only as the war continued was the British Commonwealth given some $31 billion in supplies and the Soviet Union some $11 billion. Furthermore, ultimate repayment would not necessarily be made in money or even in goods in kind, but would rather involve the abolition of the British commercial system of imperial preference, by which the Commonwealth nations and over twenty countries in Europe and Latin America had levied discriminatory tariffs against American goods.

## Military Confrontation Begins

Early in April Roosevelt signed an agreement with the Danish government-in-exile that permitted the United States to occupy Greenland. Although the action ran counter to conventional international procedure, the administration defended the move as a vital defense measure, warning that hostile planes could use Greenland as a launching pad with which to strike at New York. Conversely, in friendly hands, the island was invaluable, being able to expedite the delivery of short-range aircraft to Britain.

On April 18, 1941, FDR announced a Western Hemisphere Neutrality Patrol in the western Atlantic, settling on a North–South line down the twenty-sixth meridian that ran halfway between Brazil and West Africa and included the Azores and most of Greenland. By flashing locations of German U-boats, of course, the patrol would alert merchantmen to veer away while inviting British cruisers and destroyers to attack. The president compared the patrols to escorts of a wagon train on the American frontier, but he was obviously ignoring the severe risks involved.

Iceland was the next site of American action. On July 7, a brigade of nearly 4,000 Marines arrived to relieve British and Canadian troops who had occupied Iceland for a year. In defending his decision, FDR warned that hostile naval and air bases there would menace American-occupied Greenland and threaten US shipping in the North Atlantic, thereby interrupting the steady flow of munitions. In friendly hands, however, it could provide indispensable refueling bases for convoys and dominate the Denmark Strait, a passage between Greenland and Iceland where German ships had been active.

As in the case of the destroyers-for-bases deal and lend-lease, the moves in Greenland and Iceland raised fundamental questions concerning presidential power. Senator Robert A. Taft (Rep.-Ohio) commented that if the occupation of Iceland was defensive, then any act the president cared to order could be deemed defensive.[10]

Beyond such activity, however, Roosevelt appeared to be foundering. As historian James MacGregor Burns notes, FDR still lacked the comprehensive strategy needed to attain Allied victory. The president, argues Burns, never really integrated global diplomatic, political, and economic factors with military ones, neglected long-run war and postwar security needs, and always left the initiative to the Axis. As he said in mid-May to Treasury Secretary Henry J. Morgenthau, Jr., "I am waiting to be pushed into the situation."[11]

By the summer of 1941, the yearlong term limit for draftees was coming to an end. The fear existed that much of the new embryonic army would simply melt away. On July 21, Roosevelt warned Congress that within two months disintegration would begin. On August 7, by a comfortable margin, the Senate legislated an 18-month extension, provided for a pay raise after one year's service, and sought to expedite the release of men over age 28. On August 12, the House passed the same bill by a one-vote margin – 203–202. Even, however, had the House turned the 18-month extension down, historians Garry R. Clifford and Samuel R. Spencer, Jr., find that a compromise still would have been reached and draftees would still have needed to serve from 6 to 12 more months.[12] During the debate, many anti-interventionists had balked. Troop morale, they claimed, was already bad enough without breaking faith with men who were told their service would terminate at the end of the year.

Besides, FDR's critics argued, such a massive number of troops was not needed, particularly since an entirely new factor had undoubtedly changed the nature of the war: Hitler's invasion of the Soviet Union. On June 22, 1941, 3.2 million German troops, organized in 148 divisions, attacked along a 1,000-mile frontier extending from the Arctic Circle to the Black Sea. To anti-interventionists an alliance with Stalin's dictatorship would make a travesty of any war against totalitarianism. Furthermore, they claimed that the Russians were tying down the great bulk of the German army, thereby giving Britain a greater chance of survival without full-scale American participation.

In November, after Congress had overwhelmingly voted down a measure prohibiting aid to Russia, FDR declared the Soviet Union eligible for lend-lease assistance. Thanks to a fact-finding mission in August by presidential emissary Harry Hopkins, Roosevelt ignored the pessimistic analyses of his military advisers (which were shared by much of the public as well). Patrick J. Maney argues that the first shipment of lend-lease offered the perfect opportunity for FDR to explain how national self-interest required a walk with the devil. Instead, FDR glossed over some unpleasant facts about his ally, even claiming that the Russians exercised freedom of religion, and he continued to define the war in highly idealistic terms. Edward M. Bennett claims that FDR was forced to woo Stalin because Russia was the only power strong enough to enable the democracies to hold out. Without lend-lease, claim Bailey and Ryan, the Russians probably could not have beaten Hitler on their front, at least not as soon as they did.[13]

From August 9–12, 1941, FDR met with Churchill for the first time off the Newfoundland coast, where they drafted what subsequently became known as the Atlantic Charter. The document endorsed the self-determination of nations, equal access of all states to the world's trade and raw materials, and the final destruction of Nazi tyranny, after which it envisioned the establishment of a wider, permanent system of general security. Soon after the participants departed, both Britain and the Soviet Union qualified their endorsement. David Reynolds claims Churchill found the Atlantic Charter a poor surrogate for a declaration of war, while another historian, Theodore A. Wilson, asserts that the conference did not put the requisite iron in the presidential backbone.[14]

Within a month, however, the prime minister could be more optimistic. On September 4, the American destroyer *Greer*, en route to Reykjavik with mail and passengers, exchanged shots with a German submarine 200 miles southwest of Iceland. Addressing the nation just a week later, Roosevelt claimed that the Germans had fired without cause, neglecting to mention that the *Greer* had been spotting the submarine's location for a British patrol plane. Calling German subs the rattlesnakes of the Atlantic, he added that US patrols would protect all merchant ships – not only American ships but ships of any flag – engaged in commerce in waters vital to the defense of the United States. Historian Robert McJimsey stresses that FDR was not the first president to take steps that invited war while declaring peaceful purposes. Another scholar, Robert Dallek, sees a need to mislead the country in its own interest, though finding Roosevelt's deviousness injuring the national well-being over the long run when circumstances would be far less justifiable.[15]

More sinking of US-owned ships continued. On September 11, the *Montana*, a US freighter under Panamanian registry, was sunk between Greenland and Iceland. No one was injured. Eight

days later the *Pink Star*, another American-owned vessel flying the Panamanian flag, was torpedoed in the same general locale. This time some crew were lost. In October, four more US-owned merchant ships were sunk. In addition, on October 27 German torpedoes had damaged the *Kearny*, a crack destroyer scarcely a year in service, about 400 miles from Iceland. Just two weeks later, another American destroyer, the *Reuben James*, fell victim to a German submarine 600 miles west of Iceland. Of 160 men on board, only forty-five were able to be rescued.

By then Roosevelt had urged Congress to permit the arming of American merchant ships. Speaking on October 9, he also sought to lift the 1939 ban on their entering combat zones, thereby enabling delivery of lend-lease goods directly to the ports of friendly belligerents. Anti-interventionists saw an administration effort to maneuver the US into full-scale combat. Armed convoys, some argued, remained quite unsafe, as they lacked the capacity to respond to submarine attack. Furthermore, so critics claimed, British shipping was already recovering from U-boat attacks. Hence, the administration proposal was not only dangerous, it was also unnecessary.

On October 17, the House supported the arming of merchant ships by a vote of 259 to 138 and voted 212–194 to eliminate war zones within a month. On November 7 the Senate approved of both measures 50 to 37. After his victory, however, Roosevelt remained cautious. Even though the president was empowered to send armed convoys directly across the Atlantic, only on November 25 was the administration determined to do so, at which time it decided to send unarmed vessels to Lisbon and armed vessels to the Soviet port of Archangel. Hence, the initiative remained in the hands of Hitler, who – being preoccupied with the increasingly precarious Russian front – always sought to avoid incidents.

## The Degree of Roosevelt's Commitment

Despite accusations made by Roosevelt's critics at the time, historians increasingly deny that in late 1941 the president sought a war with Germany. There were several reasons for this, according to

David Reynolds. The American public would inevitably demand that supplies to the Allies be cut back, something that might have disastrous consequences for the US itself. If the Japanese decided to attack the United States, it would immediately be forced to fight on two fronts, something that could only delay Anglo-American plans to postpone a Pacific conflict until Germany had been defeated. Furthermore, FDR sincerely believed that the massive bombing of German towns and industrial centers would make any large-scale army superfluous. As the US was already fighting surreptitiously, a formal declaration would make little difference. As Bailey and Ryan note, FDR could not tangle with any more submarines on the North Atlantic than he was doing, even if war with Germany had been officially declared.[16]

## America Faces Japan

When the United States became a full-scale belligerent, it was not because of any overt action on the part of Germany but rather because of a confrontation with imperial Japan that resulted in the major surprise attacks on Singapore, Wake, Midway, the Philippines, and above all Pearl Harbor, where much of the US Pacific fleet was located.

Upon assuming the presidency in 1933, Roosevelt announced that he would continue what was called the Stimson Doctrine, by which the United States would continue to withhold recognition from the newly created Japanese puppet state of Manchukuo. He also built up the American fleet to the limits specified by the London Naval Treaty of 1930. In December 1934 Japan gave the stipulated two years' notice that it would no longer be bound by the Five Power naval limitation established at the Washington conference of 1921–2.

Yet on the surface relations between the US and Japan remained relatively friendly, even when, in July 1937, at Marco Polo bridge, 10 miles east of Beijing, a skirmish between Chinese and Japanese troops erupted. The fracas soon grew into a major military conflict between the two nations. Admittedly, Americans soon became shocked by the indiscriminate bombing of Chinese cities, particularly the brutality exhibited in the rape of

Nanking. In a major foreign policy speech delivered in Chicago on October 5, 1937, the president spoke only in vague terms about quarantining aggressors and, on the following day, denied he was considering sanctions against Japan. When, that December, Japanese planes attacked the US gunboat *Panay* on the Yangtze River, Japan immediately apologized and paid an indemnity to the injured and relatives of the dead.

As the Japanese continued to extend their control over North China, securing the principal coastal areas, the US countered by making a $25 million loan to China's ruler Jiang Jieshi (Chiang Kai-shek) and resumed the purchase of Chinese silver, a move that gave besieged China needed time. From 1937 to 1940, the administration continually protested against Japan's bombing of civilians, damage to American holdings, and injury to its citizens. In July 1939 Roosevelt gave the needed six-month notice for the abrogation of the 1911 commercial treaty with Japan, thereby putting a mutually lucrative trade on a day-to-day basis. Although the United States still supplied petroleum and scrap iron to Japan, commerce would hence lie at Washington's mercy.

Some Americans, such as Senator Tom Connally (Dem.-Tex.), sought to sever American shipments to Japanese armies, thereby aligning national policy to moral principle. Others, such as ex-president Herbert Hoover and international lawyer John Foster Dulles, opposed any pressure at all, arguing that Japan would certainly retaliate. Furthermore, said the foes of intervention, such efforts would invariably be ineffective, for Japan possessed alternative sources of supply. Other arguments included claims that the US lacked any vital interest in Asia; that Japan was a far better customer than backward and corrupt China could ever be; that Japan lacked the means to serve as a military threat; and that, should war break out, Japan itself could never be invaded.

In the spring of 1940, Germany conquered the Netherlands and France and was engaged in massive bombing of the British Isles. The East Asian possessions of all these nations suddenly became exposed to Japanese invasion. As what Japan called the "China incident" was becoming increasingly stalemated, such colonies became most appealing, in particular French Indochina, long the rice bowl of Southeast Asia, the Dutch East Indies, with its vast stores of oil, and British Malaya, possessing extensive rubber forests.

On July 2, 1940, Roosevelt signed the National Defense Act, a bill that gave him authority to restrict certain exports. Just three weeks later, using the rationale of national defense, he imposed an embargo on the sale of high-octane fuels and top-grade scrap iron to Japan. Although the Japanese compensated by buying US medium-octane fuels sufficient for their military needs, Roosevelt had served notice that American patience was not unlimited. In September American anxieties intensified when the Vichy government, acting under pressure, gave Japan permission to occupy northern Indochina. On September 26 the United States was alarmed enough to embargo all scrap metal, not just the top-grade material, a move that severely strained Japan's war-making capability.

## The Consequences of the Tripartite Pact

Still greater consensus surfaced when, on September 27, 1940, Japan entered into what was called the Tripartite Pact. By its terms Japan recognized Germany's and Italy's leadership in creating a new order in Europe; the two European powers in turn acknowledged Japanese dominance in "Greater East Asia." All three nations agreed to cooperate militarily, politically, and economically if, in the language of the pact, one of the three contracting powers was attacked by a Power at present not involved in the European war or in the Chinese–Japanese conflict. As one clause in the treaty exempted the Soviet Union from being a target, the United States was obviously the power in mind. By signing the pact Japan had hoped to isolate the US, gain German recognition of its sphere of influence for all East Asia, and – despite the pact's disclaimer – check possible Soviet ambitions on the Asian continent. The pact backfired on what was becoming known as the Axis, however, for the Roosevelt administration now linked the British battle against Germany to Japan's activities in the Far East. The conflict was perceived as global in nature, a single struggle being fought on two fronts.

On July 24 Japan seized south Indochina, an obvious launching pad from which to invade Thailand, British Malaya, and the Dutch East Indies. Fifty thousand Japanese troops were dispatched to the area. Roosevelt immediately countered by freezing Japanese assets in the US, a move that soon – whether deliberately or not – became the instrument for ending all trade between the two nations.[17] Britain, the Netherlands, and the Philippines followed suit. With such vital materials as petroleum suddenly severed, Japan's new empire was living on borrowed time. Now the Japanese navy possessed only an 18-month supply; Japan's army had only a year's worth left. Rice, tin, bauxite, nickel, rubber were all equally threatened.

Several historians see Roosevelt acting most unwisely. Michael A. Barnhart finds the move strengthening the more militant elements within the Japanese government. To Akira Iriye, Japan and the US were reaching the point of no return. In the words of another scholar, Jonathan Utley, the embargo placed a time limit on peace in the Pacific.[18]

In an effort to break the emerging deadlock, early in August the Japanese proposed a summit conference between President Roosevelt and their prime minister, Prince Konoye Fumimaro. At first FDR seemed sympathetic but Hull remained rigidly opposed, claiming that Konoye lacked the authority to make needed concessions.

The wisdom of such a meeting is still debated. Iriye sees the possibility of a compromise that would not have betrayed Chinese interests. Similarly, a Japanese historian, Tsunoda Jun, claims that Konoye could have overridden military opposition. Other historians differ. Robert Butow notes that War Minister Tojo Hideko told Konoye that the prime minister must avoid further concessions. Waldo Heinrichs doubts whether a genuine peace could have been made by the very man who led Japan into such ventures as the war with China, the Axis alliance, and recent moves into Indochina.[19]

On September 6, an imperial conference was held. Here Japanese policymakers set the date of October 15 for successful negotiations, otherwise Japan would attack Pacific possessions of the United States, Britain, and the Netherlands. The conference drafted Guidelines for Implementing National Policies, a document that Iriye calls a virtual declaration of war.[20] Japan set most severe conditions: the US must discontinue aid to Jiang, restore full trade relations with Japan, and build no military bases in Thailand, the Dutch East Indies, China, or the Far Eastern provinces of the Soviet Union. Japan in turn would promise not to expand further in Asia, guarantee the neutrality of the Philippines, refrain from hostile action against the Soviets, and withdraw its troops from Indochina upon the establishment of a just peace in the Pacific.

Yet, when the October 15 deadline had passed, Japan did not go to war. On October 17 War Minister Tojo became prime minister. Upon taking office, he was given an imperial command to wipe the slate clean by reviewing all past decisions and working for peace. The order was unprecedented, for no emperor had ever before rescinded a decision of an imperial conference.

## Last-Minute Peace Efforts

On November 10, Ambassador Nomura Kishisaburo submitted Plan A, a proposal for a general settlement, to Roosevelt and Hull. By its terms, the United States would restore normal trade with Japan and persuade Jiang Jieshi to meet Japan's terms. If Jiang refused, the United States was to stop all aid to China. The Japanese, for their part, would not automatically attack the United States if Germany and Italy went to war but would decide any obligation entirely independently. They spoke in terms of guaranteeing an open door to trade in their empire but added that the proviso would only come into effect when other parts of the world accepted that principle. They would evacuate troops from most of China within two years of a truce while remaining in Mongolia, Sinkiang, Hainan, and, most important of all, certain parts of northern China. (Here Tojo spoke in terms of 25 years.) They would evacuate Indochina, though only after conclusion of the China incident. Japan would not honor the Tripartite Pact unless the US attacked Germany first. Such terms appeared so extreme that they met with summary rejection.

Ten days later, Nomura submitted Plan B, a strictly temporary proposal. Japan would advance no further in Southeast Asia and the western Pacific; it would withdraw from Indochina after a general settlement or the restoration of peace

with China. The United States would unfreeze Japanese assets, supply Japan with a required quantity of oil, and press the Dutch to reopen the East Indies to Japanese trade. Most important of all was the final paragraph, which demanded that the US be prepared to terminate aid to China. Historian Herbert Feis goes so far as to claim that whoever insisted on the last paragraph – Tojo and the army certainly did – insisted on war.[21]

China increasingly remained the crucial factor. Japan felt it could not immediately abandon an enterprise that had been undertaken at such cost. As Tojo told the cabinet on October 14, "If we concede, Manchuria and Korea will be lost."[22] Roosevelt's top military leadership, including General Marshall and Admiral Stark, preferred stalling the Japanese to immediate confrontation. So did Secretary of War Henry L. Stimson and Secretary of the Navy Frank Knox. Army intelligence continually stressed that the European war must remain primary, surmised that Japan was really estranged from Germany, and posited that it might even be harmful to insist upon Japan's immediate evacuation of China.

In a final desperate effort, Hull and his staff at the State Department considered a truce, a 3-month modus vivendi. Japan would withdraw from south Indochina and retain only 25,000 troops in the north. The United States would rescind the order freezing Japanese funds, although the resumed monthly oil shipments would be limited to a quantity sufficient for strictly civilian needs. The United States would be open to direct Sino-Japanese negotiations but without pressuring Jiang.

The modus vivendi proposal had no chance. The Chinese pleaded with Washington to accept no terms that might compromise their interests. The British too objected, with Churchill cabling Roosevelt: "What about Chiang Kai-shek? Is he not having a very thin diet? Our anxiety is about China. If they collapse, our joint dangers would enormously increase." Some historians concur. As Reynolds notes, at this stage in the war, when the Red Army had been driven back to the gates of Moscow, a Chinese collapse would be disastrous. Utley agrees, claiming that if Hull compromised, China might feel so betrayed that it would give up on the war.[23]

On November 26, Hull submitted a ten-point proposal strictly for the record, for the terms were almost guaranteed to elicit rejection. This time it was the Americans who were advancing a non-starter. Provisions included the withdrawal of all Japanese forces from China and Indochina, neutralization of French Indochina, and Japanese participation in a non-aggression pact with the Allies. In return, the United States would remove the freezing orders, lift the tariff on raw silk, and otherwise encourage increased trade. As Iriye notes, the US was inviting Japan to help reestablish a western-oriented brand of order in the Pacific. If Japan refused to do so, then no compromise could be achieved. Another historian, Norman A. Graebner, agrees, stressing that Roosevelt and his advisers preferred war to any successful assault on the treaty structure erected at the Washington conference of 1921–2. FDR, he continued, was never able to establish goals in the Far East, which reflected the nation's limited interests, its lack of available strength, and its desire to avoid war.[24]

On December 1, 1941, as the Japanese strike force was already on its way to Pearl Harbor, Roosevelt told Lord Halifax, the British ambassador, that if Japan attacked British or Dutch possessions in Southeast Asia, this move would result in bringing them all together. A Japanese strike at Thailand, by moving forces through the Isthmus of Kra, also met with a possible commitment, though two days later FDR added that he needed Congressional approval for armed support.

Historians differ as to the president's intent. Raymond A. Esthus asserts that the Roosevelt administration had finally succumbed to British entreaties for assurance. Reynolds claims the British finally possessed the commitment that they had long sought. Kimball differs, finding FDR too vague in his language to be reassuring. Had the Japanese avoided any attack on American territory, Roosevelt would have been in an extremely awkward position.[25]

On December 7, what had been marked by deadlock was decisively resolved, for the Japanese attacked major bases in the western Pacific. The toll at Pearl Harbor was particularly heavy, involving the destruction of two battleships, the immo-bilization of six others, the loss of 188 military planes, and the death of over 2,400 Americans. Four days later Adolf Hitler declared war on the United States. Had the Führer exercised restraint, American public opinion might have forced Roosevelt to focus most, if not all, of his military attention on Japan, doing so at a time when the Allies were most in peril.

## The Balance Sheet

Unquestionably, in dealing with opposition, Roosevelt was most skilled in political maneuver, giving his foes no real opportunity to defeat him. To the frustration of the anti-interventionists, the president never presented the issue as one of peace versus war and so could keep the framework of the debate within his own hands. At first, he claimed that his proposals were the best means of avoiding conflict. By the middle of 1941, the president was asserting that the Germans were thrusting combat upon the United States. Not only did FDR possess a workable Congressional majority, he also used the powers of the presidency to the fullest. On his own, he made the destroyers-for-bases deal, placed Greenland under temporary US guardianship, sent American troops to Iceland, and levied an oil embargo on Japan. His administration was also successful in unfairly branding such critics as the America First Committee as potential traitors or Nazi dupes, thereby establishing a Brown Scare quite similar to the Red Scare of the 1950s.

The president could be less skilled in the international arena than the domestic. While most historians today praise Roosevelt for perceiving the dangers of German expansion, they are still divided over his Japan policy. As such the legacy remains somewhat ambivalent.

### NOTES

1 *New York Times*, September 12, 1941, pp. 1, 4.
2 Warren F. Kimball, *Forged in War: Roosevelt, Churchill, and the Second World War* (New York: William Morrow, 1997), p. 49.
3 Irwin F. Gellman, *Secret Affairs: Franklin Roosevelt, Cordell Hull, and Sumner Welles* (Baltimore: Johns Hopkins University Press, 1995), p. 201.

4  Thomas A. Bailey and Paul B. Ryan, *Hitler vs. Roosevelt: The Undeclared Naval War* (New York: Free Press, 1979), p. 96; Kimball, *Forged in War*, pp. 59–60; Robert Shogan, *Hard Bargain: How FDR Twisted Churchill's Arm, Evaded the Law, and Changed the Role of the Presidency* (New York: Scribner, 1995), chap. 14.

5  *New York Times*, October 31, 1940, p. 1.

6  Kimball, *Forged in War*, p. 8.

7  *New York Times*, December 30, 1940, p. 7.

8  Warren F. Kimball, *The Most Unsordid Act: Lend-Lease, 1939–1941* (Baltimore: Johns Hopkins University Press, 1969), p. 241; Kimball, *Forged in War*, pp. 73, 76.

9  David Reynolds, *The Creation of the Anglo-American Alliance 1937–1941: A Study in Competitive Co-operation* (Chapel Hill, NC: University of North Carolina Press, 1982), p. 166.

10  Taft, *Congressional Record*, July 10, 1941, p. 5926.

11  James MacGregor Burns, *Roosevelt: The Soldier of Freedom* (New York: Harcourt Brace Jovanovich, 1970), pp. 87, 91–2.

12  J. Garry Clifford and Samuel R. Spencer, Jr., *The First Peacetime Draft* (Lawrence, KS: University Press of Kansas, 1986), p. 233.

13  Patrick J. Maney, *The Roosevelt Presence: A Biography of Franklin Delano Roosevelt* (New York: Twayne, 1992), p. 165; Edward M. Bennett, *Franklin D. Roosevelt and the Search for Security: American–Soviet Relations 1939–1945* (Wilmington, DE: Scholarly Resources, 1990), p. 8; Bailey and Ryan, *Hitler vs. Roosevelt*, p. 113.

14  David Reynolds, *From Munich to Pearl Harbor: Roosevelt's America and the Origins of the Second World War* (Chicago: Ivan Dee, 2001), p. 148; Theodore A. Wilson, "The First Summit: FDR and the Riddle of Personal Diplomacy," in *The Atlantic Charter*, ed. Douglas Brinkley and David R. Facey-Crowther (New York: St. Martin's, 1994), p. 21.

15  Roosevelt, *New York Times*, September 14, 1941, p. 4; George McJimsey, *The Presidency of Franklin Delano Roosevelt* (Lawrence, KS: University Press of Kansas, 2000), p. 201; Robert Dallek, *Franklin D. Roosevelt and American Foreign Policy, 1932–1945* (New York: Oxford University Press, 1979), p. 289.

16  Bailey and Ryan, *Hitler vs. Roosevelt*, p. 227; Reynolds, *Creation of the Anglo-American Alliance*, pp. 218–19.

17  For the claim that Roosevelt's move was inadvertent, see Jonathan G. Utley, *Going to War with Japan, 1937–1941* (Knoxville, TN: University of Tennessee Press, 1985), pp. 151–6. For the assertion that FDR's move was deliberate, see Waldo Heinrichs, *Threshold of War: Franklin D. Roosevelt and American Entry into World War II* (New York: Oxford University Press, 1988), pp. 246–7 n.68.

18  Michael A. Barnhart, *Japan Prepares for Total War: The Search for Economic Security, 1919–1941* (Ithaca, NY: Cornell University Press, 1987), p. 271; Akira Iriye, *The Origins of World War II in Asia and the Pacific* (New York: Longman, 1987), p. 146; Utley, *Going to War with Japan*, p. 156.

19  Iriye, *Origins of World War II*, pp. 166–7; Tsunoda Jun, "On the So-Called Hull–Nomura Negotiations," in *Pearl Harbor Reexamined: Prologue to the Pacific War*, ed. Hilary Conroy and Harry Wray (Honolulu, HI: University of Hawaii Press, 1990), p. 94; Robert J. C. Butow, *Tojo and the Coming of the War* (Princeton, NJ: Princeton University Press, 1961), p. 244; Heinrichs, *Threshold of War*, p. 187.

20  Iriye, *Origins of World War II*, p. 160.

21  Herbert Feis, *The Road to Pearl Harbor: The Coming of the War Between the United States and Japan* (Princeton, NJ: Princeton University Press, 1950), p. 309.

22  Tojo quoted in John Toland, *The Rising Sun: The Decline and Fall of the Japanese Empire, 1936–1945* (New York: Random House, 1970), p. 113.

23  Reynolds, *From Munich to Pearl Harbor*, pp. 161–2; Utley, "Cordell Hull and the Diplomacy of Inflexibility," in *Pearl Harbor Reexamined*, ed. Conroy and Wray, p. 81.

24  Iriye, *Origins of World War II*, p. 181; Norman A. Graebner, "Hoover, Roosevelt, and the Japanese," in *Pearl Harbor as History: Japanese–American Relations, 1931–1941*, ed. Dorothy Borg and Shumei Okamoto (New York: Columbia University Press, 1973), p. 46.

25  Raymond A. Esthus, "President Roosevelt's Commitment to Britain to Intervene in a Pacific War," *Mississippi Valley Historical Review* 50 (1963): 28–38; Reynolds, *Creation of the Anglo-American Alliance*, p. 246; Warren F. Kimball, *The Juggler: Franklin Roosevelt as Wartime Statesman* (Princeton, NJ: Princeton University Press, 1991), p. 13.

## GUIDE TO FURTHER READING

Thomas A. Bailey and Paul B. Ryan, *Hitler vs. Roosevelt: The Undeclared Naval War* (New York: Free Press,

1979). Shows the reasons why both leaders sought to avoid all-out war while fighting a limited conflict.

J. Garry Clifford and Samuel R. Spencer, Jr., *The First Peacetime Draft* (Lawrence, KS: University Press of Kansas, 1986). Detailed account of a critical point in America's military preparation, when the sacred tradition of a volunteer army was overturned.

Hilary Conroy and Harry Wray, eds., *Pearl Harbor Reexamined: Prologue to the Pacific War* (Honolulu, HI: University of Hawaii Press, 1990). Anthology offering conflicting interpretations concerning American and Japanese diplomacy.

Robert Dallek, *Franklin D. Roosevelt and American Foreign Policy, 1932–1945* (New York: Oxford University Press, 1979). Thorough account that stresses the domestic background and often defends Rooseveltian statecraft.

Justus D. Doenecke, *Storm on the Horizon: The Challenge to American Intervention, 1939–1941* (Lanham, MD: Rowman & Littlefield, 2000). Surveys Roosevelt's foreign policy critics, stressing their underlying strategic and ideological premises.

Irwin F. Gellman, *Secret Affairs: Franklin Roosevelt, Cordell Hull, and Sumner Welles* (Baltimore: Johns Hopkins University Press, 1995). Shows the vulnerability of all three figures.

Waldo Heinrichs, *Threshold of War: Franklin D. Roosevelt and American Entry into World War II* (New York: Oxford University Press, 1988). Finds FDR as purposeful planner and sees Soviet Union as pivotal to understanding FDR's diplomacy.

Akira Iriye, *The Origins of World War II in Asia and the Pacific* (New York: Longman, 1987). Excellent in explaining Japan's motives and dilemmas.

Warren F. Kimball, *Forged in War: Roosevelt, Churchill, and the Second World War* (New York: William Morrow, 1997). Positive stress on the ability of both men while showing their limitations; *The Most Unsordid Act: Lend-Lease, 1939–1941* (Baltimore: Johns Hopkins University Press, 1969), denies Roosevelt acted as dictator but finds him lacking in candor.

William L. Langer and S. Everett Gleason, *The World Crisis of 1937–1941 and American Foreign Policy*, vol. 1, *The Challenge to Isolation, 1937–1940* (New York: Harper, 1952); vol. 2, *The Undeclared War, 1940–1941* (New York: Harper, 1953). Remains an outstanding account after over fifty years.

David Reynolds, *The Creation of the Anglo-American Alliance 1937–1941: A Study in Competitive Cooperation* (Chapel Hill, NC: University of North Carolina Press, 1982). Indicates that underlying rivalries remained during the shift in power from Britain to the US.

Jonathan G. Utley, *Going to War with Japan, 1937–1941* (Knoxville, TN: University of Tennessee Press, 1985). Stresses the role of a powerful bureaucracy in maneuvering economic warfare that led to full-scale conflict.

Theodore A. Wilson, *The First Summit: Roosevelt and Churchill at Placentia Bay, 1941* (Lawrence, KS: University Press of Kansas, rev. edn, 1991). Detailed description of the August 1941 Newfoundland conference, at which the Atlantic Charter was drafted.

# Part IV

## From Grand Alliance to Cold War

# CHAPTER TWENTY-TWO

# The Grand Alliance, 1941–1945

## WARREN F. KIMBALL

The Grand Alliance is, first and foremost, the story of one of history's most successful wartime alliances – and rumors of its death are exaggerated, for it never quite died. The Grand Alliance did not survive the Second World War, at least not in the same form, yet it was at the core of the continuance of the Anglo-American special relationship. Moreover, Great Power collaboration – the primary legacy of the Grand Alliance – provided an invaluable platform from which to launch initiatives for a lessening of Soviet–western tensions. Yet histories of the alliance and the Second World War routinely focus on the wartime rifts and tensions that created what became known as the Cold War, even while the Grand Alliance was battling and defeating a common set of enemies.[1] Preparing for the world that would emerge after the war proved problematic. But the Grand Alliance faced those problems and formulated responses that, for better or worse, lasted into the twenty-first century.

Winston Churchill dubbed the array of nations fighting Hitler's Germany (and Japan?) the Grand Alliance, then popularized and perpetuated the name by using it as the title of the third volume of his extraordinarily popular memoir, *The Second World War*.[2] As history looked at the parade of what later were called "summit" meetings among the Big Three leaders, the Grand Alliance became nearly synonymous with Churchill, Franklin Roosevelt, and Josef Stalin – and so it shall be used in this chapter.

The Grand Alliance was never formal. But its basic principles of a joint struggle and a commitment to "complete victory over their enemies" were set out in January 1942 by British Prime Minister Winston Churchill and US President Franklin D. Roosevelt in what FDR labeled the "Declaration by United Nations." Save for the name, the Declaration had nothing to do with the later United Nations Organization; rather, it was a statement of allied unity for those nations signing on to use their "full resources, military or economic," against the Tripartite Pact (September 1940) of Germany, Italy, and Japan. The Declaration also referred to the "common program of purposes and principles" that had been set out in the Atlantic Charter, agreed to by Churchill and Roosevelt in August 1941. Eventually, some forty-five governments (including, to Churchill's discomfort, India) signed on. Whatever the length of that list, the Grand Alliance – Great Britain, the Soviet Union, and the United States – together led the struggle against the enemies of all.

As a statement of the war aims for the Grand Alliance, the Atlantic Charter was intended as merely a set of guidelines – Churchill called it "not a law, but a star."[3] Both Britain and the Soviet Union had express reservations about promising to "respect the right of all peoples to choose the form of government under which they will live." After all, each had an empire to hold on to. The Russians also insisted on maintaining their neutrality regarding Japan, a sensible position with German armies at the gates of Moscow, but less understandable by 1944 with Hitler's forces in retreat. But even with such conditions, the Atlantic Charter "turned up like a copper penny throughout the war – alternately embarrassing and pleasing its designers." It was both an "idea and reality."[4]

The principles of the Atlantic Charter helped shape postwar policy, but those principles were always preempted by national interest. The phrase "national interest" seems hard-nosed and practical, but definitions of what is national interest are invariably filtered through ideology and history. For Churchill and the British, declarations supporting home rule and self-determination for all people meant that places like India and British colonies in Africa could choose to leave the British economic and political system. For the Americans, the Charter's call for so-called free trade (multilateralism) would benefit strong economies like that of the United States. For the Soviet Union, its security depended on "friendly" governments in neighboring states, and friendly meant communist regimes that followed Moscow's lead. All three leaders would have agreed with Stalin when, in 1945, he offered an axiom to the Yugoslav communist Milovan Djilas: "whoever occupies a territory imposes on it his own social system." Churchill had offered his own cynical contention that "the right to guide the course of history is the noblest prize of victory." FDR made no epigram, but insisted that the United States have a major role in places like Italy, even though Churchill had suggested that Great Britain be the "senior partner" in the occupation of that country. More important, Roosevelt consistently tried to attach the American liberal economic agenda to agreements with his alliance partners.[5]

Additional "definitions" of the goals of the Grand Alliance would come with the 1942 Anglo-Soviet Treaty, a more traditional bilateral alliance, and the "unconditional surrender" declaration made by both Roosevelt and Churchill at the Casablanca conference in January 1943. Both essentially repeated the commitment not to sign a separate peace and, in the words of the Declaration by United Nations, to insist on "complete victory."

The essential strategic understanding that made the Grand Alliance possible came early in 1941, well before either the US or the Soviet Union went to war with Germany. American–British "conversations" between the top naval officers from each country (the ABC-1 talks) concluded that, in the event of a war against both Hitler's Germany and Japan, the two nations should focus on defeating Germany, the larger military power, first. FDR never gave official approval to the strategic recommendation until after Pearl Harbor, but he read the report and gave tacit approval. That Germany-first policy, and FDR's refusal to waver on it in the dark days after the Pearl Harbor attack, were the sine qua non for the creation of the Grand Alliance.

The essence of the Grand Alliance was never on paper, but rather in the leadership and interactions of the Big Three – Churchill, Roosevelt, and Stalin. Without the careful, personal diplomacy of the three leaders, the wartime alliance easily could have disintegrated into direct Soviet–western conflict even before war's end – a frightening thought since by that time both factions had deployed vast, battle-hardened military forces in Europe and, to a lesser degree, in East Asia. Their diplomacy was complicated by ideological differences among all three nations. Soviet communism and authoritarianism ran contrary to British and American institutions. British imperialism and colonialism generated strong American opposition, and attacks on empire generated equally impassioned British defense, especially from Churchill. American unilateralism (misleadingly labeled "isolationism") and its liberal ideology of "free trade" made for unsettling postwar security issues (after all, strategic resources are just that – strategic!), and threatened the more statist economic systems of the Soviet Union and Great Britain.

Geography, language, and shared history for over 300 years made the Anglo-American relationship special. Whatever British complaints about Americans being "overpaid, oversexed, and over here," the two countries had tightly interwoven historic trade patterns, "combined" planning boards for both logistics and military strategy, extensively shared intelligence including a remarkable exchange of codebreaking secrets, and the

Churchill–Roosevelt connection. Certainly, that relationship was tighter and more trusting than their association with the Soviet Union, a revolutionary state with an ideology that threatened the social and economic institutions of its two Grand Alliance partners. The distrust was mutual and well earned by all three. British and American diplomats complained bitterly about Soviet harassment and suspicions. Nonetheless, lend-lease aid poured into Russia (eventually comprising 7 to 10 percent of Soviet war materials), intelligence sharing was significant though less detailed and extensive than that between the US and the UK, and wartime grand strategy as well as postwar planning were discussed at the highest levels. Like Churchill and Roosevelt, Stalin worked to make the Grand Alliance function – and bring it into the postwar world.

The great truth about the Grand Alliance is self-evident – Nazi Germany and expansionist Japan were defeated, although that can get ignored if the Second World War is seen merely as the origins of another war. A key strategic victory in Europe occurred before the Grand Alliance took shape. From autumn 1940 through spring 1941, Germany lost the massive air struggle that Churchill called the Battle of Britain, forcing Hitler to shelve plans to invade and occupy England. Without that British victory, the entire war would have been different. The Soviet Union, in order to survive, might well have struck another, less favorable deal with the Germans. Even if such offers were spurned by Hitler, the Russians could not have counted on any effective help. The Americans, reluctant to get involved in "Europe's wars," whatever FDR's concerns, would surely have withdrawn behind what some viewed as Fortress Atlantic, not to venture out unless Hitler threatened the western hemisphere. Moreover, German naval and aviation bases in the British Isles would have closed the Atlantic to any American attempt to provide aid to Hitler's enemies. That would have left Europe from Poland to Italy to Spain to the Netherlands under the barbaric control of Nazi Germany and its allies. We would have avoided the Cold War, but at a far more horrifying price.

But by the time of the Japanese attack on Pearl Harbor on December 7, 1941, when the Grand Alliance came into being, Britain was safe, and American military aid was beginning to trickle across the Atlantic and even into the Soviet Union. Even as the Red Army retreated from the German onslaught that had begun on June 15, 1941, Roosevelt instructed that aid be sent to the beleaguered Russians. Ignoring American and British military predictions for a quick German victory, he ordered: "Use a heavy hand – act as a burr under the saddle and get things moving. . . . Step on it!"[6] That aid had little effect on the ability of Russian forces to stop the Germans at the gates of Moscow, which they did in December 1941, but it held out the promise of more and substantial help to come. Whatever the morale boost, the key effect was to build confidence with Stalin – no small task when dealing with a revolutionary whose revolution had been directly threatened two decades earlier by British, and to a lesser degree American, military action.

## The Second Front

The decision to aid Russia was a precursor to Franklin Roosevelt's wartime policy of using the Grand Alliance to build Stalin's confidence that his alliance partners could be trusted in the postwar world. Churchill generally agreed, but occasionally swung between exhortations to confront the Soviets during the war and agreements with Stalin to recognize Soviet dominance in eastern Europe. Churchill understood that Britain's traditional policy of playing the balance-weight rather than trying to impose its will by force had been dictated by realities of physical size that could not be overcome by economic strength, even in Marlborough's era. By the 1940s, he unhappily recognized that Britain's economic power had faded, and feared it would fade further if it lost its empire as a result of the war. As for Stalin, necessity made him receptive to Roosevelt's blandishments. Yet what evidence we have from Soviet archives indicates that the Soviet leader became increasingly intrigued with the possibility that what Winston Churchill later christened "peaceful coexistence" might be possible, though only on Soviet terms.[7]

Those terms quickly became apparent. During visits to London and Washington in spring 1942,

Soviet Foreign Minister V. M. Molotov reiterated the requirements Stalin had laid out repeatedly since the German attack: recognition of Soviet boundaries that included the Baltic states and what had been eastern Poland, and the establishment of a major Anglo-American military front in western Europe – defined as "drawing off 40 German divisions (these being first-rate divisions) from the Soviet–German front" – *the* Second Front. Time and again Molotov told Churchill and then Roosevelt that the Second Front was more a political than a military question, "and as such should be solved not by generals but by statesmen."[8]

Stalin's territorial demands were awkward for the British. They had assisted in the creation of independent states in the Baltic after the First World War, and had ostensibly gone to war in 1939 to "save" Poland from the Germans. But Stalin was both sensitive to and wary of ethnic nationalism, viewing independence for Latvia, Lithuania, and Estonia after 200 years of being part of the Russian Empire as illegitimate and a threat to Soviet security. By spring 1942, the British had accepted his position on the Baltic states, leaving Polish boundaries for later. As for the Second Front, at the beginning of 1942 Soviet military needs were dire. Moscow and Leningrad (St. Petersburg) were under siege, while German forces were moving across the Ukraine, Russia's breadbasket, and would take the port of Sevastopol on the Black Sea that autumn. Molotov may have called the Second Front "political" (perhaps hinting at a separate peace), but the military need was overwhelming.

Roosevelt reacted to Stalin's territorial demands with his classic tactic – delay. Arguing that those matters should be left to the postwar peace conference, he told the British not to get into such details. A few months after Japan's attack on Pearl Harbor, with the American public clamoring for prosecution of the war against the much-reviled Japanese, was no time to risk rumors of a deal with Stalin on boundaries. That would threaten what FDR and his military advisers knew was crucial – the common Anglo-American understanding that Hitler's Germany was the primary threat. When both the British and the Americans refused to sign off on a Soviet–Polish boundary,

Stalin explained his intentions to Molotov in no uncertain terms. Ignore British refusals to guarantee Soviet boundaries, Stalin instructed, "for it gives us a free hand. . . . The question of frontiers . . . will be decided by force."[9] All this was, of course, done by the Americans and the British under the fear that Stalin would do again what he did in 1939 – make an agreement with Hitler, this time leaving his allies high and dry. That fear of a separate peace worried Churchill and Roosevelt throughout the war. Ironically, Stalin repeatedly expressed similar fears to his advisers.

*The* Second Front in 1942 would not happen, whatever Roosevelt's private assurances and public commitment to such an operation. Molotov and FDR announced that a "full understanding was reached with regard to the urgent tasks of creating a second front in Europe in 1942," but neither Molotov nor Stalin believed FDR. Soviet records show that endorsements by Roosevelt and Hopkins of a Second Front by autumn were invariably followed by expressions of doubt. "The question arises: can we do it?" the president wondered. Please tell Stalin, Roosevelt requested, "that we were *hoping* to open a second front in 1942."[10] The American military spoke in terms of air operations in the event of a Soviet collapse, hardly the Second Front the Russians needed. Moreover, the British dropped their guarded language and finally made clear their unequivocal opposition to any major invasion of western Europe in 1942. They told Molotov that any such landing on the continent in 1942 "was doomed to failure" and "would do nothing to help the Russians."[11] That constituted a veto since any invasion that year would have to be made primarily with British forces.

The decision not to launch the Second Front in 1942, combined with the "pull of the Pacific" (pressure to prosecute the war against the Japanese), prompted Roosevelt to return to an idea he had broached shortly after the United States entered the war.[12] Not only did Stalin need reassurances, but the Germany-first strategy FDR and his military had agreed upon was threatened by a growing sense of American detachment from the war against Hitler. Bloodying the troops seemed the answer. In June 1942, Churchill decided to "flip over" to Washington for talks with FDR and was delighted to find that the president had returned to his idea of an Anglo-American invasion of North Africa. The North African coast of the Mediterranean had been a persistent battleground since the start of the war. Hitler's Italian ally, led by fellow dictator Benito Mussolini, had overextended its forces in various parts of the Mediterranean littoral, forcing the Germans to bail him out in Yugoslavia, Greece, and Libya/Tunisia. French forces, presumably neutral since their country's surrender in June 1940, controlled their Moroccan colony and other parts of Northwest Africa. German forces, led by General Erwin Rommel, threatened Egypt and the Suez Canal. Even as Churchill arrived in Washington for the third of what would be a dozen Churchill–Roosevelt meetings, he learned of the surrender of 33,000 experienced British troops and the fortress at Tobruk in Libya, to a German force half that size. "Defeat is one thing; disgrace is another," Churchill later wrote.[13]

The American military was willing to offer the British tanks and supplies, but was aghast at FDR's suggestion of a North African invasion. General George C. Marshall, the US Army Chief of Staff, and his planners were adamantly committed to a major cross-Channel invasion. Mediterranean operations were a "suction pump" that would divert attention from "the main plot." Marshall muttered darkly about Roosevelt's "cigarette holder" strategizing, about British efforts to drag the Americans into a fight to restore British influence in the region rather than defeat Hitler, and even about making the war against Japan the first priority. FDR confronted Marshall, likening the general's arguments to "taking up your dishes and going away." Fighting for a bunch of islands in the Pacific "will not affect the world situation this year or next." But the collapse of Russian resistance would. Churchill and Roosevelt agreed that Germany-first meant keeping the Soviet Union actively in the war, and that meant the North African invasion – operation TORCH.

## Operation TORCH

That decision sent Churchill on the mission of "carrying a large lump of ice to the North Pole"

– explaining to Stalin why the Second Front in western Europe had been replaced by obviously more peripheral operations in North Africa. The trip, in August 1942, came at a time when supply convoys to northern Russia had been suspended following staggering losses of shipping caused by German submarine, air, and surface raider attacks. At the same time, German U-boats had disrupted the sea-supply lines from the United States to Great Britain, due in part to a loss of intelligence that came when the Germans changed their communications ciphers. Stalin had complained angrily about the cut-off of convoys, but received the news of TORCH with apparent resignation and relief – partly because he already suspected that the Second Front would be delayed, partly because Hitler had launched a summer offensive that had forced Stalin to order a strategic retreat (the only time he did so during the war). His allies would open a second front, but not *the* Second Front the Soviet leader hoped for. Still, they were not deserting him. Churchill revealed his personal preference for a Mediterranean campaign when he drew a clever sketch of a crocodile showing TORCH as an attack on the "soft underbelly" as part of an attack on the "hard snout" – Hitler's Europe. Stalin responded, "May God prosper this undertaking." The Grand Alliance was intact.[14]

But the Second Front issue, political and military, would not go away. Churchill's soft underbelly remained the Anglo-American strategic focus, just as General Marshall had feared and Stalin must have suspected. The reality was that TORCH made a major cross-Channel invasion impossible in 1943, although that postponement might well have come anyway given training and logistical challenges. Postponing the Second Front *and* not actively engaging Hitler's forces for a year (spring 1943 to spring 1944) could prompt Stalin to conclude that his allies were leaving him in the lurch. As the Soviet victory at Stalingrad that would soon come in February 1943 became obvious, US assessments of probable Soviet intentions raised concern that the Soviet Union might settle for a restoration of its 1939 boundaries and not prosecute the war against Germany. Churchill understood: "Nothing in the world will be accepted by Stalin as an alternative to our placing

50 or 60 Divisions in France by the spring of this year."[15]

But making Stalin content was not Churchill's primary concern. He had never been comfortable with the American plan for a single, massive invasion of western Europe across the English Channel. Memories of the horrifying trench warfare of the First World War and limited British manpower prompted the British prime minister to opt for a war of attrition: a series of attacks on the periphery of German-held Europe that would wear down resistance. The Anglo-American invasion of North Africa in November 1942, and a British offensive westward from Egypt, had succeeded in removing any German threat to the Suez Canal and the Middle East. Now Churchill hoped that a campaign in Italy and perhaps the Aegean Sea region would take precedence. The Normandy invasion would still take place, but it would be just one of a number of Anglo-American fronts.

But the North African campaign proceeded much more slowly than they had hoped. He and FDR met at Casablanca in February 1943, and agreed on an invasion of Sicily. The Italian island of Sicily lay only some 150 miles from the port of Tunis, making it an inviting target. For FDR, it offered a charade of continuing to engage the Germans. For Churchill, it held out the hope of a Mediterranean strategy – one that would reinstall Britain into its traditional sphere of influence. For Stalin, it was not the Second Front, but at least his allies were not deserting him – or so they hoped he would think. When Churchill and Roosevelt met in January 1943 at Casablanca, in just-liberated French Morocco, they agreed to take that step, although the Americans insisted that preparation for the cross-Channel invasion had first priority.[16]

With the Soviet Union firmly in mind, Roosevelt and Churchill also proclaimed "unconditional surrender" as their joint goal. FDR had earlier called for "victory, final and complete," a phrase that was repeated in the Declaration of United Nations, but the words "unconditional surrender" also ruled out negotiations with Hitler. That was not only a message for Stalin, but also a statement of Roosevelt's belief that German character had been so warped and distorted by

Prussian militarism and Nazism that fundamental reforms had to be imposed on Germany – in later parlance, "nation-building." Both Stalin and Churchill had some doubts about unconditional surrender, but never repudiated the policy.[17]

By early 1943 the outline of wartime Anglo-American relations with the Soviet Union had taken shape. The military engagements between the Bolshevik revolutionaries and the West, which had happened only twenty-five years earlier, were not forgotten. Nor were Bolshevik threats and condemnations. Cooperation and a degree of trust had come very recently, and then only because of a common enemy – Hitler's Germany. Neither Churchill nor Roosevelt (nor Stalin for that matter) wanted the Second World War to become the Third. How to avoid that was the question. Churchill favored creating a balance of power that would restrain the Soviets, but drew back from abandoning efforts to prolong the Grand Alliance. Roosevelt, halfway around the world from Moscow, reversed the precedence, insisting on working to bring the Grand Alliance into the postwar world, but drew back from actions that might compromise America's interests or security. The two leaders never considered allowing their differences to split Britain and the United States – a demonstration of their "special" relationship – but those differences affected all aspects of Anglo-American wartime relations. Decolonization, the fate of France, the establishment of an international organization, occupation and liberation policy, the treatment of Germany and Japan – all took different shape because of divergent views in London and Washington on how to deal with the Soviet Union. As for Stalin, while he (more than Molotov) seemed intrigued with the notion of cooperation, he never took his eye off his immediate goals of physical and ideological security for the Soviet state.

FDR's hopes of transmuting the wartime Grand Alliance into a postwar working relationship (a modus vivendi) came to dominate Anglo-American policy, especially as that cooperative policy also addressed their persistent fears that Stalin would once again strike a deal with Hitler and leave his allies to fight on alone. Whatever the arguments between London and Washington over postwar trade, empire, and influence, the

Anglo-American relationship continued to maintain the peaceful civility that had existed since the American Civil War, despite quarrels and jealousies and suspicions. But the Soviet Union was a different kettle of fish. During Roosevelt's regular meetings with State Department officials drawing up plans for the postwar world, he worried aloud that "he didn't know what to do about Russia." British Foreign Secretary Anthony Eden echoed FDR's concern, warning that the Soviet Union was "our most difficult problem," though he did not think Soviet leaders actively planned for the spread of international communism. But even if they did, "if we are to win the war and to maintain the peace, we must work with Stalin and we cannot work with him unless we are successful in allaying some at least of his suspicion."[18]

Roosevelt had come into the war with what proved to be consistent, if uncomfortably vague, views on how to restructure international relations in the postwar world. The United States would work with other nations to preserve peace, but it had to avoid commitments that would drag it into every little argument and local squabble. Woodrow Wilson's League of Nations concept had fallen into that trap, and the American public and Congress had rejected the scheme, insisting that the United States retain its freedom of action. That experience, and FDR's assessment of the causes of the two world wars, left him convinced that, since the Great Powers made world wars, only the Great Powers could maintain the peace.[19] At the same time, he believed that each of the Great Powers, the sheriffs or policemen, should pay primary attention to its own region – for the United States that meant the western hemisphere, a more palatable commitment for parochial Americans in an age before jet planes and rockets. As early as August 1941, during a meeting with Churchill, Roosevelt had suggested that the two Great Powers, the United States and Great Britain, would have to act as policemen after the war. By 1942, the list of policemen had expanded to four to include the Soviet Union and China. Disarmament would be key – "smaller powers might have rifles but nothing more dangerous," he once commented. Small nations would have to trust in the Great Powers – "another League of Nations with 100 different signatories" would mean "simply

too many nations to satisfy." He had spoken similarly to Molotov in May–June 1942, and gotten Stalin's strong endorsement: "Roosevelt's considerations about peace protection after the war are absolutely sound . . . his position will be fully supported by the Soviet Government."[20]

By mid-1943, with the Germans halted in North Africa and the tide about to turn on the Russian front, European frontiers and self-determination became a major issue. From the start, Stalin had insisted on having "friendly" governments around the Soviet periphery in eastern Europe. Roosevelt's (and Churchill's, at least most of the time) dreams of persuading Stalin to be a cooperative participant in the postwar world required that the Soviet leader feel secure, satisfied, and sure of Anglo-American reliability. But since self-determination meant independence for the Balts and the establishment of an anti-Russian (and anti-Soviet) government in Warsaw, how then to avoid the obvious? Both Roosevelt and Churchill had tried to create a good postwar relationship with the Soviet Union even before the Stalingrad battle demonstrated the likelihood of Red Army occupation of the territory Stalin demanded. What options were left to London and Washington? Not military confrontation, at least not with Anglo-American forces still struggling in North Africa and 15 months away from an invasion of western Europe. More to the point, what were the long-term prospects for peace if the United States and Britain chose to confront the Russians? More frightening, what if getting tough with Stalin pushed him into making a deal with Hitler? After all, Stalin had complained, accurately, that the North African campaign was no substitute for the Second Front. The atomic bomb could change the dynamic, but that weapon was still only a project, not a reality until after the Germans surrendered. Then there was Japan to be defeated – a campaign that all agreed would take some two years. Rather than fruitlessly opposing any and all expansion of Soviet power in eastern Europe, the Anglo-Americans opted to continue to promote long-term cooperation. As Roosevelt and Under-Secretary of State Sumner Welles told Anthony Eden, "the real decisions should be made by the United States, Great Britain, Russia and China, who would be the powers for many years to come that would have to police the world."[21]

All this came in the atmosphere of suspicion created by German disclosures in mid-April 1943 that the Soviet Union had executed some 4,400 Polish officers and men when the Red Army took eastern Poland late in 1939 as part of the agreements in the Nazi–Soviet Pact. Churchill found reports of the massacre persuasive, but both he and Roosevelt put first things first and refused to let the issue divide the Grand Alliance. It was the beginning of a "litmus test" – the independence of Poland from Russian/Soviet control – that would spell the disintegration of the Grand Alliance.[22]

By autumn 1943, the Soviet military situation had improved significantly, eliminating Hitler's offensive threat by destroying the bulk of the German tanks and mobile artillery. The Red Army had faced, and won out over, the bulk of German military forces, while the Anglo-Americans were still nibbling around the edges in North Africa and Italy. Yet Stalin still needed the Grand Alliance, for the Germans remained a powerful defensive force that could reconstitute its ability to go on the attack if the growing pressure in the west slacked off. But the political dynamic was shifting, and that made a meeting of the Big Three – Churchill, Roosevelt, and Stalin – desirable, even necessary. Roosevelt, with Churchill's agreement, backed off from suggestions of Alaska, North Africa, Cairo, and Baghdad, and agreed to meet in Teheran, Iran – which was as far outside the Soviet Union as Stalin would travel.[23]

## The Teheran Conference

In theory, the Second Front decision remained in play for the conferees. Churchill made his case for an expanded Italian campaign, but the painfully slow advance up the Italian peninsula, even after Italy's surrender, had made those arguments non-starters. As Stalin had accurately put it, the Germans would keep "as many allied Divisions as possible in Italy where no decision could be reached" – which is precisely what Hitler did. When the Soviet leader made clear his insistence on a major cross-Channel invasion, the debate ended. Churchill railed about "the dangers of

spelling the word OVERLORD T-Y-R-A-N-T."[24] But the decision had been made. An Italian campaign would not replace a single, massive cross-Channel invasion. Angry and feeling isolated, Churchill privately threatened to get drunk and go home, but there was no chance of that happening once the conference got down to the business at hand – immediate and longer-term postwar settlements.

The Teheran conference marked the apogee of the Grand Alliance. The discussions were friendly, and their agreements general enough to avoid the devilish details. All three felt comfortable with their specific as well as the overall military situation, even if the Russians still bore the brunt of the fight against Germany. Despite Churchill's frustration at the dismissal of his peripheral approach, the Germans no longer threatened Egypt and the Suez Canal. Stalin thrilled the Americans when he repeated a commitment made a few weeks earlier (at a meeting in Moscow of the UK, US, and Soviet foreign ministers) to attack Japan six weeks after Germany's surrender. American campaigns in the Pacific had secured the Southwest Pacific, and the island-hopping campaign against Japan was about to start. The Anglo-Americans promised the Soviets a portion of the captured Italian fleet. But even Stalin knew that they had gathered at Teheran to talk about politics, not military issues – he had left his military staff back in Russia.

All politics is related, but two issues stood out. One was an opportunity – establishing a postwar international structure that could preserve the peace. The second was a challenge – to reconstitute European nations and boundaries in the wake of Hitler's disruption and destruction. That challenge, labeled "self-determination" by the western powers, quickly became a contest between the Big Three to implement Stalin's axiom – "whoever occupies a territory imposes on it his own social system." A subset of that challenge, also embraced by the term "self-determination," was the decolonization of European empires, particularly in South and Southeast Asia. As it turned out, the challenge trumped the opportunity, while the colonized sought their own solutions.

The opportunity was the creation of an international system, a set of relationships, that would avoid, evade, and even prevent another great war.

Both Churchill and Stalin saw FDR's Four Policemen as a regional system, leaving them in charge of what they viewed as their spheres of influence – Great Britain in western Europe and the Mediterranean, Russia in the Balkans and Europe east of Germany. When Roosevelt sketched his concept of the Four Policemen to Stalin, the Soviet leader questioned having China play a role in European affairs. FDR, always concerned about a rebirth of so-called isolationism, warned that the United States could not participate in an exclusively European grouping that might try to force the dispatch of American troops to Europe. When Stalin wondered how the United States would respond to a request for military assistance from another Policeman, the president evasively spoke of quarantines and using only ships and airplanes – not troops.

Stalin agreed that any international organization should be worldwide, not regional, but he also heard the clear message that the Americans would not be militarily involved in policing Europe. The Cold War confrontation had not begun – cooperation within the Grand Alliance remained the watchword. There were no further significant discussions of the postwar structure. Working out the details could derail the concept, especially with the disposition of Germany waiting in the wings. Yet all three delegations had taken to referring to some sort of postwar organization as "the United Nations."[25]

The challenge of boundaries and political reconstruction centered on central Europe, specifically Germany and Poland. All three leaders agreed that Germany should be broken up (Soviet officials and historians later denied that Stalin had supported dismemberment). But no one was ready to get into the messy details of boundaries and specifics of governance lest that threaten the cooperative atmosphere or limit their freedom of action. Instead, they created the European Advisory Commission (EAC) to study such issues. As it turned out, by the time of the Yalta conference 14 months later, that commission's proposals became by default the guiding principles – setting "temporary" occupation zones of Germany that lasted for a half-century.

Stalin's initial proposal for Poland found quick agreement from Churchill. Whatever the details, the basic agreement was crystal clear. In Churchill's words: "he would like to see Poland moved westward in the same manner as soldiers at drill execute the drill 'left close' and illustrated his point with three matches representing the Soviet Union, Poland and Germany." Churchill's instinctive reaction to the possibility of postwar confrontation with Russia was to establish clearly defined boundaries and spheres of influence. Such Victorian arrangements had worked in the nineteenth century, why not again? The Great Powers of Europe would, he hoped, seek their own interests and create a great peace. "I did not think we were very far apart in principle," he told Stalin.[26] Ten months later, during his talks in Moscow with Stalin, the British prime minister would take the next step and spell out in clear, certain terms just who would get what.

Whatever the domestic problems Churchill's "left close" maneuver for Poland might generate for FDR, Great Power cooperation came first. He had, like Churchill, agreed earlier that the Baltic states were an integral part of the Soviet Union. "Do you expect us and Britain to declare war on Joe Stalin if they cross your previous frontier?" he told the Polish ambassador (he repeated the story to Stalin). "Even if we wanted to, Russia can still field an army twice our combined strength, and we would just have no say in the matter at all." Churchill made a similar comment a few weeks later.[27] The same was true for Poland.

Yet Poland eventually became the litmus test for Soviet intentions, despite what seemed a clear understanding that independence and freedom of action depended on Soviet self-restraint, not Anglo-American guarantees. Why? Partly because Stalin acted with such harsh brutality; partly because Churchill and Roosevelt both failed to prepare their publics and their parliaments for something less than a perfect solution – leaders could not speak of geopolitical compromises in a "People's War" fought for principles; partly because Polish leaders-in-exile in England rejected any compromise. Self-determination for Poles meant an anti-Soviet/anti-Russian regime in Warsaw. Stalin had no intention of allowing that to happen, any more than the Americans and British would stand by while Italy or Greece or

France were reconstructed in ways that went against Washington or London.

Operation OVERLORD, the Allied cross-Channel invasion of western France in June 1944, quickly followed as it was by a promised Red Army offensive, should have been the Grand Alliance's greatest moment. It was, on the surface. The full defeat of Germany had become only a matter of time. But that also meant that the Big Three could no longer postpone agreement on postwar geopolitical issues. Whether or not the attack was militarily necessary to defeat Hitler was hardly discussed. The Anglo-Americans had made a promise, and they would keep it! Not to do so would only have confirmed Stalin's persistent suspicions that his allies would turn on the Soviet Union once the war ended.

Yet there is an undertone of politics in OVERLORD. The Americans had long entertained an operation, codenamed RANKIN, that expressly called for an emergency insertion of British and American forces into western Europe in the event of a Soviet breakthrough. Why? Stalin's axiom governs. If the Anglo-Americans were not on the continent to liberate western Europe, how could they ensure that their "social system" would prevail? In Italy, the British and Americans had excluded the Soviet Union from any meaningful role in reconstruction, then quarreled themselves about whether or not Italy should be a "constitutional" monarchy (Churchill) or a public democracy (FDR). Anglo-American conceptions of democracy and freedom may have been superior to those of the Soviet Union, but geopolitical positioning also played a role. The Normandy invasion was more than just a heroic effort to eliminate Nazism. But a "People's War" requires grand themes and high purposes. Geopolitics sits uncomfortably in that seat.

By August 1944, the Polish resistance in Warsaw had concluded that it had to liberate the city before the Red Army could do so. Hitler responded predictably, ordering that the uprising be crushed. Soviet forces near Warsaw did not attack, and Stalin rejected Anglo-American gestures to send what would have been meaningless aid and thus avoid embarrassment at home. Perhaps Soviet actions in autumn 1944 indicated that the Grand Alliance had collapsed. But perhaps

Poland, which had been forced to "migrate" westward for some 600 years, and whose leaders had played a dishonest political game since 1919, was not a valid litmus test.

## Planning for Postwar: Poland and Percentages

By autumn 1944, full-fledged postwar planning had broken out. FDR assumed that geography and "isolationism" dictated that the United States operate at a distance. American planners focused on internationalizing New Deal economic planning with grand trade agreements. Wheat and oil were just the start. A "world bank" and international monetary agreements (the Bretton Woods conference) were keys to a better world. They would, of course, provide economic advantage for the United States. That, along with the creation of what became the United Nations Organization (at the Dumbarton Oaks conference), would ensure long-term US involvement on the international scene (though it would not ensure the victory of internationalism over unilateralism).

But Churchill and Stalin had to think in terms of details. Britain and Russia would look at each other across the European continent, and who controlled/influenced what was a crucial detail. Politics is principle. The Warsaw Uprising did not prevent Churchill from traveling to Moscow two months later (the TOLSTOY conference) to work out a political arrangement he thought could avoid a confrontation with the Soviet Union. The now famous "percentages" agreement ignored Poland – the matchsticks had already been moved westward. Percentages of influence (Britain 90 percent in Greece, the Soviets 90 percent almost everywhere else), a bizarre concept, were an attempt by both parties to avoid confrontation while implementing Stalin's axiom. The 50–50 split in Yugoslavia was more a concession to the strength of Tito's regime than anything else. Stalin ignored his 10 percent in Greece; Churchill did the same for the rest of the South Balkans except in Yugoslavia, where neither East nor West prevailed.

In December 1944, FDR, in a message to Stalin (repeating a State Department statement), asserted that the United States was committed to "a strong, free, independent and democratic Poland." He went on to state the American preference for boundary questions to be settled at a postwar peace conference, then dropped the other shoe. It would be acceptable to arrive at boundary decisions and to transfer "national groups" so long as the "Government and people of Poland" agreed.[28] On the surface it said all the right things. But Roosevelt, Churchill (who agreed with the message), and Stalin – as well as the Polish leaders in London – all knew full well what it meant. Any Polish government "friendly" to the Soviet Union would agree to moving the boundaries and "national groups" (i.e., Poles and Germans) westward to fit into the new Polish boundaries – and Roosevelt knew that Stalin was about to recognize just such a "friendly" government, the so-called Lublin Poles.

So where did it all go wrong? Certainly not at Yalta. When the Grand Alliance leaders met for the last time before Germany surrendered (unconditionally), the basics of a political settlement had been decided. Germany would be occupied along boundaries recommended by the EAC, with its future to be decided. Eastern Europe, save for Greece, would be in the Soviet sphere of influence. Great Britain, assisted at its request by France, would handle the reconstruction of western Europe. The United States would be in charge of the western hemisphere, but had its fingers in everyone else's pie through the various international economic institutions being established. And the Grand Alliance – the Great Powers – would live on as the UN Security Council where they could continue to work things out, safe from unwanted influence from others thanks to the veto.

But the Yalta agreements became a symbol in the United States and Britain of corrupt, even conspiratorial, power politics. Neither Churchill nor Roosevelt believed they could admit to their publics or their political opponents that they had consigned the Baltic states, Poland, and much of the South Balkans to the tender mercies of Soviet control. Neither could admit that they had made concessions in Northeast Asia that restored Russian economic and political influence in Manchuria and northern Korea. In each case the reasons were mixed, but establishing a cooperative rather than confrontational relationship with the Soviet Union was the overriding motive. It was sometime a case of making a silk purse out of a sow's ear, especially in places like the Baltic states, but better that than playing dog-in-the-manger and getting suspicion and enmity in return. The Declaration on Liberated Europe, agreed to at Yalta, called for the kind of openness and political freedom enjoyed in the United States and Britain. But that was no rhetorical "victory" over the Soviet Union. Rather, it served to raise expectations for the war's outcome to unrealistic levels, and helped guarantee that American and British frustrations and disillusionment would, as after the First World War, intensify tensions. Only this time it became the Cold War.[29]

The conventional wisdom is that the Grand Alliance was collapsing by March/April 1945. But that confuses difficulties with disaster. Stalin took a hard line in Poland and eastern Europe, consolidating his control with ruthless brutality. FDR and Churchill had fully expected the Soviet Union to impose firm control, but had hoped for at least the cosmetics of plebiscites in the Balkans (which pro-Soviet elements were bound to win with the Red Army standing by), and with a superficially independent Polish government. But no Polish political group that was "friendly" to the Soviet Union could get elected, so Stalin installed his own set of puppets. Churchill hoped to have things both ways. Even while he tried to persuade Roosevelt to get tough with Stalin, the prime minister instructed his government not to complain since Stalin was living up to his commitment about leaving Greece to Britain. Cooperation remained an objective. The Grand Alliance – international leadership by the Great Powers – still existed, and would continue to do so until the end of the Cold War.

Perhaps Stalin's most prescient comment, however dubious his history, on the nature of the postwar world sums up the problems faced by the Grand Alliance:

[A]fter this war all States would be very nationalistic. . . . The feeling to live independently would be the strongest. Later, economic feelings would prevail, but in the first period they would be purely nationalistic and therefore groupings would be unwelcome. The fact that Hitler's regime had developed nationalism could be seen in the example of Yugoslavia where Croats, Montenegrins, Slovenes, &c. all wanted something of their own. It was a symptom.[30]

It was more than a symptom; it was a fact. It took Germans and Czechs and Poles and Balts and Slovaks and others a half-century to achieve their nationalist aspirations, but it was they who caused the collapse of the Soviet Empire.

FDR's death quickly ended cooperation as the watchword as the new president, Harry Truman, took advice from those advisers of FDR who had swung to a get-tough approach to the USSR. That did not cause the Cold War, which had antecedents that stretched from 1917 to the Polish independence crisis. But it did create a meaner, more confrontational, scarier world.

## NOTES

1   Grand sweeping histories like this *Companion to the International History of the Twentieth Century* depend on periodization to create intellectually digestible pieces of related information. But some chronologically short chunks of important, world-shaping history do not fit comfortably or logically into either the period before or the era that follows. The brevity of the Second World War – a massive, worldwide struggle – has made the international history of the Second World War begin to disappear, particularly under the icy onslaught of the Cold War. For a fuller discussion see Warren F. Kimball, "The Incredible Shrinking War: The Second World War – Not (Just) the Origins of the Cold War," *Diplomatic History* 25 (2001): 347–65.

2   Whether or not Churchill used the phrase during the Second World War, it gained no currency until after the publication of his memoir/history. He obviously took the term from the successful diplomacy of his forebear John Churchill, the 1st Duke of Marlborough, who had, in the 1690s, created what became known as the Grand Alliance against Louis XIV of France. Winston Churchill, who thought of Marlborough as a model, always thought in terms of personal diplomacy and used the term to describe the Big Three leaders and their states – the United States, the USSR, and Great Britain – whatever his references to the

British War Cabinet being "at once surprised and thrilled by the scale on which the Grand Alliance was planned." The quotation, which is from Churchill, *The Second World War* [*SWW*] 6 vols. (Boston: Houghton Mifflin, 1948–53), vol. 3, *The Grand Alliance*, p. 665, is the only use of that term, other than the volume title, found in any of the six volumes. For the history of that history, see David Reynolds, *In Command of History* (London: Allen Lane/Penguin, 2004).

3   Churchill's comment is in his *SWW*, vol. 6, *Triumph and Tragedy*, p. 393. The context and details of the Atlantic Conference and Charter of August 1941 can be found in Douglas Brinkley and David Facey-Crowther, eds., *The Atlantic Charter* (New York: St. Martin's, 1994).

4   The quotes are from Theodore Wilson, *The First Summit* (Lawrence, KS: University Press of Kansas, rev. edn, 1991), p. 149, and Lloyd Gardner, "The Atlantic Charter: Idea and Reality, 1942–1945," in *The Atlantic Charter*, ed. Brinkley and Facey-Crowther, pp. 45–81.

5   Djilas quoting Stalin as cited in Georg Schild, *Bretton Woods and Dumbarton Oaks* (New York: St. Martin's, 1995), p. 175; Churchill as quoted in Raymond Callahan, *Churchill: Retreat from Empire* (Wilmington, DE: Scholarly Resources, 1984), p. 185. Churchill wrote similarly to Eden in January 1942; Churchill, *The Grand Alliance*, p. 696.

6   Roosevelt to Wayne Coy, August 2, 1941, *F.D.R. His Personal Letters, 1928–1945*, 3 vols., ed. Elliott Roosevelt (New York: Duell, Sloan, and Pearce, 1950), vol. 2, pp. 1195–6.

7   Churchill genially lifted the phrase from a speech by his foreign secretary and inserted it in a speech to the House of Commons on July 12, 1954; Geoffrey Best, *Churchill and War* (London and New York: Hambledon, 2005), p. 240.

8   Oleg A. Rzheshevsky, ed., *War and Diplomacy: The Making of the Grand Alliance* (Amsterdam: Hardwood Academic, 1996), doc. 70 (record of talks between Molotov and Roosevelt, May 29, 1942), pp. 177–8.

9   Rzheshevsky, *War and Diplomacy*, doc. 38 (Moscow to Molotov, May 24, 1942), p. 122.

10  See all the documents in Rzheshevsky, *War and Diplomacy*, pp. 163–261, but especially docs. 71, 72, 81, 83, 94, and 100. Italics added. *Molotov Remembers*, ed. Felix Chuev and Albert Resis (Chicago: Ivan R. Dee, 1993), pp. 45–6.

11  Warren F. Kimball, *Forged in War* (New York: Morrow, 1997), p. 142; Martin Gilbert, *Road to*

*Victory* (Boston: Houghton Mifflin, 1986), p. 121.

12 The "pull of the Pacific" was heightened by American naval victories in the Pacific. In fact, by June 1942, US forces had halted the Japanese advance in the Southwest Pacific, ended Japanese carrier-based air superiority in the Pacific, and regained the balance of sea power in that theater of operations.

13 Churchill, *SWW*, vol. 4, *The Hinge of Fate*, p. 383.

14 The short quotes in the preceding two paragraphs are taken from various sources cited in Kimball, *Forged in War*, pp. 148–59, plus one from Churchill, *The Hinge of Fate*, p. 481.

15 Churchill as quoted in Gilbert, *Road to Victory*, p. 313.

16 If the conquest of Sicily went well and quickly, Italy would be next – although Churchill pushed so hard for a formal commitment that Roosevelt got annoyed and, according to Stimson, told the prime minister that he had better "shut up." Kimball, *Forged in War*, p. 214.

17 Arguments that unconditional surrender was a tragedy and that it lengthened the war are premised on a canard – that a strong Germany at the end of the Second World War would have somehow prevented Soviet occupation of eastern Europe and won the Cold War even before it started. In reality, the likely result of an Anglo-American settlement with the German generals (assuming the unlikely prospect of a successful coup against Hitler) that excluded the Soviets would have been either Europe engulfed by a Soviet–German war or a Soviet–German alliance.

18 Eden to Halifax, January 22, 1942, FO 954/29xc/100818, Public Record Office (PRO); E. L. Woodward, ed., *British Foreign Policy in the Second World War* (London: HMSO, 1971), vol. 3, pp. 9–10; US Department of State, *Foreign Relations of the United States* (hereafter *FRUS*) (Washington: USGPO, 1862–), 1943, vol. 3, p. 13; Robert E. Sherwood, *Roosevelt and Hopkins: An Intimate History* (New York: Harper, rev. edn, 1950, pp. 708–9); Department of State [Harley Notter], *Postwar Foreign Policy Preparation, 1939–1945* (Washington: USGPO, 1950), pp. 92–3, 96–7; and *Post World War II Foreign Policy Planning: State Department Records of Harley A. Notter* (microform: Bethesda, MD, 1987), file 548-1 (a summary of contacts with the president).

19 As quoted in John L. Harper, *American Visions of Europe* (New York: Cambridge University Press, 1994), p. 113.

20 For the Molotov–Roosevelt conversations of May–June 1942 and Stalin's strong endorsement of FDR's thinking, see Rzheshevsky, *War and Diplomacy*, docs. 68, 77, 82, 83; and *FRUS*, 1942, vol. 3, pp. 573–4. Citations to the other quotes can be found in Kimball, *Forged in War*, p. 368 n.11. For more references to the "policemen" idea, see Warren F. Kimball, "The Sheriffs: FDR's Postwar World," in D. Woolner, W. Kimball, D. Reynolds, eds. *FDR's World: War, Peace, and Legacies* (New York: Palgrave Macmillan, 2008), 91–121.

21 *FRUS*, 1943, vol. 3, p. 39.

22 The so-called Polish Question is far too complex and lengthy to cover in this essay. Suffice to say that nationalism, religion, and politics all combined to make an inflammatory mix. The realities of war, Polish intransigence, and the need to maintain the Grand Alliance and extend it to Japan prevented the Anglo-Americans from giving the Poles anything more than private and empty reassurances.

23 Too much has been made of FDR's acceptance of Stalin's invitation to stay at the Soviet embassy. Even Churchill agreed that travel through Teheran's streets by FDR should be avoided, while both men correctly assumed that their quarters were "bugged" with Soviet electronic listening devices. The conference met from November 28 through December 2.

24 Kimball, *Forged in War*, p. 259. Field Marshal Lord Alanbrooke, *War Diaries, 1939–1945*, ed. Alex Danchev and Daniel Todman (Berkeley and Los Angeles: University of California Press, 2001), p. 480.

25 *FRUS, Tehran Conference*, pp. 530–2, 595–6, 622; Kimball, *The Juggler: Franklin Roosevelt as Wartime Statesman* (Princeton, NJ: Princeton University Press, 1991) p. 110; Earl of Avon, *The Reckoning* (London: Cassell, 1965), p. 437.

26 Churchill, *SWW*, vol. 5, pp. 395–7; *FRUS, Tehran Conference*, pp. 512, 599. Stalin's firm preference for dismemberment of Germany is one of the few instances where the British and American records are not seconded by the published Soviet record.

27 FDR is quoted in Dallek, *Franklin D. Roosevelt and American Foreign Policy* (New York: Oxford University Press, 1979), pp. 436–7. Churchill to Eden (January 7, 1944) as quoted in Gilbert, *Road to Victory*, p. 641.

28 The State Department statement is printed in USSR, Ministry of Foreign Affairs, *Stalin's Correspondence with Roosevelt and Truman, 1941–*

*1945* (New York: Capricorn Books, 1965), p. 176.

29   This summarizes arguments I have made in "The Sheriffs."

30   Minutes of the TOLSTOY conference as quoted in Gilbert, *Road to Victory*, p. 1026.

## GUIDE TO FURTHER READING

Edward M. Bennett, *Franklin D. Roosevelt and the Search for Victory: American–Soviet Relations, 1939–1945* (Wilmington, DE: Scholarly Resources, 1990). An important study of US–Soviet relations during the Second World War.

Douglas Brinkley and David Facey-Crowther, eds., *The Atlantic Charter* (New York: St. Martin's, 1994). Essays by leading scholars on this aspect of the Anglo-American relationship.

David Carlton, *Churchill and the Soviet Union* (Manchester: Manchester University Press, 2000). An intriguing study of Churchill's changing attitudes toward the Soviet Union.

Robert Dallek, *Franklin D. Roosevelt and American Foreign Policy* (New York: Oxford University Press, 1979). A solid broad survey of Franklin Roosevelt's foreign policies.

Lloyd C. Gardner, *Spheres of Influence: The Great Powers Partition Europe from Munich to Yalta* (Chicago: Ivan R. Dee, 1993). A succinct, focused look at the Grand Alliance and wartime diplomacy related to peacemaking.

Martin Gilbert, *Road to Victory* (Boston: Houghton Mifflin, 1986). The Second World War volume in the official Churchill biography.

Warren F. Kimball, *The Juggler: Franklin Roosevelt as Wartime Statesman* (Princeton, NJ: Princeton University Press, 1991) and *Forged in War* (New York: Morrow, 1997). Essays on FDR's foreign policies, and a more general study of the Grand Alliance.

Wm. Roger Louis, *Imperialism at Bay* (New York: Oxford University Press, 1977). The best in-depth survey of the wartime pressures on the British for decolonization.

David Reynolds, *In Command of History* (London: Allen Lane/Penguin, 2004). The definitive study of the writing of Churchill's war memoir, and of how that written history squared with the events.

Oleg A. Rzheshevsky, ed., *War and Diplomacy: The Making of the Grand Alliance* (Amsterdam: Hardwood Academic, 1996). A collection of previously unpublished and unavailable documents from Soviet sources, this invaluable collection explains much of Stalin's thinking in the 1941–3 period.

Georg Schild, *Bretton Woods and Dumbarton Oaks* (New York: St. Martin's, 1995). A solid, useful summary of two conferences that laid out much of the postwar economic structure and set up the United Nations Organization.

Theodore Wilson, *The First Summit* (Lawrence, KS: University Press of Kansas, rev. edn, 1991). A broadly conceived study of the Atlantic Conference between Churchill and Roosevelt, the meeting that set the parameters for the Anglo-American wartime alliance.

# CHAPTER TWENTY-THREE

# A Bipolar World

## SAKI RUTH DOCKRILL

A bipolar world is used as a shorthand description of the world during the Cold War. By 1950, Europe and some parts of Asia were roughly divided into two blocs, one supporting the western liberal democratic capitalist system, the other pursuing the creation of a pan-communist world. Each side feared the expansionist aims of the other, a fear which was fed by mutual misperceptions and a lack of understanding of each other. This meant that each side tended to depict the other in the worst possible light, which in turn created a situation whereby both sides misread the other's intentions and overestimated each other's capabilities. The possession of nearly 50,000 nuclear weapons by the two superpowers made the confrontation deadly, while the East–West ideological competition added to the dynamic to expand, and intensify, the Cold War worldwide. One of the most striking images of a bipolar world can be found in a conversation between the American president, Ronald Reagan, and the Soviet leader, Mikhail Gorbachev, at Geneva in November 1985. Reagan told Gorbachev that: "Here you and I are, two men in a room, probably the only two men in the world who could perhaps bring about peace in the world . . . Mr. General Secretary, we don't mistrust each other because we are armed; we are armed because we mistrust each other."[1]

The superpowers attempted to regulate their activities in the nuclear sphere and "cooperated" in an effort to moderate the threat caused by their ability to destroy the world with their nuclear weapons. Moreover, they also competed with each other in waging "peace" – an attempt to outdo each other by winning international support for their respective causes, as instanced by a series of so-called peace offensives launched by the post-Stalin Kremlin leadership in the mid-1950s. With some notable exceptions, they also refrained from meddling in each other's spheres of influence for fear that this might provoke the other side to embark on a general war – indeed, the Cuban missile crisis demonstrated the extreme danger of such meddling. Furthermore, Washington and Moscow had to some extent shared a political interest in avoiding responsibility for intensifying the Cold War, although they blamed each other for creating difficulties in the way of achieving world peace. Thus, mistrust, hostility, tension, cooperation, and competition were the tidal patterns of the Cold War. Invariably a period of rising superpower tension was followed by a thaw, while often a thaw was followed by another tense period. The short-lived Geneva détente, for instance, preceded the Berlin and Cuban missile crises, which were followed by a relatively quiet period in Europe in the 1960s, by détente in the early 1970s, then a further phase of rising superpower tension in the Third World by the mid-1970s. In September 1989, Deputy Secretary of State Lawrence Eagleburger declared that: "For all its risks and uncertainties, the Cold War was characterized by a remarkably stable and predictable set of relationships among the great powers."[2]

## Differences between the Western and Eastern Blocs

The image of bipolarity masked the differences between these two blocs, however. The Soviet Union had never been co-equal with the United States: not only were there disparities of economic and military power between them, but their very different ideologies and histories created profoundly different states, each of which led a bloc – one consisting of mostly liberal democratic capitalist societies, the other of authoritarian socialist state regimes. Confrontation between the blocs was most conspicuous in Europe, where the Soviet threat helped to unify, and maintain, a coherent outlook on the part of the Atlantic alliance, and where the fear of Soviet coercive power pulled the Warsaw Pact together.

The US, born out of revolution and war, regarded itself (like the Soviet Union) as an anti-colonial and an anti-imperialist power, and retained a deep sense of "vulnerability to external pressures in a world of scheming nations." This, combined with the United States' earlier experiences with the European imperial powers, codified its mental map in the form of isolationism, which was expressed in the early part of the twentieth century as preferring neutrality and avoiding close entanglement with European powers. The sense of vulnerability to external threats and the rejection of European interventionism further cultivated America's incentive to pursue bona fide independence and to achieve "national greatness."[3] Even after 1945, when the US was increasingly taking on global responsibilities from the former European imperial powers, there remained a strong feeling in Washington that America's commitment to European security was a stopgap solution. Once western Europe had recovered from the economic exhaustion caused by the previous war, Washington assumed that Europeans should take the chief responsibility for the defense of western Europe. The exigency of the Cold War compelled the US to lead a peacetime alliance with western Europe under the North Atlantic Treaty Organization (NATO), but the word

"Europe" was omitted from the title to pacify the Euroskeptics in Congress.[4] Once the Soviet Union was identified as the source of the threat to the western world, the Americans fought the Cold War on the assumption that "if you are not with us, you are against us," an assumption that figured more prominently in American society than in its western European counterparts. Ronald Reagan called the Soviet Union an "evil empire," while the current US president, George W. Bush, has defined all terrorism as "evil."[5]

Europeans invariably exhibited different ideologies and methodologies in tackling the Cold War. At the outbreak of the Cold War, France and Britain sought to achieve an independent western Europe as a "third force" by utilizing the resources of Europe's colonial possessions in Africa and the Middle East. It was important for them to recover their Great Power status, and such a third power bloc might become strong enough to withstand the Soviet monolith and to keep the Soviet–US confrontation at arm's length. These European powers regarded the US as an isolationist country, which could not be relied upon in peacetime. For example, the British Foreign Office envisaged in March 1944 that in the case of a future collaboration with the United States, the Americans were bound to follow "our lead," as Britain had "the capacity to guide and influence them." Admittedly the United States was now an "enormous power," but this acceptance was qualified by the statement: "it is the power of the reservoir behind the dam, which may overflow uselessly, or be run through pipes to drive turbines."[6]

After 1945, European leaders foresaw a competitive and anarchic world system where national and territorial rivalries would continue, and in the process they feared that they might be forced to take up arms again against Germany and/or the rising power, the Soviet Union. What proved to be a "long peace" since 1945 was not readily foreseen by the Europeans.[7] The two devastating world wars, which had ruined the European continent, were constantly in the minds of the Europeans. Moreover, war in the atomic age was no longer seen as a practical means of resolving national differences. With or without the Cold War, European leaders were looking for ways to avoid military conflicts and to manage the new

(Soviet) and old (German) security threats by non-military means. During the Cold War, the Europeans were thus more concerned to reduce rather than eradicate the Soviet threat, and looked for a window of opportunity in which to employ diplomacy to alleviate the Soviet fear of the West. They preferred an unostentatious and slow process of détente with the East as the best strategy.

Britain had good reason to feel proud in 1945. Despite its economic exhaustion, the Second World War had left Britain's institutions largely intact. It was not until 1949 that Whitehall formally adopted Atlanticism with Anglo-American relations at its core. This was the framework on which Britain's strategies were constructed throughout the Cold War years. Anglo-American relations provided London with an opportunity to participate in, and influence, Washington's decision-making, and this was reckoned to be more economical and feasible than increasing Britain's commitment to the security of western Europe.[8] France was another proud nation, but was in most Cold War years obsessed with the possible adversarial effects on its national security if a defeated Germany, once recovered, began to flex its muscles in Europe. France believed that the wartime Big Three had divided up Europe in the absence of France, and was even more resentful at the domination of postwar Europe by the superpowers. The perceived Soviet threat compelled Paris to agree to NATO, but it feared that the new organization might quicken the process of remilitarizing western Germany like "the yoke of the egg."[9] France wanted a Europe governed by Europeans and led by the French, and free of any single or combined hegemonic control either by the Soviet Union, Germany, or the United States. When the Cold War intensified, the United States took a more heavy-handed interventionist approach toward Europe, which the French resented. On the other hand, when East–West relations relaxed, as in the early 1970s, there was the possibility that the Germans might start thinking about reunifying their country, a prospect which the French regarded with trepidation.

The Federal Republic of Germany felt that its European allies and the Soviet Union had long denied Bonn the option of reunifying its country.

It presented itself as the major victim of the Cold War. It wanted a proper postwar settlement, full independence, and the eventual reunification of Germany in a climate of deep détente with the East, although by the 1980s this possibility was regarded as too remote to contemplate. Two important and often competing priorities governed West Germany's foreign policy throughout the Cold War: the transatlantic relationship and the Franco-German rapprochement, both of which provided Bonn with security, power, and influence in postwar Europe.

In the main, the West fought the Cold War with two main strategies: deterrence and containment. After the Cuban missile crisis, détente also became part of a formal NATO strategy to promote an improvement in East–West relations. After the death of Josef Stalin in 1953, NATO was inclined to believe that the prospect of a Third World War was unlikely except by accident or miscalculation. Nevertheless, there was still great uncertainty in the West concerning Soviet military intentions. At the time of the Soviet invasion of Afghanistan in 1979, a famous theorist of international relations, Hans Morgenthau, gloomily predicted that "the world is now moving ineluctably towards a third world war – strategic nuclear war. I do not believe that anything can be done to prevent it."[10] As another scholar has recently put it: "On a medical analogy, the West by the 1980s had become well informed about Soviet anatomy and physiology; but the windows to the antagonist's mind remained largely opaque."[11]

Perhaps the main strength of the West was its belief that the Soviet system would eventually decay and that democratic/capitalist values would eventually prevail. If this seemed ideologically complacent, it was supported by reality. Economic globalization, especially after the 1970s, continuously expanded, almost "leading a life of its own."[12] The United States and other industrialized countries in the West were the leaders of the "information revolution" in the 1980s. In other words, capitalism and democracy were two existing currencies of the western order. Despite occasional difficulties in balancing the public sector against the private within the market economy, the West had long practiced this method and was not looking for an alternative. As far as the West was concerned, the Cold War was a waiting game that they were bound to win in time. By contrast, the eastern bloc was handicapped by the fact that it was experimenting with the application of Marxist-Leninist theory.

The Soviet Union, born out of the October 1917 Bolshevik Revolution, was ideologically driven to weaken its capitalist competitors and to promote socialist revolutions elsewhere in the world. The Kremlin assumed that its ideology put it on the right side of history, whereas the capitalist countries were bound to quarrel with each other and eventually collapse. Stalin, Nikita Khrushchev, Leonid Brezhnev, and Gorbachev all believed in Marxism-Leninism. During the Stalin years (1928–53), attention to geopolitics and security became equally important in his calculations, but ideology occasionally reared its ugly head as a morale booster. It invariably emboldened Stalin's approach to the West, and in other times it helped the Soviet leader to underestimate the West's determination to respond to the perceived Soviet threat.

If Stalin was a complicated, ruthless, but immensely insecure dictator, Khrushchev in the 1950s tried to make some adjustments to the Soviet system which would make it more faithful to Marxism-Leninism. In doing so, Khrushchev needed to be optimistic, and what he believed became almost what he saw. In 1961 he raised hopes when he declared that Soviet socialism was so advanced that by the end of the next decade it would surpass the production of the United States and be in a position to construct a true communist society. His successor, Brezhnev, was a man who believed in using military might as a tool to challenge the West. This did not make the ideological goal of achieving a communist society any easier, however. Twenty years after Khrushchev's speech, Brezhnev had to tone down his predecessor's rosy prediction and substitute the rhetoric of gradual progress. In Brezhnev's words, Soviet society was "proceeding to communism through the stage of 'developed socialism'" and was one step behind "advanced" socialism. By 1987 references to "developed socialism" were dropped and replaced by "developing socialism," suggesting that the creation of a communist society remained

a long way off.[13] Similarly, the idea of exporting Soviet-style socialism encountered some difficulties: China, Yugoslavia, and Albania had decided to depart from Moscow's version of Marxism.

The Soviet Union and the eastern bloc were also aware that NATO's strategy was defensive, but this did not dispel the fear that NATO might attack the East. Prior to his decision to invade Czechoslovakia in 1968, Brezhnev, fearing that Soviet repressive measures might provoke the West into war against Moscow, took refuge in heavy sedation, which became a permanent habit.[14] It was a great relief to him when the West did not react adversely to the Warsaw Pact's invasion of Czechoslovakia, which he attributed to the growing military power of the Soviet Union. Just as the West viewed the Soviet Union as the main threat to western civilization, the Soviet Union saw the East–West contest as an "irreconcilable" struggle; just as Washington interpreted American gains as Soviet losses, Moscow interpreted pro-Americanism as anti-Sovietism.

Nevertheless, within the communist bloc there were significantly different approaches to, and perceptions of, the world. Their leaders imposed their own rules on their citizens and the stability of the bloc depended upon the elimination of actual or potential anti-establishment individuals. There was no rule of law, since the Communist Party was above the law. The Warsaw Pact was initially a strategic response to the West's idea of rearming West Germany within NATO, but thereafter served to keep eastern Europe together under the sole leadership of the USSR. Its unity owed much to Soviet coercive power, which culminated in the Brezhnev Doctrine in 1968 and, to a lesser extent, to ideological cohesion under the slogans of "proletarian solidarity" and "socialist internationalism." When Gorbachev reduced the role of ideology and made deep cuts to the Soviet military, and when "popular resentment" against Soviet imperialism "outweighed the lingering public concerns about Germany," the *raison d'être* for the Warsaw Pact no longer existed.[15]

While both sides appreciated the need to avoid a final battle between them if the globe was to survive, the Cold War was far from a "long peace." The Cold War world was unstable, unpredictable, and not always peaceful; certainly, few foresaw that the bipolarity that characterized it would disappear peacefully.

## The Emergence of the Bipolar World, 1944–1950

While the emerging bipolarity was foreseen during the Second World War, this was initially a contest between the British and the Soviets over the distribution of power in postwar Europe. In advance of the war's end, British Prime Minister Winston Churchill made "percentage" agreements with Stalin in 1944 to assign spheres of influence whereby the Soviet Union would have a 90 percent predominance in Romania, 75 percent in Bulgaria, 50 percent in Yugoslavia and Hungary, with Britain having 90 percent predominance in Greece. At the end of the Second World War, Stalin was satisfied with the broad acknowledgment by the US and Britain of the "gains" that the Soviet Union had made in eastern Europe.[16] During the Yalta conference in February 1945, the American president, Franklin D. Roosevelt, sought an early US withdrawal from Europe once its occupation duties were completed, and probably within two years. He was more concerned about ameliorating the clashes over spheres of influence between the British and the Soviets, but assumed, as the British Foreign Office did, that the eastern European countries occupied by the Red Army were likely to remain under the Kremlin's control.[17]

There existed a curious mixture of hope and anxiety in the major capitals in the aftermath of the Second World War. Boosted by his perception that the Grand Alliance of the war years elevated the status of the Soviet Union as a great power, Stalin was hopeful that the United States and Britain would be able to help the Soviet Union to recover its wartorn economy, but if not, Stalin would gain by exploiting the rift between Britain and the United States. At issue was how long the West would continue to remain generous about Stalin's demand for security.[18]

Once the dust of the Second World War settled down, Washington was able to engage in critical thinking about the role of the Soviet Union in the postwar world. In February 1946, George Kennan, the architect of American containment

policy, sent his famous long telegram to Washington urging American policymakers to adopt a vigilant attitude toward the Soviet Union, whose interests were incompatible with those of the West. Winston Churchill, during his trip to the US, made his equally famous "iron curtain" speech, pointing out that while the Soviets did not want war, they desired the "fruits of war and the indefinite expansion of their power and doctrines."[19] In 1946, faced with Stalin's ambitions in the Mediterranean (Britain's important security zone), the United States was by this time more determined to resist Soviet pressure in that region. Pressed by Britain to deal with the communist-led guerrilla movement in Greece and the Soviet threat to Turkey, the US in March 1947 announced – as part of the "Truman Doctrine" – that "it must be the policy of the United States, to support free peoples who are resisting attempted subjugation by armed minorities or by outside pressure." This was quickly followed by the Marshall Plan designed to facilitate Europe's economic recovery, thereby rendering it less vulnerable to the communist threat. The defining thrust of the plan was to force the Soviet Union to choose whether or not it wanted to be included in it. Stalin eventually rejected it, as he decided that it was an American attempt to control Europe. The Marshall Plan was, for Moscow, a challenge which Stalin decided to counter with determined opposition.[20] The world was now increasingly divided between the two hostile blocs, led by the United States and the Soviet Union.

The crucial question was the future of a defeated Germany, for both sides had good reason to fear that the other side wanted control of the whole of Germany on its own terms. The final break-up of the Council of Foreign Ministers over Germany at the end of 1947 was followed by a communist coup d'état in Czechoslovakia in February 1948, the subsequent Norwegian fear that the Soviets were about to take over their country, and finally the Berlin crisis of 1948–9. These events helped western Europe, led by Britain, to persuade the US to be included in a peacetime alliance, leading to the treaty that established NATO in April 1949.

The East–West confrontation intensified in 1949 when the successful Soviet test explosion of an atomic bomb in August precipitated America's development of its hydrogen program. In the autumn, two German states were formed: the Federal Republic of Germany (FRG) led by the West, and the German Democratic Republic (GDR) under Soviet control. By then eastern Europe was in a Stalinist straitjacket (with the exception of Yugoslavia, which had rejected Stalin's exclusive control and seceded from the Cominform in June 1948). During these years, the Soviet Union realized that its expansionist policy in Europe had been steadily undermined by western resistance, and this in turn resulted in the opening of the "unwanted Cold War."[21]

## The Globalization of the Bipolar System, 1950–1963

While the East–West confrontation began in Europe, it soon spread to Asia, with the establishment of the People's Republic of China under Mao Zedong in October 1949, followed by the outbreak of the Korean War in June 1950. China was where Lenin's notion of a Communist–Nationalist fusion did not succeed in the late 1920s, and since then Moscow had lost much of its control over the political situation there. The success of communist revolution in China in 1949 was the consequence of the rise of Mao Zedong's CCP and the failures of the corrupt and feeble Nationalist Chinese led by Chiang Kai-shek.

The Korean peninsula was regarded as an important security buffer zone for the Soviet Union. After the Second World War, the former Japanese colony was divided at the 38th parallel, initially for occupation purposes, between the United States in the south and the Soviet Union in the north, but it soon became clear that there could be no superpower agreement on the unification of Korea. By the end of 1948, two independent states were formed: the Republic of Korea (ROK) organized by the anti-communist Syngman Rhee in the south, and the Democratic People's Republic of Korea (DPRK) in the north led by Stalin's protégé, Kim Il Sung. Kim pressed Stalin to accept his plan to unify the country by open war, and Stalin gave the green light to this in the spring of 1950. The Soviet leadership calculated that the United States, having withdrawn its

troops from South Korea in 1949, would be most unlikely to return to the peninsula. Although Stalin continued to dread the possibility of American intervention if Kim went ahead with his military adventure, he hoped to expand the buffer zone along his border, to create a springboard against Japan which could be used in a future global conflict, to test American resolve, to intensify the hostility between Beijing and Washington, and finally – and most importantly – to draw US power away from Europe (and the German question), and test the Western Alliance.[22] However, the North's invasion provoked a swift intervention by American-led troops under a UN mandate, which in turn led China to join the war on the side of North Korea. All this turned the Korean conflict into one of the most horrendous hot wars during the Cold War.

Stalin had mistaken NATO as an American political tool designed to prevent the collapse of the capitalist system, and had not taken it seriously when it was formed.[23] However, the Korean War confirmed the suspicions of westerners that Stalin was embarking on a new offensive, and they enhanced the morale of the Atlantic alliance under Washington's firm control.[24] The US now urged its European allies to rearm, increased American troops and assistance in Europe, and established the Supreme Allied Headquarters Europe (SHAPE) in 1951, which was headed by American wartime hero General Dwight D. Eisenhower as Supreme Allied Commander in Europe (SACEUR). NATO was enlarged eastwards with Greece and Turkey joining the organization in 1952. In return for America's much deeper commitment to the defense of Europe, Europeans also agreed to begin negotiations with West Germany about a military contribution, first in the abortive European Defense Community (EDC), and later directly into NATO in 1955.

The German question remained the key to the shape of the Cold War in Europe. Stalin offered, in March 1952, to create a unified, rearmed, and neutral Germany, thereby preparing to abandon East Germany if he could prevent the FRG from being rearmed within NATO. The West, haunted by the memories of the Rapallo Treaty of 1922 (the normalization of relations between the Soviet Union and Germany), with the perceived ganging up of the two countries against the West, as well as by memories of the recent war against the Germans, vehemently objected to a neutral and unified Germany, which might play off the East against the West. It seems that Stalin's offer was somewhat tentative and, as the West suspected, had more to do with his anxiety to thwart NATO's plan for West German rearmament than with the pacification of Europe.[25]

By the time Stalin died, the Cold War was firmly entrenched in the minds of western leaders. The incoming American president, Eisenhower, regarded the Cold War as a long-term, tenacious, and predictable threat to American security, and was determined to fight it through until the Soviet Union changed its system and abandoned its ideology.[26] To be sure, Stalin's death and the subsequent mood of East–West relaxation allowed for the end of the Korean War in July 1953 and the conclusion of the Austrian State Treaty in May 1955. Khrushchev tried to divorce himself from Stalin's repressive rule by making his "de-Stalinization" speech during the 20th Party Congress in 1956, while encouraging eastern Europeans to take their "separate paths to socialism." The Soviet leader upheld the concept of "peaceful coexistence" with capitalism in the age of nuclear weapons, and sought détente with the West, which might give the Soviet Union time to reinvigorate its economy and perhaps enable it to establish its legitimacy as an alternative to the US-led capitalist bloc. It was a different way of challenging the West from the Stalin years, backed by the same aim of weakening, and possibly destroying, NATO. His erratic and often autocratic leadership style did not earn credibility at home or confidence in the West.

In May 1955, the Soviet Union formed the Warsaw Pact (or the Eastern European Assistance Treaty) in order to counter NATO. After all, most eastern European countries were under the Kremlin's exclusive control, and the Soviet Union did not need a collective organization to confirm that. After having failed to prevent West Germany from becoming a member of NATO, Khrushchev came up with numerous grandiose disarmament plans, including the formulation of a comprehensive new European security system. Once this was accepted, the Soviet leader calculated, the new

security arrangement would replace NATO and the Warsaw Pact. The Warsaw Pact was extended to East Germany in 1956, and it also replaced in 1956–7 Moscow's previous bilateral agreements with the signatory countries (Albania, Bulgaria, Czechoslovakia, Hungary, Poland, and Romania) which sanctioned the Soviet military presence in these countries. In the same year, the pact's political committee and joint military staff were also established in Moscow.

Khrushchev's de-Stalinization backfired in eastern Europe and exposed the limitations of his policy to the world. The uprisings of 1953 in East Germany and 1956 in Hungary were suppressed with the help of the Red Army. In 1955, Khrushchev established diplomatic relations with Yugoslavia, but the latter continued to stay outside the pact. At the end of 1961 Albania, "Stalin's most loyal ally," chose to align itself with Communist China and formally withdrew from the Warsaw Pact in September 1968. Romania also adopted a separatist path after 1956 and resisted Moscow's attempts to control its economy.[27] In 1957, the Polish foreign minister proposed to the UN the creation of nuclear-free zones in West and East Germany, Poland, and Czechoslovakia, assuming that a successful outcome of the plan would help to restrict Soviet military control over these socialist countries. All this demonstrated that the Soviet grip on eastern Europe was weakening.

Khrushchev's relations with Mao Zedong also suffered after his de-Stalinization speech. China had enhanced its prestige and power by its role in the Korean War, and became more confident about dealing with the Soviet Union as an equal partner. Convinced that the western capitalist world was now weaker than that of the communist camp, Mao took an assertive approach toward achieving China's security concerns, resulting in Beijing's attack on the Taiwan offshore islands of 1958, the suppression of the separatist Tibetan rebels, and growing tensions with India. The Soviet Union found an increasingly militant and independent China difficult to deal with, and the relationship between the two powers irrevocably broke down in the early 1960s.[28]

In the West, the transatlantic relationship was strained by the Suez crisis and by America's interest in reducing troops in Europe, but NATO managed to develop a more pragmatic strategy to cope with the growing Soviet nuclear threat. Conventional rearmament imposed by the Korean War was increasingly seen by the European member states as too expensive to achieve, especially in the climate of the 1950s détente. European NATO powers were instead inclined to rest their security on America's extended nuclear deterrence. NATO strategy had incorporated nuclear weapons after 1954 in its planning, but the idea of defeating the Soviet Union increasingly looked apocalyptic (Moscow launched the world earth satellite, the Sputnik, in October 1957, ushering in the missile age). Accordingly, NATO's post-Sputnik strategic aims became less ambitious, limiting its war aims to the preservation of NATO territory.[29]

These moves were not comprehended by the Kremlin. Eisenhower's massive retaliation strategy and his interest in sharing nuclear weapons with the Europeans raised the Kremlin's fear of the nuclearization of West Germany. Partly to prevent this, and also pressed by the East German leader, Walter Ulbricht, to increase his control over West Berlin, Khrushchev sent the West an ultimatum in November 1958, demanding the withdrawal of the western occupation troops from West Berlin and the conclusion of a peace treaty with East Germany. If not, Moscow would be prepared to fight for its ally. The second Berlin crisis, symbolized as it was by the building of the Berlin Wall in central Europe, hardened the division of Europe.[30]

In the Third World the situation was now fluid, with rising numbers of newly independent states as a result of the first wave of postwar decolonization in the Middle East, Africa, and Asia. In 1955, Khrushchev identified the Third World as an area of new competition between the capitalist and communist blocs and reverted to Lenin's dictum of increasing contacts with nationalist elites, who were now regarded as taking a "progressive role" in eventually leading their countries to socialism.[31] Under the banner of Khrushchev's 1961 declaration of "wars of national liberation," the Soviets at first supported the Pathet Lao, but Khrushchev later reached agreement with American President John F. Kennedy for a neutral Laos. However, Moscow's relations with Havana (which began hesitantly, since it at first regarded Castro as an "authentic leader of the leftist bourgeoisie") led to the most memorable superpower crisis of the time when, in October 1962, an American spy plane discovered Soviet nuclear missiles on Cuba (some still were on the way). Khrushchev apparently had numerous motives: to defend the island from what Moscow perceived to be a likely invasion from the United States, to keep the island closer to Moscow (rather than to Beijing), and to use the missiles as a bargaining counter to remove American missiles from Turkey as well as to extract more concessions over Berlin.[32] Ironically, in initiating both the Berlin and Cuban crises, the Soviet Union was not seeking confrontation but wanted to maintain détente with the West. However, the Cuban crisis shows how rational calculations and misperceptions spiraled into the most dangerous confrontation in the nuclear age, which came, in the words of Kennedy's Defense Secretary Robert McNamara, "very, very close" to a superpower nuclear war.[33]

## The Relaxation of Bipolarity, 1963–1979

With the shock of the Cuban missile crisis in 1962, the superpowers began to regulate their activities in the nuclear sphere and to cooperate in an effort to moderate the threat caused by their ability to destroy the world. Following the conclusion in 1963 of the Nuclear Partial Test Ban treaty came the signature of the Nuclear Non-Proliferation Treaty (NPT) in 1968 between the United States, Britain, and the Soviet Union, which was eventually joined by fifty-nine countries. The two superpowers then agreed to achieve a "stable mutual strategic deterrence" by entering into the Strategic Arms Limitations Talks (SALT) in 1969.[34]

During these years (1963–8) the US became heavily involved in fighting the Vietnamese communists. Kennedy's aim was initially to win credibility in the Third World, and to him "Vietnam look[ed] the place."[35] The US sought to make pro-West South Vietnam sufficiently strong to resist Ho Chi Minh's North, but this goal proved to be hard work and eventually became untenable.

While the Americans became trapped in the jungles of Southeast Asia, the Europeans saw an opportunity for détente in Europe. Nobody by then believed in the likelihood of Soviet military aggression. The Europeans reasoned that the Soviet Union was licking its wounds after its failure to "make significant gains by their tough tactics in Berlin and Cuba," was suffering from the recent collapse of the agricultural reform program, and was strained by the increasingly acrimonious Sino-Soviet relationship.[36] By contrast western Europe had, in 1957, successfully created the European Economic Community (EEC), backed by a degree of stability on the basis of the division of Germany.

The first move toward détente came from President Charles de Gaulle of France. He wanted to reduce the United States' control over western Europe and to create favorable conditions for pan-European cooperation. NATO increasingly looked like an obstacle to his plans, and in 1966 France withdrew from NATO's integrated command (although it remained a member of the alliance) and its headquarters were moved from Paris to Brussels. Unfortunately for de Gaulle, the Soviet Union wanted to continue its military build-up and was not disposed to listen to de Gaulle's anti-bloc approach.[37] NATO, however, survived de Gaulle's challenge reasonably well. Despite its close attention to Vietnam, the Lyndon Johnson administration resolved the question of NATO's nuclear sharing by setting up the Nuclear Planning Group (December 1966), accepted in 1967 the new strategy of flexible response, which included options preferred by both Europe and the US, and secured NATO's adoption of the Harmel Report (December 1967) calling for détente and defense, a strategy that served to increase western Europe's pressure for détente in the 1970s.

The Warsaw Pact countries were not so lucky. Their war plans (in the event of the West's attack) continued to aim at defeating and annihilating the NATO powers at all costs. Obsessed with the memories of western invasions (such as during the Russian Civil War and the German attack in 1941), Soviet military planners were determined to carry the battle into enemy territory and were even thinking about the "need to forestall such an invasion" preemptively.[38] After the building of the Berlin Wall in 1961, the Warsaw Pact introduced joint military maneuvers in order to boost morale in the wake of the embarrassing defection of Albania. Under the Soviet operational plan, eastern European troops would chase western Europeans "as far as the Pyrenees, English Channel, and North Sea" with the generous use of nuclear weapons. Romania was scared of such a nuclear outcome, and after the fall of Khrushchev in the autumn of 1964, Bucharest prohibited the use of the country for future Warsaw Pact military exercises and urged the Soviet Union, as Poland had done in the 1950s, to rotate the command of the Warsaw Pact among its member states.

The new secretary general, Leonid Brezhnev, however, took NATO's adoption of the strategy of flexible response as raising the prospect of conventional fighting in Europe, thereby making war more likely. This increased Moscow's incentive to expand conventional (naval and air) capabilities, together with the building up of its nuclear arsenals. However, a militarily strong Soviet Union did not earn much respect from the Warsaw Pact countries, and its first job, as it turned out, was not to defend East Europe against the West but to invade Czechoslovakia in order to suppress liberalization there in August 1968. The death of the "Prague Spring" marked the decline of the legitimacy of communist rule throughout eastern Europe, while the Soviet Communist Party had lost its appeal to fellow communists in western Europe. The younger generation of eastern European intellectuals began to search for a "European" identity as an alternative to subordination to Moscow, although many of their rulers had no choice but to return to conservatism (or "normalization") by closing the doors to the modernization of the communist socioeconomic systems, a situation which persisted into the middle of the 1970s.[39]

The 1970s détente was built around the regional détente in Europe and by a series of American initiatives designed to reduce US tensions with Communist China and the Soviet Union. The subsequent Sino-US rapprochement led to a significant reduction of East–West tension in Asia, ending bipolarity in that part of the world. The Soviet–US détente culminated in the conclusion of the first superpower strategic arms control limitation talks, SALT I. The détente was the result of American President Richard Nixon's skillful exploitation of the widening rift between Beijing and Moscow, and of the West's encirclement of Soviet Russia by bringing China into the western bloc.

In Europe, NATO's strategy for détente helped West Germany to adopt a more assertive policy by breaking the stalemate created by the Berlin Wall. German Chancellor Willy Brandt's Ostpolitik stressed the normalization of West Germany's relations with the Soviet Union and the countries of eastern Europe, including East Germany, and thus meant the renunciation of the Halstein Doctrine of the 1950s. Ostpolitik confirmed the status quo of the two Germanies and the division of Europe, and was therefore welcomed by the Soviet Union. The other aspect of Ostpolitik, that is, change through rapprochement (*Wandel durch Annäherung*), was an attempt to "roll back" communism in eastern Europe in stages. The August 1975 signature of the Helsinki Act by thirty-three eastern (except for Albania) and western European countries as well as the United States and Canada represented the culmination of European détente which began in the late 1960s. The détente provided western Europe with the potential to melt down the Iron Curtain by stealth: increasing trade, cultural, and human contacts with its eastern counterparts would expose eastern Europeans to western democratic and liberal ideas, better consumer goods, and more sophisticated technology, thereby loosening the cohesion of the Soviet bloc. The West rested its hope of breaking down East–West barriers in Basket III of the Helsinki Act, which contained a joint East–West pledge to respect human rights in individual countries. The Soviets accepted the provision, assuming that "no one could seriously expect them to honour" it,[40] but Czech intellectuals tried to persuade the government to defend the human rights of individuals. They produced their manifesto in January 1977, "Charter 77." We now know that the Helsinki accords helped to soften the rigidity of the state socialist system in eastern Europe, while they also encouraged pro-western Soviet thinkers to promote reforms at home.[41]

The Helsinki accords can be seen as part of the "rollback" strategy, utilizing "soft power" in order to reach out to the minds of the peoples behind the Iron Curtain.

By contrast, and in all fairness to the regularities of the bipolar world managed by the superpowers, the 1970s détente took place against a background whereby their power base had begun to erode. While they continued to dominate the military and nuclear fields, their dominance had become less pronounced in other areas. The economic rise of western Europe and of East Asia during the 1960s meant that Britain, Germany, France, and Japan were able to occupy crucial positions in international trade and finance. These changes demanded a new international financial system. In 1973, the US decided to end the dollar's link to gold and to float the dollar against other major currencies. This marked the end of the Bretton Woods system. The superpower 1970s détente largely derived from America's anxiety to decouple Vietnam from the Cold War by appeasing the two communist great powers, China and the Soviet Union, while a relaxation of tension might help the US to fight the Cold War more cheaply.

Détente provided the USSR with another opportunity to confirm its position as a superpower, and Moscow welcomed the West's recognition of the legitimacy of the Soviet Union and its security interests in eastern Europe. The American initiative on détente was beneficial to the Soviet Union: the SALT I treaty gave Moscow an advantage in certain areas, and economically, it received generous American credits and much-needed American grain imports. However, the détente remained limited to Europe and to superpower arms negotiations. It did not apply to Soviet/Cuban activism in Africa, Central America, and elsewhere. It eventually disappeared altogether when the Soviet Union invaded Afghanistan in 1979.

## The Bipolar System under Stress, 1979–1984

The 1970s détente was soon followed by the deterioration of East–West relations. In retrospect, the reasons for this were not difficult to comprehend. Both sides wanted détente in the 1970s, but neither gave up the idea of competition with each other and the desire to prevail over the other.

The Kremlin's optimism that détente would revive after the initial "shock" of the Soviet–Afghan War had subsided was premature. Moreover, it was unfortunate that Moscow had to deal with the newly elected and staunch anti-communist and conservative Republican president, Ronald Reagan, who entered the Oval Office in January 1981. The new president adopted a much tougher stance toward the Soviet Union than had his predecessor, describing it as an "evil empire" and embarking on a major rearmament program. Reagan's angry and desperate mood was reflected not only in government circles but also in public opinion. The United States had been humiliated by the continued captivity of the American hostages in Iran, while America's backyard in Central America was also in turmoil. In Washington's view, it was the Soviet Union who had exploited America's willingness to achieve détente and arms control negotiations, and as a result it must be countered from a position of strength.

In 1983, Reagan launched the Strategic Defense Initiative (SDI) or "Star Wars" – an anti-ballistic missile defense system in space. A successful SDI would intercept and destroy incoming Soviet missiles before they reached the US, thereby nullifying the nuclear deterrent power of the Soviet Union. The SDI deepened the Kremlin's concern about the fate of future arms negotiations with the United States, which were in turn adversely affected by the Soviet shooting down of the South Korean airliner KAL 007 in September 1983.

In Europe, a nuclear crisis began mainly as a result of the introduction of new generations of Soviet missiles in Europe in the mid-1970s. This situation was further complicated by the growing anti-nuclear movements in the major capitals in western Europe. If the United States was unable to address the fear of a nuclear war in Europe by supplying American missiles to counter the Soviet Union's nuclear capabilities there, the White House feared that the situation might lead to "Finlandization," the possibility that West Euro-

peans "might well shrink from actions unpalatable to the Soviets."[42] However, the superpower negotiations over the European missiles or the Intermediate-range Nuclear Forces in Europe (INF) had stalemated and NATO decided to go ahead with the deployment of new American missiles, which began to arrive in Europe in December 1983. In response, the Soviet Union walked out of the superpower nuclear arms negotiations talks; this deteriorating relationship heightened Moscow's fear of a possible military confrontation – the so-called "war scare" of 1983.[43] Thus the picture presented here suggests that the Cold War had once again become the fulcrum of deepening East–West mistrust and anxieties.

However, Reagan's tough approach toward Moscow was gradually softening as early as 1983, and once he had placed his rearmament program in train, he felt confident that he could deal with the Soviet Union. After all, the United States sought to reduce the fear of a Soviet surprise attack, and this could not be attained if East–West relations remained strained. At the end of the 1970s, western Europeans were enjoying the fruits of détente and did not want to see détente collapse as a result of Reagan's hardline approach. Europe's desire for the continuation of détente was reflected in the convening of a conference in Madrid on security and cooperation (CSCE) to uphold the Helsinki accords between 1980 and 1983, while another pan-European negotiation on Mutual and Balanced Force Reductions (MBFR), which had begun in 1973 in an effort to reduce the threat of the Red Army in eastern Europe, also continued into the 1980s. Moscow did not want to increase East–West tension either. The Kremlin wanted to disengage from Afghanistan when conditions there stabilized, while in any case it was more the consequence of Cuban ambitions rather than of Soviet initiative that some of the Third World conflicts intensified in Central America and which had so alarmed many American conservatives in the early 1980s.

Thus, although the Cold War had intensified in the early 1980s, this was contrary to the will of all the key players. Most powers wanted to see the nuclear weapons possessed by both superpowers reduced in number. Washington, despite its rhetoric, was not prepared to fight the Cold War outright at the cost of undermining the credibility of America's global leadership. Reagan's new Cold War policy had its limits and was largely restrained by Congress and the American people, who still suffered from the "Vietnam syndrome." In 1985 the West finally found in the new Soviet leader someone who was prepared to accept that Moscow's interests could be met most effectively by reducing East–West tensions.

## Conclusion: The End of the Bipolar World

The final stage of the bipolar world saw the collapse of communism as a political force. In the process, the Soviet Union, as the leader of the international socialist movement, was much weakened and eventually was unable to exercise control over its spheres of influence in eastern Europe and elsewhere. The country itself disintegrated from within, and collapsed at the end of 1991. Gorbachev was not, of course, seeking to abandon eastern Europe or destroy his own country, let alone concede the Soviet Union's defeat in the Cold War. However, the path he chose, or was sometimes compelled to take, led to the collapse of the Soviet empire in Europe, Moscow's withdrawal of support from its Third World clients, and deep cuts in Soviet nuclear and conventional arms. He also abandoned the international class struggle and resigned as general secretary of the Communist Party of the Soviet Union in August 1991. Overall, he removed the very foundations on which the Soviet Union had exerted its power and influence in the world, and this resulted in the end of the Cold War, thereby the disappearance of the bipolar world.

The rapidity with which the bipolar world disappeared took everyone's breath away. From the outset, Europe was central to the bipolar structure of the world. In the end, it was NATO that came out of the Cold War in remarkably good shape. The fundamental structure of western Europe had hardly undergone any major change in the immediate aftermath of the end of the Cold War. The plans which were put in place before that end were implemented without major alterations, and while the richest country, Germany,

was beset with severe problems in its efforts to absorb eastern Germany into the former Bonn Republic, there were no major upheavals in western Europe as a result of the reunification of Germany. On the contrary, this even helped to give an additional momentum to the French and German leadership to strengthen EC institutions, thereby allowing for more progress in this direction. It was the Soviet Union that held the key to the end of the Cold War in Europe, but in an actual sense it was the Soviet Union that *had to* come around to adopting western values if it sought friendship rather than confrontation with the West. This was why the West was not enthusiastic about Gorbachev's "common European home," which in effect demanded the end of the Cold War "symmetrically," through mutual concessions and an equal role for the Soviet Union with the United States in Europe.[44] The sinews of the bipolar system meant that the solution to the division of Europe could not be found in the establishment of a halfway house. The end of the bipolar world demonstrated that this indeed was the case.

### NOTES

The author is grateful to the British Academy for its generous grant, which enabled her to undertake research in the United States in relation to this chapter.

1  Ronald Reagan, *An American Life* (New York: Simon & Schuster, 1990), p. 13.
2  Michael R. Beschloss and S. Talbott, *At the Highest Levels: The Inside Story of the End of the Cold War* (London: Warner, 1994) p. 106.
3  Richard Crockatt, *American Embattled: September 11, Anti-Americanism and the Global Order* (London: Routledge, 2003), p. 11; Michael Hunt, *Ideology and US Foreign Policy* (New Haven, CT: Yale University Press, 1987), p. 28.
4  Lawrence Kaplan, "Alliance," in *Palgrave Advances in Cold War History*, ed. Saki Ruth Dockrill and Geraint Hughes (Basingstoke: Palgrave Macmillan, 2006), p. 116.
5  Saki Ruth Dockrill, *The End of the Cold War Era: The Transformation of the Global Security Order* (London: Hodder Arnold, 2005), pp. 203–28; Jeffrey Record, "Threat Confusion and Its Penalties," *Survival* 46 (2004): 52–3.

6 "The Essentials of an American Policy," March 21, 1944, FO (Foreign Office) 371/28523, the National Archives (hereafter cited as TNA), Kew, England.

7 The concept was coined by John Lewis Gaddis; see his *The Long Peace: Inquiries into the History of the Cold War* (New York: Oxford University Press, 1987).

8 Saki Dockrill, *Britain's Retreat from East of Suez: The Choice between Europe and the World?* (Basingstoke: Palgrave Macmillan, 2002), pp. 11–12.

9 Pierre Mélandri, *Les États-unis face à l'unification de l'Europe, 1945–1954* (Paris: Pedone, 1980), p. 289.

10 John Mueller, *The Remnants of War* (Ithaca, NY: Cornell University Press, 2004), p. 81.

11 Peter Hennessy, *The Secret State: Whitehall and the Cold War* (London: Allen Lane, 2002), p. 5.

12 Ian Clark, *Globalization and Fragmentation: International Relations in the Twentieth Century* (New York: Oxford University Press, 1997), p. 172.

13 Stephen White, *After Gorbachev* (New York: Cambridge University Press, 1993), pp. 224–5.

14 Vladislav M. Zubok, "The Brezhnev Factor in Détente, 1968–1972," in *Cold War and the Policy of Détente: Problems and Discussions*, ed. N. I. Yegorova (Moscow: Russian Academy of Sciences, 2003), pp. 291–2.

15 Mark Kramer, "Ideology and the Cold War," *Review of International Studies* 25 (1999): 552–3.

16 Alan Bullock, *Hitler and Stalin: Parallel Lives* (London: HarperCollins, 1991), p. 867.

17 John Kent, "British Postwar Planning for Europe, 1942–45," in *The Failure of Peace in Europe, 1943–48*, ed. Antonio Varsori and Elena Calandri (Basingstoke: Palgrave Macmillan, 2002), pp. 22–3.

18 Vladislav Zubok and Constantine Pleshakov, *Inside the Kremlin's Cold War: From Stalin to Khrushchev* (Cambridge, MA: Harvard University Press, 1996), p. 30.

19 Martin Gilbert, *Never Despair: Winston S. Churchill 1945–1965* (London: Heinemann, 1988), p. 202.

20 Zubok and Pleshakov, *Inside the Kremlin's Cold War*, pp. 104–8; Mikhail M. Narinskii, "The Soviet Union and the Marshall Plan," in *Failure of Peace in Europe*, ed. Varsori and Calandri, pp. 275–86.

21 Vojtech Mastny, *The Cold War and Soviet Insecurity: The Stalin Years* (New York: Oxford University Press, 1996), p. 23.

22 For the outbreak of the Korean War, see Kathryn Weathersby, "'Should We Fear This?' Stalin and the Danger of War with America," *Cold War International History Project* (hereafter *CWIHP*) *Working Paper* 39 (2002); and Weathersby, "Soviet Aims in Korea and the Origins of the Korean War, 1945–1950," *CWIHP Working Paper* 8 (1994). See also James Hershberg, "Russian Documents on the Korean War, 1950–1953," *CWIHP Bulletin* 14/15 (2003–4): 369–84.

23 N. I. Egorova, "Soviet Leaders' Perceptions of NATO and the Decision-Making Process," in *L'Europe: de l'Est et de l'Ouest dans la Guerre froide, 1948–1953*, ed. Saki Dockrill et al. (Paris: Presses de l'Université Paris-Sorbonne, 2002), pp. 217–26.

24 Saki Dockrill, *Britain's Policy for West German Rearmament, 1950–1955* (Cambridge: Cambridge University Press, 1991), pp. 21–2.

25 See, for example, Gerhard Wettig, "Stalin's Note of 10 March 1952: Historical Context," in *L'Europe: de l'Est et de l'Ouest*, ed. Dockrill et al., pp. 137–49; Charles S. Maier, *Dissolution: The Crisis of Communism and the End of East Germany* (Princeton, NJ: Princeton University Press, 1997), p. 16.

26 Saki Dockrill, *Eisenhower's New Look National Security Policy, 1953–1961* (Basingstoke: Macmillan, 1996), pp. 25–49.

27 R. J. Crampton, *Eastern Europe in the Twentieth Century and After* (London: Routledge, 1997), pp. 308–13.

28 Zubok and Pleshakov, *Inside the Kremlin's Cold War*, pp. 211–35; Odd Arne Westad, "Introduction," in *Brothers in Arms*, ed. Westad (Stanford, CA: Stanford University Press, 1998), pp. 7–32ff.

29 Beatrice Heuser, "Victory in a Nuclear War? A Comparison of NATO and WTO War Aims and Strategies," *Contemporary European History* 7 (1998): 315–18.

30 Harrison Hope, *Driving the Soviets up the Wall: Soviet–East German Relations, 1953–1961* (Princeton, NJ: Princeton University Press, 2003), pp. 97–132ff.

31 Wayne P. Limberg, "Soviet Military Support for Third-World Marxist Regimes," in *The USSR and Marxist Revolutions in the Third World*, ed. Mark N. Katz (New York: Woodrow Wilson International Center for Scholars, 1990), p. 60.

32 Piero Gleijeses, *Conflicting Missions: Havana, Washington, and Africa, 1959–1976* (Chapel Hill, NC: University of North Carolina Press, 2002), p. 18.

33  James G. Blight and Janet M. Lang, eds., *The Fog of War: Lessons from the Life of Robert S. McNamara* (London: Rowman & Littlefield, 2005), p. 196.

34  Christoph Bluth, "Strategic Nuclear Weapons and US–Russian Relations: From Confrontation to Co-operative Denuclearization?" *Contemporary Security Policy* 15 (1994): 80.

35  Lawrence Freedman, *Kennedy's Wars: Berlin, Cuba, Laos, and Vietnam* (Oxford: Oxford University Press, 2000), p. 317.

36  Dockrill, *Britain's Retreat*, p. 27.

37  Frédéric Bozo, "Détente versus Alliance: France, the United States and the Politics of the Harmel Report (1964–1968)," *Contemporary European History* 7 (1998): 343–60.

38  Heuser, "Victory in a Nuclear War?," p. 320.

39  Arne Odd Westad, "Introduction," in *The Soviet Union in Eastern Europe 1945–89*, ed. Westad, Sven Holtsmark, and Iver B. Neumann (Basingstoke: Macmillan, 1994), p. 5.

40  Vojtech Mastny, *Helsinki, Human Rights, and European Security: Analysis and Documentation* (Durham, NC: Duke University Press, 1986), pp. 7–8, 11.

41  Robert English, "The Road(s) Not Taken: Causality and Contingency in Analysis of the Cold War's End," in *Cold War Endgame*, ed. William C. Wohlforth (University Park, PA: Pennsylvania State University Press, 2003), p. 251; Jussi Hanhimäki, "Ironies and Turning Points: Détente in Perspective," in *Reviewing the Cold War: Approaches, Interpretations, Theory*, ed. Odd Arne Westad (London: Frank Cass, 2000), pp. 326–38.

42  Fraser Harbutt, *The Cold War Era* (Oxford: Blackwell, 2002), p. 274.

43  Anatoly Dobrynin, *In Confidence: Moscow's Ambassador to America's Six Cold War Presidents* (New York: Random House, 1995), pp. 528–30; Aleksandr' G. Savel'yev and Nikolay N. Detinov, *The Big Five: Arms Control Decision-Making in the Soviet Union* (Westport, CT: Praeger, 1995), pp. 163–5.

44  Stephen G. Brooks and William C. Wohlforth, "Economic Constraints and the End of the Cold War," in *Cold War Endgame*, ed. Wohlforth, p. 306.

## GUIDE TO FURTHER READING

Malcolm Byrne and Vojtech Mastny, eds., *A Cardboard Castle? An Inside History of the Warsaw Pact, 1955–1991* (New York: Central European University Press, 2005). The first major comprehensive story of the Warsaw Pact throughout the Cold War.

Richard Crockatt, *The Fifty Years War: The United States and the Soviet Union in World Politics, 1941–1991* (London: Routledge, 1996). A sound analysis of superpower relations.

Anatoly Dobrynin, *In Confidence: Moscow's Ambassador to America's Six Cold War Presidents* (New York: Random House, 1995). A veteran Soviet ambassador's view on the superpower relationship during the Cold War.

Saki Ruth Dockrill, *The End of the Cold War Era: The Transformation of the Global Security Order* (New York: Oxford University Press, 2005). An interpretive account of international history leading to the termination of the Cold War; with Geraint Hughes., eds., *Palgrave Advances in Cold War History* (Basingstoke: Palgrave Macmillan, 2006), a collection of essays with emphasis on the key ideas and concepts relevant to the Cold War.

J. L. Gaddis, *We Now Know* (New York: Oxford University Press, 1997). An interpretive account of the Cold War, 1945–63.

Raymond L. Garthoff, *The Great Transition: American–Soviet Relations and the End of the Cold War* (Washington, DC: Brookings Institution, 1994). A detailed and fascinating account of the end of the Cold War.

Jussi M. Hanhimäki and Odd Arne Westad, *The Cold War: A History in Documents and Eyewitness Accounts* (New York: Oxford University Press, 2003). A useful collection of documents and witness history.

Fraser Harbutt, *The Cold War Era* (Oxford: Blackwell, 2002). An American perspective on the Cold War and its impact on American society.

Beatrice Heuser, "Victory in a Nuclear War? A Comparison of NATO and WTO War Aims and Strategies," *Contemporary European History* 7 (1998): 311–27. A strategic dimension of the Cold War with emphasis on NATO and the Warsaw Pact.

Wilfried Loth, *Overcoming the Cold War* (Basingstoke: Palgrave Macmillan, 2001). A European interpretation of détente as a way of overcoming the Cold War.

Georges-Henri Soutou, *La Guerre de Cinquante Ans: Les relations Est–Ouest 1943–1990* (Paris: Fayard, 2001). A well-researched study of the Cold War in Europe.

Odd Arne Westad, *The Global Cold War: Third World Interventions and the Making of Our Times* (Cambridge: Cambridge University Press, 2005). A well-researched study examining both superpowers' interventionism in the Third World.

N. I. Yegorova, ed., *Cold War and the Policy of Détente: Problems and Discussions* (Moscow: Russian Academy of Sciences, 2003). A collection of essays discussing the politico-strategic dimension of the East–West confrontation.

Vladislav M. Zubok and Constantine Pleshakov, *Inside the Kremlin's Cold War: From Stalin to Khrushchev* (Cambridge, MA: Harvard University Press, 1996). A revisionist account of the middle years of the Cold War as seen from the Soviet Union.

# CHAPTER TWENTY-FOUR

# A Third World?

## NORRIE MACQUEEN

The membership statistics of the United Nations in the post-1945 decades provide a telling insight into the development of the international system after the Second World War. Fifty-one states signed the United Nations Charter at San Francisco in April 1945. Of these, only three were African and eleven from the Asia-Pacific region (including the Middle East). By 1960 there were 100 members of the UN, with the fifty-two Afro-Asian states constituting a slim majority. Twenty years later the United Nations had 150 members of which ninety-one were either African or Asian-Pacific countries. Africa, with fifty-one member states, now formed the largest regional bloc. Over the period, therefore, the Afro-Asian membership of the UN rose from 27 percent to 61 percent of the total. In these thirty-five years the political power of this group of international actors, largely the product of European decolonization, waxed and waned dramatically. At the mid-point the influence of the so-called "Afro-Asian bloc" was at its zenith and its impact on the international relations of the 1960s was considerable. By the beginning of the 1980s, however, although the group had continued to grow in numerical strength, its diplomatic leverage was rapidly declining.

The purpose of this chapter is to trace and account for this trajectory. Our starting point will be to look at the origins of what would come to be known as the "Third World" in the years after 1945. How was the grouping defined? What were

its boundaries? How did it expand and how did it first exert its influence on the bipolar structure of world politics during the Cold War? We will then explore the "institutionalization" of the Third World "movement" in world politics through the agency of the Non-Aligned Movement and in its joint ventures within the United Nations system. Finally, we will pose some questions (even if we cannot answer them wholly satisfactorily) about the Third World, so far as such a thing can still be said to exist in its original form, in the post-Cold War era.

## The Emerging Third World in the 1950s: A Question of Leadership?

The first use of the term "Third World" is usually ascribed to the radical French economist Alfred Sauvy, who wrote in 1952 of a "*tiers monde*."[1] The expression was used by Sauvy as a deliberate parallel with the social structure of pre-revolutionary France. This consisted of "First and Second Estates" composed of the monarchy, nobility, and clergy, and the "Third Estate," which included everyone else whether middle class, peasant, or urban poor. Like the Third Estate, Sauvy argued, the "Third World" aspired to a greater and more respected role in an (international) realm hitherto dominated by a privileged minority (of states). As the Cold War deepened during the 1950s the term evolved to take on a different connotation. The expression was increasingly used in a diplomatic sense to describe a "third force" between the "First World" composed of the capitalist West, and the "Second World" of the communist bloc. This political usage dominated the "discourse" of the Third World throughout the 1950s and 1960s, though by the 1970s the sense of economic weakness and exploitation present in Sauvy's original coinage was gradually reappearing.

The Afro-Asian states that rapidly filled the UN General Assembly as the wave of decolonization grew in the 1950s and 1960s formed only one part of the Third World as it was to emerge. Another component part was already present in the United Nations from the outset, though without the same sense of global self-identity. This was Latin America, twenty countries of which were founder members of the UN. On their own, however, they would have been much slower to develop as a distinct group of actors in world politics. There were two basic reasons for this, economic and political. Firstly, the states of Latin America covered a wide spectrum of economic development. At one end of this were countries like Chile and Argentina, whose ruling elites at least would have identified themselves as part of the "developed" world with economies based to a significant degree in industrial production. At the other were unambiguously underdeveloped countries like Guatemala and Honduras, with economies reliant on "monoculture" (a single cash crop like coffee or bananas). Secondly, at the political level, the western hemisphere as a whole had long been regarded as lying within the sphere of influence of the United States. This had been laid down semi-formally in the "Monroe Doctrine" (named for the fifth president of the United States, James Monroe) in 1823. This declaration by the United States of exclusive interests in the region was intended originally to discourage European imperialist designs on the Caribbean and Latin America. With the beginning of the Cold War the warning was redirected toward the supposed "expansionism" of the Soviet Union. American policy in the region was designed to maintain "friendly" regimes and discourage any left-wing political developments which might open the door to wider communist influence. But with the expanding roll-call of

independent Afro-Asian states in the 1950s and 1960s, a sense of Third World identity became increasingly global and Latin American countries eventually joined in what was described (by Fidel Castro, perpetual bane of the Monroe Doctrine) as a "tricontinental" movement.

The early stages in the development of this movement were exclusively Afro-Asian in inspiration and participation, however. In April 1955 twenty-nine states (representing more than half of the world's population) met in the city of Bandung in Indonesia. Reflecting the uneven nature of decolonization at this stage, only six of the participants were African, though this imbalance in what was to emerge as an "Afro-Asian bloc" would soon be redressed as increasing numbers of black African states became independent and therefore free diplomatic actors. The significance of Bandung was symbolic rather than concrete, though none the less real for that. But the mix of participants at this first "Third World summit" was such that firm agreement on some of the most pressing issues of the time would not be possible. Asian participants included, on one side, Communist China, at that time still a close ally of the Soviet Union, and radical Indonesia. On the other there were dependable allies of the United States like Thailand and the Philippines. Yet overall Bandung was an immensely important stage, emblematically and psychologically, in the forging of a non-aligned identity among the states of the new Third World. Its success in this could be gauged by the diplomatic disquiet that the conference caused in western capitals, throwing into doubt some of the assumptions about the continued diplomatic "loyalty" of the ex-colonial world. In nothing else, Bandung was a shot across the bows of this complacency.

The conference also provided an opportunity for a number of powerful and charismatic national leaders to come together, take the measure of each other, and judge the extent of national advantage in international cooperation. Many of these leaders were still inexperienced and from countries in regions which were inherently unstable in the dying days of colonialism. The opportunity to meet and confer with others in the same circumstances reduced their sense of vulnerability to global forces and held out the tantalizing possibility of a wholly new type of international alliance, one strong enough to confront the Cold War blocs on equal terms. Dominant among these leaders were Nehru of India, Nasser of Egypt, Sukarno of Indonesia, and Nkrumah of Ghana. Later, as the potential for a more permanent diplomatic third force became clear after Bandung, President Tito of Yugoslavia was brought in to the group to emphasize its non-aligned – as opposed to its merely Afro-Asian – character. The diplomatic and ideological aspirations of these five differed enormously. They were able nevertheless to present a unified global vision and to represent a particular sectional interest within it. Their success in working together was undoubtedly aided by the fact that their respective countries occupied widely dispersed regions of the world, and therefore their immediate national interests did not clash in any way. But their achievement was considerable nevertheless.

Jawaharlal Nehru was India's first prime minister. During his long period in office, from independence in 1947 until his death in 1964, he dominated the politics of the subcontinent as well as playing a major role in world politics. The end of Britain's Indian empire was a key event in shaping the post-1945 international system. In the years immediately following the Second World War the end of imperial rule in India and the consequent creation of four new states (India, Pakistan, Ceylon, and Burma) created an entirely new geopolitical region in South Asia. But it also had a larger, symbolic importance, which had global implications. By giving up the "jewel in the crown" of its empire in 1947, effectively without resistance or protest, Britain had signaled the coming end of its imperial role in its entirety. And if Britain, the largest of the European imperialists and the only one which could realistically be described as a wartime victor, was resigned to the end of its empire, the writing was clearly on the wall for the French, Belgian, Portuguese, and Spanish. The political and diplomatic stance of the new Republic of India, the largest and most significant of the successor states in South Asia, would be critical in setting the terms of post-imperial international relations, not only within Asia but also between Asia and the rest of the world.

The initial omens were not encouraging. Independence had come with the partition of the component parts of the "Indian" empire, and relations between the new, predominantly Hindu, India and its new northern neighbor, Muslim Pakistan, began amidst intercommunal massacres on the common border. They were further blighted by territorial conflicts, particularly in relation to Kashmir (which despite having a Muslim population had remained part of India after independence), over which the two countries quickly found themselves at war in 1948. That independent India emerged from these difficulties not only intact but also as a significant and respected international actor was due in great part to Nehru himself. A leading nationalist activist in the last phase of British rule and a close lieutenant of Mohandas Gandhi, Nehru was nevertheless a pragmatic politician whose considerable natural authority and patrician bearing allowed him to integrate easily into the mainstream of international diplomacy. He played a crucial part in Britain's postcolonial adjustment by providing a bridge between the "old" Commonwealth of the white dominions (Australia, Canada, New Zealand, and South Africa – the "colonies of settlement") and the emerging "new" Commonwealth made up predominantly of new states in Asia, Africa, and the Caribbean (the former "colonies of exploitation"). More than some of his fellow Third World leaders, Nehru saw the burgeoning movement primarily in terms of the contribution it could make to the peace and stability of the international system as a whole rather than as a "trade union" committed to securing maximum advantage for its members. The Third World movement which grew out of the Bandung conference should, in Nehru's view, pursue a unified international "ideology." This came to be known as "neutralism." This was quite different from "neutrality," which is a status under international law by which states decline to become involved either in wars or in military alliances. The "ism" in neutralism connotes a positive, proactive approach to potentially destructive bloc politics. The neutralist states, in other words, had a duty to resolve conflicts rather than just stay out of them. And, of course, the prevailing conflict of the 1950s and 1960s was the Cold War between

West and East. Beyond India's involvement with the Afro-Asian group (and, when established, the Non-Aligned Movement) during the seventeen years of Nehru's premiership, India also expressed this commitment to neutralism by taking a leading role in the internal diplomacy of the United Nations and became a leading participant in UN peacekeeping operations.

Gammal Abdel Nasser, president of Egypt, was a very different type of Third World leader, but in his way he had at least as great an impact on world politics as Nehru. Nasser had played a leading part in a coup against the pro-western Egyptian monarchy in 1952, eventually emerging as the unchallenged leader of Egypt in 1954. Domestically, Nasser was a modernizer, committed to pulling a backward and impoverished Egypt into the twentieth century. Regionally, he sought to lead a pan-Arab movement which would unite the various, often squabbling, states of the region. Implacable hostility to Israel was a central part of this strategy as it provided the one unifying issue in the Middle East region. In 1958 Nasser tried to give tangible political reality to the idea of Arab unity when he persuaded the Syrian leadership to create a single "United Arab Republic" (UAR) with Egypt. This was to be the first stage in a longer-term process of Arab unification which would gradually embrace the other countries of the region. But the UAR project proved to be a failure. The fragility rather than the robustness of regional relationships was emphasized when Syria, resentful at Nasser's apparent determination to dominate the arrangement, withdrew in 1961. But the UAR experiment was a measure of the grand (or perhaps grandiose) scale of Nasser's political vision.

Another component of this had already brought Nasser to world attention. The centerpiece of his modernization strategy for Egypt was a vastly ambitious plan for the construction of a high dam on the Nile at Aswan. This, Nasser was convinced, would impel the country forward to economic self-reliance by increasing food production through irrigation schemes and generating enormous hydroelectric capacity which would serve the industrialization of the Egyptian economy. The scheme was to be funded by loans from the World Bank guaranteed by the United States and other western powers. In 1956, however, Nasser's growing diplomatic warmth toward the Soviet Union caused the American administration, on the urging of its secretary of state, the inveterate Cold Warrior John Foster Dulles, to stop the project in its tracks. In response Nasser nationalized the Suez Canal, expropriating it from the Anglo-French company which had owned it. In one stroke, as he conceived it, an alternative source of funding for the Aswan project had been created (from the dues paid by shipping using the canal) and an offensive residue of European imperialism had been summarily removed from Egypt (and, by extension, the former colonial world as a whole). The ensuing crisis reverberated through the international system. The western bloc was split. Britain and France conspired with Israel to "create" a war in the region which would provide an excuse for an Anglo-French invasion. For their part, the Americans were horrified at this imperial reflex and made no secret of the fact. Washington was much more aware than the old imperial capitals of London and Paris of the damage that could be inflicted on the West's prestige and credibility in the emerging Third World by such a backward-looking response to a perceived post-imperial slight. The United States was quicker than its European allies to comprehend the developing competition between East and West for prestige and influence in the new Third World.

The crisis was eventually resolved by the intervention of UN peacekeepers and the withdrawal of foreign forces from Egyptian territory. In the aftermath Nasser was able to present himself as both victim and victor, and his standing as a leader of the new Third World was greatly enhanced. Like Nehru, Nasser's period in power was a long one, ending only with his death in 1970. But the two men had fundamentally different views on the purpose of the Third World movement. While Nehru sought to position the Third World as a positive force for world peace, Nasser saw it as a diplomatic instrument with which the ex-colonial world could secure reparation for past crimes and exploit the bipolar competition between West and East to extract maximum benefit for the South.

The host of the Bandung conference, President Sukarno of Indonesia, lay closer to Nasser in his vision of the Third World, but in most respects was a less much less impressive figure. Unlike Nehru and Nasser, who both died while still in office after long periods in power, Sukarno was effectively overthrown by his own military in 1966 and his political passing was little mourned in the wider world. From the time of Indonesia's independence in 1949, however, he had led one of the largest and most populous countries in Asia and had, in his later years in office, proved a major thorn in the side of the West. During the 1920s and 1930s he had been a charismatic leader of the growing movement of opposition to Dutch colonialism in the Netherlands East Indies, the vast Asia-Pacific archipelago which eventually formed post-independence Indonesia. His political activities had led to his imprisonment for two years in Bandung, an autobiographical detail which may well have influenced the choice of the Javanese hill town as the venue for the Afro-Asian summit in 1955. Having declared Indonesia independent in 1945 after the withdrawal of the wartime Japanese occupation, Sukarno led the resistance to Dutch attempts to reestablish European rule, efforts which Holland abandoned four years later.

In the post-independence period the uncertain borders of Indonesia, along with Sukarno's equally uncertain temperament, did not endear Indonesia to its neighbors. During the 1950s and early 1960s Sukarno's government violently pursued territorial expansion at the expense of both Malaya and the Philippines. The most politically and diplomatically significant target of Sukarno's expansionist instincts was Holland, however. When it finally agreed to Indonesia's independence the Netherlands had insisted on retaining its control over West New Guinea, located at the eastern end of the old Netherlands East Indies, whose Melanesian people had little in common culturally with Indonesia. It was a measure of the diplomatic leverage that the Afro-Asian group could exert when, in 1962, the United Nations was drawn into a process which legitimized the transfer to Indonesia of West New Guinea with little consideration given to the interests of its inhabitants. At this time the anti-colonial card, if used adeptly by

a major player, could trump prior considerations of self-determination and natural justice.

In positioning himself among the leaders of the movement of Third World states, Sukarno acquired a global credibility that he would otherwise have been hard put to achieve. By about 1964, however, his credit with the West was badly depleted. Increasingly unpredictable in his pronouncements and actions, he became vociferously anti-American and pro-Soviet, appearing to depart from any semblance of non-alignment. His ever-closer association with the large Indonesian Communist Party led directly to the army intervention which ended his presidency in an orgy of bloodshed throughout the country.[2] Although perhaps half a million communists and other radicals were killed by the army during and immediately after the coup, Sukarno himself died quietly in retirement in 1970.[3]

If Nehru saw the emerging Non-Aligned Movement in the Third World as an honest broker between East and West, and Nasser saw it as a means of achieving post-imperial reparation, then Sukarno, as far as a cohesive position can be discerned from his politics, saw it as an *alternative* to the existing power structure in the international system. His views were summed up in two acronyms of his own coinage. "Nekolim" stood for the dying forces of "neocolonialism, capitalism, and imperialism," while "Nefo" were the "new emerging forces" of the Third World which would triumph over the old and exhausted powers of the global North.

The most vocal among the sub-Saharan African leaders at Bandung was Kwame Nkrumah, who went on to play a prominent role in the subsequent development of the Third World movement as a whole. Nkrumah was the highly charismatic leader of the nationalist movement in what was, at the time of Bandung, still the British colony of the Gold Coast but which was already set to become the new state of Ghana two years later. Like Sukarno, Nkrumah succumbed to a military coup after his initially inspirational leadership faltered and declined into authoritarianism and the neglect of the detail of national governance. Showing great intellectual promise from an early age, Nkrumah, unusually for Africans from British colonies, went to university in America.

Returning to Ghana in the 1940s, he quickly became involved in the already well-established nationalist agitation in the Gold Coast. Professing both Christian and Marxist beliefs, he dominated the more radical wing of the anti-colonial movement and became the first post-independence prime minister of Ghana in 1957. He became president three years later after fashioning a new, executive-dominated constitution.

In the early 1960s Nkrumah, like Nasser in the Middle East, became a driving force for regional unity. But if the prospects for a successful pan-Arab movement were unpromising, there was much less likelihood that the continental vastness of black Africa with its constellation of different religions, cultures, and economic possibilities was ready for meaningful political unification. Like Nasser, though, Nkrumah used his domination of regional international relations to launch himself onto the larger global stage. Here – admittedly against very limited opposition, as few sub-Saharan African countries were yet independent in 1960 – he drew considerable attention as the voice of the new Africa. His influence in Third World politics in the early 1960s therefore was substantial, indeed perhaps disproportionate, as he could claim to be a tribune of black Africa in its entirety.

The last member of this quintet of "Third World" leaders, Josip Broz Tito of Yugoslavia, stood apart from the others in a number of respects. For one thing, of course, he was not a Third World leader at all, but president of a European country (albeit one with a Third World level of development in places). Moreover, Yugoslavia was a communist state ruled by a single vanguard party presiding over a Marxist command economy. Crucially, however, Yugoslavia was emphatically not part of the Soviet bloc in the sense that, say, Hungary, Poland, Bulgaria, and the other post-Second World War "satellite" states were. Tito was not a figure who would willingly take second place to any other leader nor permit Yugoslavia to orbit another power. As a communist activist in the 1930s, he had fought on the Republican side in the Spanish Civil War. His most celebrated role, however, had been at the head of Yugoslavia's partisan resistance to German occupation during the Second World War. With the end of the war

there was no question of a reversion to the political status quo ante in Yugoslavia. The monarchy installed when the country was created after the First World War did not return and Tito led the Communist Party into peacetime government.

While Communist Yugoslavia inevitably stood apart from the rest of capitalist western Europe and the increasing momentum of its economic and political cooperation in the postwar years, its rejection of a subordinate relationship with Moscow left it outside of the eastern bloc as well. It is in this sense that Yugoslavia could claim to be truly non-aligned. Tito had to find his friends, and his international role and identity, outside of Europe. The emergence of an Afro-Asian grouping with an ambition to expand into a unified third force in global politics therefore provided him with an ideal opportunity to assert an international identity for Yugoslavia which otherwise might remain an insignificant historical and political curiosity between the two European power blocs.

These five leaders and their countries were not, then, united by either local political aims or by ideological outlook. They came from wholly separate international regions of the world and from countries facing quite different political and economic challenges. What united them, and what therefore galvanized the creation of a Third World movement, was a shared impulse to find a role and a voice in international politics for a class of states in danger of being squeezed between the ideological and economic poles around which global power had begun to accrete after 1945.

## The Third World Institutionalized: The Non-Aligned Movement

The next major stage in the development of the neutralist movement came in 1961 when President Tito hosted a summit of non-aligned leaders in the Yugoslav capital, Belgrade. Twenty-five states were represented at Belgrade, slightly fewer than at Bandung six years previously. The states invited to the meeting by Tito lay more at the Nasser–Sukarno end of the non-aligned spectrum than that represented by Nehru. The meeting was held against the backdrop of rapidly deteriorating East–West relations. The superpowers were locked in one of the most serious of their regular confrontations over divided Germany (1961 was the year of the construction of the Berlin Wall). The nuclear arms race appeared to be spinning out of control and there was a pervasive pessimism about the future. Two other areas of crisis lay close to Third World concerns. Since its revolution in 1959 Cuba had been at the center of a vicious cycle of power politics in which its dependency of the Soviet Union grew in step with the mounting hostility of the United States. The Castro regime in Cuba – which was represented at Belgrade – was therefore testing the Monroe Doctrine to destruction, a situation which threatened to flare into a major international crisis (as indeed it did with the "missile crisis" the following year). Secondly, the long, violent conflict in the Congo had mutated into a Cold War confrontation where the West was accused by a number of the more radical Third World states – with the Soviet Union urging them on from the sidelines – of neocolonial maneuvering. Despite the gravity of the world situation, however, Nehru's attempts to use the Belgrade meeting as a launch for a much needed mediation between East and West came to nothing. The tone of the summit was an uncompromisingly anti-colonialist one which, by default, was distinctly more anti-western than anti-Soviet. Moscow's misdemeanors were, after all, mainly committed in Europe while its broader foreign policy rhetoric was unimpeachably anti-imperialist.

The most concrete outcome of the Belgrade summit was the transformation of the disparate non-aligned states that had gathered there into a formal Non-Aligned Movement (NAM). As an institution the NAM was to lie at the "minimalist" end of the scale of international organizations. In contrast to the United Nations, for example, the NAM was to have no permanent headquarters, no full-time secretariat, and, crucially, no written constitution comparable to the UN Charter. The sole qualification for membership was that a state should not be in alliance, or be party to defense pacts, with either West or East. This would not, in principle, have excluded the European neutrals of the time, like Ireland, Switzerland, and Austria, but these states showed no inclination to seek membership of what was

overwhelmingly a movement of the Third World. Aside from Yugoslavia, the only European country to join the movement was Cyprus whose recent colonial status clearly put its historical and geographical positions at odds with each other. The supreme decision-making organ of the movement was to be its regular summit meetings, the Conferences of Heads of State or Government, which were supposed to be held every three years. The member hosting the summit would preside over the movement until the next meeting and provide the necessary administrative support in this period.

| Summit | Year | Venue |
|--------|------|-------|
| I | 1961 | Belgrade, Yugoslavia |
| II | 1964 | Cairo, Egypt |
| III | 1970 | Lusaka, Zambia |
| IV | 1973 | Algiers, Algeria |
| V | 1976 | Colombo, Sri Lanka |
| VI | 1979 | Havana, Cuba |
| VII | 1983 | Delhi, India |
| VIII | 1986 | Harare, Zimbabwe |
| IX | 1989 | Belgrade, Yugoslavia |
| X | 1992 | Jakarta, Indonesia |
| XI | 1995 | Cartagena, Colombia |
| XII | 1998 | Durban, South Africa |
| XIII | 2003 | Kuala Lumpur, Malaysia |
| XIV | 2006 | Havana, Cuba |

## Conferences of Heads of State or Government of the Non-Aligned Movement, 1961–2003

The agendas and communiqués of the Non-Aligned summits of the 1960s and 1970s mapped the changing preoccupations of the Third World throughout these two fraught decades.[4] At Cairo in 1964 a major focus of discussion was imperialism and racism. This reflected the concerns of the great inflow of African states to the movement after the especially intense phase of decolonization throughout the continent since the Belgrade summit of 1961. Both the situation of those parts of Africa still under colonial rule and the affront to African political sensibility of the white minority regime in South Africa were dominant concerns in what was, after all, a conference held in an African state, even if not of the sub-Saharan region. Significantly, issues of development and international economic equity did not yet feature largely. In 1964 the economic problems that would eventually afflict the Third World in general and Africa in particular were just beginning to make themselves felt in what was still the relatively favorable climate of the global economy at the time.

This environment had changed by the time of the next summit, which met six years later in sub-Saharan Africa, in Lusaka, the capital of Zambia. Here, though, the tone was not despairing. Economic self-reliance was a major point of discussion in Lusaka, a theme with a strong regional resonance. In 1967 Julius Nyerere, the leader of Zambia's neighbor Tanzania and by then a major figure in the broader Third World movement, had enunciated the famous Arusha Declaration, which laid down a blueprint for a distinctly African socialism. This was to be based on meeting essential needs on the basis of small-scale production as against the grand schemes for European-style industrialization that had dominated development thinking hitherto. Three years later, at the next summit in Algiers, the economic theme predominated, but in less optimistic terms. The year 1973 brought war in the Middle East and the first of the decade's two oil shocks (the second coming after the Iranian Revolution in 1979). The global economic climate was no longer nearly as benign as it had been. By this point the Non-Aligned Movement had shifted decisively from being the primarily political organization envisaged (though in different ways) by Nehru and Tito, and was assuming the shape of a pressure group of the poor.

It was a transition that was confirmed at the next summit in Colombo in Sri Lanka three years later. Here the global axis of interest was exclusively North–South, with virtually no attention given to issues of East–West relations where they did not impinge directly on Third World economic interests. By the mid-1970s the predominant strand of economic thinking in the NAM derived in the main from neo-Marxist "dependency" theories, which saw a world composed of a dominant "core" (the global North) and a dependent "periphery" (the South or Third World) whose underdevelopment was intentionally maintained by the core in the interests of its own

continued prosperity.[5] It was an attractive theory which conveniently excused the leaders of the Third World of responsibility for their countries' difficulties. But it was also one which proposed no viable way forward from diagnosis to remedy other than a vaguely conceived revolution; a political dead-end now seemed to be beckoning the NAM.

The next summit was held in 1979 in Havana, a date and a venue that together were to prove toxic to the cohesion and therefore to the future prospects of the Non-Aligned Movement. Throughout the 1970s there had been a partial but nevertheless real suspension of hostilities in the Cold War. This was the period of so-called détente, which had its origins in the mutual realization by the superpowers of the likely consequences of the Cold War turning hot. The Cuban missile crisis in 1962 had concentrated minds in this regard when it became clear that the nuclear conflict, which at points during that autumn looked more likely to occur than not, would lead inevitably to the destruction of both sides. This was in essence a function of technology, but it had real political consequences. Both superpowers now possessed "second strike capability" which would allow them to retaliate (from submarines or missile silos deep in deserts) to an attack that may already have wiped out whole cities. In other words, a condition of "mutually assured destruction" (MAD) prevailed, and policymakers had to respond to its political logic. By the end of the 1960s this response had begun to take the shape of enhanced respect for spheres of influence and of superpower cooperation in the management of regional crises to prevent their escalation. (The joint response of Washington and Moscow to the 1973 Middle East war was an example of this.) Détente was a mixed blessing for the Third World. On the positive side, the lessening of East–West tensions permitted greater focus on the economic aspects of North–South relations. As the economic travails of the Third World mounted at this time, that was a welcome development. But, inevitably, greater mutual understanding between the superpowers meant a reduction of the leverage which Third World states could apply to East and West in their own interests.

Whatever the balance of advantage in it for the Third World, détente was not to prove a permanent feature of global relations. From the middle of the 1970s it came under growing pressure, mostly from developments in the Third World. The sudden end of the Portuguese empire in Africa in 1975 brought pro-Moscow Marxist regimes to power in Angola, Mozambique, and Guinea-Bissau. The same year saw the final victory of North Vietnam over the South and the seizure of power by the communist Khmer Rouge in Cambodia. In the Third World at least, communist influence seemed to be advancing on all fronts. In the face of this, American policymakers were inclined to rethink the assumptions of the past decade, and détente began to unravel into what has been described as the Second Cold War. The Havana Non-Aligned summit took place three months before what was perhaps the tipping point of this process – the Soviet invasion of Afghanistan in December 1979 – but the signs were already many and clear. Had the conference been held in a less politically problematical venue then this difficult wider background might not have been so significant. But Cuba was perhaps the Soviet Union's closest ally in the Third World. Indeed, others in the Non-Aligned Movement questioned its qualifications for membership, though Havana could justifiably point out that it was not in any formal military alliance with Moscow. Cuban troops were, however, deployed throughout pro-Soviet Africa at this time, most notably in Angola and Ethiopia (where their presence had in fact been an important factor in the breakdown of détente). And it was not simply a question of a single conference at which the Cuban leader Fidel Castro could abuse the United States and praise the Soviet Union. The rules of the Non-Aligned Movement, it will be recalled, meant that Cuba would be its president for the following three years.

The Havana summit crystallized what had become the critical – and ultimately insoluble – difficulty confronting the Non-Aligned Movement. By 1979 the movement had 106 members, considerably more than half of all the states in the international system at that time. These represented an enormous range of political positions on the issues the movement was established to

confront. At one end of the spectrum were states like Cuba and Vietnam, which were to all intents and purposes diplomatic creatures of the Soviet Union. At the other were countries like the Philippines and Chile, which at that time were close and faithful friends of the United States. The shift in the movement's attention in the 1970s from the political to the economic had allowed it to evade some of the hard questions that this situation posed (even though the revolutionary language of dependency theory which went with that shift was uncomfortable for some). But the end of détente and the return to a level of East–West antagonism – which would have seemed unusual even during the First Cold War – changed all that. To this extent, therefore, the 1979 summit in Havana did not create a crisis in the movement, it simply forced an acknowledgment of an elephant in the room which had been there for some time.

## The Third World at the United Nations: UNCTAD and the New International Economic Order

We will return to the Non-Aligned Movement in the 1980s and the possibly terminal crisis of identity which it faced with the end of the Cold War in due course. Before this, though, we remain in the 1960s and 1970s with the experience of the Third World as a "movement" within another, larger international organization, the United Nations. We began by using UN membership as a measure of the expansion of the Third World, particularly in the 1950s and 1960s. As the number of these new states grew, the automatic majority in the General Assembly enjoyed by the western powers evaporated, and the UN became something of a radical force in the global anti-colonial and anti-racist movement of the 1960s. This eventually set up a certain tension in the United Nations between the Assembly, which represented all members, and the Security Council, which was dominated by the big powers. The United States in particular complained of the supposed unrealistic nature of General Assembly statements and resolutions at this time. Perhaps the high point of this Afro-Asian influence on the politics of the United Nations was the adoption by the General Assembly in 1960 of the Declaration on Granting Independence to Colonial Countries and Peoples, which effectively pronounced colonialism to be illegal.[6] Third World activism in the UN was evident in the economic and development areas as well as in political matters. The UN General Assembly in fact became a forum for deliberation and decision on the economic plight of Third World states some time before the Non-Aligned Movement began to focus on it.

The principal vehicle used by the states of the Third World to discuss and disseminate concerns and proposals about economic equity was the United Nations Conference on Trade and Industry (UNCTAD).[7] The first meeting of what was to become a permanent component of the UN system was held in Geneva in 1964. From this there emerged a so-called "Group of 77" countries which committed itself to reaching a common Third World position in matters of trade and aid. The most celebrated achievement ascribed to UNCTAD and the Group of 77 was in fact the result of a joint effort with the Non-Aligned Movement. As we have seen, the 1973 NAM summit was preoccupied with the economic concerns of the membership. One of the Third World's immediate economic woes at this time, however, seemed to point to an opportunity as well as being a source of difficulty. The 1973 oil crisis was the result of joint action by Middle East producer states to bring pressure on the West to moderate its automatic support for Israel in the region during and after the war of that year. This successful cartel action encouraged a new confidence in the Third World generally about the possibility of shifting the balance of economic power, which had always been to the advantage of the global North. Third World states were of course already well aware of their voting power in the General Assembly and the result was a new assertiveness on economic issues. In the wake of the NAM summit its host (and therefore chair for the following three years), Algeria, consulted with the Group of 77 (almost all of which were members of the NAM anyway). Consequently, a Special Session of the UN General Assembly was held in April and May 1974 at which a Declaration on the Establishment of a

New International Economic Order (NIEO) was adopted.[8]

The NIEO consisted of a series of aspirations and targets which, if achieved, would have fundamentally changed the terms of North–South economic relations. On trade, the NIEO called for the reduction of tariffs on the import of Third World goods by countries of the North and for mechanisms to give stability and buoyancy to commodity prices on which many Third World economies were dependent. It also proposed the movement of some sectors of industrial production from the North to the South and a general technology transfer which would facilitate advanced manufacturing in the Third World. On aid, the key proposal was that the developed countries should commit themselves to an annual contribution of 7 percent of their gross national product (GNP) to Third World development. Additionally, an international food security program was proposed to reduce the risk of shortages and famine which regularly destroyed the economic prospects of Third World countries, particularly in Africa.

In the event, the NAM and Group of 77 overestimated the pressure they could bring to bear on the developed world. Although Third World voting strength in the General Assembly could guarantee the adoption of the NIEO as a set of principles, it was another thing to ensure its implementation. The established Bretton Woods institutions – the International Monetary Fund and the World Bank – continued to dominate the regulation of the world economy, and they in turn continued to be dominated by the countries of the North. Although a general commitment to the NIEO was reaffirmed at successive sessions of UNCTAD throughout the 1970s and 1980s, this amounted to little more than lip-service. The seductive example of the oil cartel proved inapplicable to the broader range of primary products (many "substitutable" in a way that oil was not) that were produced in the Third World. In reality, the comparative value of such exports from the South fell rather than rose in relation to the cost of manufactured imports from the North in the coming decades. While a very few countries did achieve the 7 percent of GNP target for aid, it is unlikely that the NIEO was instrumental in this, and the richest did not. The net result of the NIEO therefore was a negative one for the Third World: it merely underlined the weakness rather than the strength of the South in its economic and political relations with the North.

## The Third World and the End of the Cold War

We left the Non-Aligned Movement in some disarray after the Havana summit in 1979 as the new Cold War deepened and the fissures among the movement's membership widened. While the sudden end of the Cold War at the end of the 1980s took most of the world by surprise, the NAM was, in a rather despondent way, perfectly prepared for it. The fact was that when the structural *raison d'être* for a third force in global politics disappeared with the end of the bipolar system, that third force had already ceased to exist as an effective actor. The impossibility of forging a meaningful and cohesive program among such a large and disparate membership was only the most serious of the NAM's problems. The world of the 1980s was quite different in many respects from that of the 1960s. For one thing, the quality of leadership which had overseen the creation of the movement was no longer present. Nehru, Nasser, Sukarno, Nkrumah, and Tito were far from being paragons of political or personal morality. For the most part they were politicians who had emerged at the top of political systems in which high standards of idealism and ethical behavior were not usually associated with success. But they had levels of drive, commitment, and charisma which were not common in their successors. These successors were also faced with difficulties, particularly economic ones, which did not trouble the first generation of Third World leaders, however. This had an impact both on the attention that leaders could devote to collective action and, simultaneously, on the leverage that such action could exert on the larger international system. As a result, by the late 1970s the optimism which had characterized the early days of the Third World movement had mostly evaporated.

The decline of the Non-Aligned Movement and the failure of the Third World to reshape the world economy through the United Nations did not mean that states in the South lost all voice in global international relations. The unwieldy size of the NAM had vitiated its performance as a unified actor in international relations, but these states had in the meantime found other, more viable means of collective expression. Regional organizations had become a prominent feature of diplomacy by the end of the Cold War. In Africa the venerable Organization of African Unity was reconstructed and revived at the beginning of the new century in the form of the African Union. More locally still, bodies like the Economic Community of West African States and the Southern African Development Community provided an alternative and more productive focus for mutual support and diplomatic empowerment to the NAM in its decline. In Asia the Association of Southeast Asian Nations proved even more successful than its African counterparts in bringing collective political and economic benefits to its members.

This quickening pace of regionalism in the South was in many respects the logical response to the end of the Cold War. As global bipolarity, which offered certain opportunities for the South, was supplanted by the economic and cultural forces of globalization, which did not, the best collective defense among the most vulnerable states was a local one. And, even if the bipolar configuration of the Cold War system had persisted, the global-level response to it in the South as represented by the Non-Aligned Movement had already proved itself too cumbersome and too much tied to a past era to remain effective. The end of the Cold War may have rendered the concept of a Third World irrelevant, but the category had already become too large to be meaningful. Differential rates of development between different regions and cultures, and different regional histories had already begun to raise questions about the Third World identity of some countries in regions like Southeast Asia and Latin America. Meanwhile, development economists began to talk of a "Fourth World" in relation to much of sub-Saharan Africa. By the new century, in short, the Third World was a category without meaningful criteria and a movement without a feasible cause.

## NOTES

1  *L'Observateur*, August 14, 1952.
2  The role of the United States in the overthrow of Sukarno was long argued about after the event. Some interesting insights on Washington's position can be drawn from a series of State Department communications from 1965 now available on the US State Department website at www.state. gov/r/pa/ho/frus/johnsonlb/xxvi/4445.htm.
3  In 2001 Sukarno's daughter, Megawati Sukarnoputri, became president of Indonesia in the process of democratization that followed the downfall of her father's nemesis, President Suharto. She was defeated in the election of 2004.
4  A concise outline of the agendas of the successive NAM summits of the 1960s and 1970s is provided in Gwyneth Williams, *Third-World Political Organizations: A Review of Developments* (London: Macmillan, 1981), pp. 46–65.
5  The classic presentations of dependency theory at this time whose influence spread throughout the Third World include: André Gunder Frank, *Capitalism and Underdevelopment in Latin America: Historical Studies of Chile and Brazil* (New York: Monthly Review Press, 1968); Immanuel Wallerstein, *The Modern World System: Capitalist Agriculture and the Origins of the European World Economy in the 16th Century* (New York: Academic Press, 1974); Samir Amin, *Accumulation on a World Scale: a Critique of the Theory of Underdevelopment* (New York: Monthly Review Press, 1974).
6  General Assembly Resolution A/RES/1514(XIV), December 14, 1960.
7  For a detailed account of the first UN Conference on Trade and Development (UNCTAD-I), see Williams, *Third-World Political Organizations*, pp. 1–25.
8  Resolutions adopted by the General Assembly during its Sixth Special Session, April 9–May 2, 1974, General Assembly Document A/9559.

## GUIDE TO FURTHER READING

Said K. Aburish, *Nasser: The Last Arab* (New York: Thomas Dunne Books, 2004). An up-to-date political biography of the Egyptian leader and key figure in the Non-Aligned Movement.
Roy Allison, *The Soviet Union and the Strategy of Non-Alignment in the Third World* (Cambridge: Cambridge University Press, 1989). An exploration of the Soviet position on Third World non-alignment during the Cold War.
David Birmingham, *Nkrumah: Father of African Nationalism* (Athens, OH: Ohio University Press, 1998). A sympathetic study of the leading black African figure in the Third World movement.
Judith Brown, *Nehru: A Political Life* (New Haven, CT: Yale University Press, 2003). A study of the political contribution of one of the most important figures in the development of Third World non-alignment.
Milovan Djilas, *Tito: The Story from Inside* (London: Phoenix Press, 2001). A portrait of Tito as both a Yugoslavian and a world politician written by a former "insider" turned critic.
Louise Fawcett and Sayigh Yezid, *The Third World Beyond the Cold War: Continuity and Change* (Oxford: Oxford University Press, 2000). A study of the impact of the end of the Cold War on the place of the Third World in the international system.
Richard Jackson, *The Non-Aligned, the UN and the Superpowers* (Westport, CT: Greenwood Press, 1987). A view of the changing place of the Non-Aligned Movement in international politics written during the last phase of the Cold War.
Keith Kyle, *The Suez Crisis: Britain's End of Empire* (London: I. B. Tauris, 2002). A searching and highly readable account of a key event in the development of Third World consciousness and the development of non-aligned solidarity.
John D. Legge, *Sukarno: A Political Biography* (London: Butterworth Heinemann, 2003). A biography of one of the more controversial leaders of the early Third World movement.
Evan Luard, *A History of the United Nations*, vol. 1, *The Years of Western Domination, 1945–55* (London: Macmillan, 1982); vol. 2, *The Age of Decolonization, 1955–65* (London: Macmillan, 1989). A highly authoritative, detailed history of the first two decades of the United Nations which gives particular attention to the place of the Third World in the development of the organization.
Jamie McKie, *Bandung 1955: Non-Alignment and Afro-Asian Solidarity* (Singapore: Archipelago Press, 2005). A recent interpretation of the "seminal" conference of the Afro-Asian bloc.
Mike Mason, *Development and Disorder: A History of the Third World since 1945* (Lebanon, NH: University Press of New England, 1997). A general history of Third World politics since the Second World War.
Paul Nugent, *Africa since Independence: A Comparative History* (London: Palgrave Macmillan, 2004). A concise and accessible history of contemporary sub-Saharan Africa.

Norman G. Owen, *The Emergence of Modern Southeast Asia: A New History* (Honolulu, HI: University of Hawaii Press, 2004). A general history of the Southeast Asian region and its place in the international system.

Ian Roxborough, *Theories of Underdevelopment* (London: Macmillan, 1979). A short survey of the main political and economic theories which claimed to explain the failure of development in the postcolonial world.

Alvin Z. Rubenstein, *Yugoslavia and the Nonaligned World* (Princeton, NJ: Princeton University Press, 1970). A study of Yugoslavia's non-aligned foreign policy and its relations with the Third World.

John Springhall, *Decolonization since 1945: The Collapse of the European Overseas Empires* (London: Palgrave Macmillan, 2001). A concise account of both the underlying and immediate causes of Europe's retreat from empire.

Tom Tomlinson, *The Third World in the Twentieth Century* (London: Edward Arnold, 2001). A history of the Third World both during and since the Cold War.

Marc Williams, *Third World Cooperation: The Group of 77 in UNCTAD* (London: St. Martin's, 1991). A study of Third World solidarity in the key development organs of the UN.

# CHAPTER TWENTY-FIVE

# Making the New Europe: European Integration since 1950

## PIERS LUDLOW

The first decade after the Second World War was not an easy one for Europe. The widespread physical destruction caused by six years of intensive warfare was soon compounded by the disruptive effects of East–West division. Within less than five years of VE day, "liberated Europe" had effectively been split in two, with the states to the east of what Churchill termed the "iron curtain" being forced to establish the uniform political and economic structures of Stalinism. Nor could western Europe feel secure. Not only was it incapable of defending itself militarily should the Red Army decide to march westwards, but the presence of large and electorally successful communist parties within countries like France and Italy suggested that parts of western Europe might turn to Moscow voluntarily unless the quality of life of its citizens rapidly improved. At a time of severe economic underperformance, made worse by the particularly harsh winter of 1946/7, this would not be an easy task. Also preoccupying to western European governments were the growing difficulties they were experiencing in their vast worldwide empires. In the immediate postwar period, there had been some hope that it would be thanks in part to the resources and markets of these last that Europe might rebuild its prosperity. And it was certainly believed in both Paris and London that the only way in which medium-sized countries like France and Britain could compete with the emerging superpowers was by mobilizing the capacities of their extensive empires. But all of the

colonial powers were to find it ever harder to contain nationalist discord within their overseas territories. By the early 1950s, the Dutch had thus been forcibly ejected from their Southeast Asian empire, the French were embroiled in a bloody conflict in Indochina and on the defensive in North Africa, and the British had relinquished India and Palestine and were engaged in low-level battles in Malaya and Kenya. Few Europeans, admittedly, would have anticipated quite how quickly their empires would fall away (by the mid-1960s only Portugal retained a colonial empire of any note), but the confident assumptions of 1945 were already looking naïve well before ten years had elapsed.

It was against this somber backdrop that the process of European integration began. The idea of European unity or European cooperation was not entirely new, of course. It had been talked of by intellectuals and political visionaries long before the twentieth century. In the interwar period a number of abortive schemes had been launched which were designed to bring a fractured continent together – notably the Briand Plan of 1930. The establishment of some larger European entity was also the subject of some debate amongst both sides during the Second World War itself. Yet it was only after 1945 that meaningful institutions began to be built and it would take until 1950 before the true foundations of today's European Union were laid.

The first serious institutional attempt to bring Europe closer together was the Marshall Plan launched in 1947. Although the European Recovery Program (ERP) – to give the initiative its official name – is now more often remembered as a financial aid package, designed to allow wartorn Europe to get back onto its feet economically (and thereby banish the danger of a voluntary turn to communism), it is quite clear that its US originators hoped that the scheme would also encourage Europe to unite. It was for this reason that the Americans insisted that the prospective European beneficiaries of their largesse gather together in order to discuss their collective needs. And it was also with this end in mind that the US pressed for the temporary Conference on European Economic Cooperation (CEEC) – the forum where European governments came together to discuss what they needed from the US – to be replaced by the more permanent Organization for European Economic Cooperation (OEEC). But despite the general plaudits won by the American rescue effort, it was a failure in terms of uniting Europe. For while the OEEC did take a number of useful, if limited, steps toward facilitating trade within western Europe, it fell well short of its initial goals and remained a weak institution, easily blocked by countries such as the United Kingdom that were ambivalent about too much European cooperation. Indeed, amongst those who would go ahead and pioneer the European communities of the 1950s and 1960s, the OEEC had become a byword for institutional ineffectiveness and decision-making paralysis. Likewise, the Council of Europe, launched by the French in 1948 and established a year later, also proved too weak institutionally to hold the states of Europe together.

The true start of European integration was thus the Schuman Plan, the idea of pooling the French and German coal and steel industries announced by the French foreign minister on May 9, 1950. This was a breakthrough in at least two ways. First of all, the scheme launched by the French was to be supranational – in other words, it was designed to set up a level of governance that would be binding on all of those taking part. Countries would thus no longer be able to opt out of or ignore aspects of cooperation that they disliked. Second, it marked the moment when

France accepted that it was in its national interest to build an integrated Europe with Germany but without Britain. The United Kingdom was invited to take part – indeed, many within the French political elite sincerely hoped that London would respond favorably to their invitation. But Schuman and Jean Monnet, the latter the key originator of the Plan, were both adamant from the outset that France and Germany would go ahead together *irrespective* of who else chose to join them. They were thus undeterred by British ambivalence and did not allow their ideas to be watered down in the manner that the earlier Council of Europe plan had been. It was thus only six countries – France, West Germany, Italy, Belgium, the Netherlands, and Luxembourg – who gathered in Paris in the summer of 1950 to begin to design what would become the European Coal and Steel Community (ECSC). The same six countries would remain at the heart of the European integration process until the first enlargement of the European Community in 1973.

Their next collective attempt, admittedly, was to be much less successful. Between the autumn of 1950 and the summer of 1954, the fortunes of the integration process seemed to have become entirely wrapped up in the attempt to create a European Defense Community (EDC). This was another French idea, intended to allow German troops to participate in the defense of western Europe without the need to reconstitute a German army. Instead, all of the armed forces of the Six were to be amalgamated into the EDC. Almost at once, however, the plan encountered a level of difficulty that the Schuman Plan had escaped. The Germans justifiably disliked the elements of discrimination to which they would be subject within the proposed European structures; many military leaders believed the project to be inoperable; and the French soon began to suffer severe qualms about the plan they themselves had launched. Apart from anything else, the Cold War anxieties of imminent Soviet invasion which had given urgency to the debate about German rearmament, especially after the start of the Korean War in June 1950, faded significantly once Stalin died in the spring of 1953. In August 1954 the French National Assembly thus refused to ratify the treaty which would have brought the EDC into existence. Supranational European integration amongst the Six appeared to have died a mere four years after its appearance. This was all the more so since the successful quest for an alternative mechanism by which German troops could be brought into NATO was led by the British and culminated in the creation of the Western European Union. The 1950 rift between the UK and the Six seemed to have been mended by the Paris Agreements of 1954.

Within months it had opened up again. In June 1955, the six member states of the ECSC met in Messina in Sicily to discuss new cooperative schemes. The British had been invited but chose not to attend. And while a British representative did fleetingly participate in the follow-up deliberations over the next few months, by November 1955 he had been withdrawn. It was thus the same six countries as had participated in the Schuman Plan talks which were to devise together the Treaties of Rome. Signed in the Italian capital in March 1957, these brought into being the European Atomic Energy Community (normally known as Euratom) and, more importantly, the European Economic Community (EEC). This last was designed to link the economies of the Six, establishing a European customs union (i.e., an area with no internal tariff barriers and a common external tariff toward all non-members) bolstered where necessary by common policies – notably a common agricultural policy (CAP). It would be run by a quartet of institutions adapted from those which had been devised for the ECSC. A central European Commission would thus draw up policies, but would be controlled by a Council of Ministers bringing together member-state representatives, a European Parliamentary Assembly, and a Court of Justice. These institutions are still recognizably those that exist within today's European Union (EU), and the Treaty of Rome remains at the heart of the Union's operation.

## The Causes of Integration

Early explanations of how the Six had taken these steps were grounded in the numerous recollections of participants and gave a quasi-heroic air to all that had happened. Schuman, Monnet, the

German chancellor Konrad Adenauer, and all of the others involved had been driven, it was claimed, by the desire to cement peace in western Europe and to prevent a recurrence of the tragedies of 1914 and 1939.[1] They had thus laid aside narrow national interest and devoted themselves to building structures that would make war amongst Europeans impossible and which would, in due course, lead on to much greater European unity. Jean Monnet indeed had famously outlawed any talk of national interest in the course of the ECSC negotiations in 1950. Similarly, Paul-Henri Spaak, the Belgian statesman who had chaired the key negotiating committee behind the Treaties of Rome, had shown little patience for those who had sought to protect petty national concerns at the expense of the wider common interest. In one celebrated instance, he had broken a deadlock which had occurred over the exact tariff rules to be applied to bananas imported into the future EEC by telling the negotiators that unless they settled their differences within two hours, he would convene a press conference at which he would announce that the unification of Europe had broken down over a squabble about bananas. Unsurprisingly, by the time he returned to the room two hours later, a compromise had been hammered together.[2] The overall message of early writing about European integration was thus that this was a manifestly political project, in which the primarily economic measures initially employed were merely stepping stones to the more grandiose objectives of European peace and outright political federation. As the first president of the European Commission, Walter Hallstein, was fond of claiming: "we are in politics, not business."[3]

Unsurprisingly, this foundation story has come under sustained historical criticism over the last twenty years. Few historians were likely to be fully comfortable with the implied outbreak of collective altruism and political selflessness on the part of politicians that the traditional account implied. Instead, the gradual opening of government and Community archives has allowed a number of competing explanations to emerge, each of them solidly grounded in the more familiar idea that national politicians are normally motivated by their perception of the national interest. Thus for the majority of continental historians, the key factor behind both the French efforts to launch the integration process and the favorable response which it received from Germany, Italy, Belgium, the Netherlands, and Luxembourg was a series of political calculations. The Schuman Plan, for instance, was a means for France to seize the diplomatic initiative in western Europe, after a period during which the United States and Britain had shaped western policy, and devise a solution to the German problem of its own making.[4] For Bonn, meanwhile, the scheme offered a very welcome escape from the pariah status of the Federal Republic after the Second World War, a useful first step toward reconciliation with France, and, perhaps most importantly, a mechanism to bind West Germany firmly to the western camp. This last would protect the Federal Republic both against any deal with Moscow that its allies might be tempted to strike and against a choice by Adenauer's successors to negotiate with the eastern bloc rather than remaining loyal to the West.[5] In similar fashion, the EEC was perceived by Paris as a means of "curing French impotence" at a time of colonial retreat and generalized foreign policy crisis, while for both the Germans and the Italians it represented a useful further stage in their postwar rehabilitation and a framework within which they could regain power and influence without threatening their neighbors.[6] The longer-term political and strategic perspectives opened up by the notion of "ever closer union" were also particularly attractive to the powers of western Europe in the aftermath of the Suez crisis in 1956, which had dramatically underlined the weakness of European powers within the new world order and the fickleness of American support. "Europe will be your revenge," Adenauer is said to have commented to the French prime minister, Guy Mollet, as the two leaders met in Paris just days after the Suez debacle and struck a deal which broke the deadlock in the Treaty of Rome negotiations.[7]

Other historians, led by the British economic historian Alan Milward, have preferred to emphasize the economic motives which underpinned both the Schuman Plan and the EEC. The former was, according to this view, a French move designed to address the short-term crisis in the French steel industry caused by its dependence on German supplies of coke. Prior to 1950 this had not mattered greatly since Germany's own steel production had been tightly controlled by the occupying powers. There had thus been plenty of German coke available to France and some prospect of the French steel industry being able to establish itself as a major force within continental Europe. But with Allied controls on West German production being steadily lifted from 1949 onwards, France faced the danger of renewed German competition. To make matters worse, the mines which produced the coke needed by France were more often than not owned by the same German steel producers against whom French companies had to compete. In free market conditions, the German producers would hence have found themselves in a very strong position vis-à-vis their French rivals. Paris thus decided to seek a reimposition of controls on German industry, this time administered not by the occupying powers whose prerogatives were fast disappearing, but instead by a neutral European authority whose remit would extend to France as well as Germany.[8] The French, in other words, were prepared to make their own industry subject to a supranational authority provided that this also limited the capacity of the German steel industry to realize its potential to become the dominant producers within continental Europe. The integration of western Europe thus began with a French attempt to stop the reemergence of an economically powerful West Germany from disrupting its own postwar economic recovery.

For Milward and his followers, the formation of the EEC is also explicable primarily in economic terms. In this instance the initial impetus came not from France but from the Netherlands. Throughout the early postwar period, the Dutch were deeply worried about the danger that western Europe might once more lapse into the type of economic protectionism which had characterized the 1930s. This would be particularly damaging to a highly industrialized country like the Netherlands with a small domestic market. The Dutch thus made a number of proposals designed to make the process of tariff reductions and trade liberalization already under way in western Europe absolutely irreversible. It was one such proposal, put forward by Foreign Minister Jan-Willem

Beyen in 1953 and initially intended to be part of the EDC, which was picked up again in 1955 and became the heart of the EEC project.[9] The scheme which underpinned the European Economic Community was thus fundamentally an economic one and had little to do with the geopolitical explanations favored by many other historians. Similarly, the reasons why the French in particular were prepared to countenance the idea of a customs union despite the tendency toward protectionism of governments during the fourth republic was their realization firstly that France would not be able to complete its process of economic modernization without a degree of trade liberalization, and secondly that liberalization was unlikely to come in a much more congenial form than that available through the EEC. Not only would France dismantle its tariffs merely toward five other countries. Within the proposed Community, liberalization would also be conducted within an institutional framework in which the timetable could be slowed down should France experience difficulties. Reductions to industrial tariffs could be mitigated by measures such as a common agricultural policy or the association system for French Africa designed to share out the costs of supporting empire and French farmers amongst all of those countries taking part in the EEC.[10] The French and Dutch examples therefore both serve to prove, Milward maintains, that the urge to integrate western Europe was only political insofar as democratic governments were forced to engage in such economic integration in order to supply the economic prosperity which their voters demanded and without which they would soon have been voted from office. "The true origins of the European Community are economic and social," Milward claims in the preface to his influential study, *The European Rescue of the Nation-State*.[11]

This redirection of attention away from the tale of altruism and selflessness implicit in the original memoir account and toward distinctly more credible political and economic factors is generally welcome. The arguments now advanced to explain why, in the course of the 1950s, some of the states of western Europe went further and faster than any other group of nations at any other time in history toward pooling their sovereignty and binding themselves into far-reaching cooperative arrangements are much more sophisticated and satisfactory than they once were. Equally important have been the historiographical advances in explaining – without condemning – why some European countries, such as Britain, chose not to take part in the initial phases of integration. These reject the once-dominant idea that such countries "missed the bus" through a combination of complacency, myopia, and arrogance and instead emphasize the degree to which the circumstances of those countries that chose to stay aloof did not appear to justify the radical step of integration in 1950 or 1955.[12] It was thus only when their circumstances changed and some of the reasons behind their early decision to abstain disappeared that Britain, Denmark, or Sweden found themselves belatedly applying to join the integration process. Participation in the EC/EU was, in other words, a step that countries only took when they needed to do so, rather than the type of purely ideological choice that Monnet, Spaak, and some of the other founders had seemed to imply.

What has been less well captured by historians so far, however, is the way in which the integration process has always reflected a multiplicity of differing national needs, aspirations, and anxieties, which in turn can evolve considerably over time. Thus even the most convincing explanation of why an official in the Dutch Ministry of Economics supported a customs union plan in the early 1950s stands little chance of also elucidating why an Italian Christian Democrat voted in favor of the Treaty of Rome or clarifying the position toward the EEC adopted by a French centrist with close links to the farming community. Each harbored radically different views about what "Europe" should be and where it should lead. But each believed that their vision could be advanced by the set of institutions and mechanisms set up by the Treaty. It is thus the sheer variety of different motivations that needs to be emphasized in explaining how a process like European integration was able to generate the momentum necessary to begin, rather than too much effort being wasted in a fruitless quest to unearth a single explanatory factor.

This is all the more true once the focus is shifted from the origins of the current EC/EU to its evolution and development over the last fifty years. Monnet of course has been proved partly right with his emphasis on the enduring nature of institutions.[13] European integration has not persisted simply because it has been institutionalized, however. Instead, it has endured and progressed because each generation of European politicians and leaders since the 1950s has discovered new tasks which could be usefully pursued by means of the collective institutions it had inherited. In the 1960s, for example, the EEC was variously seen as an important component of the enduring trade boom within western Europe, as a means of solving the crisis of the French peasantry, as a political stepping stone to the reassertion of a more audible European voice on the world stage, and even, toward the latter half of the decade, as a framework for containing unpredictable Gaullist France. In the 1970s, by contrast, attempts were made to use the Community mechanisms to create an island of European monetary stability in the increasingly turbulent sea of world currency movements, as a forum for coordinating Europe's responses to the world energy crisis, and as a tool for ensuring that the states of western Europe adopted similar positions during the Conference on Security and Cooperation in Europe. And in the following decade the priorities shifted once more, with the EC at the heart of an attempt to break out of economic stagnation and respond to the competitive challenges posed by the United States and Japan, but also being used to redistribute substantial sums of money so as to encourage some of the poorer parts of Europe to catch up with their neighbors, to respond to the new environmental concerns of Europeans, and to provide a solid enough political context to permit the reunification of Germany to occur without any serious damage being done to the European balance of power. By no means were all of these endeavors successful. But the fact that so many, highly different, ambitions were sought using the same institutional instruments does serve to underline the way in which one of the strengths of European integration and one of the sources of its longevity has been its flexibility and its ability to adapt to the shifting political priorities of successive European leaders. Rather than the answer to one single problem and hence liable to

being wound up as soon as that problem was resolved, the process of European integration was instead a response to multiple needs and has gone on discovering new rationales and *raisons d'être* throughout its five decades of existence.

## The Mechanisms of Integration

Supranational integration was initially conceived as a process within which most power would reside with a single central executive. Monnet's ideas, as set out in the 1950 Schuman Plan, were notoriously short on the detail of how exactly the proposed new body would work. What was made clear, however, was that the planned High Authority would be a powerful entity, able to impose its will upon national governments and free from their control. Only in this way could the French be sure that the new European controls which they envisaged would be enforceable on Germany and thus strong enough to avert the crisis which otherwise threatened French steel production. But the impression of the centrality of the High Authority, and then of the European Commission, which Schuman's declaration had given was only reinforced throughout most of the early reporting about and writing on the European integration process. To most observers, whether journalists or academics, the new "executives" appeared the most original and innovative of the new institutions and both Monnet himself, as the first High Authority president, and then Hallstein at the EEC Commission, had enough flair for self-publicity to ensure that they became seen as the embodiments of the integration process. Both were periodically dubbed "Mr. Europe" by the American press. Flattering patronage from the US government also helped – a symptom of the enduring US support that was a vital precondition for the early success of European integration. John Foster Dulles, President Eisenhower's secretary of state, made Monnet's Luxembourg headquarters his base during a 1953 visit to Europe, while Hallstein was repeatedly received in Washington with honors normally reserved for visiting heads of state. It was thus easy for both casual observers and those devoting more detailed attention to the making of the new Europe to assume that the High Authority and the European Commission were the central organs of the integration process.

In fact, however, the ink was barely dry on the Schuman Declaration itself before the dominant position foreseen for the High Authority began to be chipped away. In the Treaty of Paris negotiations that gave substance to the Schuman Plan, a strong central authority was certainly created. But it was flanked by three other institutions intended to exercise some degree of oversight: a Court of Justice, a Parliamentary Assembly, and a Council of Ministers. And while in theory none of these was to possess the power to challenge the High Authority in most of what it did, it quickly became apparent that for most controversial decisions the High Authority only felt able to act once it was certain of the approval of the Council of Ministers. Supranational authority could not, in other words, be exercised in the teeth of member opposition. The practical operation of the ECSC was hence much less dominated by the High Authority than a strict reading of the Treaty might have implied. This trend away from centralized power was accentuated during the negotiations that were to lead to the Treaty of Rome. Influenced no doubt by the French rejection of the EDC, the treaty framers deliberately made the powers of the European Commission less extensive than those of the ECSC High Authority and increased those of the Council of Ministers. The central "executive" would no longer be able to take most decisions itself, subject only to "consultation" with the Council; it would need clear Council consent before any of its significant decisions became law. The legislative whip hand had thus passed from the Commission, which would now merely "propose," to the assembled national ministers, who would "dispose." Furthermore, while provision was made for the Council eventually to take decisions by majority vote, the treaty made clear that key decisions were always likely to require unanimous backing amongst the member states. Each member-state government thus retained a substantial ability to influence, and on occasion to block, policy developments within the EEC.

The Community's development during its formative years only confirmed this reality. Traditionally, the imposition of member-state control over the integration process has been associated with the 1966 Luxembourg compromise – the moment when General de Gaulle's French government bullied its partners into signing an agreement which further cut the power of the European Commission and which ruled out any use of majority voting for issues deemed to be of "vital interest" by any member state. According to one of the early Commissioners, Robert Marjolin, this marked the victory of Gaullist Europe over the supranational vision of Monnet.[14] But a careful study of the Community's evolution during the 1960s would suggest that the manner in which the EEC operated was not brutally altered by de Gaulle. Instead, what was brought to the surface by the so-called empty chair crisis of 1965–6, and the Luxembourg compromise that ended the crisis, was a pattern of institutional development which had been under way since 1958 and which led the Community away from both Gaullism and federalism in their purest forms. The reality of EEC operations was not significantly altered; all that changed was that a layer of rhetoric about the Community's degree of supranationalism was stripped away.

Within this hybrid EEC, power was shared between the European Commission and the Council of Ministers. The former was certainly not reduced to the mere secretariat of which de Gaulle sometimes spoke. It remained, by contrast, a key player, vital as both a source of policy ideas and a builder of member-state coalitions in favor of its proposals. Commission contributions to discussions in the Council of Ministers could frequently exercise a decisive influence on the final decisions reached. And the European Commission was also allowed to develop a significant international role, most notably as the main European negotiator within international commercial discussions under the General Agreement on Tariffs and Trade (GATT). But it was not, despite the delusions of its first president, a European government-in-the-making.[15] For real power and control within the early Community was concentrated ever more clearly within the hands of the member states and exercised collectively through the Council of Ministers and its various subordinate bodies. It was thus national ministers who gathered to finalize all of the key legislative breakthroughs of the Community's formative years, national representatives who established most of the key Community positions in the Kennedy Round negotiations in the GATT, and member-state delegates who determined the stance that the EEC was to adopt vis-à-vis those numerous countries who applied to either join or associate with the EEC during the 1958–73 period. So great indeed did the ministerial workload become that it quickly became too much for the foreign ministers alone to handle. As the EEC developed, it thus began to involve a growing number of other ministers and officials, with ministers of agriculture, finance, and trade gathering in Brussels on increasingly regular occasions. Such ministerial-level meetings, moreover, were prepared by ever more frequent gatherings of national civil servants. And from the mid-1970s this whole pyramid was topped by regular meetings of the European Council which brought together the heads of state and government – in other words, the prime ministers and presidents who alone had the political clout to direct the Community's overall development. Member-state control of the integration process had never been greater.

To some ardent pro-Europeans this steady increase in Council and member-state control was a disappointment or even a betrayal of European integration's original purpose. There was thus a vocal minority who denounced the start of regular European Council meetings in 1975 despite the fact that it had been partly at the suggestion of Jean Monnet that French President Valéry Giscard d'Estaing had proposed the idea. More realistically, however, this growth of member-state control over the integration process should probably be viewed as an inevitable corollary of the other transformation that had occurred during the same period, namely, the shift from a narrow process of European cooperation which affected only a minor part of each state's sovereignty to a much broader integration process involving multiple aspects of national sovereignty. In a crisis situation such as that of 1950, it had been feasible to expect member states to hand over almost all of their power over two relatively contained, if important, sectors of their economy to a supranational bureaucracy that in theory they were not allowed to control. But no nation-state was likely to have gone on relinquishing sovereignty indefinitely

over numerous other fields of state action. European integration has thus only been able to evolve from a phenomenon that directly affected solely the coal and steel industries into today's EU, which is involved in everything from monetary policy to humanitarian aid and from student-exchange schemes to rules for concerted police action, because the nations taking part have believed that they will go on being able to have an important voice in the formulation of these joint policies. Integration has never really been about the surrender of sovereignty; instead it has been about the agreement between states to exercise collectively some of their sovereignty so as to be better able to deliver results that would be beyond them individually. And such a collective exercise of power could only happen in a system which placed all of the member states at the very heart of the decision-making process. The greater use of majority voting from the mid-1980s onwards and the parallel growth in the influence and responsibility of the European Parliament, while not unimportant, have not significantly altered this reality.

## Deepening and Widening

The centrality of member-state power and influence to the process also helps explain the evolution of the Community's policy agenda from the initial narrow concerns of the "Common Market" to that of today's much broader and multifaceted EU. The earliest school of political analysts to write about the integration process – the so-called neofunctionalists – had predicted that the key mechanism by which integration would broaden its range and scope would be through something which they dubbed "spill-over."[16] In essence this was the belief that European-level action in one policy area would create substantial pressures for similar European-level actions elsewhere. Thus, for instance, joint European policies on heavy industries such as coal and steel would make it increasingly anomalous for the control of the transport facilities so vital for such industries to remain entirely under national or local control. Instead it would be much more logical to Europeanize transport arrangements also. This in turn would then create further pressure for integration to be spread to new sectors of the economy.

And so the whole process would grow. But while it is undoubtedly the case that the integration process has at times acquired a momentum of its own, with each success creating pressures for further advance – thus the steady rise since the late 1980s of European action in the field of justice and home affairs does seem to have resulted, to some extent at least, from the removal of most frontier checks as part of the effort to establish a full internal market within western Europe by the end of 1992 – spill-over has not proved to have been as widespread or as inexorable as the neofunctionalists predicted. There has thus been little to suggest that the integration process, once begun, has become automatic to the extent that its spread was inevitable regardless of the sentiments of its member states. The neofunctionalists indeed soon fell from favor in the mid-1960s when Gaullist France appeared to demonstrate that determined national leaders could defy the pressures for further integration and throw the whole process into reverse if they so chose.[17]

It makes much more sense to try to explain the broadening agenda of the EEC, then the EC, and finally the EU primarily in terms of the evolving priorities of member states. At least three different dynamics can be seen to have been at work. In the first and most simple, the range of Community activities has grown because member states have decided to employ the European mechanisms at their disposal to address policy issues and problems which no longer seem amenable to a strictly national approach. Environmental policy would be a good example of this, since tackling pollution or seeking to improve the quality of water in Europe's seas and rivers are not tasks easily realized by individual countries acting on their own. Neither rivers nor sea water are likely to respect national frontiers. Pan-European action, devised and enforced by the existing European institutional framework, is much more likely to have an impact.

The second factor explaining the expansion of the European agenda has been the way in which changes in Europe's international context have obliged European states to develop a collective response. In the late 1960s and early 1970s, for instance, the collapse of the Bretton Woods monetary system and the prospect of widespread volatility in currency values across the developed world encouraged the members of the EEC to turn their attention to the way in which the existing institutions might be used to develop monetary integration within Europe. Doing so did not prove easy. The first big European effort in this direction, the 1970 Werner Plan with its ambition of establishing economic and monetary union by 1980, soon proved utterly unrealizable. But by the end of the 1970s, the European Monetary System had been created, establishing a mechanism to limit the fluctuations of most European currencies against each other. In other words, Europe's states had responded to a global problem by acting at a European level in order to devise a solution intended to shelter western Europe from the worst effects of world currency instability. In so doing they had also entered an area of policy-making which has gone on to become central to the whole integration process, with Economic and Monetary Union (EMU) and the launch of the single currency in 2002 becoming the flagship policy of the EU in the way that the CAP had been in the 1960s.

The third major reason behind the spread of European integration into new policy areas has been the growth in the membership of the EC/EU. Each new wave of member states has inevitably brought new policy concerns and priorities to the Council table, and with time these have often found themselves reflected in the policy development of the Community/Union. The way in which redistributive policies became so important during the 1980s and early 1990s, for example, with very sizable amounts of money being channeled, through Community mechanisms, from the wealthier parts of western Europe to the poorer was clearly a consequence of Community enlargement. The original six member states had been relatively homogeneous in terms of wealth, with only southern Italy lagging far behind the European norm. The initial Community agenda did not therefore include any significant measure designed to help the poorer regions of the EEC catch up with the more advanced. But the subsequent entry of Ireland, then Greece, and finally Spain and Portugal made wealth disparities a much less marginal concern and helped create a substantial constituency within the Brussels institutions in favor of an EC effort to tackle the problem. The emergence of the structural and cohesion funds during the 1980s and early 1990s was the result.

This last argument draws attention to another facet of the integration process which deserves to be highlighted, namely, the growth in the membership of the EC/EU. The first enlargement of the Community occurred in 1973 when Britain, Denmark, and Ireland joined the original Six. In 1981 Greece then joined, followed in 1986 by Spain and Portugal. Sweden, Finland, and Austria became members in 1995. And, most recently, in May 2004, ten new countries took their place within the EU: Poland, the Czech Republic, Slovakia, Slovenia, Hungary, Estonia, Latvia, Lithuania, Cyprus, and Malta. What had started off as a process involving a mere six countries concentrated in the western portion of the European continent has thus grown to a twenty-five-nation entity stretching from the eastern Mediterranean to the Arctic circle and from Portugal to the borders of Russia. Nor is this likely to be the end of the membership growth. Bulgaria and Romania are both set to join in 2007, with Turkey, Croatia, Serbia, Albania, and the Ukraine all having either submitted membership applications or giving serious thought to the possibility of doing so. The increase in size of the EC/EU has been possibly the most remarkable aspect of its entire development and one which has almost certainly advanced beyond the expectations of almost all of those who were involved with the start of the process in 1950.

The reasons for which all of these countries have decided to seek Community membership are still more varied and multifarious than the motivations of the six founding member states. The economic desires to have unrestricted access to the markets of the EC/EU, to be able to export surplus labor to the rest of Europe, or to benefit from the type of redistributive policies which had helped both Ireland and Spain catch up with and overtake many of their European counterparts have thus been flanked by a number of much more political calculations. These have ranged from the desire to consolidate democracy – crucial not just for the former Warsaw Pact countries which joined in 2004 but also for Greece, Spain, and Portugal,

all of which had only recently escaped from autocratic rule when they entered the EC – to the quest for greater security, or the hope of exercising greater influence over the internal deliberations of the EC/EU. Particularly striking in this last respect are the cases of the three countries which joined in 1995, since all three were not only wealthier than the EU average but also enjoyed extensive economic access to European markets as members of the European Economic Area. They nonetheless decided that actually to join the Union and thereby gain a voice in the collective decision-making process was preferable to sitting on the margins, deeply affected by whatever was decided in Brussels but largely powerless to shape European legislation. As one Swedish diplomat put it, full membership entailed a far lesser diminution of national sovereignty than the prospect of remaining what he dubbed "a mailbox democracy," all but bound to follow European rules devised in Brussels with minimal Swedish input.[18]

Equally intriguing have been the effects of these waves of enlargement on the EU itself. At every stage of the EC/EU's development there have been those amongst the existing member states who have lamented the approach of others, predicting that new members would either paralyze decision-making or rule out any hope of developing new areas of Community or Union activity.[19] The widening of EC/EU membership – it has frequently been claimed – is incompatible with deepening the integration process. In practice, however, such dire predictions have seldom come true. On the contrary, new members have more often added impetus to the EC/EU's development than they have held it back, whether by providing new sources of leadership, new policy issues for the institutions to tackle, or by forcing the EC/EU as a whole to reconsider its mode of operation so as to be able to function with an enlarged membership. The increase in the size of the European market has also been an important factor, especially in an era when the world economy has become ever more fixated on the rise of huge population centers such as China or India. And well before actual membership is realized, the prospect of EC/EU membership has given the existing member states an extraordinary degree of collective influence and leverage over the internal development of states aspiring to join the Union. Both Turkey and Croatia, for example, have recently taken a number of political/judicial decisions that are all but impossible to explain without reference to the fact that both states are intent upon proving their European and democratic credentials in the hope of hastening their entry into the EU. The prospect of enlargement, to put it another way, has proved by far the most effective instrument in the EU's somewhat uphill struggle to develop an effective common foreign policy.

## Conclusions

The process of European integration has been one of the most remarkable features of the six decades that separate us from the end of the Second World War. Nowhere else in the world have independent states gone quite so far in pooling their sovereignty and taking a wide range of decisions in different policy areas collectively rather than individually. Nowhere else has so complex a supranational institutional system been created. And in no other part of the world has so large a body of shared legislation been drawn up, enforceable by courts across Europe, directly affecting the lives of all of Europe's citizens and taking precedence over laws devised within individual member states. Such uniqueness would of itself justify a closer investigation of why Europe has gone so far down a path only tentatively followed elsewhere. The fact that this course of action has also been inextricably tied up with the continent's economic and political recovery from the traumas of the Second World War makes it doubly important to examine in detail and to explain.

The integration process emerged out of the dire circumstances faced by western Europe in the immediate postwar period. Its radicalism reflected the seriousness of the situation then faced by France, Germany, Italy, the Netherlands, Belgium, and Luxembourg. Yet, while some early accounts suggested that the gravity of the position in which these countries found themselves prompted national politicians to set aside traditional calculations of national interest and throw themselves into an idealistic attempt to transcend the nation-state, it is now widely recognized that it was

actually for national motives, both political and economic, that they chose to devise cooperative institutions and to confront some of their problems collectively and not individually. And such hard-headed calculations of national interest have remained at the heart of the integration process ever since. The EC and then EU have thus developed largely in accordance with the wishes of their member states, taking on new tasks as required and evolving to respond to the altered circumstances in which the states of Europe have found themselves. The gravitational pull, both economic and political, of the EC/EU has meanwhile ensured that the number of countries involved has grown continuously, with each new entrant able in turn to raise its priorities and concerns within the collective decision-making process.

Fifty years on from its creation, the Union does admittedly face a number of serious concerns. The years since 2000 have thus been marked by a dearth of strong political leadership within the EU, a crisis of public legitimacy (epitomized by the negative votes in the French and Dutch referendums of 2005), and a sense of gloom at the recent economic underperformance of several of the larger member states, notably France and Germany. So numerous, however, are the national interests wrapped up in the integration process that it seems improbable that Europe's leaders will let the EU drift for long, still less abandon the endeavor entirely. Instead, the likelihood is that, faced with a new set of problems, the member states of the EU will turn once more to their common institutions and seek again to employ them as a mechanism to address the crisis. The institutions and the structures of the EC/EU have proved too good a tool throughout the last five decades to be left unused as Europe comes to terms with the challenges of a new century.

### NOTES

1  Jean Monnet, *Memoirs* (London: Collins, 1978), pp. 264ff.
2  Paul-Henri Spaak, *Combats inachevés* (Paris: Fayard, 1969), vol. 2, p. 89.
3  For a somewhat more sophisticated formulation of this view, see his speech to the British Institute of

International and Comparative Law, March 25, 1965. European Community Historical Archives, Brussels, speeches collection.

4   Raymond Poidevin, *Robert Schuman: homme d'état, 1886–1963* (Paris: Imprimerie Nationale, 1986), pp. 244–74.

5   Hans-Peter Schwarz, *Konrad Adenauer: A German Politician and Statesman in a Period of War, Revolution, and Reconstruction* (Providence, RI: Berghahn Books, 1995), vol. 1.

6   Ennio di Nolfo, ed., *Power in Europe? II. Great Britain, France, Germany and Italy and the Origins of the EEC, 1952–57* (Berlin: Walter de Gruyter, 1992).

7   Cited in Christian Pineau, *1956: Suez* (Paris: Robert Laffond, 1976), p. 191.

8   Alan Milward, *The Reconstruction of Western Europe, 1945–51* (London: Methuen, 1984), pp. 362–80.

9   Alan Milward, *The European Rescue of the Nation-State* (London: Routledge, 1992), pp. 173–96.

10  Frances Lynch, *France and the International Economy: From Vichy to the Treaty of Rome* (London: Routledge, 1997), pp. 169–85.

11  Milward, *The European Rescue*, p. xi.

12  See, e.g., Alan Milward, *The Rise and Fall of a National Strategy 1945–1963* (London: Frank Cass, 2002).

13  Monnet famously claimed that while men died taking their experience with them, institutions would endure. *Memoirs*, p. 384.

14  Robert Marjolin, *Le Travail d'une vie. Mémoires 1911–1986* (Paris: Robert Laffond, 1986), p. 343.

15  For a flavor of Hallstein's institutional ambitions, see Walter Hallstein, *Europe in the Making* (New York: Norton, 1973).

16  See, for example, Leon Lindberg, *Political Dynamics of European Economic Integration* (Stanford, CA: Stanford University Press, 1963).

17  Stanley Hoffman, "Obstinate or Obsolete? The Fate of the Nation-State and the Case of Western Europe," *Daedalus* 95 (1966): 862–915.

18  Comment by the Swedish permanent representative to the EU at a Center for European Policy Studies Seminar, Brussels, 1994.

19  The French case against British membership in the 1960s was the first manifestation of this trend.

## GUIDE TO FURTHER READING

Anne Deighton and Alan Milward, eds., *Widening, Deepening and Acceleration: The European Economic Community 1957–1963* (Baden-Baden: Nomos, 1999). One of several edited volumes so far published providing a multilingual flavor of current research on the EEC's early development.

Jeffrey Giauque, *Grand Designs and Visions of Unity: The Atlantic Powers and the Reorganization of Western Europe, 1955–63* (Chapel Hill, NC: University of North Carolina Press, 2002). A flawed but stimulating attempt to provide a very political reading of the EEC's origins and early development.

William Hitchcock, *France Restored: Cold War Diplomacy and the Quest for Leadership in Europe, 1944–1954* (Chapel Hill, NC: University of North Carolina Press, 1998). A good study, emphasizing the political roots of the Schuman Plan and the EDC; *The Struggle for Europe: The Turbulent History of a Divided Continent* (London: Profile, 2003), a decent textbook on postwar Europe, placing the integration process in its wider context.

Michael Hogan, *The Marshall Plan: America, Britain, and the Reconstruction of Western Europe, 1947–1952* (Cambridge: Cambridge University Press, 1986). The best account of US motivations in launching the Marshall Plan.

Wilfried Loth, ed., *Crises and Compromises: The European Project 1963–1969* (Baden-Baden: Nomos, 2001). The sequel to the Deighton/Milward volume.

N. Piers Ludlow, *Dealing With Britain: The Six and the First UK Application to the EEC* (Cambridge: Cambridge University Press, 1997) and *The European Community and the Crises of the 1960s: Negotiating the Gaullist Challenge* (London: Routledge, 2006). Two detailed monographs that try to chart the development of the EEC in its first decade.

Alan Milward, *The Reconstruction of Western Europe 1945–51* (London: Methuen, 1984). The first of three revisionist volumes, emphasizing the economic roots of European integration; *The European Rescue of the Nation-State* (London: Routledge, 1992), the sequel, focusing on the launch of the EEC.

Andrew Moravcsik, *The Choice for Europe: Social Purpose and State Power from Messina to Maastricht* (Ithaca, NY: Cornell University Press, 1998). The most controversial attempt by a political scientist to review the development of the EEC since 1958.

Ennio di Nolfo, ed., *Power in Europe? II. Great Britain, France, Germany and Italy and the Origins of the EEC, 1952–57* (Berlin: Walter de Gruyter, 1992). A reasonable selection of essays on national motivations behind the EEC's launch.

Craig Parsons, *A Certain Idea of Europe* (Ithaca, NY: Cornell University Press, 2003). Another political science attempt to tackle the EEC's past, this time focusing on France.

Enrico Serra, ed., *The Relaunching of Europe and the Treaties of Rome* (Brussels: Bruylant, 1989). A further collection of essays on the EEC's origins.

Peter Stirk, *A History of European Integration since 1914* (London: Continuum, 2001). A useful textbook which gives an overview of both the interwar and postwar development of integration.

Derek Urwin, *The Community of Europe: A History of European Integration since 1945* (London: Longman, 2nd edn, 1995). Although a little dated, this is still probably the best textbook on post-1945 integration.

Antonio Varsori, ed., *Inside the European Community: Actors and Policies in the European Integration 1957–1972* (Baden-Baden: Nomos, 2006). The most recent shop window on research across Europe on integration history.

# CHAPTER TWENTY-SIX

# The Making of Modern Southeast Asia in the Age of Decolonization and the Cold War

## KEVIN RUANE

One way to appreciate the tremendous impact of the Second World War on the political geography of Asia is to compare two maps, the first depicting the area in 1939, the other as it stood just ten years later. Even the casual observer of the 1939 map could not fail to notice the expanse of imperial red denoting the extent of British rule. India under the Raj dominated South Asia, with Burma and Sri Lanka (Ceylon) important adjacent interests. Further east, British economic penetration of China and control of Hong Kong had created a vibrant hub of commercial activity; indeed, China was prey to a conglomeration of powers, among them Britain, Russia, Japan, and the United States, which controlled much of the country's commercial life. In Southeast Asia, the main focus of this study, the British position centered on Malaya and Singapore. But other European powers also held sway in the region, notably the Dutch in Indonesia (Netherlands East Indies) and the French in Indochina (Vietnam, Laos, and Cambodia). In fact by 1939, only two Asian countries, Japan and Thailand (Siam), could lay claim to any degree of genuine independence.

Apart from the imperial coloration, it is perhaps the geographical enormity of China that is the most striking feature of the earlier map. Revolution had swept away the Chinese imperial order in 1911–12 but exercising control over so vast a country proved beyond the power of the republic's first administrations until, in 1928, the Guomindang (Kuomintang) nationalists established a

government in Nanjing (Nanking). Led by Jiang Jieshi (Chiang Kai-shek), the Guomindang (GMD) sought to create a united China and, in the process, reassert national sovereignty by ending foreign exploitation. In the 1930s, however, GMD political primacy was increasingly challenged by the Chinese Communist Party (CCP) and by mid-decade civil war beckoned.

A further observation occasioned by the 1939 map relates to the contrast to be drawn between China and Japan and, in particular, to the way in which Japan, though much smaller in geographical scale and seriously deficient in the natural resources needed to maintain a modern economy, had nonetheless emerged as the leading regional power. Successful wars against China (1894–5) and Russia (1904–5) had brought Japan significant territorial gains, including Taiwan (Formosa) and Korea, as well as a privileged economic position in Manchuria. Japan was thus an imperial power in its own right even before the 1930s when its powerful military, naval, and bureaucratic elites set the country on an aggressively expansionist course. In 1937, full-scale war broke out between Japan and China, the GMD and CCP uniting (albeit uneasily) in the face of the common enemy. In December 1941, the Japanese attack on Pearl Harbor was the prelude to a major military offensive in Southeast Asia intended to drive out the Europeans (as well as the Americans from the Philippines), seize the area's natural resources, and create the economic basis for future regional hegemony. The Sino-Japanese War continued as of old but was now incorporated into this wider conflict.

## The Impact of the Second World War

To what extent did the Second World War in Asia, in tandem with other factors, contribute to the emergence of a "new" Southeast Asia in and after 1945? This question is best answered by focusing largely (though not exclusively) on Vietnam, a country whose violent postwar history is for many people synonymous with the history of modern Southeast Asia as a whole. Beyond this, Vietnam is an apposite study insofar as the "quivering kaleidoscope of international relations early acquired and still in part retains a distinctively Indochinese rhythm to complicate its shifting patterns," not least in Iraq in 2003–6.[1]

The juxtaposition of the 1939 and 1949 maps would certainly appear to confirm the Second World War's catalytic properties: while much of prewar Southeast Asia had been dominated by western imperialism, the events of 1941–5 gave rise to militant anti-colonialism and ultimately decolonization. Before 1941, the European powers, weakened by the First World War, had begun to envision a transition (admittedly long-term) to self-government and ultimately independence for many of their colonies. The problem was that in 1945 the Europeans "lost control of the process": the spectacular Japanese victories over the British, French, Dutch, and Americans in 1941–2, and Japan's subsequent occupation of much of Southeast Asia, had spawned radical strains of revolutionary nationalism whose leaders rejected independence on an installment plan in favor of immediate freedom at the end of the war.[2]

To nationalists like Ho Chi Minh in Vietnam and Achmad Sukarno in Indonesia, the Japanese occupation, in arousing widespread anti-Japanese sentiment and contributing to a heightening of popular nationalist consciousness, created a potential mass political constituency. Though Ho and Sukarno were markedly different nationalists – the former a communist who resisted the Japanese, the latter a non-communist who cooperated

with them – they both recognized that this constituency could fuel the drive for independence after the war. Therefore, even though Japan was defeated in 1945, its earlier military triumphs had exposed the myth of white European supremacy and bequeathed to a generation of nationalists the confidence to oppose a return to the old colonial order. Significantly, in a number of instances – Vietnam, Indonesia, Burma, the Philippines – communists were prominent in the rise of revolutionary nationalism. In 1949, the US secretary of state, Dean Acheson, argued that "All Stalinists in colonial areas are nationalists."[3] Acheson was partly correct: by playing the patriotic card, communists could appeal to a far larger audience than if they confined themselves to extolling the virtues of Marx and Lenin. In Vietnam, however, Ho Chi Minh and the Indochinese Communist Party (ICP) seem to have been inspired by genuinely nationalist ideals as well as by socialist principles, and the Vietminh Independence League, though formed on the initiative of the ICP in 1941, was politically pluralistic and no mere communist "front" organization. Ho remains a controversial figure, his political motivation a matter of intense historical debate. But while fitting Acheson's template, Ho was surely only as successful as he was because his nationalism stemmed from conviction rather than political expedience.[4]

The burgeoning of revolutionary nationalism and the start of decolonization were the two most critical consequences of the war in Southeast Asia and, by extension, two of the key distinguishing features of the "new" Southeast Asia. However, before looking more closely at these developments, it is necessary to offer a word of caution against overly loose employment of the terms "nationalism" and "decolonization." Decolonization was never a uniform process. Leaving aside differences in the British, French, and Dutch experiences in Southeast Asia, there were also discontinuities in the British decolonization process across Asia, to say nothing of the contrast to be drawn with British policy in Africa or the Middle East. "Decolonizations," therefore, might be a more accurate term. Nationalism, too, could benefit from redefinition in the plural since the term suggests homogeneity while masking divisions. In Southeast Asia, ethnic, regional, and class rivalries produced within individual countries a great diffusion of nationalist movements and a sometimes violent competition between them to determine who would govern in the postcolonial era.[5] Historians cannot avoid generalizations – as the remainder of this survey will confirm – but they can remind their readers that behind every generalization lies a complexity deserving further investigation.

## Decolonization in Southeast Asia, 1945–1950

It was the British who set the pace of European decolonization when, in August 1947, India and Pakistan were granted independence. Freedom for Sri Lanka and Burma followed in 1948. Notwithstanding a vibrant historiographical debate in which these events are explained inter alia in terms of British postwar economic weakness, the mobilization of indigenous nationalism, or international pressures, the simple fact is that the Labour government had neither the power nor the inclination to maintain the Raj. "If you are in a place where you are not wanted, and where you have not got the force to squash those who don't want you," opined Hugh Dalton, chancellor of the exchequer, "the only thing to do is to come out."[6] In a throwback to the Victorian ideal of "trade without rule where possible, rule for trade where necessary," Britain sought to establish a new relationship with these countries within a broadened multiracial Commonwealth, substituting influence for control and seeking to maximize economic benefits.[7] It follows that terms like "retreat from" or "abandonment" or "liquidation" of empire, though common in the historiography, are misleading: "transformation" is a more accurate expression of British intent. Nor was the transfer of power on the subcontinent meant to presage a similarly swift process of decolonization in Britain's Southeast Asian empire. On the contrary, independence for India, Pakistan, Sri Lanka, and Burma – countries wherein commercial gain stood to be swamped by security costs – represented a streamlining of the imperial enterprise in an effort to make the remainder run more profitably as Britain

embarked on the mammoth task of postwar reconstruction.

Southeast Asia, as a geographical term, only gained currency during the Second World War as the area falling under the responsibility of the Southeast Asia Command (SEAC), formed in 1943. This wartime delineation survived into the postwar period when Southeast Asia was generally deemed to comprise the Philippines, Indonesia, Burma, Vietnam, Laos, Cambodia, Thailand, Malaya, and Singapore. Given the area's structural artificiality and the pronounced nationalist outlook of its individual countries, it is hardly surprising that a cohesive regional identity or outlook was slow to emerge. Arguably, the first significant step in this direction came only in 1967 when the Association of Southeast Asian Nations came into being. Until then, the history of modern Southeast Asia is the history of individual states of singular character undergoing sometimes comparable but often differing political, economic, and social development, hence regional generalization can be risky. Decolonization is a case in point: beyond the common desire to be free, the process by which colonial territories achieved their independence was a varied one.

As already observed, the pace of British decolonization in Southeast Asia was slower than in South Asia, partly because of the absence of mass-supported nationalist movements pressing the case for early independence, and partly because the strategic importance of Singapore and the great dollar-earning value of Malaya remained imperial assets at a time when the subcontinent offered only mounting liabilities. The Attlee government's decision to maintain colonial rule in Southeast Asia (albeit diluted by significant concessions to moderate Malay nationalism) was also based on the twin assumptions that Britain's continued Great Power status depended on global reach and that the "special relationship" with the United States required Washington to value Britain as an ally on the world, not just the European, stage. For their part, the Americans had moved quickly to finalize independence for the Philippines (July 1946), though not before they had ensured the preservation of their economic stake and military bases in the country in such a way that for many years Washington's relations with Manila displayed the hallmark of informal imperialism.

Indonesia, the largest and most populous country in Southeast Asia, had been occupied by Japan in 1942. Local nationalists, among them Sukarno, were initially seduced by Tokyo's clarion call of "Asia for the Asians" and willingly cooperated with the Japanese in maintaining civil administration. Over time, though Indonesian resentment grew as it became clear that Tokyo's real aim was "Asia for Japan," Sukarno took the pragmatic view that continued collaboration offered an opportunity to lay the political and military groundwork for future independence. It was an approach that bore fruit in August 1945 when, on the heels of the Japanese surrender, Sukarno declared Indonesia independent. Over the next year, however, the weak Indonesian Republic was unable to resist the gradual reimposition of Dutch control over much of the archipelago. Negotiations then ensued during which The Hague offered semi-independence (with Java and Sumatra ceded to the Republic), but accompanying proposals for an overarching federal political structure were transparently designed to preserve de facto Dutch authority. The refusal of The Hague to make further meaningful concessions provoked clashes between nationalist and Dutch forces and led to two brutal Dutch "police actions" in 1947–8 that aroused widespread international condemnation.

Against this torrid backdrop, the United States declared itself in favor of total independence for Indonesia. The Truman administration's approach to decolonization was framed in response to the exigencies of the Cold War. In cases where America's European allies faced nationalist movements led or strongly influenced by communists – in Indochina, for example – anti-communism trumped anti-colonialism and the United States opted for a coalition with imperialism. In Indonesia, however, Sukarno's crushing of a major communist revolt on Java in 1948 suggested that Indonesian nationalism was in safe anti-communist hands and Washington felt free to vent its anti-colonial spleen. But the Americans were also concerned lest the Dutch become sucked into a full-scale war of reconquest that would

denude their contribution to the economic recovery and security of western Europe, both US priorities. The United States thus pressed the Dutch hard on the independence issue, even threatening to suspend Marshall Plan appropriations. In the end, as one American diplomat put it, "money talked," and in December 1949 Indonesia became fully independent.[8]

The Dutch had shown themselves to be graceless decolonizers but the level of violence in Indonesia still fell short of full-scale conflict. This was also the case in Malaya where the British faced a communist insurgency, one of several to break out in Southeast Asia in 1948.[9] Although the Malayan "Emergency" officially lasted twelve years, the communist threat had been effectively contained by the mid-1950s. Some historians have argued that the "Emergency" was convenient to the British in that it served as justification for protracted control over a wealth-generating colony. This view in turn highlights the wider historiographical argument that Britain, with America's acquiescence, invoked Cold War necessity to legitimize a continuation of direct or indirect imperial rule in Southeast Asia, the Middle East, and Africa; air bases in Iraq, for instance, would be crucial to any air offensive against the southern USSR, while Singapore's naval installations were valuable in the context of communist containment in Southeast Asia.[10] There is some merit in this view, but it underrates the readiness of the British to bow before the force of local nationalism as they did in negotiating the Suez base agreement with Egypt in 1954. Moreover, in Malaya it was Britain's repeated promise of ultimate independence – made good in 1957 – that helped secure the support, or at least neutrality, of the Malay population in the struggle against a Malayan Communist Party mainly recruited from the ethnic Chinese community. The British were also inclined to draw unfavorable comparisons between their own flexible approach to colonial transformation and the unreconstructed imperialism of the Dutch and the French which, by generating regional instability, endangered London's broader objective of a new economic and security partnership between the West and Southeast Asia. Most damaging in this regard was the Indochina War.

## The Indochina War

French imperial expansion in Southeast Asia had climaxed in 1887 with the creation of the Union of Indochina – Laos, Cambodia, and Vietnam. Notwithstanding periodic anti-colonial eruptions, French rule continued uninterrupted until June 1940 when defeat in Europe by Germany severed the link between the metropole and its Southeast Asian empire. A predatory Japan quickly took advantage of Vietnam's isolation, occupying the country in stages between July 1940 and July 1941. Thereafter, in a move atypical of Japanese occupation policy in European territories, the French colonial regime was recruited to maintain civil administration. Meanwhile, in May 1941, the ICP had established the Vietminh as a vehicle for channeling anti-Japanese feeling into nationalist action. For the next four years, the Vietminh organized and proselytized in anticipation of *thoi co* – literally, "seizing the right opportunity."[11] That opportunity arrived in August 1945 when, following the Japanese surrender, the Vietminh took control of the principal centers of power. The defeated Japanese put up no resistance, while French colonial officials languished in jail, prisoners since the previous March when the Japanese had terminated their collaborationist relationship. On September 2, 1945, Ho Chi Minh declared the birth of an independent Democratic Republic of Vietnam (DRV).

Vietnam's independence lasted roughly two weeks. In mid-September, British-led Indian forces arrived in Saigon to oversee the Japanese surrender. Bypassing the Vietnamese administration, the British released the French from jail and then assisted them in driving the Vietminh from the city. Though reconciled to Indian independence, the Labour government was not yet ready to relinquish its Southeast Asian empire and, in this connection, feared the encouragement that a Vietminh state would give to nationalists in British territories. By the end of 1945, the French had regained control of the south, but in the north the Nationalist Chinese, under cover of taking the surrender of Japanese forces, seemed bent on annexing the area. Reluctantly, the Vietminh accepted that a French return to the north was the only way to ensure Chinese evacuation.

Convinced that European colonialism was dying, Ho reasoned that the French "can stay for only a short time" whereas the last time the Chinese came "they stayed a thousand years."[12] In March 1946, the French, having first agreed to negotiations on Vietnam's future, returned north, but the subsequent talks got nowhere mainly because unqualified independence, though at the top of Ho's agenda, was at the bottom of France's. At the end of 1946, France resorted to military force to drive the Vietminh out of the main northern cities and, in the process, triggered the first Vietnam War. Importantly, the French would eventually secure an advantage denied the Dutch in Indonesia, namely American backing. Indeed, while the United States worked to undermine the Dutch empire in Southeast Asia, it would help preserve the French imperial position in Indochina, an inconsistency explicable by reference to the Cold War and the evolving US concept of national security.

Following the promulgation of the Truman Doctrine in 1947, the French increasingly depicted the struggle in Vietnam as a contest between the Free World and Soviet communism in the hope of securing military assistance from Washington. To the Americans, however, the war remained as much a colonial as a Cold War issue and a decision on aid was deferred until, in 1949, the end of the Chinese Civil War and the birth of the People's Republic of China (PRC) altered US strategic priorities and raised fears for the future of Japan in particular. In order for Japan to be economically self-sustaining – a goal of US policy – it required an alternative source of raw materials and trading options to its traditional (but now communized) China market. Southeast Asia fitted the bill. Hence, by propping up the French in Indochina, the US could ensure the stability of Southeast Asia generally and simultaneously insure against the risk of Japan being drawn into the PRC's economic, and even political, orbit. The winter of 1949–50 also saw the Truman administration subjected to such fierce domestic criticism over its failed China policy that a "do nothing" approach to Southeast Asia was politically impossible. In any event, the revised US Cold War strategy contained in NSC-68 (April 1950) emphasized the importance of decisive action. Accordingly, in May 1950, the US government announced the start of a military assistance program for France in Indochina. But just as the Americans were aligning themselves with the French – and providing military assistance to Burma, Indonesia, and Thailand in keeping with their new interest in Southeast Asian security – so the PRC was committing itself to the Vietminh. By spring 1950, the Indochina conflict had become a Sino-American war by proxy.

## The Cold War in Asia

The emergence of the PRC opened up a second major front in the Cold War. Initially, the US State Department entertained some hope that the CCP's pronounced nationalism would make it a reluctant follower of the USSR and that international communism might yet be an enemy divided. In London, too, the Labour government discerned an opportunity for the West to drive a wedge between Moscow and Beijing, and this consideration, coupled with the need to protect its economic stake in China, explains the Attlee administration's decision to accord early *de jure* recognition to the Central People's Government in January 1950. The Truman administration might have followed suit when, as Acheson put it, the "dust had settled" on the domestic tumult caused by the Soviet A-bomb test, the communist victory in China, and the first McCarthyite allegations.[13] But the outbreak of the Korean War in June 1950, and especially PRC entry into the conflict a few months later, meant that the dust never had a chance to settle and that Sino-American relations would be marked by hostility and an absence of diplomatic relations for a further three decades.

Research has since confirmed the existence of deep tensions from the very outset of the Sino-Soviet partnership. In February 1950, the signature of the Sino-Soviet Treaty seemed to many western observers to betoken a united Euro-Asian communist bloc, but in reality the treaty was the result of difficult and protracted negotiations during which Mao Zedong was brow-beaten by an imperious Stalin determined to assert his leadership of world communism. Mao tolerated this treatment because of the PRC's dependence on Soviet economic and military assistance as well as diplomatic support for admission to the United Nations (UN) and the return of Taiwan. Yet for all the fractiousness of Sino-Soviet relations, it is also clear that Beijing's ideologically driven hostility toward the United States was so pronounced that even if the latter had chosen the path of accommodation, the PRC would have continued, as Mao put it, to "lean to one side."[14] Interestingly, one of the few matters on which Stalin and Mao were in accord was that chief responsibility for aiding the Vietnamese communists should be China's, partly because of geography and partly because, in Stalin's view, Ho's nationalism made him a potentially troublesome ally. In early 1950 a Chinese Military Advisory Group was established as the conduit for PRC aid to the Vietminh, an initiative personally supported by Mao as a means of buttressing PRC security to the south.

The Korean War provides a further example of this PRC security imperative. After enjoying great early success in the summer of 1950, the North Koreans had been driven back to the 38th parallel, the border between North and South Korea, by American-led UN forces. In October, UN troops crossed into North Korea with the aim of liberating the country from communist rule. Viewed from Beijing's standpoint, this move appeared to be part of a coordinated assault on PRC security: since the outbreak of the Korean conflict, the United States had made itself the protector of the Nationalist Chinese regime on Taiwan, increased military assistance to the French in Indochina, and was evidently bent on restoring Japanese sovereignty and recruiting Japan into a Cold War alliance. In November 1950 the PRC hit back, Chinese troops entering North Korea in force and halting, then reversing, the UN advance. By spring 1951, the fighting had stabilized around the 38th parallel and ceasefire talks began. Two years on, in July 1953, an armistice confirmed the partition of Korea on much the same geographical basis as had existed before the war.

## Indochinese Climacteric

As the Korean War waned, so the Indochina War waxed. By the end of 1953, US dollars were paying for nearly 80 percent of the cost of the French war effort, yet it was the Vietminh that was in the ascendant. In an attempt to wrest back the military initiative, the French constructed a fortress at Dien Bien Phu, a remote valley in northwest Vietnam deep inside enemy territory. The aim was to draw the Vietminh into a set-piece battle in which superior French firepower might for once prove decisive. But any such optimism evaporated once the battle opened on March 13, 1954. The Vietminh pitted over 40,000 troops against the 12,000-man garrison (rising to 15,000 with emergency reinforcement), while Vietminh artillery quickly destroyed the airstrip, the garrison's lifeline. At the end of March, the Vietminh commander, General Vo Nguyen Giap, abandoned his initial but costly "human wave" tactics in favor of attritional siege warfare.

In Washington, US policymakers feared that a French defeat would lead either to a general military collapse in Vietnam or, by exacerbating war-weariness in France, to a diplomatic sell-out at the Geneva conference on Asian Cold War problems that was scheduled to begin on April 26. Either scenario would constitute a communist triumph and an American, as well as a French, humiliation. At the end of March, the Eisenhower administration publicly announced its crisis solution: "united action." A coalition of the United States and like-minded powers (in the first instance Britain, France, Australia, and New Zealand) would intervene in Vietnam to strengthen the French position beyond Dien Bien Phu and so ensure that the loss of one battle did not lead to the loss of the war. In trying to sell "united action" to the American public, President Eisenhower coined the term "domino theory" to describe the geopolitical consequences that would flow from a Vietminh success, but the US Congress, to which Eisenhower turned for war powers, was less susceptible to apocalyptic rhetoric and made approval of "united action" contingent upon two key prerequisites: first, that there was genuinely wide allied support; and second, that the French commit themselves to total independence for Vietnam. In the event, neither precondition was fulfilled and, in consequence, there was no US-led military intervention. Left to its fate, the French garrison at Dien Bien Phu finally surrendered on May 7, the day before the Geneva conference formally turned its attention to Indochina.

Britain, America's closest ally, had refused to countenance any kind of military solution before or during the Geneva negotiations, a stance that clearly influenced Australia and New Zealand. Fearful that armed intervention would be met by Chinese counter-intervention on the Korean model and that the conflict might even escalate into a Third World War, the Churchill government preferred to seek a political solution based on partition of Vietnam. The French, meanwhile, prevaricated over Vietnam's political future until June when the anti-war politician Pierre Mendès-France was elevated to the premiership. Mendès-France met American requirements by his advocacy of Indochinese freedom but, crucially, he was at one with the British in favoring a peaceful settlement. On July 21, 1954, an agreement was finally reached at Geneva that provided for an armistice in Vietnam, the temporary division of the country at the 17th parallel (the Vietminh regrouping north and the French south of that line), and nationwide elections in 1956 after which Vietnam would be reunited and its independence confirmed.

In America, this dénouement was condemned in right-wing circles as communist appeasement but the Eisenhower administration was more measured in its verdict. As Under-Secretary of State Walter Bedell Smith reflected, "diplomacy is rarely able to gain at the conference table what cannot be gained or held on the battlefield."[15] From a Vietminh standpoint, however, the settlement involved substantial concessions, including the retrocession of 20 percent of territory (and more than a million people) previously under their control. Evidence available since 1979 confirms that the Lao Dong (or Vietnam Workers' Party, as the ICP restyled itself in 1951) was pressured to compromise by its powerful communist patrons. Neither the USSR nor the PRC was prepared to back the Vietminh's claim to all or even most of Vietnam, if by so doing the conference collapsed, the war continued, the US intervened, and the conflict escalated in a way that threatened to draw in both communist giants. Moreover, from the PRC's perspective, its security would be more than adequately guaranteed by Vietminh control of just northern Vietnam, hence it was Beijing that took the lead in levering the Lao Dong into accepting a settlement that promoted Sino-Soviet strategic interests at the expense of Vietnamese nationalist goals.[16]

US policymakers were probably better pleased by the Geneva accords than Ho and his followers, particularly as the southern half of the trigger-domino of Southeast Asia remained free when at one point all of Vietnam seemed in jeopardy. Building on this positive outcome, in autumn 1954 the Eisenhower administration launched a "nation-building" program designed to create a separate, anti-communist state in southern Vietnam and, as an intended consequence, to render partition permanent. The man chosen to lead the enterprise was Ngo Dinh Diem, a Vietnamese nationalist with impeccable anti-communist credentials. In 1955, with US backing, Diem rejected the Geneva proposal for all-Vietnam elections and installed himself as president of a new state, the southern-based Republic of Vietnam (RVN). The RVN was given protection against external threats by the Southeast Asia Treaty Organization (SEATO); established in September 1954, SEATO comprised the United States, Britain, Australia, New Zealand, France, Thailand, Pakistan, and the Philippines, and took responsibility for the security of Laos, Cambodia, and southern Vietnam.

## The New Asia in and after 1955

By 1955 a new Southeast Asia had emerged from its colonial cocoon. Leaving aside Thailand (which had never been colonized), Indonesia, Burma, the Philippines, Laos, and Cambodia had all attained their freedom. In Vietnam, the northern half of the country – the Democratic Republic of Vietnam – was already independent; in the south, independence arrived with the withdrawal of the residual French presence and the establishment of the RVN in the autumn of 1955. Colonialism endured in Malaya, Singapore, and the Borneo territories, but even here Britain was working to a timetable that would see Malaya independent in 1957, Singapore self-governing in 1959, and both territories, along with North Borneo, merged into

a new independent construct, the Malaysian Federation, in 1963.

Decolonization, like the Second World War, at first sight appears to be a common denominator in the region – an experience undergone by most of the countries of the area and, as such, a potentially unifying development. The problem is that the *way* in which individual countries experienced both the war and the end of colonial rule varied so greatly that even in 1955 "Southeast Asia" remained little more than a catch-all term for a grouping of geographically proximate but otherwise disparate states. Whereas in western Europe after 1945 a strong regionalism developed out of a mainly common political culture – parliamentary democracy – the newly independent countries of Southeast Asia were politically eclectic and initially more concerned with nation-building than inter-nation cooperation. For two decades after 1955, Vietnam encompassed both communist dictatorship and right-wing authoritarianism; in Cambodia and Laos, royalist governments clung to power in the face of left- and right-wing pressures; in Thailand, though the monarchy remained intact, real power lay with a military-backed right-wing political clique; in the Philippines, and to some degree in Malaya/Malaysia, governance oscillated between real and sham democracy; and in Burma, military dictatorship became the established order. In Indonesia, Sukarno substituted "guided democracy" for parliamentary rule in 1959, a political experiment that went so awry that he was forced to try to contain the ensuing domestic unrest, exacerbated by a deteriorating economic situation, by conjuring up an external threat in the form of the new Malaysian Federation. The ensuing "Konfrontasi" with Malaysia lasted from 1963 to 1966 and only ended when Sukarno was overthrown by the Indonesian military.

In the mid-1950s Southeast Asia found itself in the eye of the Asian Cold War storm. With the European front largely stabilized, the East–West struggle had shifted to the Third World where the capitalist and communist powers engaged in vigorous competition for the allegiance of recently independent nations. In Southeast Asia, US national security concerns led to unprecedented levels of engagement: political support for the

Indonesian Republic was followed by military and economic aid until, in the early 1950s, Jakarta gravitated toward Cold War neutrality and relations with Washington deteriorated; American assistance for France in Indochina was succeeded by extensive military and economic aid to the RVN; new US military bases were established in Thailand; and a 1951 security treaty with the Philippines – a crucial link in the US "offshore island defense chain" running from Alaska through Japan to the Ryukyus – guaranteed retention of existing bases in that country. SEATO, meanwhile, provided a wider security context for America's emergence as a regional power. It was, however, the defense of South Vietnam that became America's top priority, the escalating commitment to the RVN a "logical, if not inevitable, outgrowth of a world view and a policy, the policy of [communist] containment, which Americans in and out of government accepted without serious question for more than two decades."[17] In national security terms, the RVN was the domino that could not be let fall. But it was also an American creation – "our offspring," as John F. Kennedy once put it – and the obligation to protect it from internal and external threats ran deep.[18]

For many ordinary Southeast Asians, however, the Cold War struggle took second place to the daily struggle for food, shelter, and a basic living. The poverty in which the masses in most countries lived provides a continuity between the new and old Southeast Asia, albeit one that Commonwealth foreign ministers, meeting in Colombo in January 1950, were determined to sever by launching the so-called Colombo Plan to foster economic development in South and Southeast Asia. Beyond the moral imperative of improving living standards and increasing food production, the plan possessed a Cold War dimension insofar as communism was thought to breed like a disease in conditions of poverty. The Attlee government, while accepting the need for a degree of conventional security as a deterrent to PRC adventurism, believed that victory in the Asian Cold War depended on imaginative social and economic programs that negated the popular appeal of communism. From the outset, Britain and its Commonwealth partners understood that the success

of the Colombo Plan hinged on a major injection of "new money," especially US dollars. The Truman administration, however, fixated on the conventional military threat that Communist China was deemed to pose, was initially noncommittal. Then came the Korean War and, with it, a growing American appreciation that the Colombo Plan, if it helped to contain communism at "rice-roots" level in Asia, would complement US efforts to contain communism at the main-force military level. The United States subscribed to the plan in 1951 and over the next five years contributed $2 billion in economic and technical aid; by 1983, of the $72 billion in aid channeled into the plan during its near-quarter-century existence, over 50 percent ($41.2 billion) had come from American sources.[19]

By 1955, all the countries of Southeast Asia, except divided Vietnam, were involved in the Colombo Plan, which thus served as a much-needed forum for regional cooperation. But while the Americans and British viewed Southeast Asian unity primarily through a Cold War lens, the Indian leader, Jawaharlal Nehru, increasingly saw it as a guarantee of the area's independence from both communist and neocolonialist threats. Since gaining independence, India had emerged as a pole of attraction for other Asian states that shared not only Nehru's determination to avoid entanglement in the Cold War but also the *panchsheel* (or five principles of his foreign policy), namely, mutual respect between states for their territorial integrity and sovereignty; non-aggression; non-interference in the internal affairs of other states; equality of status between states; and peaceful coexistence. In April 1954, the *panchsheel* had formed the basis of a declaration issued by the Colombo Powers – so-called because of the venue of a gathering of Indian, Indonesian, Pakistani, Sri Lankan, and Burmese leaders – in response to the crisis in Indochina. The Colombo Powers also proposed a further meeting encompassing all Afro-Asian states in order to forge a collective voice on international affairs. A year later, in April 1955, this idea was realized at the Bandung conference. In all, twenty-nine states, including Communist China (deemed by Nehru to be Chinese first and communist second), attended. But common ground was hard to find. The term

"Afro-Asian" implied a degree of unity that simply did not – nor could not – exist given the widely diverging political and economic agendas of the participating countries. What, it might be asked, did parliamentary democracies have in common with communist dictatorships, absolutist monarchies, and authoritarian regimes, all of which were on parade at Bandung? Inevitably, the conference's conclusions were generalized – acceptance in principle of the *panchsheel*, denunciation of colonialism and racism, appeals to the richer nations of the world to devote greater resources to economic development in poorer countries. Bandung did, however, prove to be the genesis of the Non-Aligned Movement (NAM). About half the conferees were genuinely non-aligned (of the remainder, most were allied with the United States and the West, with North Vietnam and the PRC the exceptions), and these states built upon this common link at a subsequent series of conferences that also attracted European, Middle Eastern, and Latin American countries and culminated in the formal launch of the NAM in Belgrade in 1961.

## Vietnam Codicil

Absent from Belgrade was North and South Vietnam, the Cold War alignment of both countries being unquestionable. Indeed, 1961 was the year when the fuse that would ignite the second Vietnam War was lit. Following the cancellation of the all-Vietnam elections, the DRV concentrated on nation-building in the north but never lost sight of the goal of national reunification and eventually, in late 1960, shifted strategy to elevate liberation of the south to a status equal to defense of the north. With Hanoi's encouragement, the National Liberation Front (NLF) for South Vietnam was established to direct political opposition to the US-sponsored government in Saigon. Like the Vietminh before it, the NLF attracted non-communists as well as communists, although the latter exercised a subtle but controlling influence. In early 1961, the People's Liberation Armed Forces (PLAF) was established as the military wing of what soon became a full-scale insurgency against the Diem regime. The Kennedy administration responded by increasing military

and economic aid and by dispatching over 15,000 military advisers to work with the RVN armed forces.

The story of the second – American – war in Vietnam is familiar to most students of international history, though it is often told through the distorting prism of a historiography dominated by US historians seeking explanations for US involvement and US defeat. Hence we are provided with the failure of the Kennedy administration's efforts to arrest the decline in RVN political and military fortunes; President Johnson's decision to deepen US involvement in 1965, first by launching an air war against North Vietnam in the hope of forcing Hanoi to end its support for the southern insurgency, and then by the commitment of US ground troops to hold the line in South Vietnam while the air war was given time to achieve its coercive objectives; the ensuing massive US military escalation as North Vietnam refused to buckle and the PLAF proved to be an elusive but deadly adversary; the shock of the Tet Offensive of 1968, which showed that, after three years of escalation, the communists were no closer to defeat nor therefore the US any nearer to victory; the Johnson administration's post-Tet decision to seek a negotiated exit and its endorsement in 1969 by Richard Nixon's Republican administration; the tortured American pursuit of "peace with honor" culminating in the signature of the Paris Peace Accords in January 1973 and the US military withdrawal; the North Vietnamese offensive against the south in 1974–5 and the Ford administration's refusal to reopen US involvement; and finally, the fall of Saigon in April 1975 and Vietnam's emergence from the fog of war as a united, independent, and communist state.

Over the last fifteen years, however, the American emphasis in Vietnam historiography has been leavened somewhat by research into the conflict from "the other side" – from the communist perspective. As a result, it is now possible to construct a more rounded appreciation of the Vietnam wars.[20] One feature of this "new" Vietnam history has been greater scrutiny of PRC and Soviet policy. To some extent, the work of Chen Jian, Qiang Zhai, and Ilya Gaiduk (to name but three of the historians working in this field) has merely confirmed what was already known, namely, that

Moscow and Beijing were engaged in fierce competition for the loyalty of Hanoi, that they sought to buy that loyalty through huge grants of military and economic assistance, but that the DRV's leaders skillfully exploited this competition to North Vietnam's ultimate gain. In the process, however, these writers have added tremendous detail as well as interpretive nuance and subtlety.[21] Relations between the Chinese and Vietnamese communists, for example, can now be divided into two distinct phases. During the 1950–68 period, when the PRC viewed the United States as the major threat to its security, cooperation with the DRV was Beijing's priority. Staggering amounts of Chinese military supplies not only ensured the Vietminh triumph over the French in 1954 but, a decade or so later, helped North Vietnam survive the onslaught of the American air war. Between 1968 and 1975, however, the PRC moved toward containment of North Vietnam. This was the period when Beijing came to regard the Soviet Union as its main adversary and when the DRV, increasingly reliant for its defense on sophisticated Soviet-supplied military hardware, gradually abandoned its policy of not taking sides in the Sino-Soviet dispute and gravitated toward the USSR. Concurrent efforts by Hanoi to extend its influence into neighboring Laos and Cambodia conjured up for Beijing a troubling vision of a future Indochina controlled by a united Vietnam in alliance with Moscow – a vision that came close to realization with the DRV victory in 1975. No amount of PRC aid and advice could overcome the age-old Vietnamese mistrust of all things Chinese or even dent the determination of the Lao Dong's leaders that Vietnam would never be a satellite of the PRC in the way that, a thousand years earlier, it had been a vassal state of Imperial China.

The USSR provides the other side of this story. Between 1950 and 1964 Moscow was content to allow the PRC to take the lead in Vietnam, but following the start of US military action against North Vietnam in 1964–5 Soviet policy became more proactive. With its claim to leadership of the world communist movement increasingly challenged by China, the USSR had little choice but to respond to this threat to a fraternal socialist state. Interestingly, however, while Soviet military aid to North Vietnam increased markedly from 1964, the Kremlin repeatedly urged Hanoi to think in terms of a peaceful settlement. For the Soviets, the Vietnam War was a balancing act. On the one hand it was essential to defend the DRV; on the other, the risk of a prestige-engaging showdown with the US on the Cuban model of 1962 had to be avoided. When North Vietnam's leadership agreed in the aftermath of the Tet Offensive to enter into negotiations with the United States, the USSR appeared to have secured its desiderata: not only had the DRV been preserved, but also a political settlement, the Kremlin's preferred outcome since 1965, now beckoned. The reality, though, was rather different, and evidence shows that Hanoi's decision was based less on Soviet pressure than on the Lao Dong's own assessment of what was right for the DRV. The USSR, as much as the PRC, learned the hard way that military aid bought little influence over Vietnamese decision-making.

North Vietnam's involvement in the Paris peace process in 1968 was in defiance of PRC advice to maintain the military offensive and thus further damaged already brittle CCP–Lao Dong relations. Before long the PRC would itself be attempting to negotiate a Sino-American axis in Asia to counteract the perceived Soviet threat, a development that North Vietnam, still at war with America, viewed with repugnance. After 1975 the Sino-Vietnamese schism intensified and in 1979 the two countries went to war – briefly and inconclusively – following Hanoi's toppling of the Khmer Rouge regime in Cambodia, which Beijing had hitherto backed in an effort to dilute Vietnam's Indochinese hegemony. The USSR stood aside from this "third" Vietnam War but derived satisfaction from PRC discomfiture. Indeed, given that the security imperative had so strongly informed Beijing's policy since 1950, the result of the war – the presence on its southern frontier of a united Vietnam in league with the USSR – makes it hard to regard China as anything other than a loser in the Vietnam context. Yet it does not follow that the Soviet Union was a winner. As Gaiduk has shown, Moscow drew seriously erroneous lessons from the American debacle; in thrall to Marxist-Leninist ideology and convinced that it could succeed where US "imperialism" had failed, the Kremlin became more interventionist in the Third World, an approach that led directly to the "tragedy of Afghanistan" and indirectly to the destruction of the Soviet Union itself.[22]

## Conclusion: Southeast Asia Yesterday, Today, Tomorrow

"The term Southeast Asia," wrote one informed observer in 1946, "is a convenient geographic expression, but is it anything more?"[23] Nearly a decade later, another regional commentator declared: "I do not believe there is such a thing as Southeast Asia except for cartographic purposes."[24] One of the themes of this essay has been the way in which "regionalism" was slow to develop in Southeast Asia. Externally generated initiatives like the Colombo Plan and SEATO possessed marginal value as unifying mechanisms, as did the Bandung process. In fact, it was not until 1967 that the first meaningful moves were made in this direction with the formation of the Association of Southeast Asian Nations (ASEAN). Against the backdrop of the escalating war in Vietnam, five non-communist countries – Thailand, Indonesia, Singapore, Malaysia, and the Philippines – came together to enhance their security and coordinate their economic development. Even then it was a halting first move. Another nine years would pass before the inaugural ASEAN heads of government summit, at which point – 1976 – it was agreed that economic cooperation, previously an aspiration, was now a necessity. Over the following decade, the organization's positive contribution to regional stability helped inspire international business confidence and, with it, mounting levels of inward investment that in turn triggered impressive export-led economic growth amongst member states. In 1984 Brunei joined the association, followed, in 1995, by the Socialist Republic of Vietnam. The accession of Vietnam confirmed the altered political outlook of ASEAN in the post-Cold War world, while for Hanoi the motivation was partly security – the ever-present threat from the PRC – and partly economic. By the turn of the century, Laos, Myanmar (Burma), and Cambodia had boosted ASEAN membership to ten.

Is ASEAN today anything more than a loose grouping of states with certain shared economic and security concerns? Or are its members now thinking regionally and integratively? The answer lies somewhere in between. As recently as 1997, the *Southeast Asian Affairs* review of the year discerned only a "tentative regionalism" at work, but it was evident that greater integration was the sine qua non if ASEAN, hence Southeast Asia, was to realize its full economic potential.[25] There has since been movement in this regard, notably the establishment of an ASEAN Free-Trade Area covering all ten states, though the economies of the newest members have yet to be fully incorporated. Meanwhile, Vietnam has become ASEAN's greatest economic asset. In 1986, Hanoi launched an economic reform program (*doi moi* or "renovation"), which paved the way for the introduction (or reintroduction) of free market practices. The reforms were slow to make an impact but in the early 1990s the Vietnamese economy achieved lift-off and has since proved "unstoppable," maintaining an annual GDP growth of 7–8 percent since 1997. Meanwhile, following normalization of diplomatic relations, trade between Vietnam and the United States rose from $451 million in 1995 to $6.4 billion in 2004, testimony to the desire of both countries to bury the past. But US–Vietnam relations have also become closer in the security sphere, mainly as a reaction to the growing military might of Communist China.[26] All of which may yet see Vietnam emerge as primus inter pares within ASEAN – an ironic prospect given that ASEAN was originally formed in large measure as a reaction to the dangers posed by Vietnamese communism.

As to whether ASEAN can become a regional organization on the lines of the European Union, this will depend on the member states achieving a level of political cohesion to match their increasing economic interdependence. This, though, is doubtful in the near future in view of Vietnam's continued commitment to state socialism and one-party rule. Nor has the prospect of democracy acting as a common political currency elsewhere in Southeast Asia been enhanced in the post-9/11 era by the Bush administration's recruitment of allies in the "war on terror" through grants of economic and military assistance without accompanying pressure to perfect democratization – an approach redolent of US Cold War recruitment strategy when the enemy was international communism rather than international terrorism.[27] Nevertheless, just as it is now possible to think of Vietnam as a country – and not as a war – it is clear that, whatever the future holds, Southeast Asia is no longer merely a "convenient geographical expression."

## NOTES

1  James Cable, *The Geneva Conference of 1954 on Indochina* (London: Macmillan, 1986), p. 1; Melvin Laird, "Iraq: Learning the Lessons of Vietnam," *Foreign Affairs*, November–December (2005): 22–43.

2  P. Kratoska, "Dimensions of Decolonization," in *The Transformation of Southeast Asia: International Perspectives on Decolonization*, ed. M. Frey, R. Pruessen, and Tan Tai Yong (New York: Sharpe, 2003), p. 3.

3  *The Pentagon Papers: The Defense Department History of United States Decisionmaking on Vietnam* (Boston: Beacon Press, 1971), I, p. 51.

4  In general W. Duiker, *Ho Chi Minh: A Life* (New York: Hyperion, 2000).

5  A. Stockwell, "Southeast Asia in War and Peace: The End of European Colonial Empires," in *The Cambridge History of Southeast Asia*, vol. 2, part 2, *From World War II to the Present*, ed. N. Tarling (Cambridge: Cambridge University Press, 1999), p. 20.

6  D. Judd, *Empire: The British Imperial Experience from 1765 to the Present* (London: Fontana, 1997), p. 328. In general, see J. Darwin, *The End of the British Empire: The Historical Debate* (Oxford: Blackwell, 1991).

7  W. R. Louis and R. Robinson, "The Imperialism of Decolonization," *Journal of Imperial and Commonwealth History* 22 (1995): 463–4.

8  R. McMahon, *The Limits of Empire: The United States and Southeast Asia since World War II* (New York: Columbia University Press, 1999), p. 33.

9  Burma, Indonesia, and the Philippines were the others.

10  See in general Louis and Robinson, "Imperialism of Decolonization."

11  W. Duiker, *Sacred War: Nationalism and Revolution in a Divided Vietnam* (New York: McGraw-Hill, 1995), p. 42.

12  Duiker, *Ho*, p. 361.

13  R. Schulzinger, *US Diplomacy since 1900* (Oxford: Oxford University Press, 1998), p. 224.

14  Chen Jian, *Mao's China and the Cold War* (Chapel Hill, NC: University of North Carolina Press, 2001), p. 40.

15  *Pentagon Papers*, I, p. 176.

16  Qiang Zhai, *China and the Vietnam Wars, 1950–1975* (Chapel Hill, NC: University of North Carolina Press, 2000), pp. 46–64.

17  G. Herring, *America's Longest War: The United States and Vietnam, 1950–1975* (New York: McGraw-Hill, 1986 edn), p. 12.

18  R. Buzzanco, *Vietnam and the Transformation of American Life* (Oxford: Blackwell, 1999), p. 64.

19  M. Berger, *The Battle for Asia: From Decolonization to Globalization* (London: Routledge, 2004), p. 44.

20  F. Logevall, "Bringing in the 'Other Side': New Scholarship on the Vietnam Wars," *Journal of Cold War Studies* 3 (2001): 77–93; K. Ruane, "Putting America in its Place? Recent Writing on the Vietnam Wars," *Journal of Contemporary History* 37 (2002): 115–27.

21  Qiang Zhai, *China and the Vietnam Wars*; Chen Jian, *Mao's China*; I. Gaiduk, *Confronting Vietnam: Soviet Policy toward the Indochina Conflict, 1954–1963* (Stanford, CA: Stanford University Press, 2003); idem, *The Soviet Union and the Vietnam War* (Chicago: Ivan R. Dee, 1996).

22  Gaiduk, *Soviet Union and the Vietnam War*, p. 250.

23  A. Vandenbosch, "Regionalism in Southeast Asia," *Far Eastern Quarterly* 5 (1946): 427.

24  N. Peffer, "Regional Security in Southeast Asia," *International Organization* 8 (1954): 311.

25  J. Clad, "Regionalism in Southeast Asia: A Bridge Too Far?" *South East Asian Affairs 1997* (Singapore: ISES, 1997), pp. 3–14.

26  *The Economist*, "Vietnam's Economy: The Good Pupil," May 6, 2004; idem, "America and Vietnam: One chapter ends . . . ," June 23, 2005.

27  J. Öjendal, "Back to the Future? Regionalism in South-East Asia under Unilateral Pressure," *International Affairs* 80 (2004): 532–3.

## GUIDE TO FURTHER READING

Chen Jian, *Mao's China and the Cold War* (Chapel Hill, NC: University of North Carolina Press, 2001). Drawing on recently available Chinese communist sources, Chen Jian has written a fine study that examines the interplay of domestic political and economic factors with ideological and security imperatives in the making of Chinese Cold War policy and demonstrates the centrality of Mao Zedong in Beijing decision-making.

C. Christie, *A Modern History of Southeast Asia: Decolonization, Nationalism and Separatism* (London: Tauris, 1996). In this important work, Christie examines decolonization in Southeast Asia from the perspective of ethnic and social minorities whose interests were marginalized rather than secured by independence – the Penang Chinese, the South Moluccans, and Acehnese in Indonesia, the Karens and Arakanese in Burma, the Montagnards in Vietnam, and the Malays of South Thailand.

W. Duiker, *Sacred War: Nationalism and Revolution in a Divided Vietnam* (New York: McGraw-Hill, 1995). In addition to offering a lucid and thoughtful discussion of Vietnamese communist decision-making during the Vietnam conflicts, Duiker expertly integrates the American perspective in one of best and most rounded accounts of modern Vietnamese history.

M. Frey, R. Pruessen, and Tan Tai Yong, eds., *The Transformation of Southeast Asia: International Perspectives on Decolonization* (New York: Sharpe, 2003). An excellent sequence of essays – with an important initial overview chapter by Paul Kratoska – that brings recent scholarship to bear on the subject of decolonization and offers both country-specific and comparative analyses.

I. Gaiduk, *Confronting Vietnam: Soviet Policy toward the Indochina Conflict, 1954–1963* (Stanford, CA: Stanford University Press, 2003); and *The Soviet Union and the Vietnam War* (Chicago: Ivan R. Dee, 1996). In these books, Gaiduk, employing Soviet primary sources that became available in the years following the dissolution of the USSR, offers the best available account of Moscow's approach to the Vietnam conflict and shows, inter alia, that in addition to military support for North Vietnam in the 1960s, the Soviets privately sought to broker a political settlement between Hanoi and Washington.

A. Iriye, *The Origins of the Second World War in Asia and the Pacific* (London and New York: Longman,

1987). This book, which has become something of a "classic," is required contextual reading for anyone interested in modern Southeast Asia; it provides the "big picture" accompaniment to the "small picture" developments in Vietnam, Indonesia, Burma, the Philippines, and elsewhere.

R. McMahon, *The Limits of Empire: The United States and Southeast Asia since World War II* (New York: Columbia University Press, 1999). McMahon examines the impact of the United States' emergence as a de facto Southeast Asian power in and after the Second World War, and offers an important corrective to those works that assume that Vietnam was America's sole regional interest in the postwar period.

M. Osborne, *Southeast Asia: An Introductory History* (London: Allen & Unwin, 1998). This book, which has gone through several editions, remains an important, readable, and accessible overview of Southeast Asia's history and more recent development. A good starting point for further study.

Qiang Zhai, *China and the Vietnam Wars, 1950–1975* (Chapel Hill, NC: University of North Carolina Press, 2000). A complement to Chen Jian's work on China and the Cold War (see above), this book, drawing on Chinese communist sources, offers a wealth of detail on PRC decision-making on Vietnam and suggests that the emergence in 1975 of a hostile Socialist Republic of Vietnam allied to the USSR renders China almost as great a "loser" in Vietnam as the United States.

K. Ruane, ed., *The Vietnam Wars* (Manchester: Manchester University Press, 2000). A collection of key primary sources on the conflict from all perspectives, Vietnamese and international, accompanied by a series of essays charting the origins, course, and consequences of the Vietnam wars.

N. Tarling, ed., *The Cambridge History of Southeast Asia*, vol. 2, part 2, *From World War II to the Present* (Cambridge: Cambridge University Press, 1999). An important collection of essays exploring in detail, and with great sophistication, Southeast Asia's modern history – though better as a follow-up to Osborne (see above) than as a starter text.

# CHAPTER TWENTY-SEVEN

# The Middle East, 1945–1991:
# The Making of a Mare's Nest

## *SAUL KELLY*

The trouble with much of the literature on the international history of the Middle East during the latter half of the twentieth century is that it is dominated by Cold War studies which have imposed a superpower straightjacket on our understanding of this subject.[1] This has influenced the way we have looked at the motives and actions of the principal Great Power in the region, namely, Great Britain, and its interaction with the local states from the end of the Second World War in 1945 to the Suez crisis in 1956. Whereas the former is usually portrayed as a wicked imperialist, the latter are cast as nations struggling to be free, looking either to the United States or the Soviet Union for aid and succor. This tells us much about the obsessions of American historians but little about the real reasons for developments in the region in this period, namely, the mutual desire of both the superpowers and the local powers to further their own various interests by humbling Britain.

An indecent desire to read the obsequies for Britain in the Middle East after the Suez crisis, in order to concentrate on the bipolar struggle, has led many American historians to neglect the role, admittedly a reduced one, that Britain continued to play in the region until finally deciding in 1966 to withdraw from east of Suez. It is only after that date that one can begin to talk of a bipolar rivalry in the Middle East, but even here American historians have tended to exaggerate it, and the degree of influence which the superpowers had

over their local "client" states. If anything it was the latter who succeeded in enlisting US or Soviet support to further their conflicting regional ambitions.[2] This did not stop with the end of the Cold War in 1991, following the collapse and break-up of the Soviet Union, which coincided with the Gulf War, or, to be more terminologically exact, the Kuwait War. One has only to look at how Saddam Hussein succeeded in dividing the UN Security Council over sanctions and war, or how Iran has played off all and sundry in order to try to secure its nuclear program, to understand the continuity in the nature of relations between local states and the Great Powers. However, this chapter will concentrate on the international history of the Middle East during the Cold War era, from 1945 to 1991.

## The Erosion of British Paramountcy, 1945–1956

With the end of the Second World War Britain seemed to be the paramount power in the Middle East, having defeated its two wartime adversaries in the region, Italy and Germany. The collapse of its main prewar rival, France, had led to the latter's eviction from its mandated territories of Syria and Lebanon and its retreat to the western Mediterranean. The United States seemed only to be interested in exploiting its oil concession in Saudi Arabia. The Soviet Union appeared to be concerned only with erecting a defensive cordon on its southern flank, which involved securing agreements from Turkey and Iran. Britain seemed set to dominate the region through its newly created organizations, politically through the Arab League and economically through the Middle East Supply Centre. Even the Arab nationalists, many of whom had cooperated with the Axis powers, maintained an embarrassed silence as they came to grips with Britain's imposing postwar presence in the Middle East. Within ten years, however, Britain's position had been fatally undermined, losing Egypt, Iraq, Palestine, and Transjordan, while managing to keep footholds only on the periphery of the Middle East, in Libya (independent but under British influence), Aden and the Gulf sheikhdoms, and Cyprus (which was itself convulsed by civil war between Greeks and Turks). What had happened to bring about such a swift collapse of not only British but western predominance in the region?

The most popular explanation given is that Britain failed to come to terms with the rising tide of nationalism in the Middle East. Certainly, Britain could not resolve peacefully the conflicting claims of Jewish and Arab nationalism in its Palestine mandate, and had to hand back responsibility to the United Nations in 1947. Egyptian nationalist demonstrations played a part in preventing agreement in 1946 between the Egyptian and British governments over the future of Britain's main base in the Middle East, in the Suez Canal Zone, and over the Sudan. Similarly, Iraqi nationalist demonstrations contributed to the rejection of the Shayba/Habbaniya base agreement in 1948.[3] It could be argued, however, that the terrorist acts and street demonstrations were not caused by the articulation of widespread nationalist feeling but were the responsibility of factions who were pursuing their own narrow political agendas. If the British, or their client regimes, had confronted them resolutely, the opposition might well have disappeared.[4] Was the new British Labour government inclined to do so? Did leading elements in it actually favor Arab and Jewish nationalism and were they anxious either to encourage it or at least placate it? Moreover, were they worried what American liberal and world opinion, as represented in the United Nations, would think? Was there a conscious rejection by Labour of the old ways of imperial control and compulsion in favor of cooperation and consent?

Another explanation for the loss of British paramountcy in the Middle East is that once India had been "lost" in 1947, the whole *raison d'être* for a presence in the Middle East had disappeared. Britain had become involved in the Middle East in the first place in order to protect the routes to India through the Red Sea (Egypt and Aden) and overland through Palestine, Jordan, and Iraq to the head of the Gulf. It was to guard the northwestern approaches to India that it had become involved in the defense of the Gulf and Iran. Once the British had left India, there was no reason for them to stay in the Middle East, to maintain those "barbicans" and "sally-ports" of empire to which Lord Curzon had referred.[5] Certainly, the new Labour prime minister, Clement Attlee, thought so. He believed that the British position in the Mediterranean and the Middle East was indefensible in the new age of air power and the atomic bomb. His own foreign secretary, Ernest Bevin, and the British chiefs of staff argued against this, however, pointing out that Britain's sea and air routes to its Far Eastern empire and Australia and New Zealand still passed through the Middle East and that its economic recovery after the war depended on Iranian and Iraqi oil. Moreover, its presence in the region acted as a counter to increasing communist influence in southern Europe, shoring up the sagging underbelly of that continent. Lastly, and most persuasively, bases in the region provided the only means by which British bombers could reach the Soviet Union in the event of war.[6] So a new *raison d'être* for Britain remaining in the Middle East had begun to evolve after the war.

Another reason given for the British retreat from the Middle East is that the war had effectively left them bankrupt and that they could not afford to stay. They had liquidated a goodly proportion of their overseas investments and borrowed heavily to pay for the war effort. Not only had the Labour government to find ways of paying for reconstruction, but also it had committed itself to building the New Jerusalem, the welfare state, in Britain. At the same time, it had a million men under arms posted around the world.

Sacrifices had to be made and in the harsh winter of 1946–7 it was decided that it should be the commitments to Greece, Turkey, India, and Palestine.[7] Bankruptcy, the loss of India, and nationalism were all, no doubt, contributory factors to the erosion of British paramountcy after the war. But what about the human factor? The decisions about how to deal with these problems were taken by cabinet ministers on a balance of calculations as to how best to defend British interests. What one has to do is to assess whether these calculations were based on accurate information and to what extent personal and political factors influenced the interpretation of this information and the eventual decisions.

Bevin sought in the Arab Middle East to safeguard British strategic interests (oil and communications) and also to erect a defensive shield for Africa, which both he and Attlee saw as the new economic heart of the empire now that it was clear that Britain would have to leave India. Bevin tried to achieve this in two, complementary ways: through a military confederation under British leadership, which would protect the region from the perceived Soviet threat, and through a program of economic development, again British-led, which would benefit the Arab peoples. The buzzword was "partnership," but with the peasants and the moderate Arab nationalists rather than with the pashas, the old ruling class in the Middle East.[8] This was in line with the working-class sympathies and internationalist outlook of Bevin and the Labour Party.

This regional approach was fundamentally flawed given the differences and longstanding rivalries among the local powers in the region, especially Egypt and Iraq. Its purposes were too vague and Britain was simply not up to providing the necessary economic aid because it had been bankrupted by the war. The idea of developing Africa as an economic alternative to India was overplayed. Lastly, there must be doubts about the negotiating strategy adopted by Bevin to bring about the establishment of these regional military and economic organizations, namely, a bilateral approach. The failure between 1946 and 1948 to secure new defense agreements with Egypt and Iraq, and to stay in Palestine, seriously weakened the British military position in the

Middle East. How was Britain to defend its strategic interests in the region in the future without bases? It can be argued that Bevin and the Foreign Office were largely responsible for Britain's unenviable predicament by actually undermining the old treaties in seeking to revise them. The 1936 treaty with Egypt still had ten years to run when Britain made its fatal gesture and agreed to evacuate Egypt. Any future negotiations had to start from this point, and this is indeed what happened after Egypt denounced the treaty in 1951. The eventual Anglo-Egyptian agreement of 1954 provided for British evacuation of the Suez base along the lines of the 1946 agreement. Although Britain still had bases and troops in Jordan and Iraq, and acquired new ones in newly independent Libya, it was clear that its retention and use of them was entirely dependent upon the goodwill of the host country. Britain had lost that all-important element of control which it had had under the 1930s treaties and which had underpinned its position in the Middle East. The implications of this were to become all too clear in the 1950s.[9]

If the Attlee government's hapless diplomacy helped undermine the British position in the Middle East, what role did the Americans play? It has been said that "if the USA did little to support Britain it did little to undermine the British position either."[10] Is this true? What about the Soviets? Were their demands for control of the Turkish Straits and northern Iran in 1945–6 only part of a clumsy attempt to set up a defensive buffer on their southern flank in much the same way as they were doing in eastern Europe? Is it correct to say that there is no evidence that they sought a warm water port on the Indian Ocean or to penetrate the Mediterranean?[11] If the sole purpose of the Soviets was to close the Straits to foreign warships, however, why did they seek a trusteeship of Tripolitania (the Italian colony in western Libya captured and occupied by the British during the Second World War), back the Yugoslav claim to Trieste, and express an interest in the Dodecanese on the grounds that they needed a port in the Mediterranean for their tiny merchant fleet?[12] It is often overlooked that Stalin dreamt of creating an ocean-going battle fleet in 1945–6.[13] Moreover, control of northern Iran would have undermined British influence in the south of the country and allowed the Soviets to fill the vacuum and reach the northern shore of the Persian Gulf. It was the realization of this, and Britain's perceived inability to resist it, given its bankruptcy, that led the British government in 1946 to slough off responsibility for resisting Soviet pressure on Iran, Turkey, and Greece to the Americans. The Truman administration was reluctant to assume such responsibilities, given the lack of obvious American interests, but a growing perception among some influential policymakers in Washington that Soviet expansionism needed to be contained led to a ringing declaration in March 1947, in the Truman Doctrine, that the US would lend support to any state whose independence was threatened by communist aggression. Actual material aid, rather than diplomatic grandstanding, however, was slow in coming.[14]

If the Americans were prepared to provide some diplomatic support to the British over Greece and the Northern Tier, they were more of a hindrance in the Arab Middle East. American behavior before and during the Suez crisis summed up their ambivalent attitude toward Britain in the Middle East, and France in North Africa. The crisis had been sparked off by Egyptian President Gamal Abdul Nasser's nationalization of the canal, in retaliation for the withdrawal of Anglo-American-sponsored funding for the new Aswan High Dam, which had originally been intended to win Nasser over to the West, after his Czech/Soviet arms deal in 1955. The crisis was brought to a head by the elaborate "collusion" by Britain, France, and Israel to seize the canal and replace the Egyptian leader, which was thwarted by US–Soviet cooperation in the UN. On the one hand, the Americans wanted Britain to take the lead in the defense of western interests in the region, yet they were not prepared to give Britain the necessary political and military support to make this possible (either during the Suez crisis or by joining the Baghdad Pact, of Britain, Turkey, Iraq, and later Iran and Pakistan), since they did not want to be tarred with the colonialist brush.[15] Another factor was the growing American trade and commerce in the region, and particularly the growing importance of oil interests and jealousy of their British rivals. This was perfectly illustrated during the Iranian oil nationalization crisis (itself sparked

by ARAMCO's 50/50 royalties deal with Saudi Arabia) that ended with the American-brokered 1954 agreement which gave US oil companies the lion's share of Gulf oil.[16] The Americans had also been under the illusion that they could win over the Arab nationalists on an anti-colonialist ticket, not realizing that US support for the foundation of the Jewish state of Israel in 1948 had alienated Arab opinion. American and British illusions about Arab nationalism and their pursuit of the chimera of Arab goodwill had led them both to surrender military control of the Middle East and had allowed the Soviet Union, from 1955 onwards, to place itself at the heart of the region: the very thing Britain and the US had sought to prevent since 1945. This represented a huge failure of western policy toward the region. Illusion, incompetence, and loss of will were largely responsible for the erosion of British paramountcy in the Middle East between 1945 and 1956.

## America Intervenes, Britain Retreats: 1957–1968

President Eisenhower and his secretary of state, John Foster Dulles, were certainly concerned that the defeat of Britain and France at Suez had created a power vacuum in the Middle East which might be filled by the Soviet Union. Instead of taking the logical option by joining the Baghdad Pact, Dulles came up with the anti-communist Eisenhower Doctrine in January 1957, which offered military and economic assistance to any state in the Middle East that asked for aid against "armed aggression from any country controlled by international communism." As has been pointed out, it was "a very political document, hastily cobbled together" to satisfy calls both at home and in the region for the US to react.[17] It was hoped that the tone would be bold enough to enable the US to avoid becoming involved in regional entanglements, but this proved to be a barren hope.

The Americans were skeptical about British claims that Egypt and Syria, which had formed the United Arab Republic (UAR) in February 1958, were interfering in the Lebanon, where civil disorder had broken out in May and the pro-western Lebanese president, Camille Chamoun, had appealed to the UN. They were sufficiently worried, however, that the unrest might be communist-inspired to draw up military contingency plans for joint intervention in the Lebanon and Jordan with the British if necessary. In the event it was the Iraqi Revolution of July 14, 1958, which prompted the Americans to intervene militarily in the Lebanon, in response to a request from Chamoun, to prevent another revolt occurring. With the murder of King Faisal II and the overthrow of the Hashemite dynasty in Iraq, the strategy of the British prime minister, Harold Macmillan, of relying on the Iraqi alliance through the Baghdad Pact to maintain British influence (and a northern base) in the Middle East had been destroyed. Initially holding Nasser responsible for what had happened in Iraq, Macmillan wanted joint Anglo-American intervention in the region to confront Nasser and stabilize the British position. The Americans were only prepared to intervene in Lebanon, and then only unilaterally. So Macmillan had to show the British were still prepared to defend their interests in the region, alongside the US, by getting the king of Jordan to invite in British paratroops. The Americans would not send in supporting ground troops and thought the British position too exposed to contribute to the stability of the region.

Following the collapse of the Baghdad Pact, the Northern Tier alliance was reconstituted without Iraq and renamed the Central Treaty Organization, based on Turkey and Iran. Both countries had signed military assistance agreements with the US, and Turkey had allowed US Jupiter missiles to be deployed on its soil. The US and British interventions in Lebanon and Jordan seemed to calm the Arab Middle East for a while, and Macmillan even considered a détente with Nasser which would be useful to Britain in the event of the new military regime in Iraq of Brigadier Qassem posing a threat to Kuwait and the Gulf. This new strategic reality of an unpredictable Iraq eventually drove Britain and Egypt to restore diplomatic relations in January 1961. Five months later, Britain's granting of independence to Kuwait provoked a furious response from Iraq, which seemed to be planning an invasion of the emirate in furtherance of its longstanding territorial claim. It led the British government, with

Kuwaiti agreement, to send troops (later replaced by Arab League peacekeepers) to the emirate – in Operation Vantage – to preempt an Iraqi move.

A key element in Britain's continued ability to defend its position in the Gulf and east of Suez was the base at Aden. This was threatened by the outbreak of a civil war in the Yemen in September 1962 between the royalist forces of the imam and the revolutionary republican forces, which were heavily backed by Nasser in an attempt to restore his prestige in the Arab world following the collapse of the UAR in January 1961. Much to Macmillan's disquiet, the new Kennedy administration recognized the republican regime in December 1962 (although President Kennedy could not even place the Yemen on the map), fearing that continued support for the royalists would lead to a growth of Soviet and Chinese influence, a loss of supposed economic influence over Nasser, and the undermining of the Saudi and Jordanian regimes and US oil interests. The Americans continued to labor under the illusion that seeking the cooperation of radical Arab nationalist regimes in the Middle East was the best way of fighting communism there.

US recognition of the republican regime had the gravest implications for Aden since it encouraged the subversive forces in furtherance of Yemeni irredentism in the Aden Protectorates, where Britain had pursued a "forward policy" and turned the tribal fiefdoms of the conservative sheikhs into a federal union, including Aden colony, called the Federation of South Arabia by January 1963. In a far-sighted move, in the summer of 1964, following the defeat of the tribal rebellion in the Radfan, the Conservative government of Sir Alec Douglas-Home promised independence to South Arabia in an attempt to undermine the prime excuse of the radical Arab campaign of subversion, backed by Nasser, for the liberation of "South Yemen" from "the tyranny of British colonialism."[18] From then on it was a race against time to make the federation strong enough, through British military and economic aid, to stand on its own two feet at independence.

Any chance of this happening vanished with the advent of the Labour government of Harold Wilson in October 1964. "The party's doctrinal convictions about the evils of western imperialism and the foreordained emergence of socialism in Africa and Asia had led it automatically to side with the Aden nationalists from the start."[19] They saw the latter as social democratic trade unionists, rather than the anti-democratic terrorists that they were, and caricatured the rulers of the federation as anachronistic symbols of the hereditary order of sultans, sheikhs, and emirs. Labour's ignorance and delusion about the realities of South Arabian politics informed nearly every decision taken by them on the future of Aden and the federation from 1964 and ultimately sealed its fate. In February 1966, the Labour secretary of defense, Denis Healey, announced a severe reduction in the British presence east of Suez, including the withdrawal from Aden colony and base by the end of 1968 and the termination of the treaties of protection with the federal rulers. It was a total betrayal of past British undertakings, which destroyed the basis of Britain's authority in South Arabia, delighted Nasser and the nationalists, and led to a bloody struggle between rival Arab nationalist factions to see who would succeed the British. It is doubtful in the history of the British Empire whether there has been a more shameful end to British rule than the abandonment of Aden in 1967. Within 18 months of the British departure, the population of Aden shrunk from 220,000 to 80,000 (most of whom had been murdered). Another 200,000 fled from the old protectorate to Saudi Arabia in the next few years. This was the reality of the new People's Republic of South Yemen.

The Gulf sheikhs had watched with growing concern as the situation had unraveled in Aden, for the principal justification offered by successive British governments for the retention of Aden was that it was needed to underpin the British position in the Gulf. Various Labour ministers had sought in the course of 1967 to reassure the Gulf rulers about Britain's intention to stay in the Gulf to safeguard its considerable oil interests and to honor its treaty commitments to the rulers. Yet, in January 1968, the Wilson government announced that Britain intended to withdraw by 1971. Financial necessity has always been offered as the reason for this decision. But the financial crisis in the autumn of 1967 arose largely from the reduction in oil supplies from the Gulf during the Arab–Israeli War in June. The Wilson government now proposed to make it easier for those supplies to be cut off in future at the whim of Arab governments by relinquishing whatever control the British might have exerted over them by its presence in the Gulf. The sum involved in keeping the British troops in the Gulf was a paltry £12 million per annum, which was nothing when set against the value of British oil investments there. When the sheikhs of Abu Dhabi and Dubai offered to pay to keep British troops in the Gulf, they were brushed aside by Healey, who boorishly commented that "he was not a white slaver for the sheikhs" and that "It would be a very great mistake if we allowed ourselves to become mercenaries for people who like to have British troops around"[20] – though this did not stop Britain taking financial contributions toward maintenance of the British army of the Rhine. Labour's decision was to have far-reaching consequences, not least for Anglo-American relations. The Americans, heavily engaged in Vietnam, had wanted Britain to stay in the Gulf. Their sense of betrayal at Labour's decision soured transatlantic relations. Although the Conservatives had initially pledged to reverse the decision, after winning the 1970 election they meekly followed the line set down by the permanent officials of the Foreign Office, who were in favor of keeping to the planned date of withdrawal by the end of 1971. They saw benefits for Britain in selling arms to the two main inheritors of Britain's position in the Gulf: Saudi Arabia and Iran. It was for this reason that the British government succumbed to the extortionate demands of Saudi Arabia – that it should get a large chunk of Abu Dhabi and its oil – and Iran – that it should be authorized to occupy Abu Musa and the Tunbs (none of which belonged to them) as their conditions for recognizing the new Union of Arab Emirates (UAE). Thus Britain betrayed its treaty obligations to defend the territorial integrity of these sheikhdoms and debased the value of any defense undertakings they might have made to UAE. In fact, Britain had completely betrayed its position in the Gulf over the previous 150 years for it had ceased to restrain by its presence the two local powers, Saudi Arabia and Iran, who had always been the main threat to Gulf security. Britain actually compounded its betrayal by selling arms to these regimes to encourage them in realizing their expansionist and rival aims in the Gulf.

## The Nixon Doctrine, 1969–1979

While Britain was busy withdrawing from the Gulf, the Americans were getting out of Vietnam. The searing experience of Vietnam made the Americans wary of intervening on the ground in the wars of other countries. In future, and as enunciated in the Nixon Doctrine in 1969, the Americans were prepared to provide the money and arms to countries fighting a communist insurgency or an external threat, but the war would have to be fought by that country's troops rather than American soldiers. Henceforth, the US would rely on friendly local powers to carry out the role of regional policeman, rather than carrying out the role itself. In the Middle East the two candidates nominated by the US for this role were Israel and Iran. Saudi Arabia was allotted a supporting role to Iran in the Gulf, in what became known as the "twin pillars" policy to guard the security of the Gulf.

Before the June 1967 War, Israel had been regarded by the US government as a strategic and political liability. This attitude changed with Israel's six-day defeat of the combined armies of Egypt, Syria, and Iraq, the three main regional allies of the Soviet Union. Israel had shown by its exertions that it was not only perfectly capable of defending itself but that it was the strongest military power in the Middle East that could resist Soviet expansionism in the region. Israel had become a strategic asset rather than a liability to the US. The Arabs also realized that the Israeli military triumphs were due to a great extent to the superiority of US weaponry and they wanted access to it. They did not want to have to continue to rely on inferior Soviet arms. This greatly enhanced US prestige in the region and enabled the US to counter Soviet influence by stressing that only the Americans could pressure the Israelis into making concessions to the Arabs, over returning territory captured during the June 1967 War.

The Israelis demonstrated their strategic usefulness to the US in the region when they prevented Syria and the Palestine Liberation Organization (PLO), two Soviet allies, from toppling King Hussein of Jordan, a key US ally, from his throne during "Black September" in 1970. While the Arabs were becoming increasingly disillusioned with the Soviets, the Americans were so delighted with the Israelis that they were prepared to boost military aid to Israel from $62 million in 1968 to $602 million by 1973. After the 1973 War the Israelis received $4.4 billion worth of arms and since then the aid package has run at about $3 billion a year. This lies at the heart of the US–Israeli "special relationship."[21]

However, tensions in the US–Israeli relationship arose in 1973 during the Yom Kippur War. After the Israelis defeated the Egyptians in Sinai and drove across the canal, the US joined with the Soviets in the UN to secure a ceasefire; when this broke down and the Soviets seemed about to intervene militarily on behalf of the Egyptians, the US managed to deter the intervention only by putting its forces on a worldwide nuclear alert. The US successfully forced the Israelis to accept a ceasefire on October 25 as their forces surrounded the Egyptian Third Army on the eastern bank of the canal. Determined to win a defeated and dispirited Egypt away from the Soviets, US Secretary of State Henry Kissinger prevented the Israelis from starving the Third Army into submission and traveled to Cairo in November to persuade Sadat to kick the Soviets out of Egypt and the Middle East. Kissinger planned to do this through the two disengagement agreements of 1974 and 1975 which separated the rival armies in the Sinai and sought to turn Egypt into a strategic ally of the US in the region, alongside Israel. Kissinger and the new US president, Gerald Ford, achieved this through the time-honored method of withholding military and economic aid from Israel until it agreed to enter negotiations with Egypt and reach agreement on disengagement. It seemed a great victory for the US, which had lured Egypt away from the Soviets and showed that it was Washington rather than Moscow which was more likely to solve the Arab–Israeli dispute. Yet it owed a great deal to Sadat's willingness to leave the Soviet fold and to the blow to the Israelis' overweening self-confidence dealt by the early Egyptian successes. It was clear to the

Israelis that they would have to seek a peaceful solution to the Arab–Israeli dispute.

The Camp David peace process, which led to the signing of a peace treaty between Egypt and Israel in Washington in 1979, was not the unalloyed success that the American public have been led to believe.[22] It provided for peace between Egypt and Israel but it did not solve the Palestinian problem, which was to continue to plague Arab–Israeli relations. A close analysis of the peace process also shows that it was essentially driven by the desire of Egypt and Israel for peace, although the US president, Jimmy Carter, helped smooth over difficulties in the negotiations. America's biggest contribution was its promise of massive economic and military aid to both countries, in effect bribing them to keep the peace. By doing so, the Americans hoped that other Arab countries would follow the lucrative path to peace.

Under the "twin-pillar" strategy of the Nixon Doctrine, the Americans supplied arms and technical expertise to Iran and Saudi Arabia as part of their security commitment to the region. Not only was the heavy American arming of the shah undermining his position at home, by diverting much-needed funds from social and economic reform, it was also encouraging his hubris abroad. The British departure from the Gulf had encouraged the shah, first in 1969, to renounce the 1937 agreement with Iraq on the Shatt-al-Arab (which gave Iraq control to the eastern bank), and then, in 1971, to demand the median line and to seize Abu Musa and the Tunbs at the mouth of the Gulf. This so alarmed the Iraqis that they signed a defense agreement with the Soviets in 1972. In other words, the shah's expansionist activities had brought the Soviets into the Gulf, the very thing the Americans wanted to avoid. Nor was this all. Five months after Nixon visited Teheran in 1972, the shah went to Moscow and issued a joint communiqué with the Soviets calling for the Americans to stay out of the Gulf (they had a small naval force based at Jufair in Bahrain). The shah was worried that the American naval force might impede further Iranian expansionism. He was emboldened to do it by America's enfeeblement in Vietnam. He would not have dared to make such a statement to the Soviets, who had naval

base facilities at Umm Qasr in Iraq. Moreover, the shah had no qualms about signing economic and arms agreements with the Soviets in the 1960s and 1970s. The Soviets were quite happy to encourage the shah's grandiose ambitions in the Gulf: it helped to destabilize not only Iran itself but also the region as a whole and thus the American position generally. The Soviets believed that they would benefit from this situation, as they had in Iraq.

Just as the Americans were falsely congratulating themselves in 1973 on the success of the Nixon Doctrine, the Yom Kippur War broke out and the Arab Gulf states restricted oil exports to the US and the European supporters of Israel. At one fell swoop, the US policy of keeping the politics of the Gulf separate from the Arab–Israeli conflict had been destroyed. By late 1974 the Organization of Oil Exporting countries (OPEC), supported by America's "twin pillars," Iran and Saudi Arabia, had increased the price of oil fourfold. What followed was a massive transfer of the financial resources of the West to the Middle East. In turn the Saudis and the Iranians spent some $30 billion on US arms from 1973 to 1980. They also invested heavily in western financial markets. This created a strong economic interdependence between western and Gulf economies which has lasted into the twenty-first century.

The heavy militarization of the Gulf, as we have seen, did not have the intended effect of making it more stable. Just the opposite, in fact. After 1972 the US, along with Israel, secretly helped Iran to encourage a revolt among the Kurds in northern Iraq. The purpose was to put pressure on Saddam Hussein to concede the median line to Iran in the Shatt. Having achieved this in 1975, the Iranians and their western backers ceased to support the Kurds and left them to the tender mercies of Saddam. By backing Iranian expansionist ambitions in the Shatt, the US had, unwittingly perhaps, created a grievance in Saddam's mind – to which he was bound to seek redress when he saw an opportunity to do so, which would then further destabilize the Gulf.

Despite President Carter's emphasis in US foreign policy on human rights and the restriction of arms sales, US relations with Iran continued on much the same basis as they had under the

Republican administrations of Nixon and Ford. But no sooner had Carter announced that Iran was an "island of stability" in the region than the shah was overthrown in 1979 by an Islamic fundamentalist revolution under the Ayatollah Khomeini.[23]

With the fall of the shah the US strategy of building up Iran as the major pillar of its position had collapsed, and the Nixon Doctrine lay in tatters. The US had lost not only its closest ally in the Gulf but also an extremely lucrative export market for goods, services, and arms. It had lost its listening stations along the Iranian frontier with the Soviet Union. More seriously, perhaps, the price of oil went up from $13/barrel to $34/barrel, which hit the world economy very hard. The Americans were now totally dependent upon their other pillar in the Gulf, Saudi Arabia. But how secure was this pillar? In return for a number of worthless commitments from Saudi Arabia, the US committed itself to the defense of Saudi Arabia and the al-Saud family. If anything happened to that family, and there were signs of internal discontent in Saudi Arabia at the close connection between the al-Saud and the "infidel" Americans, the US position, and oil supplies, in that country and the Gulf would be put in jeopardy. The Americans rejected the alternative policy, which would have been to avoid an entangling alliance with Saudi Arabia and not to propitiate it at every turn.

## The Carter Doctrine to the Kuwait War, 1980–1991

The last two years of the Carter administration highlighted the themes that were to dominate US policy toward the Middle East in the 1980s, namely, the concern with Iran and the Islamic fundamentalist threat and the Soviet invasion of Afghanistan in December 1979. Carter's response was to make clear, in his State of the Union address in January 1980, that "An attempt by an outside force to gain control of the Persian Gulf will be regarded as an assault on the vital interests of the United States of America, and such an assault will be repelled by any means necessary, including military force."[24] This was very much a statement of intent, subsequently known as the

Carter Doctrine, since the US had only a very limited military ability to defend the Gulf at this time. There was no military draft and the US had no military bases in the Gulf. So Carter announced the setting up of a "Rapid Deployment Force," which took some years to complete, later becoming the US Central Command. The question remained, however, whether the US was assuming the mantle of guardian of the Gulf, cast off by Britain in 1971. This question became of more than passing interest following Iraq's sudden and massive attack on Iran in September 1980. With Iran consumed by revolutionary turmoil and cut off from the US, its former patron and arms supplier, Saddam Hussein had seen this as an excellent opportunity to grab back control of the Shatt from Iran, seize the oil-bearing Sunni Arab province of Khuzistan, counter Iranian attempts to stir up the Shiite tribes of southern Iraq, and become the dominant power in the Gulf. It was left to Carter's Republican successor, Ronald Reagan, to fashion a response to this.

One commentator has remarked on "Reagan's inability to grapple with the complexities of Lebanon" (where the US, and their Israeli allies, intervening against the PLO, had been defeated in 1984 by the Syrians and the Iranian-backed Hezbollah), contrasting it with his "more purposeful strategy in the Gulf."[25] Certainly, Reagan initially continued Carter's policy of virulent hostility toward both Iraq and Iran, which manifested itself in a studied neutrality and ban on arms sales to both countries. Americans hoped that, as Kissinger put it, "both sides would lose." Iraq was viewed as a Soviet satellite and Iran as a potential one. Reagan also continued Carter's policy of building up the capability of the US to intervene militarily in the Gulf, signing cooperation agreements with Morocco, Egypt, Kenya, Oman, and even Somalia. Diego Garcia was developed as a naval and air base in cooperation with Britain. But the Reagan administration abandoned its neutrality in the war following the Iranian counteroffensive in 1982. Washington's fear of an Iranian military victory, the overthrow of Saddam Hussein, and the spread of Islamic fundamentalism throughout the Gulf overcame its previous fear of an Iraqi victory and the spread of Soviet influence in the Gulf. In the next two years, the Americans allowed the Iraqis to purchase commodities on credit and gave them political support. Then, in 1984, the US resumed arms sales to Iraq and two years later restored diplomatic relations after a seventeen-year gap. However, when Iraq resumed the offensive against Iran, the Reagan administration was split between those, like Casper Weinberger in the Pentagon, who wanted to continue to give full support to Iraq in order to contain Iran and those, like the succession of national security advisers, who believed that Iran was more hostile to the Soviets than the Americans, and wanted to sell arms to Iran to encourage the Iranian moderates and secure the release of American hostages in the Lebanon. When it was revealed, in the Irangate or the Iran–Contra scandal (because the US was also illegally selling arms to Contras fighting the Sandinista in Nicaragua), what some rogue elements in the Reagan administration had been up to, Congressional opinion forced the administration to abandon its policy of covert arms sales to Iran. The policy had been counterproductive in any case because it had mistakenly convinced the Iranians that they could put pressure on the Americans to make concessions and tilt against Iraq when necessary. US covert policy had the effect of prolonging the Iran–Iraq War.

In fact, the Iranian seizure of the Fao peninsula, controlling Iraqi access to the Gulf, followed by Iranian attacks on Kuwaiti tankers (Kuwait was Iraq's main backer in the war) in 1986, led the Americans to tilt back toward Iraq and intervene more actively in the Gulf from 1987, becoming the ultimate guarantor of Iraq's security. It was largely manipulated into this by the Kuwaitis, who had appealed to both superpowers to protect its tankers. As the Kuwaitis expected, the Americans refused to cooperate with the Soviets, thus letting them into the Gulf, and took on the responsibility of reflagging eleven Kuwaiti tankers themselves and providing them with naval escorts. Britain and France also provided naval escorts for Kuwaiti tankers. Following an Iraqi missile hitting the *USS Stark* in 1987, which showed just how dangerous the Gulf had become, the US threw all its weight behind Iraq, even attacking the Iranian Sirri oil platform, in order to drive Iran to the negotiating table. America's manifest bias against

Iran had the initial effect of making the ayatollahs more intransigent in the peace negotiations and it was only the brutal use by the Iraqis of chemical weapons against civilian targets in Iran that led the Iranians to accept a ceasefire in July 1988. The Iran–Iraq War was the longest and costliest conflict, in money and blood, since the Second World War, and it solved nothing. Both sides felt cheated of their goal, victory and the overthrow of their opponents; both blamed the Americans, the Iraqis for not receiving the US support necessary to pursue the war to the finish, the Iranians for US intervention on behalf of the Iraqis, which prevented an Iranian victory. The enmity between Iran and Iraq, and between Iran and America, was even greater after the war than it had been before it. Moreover, the US now regarded Iraq as the main arm of its containment of Iran in the Gulf. The only upside of the war was that Saudi Arabia and the Gulf sheikhdoms had survived and the price of oil had gone down. This was the only thing on the credit side of the Reagan administration's balance sheet, which had seen the disaster in the Lebanon, lack of progress on the Arab–Israeli issue (because of the refusal of the US, the Israelis, and the PLO to talk peace), and an uncertain future in the Gulf.

After the Iran–Iraq War, Reagan, and then his successor as president, George Bush, Snr., convinced themselves that Iraq had now become a bastion of regional stability, guarding US and western interests in the Gulf against the Iranian threat, and that it would turn to economic reconstruction and pursue moderate policies in the Middle East, especially on the Arab–Israeli conflict. Saddam's seizure of Kuwait on the night of August 2/3, 1990, therefore, not only exposed the myth that the Arabs could deal with their own problems peaceably but also shattered the American illusion that they could do so, and thus the basis of US policy in the region. Saddam now posed a threat not only to the territorial order in the Middle East but also to US oil interests in the Gulf. Even then Bush's immediate response to the Iraqi *coup de main* was hesitant at best, and it took the British prime minister, Margaret Thatcher, who happened to be visiting the US at the time, to stop him, in her memorable words, from going "wobbly." With her encouragement, Bush announced that the aggression would not be allowed to stand and single-mindedly set about preparing the US and the world for war to expel the Iraqis from Kuwait. He did this against the advice of his military, still affected by the Vietnam syndrome, and his diplomats, who favored a diplomatic solution. In order to prevent Saddam from continuing his advance to the Saudi oil-fields, thus controlling 40 percent of the world's oil, Bush successfully persuaded the Saudis to allow US troops to be based in Saudi Arabia under Operation "Desert Shield." Meanwhile, the US persuaded the UN Security Council (UNSC) to pass a number of resolutions authorizing action against Iraq: 660, calling upon Iraq to get out of Kuwait, and 661, imposing economic sanctions. Although some of his advisers thought that containment and sanctions were working, Bush was determined to use force against Saddam, increasing the number of US troops in Saudi Arabia to 400,000 and securing Resolution 678 from the UNSC, which authorized the US use of force against Iraq after 45 days.

On December 29, Bush told Colin Powell, the chairman of the US Joint Chiefs of Staff, to prepare for war by the January 15, 1991, UN deadline. By then military units from some thirty countries had gathered in Saudi Arabia ready to assault the Iraqi positions in Kuwait, a testimony to Bush's diplomatic skill in forging an international coalition. Saddam Hussein threatened the "Mother of All Battles" when the US-led coalition tried to retake Kuwait. What happened when Operation "Desert Storm" was unleashed on January 16 was the "Mother of All Walk-Overs," as first the Allied air forces disrupted the military cohesion of the Iraqi forces and then the Allied land forces swept them aside as they retook Kuwait by February 28 and advanced into southern Iraq. Although the US had achieved its stated objectives, to kick Saddam out of Kuwait and restore the Kuwaiti government to power, it had not succeeded in its unstated aim, which was its hope that military defeat would see Saddam Hussein toppled from power. And when first the Iraqi Shiites in the south and then the Kurds in the north rose in revolt, Bush, who had encouraged them to do so, did not give them any support. This allowed Saddam to crush the revolts, with the Shiites

fleeing into the southern marshes and the Kurds into the mountains. Bush and his advisers were prepared to see this happen because they feared the dismemberment of Iraq, which would only profit Iran. They preferred to keep a weakened Saddam in power and contained. The question was whether the US would, or could, do this in the long term. The answer was not to come until 2003 when, following Saddam's successful division of the UNSC over the continued imposition on Iraq of sanctions and the no-fly zones and the waning of US prestige, a US-led coalition (which included Britain, but not France, Russia, and China) invaded and occupied Iraq.

## Conclusion

Although the Iraq War falls outside the sphere of this chapter, it is included in order to demonstrate one of the more enduring themes of the international history of the Middle East both during and after the Cold War era, namely, the proclivity of local regimes to involve the great powers in their affairs, often trying to play them off against each other in order to strengthen their grip on power and to further their ambitions in the region. That this has almost invariably resulted in tension, conflict, and often disaster for the regimes concerned has been detailed in the above account. The other recurring theme in the history of the region during and after the Cold War has been the long, dismal record of western and Russian intervention, based as it has been on illusion, moral cowardice, overweening greed, corruption, and incompetence. The Middle East has been a veritable mare's nest for both local and great powers in the Cold War era and after.

### NOTES

1   Most of these studies have been written by Americans; see the essay by Douglas Little, "Gideon's Band: America and the Middle East," in *America in the World*, ed. Michael J. Hogan (Cambridge: Cambridge University Press, 1995), pp. 462–500.

2   Ibid., pp. 485–98.

3   Wm. Roger Louis, *The British Empire in the Middle East, 1945–1951* (Oxford: Clarendon Press, 1984), parts 3 and 4.

4   M. E. Yapp, *The Near East since the First World War* (Harlow: Longman, 2nd edn, 1996), p. 402.

5   See Elie Kedourie's foreword to Uriel Dann, ed., *The Great Powers in the Middle East, 1919–1939* (New York: Holmes & Meier, 1988).

6   Saul Kelly, *Cold War in the Desert* (London: Macmillan, 2000), pp. 41–3.

7   See Alan Bullock, *Ernest Bevin: Foreign Secretary, 1945–51* (London: Heinemann, 1983), chaps. 6 and 7.

8   Louis, *British Empire*, pp. 15–21.

9   Yapp, *Near East*, pp. 397–400.

10  Ibid., p. 401.

11  Ibid., p. 396.

12  Kelly, *Cold War*, pp. 25–6.

13  Milan Hauner, "Stalin's Big Fleet Program," *Naval War College Review* 57 (2004): 87–120.

14  See Bruce Kuniholm, *The Origins of the Cold War in the Middle East* (Princeton, NJ: Princeton University Press, 1980).

15  N. J. Ashton, "The Hijacking of a Pact: The Formation of the Baghdad Pact and Anglo-American Tensions in the Middle East, 1955–1958," *Review of International Studies* 19 (1993): 123–37.

16  See Steven Z. Freiberger, *Dawn over Suez* (Chicago: Ivan R. Dee, 1992).

17  C. J. Bartlett, *"The Special Relationship": A Political History of Anglo-American Relations since 1945* (Harlow: Longman, 1992), p. 85.

18  Spencer Mawby, *British Policy in Aden and the Protectorates, 1955–67* (Abingdon: Routledge, 2005), p. 103.

19  J. B. Kelly, *Arabia, the Gulf and the West* (London: Weidenfeld & Nicolson, 1980), p. 21.

20  Ibid., p. 50.

21  See A. Ben-Zvi, *The United States and Israel* (New York: Columbia University Press, 1993).

22  See W. B. Quandt, *Camp David* (Washington: Brookings Institution, 1986).

23  Avi Shlaim, *War and Peace in the Middle East* (London: Penguin, 1995), p. 67.

24  Ibid., p. 70.

25  See M. Howard, "A European Perspective of the Reagan Years," *Foreign Affairs* 66 (1988): 478–93.

## GUIDE TO FURTHER READING

N. J. Ashton, *Eisenhower, Macmillan and the Problem of Nasser* (London: Macmillan, 1996). Essential reading for this period.

S. Chubin and C. Tripp, *Iran–Iraq at War* (London: I. B. Tauris, 1988). A good account of this war.

L. Freedman and E. Karsh, *The Gulf Conflict, 1990–91* (Princeton, NJ: Princeton University Press, 1992). A keen analysis of this conflict.

B. Lewis, *The Shaping of the Modern Middle East* (Oxford: Oxford University Press, 1994). A masterly interpretation.

W. S. Lucas, *Divided We Stand* (London: Hodder & Stoughton, 1991). The best book, so far, on the Suez crisis.

R. Ovendale, *Britain, the United States and the Transfer of Power in the Middle East* (London: Leicester University Press, 1996); *The Origins of the Arab–Israeli Wars* (Harlow: Longman, 3rd edn, 1999). Good overviews.

B. Rubin, *Paved with Good Intentions* (Oxford: Oxford University Press, 1980). Gives a taste of the folly of US policy toward the shah's Iran; *The Tragedy of the Middle East* (Cambridge: Cambridge University Press, 2004), explains the mare's nest that is the modern Middle East.

Y. Sayigh and A Shlaim, *The Cold War in the Middle East* (Oxford: Clarendon Press, 1997). A country-by-country analysis of the region during the Cold War by a variety of authors.

C. Tripp, *History of Iraq* (Cambridge: Cambridge University Press, 2000). The best history of Iraq.

# CHAPTER TWENTY-EIGHT

# The Sino-Soviet Alliance

## SERGEY RADCHENKO

On December 6, 1949, the chairman of the Chinese Communist Party, Mao Zedong, boarded a train for Moscow, his first ever visit abroad, and one of unparalleled significance. China had barely emerged from many years of civil war between the Communist Party and the Guomindang (Kuomintang), which ended with communist victory and Chiang Kai-shek's exile to Taiwan. Now China moved decisively in the direction of a political alignment with the Soviet Union. Mao planned to meet with the Soviet leader Joseph Stalin and work out personally the details of the emerging Sino-Soviet alliance. He expected three important outcomes from his talks: Soviet security assurances in case the United States intervened in the Chinese Civil War; Soviet economic aid in postwar reconstruction; and a Sino-Soviet treaty of alliance to mark the inauguration of a new "fraternal" relationship between Beijing and Moscow – something different in form and in essence from previous Soviet arrangements in China, something that would "look good" for Communist China as well as "taste good."[1]

This was a perfectly good plan except for the fact that Stalin already had a treaty of alliance with China – with Chiang Kai-shek's China! Signed in 1945, it was a consequence of agreements reached at Yalta between the Soviet Union, the United States, and Great Britain. Spelling out postwar arrangements, the Yalta Treaty recognized Soviet interests in the Far East, including substantial gains in China. By agreement with

Chiang Kai-shek, Stalin took back what Russia had lost to Japan after the disastrous war of 1904–5: a stake in the Changchun railroad and the right to station troops at the strategic base of Port Arthur. Despite Chiang's reservations, Stalin also pressed the issue of Mongolia's independence from China. The Chinese government had little choice but to forfeit claims to the former province, which had been under effective Soviet control since the 1920s. Thus, the 1945 Sino-Soviet Treaty was in many respects beneficial to the Soviet Union. It conferred legitimacy to Stalin's postwar "Great Power" goals; it served Soviet security needs in the Far East; and the Yalta connection of the Sino-Soviet relationship implied US recognition of Stalin's long-term interests in Asia. These were good reasons for Stalin to have second thoughts about revising the old treaty.

There were other reasons for Stalin's misgivings. In 1948 Moscow's relations with socialist Yugoslavia sharpened dramatically. Stalin was furious when the Yugoslav communist leader Josep Broz Tito, eager to assert Yugoslavia's regional leadership in southeast Europe, refused to accept Soviet-centered and strictly hierarchical lines of authority and advertised Belgrade's own importance in the communist movement. Moscow denounced the "Tito clique" for selling out to the West and broke off relations with Yugoslavia. Stalin feared that Mao, a self-made peasant revolutionary without a Soviet connection, would decline to be subordinated to his authority, and he would end up having to deal with another "Tito." Mao certainly sensed mistrust. He later recalled: "I have once pointed out to the Soviet comrades that [they] suspected that I was a half-hearted Tito, but they refused to recognize it."[2]

Mao expected that his talks with Stalin would not be easy. He thought that Stalin did not have faith in the Chinese Revolution and did not want to burn bridges to the Guomindang, which Stalin allegedly considered to be the most important force in Chinese politics. Even in the last months of the civil war, when Chiang's forces were on the brink of collapse, Stalin, in Mao's opinion, was still uncertain about his political preferences and was in no hurry to cut relations with the Guomindang. Soviet duplicity hardly encouraged Mao, but the trip to Moscow was not one he could refuse, having pushed for it for months even as Stalin procrastinated in expectation that the fortunes of the Chinese communists might suddenly be reversed.

## Mao's Talks with Stalin

Stalin was not inspired by proposals Mao put forward at their first meeting on December 16, 1949. Scrapping the old treaty with Chiang Kai-shek could give the Americans and the British a pretext to pull out from the Yalta framework and question the Soviet gains in the Far East: not only the Soviet rights in Port Arthur and Manchuria, but also claims to Southern Sakhalin and the Kurile Islands, acquired in 1945 at Japan's expense. In Stalin's view, it was better to leave the treaty intact so as not to compromise a new world order, which legitimized Soviet geopolitical interests. Mao now realized the limits of Stalin's revolutionary commitment. He was thoroughly disappointed by the Soviet refusal to sign a new treaty; and it was not his only disappointment. Stalin was also unwilling to offer direct Soviet military support in the attack on Taiwan, where Chiang Kai-shek's remaining forces held out with US backing. "What is most important here is not to give Americans a pretext to intervene," he told Mao. The Soviet Union was in no position to fight a war with the United States over the fate of China.[3]

After the first meeting, which only revealed the gap between Beijing and Moscow, Mao went to Stalin's dacha near Moscow, pending further talks. He was not in a good mood. Stalin's refusal to sign a new treaty with China was Mao's personal setback; his prestige in Beijing would suffer if he returned from the Soviet Union empty-handed. Day after day passed in uncertainty but Stalin evaded talks on the treaty, letting Mao waste his time at the dacha over the New Year. Finally the chairman threatened that he would cut short his visit and go back to Beijing – even without a treaty or any agreements with the Soviets. Unhappy with Stalin's intransigent attitude, Mao wanted to show that, besides the Sino-Soviet alliance, China had other doors open, though at that time the only doors open were those of diplomatic relations with Burma and India, possibly with the British and (Mao speculated) American recognition pending. Stalin reconsidered. In an apparent reversal of his original position, he told Mao in January 1950 that he was willing to conclude a new treaty with China irrespective of Yalta. "To hell with it!" he said – "once we have taken up the position that the treaties must be changed, we must go all the way."[4]

Why did Stalin change his mind about the treaty? He may have worried after all about western recognition of China. Stalin repeatedly advised Mao to postpone opening relations with the West – especially with the United States. And yet Soviet diplomatic reports from China regularly raised alarm over alleged pro-American inclinations in the Chinese leadership. Thus, Soviet fear of a Sino-American rapprochement had cast a shadow over the Sino-Soviet treaty talks. That fear served Mao well, for it made Stalin take a position on China after many months of procrastination. As for Mao's real intentions, in 1949 he was not in a hurry to jump trenches, and merely raised the issue of western recognition as a way to put pressure on Stalin. In fact, Mao welcomed US diplomatic withdrawal from China.

There could be other reasons for Stalin's about-face. Could he have come to think, after long meetings with Mao in late December, that he had no other options but to rebuild the Sino-Soviet relationship on an entirely new basis? Postwar expectations of Great Power collaboration gave way to the grim reality of the Cold War. The new context of Sino-Soviet relations could not be properly accommodated within the Yalta framework. Chiang Kai-shek would not have approached Stalin with requests for aid in liberating Taiwan from "reactionaries" or ask him advice on building communism in China. When he agreed to a new treaty, Stalin intended to show that ideology more than *realpolitik* was now at the basis of his China policy. On the other hand, decreasing probability of US intervention in China to restore Chiang Kai-shek to power meant that Stalin ran much less risk by reordering his relationship with Mao Zedong. One way or another, Stalin's initial procrastination did not serve the cause of the Sino-Soviet friendship: Mao was upset with what he considered humiliating treatment by Stalin. On many later occasions he recalled with bitterness how he traveled to Moscow to "quarrel with Stalin."

The decision to sign a new treaty with China put Stalin in an awkward position. He wanted to keep hard-won Soviet privileges there, but these were not very different from those won by Russia during the imperialist scramble for concessions in China in the late nineteenth century. In the end Stalin compromised on Port Arthur and the Changchun railway but produced a new list of demands in a secret protocol to the treaty, which guaranteed Soviet exclusive economic interests in Xinjiang and Manchuria. Mao was not happy with Stalin's demands, but he swallowed his pride. He had a new treaty in hand, and won a badly needed loan of 300 million dollars from Stalin. A trade agreement was signed as well, and Stalin agreed to send Soviet specialists to help reconstruct China's economy. Chinese gains from the new relationship were substantial even if they came at a hard bargain. As for the Soviet side of the bargain, by making demands that clearly compromised China's sovereignty, Stalin sowed seeds that produced a bad harvest a decade later, when Chinese ideologues accused Moscow of imperialist ambitions in China.

Despite mistrust on both sides, the Sino-Soviet alliance rested partly but firmly on "revolutionary" principles – to overlook that larger picture is to miss the whole point of the new relationship

between Moscow and Beijing. Mao appreciated Stalin's role at the helm of the world revolutionary movement, and recognized his own role beside – and slightly below – Stalin. Stalin, in turn, whether or not he recognized the virtues of Mao's Marxism, accepted the division of "revolutionary" responsibility. Mao was to take the lead in supporting revolutions and national liberation movements in Asia, especially in Korea and Vietnam. The Sino-Soviet Treaty of Alliance was signed in Moscow on February 14, 1950, amid much fanfare. A song was composed to celebrate the new Sino-Soviet friendship:

> Volga hears the voice of Yangtze
> The Chinese see the Kremlin's shining
> We are not afraid of the thunder of war
> The will of the peoples is stronger than thunder!

These words were tested before the year was out, in the storm of the Korean War.

## Sino-Soviet Relations and the Korean War

"Liberating" South Korea was an idea put forward by North Korea's leader Kim Il Sung. Stalin did not at first share Kim's enthusiasm and turned down Pyongyang's appeals for support on several occasions in 1949. The Soviet leader was afraid of US intervention in a conflict in Korea, but he suddenly changed his mind in January 1950 and, in a cable to Pyongyang, essentially approved Kim's gamble. Some months later he explained his new policy by reference to a "changed international situation." What had changed? Prospects for US intervention on the Asian mainland had weakened after Secretary of State Dean Acheson excluded the mainland from the US "defensive perimeter" during a press conference in January 1950. Now, alliance with Mao's China promised Stalin additional safeguards against American moves. In the worst-case scenario, if Kim Il Sung's gamble failed, Stalin counted on China to help Pyongyang fight the war on behalf of the Soviets.

When Stalin sanctioned Kim Il Sung's attack on South Korea, he told him to ask permission from Mao beforehand. By keeping Mao involved in the decision-making, Stalin tried to shift inherent risks of Kim's enterprise to China's shoulders, and wisely so, for Kim's offensive collapsed in September 1950 after an unexpected US intervention in the war. Stalin urgently cabled to Beijing to send reinforcements, and Mao Zedong obliged. For Mao, supporting North Korea's questionable pursuits was a natural and necessary proposition – a part of what it meant to be a "revolutionary" and a leader of a great nation that had historically "helped" Korea. Mao was also concerned lest Kim's failure would bring US forces right up to the PRC's border and menace China's security in the northeast.

The Korean War showed how robust the Sino-Soviet alliance was after all. Before the war Moscow and Beijing issued joint statements and spoke of unbreakable friendship, but Kim's failures harnessed the Soviets and the Chinese in one horse cart – cooperation became a practical day-to-day necessity. Moscow and Beijing worked closely in defining the strategic goals of the war. On the battlefield, Soviet and Chinese commanders at times imposed their will on the reluctant North Koreans. China shouldered combat on the ground with only auxiliary Soviet air support. The Chinese army pushed back and almost defeated US-led forces albeit at tremendous cost. Chinese victories raised Beijing's "revolutionary" merit and Mao's personal prestige. Just as Soviet defeat of fascism bolstered Stalin's international authority, so China's ability to stand up to "US imperialism" after many years of humiliation by foreign powers made China into an equal of the Soviet Union and Mao into an equal of Stalin – at least as seen from Beijing. The Korean War overturned the stigma of a father–son relationship between the Soviet Union and China that existed in the early months of the alliance.

Yet the Korean War also deepened Mao's mistrust of Stalin. The chairman was unhappy with being left out of negotiations leading to the outbreak of the Korean War. He complained bitterly that he was "not consulted in a sufficient way" by the Soviets. When Kim went to ask for Mao's permission, Stalin had already approved the plan in general terms, and the Chinese were left with little choice but to follow suit. Moreover, once the fronts stabilized, Stalin evidently liked the idea of low-intensity warfare, while the Chinese suffered the brunt of casualties. But – the greatest outrage of all – the Soviets billed China for weapons shipments to fight a war in Korea, which made Stalin appear at best like an arms merchant. Mao temporarily buried his concerns about Stalin's duplicity. When the Soviet dictator died in March 1953, the bond between Beijing and Moscow seemed stronger than ever.[5]

## Dynamism and Tensions

In September 1954 Nikita Khrushchev, now first secretary of the Soviet Central Committee, traveled to Beijing on his first trip abroad in his new capacity. Unquestionably aware of Mao's misgivings about Stalin's quasi-imperialist insistence on special privileges in China, Khrushchev offered to pull out Soviet troops from Port Arthur and scrap agreements on Soviet co-ownership of four enterprises in China. He also offered generous economic aid – so generous, in fact, that Khrushchev's colleagues in the Presidium had second thoughts as to whether the Soviet Union could afford to spend so much on China. Moscow initiated a massive technology transfer, aiding in the construction of hundreds of industrial enterprises. Blueprints for entire factories were handed over to China at no charge (except for photocopying). Assembly lines were set up across the country to produce trucks and tractors, but also missiles and MIG fighter aircraft. The number of Soviet advisers in China – already at around 400 in early 1954 – multiplied to an unknown number (in the thousands) after Khrushchev's visit.

Soviet economic aid was an important element of China's industrialization effort, and Mao recognized that. The legacy of old China, he told Khrushchev at their first meeting in Beijing, came down to three things: the Beijing duck, mah jong, and Tibetan medicine. The rest had to be built up from the ground. But China's untapped human potential, and enthusiasm of the masses, strengthened Mao's confidence in the success of his economic reforms. In the early 1950s, as China rapidly moved toward collectivization of agriculture and full-blown industrialization, Mao looked to Moscow for moral and material support and Khrushchev gave it. His commitment to China cost the Soviets millions of rubles and lost opportunities for economic development at home, but money was a secondary issue. What mattered was that the Chinese were not just "friends" but "brothers" – and stinginess was not appropriate for fraternal relations.[6]

Yet for all of the outward signs of vitality and dynamism of Sino-Soviet relations, tensions were brooding beneath the surface. Mao complained that Khrushchev failed to consult with him on important theoretical issues, none being more important than Stalin's legacy. In February 1956 Khrushchev denounced Stalin's crimes in a secret speech at the 20th Party Congress without discussing the issue with the Chinese beforehand. His speech, which was shortly thereafter leaked to the press, sent shockwaves throughout the international communist movement, ultimately undermining Soviet authority and stirring unrest in eastern Europe. In Mao's view, Khrushchev miscalculated badly in his condemnation of Stalin's legacy. Stalin had committed mistakes, Mao thought, but he was still a great revolutionary figure.

Of course, Mao defended Stalin not out of the goodness of his heart but because Khrushchev's denunciation of Stalin eroded the Chinese leader's own authority at a time when he needed blind devotion of the masses to move forward radical economic reforms. Mao valued the role of class struggle and international tensions as catalysts for mass mobilization, while Khrushchev initiated measures to rehabilitate Stalin's victims, weaken the power of the state security apparatus, and loosen the screws on the intelligentsia. Although these ideological and policy differences between Beijing and Moscow were important in the context of Mao's revolutionary visions, they should not be overstressed. Differences over Stalin's legacy and the like – the most visible part of the Sino-Soviet split to the western observers – obscured other problems of no lesser importance for the Sino-Soviet relationship.

An unquestionable problem for Mao was Soviet "arrogance." He complained that the Sino-Soviet relationship was like that "between father and son or between cat and mouse." The Soviets never believed in the Chinese Revolution, and were still skeptical about China's abilities even in

the 1950s. In 1958 Mao concluded that the Chinese economic plan, drawn up with Soviet help, was too conservative, that it did not take into account the enthusiasm of the masses. He decided to boost the speed of economic construction across the country, with an eye on jumping into communism ahead of the Soviet Union. Inflated projections and bizarre economic experiments surprised the Soviet specialists who sent warning signals back to Moscow. But Soviet skepticism with regard to the Great Leap Forward only annoyed Mao. He accused the Soviets of lack of faith, conservatism, and ideological capitulation.[7]

Unaware of Mao's growing frustration with Khrushchev's "arrogance," the Soviets continued to push for closer cooperation with China in the military sphere. In July 1958 the Soviet ambassador proposed to Mao to create a joint Sino-Soviet submarine fleet and construct a long-wave radio station on China's territory for communication with Soviet ships in the Pacific. Mao was outraged.

> You never trust the Chinese!, he told the dazzled Ambassador, You only trust the Russians! [To you] the Russians are the first-class [people] whereas the Chinese are among the inferior who are dumb and careless. Therefore [you] came up with the joint ownership and operation proposition. Well, if [you] want joint ownership and operation, how about have them all – let us turn into joint ownership and operation our army, navy, air force, industry, agriculture, culture, education. Can we do this? Or, [you] may have all of China's more than ten thousand kilometers of coastline and let us only maintain a guerrilla force.[8]

Mao interpreted the Soviet proposal as an attempt to control China or even turn it into a Mongolia-type satellite. In fact, this was not Khrushchev's aim. He did have unquestionable enthusiasm for his treasured alliance with China; compelling fraternal sentiments overshadowed the nuts and bolts of diplomacy, or else it would have occurred to him at some stage that Mao priced China's sovereignty higher than friendship with the USSR. Mao's revelations struck Khrushchev like a thunderbolt from a clear sky. He flew to China immediately to assure the chairman that the Soviets had nothing in mind like a joint submarine fleet. Mao agreed to settle the issue. Yet the conflict over the "joint ownership" proposal caused considerable bitterness and misunderstanding. Khrushchev had to bend over backwards to argue that the Soviets were not "red imperialists," but Mao was never really convinced.[9]

Even less convincing was Khrushchev's policy of "peaceful coexistence" with the United States that culminated in meetings between Khrushchev and US President Dwight D. Eisenhower at Camp David in 1959. Mao suspected that the "spirit of Camp David" was a superpower accord, which left China out in the cold. Khrushchev and Eisenhower agreed to disagree, but China was not a party to the agreement; Mao was not even consulted ahead of the talks. To add insult to injury, Khrushchev flew to Beijing straight after his meetings with Eisenhower. In heated exchanges he pressured the Chinese to turn over five US citizens held in the PRC on allegations of espionage. His awkward mediation efforts only embittered the Chinese. The Soviet leader lacked the tact to understand that Mao needed no one, least of all Khrushchev, to deal with the West.

To make matters worse, in 1959 Khrushchev reneged on his previous commitment to supply China with a prototype nuclear bomb. He was never enthusiastic about the prospect of a nuclear-armed China and talked his way out of a hard engagement when Mao raised that issue in 1954. In 1955 Beijing and Moscow reached an agreement on cooperation in the use of nuclear energy for peaceful purposes, and two years later Khrushchev finally gave in and promised to deliver an actual bomb. Promised, but never did. Khrushchev's cancellation of the agreement was too little and too late to delay substantially China's nuclear weapons program, but enough to make Mao think that Khrushchev was trying to "tie China by hands and feet." Nuclear capability symbolized for Mao socialist China's power and he resented the Soviet efforts to sabotage the Chinese nuclear program.

The Sino-Soviet alliance appeared to be a robust colossus in the late 1950s but it had feet of clay. The key players were increasingly at odds: Mao was bitter with Khrushchev's efforts to

"control" China, and Khrushchev was unhappy about Mao's militancy and unpredictable moves. Although tensions plagued the alliance, the split was not inevitable but the product of particular circumstances: de-Stalinization in the Soviet Union, and radicalization of Chinese domestic politics. It was also a result of misperceptions, cultural stereotypes, and ideological convictions of the Soviet and Chinese leaders. Indeed, the split was a complex, multilayered process, which was understood very differently in Moscow and Beijing.

## The First Violin

While Chinese leaders privately accused the Soviets of pressuring and subverting them and of aiding their enemies, public polemics, which flared up in the early 1960s, explored more general propositions – about war and peace, national liberation movements, and the building of communism. Yet Khrushchev did not think that ideology was the problem of the Sino-Soviet alliance. Simply put, Khrushchev thought that Mao was jealous of the Soviet leadership in the communist movement and wanted to unseat Khrushchev from the top. He wanted to "play the first violin."[10] The Soviets were not happy with growing Chinese influence in the communist movement. The Chinese example made it easier for countries like Romania and Poland to defy Soviet authority and even mediate between Moscow and Beijing. Albanian leadership indeed openly cursed Khrushchev, and won Chinese support for doing so. North Vietnam and North Korea followed China in accusing the Soviet leaders of revisionism. Foreign communist parties sent delegations to meet with Soviet and Chinese leaders and find out what the argument was all about. By 1963 the fabled "unity of the socialist camp" was as good as gone.

Khrushchev resented Chinese efforts to undermine his influence. As he explained to his colleagues, "Even, say, among friends, 5–10 people are friends and one of them is the chief; they do not elect him, they simply recognize him for some sort of qualities. [. . .] [T]here will be different colors and different characters, and different mental capabilities among people, there will be inequality as in all species of nature." The Soviet Union and China could not be put on the same level: the Soviets were there first – first to have a socialist revolution, to industrialize, to defeat Germany, to launch a rocket into space. The Soviet Union provided a nuclear umbrella for the socialist camp, and aided national liberation struggles. And as for Mao's criticism of Soviet policies, it showed only his "arrogance and some kind of nationalist symptoms."[11]

Mao for his part was not satisfied with the existing alignment of authority, centered on Moscow, under Stalin or Khrushchev. But at least Stalin commanded authority – at home and abroad. On the other hand, Khrushchev was a shadow of Stalin, while Mao was an experienced revolutionary, a theorist and a practitioner of class struggle, closer to Marx and Lenin than to mortals walking this earth. And if Mao's China was still backward and economically insignificant, Mao felt he had an upper hand over Khrushchev in matters of Marxist-Leninist theory. Materially, the Soviets were richer and more advanced, but China was more revolutionary. So Mao did not think that ideological barrage was a waste of time, nor that ideological disagreements between Moscow and Beijing were unsubstantial. Criticizing Khrushchev for allegedly abandoning class struggle at home and accommodating imperialists abroad was a matter of principle to Mao.

Indeed, while Khrushchev was anxious to end the barrage of mutual accusations and hammer out differences in private, polemics served Mao's purposes. After the Great Leap Forward failed disastrously in 1959, Mao retreated to the background, allowing more pragmatically minded Liu Shaoqi and Zhou Enlai to steer China through a period of "adjustment," i.e., reversal of ultra-leftist Great Leap policies. Communization of the countryside was basically abandoned, peasants were allowed private plots and given incentives to produce, while expansion of heavy industry was put on the back burner. Although he endorsed "adjustment" for lack of alternatives, Mao did not give up his vision of impending revolutionary changes in China. He was afraid that the so-called adjustment could in the end derail China from revolutionary tracks, and that many of his comrades-in-leadership did not have enough fervor to

persevere in the struggle for a communist society. Inasmuch as in Chinese propaganda Khrushchev came under fire for abandoning class struggle and "restoring capitalism" in the Soviet Union, Mao could use criticism of Khrushchev to undermine influence of adjustment architects, especially Liu Shaoqi. In this sense the Sino-Soviet split was but a component of Mao's long-term policy of furthering the Chinese Revolution.

Polemics also helped export Mao's revolution. Chinese propaganda about Khrushchev's sell-out to the West found an eager audience in the ruins of colonial empires and put China at the head of the "Afro-Asian solidarity movement." But in the short term, the revolutionary potential of the Third World inspired Mao; the Afro-Asian revolutionary upheaval under China's leadership towered over Khrushchev's awkward efforts to pull the blanket from the United States. In January 1963 Mao wrote a poem to reflect upon Khrushchev's insignificance and the global importance of the Chinese Revolution:

On this tiny globe
A few flies dash themselves against the wall
Humming without cease . . .
Desirous of becoming Kun-Peng have no wings
And mayflies lightly plot to topple the giant tree . . .
A universe of deeds cries out to be done . . .
Seize the day, seize the hour!
Revolutionary spirit turns up the Four Seas,
Workers and peasants leap with halberds
Away with all pests!
Our force is irresistible![12]

The Sino-Soviet polemics put Khrushchev on the defensive. He responded, inconsistently, with fiery statements, but periodically retreated and offered peace to China. The last time Khrushchev extended a hand to his Chinese critics was in November 1963: he wanted to stop polemics and improve economic ties with China, and offered to return specialists. "We are not fools," Mao commented, and intensified the polemical onslaught. Propaganda was to target Khrushchev specifically: "he loves talking, plays a hero, he is at the first place, talks the most and the rudest; if one is to grab a braid of hair, one should grab the largest," the chairman remarked with obvious disdain for Khrushchev. Realizing that he was the target of

Chinese criticism, the Soviet premier was certain of his ability to outlast his critics.[13]

## Change of Guard

Khrushchev's confidence proved unfounded. In October 1964 his comrades conspired to remove him from power. The list of complaints was a long one: economic mismanagement, reckless foreign undertakings, and violations of party democracy. Khrushchev was also criticized for his handling of the dispute with China, though it was not among the main reasons for his removal from power. The Chinese were carefully optimistic, and volunteered to send a delegation to Moscow to "establish contacts" with the new leadership, headed by Leonid Brezhnev (as the first secretary of the Party) and Aleksei Kosygin (as the prime minister). In November 1964 Prime Minister Zhou Enlai held a round of talks with them. The Soviets offered to mend fences, blaming bad relations on Khrushchev and downplaying differences with China, but Zhou was looking for signs of major shifts in Moscow's foreign policy. The talks went badly wrong when, during a reception on the occasion of the anniversary of the Bolshevik Revolution, Soviet Defense Minister Rodion Malinovskii (reportedly drunk) proposed that the Chinese depose Mao Zedong, as the Soviets deposed Khrushchev. The final few days of negotiations came down to Soviet efforts to persuade the Chinese comrades that Malinovskii did not speak for the rest of the leadership.[14]

Although the Sino-Soviet talks failed to produce results, the new Soviet leadership did not lose hope of winning back friendship with China. It did not make sense that China and the Soviet Union, two communist countries, could not overcome their disagreements. Kosygin in particular was confident of his ability to repair relations by frankly discussing matters with Mao. He thought that the split with China was to some extent Khrushchev's fault, and with Khrushchev out of the way, the fortunes of the alliance would improve. So would Kosygin's personal prestige. He had made a name as an able economist, but lacked credentials in foreign affairs. Rapprochement with China offered great possibilities for making political capital at a time when the power

struggle among the new Soviet leaders was only beginning to be revealed. The escalating war in Vietnam offered particularly bright prospects for mending fences with China. Kosygin was convinced that in the face of blunt imperialist aggression, Mao would set his differences with the Soviets aside and join efforts in helping Vietnam. Anticipating successful talks with the Chinese, Kosygin landed in Beijing on February 10, 1965.

When Mao received Kosygin on February 11, he put on great airs, and talked philosophy for two and a half hours, puffing a cigarette and looking into the distance over the heads of dazzled Soviet visitors. Kosygin for his part desperately tried to turn the conversation to practical issues. He stressed the Soviet commitment to Hanoi and asked China to join forces with the Soviet Union in resisting US moves in Vietnam. Mao was skeptical and blamed the Soviets for abandoning Vietnam and selling out to US imperialism. The results of the meeting were disappointing. Mao promised that the Chinese struggle against Soviet revisionism would last for another 10,000 years. On his way back to Moscow, Kosygin looked over his notes on the meeting with Mao and asked his advisers to dress things up a little bit to make it appear in Moscow that his trip was not a failure. But Mao's intransigence stood out one way or another. Kosygin gave up on the transcript. The Sino-Soviet rapprochement did not materialize.

Soviet efforts to have "joint actions" with China over Vietnam continued for several months. Moscow offered to call meetings with Beijing and Hanoi, and convene an international conference to settle the problem. The Soviet ambassador in Beijing, Stepan Chervonenko, was replaced with a hardliner, Sergei Lapin. Moscow even proposed to deploy its aircraft in southern China to provide air cover for North Vietnam. All these efforts proved futile. The Chinese angrily denounced the Soviet request for an air force base as a disguised plot to "put China under control." In Moscow, Chinese accusations were received with some incredulity – how could a handful of MIGs control vast China? The Soviet leaders clearly underestimated Beijing's sensitivity to even a semblance of foreign military presence on Chinese soil. Far from taking "joint actions" with the USSR,

Beijing intensified its propaganda in the summer and fall of 1965, accusing the Soviets of using Vietnam as a "trading chip" to strike a bargain with the United States.

## Containment and Crisis

However, Chinese propaganda was no longer much of a menace to the Soviet Union. Moscow's pragmatic foreign policy won the approval of China's staunch allies, North Vietnam and North Korea, which, to be sure, drifted in the Soviet direction only inasmuch as Brezhnev and Kosygin were willing to provide weapons and economic aid – and this they were willing to do much more than Khrushchev. Certainly, China still commanded authority in split-off factions in the international communist movement, but that authority was waning as China itself turned further and further inwards, preoccupied with internal problems. In January 1966 Brezhnev traveled to Ulaanbaatar to sign an essentially anti-Chinese agreement with Mongolia. That agreement marked a decisive point in Soviet policy toward China – a policy that evolved in only a few months from attempts at rapprochement to outright containment.

In the meantime, China slipped toward chaos as Mao prepared to unleash a new stage of ideological struggle – the Cultural Revolution. Mao worried that the Communist Party itself had succumbed to Khrushchev-style revisionism from within, that party leaders lacked the courage and the will to further revolutionary goals and inevitably turned into reactionary bureaucrats. Mao also feared that he was becoming irrelevant, as other party cadres gained greater prominence at his expense. Determined to reverse a revolutionary low tide in China, Mao supported leftist radicals in attacking the Communist Party itself in order to root out revisionist elements and undermine those leaders who, like Khrushchev, had taken the "capitalist road." Among these capitalist "roaders" were Beijing mayor Peng Zhen, head of state Liu Shaoqi, and general secretary of the Communist Party Deng Xiaoping. The Soviets were slow to understand the latest turn of Chinese politics. After all, the so-called Chinese "Khrushchevs" were the staunchest critics of Khrushchev's

"revisionism." How could they be accused of being Soviet allies in China? Unable to follow these twists and turns, the Soviets were utterly unprepared for the upheaval of the Cultural Revolution and a new crisis in Sino-Soviet relations.

On August 20, 1966, Soviet diplomats in Beijing witnessed a bizarre procession beyond the mission gates. Thousands upon thousands of Chinese students, "revolutionary" Red Guards, marched past the embassy chanting anti-Soviet slogans and trashing the street with big-letter posters. The Chinese authorities did nothing to control the mob and blamed the Soviets for "insulting the revolutionary masses." In Moscow, it was feared that the demonstrations were instigated from above to prepare the Chinese public for a war with the USSR.

A war between China and the Soviet Union – unthinkable? Not any longer. The Soviet leadership had been concerned for several years with growing tensions on the Sino-Soviet border. In the past, occasional Chinese fishermen and nomads regularly crossed the vast frontier, usually by accident. Before relations between China and the Soviet Union turned sour, such border incidents were easily solved in the spirit of mutual concessions. But in the early 1960s crossings no longer appeared incidental. Soviet guards believed that the Chinese deliberately provoked unwanted encounters. By August 1963, just as polemics between the Soviet Union and China flared up, the Chinese made claims to the effect that Moscow was putting China under military pressure.

All of that seemed bewildering to the Soviet leaders who continued to insist that there was no "border question" between China and the Soviet Union. Why, as Khrushchev said: "all socialist countries have their borders from former tsars, emperors and kings. If we build our relations on this basis, how far would this take us?"[15] Mao Zedong hinted just how far he was willing to go when on July 10, 1964, he suddenly announced to a visiting Japanese delegation that China was still to present a "bill" for territories annexed by the Russian tsars in the nineteenth century. Mao's unsettled bill dazzled Khrushchev. Chinese criticism of Soviet "revisionism" was bad enough, but now Mao raised territorial issues, threatening underpopulated but strategically and economically important Soviet possessions in the Far East. Khrushchev decried hideous Chinese designs and compared Mao to Hitler on one occasion in September 1964. For several weeks the Soviet press was flooded with articles under titles like "Insolent Chauvinism," "Dark Designs," and "Monstrous Pretensions of the Chinese Splitters."

Khrushchev may have overreacted to Mao's démarche. Mao's claims may have aimed at raising border tensions, which served his long-term purpose of mobilizing the Chinese masses for a new revolutionary upheaval. Nevertheless, the veiled threats were taken very seriously in Moscow. There was no immediate prospect of war, but the Soviets ordered a gradual build-up of forces in the Far East and in early 1966 agreed in principle to station military forces in Mongolia. Yet it was not until the embassy crisis of 1966–7 that the Soviet leaders grasped the seriousness of the situation. With diplomats besieged by the mob in Beijing, and tensions brooding on the border, an outright war with China became a distinct and frightening possibility. For that reason on February 4, 1967, the Politburo adopted measures to increase Soviet military presence in Zabaikal'ye, Far East and Eastern Kazakhstan, to send troops to Mongolia, and to build protected command centers.

In China, the Soviet build-up was viewed with growing apprehension, particularly after the August 1968 Soviet invasion of Czechoslovakia. The appearance of Soviet tanks in Prague had a bombshell effect in Beijing. Could China be the next victim of the Soviet efforts to "save socialism"? Zhou Enlai condemned the Soviet action as a "barbaric aggression" and warned that "one could expect anything from the Soviet Union, including an attack on China."[16] Mao was also worried that both the United States and the Soviet Union were "preparing to spread the war."[17] The Chinese Central Military Commission (headed by Mao) issued a set of instructions for the border guards, calling for vigilance in the face of Soviet military pressure and for a "tit-for-tat" response in case of Soviet provocations.[18] Ironically, the fear of war and the Chinese efforts to deter the perceived Soviet aggression by show of strength led to a series of military clashes on the Sino-Soviet border, which brought the two countries to the brink of war. On March 2 and

15, 1969, Soviet and Chinese border guards exchanged fire at Zhen Bao Island, near the Chinese bank of the Ussuri River. The first incident was instigated by the Chinese in a miscalculated attempt to "teach the Soviets a lesson." The Soviet military retaliated against the Chinese positions with massive artillery strikes.[19]

Despite the deadly border skirmishes, the Chinese policymakers initially downplayed the prospects of a major war with the USSR. A special report prepared on July 11, 1969, by four Chinese marshals on Mao's instructions indicated that the Soviets focused their attention on Europe, and a war with China would be logistically difficult to implement. The Chinese policymakers took their time in responding to requests for negotiations in order to exploit the uncertainty and tensions in the task of mobilizing the masses in China. But by August 1969, Mao became concerned that the extent of the Soviet danger had been underestimated. Another armed clash occurred on the Sino-Soviet border in Xinjiang on August 13 and later that month Moscow made veiled threats of a nuclear strike against China. It is extremely unlikely that a nuclear strike was indeed considered by the Soviet policymakers as a viable option, but the hint was not lost on China. Amid a heightening war scare in Beijing, the Chinese leaders agreed at last to the Sino-Soviet talks.

Kosygin and Zhou Enlai met at Beijing airport on September 11, 1969, in a tense atmosphere. Zhou stressed to the Soviet premier that China had absolutely no intention of fighting a war with the USSR. Kosygin in turn reassured Zhou that the Soviets would not launch a preemptive strike on China. The two sides agreed to reopen talks on the border issue and take a series of measures to lessen bilateral tensions. The talks began in Beijing in October 1969, and lasted without visible result for over a decade. Of course, meetings of the Chinese and the Soviet diplomats played a positive role: a dialogue was maintained despite hostility, and further border skirmishes were avoided. At the same time, fear of war with the Soviet Union prompted the Chinese leaders to reappraise foreign policy priorities and build bridges to the outside world in the hope of avoiding a one-on-one confrontation with Moscow. The 1969 Sino-Soviet border clashes thus paved the way for closer relations between Beijing and Washington in the 1970s.[20]

## Conclusion

In the meantime, in the Soviet Union, policymakers and academics scratched their heads to solve the baffling puzzle: what went wrong with the Sino-Soviet relationship? The alliance was from the beginning what the Soviet leadership would have called "a scientific undertaking." Based on the presumed affinity of views in Beijing and Moscow, on the adherence of both sides to "revolutionary" principles, it was not meant to be a marriage of convenience. The Soviet propaganda explained the Sino-Soviet alliance in Marxist terms to a skeptical western audience, inclined to suspect Moscow of expansionist designs in China. But the Soviet leaders believed their own propaganda. Khrushchev, for all his pragmatism, held an unwavering commitment to socialism and his commitment to the Sino-Soviet alliance was equally firm. In the early 1960s Khrushchev consistently tried to repair relations with Mao, despite the evidence of the Chinese unwillingness to reciprocate the Soviet goodwill. Khrushchev's successors renewed Moscow's efforts to find a compromise with Beijing on the premise that two communist countries were natural allies. The Soviet ideological conceptions did not suffice to explain the depth of the Sino-Soviet rift. A search for better explanations produced a thesis about Mao's anti-Soviet, even anti-Russian, inclinations.

The chairman's "anti-Sovietism" manifested itself in relentless attempts to "subvert" the Soviet influence in the international communist movement – for instance, in North Vietnam and North Korea. That was already a major problem in the eyes of the Soviet leaders. But being "anti-Russian" – not on account of disagreements with Moscow's "revisionist" policies but for nationalist or racist reasons – was a more serious charge.

This unlikely proposition squared well with Mao's peasant background, his obsessive concern to keep China free from Soviet military control, his persistent claims to neighboring Mongolia and to the Soviet Far East. The thinly disguised racial constructs of the Soviet leadership heightened the

sense of fear and insecurity in the face of the Chinese "danger." By the late 1960s, the first concern of Soviet leaders was not Chinese ideological "subversion" but the prospect of war with China. Inability and unwillingness to understand Chinese culture and traditions in Soviet policymaking circles fed the feeling of mistrust and perception of the Chinese as cunning, crafty, and aggressive. Moscow's failure to decipher the events in China at the time of the Cultural Revolution deepened Soviet suspicions of its neighbor's policies as anti-Russian at their core.

In the Chinese view, it was the Soviets who triggered the Sino-Soviet split with their sheer arrogance and Great Power policies in China. From Stalin's efforts to set up "half-colonies" in China, to Khrushchev's joint fleet proposal, to Brezhnev's and Kosygin's ambitions to "pressure," "control," and even "encircle" China – Soviet policies from the Chinese perspective manifested with striking consistency a tendency to look down on China and poured oil on the fire of pride and prestige of the Chinese leadership. Mao also became disappointed by the Soviet "betrayal" of the revolution. Moscow's skepticism about China's Great Leap Forward and Khrushchev's de-Stalinization convinced Mao that the Soviet leadership had abandoned Marxism. Association with the Soviet Union could even be harmful for Beijing, as the contagion of "revisionism" spread outwards. Mao believed that Chinese – not Soviet – socialism was on the winning side of history. The chairman's revolutionary visions were frequently misunderstood by his own colleagues in the Chinese leadership. Unsurprisingly, the Soviet leaders also missed the significance of Mao's ideological conceptions for the fate of the alliance.

It was only when Chinese and Soviet leaders took steps to overcome the baggage of mutual misperceptions and suspicions that a confrontation faded amid calls for a strategic partnership. Yet the unfortunate fate of the Sino-Soviet alliance speaks to the lasting nature of distorted stereotypes that feed misperceptions between peoples and leaders. Who knows what kind of revolutionary visions or personal grievances might tip the scales back? China was a puzzle the Soviet leaders were never able to solve. But for the

Chinese leadership, the Soviet Union was just as much of a puzzle. Both sides put their pieces together in the wrong order, arriving at grotesque caricatures. The Sino-Soviet alliance was meant to become a showcase for brotherly relations between states. Instead, it became a dialogue of the deaf. The disintegration of the alliance speaks to the potent force and the poignant consequences of ideas and perceptions in the history of international politics.

## NOTES

1 Cited in Dieter Heinzig, *The Soviet Union and Communist China, 1945–1950: An Arduous Road to the Alliance* (Armonk, NY, and London: M. E. Sharpe, 2004), p. 276.

2 Cited in Zhang Shu Guang and Chen Jian, "The Emerging Disputes Between Beijing and Moscow: Ten Newly Available Chinese Documents, 1956–1958," *Cold War International History Project Bulletin* 6–7 (1995/6): 148.

3 "Stalin's Conversations with Chinese Leaders," *Cold War International History Project Bulletin* 6–7 (1995/6): 4–9.

4 Ibid.

5 Dieter Heinzig, "Stalin, Mao, Kim and Korean War Origins, 1950: A Russian Documentary Discrepancy," *Cold War International History Project Bulletin* 8–9 (1996/7): 240.

6 Dmitrii Shepilov, *Neprimknuvshii* (Moscow: Vagrius, 2001), p. 318.

7 Cited in Merle Goldman and Leo Ou-Fan Lee, eds., *An Intellectual History of Modern China* (Cambridge: Cambridge University Press, 2002), p. 457.

8 "Conversation between Pavel Iudin and Mao Zedong" (March 22, 1958), *Cold War International History Project Bulletin* 6–7 (1995): 155.

9 Vladislav Zubok, "The Khrushchev–Mao Conversations, 31 July–3 August 1958," *Cold War International History Project Bulletin* 12–13 (2001): 251.

10 Aleksandr Fursenko, ed., *Prezidium TsK KPSS: 1954–1964* (Moscow: Rosspen, 2003), p. 720.

11 Ibid.

12 *Ten More Poems of Mao Zedong* (Hong Kong: Eastern Horizon Press, 1967), pp. 20–2, with author's corrections.

13 Wu Lengxi, *Shinian Lunzhan, 1956–1966: Zhong Su Guanxi Huiyilu* (Beijing: Zhongyang wenxian chubanshe, 1999), pp. 660–2.

14 Alexander Lukin, *The Bear Watches the Dragon: Russia's Perceptions of China and the Evolution of Russian–Chinese Relations since the 18th Century* (Armonk, NY: M. E. Sharpe, 2003), p. 130.

15 Nikita Khrushchev, *Vremia, Liudi, Vlast* (Moscow: Moskovskie Novosti), vol. 2, p. 202.

16 Boris Kulik, *Sovetsko-Kitaiskii Raskol: Prichiny i Posledstvi'ia* (Moscow: IDV RAN, 2000), p. 14.

17 "Conversation between Mao Zedong and E. F. Hill" (November 28, 1968), *Cold War International History Project Bulletin* 11 (1998): 159.

18 Yang Kuisong, "The Sino-Soviet Border Clash of 1969: From Zhenbao Island to Sino-American Rapprochement," *Cold War History* 1 (2000): 27; Sergei Goncharov and Viktor Usov, "Peregovory A. N. Kosygina i Zhou Enla'ia v Pekinskom Aeroportu," *Problemy Dalnego Vostoka* 5 (1992): 43.

19 Yang, "Sino-Soviet Border Clash," pp. 23–4.

20 Goncharov and Usov, "Peregovory A. N. Kosygina i Zhou Enla'ia," p. 43.

## GUIDE TO FURTHER READING

Barbara Barnoin and Yu Changgen, *Chinese Foreign Policy During the Cultural Revolution* (London and New York: Kegan Paul International, 1998). An excellent background to China's foreign policy in the mid-1960s.

Chen Jian, *Mao's China and the Cold War* (Chapel Hill, NC: University of North Carolina Press, 2001). One of the best accounts of Chinese foreign relations and China's involvement in the Korea and Vietnam wars, in the context of Mao's revolutionary visions.

Sergei Goncharov, John Lewis, and Xue Litai, *Uncertain Partners: Stalin, Mao and the Korean War* (Stanford, CA: Stanford University Press, 1993). A groundbreaking work on the impact of Sino-Soviet relations on the Korean War.

Dieter Heinzig, *The Soviet Union and Communist China, 1945–1950: An Arduous Road to the Alliance* (Armonk, NY, and London: M. E. Sharpe, 2004). By far the most detailed account of the making of the Sino-Soviet alliance.

Sarah Paine, *Imperial Rivals: China, Russia, and their Disputed Frontier* (Armonk, NY: M. E. Sharpe, 1996). This book puts Sino-Russian relations in the broader historical context of an uneasy relationship between the Russian and the Chinese empires.

Odd Arne Westad, ed., *Brothers in Arms: The Rise and Fall of the Sino-Soviet Alliance, 1945–1963* (Washington, DC: Woodrow Wilson Center Press, 1998). By far the best work on the Sino-Soviet alliance and split, with new evidence from Russian and Chinese archives.

Donald Zagoria, *The Sino-Soviet Conflict, 1956–61* (Princeton, NJ: Princeton University Press, 1962). A classic study of the Sino-Soviet split by a western Kremlinologist.

Vladislav M. Zubok and Constantine Pleshakov, *Inside the Kremlin's Cold War: From Stalin to Khrushchev* (Cambridge, MA: Harvard University Press, 1996). One of the best existing accounts of Soviet foreign policy in general with a generous commentary on Sino-Soviet relations.

## INTERNET RESOURCES

*Cold War International History Project Bulletin* is an invaluable source for any research on the history of the Cold War. The Sino-Soviet split is covered extensively in translated documents and scholarly commentaries. See in particular issues 6–7 (Stalin's conversations with Mao Zedong in 1950) and 12–13 (Khrushchev's conversations with Mao Zedong in 1958 and 1959) with commentaries by Chen Jian, Odd Arne Westad, Vladislav Zubok, and others. Bulletins are available in the publications section of the CWIHP website, www.cwihp.org.

# Part V

# A New World Order?

# CHAPTER TWENTY-NINE

# The Collapse of the Soviet Union and the End of the Cold War

## MARTIN MCCAULEY

The collapse of the Soviet Union, in December 1991, was as unexpected as it was astonishing. A superpower simply disappeared from the map. A civil war or external war can lead to the demise of a state. However, this did not occur as the Soviet Union expired peacefully. So why did it collapse? At a meeting of the ruling Politburo of the Communist Party of the Soviet Union (CPSU), on March 11, 1985, Andrei Gromyko, the veteran foreign minister, listed the qualities of the new general secretary (Gensek), Mikhail Gorbachev. The new leader possessed "unquenchable energy; he desired to do and achieve more; he was good with people; he always put the interests of the Party, society and people before his own; he had a great amount of Party experience; he was a good chairman of Party meetings." Eduard Shevardnadze, soon to be the Gensek's foreign voice, launched into a eulogy. Gorbachev thanked everyone for their support. We "are living through a very difficult period of transition. Our economy needs to be revitalized as does our democracy and foreign policy . . . we must move ahead, identify weaknesses and eliminate them."[1] Could the new Gensek live up to expectations? He knew that economic reform was necessary but not urgent. He had participated in seminars during the early 1980s and was aware of many problems awaiting solutions. A participant judged him to be very indecisive and incapable of formulating his thoughts precisely. This was an ominous warning that he was going to have difficulty in perceiving

what had to be done and in what sequence. Actually the economy was growing at less than 2 percent annually, about half the official rate. Since the population was increasing at about 0.9 percent annually, living standards were stagnating. The planners looked forward to matching American industrial output by 2000. The recipe to achieve this was rapid scientific-technical progress with investment in the machine-building industry to double. Gorbachev was an impatient leader. He worked according to the principle that willpower, determination, and commitment to Party goals could solve any problem. He was ill-qualified to regenerate the Soviet economy. Before becoming Gensek, he had been the top official monitoring Soviet agriculture. Blessed with much fertile land, the country still found it necessary to import food from the West. The new Gensek had little expertise in industrial matters. He believed that the planned economy was infinitely malleable. Reforms could be adopted and the net result would be beneficial. As a result he got carried away from time to time. In Tolyatti, in 1986, in a large car plant, he demanded it attain and surpass world automobile standards. Any engineer knew that this was nonsense.

At a Politburo session in April 1985, the Gensek waxed eloquent about the evils of drink and its impact on future generations. Production had to be sharply curtailed. It was pointed out that alcohol sales brought in billions of rubles a year. There was no way the budget could recoup this elsewhere. In May, a decree was adopted which aimed at turning the country into a "dry zone." Vines in Armenia, producing the best cognac in the country, were ripped up. Retail outlets were closed down. As someone observed, a Russian and his vodka cannot be parted. If the state did not produce the alcohol, the black market would. The result was a vast increase in illegal production. Sugar began disappearing from the shops, as did sweets and tomato paste. Everything was being turned into alcohol. Organized crime expanded rapidly as demand for alcohol rose. As prices doubled or trebled, vast revenues flowed into the black market. The state budget deficit grew and grew.

The new Gensek needed to replace incumbent officials with his own appointees. Most officials used their positions for personal gain. This meant that a case could be fabricated against practically anyone. The Ministry of Foreign Affairs was targeted. Diplomats in Tokyo had been purchasing Japanese consumer goods and shipping them back to Moscow in containers. They were then sold on the black market at high prices. Diplomats in other countries did the same. Eventually they accumulated so much money they could not launder it at home. They began taking it out of the country and selling it for dollars. The CIA began buying large quantities to fund their "friends" in the Soviet Union. Inevitably, the KGB picked this up. Many diplomats were dismissed, arrested, and jailed.

Then there was the Uzbek cotton scandal. For years, the Uzbek leadership had been working a scam which entailed delivering fictitious cotton to the state. One estimate is that it entailed five million tonnes of non-existent cotton which brought in over three billion rubles. The head of the KGB began delving into matters in Stavropol krai, Gorbachev's former base. The material was so embarrassing that Gorbachev engineered his removal, in January 1986. There was one unintended consequence of the anti-corruption campaign. It broke an informal contract between Moscow and the non-Russian republics. The center was aware that the republican elites had been embezzling large sums. Moscow had paid to cement their loyalty and subordination. Now these elites were being arrested, humiliated, and

sent to prison. The republics began to exact revenge. It was already clear, in late 1986, that Moscow was facing rising nationalism. The center was no longer a friend but an enemy to be ruthlessly exploited. Gorbachev was to pay a heavy price for his anti-corruption campaign.

The perception began to grow among the Soviet population that middle-level Party officials were holding up the regeneration of the country. This was reflected in a flood of letters to the Gensek. A radical solution was proposed by Aleksandr Yakovlev, who became known as the father of glasnost. He proposed, in late 1985, a two-party system based on the CPSU, the election of a Soviet executive president, a democratic transformation of the country, and pro-market economic reforms. The Gensek did not find these palatable at the time but later adopted most of them. However, he did reveal that he had democratic instincts. He regarded the evolution of an opposition as inevitable. He was confident he could hold his own. One can say that he consciously began to dismantle the totalitarian system from 1986 onwards. Gorbachev needed to refashion the Politburo to push through his policies. Egor Ligachev was elected and became the Gensek's number two. As such he became the leading voice on ideology, always a key policy area. Nikolai Ryzhkov, soon to become prime minister, and Viktor Chebrikov, KGB chief, also joined. The Gensek needed his own team of advisers. They drafted many of his proposals, decrees, and speeches. An unofficial member of the Gensek's team was his wife, Raisa. In order to keep control, Gorbachev set up commissions and bureaux with overlapping functions. This led to policy disputes. A strong, decisive leader was needed to manage such a system.

In June 1985, Gorbachev proposed to Andrei Gromyko that he take up the vacant post of president. Gorbachev could now appoint his own minister of foreign affairs. He chose Eduard Shevardnadze, the Georgian Party leader. He had an imperfect command of Russian and no diplomatic experience. Quite clearly, Gorbachev was going to be his own foreign minister. In December 1985, Boris Yeltsin became the new Moscow Party boss. Gorbachev soon had a clear majority in the Politburo.

A Party Congress offered a Gensek the opportunity to make radical changes. The 27th Congress opened on February 25, 1986, the same day as the 20th Congress which had shaken the world twenty years before. Khrushchev had then dethroned Stalin. Would something similar occur? The Gensek thought the country was overcome by inertia. Perestroika was the new slogan to revitalize the country. What was perestroika? It translates as "restructuring." But what did it mean? The Gensek never succeeded in explaining it clearly. More openness or glasnost was needed to highlight shortcomings. Everyone should become more self-critical. The masses should be consulted and listened to. This was democratization. Then he dropped a bombshell. "It is impossible to win the arms race," he declared. This stunning admission meant that the Soviet Union had lost the arms race with the United States. The burden of defense – about 40 percent of national wealth was poured into defense – had proved too onerous. The first Gorbachev–Reagan summit, in Geneva, was a success. It broke the ice between the superpowers. However, it did not change American policy.

## Chernobyl

On Saturday April 26, 1986, reactor number four of the Chernobyl power station in Ukraine exploded. A government commission immediately went to the scene. It estimated that an area of 600 square kilometers had been contaminated by radiation. The situation was getting worse by the day. Astonishingly, the May Day parades in Kyiv (Kiev), the Ukrainian capital, and other cities within the contamination zone went ahead. Official silence was observed until May 14, when Gorbachev finally appeared on television to report on the disaster. His speech was halting and unimpressive. Public anger mounted and confidence in the comrades in the Kremlin declined. The Soviet budget deficit, in 1985, was 17 billion rubles; in 1986, it was three times as much. One quarter of enterprises failed to fulfill their plan. What was to be done? However, Chernobyl had one positive outcome. There had to be glasnost right up to the top. Openness, however, was a two-edged sword. It would reveal how corrupt the Soviet establishment was.

Gorbachev always returned depressed from his visits around the country. He moaned that no one was implementing perestroika. The dead hand of bureaucracy was holding back popular participation in restructuring. Abuse poured into the Gensek's office. "Your utopian projects to save Russia are leading to total disillusionment with Party policies . . . Corruption and speculation surround us everywhere," wailed one Muscovite. Gromyko was appalled at the direction perestroika was taking. The Politburo split on whether to raise prices or not. Gorbachev and Ryzhkov, the prime minister, were strongly in favor but Ligachev and Shevardnadze were passionately against. The latter argued that it was impossible to raise prices at a time when 25 million citizens were living on a monthly income of 50 rubles per capita; 50 million were on less than 80 rubles. The issue was shelved.

In December 1986, Ryzhkov discussed the proposed law on the socialist enterprise. This would permit the election of managers and the setting up of workers' collectives. Full self-financing and self-accounting were envisaged. All this did not make much sense as prices were low and inputs regulated by the government. Who should be manager? Workers, of course, would plump for a comrade who made life easy for them. Not surprisingly, production declined. This law proved to be one of the most ill-advised economic reforms. It just made matters worse. It revealed that the prime minister lacked a basic grasp of economics and finance. In his defense, one can say he was an engineer and had no training in these matters. One of the problems was that he was unaware of this. Who was responsible for the mess the country was in? At a Politburo meeting in January 1987, Boris Yeltsin was very provocative. The present members of the Politburo were responsible. He proposed awarding them marks out of ten. Naturally this did not go down very well. Gorbachev put the blame on cadre policy and the command-administrative system. Afterwards, he complained to another member that little had changed for the better under Yeltsin in Moscow. One can see here the beginning of the fatal split between the Gensek and Boris.

Historians and writers grasped the opportunity offered by glasnost to paint the past in dark colors. The Party's ideological control was being weakened. Many poets and writers were rehabilitated. Journals, such as *Ogonek*, published sensational material on Stalin's crimes. Attempts were made to present the pre-Stalin period as a golden era when socialism had taken a wrong turn. However, Lenin was not sacrosanct. Vladimir Soloukhin, the novelist, presented the founding father as cruel and the begetter of the gulag. A Politburo commission was set up in November 1987 to rehabilitate the victims of repression. It had two functions: to uncover the dark truths about the past and to accord justice to the victims. Gorbachev had the opportunity, on the occasion of the seventieth anniversary of the revolution in November 1987, of breaking with the past. He declined to do so and alienated many progressives. This underlined one of his intellectual characteristics: indecisiveness.

Ryzhkov had nothing positive to report about the economy in 1987. Gorbachev was desperate for economic advice. As his previous advisers, such as Abel Aganbegyan, had proved so disappointing, he listened to more radical advisers. The central distribution of resources was to end. Some military enterprises were to be switched to civilian production. The cooperative movement was to receive a boost. These were very radical departures. There is little evidence that the leadership was aware of the consequences of ending the central distribution of resources, for instance.[2]

In September 1987, Ligachev chaired a Politburo meeting as Gorbachev was on holiday. He launched a furious attack on Yeltsin. The emotional Yeltsin now snapped. He wrote to Gorbachev offering his resignation as Moscow Party boss and as a candidate member of the Politburo. The Gensek was annoyed as he was in Crimea putting the finishing touches to his book, *Perestroika: New Thinking for Our Country and the World*. Things came to a head in October 1987. Politburo members severely criticized Boris. Gorbachev was even more offensive. News reached the Gensek on November 9 that Yeltsin had attempted to commit suicide. He had stabbed himself in the chest with a pair of scissors. Despite this, he was hauled before the Moscow Party bureau, given another verbal lashing, and dismissed as Party boss. The following day he was voted off the Politburo. It was a bitter parting between the two great champions of perestroika. However, it was a Pyrrhic victory for the Gensek as Yeltsin now became the unofficial leader of the opposition. He became the champion of the downtrodden, disillusioned, and disgruntled.

## Nationalities

The Soviet Union was a multinational empire with over a hundred nationalities. The Russians were the elder brothers; everyone else was a younger brother. An unofficial agreement had developed under Brezhnev. It permitted embezzlement in the national republics. Andropov and Gorbachev had broken this understanding. The situation was exacerbated by the failure of perestroika to improve living standards. This brought the superiority of the Russians into question. The Estonians, for one, were convinced they could run their republic more efficiently than Moscow. The KGB had evidence of racial tension. In the spring of 1986, in Yakutia, Yakut and Russian university students had fought one another for three days. Then the Yakuts demonstrated in front of the Party building. Slogans such as "Yakutia for the Yakuts" and "Russians get out" made their feelings clear. In December 1986, the Kazakh Party leader resigned, under pressure from Gorbachev. Instead of appointing another Kazakh, the Gensek parachuted in a Ukrainian. This provoked protests by Kazakh university students in the capital, Almaty. They wanted a Kazakh Party boss. The protests grew and became violent. Eventually two militiamen and one demonstrator died and over 1,200 were injured, almost 800 of them militiamen.[3]

The bloodiest interethnic conflict, however, took place in Nagorno-Karabakh, a predominantly Armenian enclave in Azerbaijan. In 1986, demonstrations for its transfer to Armenia began. Moscow gave the impression it might agree. In February 1988, the local soviet passed a motion requesting the Soviet government to transfer the territory to Armenia. This provoked a sharp reaction by Azerbaijan. Nagorno-Karabakh would never be ceded. In Sumgait, near Baku, Azeris began attacking Armenians and destroying property. Officially, thirty-two died and over a hundred were injured. The local militia did not intervene. Some members of the Politburo wanted martial law but Gorbachev reminded them that force had not been effective in Afghanistan. A territorial realignment in Azerbaijan and Armenia could lead to an avalanche of claims by other nationalities. Stalin had operated according to the principle of divide and rule. This had created potentially explosive situations in many parts of the Soviet Union.[4] In June 1988, the pro-independence Sajudis movement was founded in Lithuania. National fronts were set up in Estonia, Latvia, and Lithuania. Their parliaments declared their own languages to be the official ones, replacing Russian. The republics demanded political and economic autonomy. Non-Russian elites were laying claim to power in the regions. In essence, they were saying that this was the price of loyalty to Moscow. They did not wish to secede – except in the Baltic – since they benefited financially from their relationship with Moscow. There was another factor at play in Central Asia, Tatarstan, Bashkortostan, and the north Caucasus: Islam. There had always been tension between official and unofficial Islam. The latter now saw an opportunity to expand its influence.

Very radical measures were announced at the 19th Party Conference. Gorbachev recommended that the local Party boss become the chair of the local soviet. In this way, the Party and the soviets could grow together or even fuse. The Congress of People's Deputies, which had had its heyday under Lenin, was resurrected. Fifteen hundred members were to be elected directly in multi-candidate contests and 750 nominated by social organizations, such as the Party and the trade unions. The Congress would elect 400 of its members to form a Supreme Soviet. They would be full-time lawmakers. This reform transformed the role of Chair of the Supreme Soviet. Hitherto it had been decorative. As Gorbachev wanted the position for himself, he pushed Gromyko into retirement. The conference revealed quite clearly that the Party had split into two wings: the conservatives and the radicals. One of the conservatives was the writer Yury Bondarev. He likened perestroika to a plane which after it took off had no idea where it was going to land. Hence, perestroika had no clear goals or direction. It was

destructive but put nothing constructive in its place. Yeltsin was one of the stars of the show. He proposed multi-candidate elections to all Party posts. He thundered against Party privileges and the special shops and polyclinics for these comrades. Ligachev, the main target, responded by saying that the only privilege he had was to work his fingers to the bone.

Another key decision was to take the Party apparatus out of the economy. It was no longer to be responsible for monitoring the fulfillment of plans. The local Party had been the glue which kept the system together. The Party boss, often corrupt, could usually find resources to keep enterprises working. Ministries and enterprises were now responsible. The result was growing chaos. In the absence of a market, enterprises resorted to barter. They would only fulfill their contractual obligations if they got something in return. The shadow economy expanded to meet demand.

In September, Ligachev reported that proposed changes would lead to the dismissal of 800,000 comrades. This had led to confusion and a drop in discipline. There was doubt if the governmental apparatus could assume functions previously performed by the Party apparatus. Party cadres began to regard Gorbachev as the source of all their troubles.

Gorbachev's behavior was amazing. He had mounted the nomenklatura (ruling class) ladder, rung by rung, to the top. Once there, he set out to destroy it. He did not appear to have been aware of the consequences of his actions. From now on, the Party nomenklatura, in order to survive, had to grab as much state property and resources as possible. He was losing support in the nomenklatura at a time when ordinary people were expressing openly their disappointment at his policies. Trips around the country became chastening experiences.

## Radicalism and Conservatism, 1989–1990

There were to be multi-candidate elections to the 1st Congress of People's Deputies (CPD). A huge number of officials began moving from the Party apparatus to the new Supreme Soviet apparatus.

The center of power was changing. Elections to the CPD permitted the formation of movements, national fronts, single-issue groups, and an array of social democratic and religious formations. High-profile journalists, scientists, and artists could stand in their own name. The politics of choice had returned. The dispossessed nationalities now raised their voices. Volga Germans wanted their autonomous republic, abolished in 1941, to be restored. Interethnic conflicts within republics, suppressed for decades, flared up. Georgia was a special case. In the capital, Tbilisi, on April 8, 1989, security forces decided to disperse a peaceful demonstration by using gas. Nineteen died and hundreds were injured. Gorbachev was abroad at the time. Georgians began calling for independence.

The star was Boris Yeltsin. A great populist, he traveled the country castigating the Party apparatus for the failure of perestroika. He won a landslide victory in Moscow. Academician Andrei Sakharov, the father of the hydrogen bomb and now a human rights activist, the poet Evgeny Evtushenko, Gavriil Popov, the radical economist and future mayor of Moscow, and Anatoly Sobchak, a future mayor of Leningrad (St. Petersburg), were among the celebrities elected. The election revealed the unpopularity of the Party Central Committee. Some of its members had failed to be elected even though they had been unopposed. This occurred if 50 percent of voters failed to support the single candidate. As Boris Yeltsin pointed out, it required a special type of political talent to lose an election as the only candidate.

Gorbachev was elected chair of the CPD. When it opened on May 25, 1989, the whole country stopped to watch television. The show was riveting. For the first time since the 1920s there was real debate. It was like opening Pandora's box. Every national and republican grievance was aired. Gavriil Popov announced the formation of an interregional deputies' group in the CPD. Other co-chairs were Boris Yeltsin and Andrei Sakharov. Its program included private property and greater sovereignty for, and the economic autonomy of, republics. The law on cooperatives was adopted in May 1988. They developed rapidly and, in 1990, about one million persons

were involved. They soon set up their own banks. By the middle of 1991, there were over 1,500 banks. The Russian Federation Supreme Soviet, in January 1991, legalized private property. Private enterprises could now be set up. The Russian Federation began taking over Soviet enterprises and property on its territory. The Soviet economy gradually fragmented. Food-producing regions would not fulfill state contracts. They wanted to barter their produce for something else.

## Ending the Cold War

President Ronald Reagan wanted to end the Cold War by ending the arms race. He envisaged the abolition of nuclear weapons. He had made little headway with Presidents Brezhnev, Andropov, and Chernenko. They belonged to the geriatric past. The advent of the energetic Gorbachev promised an interlocutor who would engage in real debate. Gorbachev inherited a country which had abandoned the Brezhnev doctrine in eastern Europe. The Kremlin had judged intervening militarily in Poland in 1981 to save socialism too dangerous. Hungary was developing its own economic model and moving slowly toward democratization. Gorbachev decided the best policy was to allow eastern Europe to go its own way. He was certain that these countries had irrevocably chosen socialism.

Reagan referred to the Soviet Union as the "evil empire" in March 1983. He rejected the premise of détente that Moscow had earned the right to be treated as a military, political, and moral equal. US defense spending was to double between 1980 and 1985. Soviet leaders before Gorbachev read this as preparation for an attack on their country. Actually, Reagan was attempting to force the Kremlin to the negotiating table. Gorbachev was willing to come. Reagan was a leader who could see beyond complexity to simple solutions. Gorbachev could not. Whereas the US president could see a clear path ahead toward the abolition of nuclear weapons, Gorbachev could not. The latter was always wondering which path he should take. At their first summit in Geneva they sparred, trying to gain an advantage. Reagan proposed they sit down and work out how to abolish nuclear weapons. The Strategic Defense Initiative (SDI) would render this possible. He would even share the technology with Gorbachev. Two months later Gorbachev proposed the two superpowers collaborate to rid the world of nuclear weapons by 2000. The Chernobyl nuclear disaster in April 1986 led to the promotion of perestroika and glasnost. At Reykjavik, in October, Gorbachev accepted the "zero option," which envisaged the elimination of all intermediate-range nuclear weapons in Europe. Reagan proposed the abolition of all intercontinental ballistic missiles. However, SDI could not be deployed. Reagan rejected this and it appeared that the summit had been a failure. Nevertheless, the two presidents quickly realized that they had achieved a breakthrough – they saw nuclear weapons as obsolete. At their third summit, in Washington in December 1987, they agreed to dismantle all intermediate-range nuclear missiles in Europe.

The prevailing western view was that the Soviet Union would never relinquish any part of its empire. However, Gorbachev accepted that eastern Europe could go its own way. What about Afghanistan, where Soviet forces were now bogged down? Moscow began looking for an exit strategy. It also began withdrawing troops and cutting aid to Marxist regimes in Central America and Africa. This signaled the end of the "zero-sum game," in which a country which joined the Soviet or American camp was seen as a defeat for the other side. Then Gorbachev, at the UN General Assembly in December 1988, announced the Soviet Union would cut the number of ground forces committed to the Warsaw Pact by half a million men within two years. It did not depend on the Americans reciprocating. He had taken this decision without consulting his own military. At this point President Reagan left office. Gorbachev fretted that the incoming president, George Bush, was squandering the impetus that had been built up. Both leaders became wary of the other and did not expect great breakthroughs. The White House spokesman referred to Gorbachev as a "drugstore cowboy." Events in eastern Europe gathered momentum and dragged the presidents along with them. In Hungary in June 1989, Imre Nagy, prime minister during the Hungarian revolution of 1956 and then executed

by the Soviets, was reburied ceremonially in Budapest. The Hungarian government went further. It began dismantling the barbed wire along its border with Austria. When the East Germans protested, Moscow replied that it could do nothing. Gorbachev had abdicated in eastern Europe. In elections in Poland in June, Solidarity swept the board. Poland had its first prime minister and government who were not subordinate to Moscow since 1944. China viewed events in eastern Europe with alarm. When Gorbachev visited China he was given a rapturous welcome, much to the discomfort of the Chinese leadership. Deng Xiaoping's response was to order the brutal suppression of the democracy movement in Tiananmen Square in Beijing in June 1989. This won plaudits in East Berlin but condemnation elsewhere. Nervous voices wondered if this scenario would repeat itself in eastern Europe. The only countries where this might happen were the German Democratic Republic (GDR) and Romania.

The Hungarian authorities were well aware that dismantling frontier barriers with Austria in August 1989 would lead to some Hungarian citizens choosing to emigrate. They also knew that other East Europeans, especially East Germans, would avail themselves of the opportunity to move to the West. Some East Germans did not make for Hungary but invaded the West German embassy in Prague and claimed asylum. Eventually it was agreed that special trains would ferry the East Germans to the West. East German stations were closed as the trains rolled through under the cover of darkness. Thousands of other East Germans drove to Hungary and crossed into Austria. A key reason for the inept handling of the situation was that Erich Honecker, the hard-line East German leader, was ill at that time. Gorbachev thought of giving the fortieth anniversary celebrations of the GDR in October 1989 a miss due to the lack of rapport with Erich Honecker. The latter had banned Soviet publications that provided information about perestroika and democratic change in the Soviet Union. The Soviet embassy in East Berlin simply distributed the material. Gorbachev was gratified to discover that he was as popular in East Berlin as he had been in Beijing. At the official parade, young East

Germans called on him to stay and help them. Gorbachev warned that history punishes those who get left behind. Erich did not get the message and Gorbachev afterwards confided that talking to him was like "throwing peas at a wall."[5] Protests, especially in Leipzig, recommenced after Gorbachev had returned to Moscow. The Tiananmen solution – shooting demonstrators – was now a possibility. Honecker was so arrogant and impervious to negative information that he may have authorized the security forces to open fire. He was aware that the Soviet army would not intervene. The person who may have averted a bloodbath was Kurt Masur, the conductor of the famous Leipzig Gewandhaus Orchestra. He acted as a go-between and a confrontation was averted. Honecker was pushed aside and replaced by the lugubrious Egon Krenz, a member of the GDR's Slav minority. After attending the fortieth anniversary celebrations of the Chinese People's Republic in October 1989, he concluded that the Tiananmen solution would not work in the GDR. What had started as a push for democratic socialism was now becoming a wave in favor of a united Germany. "Real, existing socialism" – Honecker had boasted that it was ahead of the Soviet Union's "developing socialism" – had lost its legitimacy. Hans Modrow, the East German prime minister, begged Gorbachev for aid. "After all," he said, "the GDR is the Soviet Union's child. Please care for us." Gorbachev advised him to apply to Bonn for a loan. However, it was too late for money to make a difference. The crass incompetence of the Krenz regime was highlighted on November 9, 1989, when Günter Schabowski, a Politburo member and former journalist, misread a decree on relaxing travel restrictions to the West. He informed journalists that GDR citizens were at liberty to leave by any border crossing. Did this include West Berlin? It did. What was to happen to the Berlin Wall? Schabowski had no coherent answer. The regime had only intended to ease restrictions but Schabowski's incompetence suggested that anyone could leave. East Berliners rushed to the Wall and the guards stood aside. "I've wasted my life," a police officer poignantly commented. He had served twenty years at the Wall. Euphoria gripped the city. I was in Berlin that day and went into East Berlin the next day.

East Berliners, usually very taciturn with strangers lest they be reported to the Stasi, the secret police, talked to one as if one were family. What was Gorbachev's reaction? "You did the right thing," he told the East German leadership. For Germans, the Cold War ended that cold, dull, November day.

Gennady Gerasimov, the suave, witty foreign ministry press spokesman, hit the right note. "You remember the Frank Sinatra song, 'My Way.' Well, Hungary and Poland are doing it their way."[6] To him, the Brezhnev doctrine had given way to the Sinatra doctrine. Eastern Europe was in free fall. In Czechoslovakia Václav Havel, the playwright and dissident, became president. In Bulgaria, Todor Zhivkov, in power since 1954, wisely stepped down before he was overthrown. In Romania the reverse happened. In December, Nicolae Ceausescu tried to dam the tide of history and adopted the Tiananmen solution. His security forces killed almost a hundred in Timisoara. He called a mass rally in Bucharest which turned into a mass protest against him. He and his wife escaped by helicopter but were arrested and shot on Christmas Day.

At his first summit meeting with President George Bush, in Malta in December 1989, Gorbachev was still reeling. However, he told Bush: "We do not regard you as an enemy any more." Eduard Shevardnadze chipped in and stated that the superpowers had buried the Cold War "at the bottom of the Mediterranean." Gorbachev was desperate for western loans. Bush told him that America would not oppose German reunification. Would the whole of Germany be part of NATO or only West Germany? Moscow would not accept a unified Germany in NATO. Poland, France, and Great Britain eyed the prospect of a unified Germany with alarm. Mrs. Margaret Thatcher, the British prime minister, told Bush that there was a danger that Germans would get in peace what Hitler couldn't get in the war. This ill-judged statement revealed her simmering suspiciousness of German ambitions. Chancellor Helmut Kohl stole a march on everyone by announcing a plan for German reunification shortly before the Malta summit. Some think this was to prevent a second Yalta agreement to keep Germany divided. Bush and Kohl pushed through reunification over the objections of their allies. It was agreed that NATO's jurisdiction would not extend into East Germany but this was forgotten after the collapse of the Soviet Union. Soviet troops would leave East Germany but American troops would remain in West Germany. Germany was reunified on October 3, 1990, less than a year after the Berlin Wall came down. This stunning chain of events saw all the Soviet Union's gains in the Second World War wiped out. The overwhelming majority of Soviet citizens and military reacted with anger and dismay. Gorbachev was berated on all sides for having "lost" eastern Europe. His consolation was the award of the Nobel Peace Prize in 1990 for ending the Cold War. He deserved it.

## New Initiatives

Gorbachev decided to set up a Russian Communist Party in the hope of countering the appeal of Yeltsin. It was a forlorn hope as a conservative was elected its general secretary. An umbrella organization, Democratic Russia, had been formed to fight the CPD elections. It quickly established itself in all major Russian cities. Yeltsin proposed the direct election of a Russian president. Gorbachev's reaction was to have himself elected Soviet president. However, it was the Supreme Soviet which elected him, not the people. He was afraid to test public opinion on this point. Article 6 of the Soviet constitution which gave the Party a monopoly on power was amended. Soon every republic wanted to elect its president.

The May Day demonstrations in 1990 revealed the depth of public anger. Thousands marched behind anti-communist banners such as "Down with the CPSU" and "Pension off Gorbachev." On June 12, 1990, the 1st Russian Congress adopted the declaration of the sovereignty of the Russian Federation. This stated that Russian laws took precedence over Soviet laws. This declaration began the process which ended with the demise of the Soviet Union. Another radical economic initiative was launched. It was called the 500-day program. It mapped out the move to a market economy.

The domestic political situation became more tense. Georgia, Lithuania, and Estonia declared sovereignty in March, Latvia in May, Russia, Uzbekistan, and Moldova in June, and Ukraine and Belarus in July. Gorbachev's solution was a Union of Sovereign States. In August, the Politburo received information that the Party apparatus and some local Party leaders were coming together to oppose the Gensek. In November 1990, Gorbachev decided that a cabinet would replace the government. It would be directly subordinate to him and not to parliament. Nikolai Ryzhkov, the prime minister, was getting quite desperate. No one obeyed him. At the 6th CPD in December 1990, about 400 voted to remove Gorbachev but he still had a comfortable majority. The most sensational event was an emotional speech by Eduard Shevardnadze. He announced his resignation and warned the country of the threat of dictatorship. There was wrangling over who should become vice-president of the Soviet Union. Gorbachev insisted Gennady Yanaev be elected. He thought that Yanaev would implement his policies. He was to be sadly disappointed.

## The Baltics

According to the head of the KGB, Gorbachev had agreed to use force against the "extremists in Latvia and Lithuania."[7] Another source states that an attempt was made to introduce presidential rule in Lithuania.[8] On January 10, 1991, Gorbachev forwarded the Lithuanian Supreme Soviet an ultimatum to implement fully the Soviet constitution there. The same day, he instructed the minister of defense, the head of the KGB, and the minister of internal affairs (MVD) to use force.[9] On January 11, Soviet security forces occupied the House of the Press in Vilnius, the capital. During the night of January 12–13, an attempt was made to seize the television center in Vilnius. In the ensuing conflict, fourteen persons died. These events provoked a furious response throughout the Soviet Union. The Vilnius tragedy revealed that the Soviet government was willing to use force to keep the Union together. It could be deployed to resolve the political crisis in Russia. Russia needed to establish its own armed forces. It was also important to conclude treaties with other republics recognizing their sovereignty.

Immediately after Vilnius, Gorbachev began planning a referendum on the continued existence of the Soviet Union. It was to take place on March 17, 1991. Voters were asked if they "deemed it necessary to retain the Soviet Union as a renewed federation of sovereign states." The referendum was an attempt to forge a third way between the old Soviet Union and independence for the republics. Russia seized the opportunity to ask if voters were in favor of a president elected by popular vote. A large majority, 76 percent, voted for the retention of the Soviet Union. However, the majority of voters in Georgia, Estonia, Latvia, Lithuania, and Moldova did not participate. In Russia, 71 percent voted for the Union. But voters in Sverdlovsk (Ekaterinburg) rejected the Union, as did half of the electorate in Moscow and Leningrad. About 71 percent of Russian voters favored a directly elected Russian president.

On March 25, the Soviet Cabinet of Ministers banned demonstrations and meetings in Moscow. On March 26, Gorbachev transferred control of the militia in Moscow and Moscow oblast from the Russian government to the Soviet MVD. When the Russian CPD convened the following day, there was a huge military presence. Communist deputies tried to engineer the dismissal of Yeltsin. Many deputies demanded that Gorbachev withdraw the military but he refused. That evening there was a huge illegal demonstration in favor of the Congress. The security forces did not intervene. The carefully elaborated plan by the communist faction in the Congress had failed. Another objective had been to introduce a state of emergency in Moscow. The military withdrew with Gorbachev the loser.

At a Central Committee plenum in April 1991, Gorbachev was sharply criticized by Party functionaries. He snapped and announced he wanted to resign as Gensek. A hastily convened Politburo meeting asked him to reconsider but he declined. The plenum now had the opportunity to dismiss Gorbachev. Members lost their nerve with only thirteen voting to remove him. There was clearly no alternative candidate even though most members opposed Gorbachev's policies. The culture of obedience to the Gensek had prevailed. The once powerful Party, which had dismissed Khrushchev in 1964, was only a shadow of its former self.

## The Union Treaty

Yeltsin was elected president of Russia on June 12, 1991. He joined other republican leaders at Novo-Ogarevo, a dacha outside Moscow, to negotiate the new Union treaty with Gorbachev. Actually only nine of the fifteen republics were represented. The draft treaty was ready on June 17. It soon became clear that the Supreme Soviet opposed the Union treaty. The last Party Central Committee plenum took place on July 25–6. A new Party program and preparations for the next Party Congress were on the agenda. Members insulted the Gensek and the level of noise precluded rational debate. The draft program was a remarkable document. It was social democratic and not communist.

Gorbachev, Yeltsin, and Nursultan Nazarbaev, Party boss of Kazakhstan, met on July 29 at Novo-Ogarevo. They agreed that Gennady Yanaev, the vice-president, KGB chief Kryuchkov, Minister of the Interior Pugo, and Minister of Defense Yazov were to go. Nazarbaev was to become prime minister and Gorbachev president of the new state. Since the KGB had bugged the dacha, they learned that they were soon to be sacked. What were they to do? The CPD and the Supreme Soviet could not dismiss Gorbachev as president since he had been elected for five years. However, if he were judged physically or mentally incapable of fulfilling his duties, he could be voted out. Gorbachev on several occasions had mentioned the need for "extraordinary measures." Then, on August 3, the day before he left for Foros, Crimea, for his vacation, he said in the Cabinet of Ministers that the situation in the country was "exceptional." It was necessary to take "emergency measures."[10]

George Bush arrived for his last summit with Gorbachev on July 30. He wanted to support the Soviet leader and keep the Soviet Union together. If the country broke up there would be four nuclear powers – the Russian Federation, Belarus, Ukraine, and Kazakhstan – instead of one – the Soviet Union. Bush then went to Kyiv and warned the Ukrainians about the dangers of nationalism. His speech did not go down well and was derided as his "chicken Kiev" dish. Kyiv could not understand why America was opposed to Ukraine gaining its independence.

## The Coup

Gorbachev was warned by the US ambassador that a coup was being planned. He was unruffled and said that he had everything in hand. On August 6, KGB chief Kryuchkov instructed two of his senior officials to undertake a feasibility study on introducing a state of emergency. Their conclusion was not encouraging. Kryuchkov refused to accept this. On August 14, he informed them that Gorbachev was mentally confused and could not work. Documents establishing a state of emergency were to be prepared. They were to be presented to Gorbachev as a fait accompli. The KGB fed him increasingly negative information about the state of affairs in the country.

In Foros on Sunday August 18 at 4.50 p.m., Gorbachev was advised that he had visitors. This was strange as he had invited no one. He picked up one of the phones on his desk. It was dead; indeed, they were all dead. A delegation representing the Party, KGB, and military entered. They informed him that an emergency committee had been set up to save the country. There were documents for him to sign. He asked who the members of the extraordinary committee were. They included the head of the KGB, the minister of defense, the prime minister, and the deputy president. If Gorbachev did not sign the document introducing a state of emergency, he was to hand over his powers to Yanaev. "Relax," he was told, "we'll carry out the dirty work and then you can return."[11] As they left, Gorbachev shook hands with each of them.

The plotters had worked out three plans. Plan A envisaged Gorbachev conceding defeat and agreeing to a state of emergency. When it was in place, the Supreme Soviet could meet and remove him as president. Plan B envisaged Gorbachev playing for time. He would remain silent during the state of emergency. He could come back to Moscow, negotiate with the plotters, and resume as president. Plan C was the least desirable. Gorbachev would strongly oppose the coup and call on everyone to overthrow the extraordinary committee. A group of Moscow psychiatrists was preparing a medical bulletin about his mental health. He could die quite suddenly.

When the plotters returned to Moscow they reported the bad news to Kryuchkov. This now meant Plan B would be adopted. The coup was announced the next morning to a confused population. They were told that a minority was bent on seizing power. A tidal wave of sex and violence threatened to engulf the motherland. Over 300 tanks and almost 4,000 troops were ordered into Moscow.

Boris Yeltsin was having breakfast at his dacha outside Moscow when the news broke. He and other Russian politicians immediately set off for the White House, the seat of the government. Amazingly, they were not arrested. They began drafting the appeal: "To the citizens of Russia." Yeltsin then went outside in a bulletproof vest, climbed on to a T-72 tank, and read out his appeal. He called for support and about 25,000 came to the White House. Would the plotters attack the White House? Orders were given but the elite units involved demanded written orders, not oral. They wanted protection if anything went wrong. No assault was ever launched. This was one of the reasons why the coup failed. The soldiers were not willing to spill Russian blood.

Gorbachev came back to a different Moscow. He made the egregious mistake of talking of the Party renewing the country. Yeltsin, the great victor, delighted in humiliating the Gensek. He pointed out that it was the Party which had betrayed him. Gorbachev resigned as Gensek and the Party was banned. He busied himself with the Union treaty. Yeltsin played along but was plotting with the presidents of Ukraine and Belarus to dissolve the Soviet Union. On December 8, 1991, in a forest outside Minsk, Belarus, the presidents consigned the Soviet Union to history and set up the Commonwealth of Independent States. On Christmas Day, December 25, 1991, Gorbachev resigned as Soviet president. The communist era was over.

## Explanations for the Collapse of the Soviet Union

❖ Economic failure: the Soviet Union revealed early economic vitality but its strength was sapped during its last three decades by the exhaustion of natural resources, negative demographic developments, and the advent of computers and advanced technology. Spying brought huge scientific benefits but the planned economy failed to make adequate use of them. For instance, the microelectronic industry was founded by American communists who fled to Moscow.

❖ A mixture of economic and political factors: the decline of economic growth over a long period; the role of the West; the role of the intelligentsia; the loss of faith in Marxism which destabilized the country; the ill-considered policies adopted by Gorbachev.

❖ Nationalism: the national problem was always dormant; it flared up under Gorbachev because of his policies of glasnost and democratization. The humiliation of national elites under Andropov and Gorbachev as a result of the anti-corruption drive broke the informal agreement between Moscow and the republics.

❖ Corruption: this accelerated under Brezhnev and Gorbachev. It penetrated the regional Party apparatus: officials linked up with enterprises and the shadow market for mutual enrichment. This promoted the view of citizens that the Party and government were corrupt; corruption weakened central control.

❖ The collapse was the result of unintended consequences of government policies: the economy played a key role here. In an attempt to stimulate a slowing economy, the leadership adopted policies which fatally weakened the political and ideological pillars that sustained the system. This brought down the whole edifice. Hence the economic crisis did not cause the collapse of the Soviet Union. Ill-advised political decision-making was the key variable.

❖ The demonstration effect of the West: glasnost revealed how backward the Soviet system was. Citizens wanted rapidly rising living standards which the command-administrative system could not deliver.

❖ The military burden was unsustainable. Arms agreements ended the fear that the West would attack: why should citizens make sacrifices if there was no real threat?

❖ The command-administrative system was not innovative enough to keep pace with world trends. Technology became increasingly obsolete. Sooner or later wholesale modernization would be needed. The existing system could not cope with this.[12]

The conclusion of this essay is that poor leadership provoked political and economic collapse. A major weakness was the Party-state system. The Party never possessed the technical expertise to run the country. The government could have run the country on its own. However, this would have resulted in a weak Party leadership. Economic reform needs time to mature but Gorbachev was impatient. He wanted instant results and, as a result, adopted more and more radical solutions. The economic advice he received was poor. There was the belief that the economy was infinitely malleable. There was no understanding of the consequences of any reform. Gorbachev naïvely believed Party officials would be the engine of change.

## NOTES

1  P. G. Pikhoya, *Sovetsky Soyuz: Istoriya Vlasti 1945–1991* (Moscow: Izdatelstvo RAGS, 1998), p. 453.

2  Philip Hanson, *The Rise and Fall of the Soviet Economy: An Economic History of the USSR from 1945* (London: Longman, 2003), p. 192 and passim.

3  Pikhoya, *Sovetsky Soyuz*, pp. 523–5.

4  Robert Service, *A History of Modern Russia from Nicholas II to Putin* (London: Penguin, 2003), p. 457 and passim.

5  Quoted in John Lewis Gaddis, *The Cold War* (London: Allen Lane, 2005), p. 245.

6  Ibid., pp. 247–8.

7  Vladimir Kryuchkov, *Lichnoe Delo* (Moscow: Olimp, 1996), vol. 2, p. 30.

8  Pikhoya, *Sovetsky Soyuz*, p. 610.

9  Ibid.

10 A. I. Lukyanov, *Perevorot mnimy i nastoyashchii* (Voronezh, 1993), p. 10.

11 Mikhail Gorbachev, *Zhizn i Reformy* (Moscow: Novosti, 1995), vol. 2, pp. 558–9. An abbreviated edition of Gorbachev's memoirs is *Memoirs* (London: Doubleday, 1995).

12 Michael Ellman and Vladimir Kontorovich, eds., *The Destruction of the Soviet Economic System: An*

*Insiders' History* (New York and London: M. E. Sharpe, 1998), pp. 3–4.

## GUIDE TO FURTHER READING

Christopher Andrew and Vasili Mitrokhin, *The Mitrokhin Archive: The KGB in Europe and the West* (London: Penguin, 1999); *The KGB and the World* (London: Penguin, 2005). Useful studies of espionage and intelligence based on KGB documents.

Archie Brown, *The Gorbachev Factor* (Oxford: Oxford University Press, 1996). The case for the defense. It is mainly a political study and devotes less attention to the weaknesses of Gorbachev's economic policies.

Anatoly Chernyaev, *My Six Years with Gorbachev* (University Park, PA: Pennsylvania University Press, 2000). The memoirs of a faithful aide to Gorbachev.

John Lewis Gaddis, *The Cold War* (London: Allen Lane, 2005). The best book on the end of the Cold War.

Jonathan Harris, *Subverting the System: Gorbachev's Reform of the Party Apparat, 1986–1991* (Lanham, MD: Rowman & Littlefield, 2004). The best study of the decline of the Party.

Martin McCauley, *Gorbachev* (London: Longman, 1998). A critical assessment of the Soviet leader.

Jack F. Matlock, *Autopsy of an Empire: The American Ambassador's Account of the Collapse of the Soviet Union* (New York: Random House, 1995); *Reagan and Gorbachev* (New York: Random House, 2004). The memoirs of an astute American diplomat.

David Remnick, *Lenin's Tomb: The Last Days of the Soviet Empire* (London: Penguin, 1994). The most detailed account of the coup and the demise of the Soviet Union in English.

Nikolai Ryzhkov, *Desyat let velikikh notryaseni* (Moscow: Proveshchenie, 1995). Provides a candid account of his years at the top.

# CHAPTER THIRTY

# War and Peace in the Global Community, 1989–2001

## LLOYD E. AMBROSIUS

At the end of the Cold War in Europe, a new era in world history began. When the Berlin Wall opened on November 9, 1989, allowing all Germans on both sides of that barrier to join together in celebration, that dramatic event reverberated around the world. The total collapse of the Soviet Union and its empire by December 1991 appeared as the final defeat of communism and the triumph of freedom. To those who had experienced the hostile divisions between the East and the West since the late 1940s, these were exciting and hopeful developments. This post-Cold War era offered the promise of a global community. No longer were the United States and the Soviet Union engaged in a worldwide rivalry for influence and control over other nations. These two superpowers had shaped international relations throughout the Cold War, forming alliances, establishing protectorates, and threatening each other's global interests. Yet somehow they avoided a war against each other. Above all, neither side had resorted to nuclear weapons during their ongoing confrontations. Now it appeared that the precarious balance between war and peace, and especially the threat of nuclear annihilation, had ceased. The end of the Cold War promised something much better than the "long peace" of the decades since the Second World War.

Visions of a new global community were not new in the West. Since the eighteenth-century Enlightenment, Europeans and Americans had dreamed of creating perpetual peace among nations. During the First World War, President Woodrow Wilson had outlined his famous Fourteen Points as the basis for peacemaking. He hoped to replace the old European system of alliances and balances of power with a new international order founded on American principles of collective security to guarantee the peace settlement, national self-determination to allow democratic nations to rule themselves, and an "open door" political economy to promote international trade and investment. These progressive principles, he believed, would enable the postwar world to enjoy both peace and prosperity. In his view, American-style democracy and capitalism were key institutions for the new order. As the Great Powers joined together with small states for their mutual protection against potential aggressors and as new nations emerged from the shackles of imperialism, they could all reduce their reliance on methods of war. They could overcome their international history of arms races, military alliances, and balances of power, and move into a new era of world peace.

This Wilsonian vision survived, although it did not become reality after 1919. The League of Nations, which the United States refused to join despite the president's advocacy of it as the key to a new world order, failed to halt aggression and keep the peace. Before long, Imperial Japan, Fascist Italy, and Nazi Germany challenged the postwar settlement. Invading other lands in Asia,

Africa, and Europe, these rising dictatorships rejected Wilsonian liberal internationalism. Especially after the onset of the Great Depression in the 1930s, they attacked their neighbors, denying them self-determination. They created autarchic economies, closing their expanding empires to foreign trade and investments. Collaborating as the Axis Powers, they relied increasingly on military force. Wilson's ideals persisted, however. President Franklin D. Roosevelt revived the former president's vision during the Second World War as the United States formed an alliance with the British and Soviet empires, and also with China and France, to halt Japanese, Italian, and German military aggression. Victory over the Axis Powers offered the Allies a second chance in 1945 to create a new world order. The victors replaced the discredited League of Nations with the new United Nations, which symbolized the postwar hope for "one world" of peace and prosperity.

Although the onset of the Cold War thwarted the realization of this renewed hope for a peaceful global community, Wilson's ideological legacy continued. It provided an alternative to the promise of communism, justifying America's long-term competition with the Soviet Union in their worldwide rivalry. The end of the Cold War created an international environment in which Wilsonian ideals might finally become the reality. What had failed after 1919, and again after 1945, now appeared achievable after 1989. Placing this new opportunity in perspective, historian Akira Iriye observed that: "The emergence of the United States as an international player at the beginning of the twentieth century was significant not simply because the nation became the leading military and economic power, but also because it introduced cultural factors into world affairs." Wilson's legacy, known as Wilsonianism, was now defining the post-Cold War world. "Because the globalizing of America has been a major event of the century, Wilsonianism should be seen not as a transient phenomenon, a reflection of some abstract idealism, but as a potent definer of contemporary history."[1]

Wilsonianism furnished the conceptual definition for triumphal Americans in post-Cold War international relations. Iriye observed that the processes of globalization had created the emerging "global community" that they heralded. The new world order was not merely the consequence of communism's failure and the Soviet Union's collapse. Cultural internationalism was already, by the 1960s, producing "the new global consciousness" that would characterize the 1990s.[2] The United Nations and its various agencies connected governments across borders in more frequent peacemaking and peacekeeping operations, in humanitarian assistance for refugees and other victims of wars and natural disasters, and in international conferences to address such issues as protecting the environment, promoting economic development, improving health conditions, and defending human rights. A global civil society also emerged, sometimes to collaborate with the United Nations and national governments, and at other times to protest against their actions. Nongovernmental organizations (NGOs) actively monitored and contributed to the UN's 1992 conference on environment and development – or earth summit – in Rio de Janeiro, Brazil, the 1995 world conference on women in Beijing, China, the 1997 conference on global warming in Kyoto, Japan, and the 2000 conference on AIDS in Durban, South Africa. In the global community that had emerged by the end of the twentieth century, international organizations linked national governments and NGOs across borders. This increasingly interdependent world challenged the traditional role of nation-states in international relations and enabled more people to participate in transnational activities. It required a different kind of global governance.[3]

Globalization created both new opportunities and new problems for states, none of which could unilaterally manage the international economy or escape its impact. Customary divisions between domestic and foreign affairs vanished during the 1990s, making it increasingly difficult for national governments to exercise their sovereignty. As journalist Thomas L. Friedman observed in *The Lexus and the Olive Tree* (1999), "Nation-states, and the American superpower in particular, are still hugely important today, but so too now are Supermarkets and Super-empowered individuals. You will never understand the globalization system, or the front page of the morning paper, unless you see it as a complex interaction between all three of these actors: states bumping up against states, states bumping up against Supermarkets, and Supermarkets and states bumping up against Super-empowered individuals." All nations operating in the global economy, Friedman asserted, were required to wear what he called the "Golden Straightjacket" and were subject to the vicissitudes of the "Electronic Herd." Unless they obeyed the strict rules of capitalism, they would be trampled by the stampeding exit of international investments and suffer the loss of economic opportunities. They would, presumably, reap the benefits by following the rules. He added that, "for better or worse, globalization is a means of spreading the fantasy of America around the world. In today's global village people know there is another way to live, they know about the American lifestyle, and many of them want as big a slice of it as they can get – with all the trimmings."[4]

Triumphal Americans believed that world history was moving toward the fulfillment of Wilsonian ideals after the Cold War. Despite occasional problems, the human race seemed to be headed in the right direction. State Department policy planner Francis Fukuyama proclaimed the "end of history." He affirmed that "the fact that there will be setbacks and disappointments in the process of democratization, or that not every market economy will prosper, should not distract us from the larger pattern that is emerging in world history." In this new era, he rejoiced, "the only form of government that has survived intact to the end of the twentieth century has been liberal democracy."[5] Only this model was viable for all countries. At the beginning of the new millennium, political scientist Michael Mandelbaum reaffirmed this optimistic, progressive interpretation of history. Despite Wilson's earlier failure to create a new order based on his ideas of peace, democracy, and free markets, this "Wilsonian triad" had apparently become the global reality by the twenty-first century. These were, Mandelbaum claimed, "the ideas that conquered the world." Wilson's ideas, he contended, were "the keys to understanding the new world that emerged when the great global conflict of the second half of the twentieth century, the Cold War, came to an end."[6] Triumphalists rejoiced over the apparent victory of Wilsonianism.

As the only remaining superpower after the Soviet empire's collapse, the United States benefited from the new world order that it had helped to establish. It gained more wealth and relatively more power. Statistics confirmed the international economy's increasing importance for the nation. Americans had fostered globalization, and now their own prosperity depended on the results. Between 1990 and 2000, US exports doubled from $393,592 million to $782,429 million, while US imports increased even more from $495,310 million to $1,222,772 million. US direct investment in other countries tripled from $424,086 million to $1,293,431 million, while foreign direct investment in the United States also tripled from $396,702 million to $1,214,254 million. US trade in goods and services as a share of the gross national product (GNP) rapidly expanded from 20.4 percent in 1990 to 26 percent in 2000. This was more than twice the 1929 peak of 11.1 percent. During the Great Depression, foreign trade had declined. It would not surpass the 1929 percentage of the GNP until the 1970s. As it continued to grow, the economic welfare of Americans more and more depended on conditions in the global community.[7]

## President George H. W. Bush

This increasingly interdependent world shaped American decisions about war and peace after the Cold War. President George H. W. Bush and his secretary of state, James A. Baker III, who deftly handled the end of the Cold War in Europe, working with Chancellor Helmut Kohl to enable German reunification in October 1990 without war, shifted the international focus to the Middle East. In this region, except for Israel, America's primary interest was oil. Along with other industrial nations in Europe and Asia, the United States relied on a steady supply of petroleum from Saudi Arabia, Kuwait, Iraq, Iran, and other Persian Gulf countries. During the Iran–Iraq War of the 1980s, President Ronald Reagan had tilted US policy to favor Iraq. He had authorized various forms of military and economic assistance to Saddam Hussein's regime, supporting it in the war against Iran's revolutionary Islamic republic. Except for the bizarre episode known as the Iran–Contra affair, which involved selling weapons to Iran and diverting the profits to the Contras who were fighting against the Sandinista government in Nicaragua, the United States continued to support Iraq. Bush abruptly reversed that policy only after Iraqi dictator Saddam Hussein launched a full-scale invasion of Kuwait on August 2, 1990. Now the president was most concerned about preventing Iraq from gaining control over the oil in Kuwait and also, potentially, in Saudi Arabia. Launching Operation Desert Shield, he and Baker began immediately to build an international coalition in the United Nations to reverse Iraqi military aggression and stop this threat to the global economy.

Bush appealed to Wilsonian ideals in defining his new policy in the Middle East. He called on the United Nations to authorize military action against Iraq and thereby to provide collective security for Kuwait. The end of the Cold War made this possible. Given the new Soviet–American relationship, the UN Security Council could act without facing a veto by one of its permanent members. For the first time since the Korean War, when the temporary absence of the Soviet delegate had allowed the Security Council to authorize collective security for South Korea against communist North Korea's surprise attack, the United Nations endorsed America's request for a multilateral military response to aggression. It granted international authorization to expel Iraq's armed forces from Kuwait. Most UN members, including the People's Republic of China and the Soviet Union, shared a common interest in protecting Kuwait's sovereignty against external aggression. Emphasizing state sovereignty rather than democracy in his concept of national self-determination, Bush avoided potentially divisive questions about Kuwait's ruling monarchy. Focusing on Iraq's invasion rather than Kuwait's internal affairs, he won the votes of other authoritarian governments in the United Nations for collective security in the Middle East.

Calling for collective security to protect Kuwait's right to national self-determination, Bush appealed to the Wilsonian vision of a global community. On September 11, 1990, he hailed "a new world order" that he expected to emerge "out of these troubled times." He envisaged "a

new era – freer from the threat of terror, stronger in the pursuit of justice, and more secure in the quest for peace." This would be "an era in which the nations of the world, East and West, North and South, can prosper and live in harmony." Peace would replace war in this emerging global community. "A hundred generations have searched for this elusive path to peace, while a thousand wars raged across the span of human endeavor. Today that new world is struggling to be born, a world quite different from the one we've known. . . . A world in which nations recognize the shared responsibility for freedom and justice. A world where the strong respect the rights of the weak."[8] By acting now to stop Saddam Hussein's aggression against Kuwait, Bush promised, the United States could help create a new global community.

Bush reiterated his postwar Wilsonian vision on January 16, 1991, when he addressed the nation to announce Operation Desert Storm, the beginning of allied military action in the Persian Gulf War against Iraq. "This is an historic moment," he proclaimed:

> We have in this past year made great progress in ending the long era of conflict and cold war. We have before us the opportunity to forge for ourselves and for future generations a new world order – a world where the rule of law, not the rule of the jungle, governs the conduct of nations. When we are successful – and we will be – we have a real chance at this new world order, an order in which a credible United Nations can use its peacekeeping role to fulfill the promise and vision of the UN's founders.[9]

That dream of 1945, still alive despite earlier failures, could be fulfilled now. Like Wilson, Bush justified war by appealing to American cultural values. This was a righteous war, he told religious broadcasters on January 28: "It has . . . everything to do with what religion embodies: good versus evil, right versus wrong, human dignity and freedom versus tyranny and oppression." While having no doubt that the war was moral, the president still sought to avoid turning it into a crusade, which would pit one of the world's major religions against another and jeopardize the international coalition against Saddam Hussein's Iraq.

He explained that "the war in the Gulf is not a Christian war, a Jewish war, or a Moslem war; it is just a war. And it is a war with which good will prevail."[10]

Bush appealed to American traditions of freedom and democracy to justify the war, yet he defined the allied coalition's war aims in more limited terms. In his State of the Union address on January 29, he reiterated: "For two centuries, America has served the world as an inspiring example of freedom and democracy. For generations, America has led the struggle to preserve and extend the blessings of liberty. And today, in a rapidly changing world, American leadership is indispensable." Emphasizing the progressive American belief in the future, the president claimed that the United States could shape its own destiny in the world. "We are a nation of rock-solid realism and clear-eyed idealism." Bush's war aims, however, were limited. "Our purpose in the Persian Gulf remains constant: to drive Iraq out of Kuwait, to restore Kuwait's legitimate government, and to ensure the stability and security of this critical region." He promised only to force Iraq out of Kuwait and restore its ruling monarchy, not to topple Saddam Hussein's regime or establish a liberal democracy in either Iraq or Kuwait. His idealism was restricted by a sense of what was realistic. He wanted "stability and security" in the Middle East, despite his rhetorical call for a new world order.[11] Once the allied coalition achieved its limited aims, Bush suspended offensive combat operations in the Persian Gulf. After six weeks of intense air attacks on Iraq and 100 hours of ground operations that devastated its armed forces, the president proclaimed "a victory for the United Nations." Kuwait was now "a free and sovereign nation." In his announcement of the imminent ceasefire on February 28, Bush hinted that he would welcome a regime change in Baghdad. He blamed Saddam Hussein, not the Iraqi people, for the war, but did not make his removal a condition for the ceasefire.[12]

Bush's realistic restraint in the Middle East conformed to his general approach to international relations. In his inaugural address on January 20, 1989, he had rejoiced that the world was moving toward liberal democracy and free market capitalism. "We know what works," he proclaimed. "Freedom works."[13] Yet the president understood the limits of US power to foster American values and institutions in other countries. Nowhere was this more evident than in the People's Republic of China. Under Mikhail Gorbachev, the Soviet Union was opening and restructuring itself, and allowing its former satellites in eastern Europe to exercise their national independence. He hoped to save communism by reforming it. In the long run, this did not work as he wanted, but meanwhile Gorbachev enabled the peaceful end of the Cold War in Europe. China's communist leaders adopted different methods, even before they witnessed his ultimate failure in the Soviet Union's collapse. Pressures for reform emerged also within China. Since 1979, Deng Xiaoping had responded by allowing more entrepreneurial activities in agricultural and industrial production and more emphasis on consumer goods. He also permitted thousands of Chinese students to go abroad to western universities, where they gained modern scientific and technical knowledge and experienced greater freedom. Returning home, many of them wanted political as well as economic change. In May–June 1989, Chinese students brought their pro-democracy movement to Beijing's Tiananmen Square, where more than a million people protested against the communist regime. Calling for freedom, they waved US flags. On June 4, China's communist rulers cracked down, sending tanks into the square to crush the pro-democracy movement. In Washington, DC, the Bush administration stood by, recognizing that it could not effectively intervene to stop the massacre or change the regime. Democratic reform would have to come from within China, not from the outside. So while the Soviet Union imploded, allowing its constituent republics from the Baltic Sea to Central Asia to become independent states, China maintained its communist system of one-party government and its national unity. Its rulers opened the Chinese economy somewhat to the outside world, but resisted fundamental political change. Bush and Baker acquiesced in this reality.

In the western hemisphere, however, the United States faced no such limits to its power. General Manuel Antonio Noriega learned this lesson the hard way. After becoming Panama's president in 1983, the former intelligence chief of its national guard had continued to cooperate with the United States to topple the revolutionary Sandinista government in Nicaragua. He cooperated with the American military and Central Intelligence Agency (CIA) to support the Contras. Shifting his allegiance, however, he joined other Central American leaders, notably Costa Rican President Oscar Arias, in seeking a negotiated peace in Nicaragua. Noriega also improved Panama's ties with communist Cuba's Fidel Castro. Now that he was no longer the CIA's loyal "asset," the American government condemned Noriega for his involvement in illegal drug trafficking and money laundering. A federal grand jury in Florida indicted him on drug charges in February 1988, presuming that US law was applicable to a foreign head of state. Panamanian elections in May 1989 left Noriega in office, but opponents accused him of fraud. In the ensuing political chaos, some Panamanian military officers staged an abortive coup in October. They failed to oust Noriega, but Bush soon succeeded in removing him. On December 20, 1989, the US president ordered an invasion of Panama, claiming that Operation Just Cause was necessary to protect American citizens and the Panama Canal, and to bring Noriega to justice on the drug charges. Within two weeks, after countless civilian deaths from the US attacks, the besieged Noriega surrendered. The Americans brought him to Miami for a trial that resulted in conviction and a forty-year sentence. The United States supported the new Panamanian president, who had lost in the earlier elections and who pledged to cooperate. Although, in his inaugural address, Bush had promised a kinder nation and gentler world, he did not hesitate to use military force when he thought US interests were at stake.

One month after the US invasion of Panama, Nicaragua held free elections. In this democratic process in January 1990, President Daniel Ortega and his Sandinista government suffered defeat. Reagan and Bush had justified US support for the Contras during the 1980s by claiming that the Sandinistas were too much like communists everywhere to relinquish power peacefully. But they nevertheless did. Ironically, the Sandinistas showed that they were more democratic than

the American government ever acknowledged. Nicaragua's decade-long civil war finally ended. The Central American peace initiative, which Noriega had joined contrary to US expectations, contributed to Nicaragua's transition from war to peace. In the post-Cold War era, Bush welcomed this outcome, which now appeared to conform to his vision of a new world order of liberal democracy and capitalism.

## President Bill Clinton

US politics changed after the Cold War. As world history seemed to be moving in the direction most Americans wanted, they shifted their attention from foreign to domestic affairs without fully recognizing the interdependence between these two facets of US involvement in the global community. They wanted the benefits of globalization without its liabilities. They wanted the United States to wield its preeminent power without paying too high a price. As the journalist-historian David Halberstam noted in *War in a Time of Peace* (2001), a "fault line in American geopolitical life" exposed profound contradictions, which expressed "America's desire to exercise great power throughout the world, but to do it in a way that caused no (or at least few) American casualties and no larger political problems."[14] News media reported less about foreign affairs and more about sensational events at home. After observing this neglect of international relations throughout the 1990s, Henry Kissinger, who had served as President Richard Nixon's national security adviser and secretary of state, posed the question in the title of his book, *Does America Need a Foreign Policy?* (2001).[15] His answer, of course, was that it did, so he prescribed one for the twenty-first century. Meanwhile, the shift in national focus from foreign to domestic affairs allowed Bill Clinton to defeat Bush in the first post-Cold War presidential election in 1992 and to win reelection in 1996 against Kansas senator Bob Dole. The new Democratic president, who had avoided military service in Vietnam, represented the national mood better than the two Republicans, both Second World War veterans, who had flourished in previous decades as Cold War politicians.

Yet this presidential transition did not change America's fundamental involvement in international relations. Wilsonian idealism influenced Clinton's foreign policy, as it had Bush's vision of a new world order. In this post-Cold War era, the clarity that seemed possible during the decades of Soviet–American rivalry, when the West stood for freedom and the East for communism, no longer existed. Nevertheless, Clinton still advocated an "open door" political economy to promote international trade and investment. He encouraged the newly democratic states in eastern Europe to exercise their national self-determination, free from Soviet control. Now they could escape the shackles of communist rule and Russian imperialism. He sought to replace the hostile alliances, which had threatened each other with nuclear war, with a new system of collective security to guarantee the peace. Adopting these progressive principles, Clinton believed, would enable the world to enjoy both peace and prosperity, along with democracy and capitalism. The Great Powers could reduce their reliance on methods of war, finally overcoming their international history of arms races and precarious military balances. They could move into a new era of world peace.

Clinton aggressively promoted globalization, believing that an open economy with relatively unrestricted opportunities for international trade and investment would benefit all nations. Bush had started negotiations with Canada and Mexico to create a free trade area in North America. The new president, continuing to give this effort a high priority, succeeded in his first year. Canada and Mexico joined the United States in signing a treaty to establish the North American Free Trade Area (NAFTA). In December 1993, Clinton secured the US Senate's approval for the treaty's ratification. The opening of NAFTA on January 1, 1994, linked the three national economies in North America closer together. One year later, on January 1, 1995, Clinton also enjoyed success with the creation of the World Trade Organization (WTO) with seventy-six initial members. During the early Cold War in 1948, the United States and other western nations had concluded the General Agreement on Tariffs and Trade (GATT) to lower commercial barriers. In the increasingly global economy of the 1990s, GATT members decided to form the WTO as the multilateral institutional framework for international trade. It would codify and enforce the trading rules, and provide the forum for resolving disputes. Other nations could join former GATT members in the WTO, if they too accepted the capitalist rules for this global system.

In this post-Cold War era, Clinton believed that economic globalization would promote democracy, contributing to peace as well as prosperity. He anticipated that erstwhile antagonists would enter the new world order. "In Asia and elsewhere," he proclaimed on November 10, 1994, "we have good reason for hope, we have good reason for progress because free markets and democracy are on the move. The new global community is taking place all around the world, enshrouding the values of tolerance and liberty and civil society. I guess I really do believe that history is on our side and we have to keep trying to push it along."[16] He pressed harder than Bush to open Asian markets to US products. In February 1994, he lifted the trade embargo against communist Vietnam, which had remained in effect since 1975. He established normal diplomatic relations with Vietnam in 1995. During the 1992 presidential campaign, Clinton had criticized Bush for failing to champion human rights in China. Yet now he muted his own unfavorable judgment to foster better commercial and financial relations. He defended most-favored-nation trading conditions for China and anticipated its entry into the WTO. The China–WTO agreement in 1999 set the terms for this Asian communist country to join the western capitalist club in December 2001. The United States, along with western Europe and Japan, also welcomed Russia and other former communist nations in eastern Europe into the capitalist international economy. Fidel Castro's Cuba, however, received no such invitation. Most, but not all, communist states were deemed eligible for inclusion in the global community.

By the late 1990s, Clinton was becoming increasingly aware that globalization created problems as well as benefits. "Today," he explained on February 26, 1999, "we must embrace the inexorable logic of globalization, that everything, from the strength of our economy to the safety of our cities to the health of our people, depends on events not only within our borders but half a world away. We must see the opportunities and the dangers of the interdependent world in which we are clearly fated to live."[17] One negative consequence was the growing gap between wealthy and poor nations. "The global community," the president warned on June 12, 1999, "cannot survive as a tale of two cities: one modern and integrated, a cell phone in every hand, a McDonald's on every street corner; the other mired in poverty and increasingly resentful, covered with public health and environmental problems no one can manage."[18] Contrary to the promise of Wilsonian ideology, globalization might exacerbate conflicts and divisions within and among nations. It might not contribute to peace. Nor would it necessarily culminate in the worldwide triumph of both capitalism and democracy.

Paradoxically, integration and fragmentation went together in the global community. Globalization made the modern world increasingly interdependent, but it also generated a backlash from people seeking to preserve their separate identities. These opposite trends both threatened democracy and increased the risk of war. "Their common thread is indifference to civil liberty," the political scientist Benjamin R. Barber noted in *Jihad vs. McWorld* (1995). McWorld represented the modernity of McDonald's fast food, Macintosh computers, and MTV, while Jihad expressed the reaction of more traditional identity politics. Barber explained that "Jihad forges communities of blood in exclusion and hatred, communities that slight democracy in favor of tyrannical paternalism or consensual tribalism. McWorld forges global markets in consumption and profit, leaving to an untrustworthy, if not altogether fictitious, invisible hand issues of public interest and common good that once might have been nurtured by democratic citizens and their watchful governments."[19] Globalization, rather than bringing world peace, created even deeper divisions between the McWorld and Jihad adversaries in the global community.

Applying the Wilsonian principle of national self-determination in the 1990s was also problematic. In Africa the United States faced the difficult question of whether to allow failed states to dis-

integrate into chaos or engage in nation-building. In December 1992, at the request of the UN Secretary General Boutros Boutros-Ghali, Bush sent US troops into Somalia, as part of Operation Restore Hope, to deliver food to that nation's starving people. Clinton continued this mission, but allowed it to shift from peacekeeping to peacemaking. The United Nations, regarding Somali warlord Mohammed Farah Aideed as the main obstacle to nation-building, supported other factions against him. After his army killed Pakistani soldiers in the UN mission, the Security Council authorized Aideed's capture. He retaliated, killing eighteen US marines on October 3, 1993. Clinton quickly decided to abandon peacemaking and nation-building and to withdraw US forces from Somalia. He understood that Americans, while relishing America's position as the world's only superpower, did not want to pay a high price in casualties for this status. Stopping genocide in Rwanda also seemed at the time too risky. Beginning on April 6, 1994, Hutu army officials in the government directed the attacks against some moderate Hutu leaders and all Tutsi people, killing some 100,000 in the next 100 days. So soon after the Somali debacle, Clinton refused to take any decisive action to stop the massacre. The United States limited its involvement in these bloody civil wars in Somalia and Rwanda. Peacemaking, nation-building, and stopping genocide in Africa would have required more than Clinton thought the American people were willing to sacrifice.

This pattern also prevailed elsewhere. Dissolution of the Soviet Union permitted new nations to emerge in eastern Europe and Central Asia. Like Gorbachev, Russian President Boris Yeltsin recognized these states, but he rejected independence for Chechnya, which rebelled in 1994. To preserve good Russian–American relations, Clinton accepted Yeltsin's determination to stop further fragmentation of the former Soviet empire. The president's restraint reflected the limits of American power to shape events in distant lands.

In Haiti, however, Clinton intervened to support the democratically elected government of President Jean-Bertrand Aristide. This former Catholic priest, who had won the presidential election in December 1990 as an advocate for the poor, had been ousted by a military coup in September 1991. Although Bush acquiesced in this restoration of the ruling elite, Clinton decided to promote democracy in Haiti. Working with the United Nations, he insisted that the military regime of General Raoul Cedras relinquish its power to Aristide. "History has taught us," Clinton announced on September 15, 1994, "that preserving democracy in our own hemisphere strengthens America's security and prosperity. Democracies here are more likely to keep the peace and to stabilize our region, and more likely to create free markets and economic opportunity and to become strong, reliable trading partners, and they're more likely to provide their own people with the opportunities that will encourage them to stay in their nations and to build their own futures."[20] He sent former President Jimmy Carter, General Colin Powell, and Senator Sam Nunn to deliver the message to Cedras that he must depart. The imminent arrival of US troops in early October 1994 finally persuaded him, thus enabling Aristide to return to Haiti as president. In this application of the principle of national self-determination, Clinton gave higher priority to democratic rule than to state sovereignty. In a way, his intervention in Haiti violated that nation's sovereignty, but for the purpose of restoring its democratic government.

## War and Peace

Dissolution of Yugoslavia at the end of the Cold War caused serious complications for the United States as it raised difficult problems of war and peace in the global community. The meaning of national self-determination was not self-evident here. Yugoslavia had emerged after the First World War, combining Serbs, Croats, Slovenes, and other nationalities in a single multinational state, which included Muslims as well as Orthodox and Catholic Christians. President Wilson had welcomed it as a new nation that fulfilled his ideal of self-determination. It remained together until the 1990s. In June 1991, Croatia and Slovenia declared their independence from Serb-dominated Yugoslavia. Bosnia-Herzegovina followed in March 1992. These new states gained

diplomatic recognition first from Germany and then from other European governments, and later from the United States. Bush only reluctantly approved this break-up of Yugoslavia. Like Wilson earlier, he favored its preservation as a multinational state. Yugoslav President Slobodan Milošević, an old communist leader who now identified himself as a Serbian nationalist, refused to acquiesce in this loss of territory. He especially wanted to keep the parts of predominantly Catholic Croatia and of Bosnia, which was even more ethnically and religiously pluralistic, where Orthodox Serbs traditionally lived. He attacked these new states to rescue his fellow Serbs and the land they claimed as their home. Collaborating with Bosnian Serbs, Yugoslav forces resorted to massacres or "ethnic cleansing" of Bosnian Muslims and some Croats. To stop the killing, the United Nations sent a peacekeeping mission (UNPRO-FOR) to Bosnia in June 1992 and established a no-fly zone in October. It also appointed former US Secretary of State Cyrus Vance to work with the European Community's representative Lord David Owen to seek a peace settlement. They saw partition of Bosnia-Herzegovina along ethnic lines as the only possible solution. Neither Bush nor Clinton welcomed this outcome, or the sacrifice by Croatia of its Serb-populated areas, not wanting to reward Serbian military aggression or violate the principle of self-determination. Yet they offered no alternative. They wanted to discourage too much fragmentation in this post-Cold War era, but they also hoped to avoid American entanglement in Balkan politics.

Eventually, however, Clinton and his secretary of state, Warren Christopher, recognized that curtailing the massacres and preventing the war from spreading beyond Bosnia and Croatia would require greater US involvement. In July 1993, the president sent 300 US troops to join UN peacekeepers in Macedonia. With his approval, the North Atlantic Treaty Organization (NATO) engaged in its first ever combat operation, shooting down two Bosnian Serb aircraft that were violating the UN no-fly zone on February 8, 1994. He also supported the UN and NATO decisions in 1994 to establish "exclusion zones" and "safe areas" that Serbian forces were prohibited from entering. The United States joined the

United Kingdom, France, Germany, and Russia in the "contact group" to seek a diplomatic settlement. While Milošević refused to compromise, Yugoslav and Bosnian Serbs continued their attacks, slaughtering hundreds of Bosnian Muslims at Srebrenica in July 1995. This massacre finally led Clinton to authorize US air strikes against Serbian forces and to launch a vigorous diplomatic initiative. In November, he invited the various parties to come together in Dayton, Ohio. At this meeting, US diplomat Richard Holbrooke succeeded in negotiating the Dayton Peace Accords, which were signed in Paris on December 14, 1995. Recent military success against the Serbs by Croatian and Bosnian forces, which acquired weapons despite the UN embargo, added to US and European pressures on Milošević. He reluctantly approved the Dayton compromise, which divided the disputed territory but nominally preserved Bosnia-Herzegovina's integrity. To implement this settlement, Clinton sent 25,000 US troops to Bosnia to strengthen the NATO forces that replaced the hapless UN peacekeepers, who had been unable to protect themselves from the Serbs, much less the victims of ethnic cleansing. French President Jacques Chirac and other European leaders contributed significantly to ending the Bosnian War, but could not do so alone. Peacemaking required the active involvement of the United States as the world's remaining superpower.

That pattern persisted in Yugoslavia. In 1990, Milošević had revoked the autonomy of Serbia's southern province of Kosovo, where ethnic Albanians greatly outnumbered Serbs. He wanted to reverse the demographics in this historic area of Serbia. Denied both economic and cultural opportunities, and excluded from political institutions, some Albanians fled and others resorted to violent resistance. The Kosovo Liberation Army (KLA) appeared in 1996, claiming credit for attacks on Serbian officials and civilians. It demanded independence for the province. Denouncing the KLA as terrorists, Milošević reacted with brutality to expel the Albanians and achieve Serbian dominance. The resulting violence, which threatened to spread, prompted the European Union (EU) and NATO to seek a diplomatic solution. The Racak massacre on January 15, 1999, convinced Americans of the urgency. Under the assertive leadership of Clinton's new secretary of state, Madeleine Albright, the Europeans and Americans convened a conference at Rambouillet outside Paris in February to force both sides to compromise. Neither the KLA, wanting independence, nor Milošević, opposing outside interference in Serbia's internal affairs, accepted the proposal for NATO peacekeepers in Kosovo. Only later, under intense American and British pressure, did the Albanians acquiesce. Milošević's final rejection of the proposal called NATO's bluff. Encouraged by Albright and supported by Chirac, and even more by the new British prime minister, Tony Blair, Clinton authorized a NATO air war against Serbia. He publicly rejected the use of ground troops, however. The Kosovo War, beginning on March 24, 1999, was the first in NATO's history. NATO commander General Wesley Clark eventually achieved victory with heavy bombing of Belgrade and other sites in Serbia, but only after the Europeans indicated the likelihood of deploying land forces. Milošević surrendered on June 10. Meanwhile, over a million Albanians fled their homes in Kosovo to escape ethnic cleansing. The air war, although ostensibly fought to protect them, had left them even more vulnerable.

New forms of collective security were obviously becoming more important in the post-Cold War world. UN peacekeepers were active in Europe as well as Africa. Bush and Clinton even invited the United Nations to participate in peacekeeping in Central America and Haiti, thereby abandoning the traditional American claim, in the name of the Monroe Doctrine, to decide unilaterally what to do in the western hemisphere. They also involved NATO in the Balkans. NATO had originated in 1949 as an alliance against the Soviet Union, but now it took on other duties. In 1993, Clinton welcomed Russia into a Partnership for Peace with NATO, seeking to convince Yeltsin that the alliance was no longer a threat to Russia. He also worked to expand NATO membership to include the Czech Republic, Poland, and Hungary. Just before NATO's fiftieth anniversary on April 4, 1999, these states joined the sixteen Cold War members in the alliance. NATO expansion mostly coincided with the EU's as the former Soviet satellites in eastern Europe looked to the West for support in protecting their democratic governments and improving their economies. NATO in its new guise came closer to Wilson's original vision of collective security as a guarantee of national self-determination, not as an alliance engaged in Great Power rivalry.

Interdependence and transnationalism made questions of war and peace increasingly complicated in the post-Cold War global community. Globalization brought diverse peoples closer together, creating more, not less, conflict. The diplomat-historian William R. Polk examined this paradox in *Neighbors and Strangers* (1997). "During the whole of the human experience," he noted, "the stranger has always been a neighbor." Interactions between them constituted the fundamentals of foreign (and also domestic) affairs as different peoples divided themselves into groups of *we* and *they*. As a result of globalization, more people experienced more interactions with others and gained greater awareness of the world's diversity. Contrary to triumphalists, who thought that history was progressing in a single direction toward a peaceful and prosperous new world order with liberal democracy and capitalism, Polk understood that the reality of living together also promoted fragmentation and war. He noted that "we find it very difficult to live with people who are different from us and in times of stress or chaos turn violently against them." He anticipated, moreover, that the general trend toward the break-up of great empires would continue with the fracturing of states into smaller nations "so that, as complex as the international system has become, it is likely to become even more Balkanized."[21]

Rapid growth in the world population brought more strangers together as neighbors. In 1999 there were six billion people on the planet, up from five billion in 1986 and four billion in 1975. It had taken all of human history to attain one billion by 1830, another century to add the second billion by 1930, and three more decades to reach three billion by 1960. Almost all of the recent growth was occurring in the poorest countries, contributing further to civil strife and war.[22] Population increases in Rwanda, Haiti, and Kosovo, resulting in greater competition for scarce resources, exacerbated conflicts in those places, for example. In the Middle East, this same pattern existed. High birth rates among Palestinians living on the West Bank and in Gaza under Israeli occupation increased their numbers at the same time as they were losing more and more land to new Israeli settlements. Demographic pressures contributed to Israeli–Palestinian hostility, which erupted into renewed violence in September 2000.

For most of the 1990s, the so-called Peace Process had kept this phase of the Palestinian and broader Arab conflict with Israel under control. It offered hope to Palestinians that Israel might relinquish at least some of their ancestral land and that they might finally have their own state. That was their dream for national self-determination. But it collided with the Zionist vision for a Jewish homeland in the same place. From the Palestinian perspective, it was as if Israelis kept cutting Palestinian olive trees to clear the way for more new roads over which to drive their modern Lexus cars. Yet brighter prospects for peace in this decade greatly reduced Palestinian terrorist attacks. Both Bush and Clinton, along with Europeans, attempted to negotiate a compromise that might accommodate both sides, requiring each to recognize the legitimate rights of the other. These neighbors, who were strangers, all desired land and peace, along with economic opportunities for themselves. Israel continued to build more settlements and connecting roads on the West Bank, while the Palestine Liberation Organization (PLO) under Yasser Arafat refused to surrender Palestinian claims to Israeli-controlled land and to promise peaceful coexistence with Israel in return for vague promises of a future state. The Peace Process failed to resolve the conflict, despite the best efforts of Bush, Clinton, and many others, including the adversaries, throughout the decade.

## Conclusion

At the beginning of the twenty-first century, fragmentation and perpetual war seemed more likely than integration and enduring peace. McWorld and Jihad still clashed. Neighbors and strangers continued to divide into diverse groups of *we* and *they*. World history was not progressing in one direction toward realization of Wilsonian ideals of liberal democracy and capitalism in a global community, despite the false claims of triumphalists. Globalization generated great wealth and power for some, but also a backlash from others left behind. Ironically, they too now had access to the tools of modernity, which enabled them as "Super-empowered individuals" to lash out against their self-proclaimed enemies. No one epitomized this new reality better than Osama bin Laden, who organized al-Qaeda and masterminded the dramatic events of September 11, 2001. These terrorist attacks on the United States signaled another new era in world history.

## NOTES

1　Akira Iriye, *The Cambridge History of American Foreign Relations*, vol. 3, *The Globalizing of America, 1913–1945* (Cambridge: Cambridge University Press, 1993), p. 72.

2　Akira Iriye, *Global Community: The Role of International Organizations in the Making of the Contemporary World* (Berkeley, CA: University of California Press, 2002), p. 114.

3　John Gerard Ruggie, "American Exceptionalism, Exemptionalism and Global Governance," in *American Exceptionalism and Human Rights*, ed. Michael Ignatieff (Princeton, NJ: Princeton University Press, 2005), pp. 304–38.

4　Thomas L. Friedman, *The Lexus and the Olive Tree* (New York: Anchor Books, 1999), pp. 14–15, 294.

5　Francis Fukuyama, *The End of History and the Last Man* (New York: Free Press, 1992), p. 45.

6　Michael Mandelbaum, *The Ideas that Conquered the World: Peace, Democracy, and Free Markets in the Twenty-First Century* (New York: Public Affairs, 2002), pp. 6, 17.

7　Alfred E. Eckes, Jr., and Thomas W. Zeiler, *Globalization and the American Century* (Cambridge: Cambridge University Press, 2003), pp. 264–8.

8　George H. W. Bush, Address Before a Joint Session of the Congress on the Persian Gulf Crisis, September 11, 1990, bushlibrary.tamu.edu/research/papers/1990/90091101.html.

9　George H. W. Bush, Address to the Nation Announcing Allied Military Action in the Persian Gulf, January 16, 1991, bushlibrary.tamu.edu/research/papers/1991/91011602.html.

10　George H. W. Bush, Remarks at the Annual Convention of the National Religious Broadcasters, January 28, 1991, bushlibrary.tamu.edu/research/papers/1991/91012800.html.

11　George H. W. Bush, Address Before a Joint Session of Congress on the State of the Union, January 29, 1991, bushlibrary.tamu.edu/research/papers/1991/91012902.html.

12　George H. W. Bush, Address to the Nation on the Suspension of Allied Offensive Combat Operations, February 27, 1991, bushlibrary.tamu.edu/research/papers/1991/91022702.html.

13　George H. W. Bush, Inaugural Address, January 20, 1989, bushlibrary.tamu.edu/research/papers/1989/89012000.html.

14　David Halberstam, *War in a Time of Peace: Bush, Clinton, and the Generals* (New York: Scribner, 2001), p. 437.

15　Henry Kissinger, *Does America Need a Foreign Policy? Toward a Diplomacy for the 21st Century* (New York: Simon & Schuster, 2001).

16　Bill Clinton, Remarks at the Edmund A. Walsh School of Foreign Service at Georgetown University, November 10, 1994, in William J. Clinton, *Public Papers of the Presidents, 1994* (Washington, DC: Government Printing Office, 1995), vol. 2, p. 2060.

17　Bill Clinton, Remarks on United States Foreign Policy in San Francisco, February 26, 1999, in William J. Clinton, *Public Papers of the Presidents, 1999* (Washington, DC: Government Printing Office, 2000), vol. 1, p. 272.

18　Bill Clinton, Commencement Address at the University of Chicago, June 1, 1999, in ibid., vol. 1, p. 934.

19　Benjamin R. Barber, *Jihad vs. McWorld* (New York: Times Books, 1995), pp. 6–7.

20　Bill Clinton, September 15, 1994, quoted in Tony Smith, "In Defense of Intervention," *Foreign Affairs* 73/6 (1994): 42.

21　William R. Polk, *Neighbors and Strangers: The Fundamentals of Foreign Affairs* (Chicago: University of Chicago Press, 1997), pp. 1, 310–11.

22　The Population Institute, Washington, DC, www.populationinstitute.org.

## GUIDE TO FURTHER READING

Madeleine Albright, *Madam Secretary: A Memoir* (New York: Miramax Books, 2003). The first-hand account of Bill Clinton's second secretary of state.

Timothy Garton Ash, *In Europe's Name: Germany and the Divided Continent* (New York: Random House,

1993). An excellent analysis of the end of the Cold War in Europe.

Andrew J. Bacevich, *American Empire: The Realities and Consequences of US Diplomacy* (Cambridge, MA: Harvard University Press, 2002). A realistic assessment of the military and other foundations of America's global power.

James A. Baker, *The Politics of Diplomacy: Revolution, War and Peace, 1989–1992* (New York: G. P. Putnam's Sons, 1995). The first-hand account of George H. W. Bush's secretary of state.

George Bush and Brent Scowcroft, *A World Transformed* (New York: Random House, 1998). The president's and his national security adviser's views on the emerging post-Cold War world.

Warren Christopher, *In the Stream of History: Shaping Foreign Policy in a New Era* (Stanford, CA: Stanford University Press, 1998). The first-hand account of Bill Clinton's first secretary of state.

Wesley K. Clark, *Waging Modern War: Bosnia, Kosovo, and the Future of Combat* (New York: Public Affairs, 2001). The NATO commander's understanding of contemporary warfare in the 1990s.

Richard A. Clarke, *Against All Enemies: Inside America's War on Terror* (New York: Free Press, 2004). A valuable critique of the American government's failures before 9/11.

Bill Clinton, *My Life* (New York: Alfred A. Knopf, 2004). The president's account of his private life and public career from Arkansas to his White House years.

Warren I. Cohen, *America's Failing Empire: US Foreign Relations since the Cold War* (Malden, MA: Blackwell, 2005). A leading historian's overview of US foreign relations in the post-Cold War era.

Steve Coll, *Ghost Wars: The Secret History of the CIA, Afghanistan, and bin Laden, from the Soviet Invasion to September 10, 2001* (New York: Penguin, 2004). A journalist's important historical analysis of US covert involvement in Afghanistan before 9/11.

Robert A. Divine, *Perpetual War for Perpetual Peace* (College Station, TX: Texas A&M University Press, 2000). A perceptive series of lectures on why the United States fought wars and often lost the peace during the twentieth century.

Niall Ferguson, *Colossus: The Price of America's Empire* (New York: Penguin, 2004). An ironic critique of Americans for failing to be good imperialists because of the price.

Lawrence Freedman and Efraim Karsh, *The Gulf Conflict, 1990–1991: Diplomacy and War in the New World Order* (Princeton, NJ: Princeton University Press, 1993). A comprehensive international history of the Persian Gulf War.

William I. Hitchcock, *The Struggle for Europe: The Turbulent History of a Divided Continent, 1945–2002* (New York: Random House, 2003). An excellent introduction to contemporary European history within a global context.

Richard Holbrooke, *To End a War* (New York: Random House, 1998). A first-hand account by the US diplomat who negotiated the 1995 Dayton Peace Accords.

G. John Ikenberry, ed., *America Unrivaled: The Future of the Balance of Power* (Ithaca, NY: Cornell University Press, 2002). A collection of essays by political scientists on the relevance of balance-of-power theory to contemporary international politics.

Chalmers Johnson, *The Sorrows of Empire: Militarism, Secrecy, and the End of the Republic* (New York: Henry Holt, 2004). A critical assessment of the ongoing costs of the American empire.

Geir Lundestad, *The United States and Western Europe since 1945* (Oxford: Oxford University Press, 2003). An excellent overview of transatlantic relations by an outstanding Norwegian historian.

Walter Russell Mead, *Special Providence: American Foreign Policy and How It Changed the World* (New York: Routledge, 2002). An interesting survey of four American foreign policy traditions that still influence US decision-making.

John J. Mearsheimer, *The Tragedy of Great Power Politics* (New York: W. W. Norton, 2001). A systematic analysis of international relations by one of the foremost realist scholars.

Don Oberdorfer, *The Two Koreas: A Contemporary History* (New York: Basic Books, new edn, 2001). A journalist's excellent history of contemporary North and South Korea.

Kenneth M. Pollack, *The Persian Puzzle: The Conflict Between Iran and America* (New York: Random House, 2004). A prominent military historian's comprehensive assessment of one of the most troubled relationships in the Middle East.

Samantha Power, *"A Problem from Hell": America and the Age of Genocide* (New York: HarperCollins, 2002). A challenging reminder of the terrible human costs of genocide in the twentieth century.

Dennis Ross, *The Missing Peace: The Inside Story of the Fight for Middle East Peace* (New York: Farrar, Straus, & Giroux, 2004). A participant's account of the peace process by a US diplomat.

Gaddis Smith, *The Last Days of the Monroe Doctrine, 1945–1993* (New York: Hill & Wang, 1994). An excellent introduction to the increasingly international context of US relations with Caribbean and Latin American countries.

Tony Smith, *America's Mission: The United States and the Worldwide Struggle for Democracy in the Twentieth Century* (Princeton, NJ: Princeton University Press, 1994). A political scientist's historical overview and theoretical advocacy of Wilsonianism as the way to peace.

Philip Zelikow and Condoleezza Rice, *Germany Unified and Europe Transformed: A Study in Statecraft* (Cambridge, MA: Harvard University Press, 1995). A first-hand account of the end of the Cold War and the unification of Germany by two insiders in the George H. W. Bush administration.

# CHAPTER THIRTY-ONE

# Globalization

## ALFRED E. ECKES

During the last two decades of the twentieth century, the word globalization entered the lexicon. A new term and concept, it focused attention on how technological innovations and economic changes combined to overcome long-standing barriers of time, distance, and lack of information. First popularized by futurist John Naisbitt and Harvard University business professor Theodore Levitt in the early 1980s, the new word spread rapidly and came to symbolize the post-Cold War era of openness and interconnectivity.[1]

So what is globalization? Simply stated, it is a complex, synergistic process in which improvements in technology (especially in communications and transportation) combine with the deregulation of markets and open borders. Vastly expanded flows of people, money, goods, services, and information result. The process integrates people, businesses, non-governmental organizations (NGOs), and nations into larger networks. Globalization thus has an impact not only on business and economics but also on culture, society, politics, and almost every aspect of human existence.

Several engines drive the modern globalization process – particularly, technological innovations, market dynamics, policy ideas, and government actions. Over the long run – especially over the course of the twentieth century – improvements in transportation and communications gradually dissolved the barriers of time, distance, and lack of information that complicated all types of long-range relationships. Some of the most important developments involved aviation, wireless radio, satellite communications, fiber-optic cables, personal computers, and, of course, the Internet and cellular phones. The private sector, directed as it is to making profits and acquiring market share, is another motor vital to globalization.

Appreciating the opportunities that new technologies presented, business successfully lobbied the public sector to commercialize technologies developed for military purposes and to reduce border barriers to trade and capital flows. As a result, global markets emerged, and corporate thinking evolved accordingly. Today most large manufacturers have devised global supply and marketing chains and serve customers far from their home base. Many medium-sized firms have done the same. Strategically, they identify with global markets and many seek to blur national identifications. For example, when speaking in Beijing about plans to expand business and sourcing, John Chambers of Cisco Systems chortled: "If I wasn't American, I would be Chinese."[2]

Of course, policy ideas also influence globalization. Among the most important has been the consensus among economists that free trade, private enterprise, and competitive markets promote efficiency and economic growth, benefiting individuals and nations. This thinking took root with the writings of influential Scottish economist and philosopher Adam Smith. His

*Wealth of Nations* (1776) remains a manifesto for free marketeers. Another important set of ideas shaping efforts to structure the globalization process has origins in the efforts of international lawyers to promote mechanisms for peaceful resolution of disputes. Many of them believe that harmonization of standards, rules, and legal systems, including the establishment of supranational dispute settlement mechanisms in agreements such as the North American Free Trade Area (NAFTA) and the World Trade Organization (WTO), help to resolve conflicts among governments and private parties.[3]

Proponents of globalization – frequently business, professional, government leaders and other opinion makers – rhapsodize about a new era in which transnational corporations integrate national markets, traditional borders fade in significance, new technologies connect people around the globe, and the synergistic process lifts billions of people out of poverty. The US Council for International Business, an affiliate of the International Chamber of Commerce, extolled the opportunities available to business in a world without borders:

> Business today operates in a truly global, networked environment. In essence, the only borders are those that are self-imposed. Interconnections are made possible by buyers and sellers brought together at the speed of light by modern technology. Huge new markets and supply sources have opened in China, India, an expanded European Union, and elsewhere. Today, as never before, global commerce has the potential to create wealth, distribute it more broadly to alleviate poverty, improve the environment and promote economic development. Sustainable capital markets and communities are within our reach.[4]

Many pro-globalization enthusiasts say the process is dynamic and transformational, promoting convergence, harmonization, efficiency, growth, democratization, and homogenization. Journalist Tom Friedman of the *New York Times* is one who celebrates the modern era of globalization and plays down its conflicts. In his 1999 bestseller, *The Lexus and the Olive Tree*, he lauded the significance of rapid information transfers and instantaneous capital movements. In contrast to the phase of globalization that preceded the First World War and the Great Depression, Friedman asserted that new technologies enabled nation-states, corporations, and individuals to "reach farther, faster, cheaper and deeper around the world than ever before." In a sequel, he excitedly explained how globalization had shrunk and flattened the world, enabling individuals in China and India to become part of the global supply chain, competing for jobs and opportunities with those in high-income countries.[5]

Other troubadours of the new age have predicted that globalization would transform political relationships as well. In a series of writings, widely circulated in the business community, Kenichi Ohmae, formerly a McKinsey and Company official in Japan, espoused the view that nation-states are "dinosaurs waiting to die." Nationality would fade, he said, in the face of consumer sovereignty, as people in every developed country sought to obtain the best products in the world. Strobe Talbott, a *Time* magazine columnist and later deputy US secretary of state in the Clinton administration, predicted that "within the next hundred years, nationhood as we know it will be obsolete; all states will recognize a single, global authority. A phrase briefly fashionable in the mid-20th century – 'citizen of the world' – will have assumed real meaning by the end of the 21st century."[6]

At the grassroots level, globalization is frequently viewed in negative terms. Anti-globalization activists – including farmers, trade unionists, professors, and employees of NGOs – have a much different interpretation, one that stresses the dark side. They assert that globalization produces severe economic and social dislocations. It also arouses anxieties about job security, distribution of economic gains, and the impact of volatility on families, investments, cultures, communities, and nations. In particular, the critics assert that the globalization process puts low-skilled but high-income workers in developed countries in a race to the bottom with cheap labor in developing countries that toils in sweatshop conditions. They also claim that the spread of transnational corporations threatens the environment, national sovereignty, and democratic decision-making. Some activists associate globalization with the worldwide expansion of American capitalism, consumerism, and pop culture, which they say threatens to drive out local cultures and replace traditional values with drugs, violence, sex, and pornography. Critics frequently blame supranational agencies such as the International Monetary Fund (IMF), the World Bank, and the World Trade Organization (WTO) for advancing the pro-globalization mega-corporate agenda. As a consequence, thousands of protesters have rallied at high-level meetings of the IMF, the World Bank, and the WTO. In 1999, they succeeded in disrupting the WTO summit in Seattle, and this opposition continued at ministerial meetings in Cancun, Mexico (2003), and Hong Kong (2005).

Proponents and opponents agree on little except that the globalization process is transformational and challenges the power of nation-states. Unlike several other important unifying themes in this *Companion to International History*, such as nationalism, internationalism, and imperialism, the new concept focuses more on individuals and networks as agents of change, and less on nation-states. The former include ordinary people, corporations, and NGOs.

For historians, globalization offers a new prism for analyzing the past. Several scholars have proposed a "new global history" treating globalization as a "definitive new area of historical study." Bruce Mazlish of Massachusetts Institute of Technology and Akira Iriye of Harvard University distinguish the new global history from both state-centered national histories and world history. They say that global forces, such as migration, innovations in communications and transport, integrated capital markets, NGOs, human rights, and transnational religious and ethnic movements, cannot be understood in a traditional nation-centered framework. Nor does world history suffice. The latter began as a post-Second World War reaction to Eurocentric national histories. While world history did consider some transnational factors, such as plagues and population movements, it often attempted to synthesize the whole of past history. Mazlish and Iriye propose a more selective approach for the new global history, focusing on themes that transcend national boundaries. They emphasize the period since the Second World War as the appropriate

period for study, referring to it as a global epoch, and advocate an interdisciplinary approach.[7]

## The First Modern Era of Globalization

To understand the globalization process and to anticipate the future, some historical background is appropriate. Although the term globalization is relatively new, the process it describes has deep roots, extending back to the early traders and explorers – including such familiar names as Marco Polo, Leif Ericson, and Christopher Columbus among many others. For them, intercontinental travel and communications were time-consuming, exhausting, and hazardous. But, in the mid-nineteenth century, a series of political and technological developments transformed the business environment and speeded up the pace of change. The end of the Napoleonic Wars ushered in a century of relative peace in continental Europe. Key inventions like the steam engine and the telegraph dramatically accelerated international transportation and communications. With coal providing a cheap and readily available source of energy, the costs of moving goods and information fell sharply and the quality of these services improved markedly. In 1900 people and goods crossed the Atlantic Ocean in five or six days, down from four to six weeks during the preceding era of sail power. Transportation costs fell an estimated 45 percentage points in the period 1870 to 1913.[8]

Meanwhile, a submarine cable linked the New York and London financial markets, and an entire network of cables joined London to its overseas empire. By the 1890s, business information traveled from London to New York in two or three minutes, effectively linking financial markets. Because of the need to retransmit messages, those sent from London to India took 35 minutes, to China 80, and to Australia about 100 minutes. By the end of the nineteenth century, adventurers even traveled around the world in as few as 60 days, beating the fictional hero of Jules Verne's 1873 classic *Around the World in Eighty Days*. As a result of these technological improvements, as well as the spread of industrialization and imperialism, European businesses invested heavily abroad. They sought overseas sources of raw materials to support industrialization and agricultural products to feed urban populations. During this phase of globalization, business historian Geoffrey Jones says, "firms rather than markets or governments" drove foreign trade and investments.[9] European nations accounted for over three-fourths of the world's stock of foreign direct investment (FDI), valued in 1914 at $14.5 billion. Britain alone had 46 percent of FDI, and it exported 7 percent of national income. Not surprisingly, by the end of the nineteenth century, British companies dominated global shipping and cable networks and controlled some of the world's richest known deposits of raw materials.

The British government also played an important role behind the scenes in supporting globalization. It provided leadership in economics and finance. Adopting free trade and adhering to the gold standard, which facilitated currency convertibility and stability, London emerged as the center of world banking. In addition, a defense policy of maintaining a navy second to none and projecting power along the world's shipping lanes helped British trade and investments flourish.

For western Europeans generally, the quality of life improved during this first modern era of globalization. With faster transportation and refrigeration, along with improved communications, people enjoyed diets richer in meat, vegetables, and fruit and a wide variety of consumer goods from all areas of the world. To some residents of London this period before the First World War was a marvelous era in which economic and social life was internationalized. Economist John Maynard Keynes reflected this sentiment:

What an extraordinary episode in the economic progress of man that age was which came to an end in August, 1914! ... The inhabitant of London could order by telephone, sipping his morning tea in bed, the various products of the whole earth, in such quantity as he might see fit, and reasonably expect their early delivery upon his doorstep; he could at the same moment and by the same means adventure his wealth in the natural resources and new enterprises of any quarter of the world, and share, without exertion or even trouble, in their prospective fruits and advantages. ... He could secure forthwith, if he wished it, cheap and comfort-

able means of transit to any country or climate without passport or other formality . . . . But, most important of all, he regarded this state of affairs as normal, certain, and permanent.[10]

As in the late twentieth century, confidence grew before the First World War that global economic, social, and technological connections had made wars unrealistic and economic integration irreversible. In 1911, the peace activist Norman Angell wrote in *The Great Illusion* that "international finance has become so interdependent and so interwoven with trade and industry that . . . political and military power can in reality do nothing."[11] Subsequent events during the summer of 1914 would prove that optimism misplaced and raise questions about the durability of future periods of hyperglobalization.

## Deglobalization?

Among historians, the prevailing interpretation is that the economic and political dislocations of the First World War and its aftermath marked the end of the first modern era of globalization and the onset of a period of deglobalization that lasted until the 1970s. Niall Ferguson of Harvard University has analyzed the unanticipated collapse of this first age of modern globalization. He attributes it to imperial overstretch, unstable alliances, and revolutionary terrorism among other factors. During and after the First World War flows of investments and trade fell sharply. Postwar instability in Europe and the rise of Bolshevism in Russia produced a climate unfavorable for private trade and investments. Growing interwar competition for oil and other critical raw materials introduced new types of uncertainty. Also, governments imposed border controls to regulate migration. For the first time governments began to require that travelers carry valid passports and obtain visas.[12]

The breakdown of globalism was not simply a consequence of the strains of the First World War. Princeton University historian Harold James shows that a backlash against trade, capital flows, and international migration, as well as policy failures, contributed to the breakdown during the Great Depression.[13]

An alternative interpretation challenges the deglobalization thesis. It emphasizes that in important respects globalization continued throughout the interwar period. This explanation, offered by historians Alfred Eckes of Ohio University and Thomas Zeiler of the University of Colorado, emphasizes that significant continuities coincided with much-discussed discontinuities in economics, finance, and politics. For example, new technological innovations in transportation and communications continued to erase physical barriers of time and distance, even as nations erected political obstacles to trade, finance, and migrants. The First World War had stimulated military aviation, and afterward former military pilots began to carry airmail and provide passenger service. Charles Lindbergh, a young American aviator, captured the public imagination when he piloted a single-engine plane 3,400 miles from Long Island to Paris in thirty-three and one-half hours. In the aftermath of the First World War, several major airlines were born – including American, British Overseas, Delta, Pan American, and United. By the late 1930s, Pan American's famous clipper ships, which landed on water, were flying from San Francisco to Hong Kong, and from New York to London and Paris. Also critical to the globalization process during this period were improvements in radio and wireless. These permitted ship-to-shore communications and, under sometimes difficult atmospheric conditions, radio-telephone between North America and western Europe.

During the interwar period the spread of American consumerism and popular culture around the world also reflected the continuing vitality of globalization. Automaker Henry Ford discovered a global demand for the famous Model-T, and soon the Ford Motor Company opened assembly facilities in Germany, Russia, Japan, and other foreign locations. With the strong backing of the US government, Hollywood films dominated foreign markets, generating as much as 35 percent of total film revenue from overseas sales. Leaping over cultural barriers and market segmentation, Hollywood created a global image of life in the fast lane, one with glittering cities, vast spaces, and extravagant consumption. Foreign cinema stars like Charlie Chaplin (Great Britain)

and Mary Pickford (Canada) moved to Hollywood in order to gain greater visibility. It was said that in the 1920s the sun never set on the British Empire, or on American films.

Paradoxically, it is possible to view the Great Depression and the Second World War as marking the nadir of deglobalization, or as a period of adversity in which visionary leaders made significant preparations for a new age of globalization. Certainly, the economic calamity and the worldwide war between the Axis and United Nations powers did disrupt private flows of trade, money, travelers, and information, and it did strengthen the hands of statist regulators. But this era was also one of continuing accomplishments. Developments in technology and diplomacy would again lay the foundation during this period for a new era of globalization. Eager to gain the upper hand in the Second World War with sophisticated weapons, the major powers invested heavily in science and technology. Radar, microwave, improvements in aircraft design, the jet engine, atomic energy, and computers all had military uses and peacetime commercial applications. Planes intended for long-range bombing missions and carrying troops to distant destinations provided the basis for dramatic postwar improvements in civilian aviation and passenger travel. The B-29 Superfortress, designed for long-range bombing raids on Japan, became the luxurious 377 Stratocruiser that Pan Am used on its Atlantic routes. The four-engine Boeing 707 passenger jet, launched in 1954, had roots in military work to develop a jet tanker and in wind tunnel experiments with jet engines during the Second World War.

While technological progress was vital, individuals and ideas also played an important role in keeping alive the international ideal. Convinced that American isolationism, nationalism, and protectionism after the First World War bore some responsibility for the breakdown of peace in the interwar period, an internationalist elite of US leaders pursued policy initiatives that would establish an institutional infrastructure for a peaceful world. They envisioned the United States leading a relatively open and economically connected world. Beginning with Secretary of State Cordell Hull's initiative in 1934 to reduce high tariff barriers through reciprocal negotiations, the executive branch strongly promoted trade liberalization. Out of the prewar reciprocal trade agreements program came the State Department's postwar planning effort to establish a multilateral International Trade Organization (ITO). As conceived by its designers, the ITO would be both a comprehensive set of rules and an organization with a bureaucracy to oversee trade negotiations and to administer the rules. Initial plans proposed an independent bureaucracy and responsibilities for a wide range of trade-related subjects, from tariffs and competition policy to employment, investments, and development for poor nations.

As it turned out, the conception was too ambitious. The US Congress did not share the Roosevelt and Truman administrations' enthusiasm for such grand designs. And so, what emerged was a more limited contractual arrangement, the General Agreement on Tariffs and Trade (GATT). Pending establishment of the ITO, the GATT would be a temporary vehicle for multilateral trade negotiations among market-oriented countries, and it would offer a limited set of rules based on the principles of non-discrimination and national treatment when goods cross borders. As a consequence of these principles, every country participating in GATT negotiations was eligible to benefit from the concessions of every other signatory, and thus gained what tariff specialists call unconditional most-favored-nation status.

On January 1, 1948, nine countries, then accounting for 80 percent of world trade, put the GATT agreement into effect. They were Australia, Belgium, Canada, Cuba, France, Luxembourg, the Netherlands, the United Kingdom, and the United States. In subsequent negotiations, GATT succeeded in reducing industrial tariff barriers to minimal levels by the late 1960s.

Important as it was to opening markets for trade in goods, the GATT proved unsuccessful in many other areas. It did not succeed in removing agricultural trade barriers, in establishing a workable dispute resolution mechanism, or in removing a host of non-tariff barriers that segmented national markets. Moreover, GATT's perceived successes involved dangerous asymmetries. The principal tariff concessions came from the advanced countries of North America and western Europe, enabling latecomers, including war-devastated Japan, to gain access to lucrative markets without offering reciprocal access to their own home markets. Despite these anomalies and asymmetries, GATT would prove an important vehicle for deregulating and opening the global economy to market forces. It also would sustain the idea for a more comprehensive and permanent organization to anchor the global trade economy.

On monetary and financial matters, there was other progress during the Second World War to build a foundation for international cooperation. Under the leadership of the US and British treasuries, technical experts fashioned plans for an International Monetary Fund and an International Bank for Reconstruction and Development (IBRD, later called the World Bank). Delegates from forty-four countries approved these designs at the July 1944 money conference in Bretton Woods, New Hampshire. Architects of the IMF proposed an international organization that would work to establish the conditions for stable rates of exchange and currency convertibility so as to facilitate the revival of international trade. Interestingly, the principal authors, economists John Maynard Keynes of Great Britain and Harry Dexter White of the United States, did not envisage capital-account convertibility. Given the magnitude of private losses during the Great Depression and the risks of investments in a war-devastated world, they did not foresee the resumption of private capital flows for direct and portfolio investments. For that the designers of the Bretton Woods system proposed a parallel institution, the IBRD, to serve as a lending agency, essentially guaranteeing private capital and investing that in reconstruction and development projects.

As it turned out, the Bretton Woods institutions were unsuited to the difficult circumstances of postwar recovery and currency stability. To address urgent conditions, governments in western Europe and Japan turned back the clock and imposed restrictions on trade and currency transfers so as to regulate currency values and conserve foreign currency earnings. Indeed, until the 1980s much of world trade and finance was managed by governments, not by market forces, and governments, not private investors, provided long-term capital for development. The emergence of Cold War tensions between the Atlantic nations, on the one hand, and the Soviet Union and China, on the other, further complicated efforts to restore the conditions for open markets and opportunities for private investors.

For a brief time after the successful recovery of western Europe and Japan in the 1960s, the Bretton Woods agencies functioned as their founders envisaged. Trade revived, currencies remained relatively stable, and national and international government institutions provided the largest share of development capital. However, by the early 1970s the Bretton Woods system had become an anachronism. The United States, the linchpin in the system, was unable to honor its obligation to convert foreign dollar holdings to gold under those arrangements, and major currencies began to float. The financial world quickly moved beyond the Bretton Woods ideal of fixed but adjustable exchange rates, with the Fund providing assistance to maintain those parities. With major currencies like dollars, pounds, francs, and marks floating in the marketplace, the Fund no longer had a significant role to play. The IMF reinvented itself. While remaining a forum for international monetary cooperation, it focused on institution-building in developing countries. The IMF trained monetary officials and provided temporary assistance to developing countries facing payments problems so that they could avoid currency instability or restrictions on payments that might impair economic growth. The death of the Bretton Woods system of fixed but adjustable currency parities, and its replacement with a system of floating rates, had another significance. It permitted monetary authorities to deregulate capital markets and to rely instead on exchange fluctuations for adjusting imbalances.

In summary, the forty-year period from the Great Depression to the 1970s was a period of divergent patterns. Technological innovations continued, and governments made considerable progress in constructing an infrastructure of institutions and rules for a more integrated world. However, an economic calamity and Great Power conflicts (the Second World War and a series of Cold War conflicts) dictated that governments

regulate trade, private capital, and immigration. As a result, levels of trade and private finance as shares of GDP remained below pre-First World War levels.

## Globalization Revitalized

Conditions favorable for a general revival of economic globalization returned in the 1970s. Developments in technology as well as initial government actions to open and deregulate markets created extraordinary new opportunities for business. Nonetheless, at the time few media observers grasped the significance of these trends. A series of high-profile political and economic events focused attention on the Vietnam War, renewed conflict between Israel and its Arab neighbors, the OPEC oil embargo, currency disruptions leading to the end of the Bretton Woods system, and rising inflationary pressures.

Among the most significant long-term developments were revolutionary innovations in transportation and communications. They continued to catalyze the globalization process and to transform the world of separate nations into what Canadian academic Marshall McLuhan called a "global village." With the appearance of long-range passenger jets in the late 1950s, the number of business and leisure travelers rose rapidly. One of the most important events in the history of aviation involved the wide-bodied Boeing 747, which made its appearance in 1970. As a passenger jet it could carry as many as 500 passengers; as a freighter it could accommodate two containers side by side, 100 tons altogether. The 747 offered lower operating costs – 45 percent less than the Boeing 707-120 introduced in 1957 – and it would soon allow business to move high-valued merchandise between any two points in the world in 24 hours or less.

Other cost reductions came with the modernization of shipping ports. For decades longshoremen who could handle 10 to 15 tons per hour had loaded and unloaded ships. During the 1960s ports began to shift to standard-size containers and soon productivity had risen to 600 to 700 tons per hour. This meant faster ship turnaround, better coordination, and lower transportation costs.

Coincidentally, improvements in communications also supported the networking of people and the integration of nations. Until the late 1950s, business had relied on cable and radio-telephones for overseas communications. The first transoceanic telephone cables, connecting Europe and North America, became available in 1957. The cables brought improved business communications, but large areas of the world remained inaccessible. Satellite communications, which became generally available in the 1970s, would end this isolation and facilitate a dramatic improvement in information sharing. With the launching of Intelsat IV in 1971, 4,000 to 6,000 voice channels became available, further facilitating information sharing. With the age of cheap and rapid air transportation and the shift to containers, business soon developed the capability to run extensive overseas empires, sourcing supplies globally and serving world markets. Computerization, another product of Cold War defense research, also enabled corporations to exchange large quantities of information with overseas suppliers, assembly facilities, and customers. Later in the 1990s cell phones and the Internet enhanced business-to-business communications. With each iteration in technology, it became easier for businesses to expand overseas, either to serve customers in fast-growing foreign markets or to access more easily less expensive labor and supplies.

Not surprisingly, the 1970s saw a revolution in business thinking about international business and overseas expansion. Prior to that decade most of the *Fortune* 500 largest firms tended to focus on the US market for growth and profits. They left overseas sales and production to autonomous operations. But with new technologies and tools to run global operations, large corporations began to invest and expand overseas. Faced with economic stagnation in the US and western Europe during the 1970s, big business lobbied for deregulation of markets in order to facilitate overseas expansion. Abroad, they hoped to achieve higher growth while lowering production costs with access to cheaper labor.

In dynamic East Asia – particularly in Singapore, Taiwan, Hong Kong, and South Korea – governments experimented with business-friendly policies to lure investments, encourage technol-

ogy transfer, and jump-start economic growth. Malaysia offers one such example. There the government offered foreign manufacturers generous benefits to assemble products for export in foreign trade zones using low-cost labor. Indeed, Prime Minister Tun Razak even traveled to the United States and actively sought out foreign investors. He told a group in New York: "I hope to convince you all that Malaysia could be the answer to your problems of spiraling wages and increasing costs of production."[14]

Labor-intensive American industries responded to these lures – particularly makers of semiconductors, consumer electronics, and computer parts – and invested in tax-exempt, export-processing zones in East Asia. By 1980, Peter Drucker, the most widely read management guru, was exhorting business leaders to pursue such production-sharing arrangements with "almost-developed countries" (ADCs) such as Brazil, Mexico, Taiwan, and South Korea.

Direct investment in foreign plants surged, quadrupling between 1970 and 1980, and nearly doing the same in each of the next decades. Three-quarters of the investment flowed to developed countries, but by the mid-1990s emerging markets – particularly in Asia – were receiving about 40 percent. While American firms led the race to overseas markets, particularly to Europe, big European and Japanese corporations were not oblivious to new opportunities. European capital began to flood the American market during the mid-1970s, as French tiremaker Michelin and German automaker Volkswagen set up plants in North America. By 1980 Europe had recovered its historic position as the world's leading investor, and its accumulated stock of foreign direct investment exceeded that of the United States. Japanese firms would join the race to globalize their operations by the mid-1980s with significant greenfield investments in US assembly facilities, such as the automotive industry.

During the 1990s, as Cold War hostilities faded and the capitalist model seemed triumphant, transnationals accelerated foreign activities. More than 60,000 transnational corporations scoured the global economy searching for business opportunities. In 2000, these transnationals employed 46 million workers abroad and had foreign sales of $15.7 billion – more than double world exports. Not surprisingly, foreign direct investment soared as business contemplated expanded overseas operations. UNCTAD data show that flows of foreign direct investment rose at a rate of 40 percent annually during the last half of the 1990s, far faster than gross domestic product (1.3 percent) and world exports (3.4 percent). The United States, western Europe, and Japan accounted for 82 percent of FDI outflows and 71 percent of inflows in 2000, a peak year.

Economic ideas and government-sponsored policy changes played an important role in the rejuvenation of economic globalization. In *The Commanding Heights*, Pulitzer Prize-winning historian Daniel Yergin and Joseph Stanislaw recount the battle between government regulators and market forces that defined much of the twentieth century. They note that as the intensity of Cold War competition declined in the 1970s, business leaders reasserted the importance of market priorities and the deregulation of national markets. With the devaluation of the dollar in 1973, the US removed restrictions on capital movements and outward flows of investment capital increased substantially. Deregulation and market opening became bipartisan when President Jimmy Carter, a Democrat, proposed airline deregulation. Prime Minister Margaret Thatcher in Britain and President Ronald Reagan in the US were the political leaders most in tune with the new pro-market thinking. Their governments enacted policies to deregulate financial markets and to push trade liberalization and privatization during the 1980s.

Trade liberalization and overseas market expansion had been goals of American policy since the days of Cordell Hull and the New Deal. One of the most important developments in the post-Second World War period occurred in 1967 with completion of the Kennedy Round of GATT multilateral trade negotiations. Over five years, as it was implemented, this agreement produced cuts of 36 to 39 percent on industrial goods, effectively opening the world's largest market – the American market – to global competition. The average US duty on dutiable goods dropped below 10 percent. For most manufactured products, tariffs were no longer a significant barrier to

the American market. Indeed, Secretary of Commerce Alexander Trowbridge warned the business community that the "American domestic market – the greatest and most lucrative market in the world – is no longer the private preserve of the American businessman."[15]

Successive presidential administrations – Democrat and Republican – sustained the momentum for trade liberalization in the GATT. The Ford and Carter administrations successfully pursued the Tokyo Round during the 1970s. The Reagan administration launched the ambitious Uruguay Round of GATT negotiations in 1986, and negotiated bilateral free trade agreements with Israel and Canada. These pacts sought to expand trade, but, unlike earlier agreements which focused on tariff issues, the new ones addressed controversial matters of domestic policy – including non-tariff barriers, market opening for trade in services, liberal investment policies, dispute resolution, government procurement, and the like. In essence, new competitive circumstances and pressure from business prompted governments to push onward with initiatives to harmonize regulatory regimes and establish the international infrastructure for the globalization of business.

Renewed attention to bilateral and regional initiatives reflected the frustration of business leaders with the tortoise-like progress of multilateral trade initiatives. The Uruguay Round, which led to the creation of the WTO, took eight years of negotiations. As more nations entered the international trading system, the priorities of developing nations had an increasing impact which slowed the negotiations. While the GATT was often described as a rich man's club, dominated by the Europeans and North Americans with the acquiescence of the Japanese, a large bloc of developing nations sought to seize control of the WTO and define its agenda. Brazil and India, long spokesmen for developing-world causes, maneuvered to organize and represent the concerns of poor countries. While demanding improved access in rich markets for agricultural and manufactured exports, they sought to protect their own infant service industries and to obtain the benefits of technology transfer. Many of them took a lax approach to protecting the transnationals' intellectual property rights in software, movies and recordings, and pharmaceuticals. As a result, the multilateral negotiations deadlocked. Still eager to reduce risk and uncertainty to their operations in emerging areas, the transnationals lobbied political leaders in high-income countries for bilateral and regional initiatives. Often labeled "free trade agreements," these pacts established rules for all types of international transactions and promised impartial dispute settlement.

Deregulation and globalization of financial markets also presented problems for the Bretton Woods monetary institutions. As private capital flows revived in the 1980s, the Bank and the IMF began to proselytize developing countries to adopt market-opening financial policies, including capital-account convertibility. That is, the IMF urged emerging-market countries to remove controls on short-term and portfolio investments so that borrowers could benefit from improved access to international capital markets. And, with fewer controls, foreign investors could move capital easily about the world in search of the highest returns. Proponents said this approach would better enable developing countries to obtain the capital and technology needed to sustain high levels of economic growth. The Bretton Woods twins thus embraced the so-called "Washington–Wall Street consensus," and became institutional facilitators for market-led globalization featuring open capital markets and free convertibility.

That the IMF was giving some developing countries inappropriate advice became apparent during the 1997 Asian financial crisis. Speculative capital flows destabilized the smaller Asian currencies – the Thai baht, the Malaysian ringit, the Korean won, and the Indonesian rupiah among others – with tsunami-like fury as the financial contagion spread. Asian countries that had ignored the IMF's advice to liberalize payments – notably Malaysia, China, and India – survived the financial catastrophe with minimal damage. But countries such as Indonesia, Korea, and Thailand, ones that had implemented the IMF's controversial recommendations, had to devalue their national currencies and succumb to harsh IMF structural adjustment plans. Critics said these shifted the burden of adjustment to little people while bailing out rich investors.

In one controversial episode, the IMF's managing director, Michel Camdessus, towered over Indonesian President Suharto in January 1998 as he fixed his name to an austerity agreement. It effectively transferred important aspects of sovereignty to the Fund's international bureaucrats who forced Indonesia to abolish subsidies for food and fuel (used by the poor). Riots resulted.

The East Asian financial crisis of 1997–8 seemed to demonstrate the inadequacy of the Fund's advice and the competency of international institutions. Despite IMF claims that free trade in capital was associated with high economic growth, subsequent analysis concluded that such advice was inappropriate for developing economies with weak banking institutions and regulatory mechanisms. Columbia University economist Jagdish Bhagwati, a vigorous proponent of free trade, blamed the IMF for succumbing to the Washington–Wall Street consensus – that free capital movements necessarily stimulated growth. And Joseph Stiglitz, formerly the World Bank's chief economist, concurred that the IMF and other institutions put "the interests of Wall Street and the financial community ahead of the poorer nations."[16]

## Globalization Backlash?

The developing-world financial crisis of 1997–8, as well as controversies surrounding trade liberalization and the WTO, awakened public interest in globalization and its consequences. At the end of the 1990s, there were mounting protests against developing-world sweatshops that supplied multinational corporations such as Nike and Wal-Mart, and against international institutions like the WTO and the Bretton Woods institutions. Thousands marched in much-publicized and sometimes violent protest rallies, wherever heads of government and corporate leaders assembled. In high-income countries, public opinion polls registered rising concerns about job losses, overseas outsourcing, and income inequality. And there were growing doubts about the competence of international institutions and governments to respond to financial and economic contagions. Had the proponents of globalization overreached?[17]

The large protests in Seattle in December 1999, at annual meetings of the Bretton Woods institutions, and at annual meetings of the elite World Economic Forum in Davos, Switzerland, where top business and government leaders gathered, seemed to signal trouble for corporate-led globalization. But while ordinary people around the world shared many of the protesters' concerns about lost sovereignty, job losses, and threats to their ways of life, reputable public opinion polls claimed that the world's public generally did not sympathize with the demonstrators or blame corporations. A Pew survey of 38,000 people in forty-four countries, released in May 2003, concluded that for the global public, "globalization is now a routine fact of their everyday lives." On the one hand, majorities in each of the nations surveyed said that "growing business and trade ties are at least *somewhat* good for their country and themselves." But, on the other hand, the survey found signs of disquiet. In every region the survey found people "deeply concerned about a range of worsening financial and social problems in their lives – a lack of good paying jobs, deteriorating working conditions, and the growing gap between rich and poor." While anti-globalization activists had not succeeded in convincing "the public that globalization is the root cause of their economic struggles," the Pew survey found that large majorities in forty-two of forty-four countries believed that "their traditional way of life is getting lost and most people feel that their way of life has to be protected against foreign influence."[18]

Nonetheless, at the dawn of the twenty-first century, transnational business had much to cheer. Standard economic indicators – such as trade, finance, and Internet usage – suggested that globalization was gaining momentum and winning popular acceptance. Benefiting from the synergistic applications of new technologies and market-opening policies, transnational business continued to establish global supply and marketing chains and to take advantage of the new technologies of communications and transportation. They marketed the same leading brands around the world – Coca-Cola, McDonald's, BMW, Mercedes Benz, Nike, Shell, Sony – as middle-income consumers developed similar tastes. As it

opened one supercenter after another in China, Wal-Mart, the world's largest private employer, set out to prove that it could even make money selling Chinese-made goods to the Chinese middle class, and thus broaden consumer choice. Public opinion polls showed that people around the world generally approved of expanding trade and new technologies – particularly the Internet and cell phones.

Nor was globalization seemingly the great threat to traditional cultures that some critics asserted. Economist Tyler Cowen offered an effective response to the cultural homogenization thesis, arguing instead that globalization had strengthened traditional cultures and expanded the menus of choice for consumers around the world. Consumers who subscribed to satellite radio found that they could listen to more than 150 different digital entertainment channels, with such diverse offerings as world music and international news programs not available in local markets. Satellite television, such as the Dish network, offered programming in eighteen languages or areas, enabling consumers to receive 24 hours of programming in Armenian, Farsi, Tagalog, Urdu, and many other languages.[19]

Nor was globalization the exclusive preserve of the rich countries, like Great Britain and the United States. UNCTAD's annual surveys of international investments found that developing countries themselves were exporting investment capital – notably Brazil, China, India, Malaysia, South Africa, and South Korea. In 2004, about one-tenth of total FDI originated in developing countries. Of the world's hundred largest corporations, a list headed by General Electric and Vodafone, four came from emerging markets. They were using direct investments to establish global brands – such as Hyundai, Samsung, Embraer, and Haier. Thus, despite the loud protests of activists, representatives of the business community and governments remained buoyant. For them the globalization process seemed inevitable and irreversible.

## Backlash?

But was further globalization really inevitable and irreversible? Historians have suggested that today's corporate and government cheerleaders may be as blind to a Doomsday scenario as their grandfathers were to the collapse of globalization in the First World War and the Great Depression. For Niall Ferguson and Harold James, there are eerie parallels. They both note a variety of signs that the present phase of economic globalization might prove no more durable and stable than the earlier one.

Among the economic perils mentioned prominently are a world financial crisis. This might result from a breakdown in China's fragile monetary system, or an emerging world financial crisis similar to the Asian collapse of 1997. Or the overburdened US dollar might melt down. For years many specialists, including this writer, have expressed alarm over America's chronic current-account deficit and its reliance on foreign borrowing to sustain its excessive consumer spending. From 1990 to 2005, the aggregate deficit was $4.1 trillion. In late 2005, America's annual deficit approached 6.5 percent of GDP, and net liabilities amounted to 25 percent of GDP, levels that had triggered financial crises in smaller countries. A sharp depreciation of the dollar and sharply higher interest rates in the United States could disrupt Asian economies dependent on export sales and reliant on American fixed-income investments for their foreign exchange earnings. In such dire circumstances, national governments might reimpose controls on capital flows and erect trade barriers, as governments did in the Great Depression.

Ferguson also identifies a series of political threats, with parallels to the First World War period. These include imperial overstretch, growing out of America's worldwide commitments, and the war in Iraq. Or Great Power rivalries could lead to the collapse of globalization. A war between China and the United States over Taiwan might bring the world's largest producer of manufacturers and the world's leading consumer into a catastrophic conflict, much like Germany and Britain in the First World War.

Then there is terrorism and weapons of mass destruction. Ferguson notes that in 1914 rogue regimes supported terrorism, and he sees parallels between Osama bin Laden and Lenin. The spread of Islamic fundamentalism might also destabilize countries as the spread of communism did after the First World War. The contemporary world, he concludes, seems "no better prepared for the worst-case scenario than were the beneficiaries of the last age of globalization, 90 years ago."

In September 2001, adopting David-versus-Goliath tactics, terrorists demonstrated the capacity to use low-tech weapons and unconventional delivery systems to attack the soft underbelly of capitalism, the global supply chain. The attacks on New York and Washington, as well as later bombings in London and Madrid, exposed the vulnerabilities of mass transportation systems to terrorists. And with millions of containers crossing borders annually, experts worried about the capacity of future tech-savvy terrorists to smuggle weapons of mass destruction that might cause hundreds of thousands of casualties. While attention focused on such threats, there was recognition that in an interconnected world, terrorists and criminals might also indulge in cyberterrorism aimed at corporate security or personal financial and health records. Another disturbing terror scenario involved possible attacks on the global food supply chain, perhaps involving tainted fruit or meat with harmful pathogens.

Concern about the transmission of a pandemic also has parallels to the First World War period. During the First World War the global spread of Spanish flu caused more deaths than battlefield casualties − over 20 million altogether. Transmission of a modern epidemic, such as SARS or the Asian avian flu, could cripple international transportation networks, overwhelm public health authorities, and lead to millions of deaths. Necessarily, the open global economy would be a casualty.

There are other dangers. Monetary historian Harold James raises questions about the competence of international organizations such as the IMF, the World Bank, and the WTO to respond to economic crises and to head off financial contagion.

Finally, there is public opinion. If ordinary people should conclude that globalization threatens existing jobs, or distributes its benefits disproportionately to the affluent, or jeopardizes traditional political, cultural, or religious values, public officials might succumb to political pressures for restrictions on trade, investments, and

migration. However, in the absence of a catastrophic economic breakdown, such as the Great
Depression, it seems unlikely that protesters will
succeed in remodeling the open global economy.

In comparison with 1914, people around the
world are much better connected than ever before.
Economic statistics provide some measures of
those connections, but they do not capture the
full extent of individual networking, via the
Internet, cell phone, and satellite communications. Information now flows easily between any
two points on the globe, via the new technologies. Ordinary people stay in touch with friends
and relatives abroad. In such circumstances, it
would seem difficult, but not impossible, for democratic governments to mobilize support for war
or unilateral restrictions.

While it is possible to imagine another breakdown of the global economy as a consequence of
war, terrorism, and disease, it seems likely that
future technological innovations – especially in
communications and transportation – will continue to bridge the remaining barriers of time,
distance, and lack of information. In particular,
the arrival of a supersonic passenger plane, successor to the Anglo-French Concorde, capable of
moving large quantities of people cheaply and
rapidly from continent to continent, would abet
the globalization process. Such innovations are
difficult to forecast, but the history of the last two
centuries is replete with examples where technological innovations created unanticipated opportunities and brought people and nations closer
together.

As the globalization process advances, leadership of that process may shift, as it did in the early
twentieth century. Before the First World War,
Great Britain is widely thought to have managed
the system, using its economic and military power
to sustain a relatively open international economy
in which people, goods, and money flowed easily.
After the Second World War the United States
prepared the way for another age of openness and
economic integration. In the distant future –
perhaps by 2050 – China and India, the two
largest countries in terms of population, might
emerge as leaders, placing a uniquely Asian stamp
on the globalization process and its institutions.
It is also possible that a united and prosperous

Europe could share in that leadership, along with
an increasingly integrated North America.

## NOTES

1  John Naisbitt, *Megatrends: Ten New Directions
   Transforming Our Lives* (New York: Warner,
   1982); Theodore Levitt, "The Globalization of
   Markets," *Harvard Business Review* 61 (1983):
   92–102.
2  "Cisco Plans Expansion in Chinese Market," *Asia
   Pulse*, June 17, 2005.
3  For a brief discussion of other relevant drivers, see
   Alfred E. Eckes and Thomas Zeiler, *Globalization
   and the American Century* (New York: Cambridge
   University Press, 2003), p. 3.
4  "Insider Trading," *The Economist*, June 24, 1995,
   p. S6; US Council for International Business: Six
   Decades of Leadership, *Annual Report* (2005),
   p. 1.
5  Thomas L. Friedman, *The Lexus and the Olive Tree:
   Understanding Globalization* (New York: Farrar,
   Straus, & Giroux, 1999), pp. xvi, 331–2; Thomas
   L. Friedman, *The World is Flat: A Brief History of
   the Twenty-First Century* (New York: Farrar, Straus,
   & Giroux, 2005).
6  Kenichi Ohmae, *The End of the Nation State: The
   Rise of Regional Economies* (New York: Free Press,
   1995), jacket; Strobe Talbott, "The Birth of the
   Global Nation," *Time*, July 20, 1992, p. 70.
7  Bruce Mazlish and Akira Iriye, eds., *The Global
   History Reader* (London and New York: Routledge,
   2005), p. 1.
8  Kevin H. O'Rourke and Jeffrey G. Williamson,
   *Globalization and History: The Evolution of a
   Nineteenth-Century Atlantic Economy* (Cambridge, MA: MIT Press, 1999), pp. 35–6.
9  Geoffrey Jones, *Multinationals and Global Capitalism: From the Nineteenth Century to the Twenty-
   First Century* (Oxford: Oxford University Press,
   2005), p. 185.
10 John Maynard Keynes, *The Economic Consequences
   of the Peace* (New York: Harcourt, Brace, 1920),
   chap. 2, p. 4. Online at www.econlib.org/library/
   YPDBooks/Keynes/kynsCP.html.
11 Norman Angell, *The Great Illusion* (New York:
   Garland, 1972, rpt. of 1911 edn), p. vii.
12 Niall Ferguson, "Sinking Globalization," *Foreign
   Affairs* 84 (2005): 64–77.
13 Harold James, *The End of Globalization: Lessons
   from the Great Depression* (Cambridge, MA:
   Harvard University Press, 2001).

14 Tun Razak quote from Mohd Ariffin, "A Fantasy Theme Analysis of Selected Speeches of Tun Abdul Razak Hussein on the Issues of New Economic Policy in Malaysia 1971–1975," MA thesis, Ohio University, Athens, Ohio, 1989.

15 US Department of State Bulletin, July 31, 1967, pp. 127–9.

16 Jagdish Bhagwati, "The Capital Myth: The Difference between Trade in Widgets and Dollars," *Foreign Affairs* 77 (1998): 6; Joseph Stiglitz, *Globalization and its Discontents* (New York: W. W. Norton, 2002), jacket.

17 Ferguson, "Sinking Globalization"; James, *End of Globalization*.

18 Pew Research Center, "Views of a Changing World 2003," June 3, 2003, and "A Global Generation Gap," February 24, 2004. Online at people-press. org/.

19 Tyler Cowen, *Creative Destruction: How Globalization is Changing the World's Cultures* (Princeton, NJ: Princeton University Press, 2002), p. 18.

## GUIDE TO FURTHER READING

Pat Choate, *Hot Property: The Stealing of Ideas in an Age of Globalization* (New York: Alfred A. Knopf, 2005). Stimulating discussion of intellectual property issues and technology transfers.

Tyler Cowen, *Creative Destruction: How Globalization is Changing the World's Cultures* (Princeton, NJ, and Oxford: Princeton University Press, 2002). Persuasive rebuttal to the claim that globalization of culture is dumbing down societies everywhere.

Alfred E. Eckes, Jr., and Thomas Zeiler, *Globalization and the American Century* (New York: Cambridge University Press, 2003). Using globalization as its focus, this volume offers a unique interpretation of twentieth-century American history.

Niall Ferguson, "Sinking Globalization," *Foreign Affairs* 84/2 (2005): 64–77. Shows how globalization disintegrated during and after the First World War, and questions the claim that globalization is irreversible.

Thomas L. Friedman, *The World is Flat: A Brief History of the Twenty-First Century* (New York: Farrar, Straus, & Giroux, 2005). Enthusiastic account of how technology and open markets flattened the global playing field, enabling 3 billion people in emerging markets to compete for work.

William Greider, *One World, Ready or Not: The Manic Logic of Global Capitalism* (New York: Simon & Schuster, 1997). Prominent reporter describes the human side of globalization, and concludes that the global economy is sowing "creative destruction."

A. G. Hopkins, ed., *Globalization in World History* (New York: W. W. Norton, 2002). Series of essays by eight Cambridge University historians supplying a valuable global and historical setting for policy debates.

Harold James, *The End of Globalization: Lessons from the Great Depression* (Cambridge, MA: Harvard University Press, 2001). Economic historian finds significant parallels between breakdown of globalization during the Great Depression and recent conditions.

Geoffrey Jones, *Multinationals and Global Capitalism: From the Nineteenth to the Twenty-First Century* (New York: Oxford University Press, 2005). Succinct interpretation placing multinational business at the heart of globalization.

Henryk Kierzkowski, ed., *Europe and Globalization* (New York: Palgrave Macmillan, 2002). Essays explore what Europe did for globalization in the past and what globalization is doing to Europe in recent times.

Bruce Mazlish and Akira Iriye, eds., *The Global History Reader* (London and New York: Routledge, 2005). Presents multidisciplinary perspectives on globalization and articulates the case for a new global history.

Joseph E. Stiglitz, *Globalization and its Discontents* (New York: W. W. Norton, 2002). Nobel Prize-winning economist's first-hand account of how the IMF and other institutions put interests of Wall Street and high finance ahead of poorer nations during the Asian crisis of 1997–8.

Alan Tonelson, *The Race to the Bottom: Why a Worldwide Worker Surplus and Uncontrolled Free Trade are Sinking American Living Standards* (Boulder, CO: Westview Press, 2000). Critic of globalization argues that globalization endangers workers in high-income countries.

Daniel Yergin and Joseph Stanislaw, *The Commanding Heights: The Battle Between Government and the Marketplace that is Remaking the Modern World* (New York: Simon & Schuster, 1998). Explains economic upheavals in the post-Cold War era as an epic struggle between free market and regulatory state.

# CHAPTER THIRTY-TWO

# Terrorism: September 11, 2001 and its Consequences

## MICHAEL BAUER

On September 11, 2001, nineteen terrorists hijacked four American passenger airplanes. Two of the planes were crashed into the Twin Towers of the World Trade Center in New York, the third hit the Pentagon in Washington, and the fourth fell down on an open field in Pennsylvania. In this devastating attack on the world's sole remaining superpower, over 3,000 people were killed. Moreover, within a few hours the vulnerability of the United States was revealed. Despite American military, political, and economic might, it seemed that terrorism – a strategy of asymmetric warfare – could deal the US a blow that would not only shatter the sense of security of the US people, but also send shockwaves around the globe. The peaceful and secure world that had been hoped for when the Cold War ended turned out to be an illusion. Simultaneously, the dream that "globalization" would produce prosperity and harmony was questioned; globalization, it seemed, was not only about economics and finance, but also about security: what was true for criminally motivated forms of organized violence proved to be true for political violence as well. By 2001, terrorism had become a global phenomenon, adapted to the possibilities that twenty-first-century logistics and communications offered. Hence, two questions lie at the heart of this chapter: first, what is particularly new about the "new" terrorism; secondly, what are the international political reactions to the terrorist menace? In order to answer these questions, this essay will consider the controversies surrounding the definition of "terrorism," will focus particular attention on the characteristics of al-Qaeda, and then deal with the impact the attacks of September 11, 2001 had on the organization of the international security architecture. Did 9/11 – as the event is called – indeed "change everything," as is often claimed?

## Approaching Terrorism

On the international political and judicial level, no generally accepted definition of "terrorism" has been established. Although a number of proposals have been brought forward by states and international bodies, none has achieved sustained and widespread acceptance.[1] Even the attacks of September 11, 2001 did not change this. Suggestions made by a high-ranking panel of the United Nations (UN) and by the European Union (EU) also failed to win recognition.[2] The main obstacle to the establishment of a consensus on what constitutes a terrorist offense is that "terrorism" is a pejorative term.[3] The labeling of a group or organization as "terrorist" implies a moral judgment not only about the legitimacy of the group's actions, but also about its motives. Especially during the Cold War and within the context of the conflict in the Middle East, the popular phrase "one man's terrorist is another man's freedom fighter" suggests the difficulty in reaching agreement on a definition of the term itself.

Nevertheless, certain groups continue to be classified as "terrorist," in spite of the absence of an agreement on a definition of "terrorism."

Given this difficulty, it seems sensible to begin by distinguishing terrorism from other types of organized violence. Is terrorism a purely "civilian" phenomenon or can it refer to the activities of governments as well? Even though totalitarian and autocratic regimes can be said to have terrorized their people, it might be sensible to avoid the use of "terrorism" to describe their activities. Sanctions against breaches of human rights by governments have been established by international treaties such as the Geneva conventions. In addition, especially since the Second World War and the Nuremberg Trials, categories such as *genocide, crimes against humanity*, and *war crimes* have been developed.[4] Although it is arguable that states have often played a role in supporting terrorist groups as a means of covert warfare, the influence they have actually exercised over such groups seems to have been fairly limited. Thus, such groups ought to be regarded as independent organizations.

Terrorism should also be distinguished from other forms of organized violence such as guerrilla groups and organized crime.[5] Terrorists and guerrillas often adopt similar methods, using assassination, bombing, kidnapping, and so on in pursuit of political aims grounded in ideological, religious, or nationalist-ethnic convictions. There are important differences, however: guerrillas often operate in large units that present themselves publicly in paramilitary outfits; they usually target military facilities; and they try to achieve control over territory. Terrorist groups do not operate in the same way and they attack civilians, politicians, and military targets alike.

While terrorists and guerrillas also share a focus on the psychological impact of their destructive acts, this psychological dimension is much more important to terrorists, who seek to grab the attention of the biggest possible audience. On the one hand, publicity is needed to generate fear among the targeted groups; on the other, as terrorists usually claim to be acting on behalf of someone else – an ethnic group, a religious community, or a social class – they need to be recognized by their alleged followers. Fundamental in

this regard is the concept of "propaganda by deed," which claims that violence has a dialectical effect, demonstrating to potential followers through what means they can achieve their aims.[6] This concept represents a basic component of every terrorist campaign; al-Qaeda employs it vigorously. Moreover, terrorist operations usually are designed as provocative acts that tempt the attacked state to retaliate on a scale that is deemed unjustified – at least from the point of view of the potential followers. This alleged overreaction is intended to create solidarity with the terrorists and diminish the legitimacy of the attacked state.

Terrorists also resemble organized crime groups in some respects. Depending on their size, the groups are organized in small units that form a network of specialized and independent cells. Generally, they operate under civilian cover. The major difference between organized crime and terrorism, of course, lies in the motivation: for organized crime material gain is an end in itself, while terrorists – although they might employ classical criminal methods – usually pursue money and other resources as a means to wider political ends. Terrorists seldom need massive resources for their operations: the costs for the preparations of the 9/11 attacks seem to have been around $500,000 (US).

There are also important aspects that shape the self-perception of terrorists. They do not perceive themselves as criminals – in fact, quite the opposite: they regard themselves as working to create a better world. Thus, at the heart of their self-conception lies the justification of the use of violence as a means to a noble end. From this self-perception it follows that terrorists do not see themselves as terrorists but as freedom fighters, soldiers, insurgents, or jihadists.

Thus, terrorism is a distinct form of sub-state violence and it is not surprising that there have been differences on how to define it. Bruce Hoffman, for instance, defines terrorism as a:

> deliberate creation of fear through violence or the threat of violence in the pursuit of political change. . . . Terrorism is specifically designed to have far reaching psychological effects beyond the immediate victim(s) or object of the terrorist attack.

... Through the publicity generated by their violence terrorists seek to obtain leverage, influence and power they otherwise lack to effect political change on either a local or an international scale.[7]

Walter Laqueur quotes Nietzsche's dictum that "only those things which have no history can be defined." Whatever the difficulties involved in defining terrorism, it has a long history and a broad spectrum of characteristics. "Today there are more varieties than existed thirty years ago, and many of them are so different from those of the past and from each other that the term 'terrorism' no longer fits some of them."[8] Let us look, then, at the historical development of terrorism.

## Terrorist Groups and Strategies – Old and New

The term "terror" was first used in the aftermath of the French Revolution. The downfall of the monarchy was accompanied by a period of instability. To reestablish public order and to ensure the success of the revolution, Maximilien Robespierre and his followers created what was called the *régime de la terreur*. Judicial and executive powers were concentrated in the hands of a tribunal that was empowered to try alleged agitators or supporters of the monarchy and execute the sentences – more often than not through the guillotine.

During the nineteenth century terrorism was used increasingly as a label to describe those who aimed at disturbing or overthrowing public order. Important theorists of this period were Karl Heinzen, Johann Most (both Germans who lived in the United States), and Michael Bakunin (a Russian).[9] All three wrote books on terrorist strategy and tactics which laid the groundwork for today's terrorist handbooks. Apart from the social revolutionary context, terrorism was used by separatist or nationalist movements in Ireland and in the Austrian-Hungarian and Ottoman empires. Probably the best-known terrorist assault of this period was the assassination of the Austrian archduke, Franz Ferdinand, in Sarajevo in 1914 by Serbian nationalists, which initiated the chain of events that ended in the outbreak of the First World War. In the aftermath of both that war and the Second World War, terrorist strategies

and tactics were employed in the anti-colonial upheavals in Asia and Africa. Some of these movements were legitimized when their countries gained their independence.

Following the Israeli victory in the Arab–Israeli War in 1967, militant Palestinian groups started a terrorist campaign against Israel. Especially important was the Palestine Liberation Organization (PLO). Similar to guerrilla groups in Asia and Africa, the PLO received strong support from the people on whose behalf it claimed to be fighting – the Palestinians – and it became, over time, a powerful political entity in the Middle East. Moreover, the Palestinian groups belonging to the PLO were the first ones to internationalize their activities by conducting hijackings, bombings, and other attacks outside the Middle East.[10] Before that the operational focus of terrorist groups had always been confined to their own lands.

Less successful than the PLO were left-wing terrorist groups such as the German "Red Army Fraction" (or Faction) that were active throughout the 1970s and 1980s in Europe. Their operations as well as their political aims were clearly rejected by the public, including those whom they were claiming to "free," i.e., the working class. At the same time, Spain and the UK witnessed a renewed increase in the terrorist activities of nationalist groups. The Irish Republican Army (IRA) tried to force British withdrawal from Northern Ireland by attacking British facilities all over Europe. In the late 1970s the Basque Fatherland and Freedom movement (Euzkadi Ta Askatasuna, or ETA) took up its fight within Spain for an independent Basque state.

In the 1980s and 1990s, however, a new form of terrorism entered the stage. Sects holding apocalyptic worldviews such as the Aum Shinrikyo in Japan, as well as a number of right-wing amateur terrorists in the US, aimed to bring about the end of the world – or whatever their abstruse aims were – by conducting acts of terror. A somewhat less apocalyptic and more political approach was the pursuit of their aims by religiously motivated groups such as the Jemahislamiah in Southeast Asia, Hamas, Palestine Islamic Jihad, and Hezbollah in the Middle East, and, with a more or less global radius, al-Qaeda.

These kinds of groups differed from nationalist or political-ideological groupings not only in their motives but also in their tactics. The operations of the former more often than not aimed primarily at gaining public attention, not physical destruction per se; indeed, in accordance with their curious logic, some of these groups narrowly defined what they considered to be "legitimate" targets. Hence Brian Michael Jenkins's assertion that "terrorists want a lot of people watching and . . . listening and not a lot of people dead."[11] Such limitations, however, seem to have evaporated in the case of religious or transcendental groups.[12] The willingness to cause high numbers of casualties among innocent people has grown considerably, as demonstrated by various terrorist attacks since the early 1990s.[13] Yet the groups inspired by fundamentalist Islam in particular differ from the secular ones in another important respect: they use suicide bombers to conduct their operations. The only non-Islamic group that has employed this tactic are the "Tamil Tigers" of Sri Lanka. On the one hand, suicide bombers increase the lethality of an attack as otherwise such operations as 9/11 would be impossible. On the other hand, their disregard for their own lives shows the unscrupulousness and decisiveness of the terrorists, thereby increasing the psychological impact of the attacks.

Osama bin Laden's network, al-Qaeda, may be distinguished from other terrorist groups, including the religiously motivated ones, because it was forged into a truly transnational enterprise which thereby posed qualitatively new threats and challenges for security policy.[14] Osama bin Laden and Abdullah Azzam, bin Laden's intellectual mentor, founded al-Qaeda ("the base") in the late 1980s to support the insurgency campaign of the mujahidin against the Soviet occupation of Afghanistan. The network's ideology was, from the very beginning, based on Wahabism – the fundamentalist version of Sunni Islam to which its two leaders adhered. Al-Qaeda's primary function at that time was to provide logistic support and training facilities in Pakistan for foreigners (mainly of Arab origin) who were willing to fight Soviet troops in Afghanistan. Especially Ayman Muhammad Rabi' al-Zawahiri, a leading figure of several Egyptian terrorist groups, was the one who, after

the death of Azzam, convinced bin Laden to transform al-Qaeda from a regional guerrilla organization into a transnational terrorist network. A particularly salient feature in this regard is the all-encompassing political agenda that al-Qaeda developed by the 1990s, after the apparent victory in the jihad against the Soviet occupation. After the Gulf War of 1991, bin Laden declared that his aims were to force the withdrawal of American troops from the Arabian peninsula and to oust the governments of Saudi Arabia and any other Muslim country that – in his view – cooperated too closely with the US and thereby betrayed Islam. He called, moreover, for the reestablishment of the Caliphate, i.e., a kind of Islamic empire that would unite the entire Muslim community (the so-called umma), as well as the destruction of Israel and the United States. Against this backdrop, al-Qaeda portrays itself as the defender of Islam against the onslaught of "Zionists," "Crusaders," and infidels within the ranks of the Muslim world itself.

The breadth and global reach of al-Qaeda's network is in clear contrast to that of secular terrorist groups as well as to other religious ones. Indeed, it allows al-Qaeda to gain both the financial and ideological support of radical Muslims all over the world, as they can identify with one or another aspect of the group's ideology or aims. Moreover, the group uses areas of conflict such as Bosnia, Chechnya, Kashmir, Palestine, Iraq, and other hotspots to convince young Muslims of the need to engage in violent jihad, thus recruiting new members in the regions and in western countries alike. Likewise, since the 1990s, al-Qaeda provides Islamic guerrilla and terrorist groups all over the world with expertise and financial support. Important in both support and recruitment activities is the decentralized structure of the network: after the withdrawal of Soviet forces from Afghanistan, many foreign mujahidin who had been in contact with al-Qaeda returned to their home countries. Fearing that they might become a destabilizing factor in domestic politics, some of these countries refused to permit the reentry of these war veterans. Significant numbers of mujahidin therefore continued their journeys to Europe, the US, or Southeast Asia where many of them served to multiply the numbers of radical

Islamists and act as the organizational linchpin. As a matter of fact, it seems to have been the deliberate practice of bin Laden to maintain envoys or even operate regional bureaux in many Arabic countries, in South and Southeast Asia, Europe, and parts of Africa. Many al-Qaeda members that were recruited and trained during the 1990s had extensive contact with veterans of the war in Afghanistan. Even though there are considerable differences in the estimates of al-Qaeda's recruitment activities, it can be taken as given that several thousand potential terrorists received training throughout the 1990s. The most important places for the education of terrorists were the camps al-Qaeda set up in Afghanistan once the Taliban took control after the Soviets withdrew. In fact, Afghanistan became the operational base for al-Qaeda, and in 1996 bin Laden moved his headquarters there. The Taliban movement that had originated in the religious schools of the refugee camps along the Pakistan–Afghan border during the 1980s and al-Qaeda fitted well together. Like al-Qaeda, the Taliban adhered to Wahabism and believed a violent jihad to be a religious duty. Moreover, the regime urgently needed support to stabilize its position in Afghanistan and therefore welcomed bin Laden and his vast financial resources. Indeed, one might argue that, while states are alleged to have supported terrorist groups such as Hezbollah and the Red Army Faction, al-Qaeda was the first terrorist organization to sponsor a state.

However, al-Qaeda was not only active as a recruiting and training organization, it also conducted terrorist attacks that displayed as much ruthlessness as organizational sophistication. In 1993 Ramsi Yousuf, allegedly trained and supported by al-Qaeda, conducted a first attack on the World Trade Center in New York; the next year he planned operation Oplan Bojinka, which was prevented by security services only by chance. Among other things, this operation had envisaged the assassination of the pope and the president of the United States during their visits to the Philippines in early 1995, as well as the bombing of eleven US passenger airplanes at the same time. In 1998 terrorists bombed simultaneously the US embassies in Kenya and Tanzania, killing 224 persons. While al-Qaeda never took official

responsibility for these attacks, the overwhelming evidence pointed to bin Laden and his network. Thus, President Clinton ordered cruise-missile attacks on a Sudanese factory as well as on al-Qaeda training camps in Afghanistan in retaliation.[15] The damage these attacks did to al-Qaeda's operational base in Afghanistan was negligible, and when it emerged that the factory in Sudan had been producing harmless medicine rather than the chemical weapons claimed by the US government, the whole reprisal turned out to be a disaster for the reputation of the US. The next two major operations of al-Qaeda failed: an attempt to blow up the Los Angeles airport as part of the so-called "millennium attacks" in 2000 was prevented when the plotter was taken into custody by US customs authorities in December 1999, and an attack on the American vessel *USS Sullivan* during its stay in the harbor of Aden failed as the boat intended to hit the destroyer sunk because it was overloaded with explosives. Al-Qaeda's next operation took place in October 2000 when a small boat loaded with explosives and controlled by at least two members of the network collided with a destroyer of the US navy, the *USS Cole*, in Aden harbor. The explosion killed seventeen US seamen and injured thirty-nine. The US identified Qaed Salim Sinan al-Harthi as the mastermind behind this attack, and succeeded in killing him in November 2002 when a missile was fired at his vehicle from a US predator-drone during a reconnaissance mission over Yemeni territory.[16]

As can be seen from this short and selective history of al-Qaeda operations before the attacks of September 11, 2001, the group had displayed both the willingness and the ability to cause immense damage and destruction. Unsurprisingly, Osama bin Laden was not content with using only conventional weapons. Asked in an interview with *Time* magazine in December 1998 about the allegation that he tried to acquire weapons of mass destruction (WMD), bin Laden declared:

> Acquiring weapons for the defense of Muslims is a religious duty. If I have indeed acquired these weapons, then I thank God for enabling me to do so. And if I seek to acquire these weapons, I am

carrying out a duty. It would be a sin for Muslims not to try to possess the weapons that would prevent the infidels from inflicting harm on Muslims.[17]

Evidence that had been collected after the US invasion of Afghanistan in late 2001 revealed that al-Qaeda had indeed tried to produce biological and chemical weapons. However, after closer examination it became clear that the group had not been very successful: they lacked both the equipment and the expertise to produce such substances. The same seems to be true with respect to their attempts to acquire nuclear materials, where it turned out that press reports of their achievements had either been exaggerated or false.[18]

## September 11, 2001

While al-Qaeda was developing into a global terrorist network during the 1990s, awareness of the group's profile and capabilities was still confined to experts in terrorism and security services. In these circles an extensive debate had evolved on the characteristics of the "new" terrorists as well as on the techniques to counter them. It was generally acknowledged that, given the extreme asymmetry of international power relations, terrorism and other kinds of clandestine warfare were the most likely threats to international security. Publicly, however, terrorism was seldom a topic of concern.

September 11, 2001 changed everything. On that day the most devastating terrorist attack in history was broadcast "live" (or shortly afterward) around the world, generating shock and fear. Given the operational capabilities an attack of that scale required, as well as the viciousness and hate in the minds of the perpetrators, nobody knew what would happen next. Therefore, when President George W. Bush addressed the nation later that evening, he appealed to the emotional firmness of the Americans: "Thousands of lives were suddenly ended by evil. These acts shattered steel, but they cannot dent the steel of American resolve."[19] Governments all over the world evinced sympathy and solidarity with the American people and condemned the attacks as abhorrent and barbarous, breaching all standards of humanity and civilization. Soon the security services identified Osama bin Laden and his al-Qaeda organization as the main suspects behind the attacks.

## First Steps in the War on Terrorism

It was hardly surprising that the events of September 11, 2001 called into question the prevailing attitude to the treatment of terrorism. Hence, on that same day, a process of interpreting the meaning of the attack began. The first question was whether 9/11 constituted an act of *war* that thereby invoked the right of self-defense or whether it was a *criminal act* that did not permit such extreme measures. While terrorism was historically regarded as a form of organized crime, al-Qaeda and 9/11 were viewed differently.[20] Given the enormous destruction, it took the US administration only hours to declare that 9/11 was an act of war. In his Address to the Nation on the evening of September 11, President Bush declared that "America and our friends and allies join with all those who want peace and security in the world, and we stand together to win the war against terrorism."[21] The US Congress followed suit and approved the administration's reading of 9/11 as an armed attack invoking right to self-defense. Moreover, Congress gave the president *carte blanche* when it authorized him to "use all necessary and appropriate force . . . in order to prevent any future acts of international terrorism against the US."[22] The interpretation of 9/11 as an act of war was confirmed shortly thereafter by the UN via Security Council Resolution 1368 of September 12, in which the Council condemned the attacks as a threat to international peace and security that brought into play "the natural right of self-defense," thus invoking Article 51 of the Charter. While the UN had repeatedly declared terrorism a threat to international peace, the application of the right of self-defense in relation to a terrorist incident was unprecedented. The principle of self-defense had previously been interpreted to apply only to an armed attack by one *state* on another. Non-state actors were dealt with individually.[23] The EU took a similar stance when it declared an American "riposte" to be justified on the basis of Resolution 1368.[24] Similarly, the North Atlantic Treaty Organization (NATO) adopted the UN's position: on September 12, it declared that if it could be established that the attack was planned outside the US, it would, for the first time in its fifty-two-year history, invoke Article 5 of the NATO Treaty, thus regarding 9/11 as an armed attack not only on the US but also on all NATO members.[25]

However, despite these declarations of support, when the US started its attack on the Taliban regime in Afghanistan – named Operation Enduring Freedom – on October 7, 2001, it did so without an explicit UN mandate (except the empowerment to self-defense according to Article 51 of the UN Charter). Nor was Enduring Freedom a NATO operation. The war in Afghanistan was primarily an American endeavor. Allies such as the UK, Germany, Japan, and France were informed in advance and did contribute some troops and other forms of support, but these were mainly symbolic and the major work was done by the US and its Afghan ally, the "Northern Alliance," a conglomerate of ethnic tribes and warlords that opposed the Taliban regime during the Afghan Civil War. After some weeks of resistance, the regime broke down and troops of the Northern Alliance moved into Kabul on November 17.

This success of the US-led intervention meant a huge blow for al-Qaeda. Hundreds of terrorists were killed or arrested, among them several high-ranking members of the organization. Those who managed to flee presumably took cover somewhere in the region – either in the border area between Pakistan and Afghanistan where bin Laden and al-Zawahiri are supposed to be hiding, or in Pakistan's metropolitan areas where the mastermind of the 9/11 attacks, Khalid Sheikh Mohammed, and other important figures of al-Qaeda were taken into custody. Moreover, the organization's infrastructure in Afghanistan is lost and the operational control of al-Qaeda over the activities of its supporters is supposed to have diminished.

After the ousting of the Taliban, the US government sought international support for its peace-building activities in Afghanistan. In December 2001, a conference on reconstruction and stabilization was held in Germany, as a result of which the UN Security Council established the International Security Assistance Force (ISAF)

whose mandate applied to all of Afghanistan and which was to support the local peace-building efforts. Since August 2003, ISAF was led by NATO, but its mandate was limited to reconstruction, whereas Enduring Freedom, the military campaign against al-Qaeda and Taliban forces in the south of Afghanistan, was an American undertaking.

NATO did, however, play a role in the campaign against terrorism before ISAF was formed. On October 26, 2001, it had begun its naval operation, Active Endeavor, to monitor shipping routes in the eastern Mediterranean. The mission's scope was gradually expanded to cover the whole of the Mediterranean, including the Strait of Gibraltar. Furthermore, as part of Enduring Freedom, planes and ships from Germany, Spain, the UK, and other NATO states patrolled the Horn of Africa, interrupting possible transit routes of al-Qaeda, detecting suspicious shipments, and ensuring the safety of civilian vessels.

Yet, Afghanistan was not the only focus of the American war on terrorism. During the preparations for Enduring Freedom the US stationed troops and set up air bases in Uzbekistan, Tajikistan, and Kyrgyzstan. US troops were also deployed in the Philippines where, from October 2001 onward, US military advisers were stationed. In 2002 and 2003, the Philippine army conducted counterterrorism maneuvers together with US troops in the southern part of the country, apparently pursuing local guerrillas and terrorists with links to al-Qaeda.[26] Moreover, in addition to their official campaigns in Afghanistan and the Philippines, the US also engaged in more or less clandestine operations hunting al-Qaeda members or other suspected terrorists all over the world.[27]

Another aspect of the new approach in dealing with terrorism concerned the handling of individuals who belonged (or were suspected of belonging) to al-Qaeda or were associated with the group. Facing terrorists who were willing to give up their lives and who were able to cause such tremendous damage even to the world's greatest military power, traditional concepts of law enforcement or, for that matter, *jus in bello* itself seemed to need some revision.[28] Thus, a number of governments introduced new domestic laws dealing with terrorism: in the US, for instance, the so-called "Patriot Act" was passed in Congress on October 25, 2001, which considerably increased the rights of the domestic security agencies. Germany, Britain, France, and other countries followed with a tightening of their regulations on domestic security. The US administration also sought ways to deal with those individuals it had arrested during the campaign in Afghanistan. From early 2002 onward, parts of the US naval base in Guantánamo Bay on Cuba were used as detention camps for these prisoners, based on President Bush's military order of November 13, 2001: "Detention, Treatment, and Trial of Certain Non-Citizens in the War Against Terrorism."[29] The US administration refused to give the detainees the status of "prisoners of war," instead labeling them "unlawful combatants" or "enemy combatants" and refusing to allow them access to legal assistance. This usage of vague legal terms and an offshore naval base to hold the suspected terrorists in custody in order to avoid the application of legal procedures that would have been required had they been held on US soil led to widespread criticism both domestically and internationally.[30] In two rulings, one in 2004, the other in 2006, however, the US Supreme Court decided that even in Guantánamo fundamental principles of US and international law were to be applied and that the sentencing of suspected terrorists by military tribunals was illegal. Hence, detainees were to be given the opportunity to challenge the allegations against them before American courts and the legal basis of the Guantánamo camps was put into question. In response to these developments, US intelligence services seem to have moved some of these prisoners to other countries: in November 2005, a *Washington Post* report accused the CIA of having established what was called "black sites," i.e., unofficial prisons, in Thailand, Afghanistan, and a number of eastern European countries.[31] Moreover, it seemed that the CIA was secretly abducting suspected terrorists in countries all over the world and transporting them by plane to these prisons. European countries had, apparently, silently ignored these practices.[32] Asked about allegations of torture in these camps and his position with regard to legislation banning torture,

President Bush felt obliged to assert that while the US administration was "aggressively" protecting American citizens, it did not engage in torture.[33] At the same time, however, Vice-President Cheney was attempting to convince Congress to exempt US intelligence officials from a general ban on torture. Unsurprisingly, the president's assertions lacked credibility.[34]

## A Doctrine of Preventive Warfare

With the unstable situation in Afghanistan, and with the growing criticism of practices at Guantánamo Bay, the US administration in early 2002 began to outline the next steps in its "war on terror." The US possessed, as the National Security Strategy (NSS) would state it some months later, "unprecedented and unequalled strength and influence."[35] President Bush was willing to use this power where and when needed and, if necessary, without allies. An overview of the missions ahead was given in the president's State of the Union address in January 2002, in which he asserted that North Korea, Iran, and Iraq constituted an "axis of evil" that threatened peace and international stability: "By seeking weapons of mass destruction, these regimes pose a grave and growing danger. They could provide these arms to terrorists, giving them the means to match their hatred. They could attack our allies or attempt to blackmail the United States. In any of these cases, the price of indifference would be catastrophic."[36] Furthermore, he vowed that in future, "I will not wait on events, while dangers gather. I will not stand by, as peril draws closer and closer." A few months later, in a speech at West Point in June 2002, he underlined his perception of the threats he foresaw: "The gravest danger to freedom lies at the perilous crossroads of radicalism and technology. When the spread of chemical and biological and nuclear weapons, along with ballistic missiles technology – when that occurs, even weak states and small groups could attain a catastrophic power to strike great nations."[37]

What the president's words meant for US policy was explained in September 2002 in the National Security Strategy of the United States. The NSS concluded that "traditional concepts of deterrence will not work against a terrorist enemy whose avowed tactics are wanton destruction . . . ; whose so-called soldiers seek martyrdom in death and whose most potent protection is statelessness. The overlap between states that sponsor terror and those that pursue WMD compels us to action."[38] If the principle of deterrence, a corner-stone of the security strategy of both the US and NATO throughout the Cold War, no longer applied, the only way to ensure national security was through preemptive action.[39] As the UN Charter forbids all applications of force, except those authorized by the Security Council or those taken in the realm of self-defense against aggression, this new interpretation of the principle of preemption was widely regarded as inconsistent with international law. What indeed was envisioned by the NSS was not a preemptive strike against an enemy that was about to attack (an operation that would have been within the pale of international law), but a preventive war irrespective of the imminence of a threat. Not only would a terrorist attack, i.e., the use of force by non-state actors, be interpreted as an armed attack that would invoke the principle of self-defense, the possibility of a development somewhere in the world *becoming* a serious threat to national security would be enough to allow the use of force.

While the US favored multilateral action, Secretary of Defense Donald Rumsfeld famously explained before meeting his NATO colleagues in December 2001 that "the mission will define the coalition. The coalition will not define the mission."[40] Rumsfeld's statement touched on two points. As the capability gap between European NATO members and the US had been an issue since the war in Kosovo in 1999, Rumsfeld under-scored what had, arguably, been the position of the US administration before 9/11: it did not see much use in an alliance that was physically inca-pable of facing today's security tasks. It seems that the European members of NATO accepted this criticism when it formulated some far-reaching plans to improve its capabilities at a summit meeting in Prague in November 2002. More fun-damental, however, was the second aspect of Rumsfeld's statement. The defense secretary made clear that the role of the US as global leader included the right to use force – regardless of

what the rest of the international community thought.

## Operation Iraqi Freedom

The US, which perceived itself as the preeminent power in the international system, but which also believed that it faced unprecedented threats, turned to Iraq as its next security challenge. From early 2002 until the start of Operation Iraqi Freedom, i.e., the invasion of Iraq in March 2003, the US and its allies (the "coalition of the willing") presented a number of justifications for their attack on Iraq. The argument most forcefully put forward was Iraq's repeated attempts to acquire weapons of mass destruction throughout the 1990s. While the mandate for UN inspections in Iraq was renewed by the UN Security Council in 1999, it was not until the US put considerable pressure on Saddam Hussein that he permitted the UN teams to begin the inspections. The fact that the inspectors found no indication of Iraqi WMD programs was countered by the US with its own intelligence reports, which concluded that Iraq did indeed have such programs which the regime had successfully hidden from the inspectors.[41] But it was not just the WMD problem that mattered. President Bush and British Prime Minister Tony Blair put forward a number of other arguments in favor of a "regime change" in Iraq: Saddam Hussein had been killing his own people and attacking Iraq's neighbors, using chemical weapons against the Kurdish minority in Iraq and against Iran in the 1980s. Hence, Iraq had become a destabilizing factor for the whole Middle East. The US administration in particular argued that it regarded regime change in Iraq as part of a broader initiative to spread democracy and respect for human rights in the Middle East; the disre-gard for these principles that was shown by numerous regimes in the Arab world was, the US argued, the root cause of terrorism.[42]

The US policy on Iraq met strong political opposition. France, Russia, and Germany rejected the US plans and refused to consent to a UN mandate for the US invasion. Instead they, along with numerous other countries, pleaded to give more time to the weapons inspectors. At the same time, high-ranking members of former US administrations or of the British Foreign Office criticized their governments for moving so quickly on the basis of weak intelligence and without either sufficient international support or a long-term plan for the whole region after the invasion.

Thus, when American and British troops invaded Iraq on March 20, 2003, they did so without a clear UN mandate and with very limited international support – either political or material. Nonetheless, in the beginning, Operation Iraqi Freedom seemed to have produced a quick victory and demonstrated that the doctrine of preventive war could be implemented successfully. The great superiority of the British–American coalition forces enabled them to defeat the Iraqi army after a few weeks. As early as May 2003, President Bush declared the "major combat operations" to be over.[43] However, it soon became apparent that the US had grossly underestimated the immediate problems of establishing security and stability in Iraq, as well as the long-term challenges of reconstructing the economy and producing a viable new political order. Since the end of major combat operations Iraq has witnessed an intensive insurgency campaign and has been a hotspot for terrorist activities. Guerrilla and terrorist attacks have claimed thousands of victims among Iraqi civilians, security forces, and foreign troops. By late 2005, more than 2,400 soldiers of the US-led coalition had been killed and over 16,000 wounded. It also became apparent that Iraq had neither been in possession of WMD nor was trying to produce such substances. President Bush's reelection in 2004 indicated that at least the American people forgave the US administration its exaggeration of the Iraqi threat. The international reputation of the US was, however, severely damaged. Facing persistent protests by their respective electorates and repeated terrorist attacks, the "coalition of the willing" dwindled. By January 2006, nine of the thirty-eight countries that had participated in the invasion had withdrawn altogether while others reduced the number of troops they had committed. US military capacity had, apparently, also reached its limit. Despite great efforts, the insurgency campaign in Iraq seemed to continue unrestrained. As Andrew Bacevich pointedly noted: "Thirty years after its defeat in Vietnam, it turns out that

the United States still does not know how to counter a determined guerrilla force."[44]

At the same time, however, the tensions between France and Germany on the one side and the US and Britain on the other began to ease, so that the international political support for the newly formed Iraqi government as well as international help for the reconstruction of the country grew. The UN Security Council agreed on a variety of resolutions supporting the political rebuilding of the country and a stronger UN involvement in Iraq.[45] Additionally, NATO established a mission assisting the new Iraqi government to train military and police personnel in 2004.

These international developments notwithstanding, terrorism was on the rise in the aftermath of the invasion in Iraq. During Operation Iraqi Freedom affiliates of al-Qaeda started to threaten and attack countries that were supporting the US in Iraq and Afghanistan. In Madrid, a terrorist assault on public transport killed 191 people and injured over 1,500 on March 11, 2003. As a reaction, the Socialist Party that won the elections that took place only a few days later withdrew the Spanish troops from Iraq. On July 7, 2005, a terrorist attack on public transport in London claimed fifty-six dead and several hundred injured. However, despite the attack and considerable domestic pressure to withdraw, Prime Minister Blair kept the UK engaged in Iraq. A group calling itself Abu Hafs al-Masri Brigade, which was unknown before the attack in Madrid, claimed responsibility for both attacks. While its relationship with bin Laden's network is unclear, the group was obviously inspired by al-Qaeda's ideology and strategy.

Generally speaking, recruitment has become easier for Islamic fundamentalists in the aftermath of the US invasion, which they portray as another attempt by the "Crusaders" to take over Muslim territory. The apparent inability of the coalition troops to overcome resistance is proclaimed to be a successful jihad, comparable to the campaign against the Soviet occupation of Afghanistan during the 1980s. Moreover, had the non-existence of WMD programs in Iraq not already discredited US policy, the scandals in the military prison of Abu-Ghraib proved to be disastrous for the reputation of the US. Pictures of US guards abusing naked Iraqi prisoners of war by forcing their victims to remain in humiliating positions caused public shock and revulsion all over the world. Especially in Muslim countries, these pictures were taken as proof of the contempt and disrespect the West showed toward Islam.

## Conclusion: Terrorism and International Relations since 9/11

The bombings in London and Madrid and the terrorist attacks in Bali, Morocco, Djerba, Karachi, Istanbul, and elsewhere signified that Islamic terrorism had not been defeated by al-Qaeda's expulsion from Afghanistan. Instead, al-Qaeda was changing its face, transforming itself from a purely terrorist network into a propaganda machine that employed a distinctive form of psychological warfare. Using the concept of "propaganda by deed," al-Qaeda is conducting a global propaganda campaign that aims at spreading its ideology and inspiring potential copycats all over the world. To achieve its ends, the group employs a very sophisticated communications strategy providing images, speeches, and short movie-sequences to international broadcasting networks like al-Jazeera and other television networks that are widely accessible in Muslim countries as well as in Europe and the US. In addition, more drastic messages and images, made for recruitment purposes, are proliferated through the Internet. The intention behind this campaign is to stage a global clash between Islam on the one side and the US and its allies on the other, presenting Osama bin Laden and al-Qaeda as the defenders of Islam. Against this backdrop, the group seeks to radicalize Muslims all over the world and encourage them to emulate al-Qaeda. Meanwhile, this process of "franchising" terrorism seems to have been uncoupled from the person of Osama bin Laden and has developed a momentum of its own: the operations of the al-Masri Brigades underscore this trend.

Thus, many of the newly formed terrorist groups copy al-Qaeda's strategy and tactics while, apparently, operating independently of it. Given the inconspicuousness of these groups, it has become extremely difficult for intelligence services and law enforcement agencies to track them. Even more worrying is that western governments apparently still lack a concept to counter al-Qaeda's propaganda campaign.

If the war on terrorism has brought about some changes for the characteristics of al-Qaeda, what are its ramifications for international relations? First, since 9/11 the international strategic landscape has experienced some modifications. America is no longer concerned about a single power dominating Eurasia. Moreover, countries that, before 9/11, were either of no importance to the Americans or the Europeans or were disregarded because of their unacceptable behavior suddenly moved to the center of attention. Stronger ties were established with countries such as Malaysia, Indonesia, Pakistan, Tajikistan, Uzbekistan, and Kyrgyzstan. Second, 9/11 has had a clear impact on international law as far as terrorism and the *jus ad bellum* is concerned. The support of the Taliban regime for bin Laden legitimized the US intervention in Afghanistan. In future, regimes that support al-Qaeda or other similarly dangerous groups are likely to be condemned by the international community – the UN Security Council, NATO, EU, and so on – and a military attack on them may be deemed legitimate. On the other hand, as became apparent in the international controversy over the legitimacy of the invasion of Iraq, the *jus ad bellum* has not been expanded in terms of preemptive or – to be precise – preventive warfare. That is not to say that an attack on a country producing WMD would never receive UN (or at least EU or NATO) blessing; the case, however, would have to be well made to gain international legitimacy.

Strategic and legal concerns notwithstanding, the question remains whether the US had, by the beginning of the twenty-first century, established itself as the hegemonic international power. Clearly, US foreign policy changed drastically after September 11 and exhibited hegemonic or – as some would rather say – imperial ambitions.[46] For the first time the United States implemented a doctrine of preventive war, ignoring the concerns of its allies and contradicting international law. Instead, President Bush and many Americans believed that US primacy was the defining feature of the world. Thus, when the president was accused of not taking advice from allies in his war on terrorism, he argued that "at some point we may be the only ones left. That's okay with me. We are America."[47]

It is questionable, however, how sustainable this ambition is. The neoconservative faction of foreign policy experts sounds confident that it is. Robert Kagan, for instance, concludes that "the collapse of the Soviet empire led to a fundamental reordering of the international system, and to the current situation in which American global hegemony is the leading factor that shapes the present and, almost certainly, the future."[48] Charles Krauthammer agrees, declaring that "the unipolar moment has become the unipolar era."[49]

At the other end of the political spectrum, Immanuel Wallerstein portrays the US as a power in decline. He argues that, while American military power remains unparalleled, the economic, political, and ideological strength of the US is shrinking. He concludes that today, the US is "a lone superpower that lacks true power, a world leader nobody follows and few respect, and a nation drifting dangerously amidst a global chaos it cannot control. . . . The real question is not whether US hegemony is waning but whether the United States can devise a way to descend gracefully, with minimum damage to the world, and to itself."[50]

The truth might lie somewhere between these two positions. When the US attacked Iraq it was widely regarded as the test case of both the doctrine of preventive war and the hegemonic ambitions of the US. US power, it turned out, failed these tests. Thus, if the National Security Strategy is pursued unilaterally, the US will soon come to the limits of its resources, both military and financial, and it will surely be confronted with an increasing number of political opponents. Such an undertaking is, however, very unlikely. Given the enormous problems in dealing with the situation in Iraq as well as the still fragile state of Afghanistan, another American unilateral intervention – in Iran, for instance – seems implausible. Instead, Europe and the US are, apparently, coordinating their policies once again – as is evident in the case of Iran. In the negotiations over Teheran's nuclear program the EU, especially Germany, France, and the UK, has taken the lead, backed by the US

administration. In the face of the strong rhetoric employed by the current Iranian President Mahmud Ahmadi-Nejad, Europeans and Americans have made determined efforts to include China as well as Russia in their coalition. On the other hand, however, the dispute with Iran highlights the unique position the US occupies in the early twenty-first century. Without US backing, European diplomacy vis-à-vis Teheran certainly would lack leverage. Moreover, in the Middle East, on the Korean peninsula, and in political trouble areas elsewhere, it is always the US that is turned to in seeking a solution. Although an international order without US leadership is unthinkable, the US is not a hegemonic power. Thus, the establishment of an enduring international order requires widespread international cooperation, or at least the cooperation of Europe and the US. Therefore, the hegemonic ambition the Bush administration displayed in the National Security Strategy is likely to prove the least lasting consequence of the terrorist attack of September 11, 2001.

## NOTES

1   For an account of the G-8 summit dealing with the topic during the 1990s, see Douglas Kash, "An International Legislative Approach to 21st-Century Terrorism," in *The Future of Terrorism: Violence in the New Millennium*, ed. Harvey Kushner (Thousand Oaks, CA: Sage, 1998), pp. 163–72.

2   United Nations, *A More Secure World: Our Shared Responsibility. Report of the Secretary High-Level Panel on Threats, Challenges, and Change* (New York: United Nations, 2004), p. 52; Council of the European Union, Council Framework Decision of June 13, 2002 on combating terrorism (2002/475/ JHA) Art. 1; the fact that until December 2005 not all EU member states had ratified this article is noteworthy.

3   Bruce Hoffman, *Inside Terrorism* (New York: Columbia University Press, 1998), p. 31; Christopher Daase, "Terrorismus und Krieg. Zukunftsszenarien politischer Gewalt nach dem 11. September 2001," in *Krieg – Instrument der Politik?*, ed. Rüdiger Voigt (Baden-Baden: Nomos, 2002), p. 367.

4   Hoffman, however, suggests differentiating between "terror" and "terrorism," the former

relating to governmental practices and the latter being reserved for non-state actors. See Hoffman, *Inside Terrorism*, pp. 24–5. Sensible as this distinction might seem, it is not adhered to in practice, as can be seen in the synonymous use of the terms in the aftermath of 9/11.

5 Hoffman, *Inside Terrorism*, pp. 41–4; for a more comprehensive account, see Herfried Münkler, *Gewalt und Ordnung. Das Bild des Krieges im politischen Denken* (Frankfurt am Main: Fischer, 1992), pp. 142–75.

6 Hoffman, *Inside Terrorism*, pp. 17–18.

7 Ibid., pp. 43–4.

8 Walter Laqueur, *The New Terrorism: Fanatics Armed with the Arms of Mass Destruction* (Oxford: Oxford University Press, 1999), p. 6.

9 Ibid., pp. 13–15.

10 Hoffman, *Inside Terrorism*, pp. 69–75.

11 Brian Michael Jenkins, quoted in ibid., p. 198.

12 Bruce Hoffman, "Terrorism Trends and Prospects," in *Countering the New Terrorism*, ed. Ian Lesser et al. (Santa Monica, CA: Rand Project Air Force, 1999), pp. 15–20.

13 A comprehensive and regularly updated overview on that subject is accessible through the database "terrorism knowledge base" compiled by the US-based *National Memorial Institute for the Prevention of Terrorism, www.tkb.org*.

14 Probably the best accounts of al-Qaeda can be found in Rohan Gunaratna, *Inside Al Qaeda: Global Network of Terror* (New York: Berkeley Books, 2003) and Peter Bergen, *Holy War, Inc.: Inside the Secret World of Osama Bin Laden* (New York: Free Press, 2001). The following paragraphs rely on these books.

15 Sudan was targeted because the Islamic regime in Khartoum had established friendly relations with bin Laden during the 1990s. Moreover, from 1992 when bin Laden was expelled from Saudi Arabia until his return to Afghanistan in 1996, Khartoum had been the home of bin Laden.

16 Seymour M. Hersh, "Manhunt: The Bush Administration's New Strategy in the War Against Terrorism," *The New Yorker*, December 16, 2002.

17 A transcript of the interview can be found at www.pbs.org/wgbh/pages/frontline/shows/binladen/who/edicts.html. Accessed February, 20, 2006.

18 Michael Bauer, *Terrorismus – Bedrohungsszenarien und Abwehrstrategien* (Munich: Hanns-Seidel Foundation, 2002), pp. 9–24.

19 Statement by the president in his Address to the Nation, Washington, September 11, 2001.

20 As already mentioned, George W. Bush's predecessor, William J. Clinton, had interpreted the bombings of the US embassies in Kenya and Tanzania in 1998 as acts of war and thought it appropriate to use military means to retaliate.

21 Statement by the president in his Address to the Nation, Washington, September 11, 2001.

22 US Congress H.J.Res. 64 Joint Resolution, September 14, 2001.

23 Magne Frostad, *Jus in bello after September 11, 2001* (Baden-Baden: Nomos, 2005), pp. 81–6.

24 Extraordinary Council Meeting, Brussels, September 21, 2001.

25 Statement by the North Atlantic Council Press Release 2001 (124), September 12, 2001; the actual confirmation of the invocation of Article 5 followed on October 2, 2001.

26 A detailed account of al-Qaeda's network in Southeast Asia can be found in Zachary Abuza, "Tentacles of Terror: Al Qaeda's Southeast Asian Network," *Contemporary Southeast Asia* 24 (2002): 427–65.

27 See, for instance, the before-mentioned operation in Yemen: Hersh, "Manhunt."

28 A detailed account of the developments regarding international law, especially *jus ad bellum* and *jus in bello*, can be found in Frostad, *Jus in bello*.

29 "President Issues Military Order: Detention, Treatment, and Trial of Certain Non-Citizens in the War Against Terrorism," Washington, November 13, 2001.

30 The Council of Europe, for instance, concluded that the "circumstances surrounding detentions by the United States at Guantánamo Bay show unlawfulness and inconsistency with the rule of law." Parliamentary Assembly of the Council of Europe, Lawfulness of Detentions by the United States in Guantánamo Bay (Resolution 1433), Strasbourg, April, 25, 2005.

31 Diana Priest, "CIA Holds Terror Suspects in Secret Prisons," *Washington Post*, November 2, 2005.

32 See, for instance, the report by Dick Marty on that subject: "Alleged Secret Detentions in Council of Europe Member States," Report to the Parliamentary Assembly of the Council of Europe, Strasbourg, January 22, 2006.

33 "President Bush Meets with President Torrijos of Panama," November 7, 2005, transcript of the press conference, www.whitehouse.gov/news/releases/2005/11/20051107.html.

34 "Torture: How to Lose Friends and Alienate People," *The Economist*, November 12, 2005.

35  "The National Security Strategy of the United States of America," Washington, September 2002, p. 1, www.whitehouse.gov/nsc/nss.pdf.

36  "President Delivers State of the Union Address," Washington, January 29, 2002.

37  "President Bush Delivers Graduation Speech at West Point," June 1, 2002.

38  National Security Strategy of the United States, p. 15.

39  Ibid.

40  Cited by Jim Garamone, "NATO Must Address Asymmetric Threats," December 18, 2001, www.defenselink.mil/news/Dec2001/n12182001_200112181.html.

41  Most famous in this regard was Secretary of State Colin Powell's address to the UN Security Council on February 3, 2003; transcript accessible at www.whitehouse.gov/news/releases/2003/02/20030205–1.html.

42  See, for instance, Secretary of State Condoleezza Rice's statement on the occasion of Princeton University's Celebration of the 75th Anniversary of the Woodrow Wilson School of Public and International Affairs, Princeton University, September 30, 2005; transcript accessible at www.state.gov/secretary/rm/2005/54176.html.

43  "President Bush Announces Major Combat Operations in Iraq Have Ended," May 1, 2003; transcript accessible at www.whitehouse.gov/news/releases/2003/05/20030501–15.html.

44  Andrew J. Bacevich, "Requiem for the Bush Doctrine," *Current History* 104 (2005): 413.

45  E.g., UN-SC Resolution 1483, May 22, 2003; UN-SC Resolution 1500, August 14, 2003; UN-SC Resolution 1511, October 16, 2003.

46  Michael Mann, for example, speaks of an *Incoherent Empire* (London and New York: Verso, 2003).

47  Quoted in Bob Woodward, *Bush at War* (New York: Simon & Schuster, 2002), p. 81.

48  Robert Kagan, "One Year After: A Grand Strategy for the West?" *Survival* 44 (2002–3): 135.

49  Charles Krauthammer, "The Unipolar Moment Revisited," *The National Interest* 70 (2003): 17.

50  Immanuel Wallerstein, "The Eagle Has Crash Landed," *Foreign Policy* 131 (2002): 60–8; pp. 63, 68.

## GUIDE TO FURTHER READING

Andrew Bacevich, "Requiem for the Bush Doctrine," *Current History* 104 (2005). Questions the sustainability of the idea of preventive military engagement after the US experience in Iraq.

Peter Bergen, *Holy War, Inc.: Inside the Secret World of Osama Bin Laden* (New York: Free Press, 2001). Provides a comprehensive overview of the development of al-Qaeda.

Philip Gordon, "NATO after September 11," *Survival* 43/4 (2001–2). Discusses the prospects of NATO as an international security institution in the post-9/11 era.

John Gray, *Al Qaeda and What it Means to be Modern* (London: Faber & Faber, 2003). Offers a sociological approach relating al-Qaeda's strategy and organizational design to the principles of modernity.

Rohan Gunaratna, *Inside Al Qaeda: Global Network of Terror* (New York: Berkeley Books, 2003). Although partly contended, probably the most detailed account of al-Qaeda.

Bruce Hoffman, *Inside Terrorism* (New York: Columbia University Press, 1998). Provides a comprehensive introduction to the study of terrorism – highly recommended.

Jolyon Howorth, "France, Britain and the Euro-Atlantic Crisis," *Survival* 45/4 (2003–4). Discusses the dispute between Paris and London over the war in Iraq and its impact on European integration and the transatlantic partnership.

Samuel Huntington, *The Clash of Civilizations and the Remaking of World Order* (New York: Simon & Schuster, 1996). A provocative and widely criticized book on cultural difference as a source of conflict.

Mark Juergensmeyer, *Terror in the Mind of God* (Berkeley, CA: University of California Press, 2000). Gives an overview on the global rise of terrorism misusing religion as justification.

Robert Kagan, "Power and Weakness," *Policy Review* 113 (2002). Points out the neoconservative perspective on the transatlantic relationship in the early twenty-first century.

Charles Krauthammer, "The Unipolar Moment Revisited," *The National Interest* 70 (2003). Explains the neoconservative concept of unipolarity after September 11.

Harvey Kushner, ed., *The Future of Terrorism: Violence in the New Millennium* (Thousand Oaks, CA: Sage, 1998). Contains an interesting collection of essays on Christian and Islamic terrorism, possible future developments, and countermeasures.

Walter Laqueur, *The New Terrorism: Fanatics Armed with the Arms of Mass Destruction* (Oxford: Oxford University Press, 1999). Offers a well-informed overview on terrorism.

Ian Lesser et al., eds., *Countering the New Terrorism* (Santa Monica, CA: Rand Project Air Force, 1999).

Focuses on the characteristics of terrorism in the 1990s.

Michael Mann, *Incoherent Empire* (London and New York: Verso, 2003). Argues that American foreign policy rests too much on military force and lacks ideological appeal as well as an economic base.

Herfried Münkler, *The New Wars* (London: Polity Press, 2004). Deals with the changing nature of warfare in the post-Cold War era. An interesting contribution not just on terrorism but also on civil wars and humanitarian interventions.

Jessica Stern, *The Ultimate Terrorists* (Cambridge, MA: Harvard University Press, 1999). Offers a broader discussion on terrorism and weapons of mass destruction.

Stephen Walt, "Beyond Bin Laden: Reshaping US Foreign Policy," *International Security* 26 (2001–2). On the transformation of the US foreign policy agenda after 9/11.

# Bibliography

Abramson, Albert, *The History of Television, 1942–2000* (Jefferson, NC: McFarland & Co., 2003).

Aburish, Said K., *Nasser: The Last Arab* (New York: Thomas Dunne, 2004).

Abuza, Zachary, "Tentacles of Terror: Al Qaeda's Southeast Asian Network," *Contemporary Southeast Asia* 24 (2002): 427–65.

Adamthwaite, Anthony, *France and the Coming of the Second World War* (London: Frank Cass, 1977).

Adamthwaite, Anthony, *Grandeur and Misery: France's Bid for Power in Europe* (London: Arnold, 1995).

Afflerbach, Holger, *Der Dreibund* (Vienna: Böhlau, 2002).

Alain, J.-C., *Agadir 1911: Une crise impérialiste en Europe pour la conquête de Maroc* (Paris: Université de Paris, 1972).

Alanbrooke, Field Marshal Lord, *War Diaries, 1939–1945*, ed. Alex Danchev and Daniel Todman (Berkeley and Los Angeles: University of California Press, 2001).

Albertini, Luigi, *The Origins of the War of 1914*, trans. and ed. Isabella M. Massey, 3 vols. (London: Oxford University Press, 1952–7).

Albright, Madeleine, *Madam Secretary: A Memoir* (New York: Miramax Books, 2003).

Aldrich, Richard, *The Key to the South: Britain, the United States and Thailand during the Approach of the Pacific War* (Oxford: Oxford University Press, 1993).

Allen, W. E. D., and Paul Muratoff, *Caucasian Battlefields: A History of the War on the Turco-Caucasian Border, 1828–1921* (Cambridge: Cambridge University Press, 1953).

Allison, Roy, *The Soviet Union and the Strategy of Non-Alignment in the Third World* (Cambridge: Cambridge University Press, 1989).

Amin, Samir, *Accumulation on a World Scale: A Critique of the Theory of Underdevelopment* (New York: Monthly Review Press, 1974).

Amin, Shahid, "Gandhi as Mahatma: Gorakhpur District, Eastern UP, 1921–2," in *Subaltern Studies III*, ed. Ranajit Guha (Oxford: Oxford University Press, 1984), pp. 1–61.

Anderson, Benedict, *Imagined Communities: Reflections on the Origin and Spread of Nationalism* (London: Verso, 1983).

Anderson, E. N., *The First Moroccan Crisis, 1904–1906* (Chicago: University of Chicago Press, 1930).

Anderson, Ross, *The Forgotten Front: The East African Campaign, 1914–1918* (Stroud: Tempus, 2004).

Andrew, Christopher M., *Théophile Delcassé and the Making of the Entente Cordiale, 1898–1905* (London: Macmillan, 1968).

Andrew, Christopher M., and A. S. Kanya Forster, *France Overseas: The Great War and the Climax of French Imperial Expansion* (London: Thames & Hudson, 1981).

Andrew, Christopher M., and Vasili Mitrokhin, *The KGB and the World* (London: Penguin, 2005).

Angelow, Jürgen, *Kalkül und Prestige. Der Zweibund am Vorabend des Ersten Weltkrieges* (Cologne: Böhlau, 2000).

Ansprenger, F., *The Dissolution of the Colonial Empires* (London: Routledge, 1989).

Antlöv, Hans, and Stein Tonnesson, eds., *Imperial Policy and Southeast Asian Nationalism 1930–1957* (Richmond: Curzon Press, 1995).

Antonius, George, *The Arab Awakening: The Story of the Arab National Movement* (London: Hamish Hamilton, 1938).

Armstrong, David, *The Rise of the International Organization: A Short History* (New York: St. Martin's, 1982).

Armstrong, David, "From International Community to International Organization?" *Commonwealth and Comparative Politics* 39 (2001): 31–50.

Armstrong, David, Lorna Lloyd, and John Redmond, *International Organization in World Politics* (Basingstoke: Palgrave Macmillan, 3rd edn, 2004).

Ash, Timothy Garton, *In Europe's Name: Germany and the Divided Continent* (New York: Random House, 1993).

Bacevich, Andrew J., *American Empire: The Realities and Consequences of US Diplomacy* (Cambridge, MA: Harvard University Press, 2002).

Bacevich, Andrew J., "Requiem for the Bush Doctrine," *Current History* 104 (2005): 411–17.

Bailey, Thomas A., and Paul B. Ryan, *Hitler vs. Roosevelt: The Undeclared Naval War* (New York: Free Press, 1979).

Baillou, Jean, ed., *Les Affaires étrangères et le corps diplomatique français. Histoire de l'administration française*, vol. 2, *1870–1980* (Paris: CNRS, 1984).

Baker, James A., *The Politics of Diplomacy: Revolution, War and Peace, 1989–1992* (New York: G. P. Putnam's Sons, 1995).

Bariety, Jacques, *Les Relations franco-allemandes après la première guerre mondiale, 10 novembre 1918–10 janvier 1925, de l'exécution à la négociation* (Paris: Publications de la Sorbonne, 1977).

Barker, A. J., *The Neglected War: Mesopotamia, 1914–1918* (London: Faber & Faber, 1967).

Barnes, William, and John Heath Morgan, *The Foreign Service of the United States: Origins, Development, and Functions* (Washington, DC: Department of State, 1961).

Barnhart, Michael A., *Japan Prepares for Total War: The Search for Economic Security, 1919–1941* (Ithaca, NY: Cornell University Press, 1987).

Barnoin, Barbara, and Yu Changgen, *Chinese Foreign Policy During the Cultural Revolution* (London and New York: Kegan Paul International, 1998).

Barnouw, Erik, *Tube of Plenty: The Evolution of American Television* (New York: Oxford University Press, 1992).

Barros, James, *The Aaland Islands Question: Its Settlement by the League of Nations* (New Haven, CT: Yale University Press, 1968).

Barros, James, *The League of Nations and the Great Powers: The Greek–Bulgarian Incident, 1925* (Oxford: Oxford University Press, 1970).

Barros, James, *Office Without Power: Secretary-General Sir Eric Drummond, 1919–1923* (Oxford: Oxford University Press, 1979).

Bauer, Michael, *Terrorismus – Bedrohungsszenarien und Abwehrstrategien* (Munich: Hanns-Seidel Foundation, 2002).

Bayly, C. A., *The Birth of the Modern World, 1780–1914* (Oxford: Blackwell, 2004).

Beasley, W. G., *Japanese Imperialism, 1894–1945* (Oxford: Oxford University Press, 1987).

Beaubois, Henry, *Airships* (New York: Two Continents, 1976).

Beckett, Ian, *The Great War, 1914–1918* (Harlow: Pearson, 2001).

Bell, Chris, *The Royal Navy, Seapower and Strategy Between the Wars* (London: Palgrave Macmillan, 2000).

Bell, P. M. H., *The Origins of the Second World War in Europe* (London: Longman, 2nd edn, 1997).

Bellavita, Emilio, *La battaglia di Adua* (Genoa: Flli. Melita, 1988).

Bender, Marylin, *The Chosen Instrument* (New York: Simon & Schuster, 1982).

Benner, E., *Really Existing Nationalisms: A Post-Communist View from Marx and Engels* (Oxford: Clarendon Press, 1995).

Bennett, Edward M., *Franklin D. Roosevelt and the Search for Security: American–Soviet Relations 1939–1945* (Wilmington, DE: Scholarly Resources, 1990).

Bennett, Edward W., *Germany and the Diplomacy of the Financial Crisis, 1931* (Cambridge, MA: Harvard University Press, 1962).

Bentley, Jerry H., and Herbert F. Ziegler, *Traditions and Encounters: A Global Perspective on the Past*, vol. 2, *From 1500 to the Present* (Toronto: McGraw-Hill, 2000).

Bergen, Peter, *Holy War, Inc.: Inside the Secret World of Osama Bin Laden* (New York: Free Press, 2001).

Berger, M., *The Battle for Asia: From Decolonization to Globalization* (London: Routledge, 2004).

Berghahn, V. R., *Germany and the Approach of War in 1914* (Basingstoke and New York: Macmillan, 2nd edn, 1993).

Bernard, Philippe, *La Fin d'un monde, 1914–1929* (Paris: Editions du Seuil, 1975).

Beschloss, Michael R., and S. Talbott, *At the Highest Levels: The Inside Story of the End of the Cold War* (London: Warner, 1994).

Best, Anthony, *Britain, Japan and Pearl Harbor: Avoiding War in East Asia, 1936–1941* (London and New York: Palgrave Macmillan, 1995).

Best, Anthony, *British Intelligence and the Japanese Challenge in Asia, 1914–1941* (Basingstoke and New York: Palgrave Macmillan, 2002).

Bilstein, Roger, *Flight in America: From the Wrights to the Astronauts* (Baltimore: Johns Hopkins University Press, 2001).

Birmingham, David, *Nkrumah: Father of African Nationalism* (Athens, OH: Ohio University Press, 1998).

Bishop, Donald G., *The Administration of British Foreign Relations* (Syracuse, NY: Syracuse University Press, 1961).

Blight, James G., and Janet M. Lang, eds., *The Fog of War: Lessons from the Life of Robert S. McNamara* (London: Rowman & Littlefield, 2005).

Blouet, Brian, ed., *Mackinder and the Defense of the West* (New York: Frank Cass, 2005).

Bluth, Christoph, "Strategic Nuclear Weapons and US–Russian Relations: From Confrontation to Co-operative Denuclearization?" *Contemporary Security Policy* 15 (1994): 80–108.

Bobilev, P. N., "Tochku v diskussii stavit; rano. K voprosu o planirovanii v General'nom shtabe RKKA vozmozhnoi voini s Germaniei v 1940–1941 godakh," *Otechestvennaia istoriia* 1 (2000): 41–64.

Borg, Dorothy, *The United States and the Far Eastern Crisis of 1933–1938: From the Manchurian Incident Through the Initial Stage of the Undeclared Sino-Japanese War* (Cambridge, MA: Harvard University Press, 1964).

Borg, Dorothy, and Okamoto Shumpei, eds., *Pearl Harbor as History, 1931–1941* (New York: Columbia University Press, 1973).

Bosworth, R. J. B., *Italy and the Approach of the First World War* (London: Macmillan, 1983).

Bosworth, R. J. B., *Mussolini* (London: Arnold, 2002).

Bosworth, R. J. B., *Mussolini's Italy* (London: Allen Lane, 2005).

Boutros-Ghali, Boutros, *An Agenda for Peace: Preventive Diplomacy, Peacemaking and Peace-Keeping* (New York: United Nations, 1992).

Boyce, Robert, *British Capitalism at the Crossroads, 1919–1932: A Study in Politics, Economics and International Relations* (Cambridge: Cambridge University Press, 1987).

Boyce, Robert, "Creating the Myth of Consensus: Public Opinion and Britain's Return to the Gold Standard in 1925," in *Money and Power: Essays in Honour of L. S. Pressnell*, ed. P. L. Cottrell and D. E. Moggridge (London: Macmillan, 1987), pp. 173–98.

Boyce, Robert, "Wall Street and the Spectre of the 'Money Power' in Small-Town America before and after the Crash of 1929," in *Etats de New York*, ed. Philippe Romanski (Rouen: Publications de l'Université de Rouen, 2000), pp. 19–31.

Boyce, Robert, and Joseph A. Maiolo, eds., *The Origins of World War Two: The Debate Continues* (Basingstoke: Palgrave Macmillan, 2003).

Boyle, Andrew, *Montagu Norman: A Biography* (London: Cassell, 1967).

Bozo, Frédéric, "Détente versus Alliance: France, the United States and the Politics of the Harmel Report (1964–1968)," *Contemporary European History* 7 (1998): 343–60.

Brands, H. W., "Woodrow Wilson and the Irony of Fate," *Diplomatic History* 28 (2004): 503–12.

Braudel, Fernand, *Afterthoughts on Material Civilization and Capitalism* (Baltimore: Johns Hopkins University Press, 1979).

Brendon, Piers, *The Dark Valley, a Panorama of the 1930s* (New York: Knopf, 2000).

Bridge, F. R., *From Sadowa to Sarajevo: The Foreign Policy of Austria-Hungary, 1866–1914* (Boston: Routledge & Kegan Paul, 1972).

Bridge, F. R., *Great Britain and Austria-Hungary 1906–14* (London: Weidenfeld & Nicolson, 1972).

Bridge, F. R., "Izvolsky, Aehrenthal, and the End of the Austro-Russian Entente, 1906–8," *Mitteilungen des Österreichischen Staatsarchivs* 29 (1976): 315–62.

Brinkley, Douglas, and David Facey-Crowther, eds., *The Atlantic Charter* (New York: St. Martin's, 1994).

Brooks, Stephen G., and William C. Wohlforth, "Economic Constraints and the End of the Cold War," in *Cold War Endgame*, ed. William C. Wohlforth (University Park, PA: Pennsylvania State University Press, 2003), pp. 273–309.

Brown, Archie, *The Gorbachev Factor* (Oxford: Oxford University Press, 1996).

Brown, Judith, *Nehru: A Political Life* (New Haven, CT: Yale University Press, 2003).

Brown, Judith M., and William Roger Louis, eds., *The Oxford History of the British Empire*, vol. 4, *The Twentieth Century* (Oxford: Oxford University Press, 1999).

Bucholz, Arden, *Moltke, Schlieffen, and Prussian War Planning* (New York: Berg, 1991).

Bullock, Alan, *Hitler and Stalin: Parallel Lives* (London: HarperCollins, 1991).

Burns, James MacGregor, *Roosevelt: The Soldier of Freedom* (New York: Harcourt Brace Jovanovich, 1970).

Busch, Briton Cooper, *Britain, India and the Arabs, 1914–1921* (Los Angeles: University of California Press, 1971).

Bush, George, and Brent Scowcroft, *A World Transformed* (New York: Random House, 1998).

Bussière, Eric, *La France, la Belgique et l'organisation économique de l'Europe 1918–1935* (Paris: Comité pour l'histoire économique et financière, Ministère des Finances, 1992).

Butow, Robert J. C., *Tojo and the Coming of the War* (Princeton, NJ: Princeton University Press, 1961).

Buzzanco, R., *Vietnam and the Transformation of American Life* (Oxford: Blackwell, 1999).

Byrne, Malcolm, and Vojtech Mastny, eds., *A Cardboard Castle? An Inside History of the Warsaw Pact, 1955–1991* (New York: Central European University Press, 2005).

Cable, James, *The Geneva Conference of 1954 on Indochina* (London: Macmillan, 1986).

Calder, Kenneth, *Britain and the Origins of the New Europe 1914–1918* (Cambridge: Cambridge University Press, 1976).

Callahan, Raymond, *Churchill: Retreat from Empire* (Wilmington, DE: Scholarly Resources, 1984).

Carley, M. J., "Behind Stalin's Moustache: Pragmatism in Early Soviet Foreign Policy, 1917–1941," *Diplomacy and Statecraft* 12 (2001): 159–74.

Carlton, David, *Churchill and the Soviet Union* (Manchester: Manchester University Press, 2000).

Cassels, Alan, *Ideology and International Relations in the Modern World* (London and New York: Routledge, 1996).

Cassels, Alan, "Ideology," in *The Origins of World War Two: The Debate Continues*, ed. Robert Boyce and Joseph Maiolo (Basingstoke: Palgrave Macmillan, 2003).

Cecil, Viscount, *A Great Experiment* (London: Jonathan Cape, 1941).

Chandler, Lester V., *American Monetary Policy, 1928–1941* (New York: Harper & Row, 1971).

Chapman, J. W. M., "Imperial Japanese Navy and the North–South Dilemma," in *Barbarossa*, ed. John Erickson and David N. Dilks (Edinburgh: Edinburgh University Press, 1984).

Charmley, John, *Chamberlain and the Lost Peace* (Basingstoke: Macmillan, 1989).

Chatterjee, Partha, *Nationalist Thought and the Colonial World: A Derivative Discourse?* (London: Zed Books, 1986).

Chatterjee, Partha, *The Nation and Its Fragments: Colonial and Postcolonial Histories* (Princeton, NJ: Princeton University Press, 1993).

Chen Jian, *Mao's China and the Cold War* (Chapel Hill, NC: University of North Carolina Press, 2001).

Chernyaev, Anatoly, *My Six Years with Gorbachev* (University Park, PA: Pennsylvania University Press, 2000).

Chevannes, B., *Rastafari: Roots and Ideology* (Syracuse, NY: Syracuse University Press, 1994).

Christie, C., *A Modern History of Southeast Asia: Decolonization, Nationalism and Separatism* (London: Tauris, 1996).

Christopher, Warren, *In the Stream of History: Shaping Foreign Policy in a New Era* (Stanford, CA: Stanford University Press, 1998).

Chung, Ong Chit, *Operation Matador: Britain's War Plans Against the Japanese, 1918–1941* (Singapore: Times Academic Press, 1997).

Churchill, Winston, *The Second World War*, 6 vols. (Boston: Houghton Mifflin, 1948–53).

Clad, J., "Regionalism in Southeast Asia: A Bridge Too Far?" *Southeast Asian Affairs 1997* (Singapore: ISES, 1997), pp. 3–14.

Clarence-Smith, Gervase, *The Third Portuguese Empire, 1825–1975: A Study in Economic Imperialism* (Manchester: Manchester University Press, 1985).

Clark, Ian, *Globalization and Fragmentation: International Relations in the Twentieth Century* (New York: Oxford University Press, 1997).

Clark, Wesley K., *Waging Modern War: Bosnia, Kosovo, and the Future of Combat* (New York: Public Affairs, 2001).

Clarke, Peter, *Hope and Glory: Britain 1900–1990* (London: Penguin, 1996).

Clarke, Richard A., *Against All Enemies: Inside America's War on Terror* (New York: Free Press, 2004).

Claude, Jr., Inis L., *Swords into Plowshares: The Problems and Progress of International Organization* (New York: Random House, 1956).

Clavin, Patricia, *The Failure of Economic Diplomacy: Britain, Germany, France and the United States, 1931–1936* (London: Palgrave Macmillan, 1996).

Clavin, Patricia, "Defining Transnationalism," *Contemporary European History* 14 (2005): 421–39.

Clifford, J. Garry, and Samuel R. Spencer, Jr., *The First Peacetime Draft* (Lawrence, KS: University Press of Kansas, 1986).

Clinton, Bill, *My Life* (New York: Alfred A. Knopf, 2004).

Cocks, J., *Passion and Paradox: Intellectuals Confront the National Question* (Princeton, NJ: Princeton University Press, 2002).

Cohen, Warren I., ed., *Pacific Passage: The Study of American–East Asian Relations on the Eve of the Twenty-First Century* (New York: Columbia University Press, 1996).

Cohen, Warren I., *America's Failing Empire: US Foreign Relations since the Cold War* (Malden, MA: Blackwell, 2005).

Coll, Steve, *Ghost Wars: The Secret History of the CIA, Afghanistan, and bin Laden, from the Soviet Invasion to September 10, 2001* (New York: Penguin, 2004).

Conroy, Hilary, and Harry Wray, eds., *Pearl Harbor Reexamined: Prologue to the Pacific War* (Honolulu, HI: University of Hawaii Press, 1990).

Coogan, J. W., *The End of Neutrality: The United States, Britain and Maritime Rights, 1899–1915* (Ithaca, NY: Cornell University Press, 1981).

Coogan, J. W., and P. F. Coogan, "The British Cabinet and the Anglo-French Staff Talks, 1905–1914: Who Knew What and When Did He Know It?" *Journal of British Studies* 24 (1985): 110–31.

Cook, Chris, and John Paxton, *European Political Facts, 1900–1996* (Basingstoke: Macmillan, 4th edn, 1998).

Cooper, Matthew, *The German Air Force, 1933–1945* (London: Jane's, 1981).

Corn, Joseph, *The Winged Gospel* (New York: Oxford University Press, 1983).

Cornwall, Mark, "Serbia," in *Decisions for War, 1914*, ed. Keith Wilson (New York: St. Martin's, 1995).

Cortazzi, Sir Hugh, and Gordon Daniels, eds., *Britain and Japan, 1859–1991: Themes and Personalities* (London and New York: Routledge, 1991).

Costigliola, Frank, *Awkward Dominion, 1919–1933* (Ithaca, NY: Cornell University Press, 1984).

Cowan, Ruth Schwartz, *A Social History of American Technology* (New York: Oxford University Press, 1997).

Cowling, Maurice, *The Impact of Hitler* (Cambridge: Cambridge University Press, 1975).

Cox, Howard, Huang Biao, and Stuart Metcalfe, "Compradors, Firm Architecture and the 'Reinvention' of British Trading Companies: John Swire & Sons' Operations in Early Twentieth-Century China," *Business History* 45 (2003): 15–34.

Crampton, R. J., *The Hollow Detente: Anglo-German Relations in the Balkans 1911–1914* (London: George Prior, 1979).

Crampton, R. J., *Eastern Europe in the Twentieth Century and After* (London: Routledge, 1997).

Crockatt, Richard, *The Fifty Years War: The United States and the Soviet Union in World Politics, 1941–1991* (London: Routledge, 1996).

Crockatt, Richard, *America Embattled: September 11, Anti-Americanism and the Global Order* (London: Routledge, 2003).

Crosby, Gerda Richards, *Disarmament and Peace in British Politics, 1914–1919* (Cambridge, MA: Harvard University Press, 1957).

Crowder, Michael, "The First World War and its Consequences," in *General History of Africa*, vol. 7, *Africa Under Colonial Domination 1880–1935*, ed. A. Adu Boahen (London: Heinemann, 1985).

Crozier, Andrew J., *Appeasement and Germany's Last Bid for Colonies* (Basingstoke: Macmillan, 1988).

Crozier, Andrew J., *The Causes of the Second World War* (Oxford: Blackwell, 1997).

d'Abernon, Lord, *An Ambassador of Peace: Lord d'Abernon's Diary*, vol. 2 (London: Hodder & Stoughton, 1929).

d'Ombrain, Nicholas, *War Machinery and High Policy: Defence Administration in Peacetime Britain 1902–1914* (Oxford: Oxford University Press, 1973).

Daase, Christopher, "Terrorismus und Krieg. Zukunftsszenarien politischer Gewalt nach dem 11. September 2001," in *Krieg – Instrument der Politik?*, ed. Rüdiger Voigt (Baden-Baden: Nomos, 2002), pp. 365–89.

Dallek, Robert, *Franklin D. Roosevelt and American Foreign Policy, 1932–1945* (New York: Oxford University Press, 1979).

Daniels, George, and Mark Rose, eds., *Energy and Transport* (Beverly Hills, CA: Sage, 1982).

Darwin, John, *Britain, Egypt and the Middle East* (New York: St. Martin's, 1981).

Darwin, John, *Britain and Decolonization: The Retreat from Empire in the Post-War World* (Basingstoke: Penguin, 1988).

Darwin, John, *The End of the British Empire: The Historical Debate* (Oxford: Blackwell, 1991).

Davenport-Hines, R. P. T., and Geoffrey Jones, *British Business in Asia since 1860* (Cambridge: Cambridge University Press, 1989).

Davidson, Eugene, *The Trial of the Germans* (Columbia, MO: University of Missouri Press, 1966).

Davies, R. G., and Philip Birtles, *De Havilland Comet* (McLean, VA: Airlife Publishing, 1999).

Davis, Calvin, *The United States and the Second Hague Peace Conference: American Diplomacy and International Organization, 1899–1914* (Durham, NC: Duke University Press, 1975).

Davis, Donald E., and Eugene P. Trani, *The First Cold War: The Legacy of Woodrow Wilson in US–Soviet Relations* (Columbia, MO: University of Missouri Press, 2002).

Davis, Richard, *Anglo-French Relations before the Second World War: Appeasement and Crisis* (Basingstoke: Palgrave, 2001).

Dayer, Roberta A., *Bankers and Diplomats in China, 1917–1925* (London and Portland, OR: Frank Cass, 1981).

De Felice, Renzo, *Mussolini il Duce: I. Gli anni del consenso 1929–1936* (Turin: Einaudi, 1974).

De Grazia, Victoria, *How Fascism Ruled Women, Italy 1922–1945* (Berkeley, CA: University of California Press, 1992).

Dehio, Ludwig, *Germany and World Politics in the Twentieth Century* (London, English trans., 1959).

Deighton, Anne, and Alan Milward, eds., *Widening, Deepening and Acceleration: The European Economic*

Community 1957–1963 (Baden-Baden: Nomos, 1999).

Del Boca, Angelo, ed., *Le guerre coloniali del fascismo* (Bari: Laterza, 1991).

Del Boca, Angelo, *Gli italiani in Africa orientale, II. La conquista dell'Impero* (Milan: Mondadori, 1992).

Del Boca, Angelo, "L'impero," in *I luoghi della memoria, simboli e miti dell'Italia unita*, ed. Mario Isnenghi (Rome: Laterza, 1996).

Dell, R., *The Geneva Racket 1920–1939* (London: Robert Hale, 1941).

Dempster, Derek, *The Tale of the Comet* (New York: McKay, 1958).

Deutscher, Isaac, *The Non-Jewish Jew and Other Essays* (New York: Oxford University Press, 1968).

di Nolfo, Ennio, ed., *Power in Europe? II. Great Britain, France, Germany and Italy and the Origins of the EEC, 1952–57* (Berlin: Walter de Gruyter, 1992).

Divine, Robert A., *Perpetual War for Perpetual Peace* (College Station, TX: Texas A&M University Press, 2000).

Djilas, Milovan, *Tito: The Story from Inside* (London: Phoenix Press, 2001).

Dobrynin, Anatoly, *In Confidence: Moscow's Ambassador to America's Six Cold War Presidents* (New York: Random House, 1995).

Dockrill, Michael J., and J. Douglas Goold, *Peace Without Promise: Britain and the Paris Peace Conference, 1919–23* (London: Batsford, 1981).

Dockrill, Saki Ruth, *Britain's Policy for West German Rearmament, 1950–1955* (Cambridge: Cambridge University Press, 1991).

Dockrill, Saki Ruth, *Eisenhower's New Look National Security Policy, 1953–1961* (Basingstoke: Macmillan, 1996).

Dockrill, Saki Ruth, *Britain's Retreat from East of Suez: The Choice between Europe and the World?* (Basingstoke: Palgrave Macmillan, 2002).

Dockrill, Saki Ruth, *The End of the Cold War Era: The Transformation of the Global Security Order* (London: Hodder Arnold, 2005).

Dockrill, Saki Ruth, and Geraint Hughes, eds., *Palgrave Advances in Cold War History* (Basingstoke: Palgrave Macmillan, 2006).

Doenecke, Justus D., *Storm on the Horizon: The Challenge to American Intervention, 1939–1941* (Lanham, MD: Rowman & Littlefield, 2000).

Dommen, Arthur J., *The Indochinese Experience of the French and the Americans* (Bloomington, IN: Indiana University Press, 2001).

Duggan, Christopher, "Francesco Crispi and Italy's Pursuit of War against France, 1887–9," *Australian Journal of Politics and History* 50 (2004): 315–29.

Duiker, W., *Sacred War: Nationalism and Revolution in a Divided Vietnam* (New York: McGraw-Hill, 1995).

Duiker, W., *Ho Chi Minh: A Life* (New York: Hyperion, 2000).

Dülffer, Jost, Martin Kröger, and Rolf-Harald Wippich, *Vermiedene Kriege. Deeskalation von Konflikten der Grossmächte zwischen Krimkrieg und Erstem Weltkrieg (1856–1914)* (Munich: Oldenbourg, 1997).

Dutton, David, *The Politics of Diplomacy: Britain and France in the Balkans in the First World War* (London: I. B. Tauris, 1998).

Duus, P., R. H. Myers, and M. R. Peattie, eds., *The Japanese Informal Empire in China, 1895–1937* (Princeton, NJ: Princeton University Press, 1991).

Edgerton, David, *England and the Aeroplane* (London: Macmillan, 1991).

Edwards, E. W., "The Far Eastern Agreements 1907," *Journal of Modern History* 26 (1954): 340–55.

Edwards, E. W., "The Franco-German Agreement in Morocco," *English Historical Review* 78 (1963): 483–513.

Edwards, E. W., *British Diplomacy and Finance in China 1895–1914* (Oxford: Oxford University Press, 1987).

Egerton, G. W., *Great Britain and the Creation of the League of Nations: Strategy, Politics and International Organization, 1914–1919* (Chapel Hill, NC: University of North Carolina Press, 1978).

Egorova, N. I., "Soviet Leaders' Perceptions of NATO and the Decision-Making Process," in *L'Europe: de l'Est et de l'Ouest dans la Guerre froide, 1948–1953*, ed. Saki Dockrill et al. (Paris: Presses de l'Université Paris-Sorbonne, 2002), pp. 217–26.

Elleman, Bruce A., "The Soviet Union's Secret Diplomacy Concerning the Chinese Eastern Railway, 1924–1925," *Journal of Asian Studies* 53 (1994): 459–86.

Ellman, Michael, and Vladimir Kontorovich, eds., *The Destruction of the Soviet Economic System: An Insiders' History* (New York and London: M. E. Sharpe, 1998).

Engel, Jeffrey A., *Cold War at 30,000 Feet* (Cambridge, MA: Harvard University Press, 2007).

English, Robert, "The Road(s) Not Taken: Causality and Contingency in Analysis of the Cold War's End," in *Cold War Endgame*, ed. William C. Wohlforth (University Park, PA: Pennsylvania State University Press, 2003), pp. 243–72.

Erickson, Edward, *Ordered to Die: A History of the Ottoman Army in the First World War* (Westport, CT: Greenwood, 2001).

Esthus, Raymond A., "President Roosevelt's Commitment to Britain to Intervene in a Pacific War," *Mississippi Valley Historical Review* 50 (1963): 28–38.

Evans, D. C., and M. R. Peattie, *Kaigun: Strategy, Tactics and Technology in the Imperial Japanese Navy, 1887–1941* (Annapolis, MD: Naval Institute Press, 1997).

Farrell, Brian, and Sandy Hunter, eds., *Sixty Years On: The Fall of Singapore Revisited* (Singapore: Times Academic Press, 2002).

Fawcett, Louise, and Yezid Sayigh, *The Third World Beyond the Cold War: Continuity and Change* (Oxford: Oxford University Press, 2000).

Feis, Herbert, *Europe: The World's Banker, 1870–1914* (New Haven, CT: Yale University Press, 1930).

Feis, Herbert, *The Road to Pearl Harbor: The Coming of the War Between the United States and Japan* (Princeton, NJ: Princeton University Press, 1950).

Fellner, Fritz, *Der Dreibund: europäische Diplomatie vor dem Ersten Weltkrieg* (Munich: Oldenbourg, 1960).

Ferguson, Niall, *The Pity of War* (New York: Basic Books, 1999).

Ferguson, Niall, *Colossus: The Price of America's Empire* (New York: Penguin, 2004).

Ferrell, Robert H., *American Diplomacy in the Great Depression: Hoover–Stimson Foreign Policy, 1929–1933* (New Haven, CT: Yale University Press, 1957).

Ferrell, Robert H., *Woodrow Wilson and World War I, 1917–1921* (New York: Harper & Row, 1985).

Ferris, John, "Image and Accident: Intelligence and the Origins of World War II, 1933–1941," in *Intelligence and Strategy: Selected Essays* (Abingdon: Routledge, 2005).

Field, Andrew, *Royal Navy Strategy in the Far East, 1919–1939* (London: Routledge, 2004).

Fieldhouse, D. K., *The Colonial Empires: A Comparative Survey from the Eighteenth Century* (London: Weidenfeld & Nicolson, 1966).

Fink, Carole, "Defender of Minorities: Germany and the League of Nations, 1926–1933," *Central European History* 5 (1972): 330–57.

Fink, James, *America Adopts the Automobile, 1895–1910* (Cambridge, MA: Harvard University Press, 1970).

Fischer, Fritz, *Germany's Aims in the First World War* (London: Chatto & Windus, 1967).

Fischer, Fritz, *War of Illusions: German Policies from 1911 to 1914*, trans. Marian Jackson (New York: W. W. Norton, 1975).

Fisher, J., *Curzon and British Imperialism in the Middle East 1916–1919* (London: Frank Cass, 1999).

Flory, H., "The Arcos Raid and the Rupture of Anglo-Soviet Relations, 1927," *Journal of Contemporary History* 12 (1977): 707–23.

Foreman-Peck, James, *A History of the World Economy* (New York: Pearson, 1995).

Förster, Jürgen, and Evan Mawdsley, "Hitler and Stalin in Perspective: Secret Speeches on the Eve of Barbarossa," *War in History* 11 (2004): 61–103.

Fox, Fiona, "New Humanitarianism: Does it Provide a Moral Banner for the 21st Century?" *Disasters* 25 (2001): 275–89.

Fox, John P., *Germany and the Far Eastern Crisis 1931–1938: A Study in Diplomacy and Ideology* (Oxford: Clarendon Press, 1982).

Frank, André Gunder, *Capitalism and Underdevelopment in Latin America: Historical Studies of Chile and Brazil* (New York: Monthly Review Press, 1968).

Fraser, Steve, *Wall Street: A Cultural History* (London: Faber & Faber, 2005).

Freedman, Lawrence, and Efraim Karsh, *The Gulf Conflict, 1990–1991: Diplomacy and War in the New World Order* (Princeton, NJ: Princeton University Press, 1993).

Freedman, Lawrence, *Kennedy's Wars: Berlin, Cuba, Laos, and Vietnam* (Oxford: Oxford University Press, 2000).

French, David, *British Economic and Strategic Planning 1905–1915* (London: Allen & Unwin, 1982).

French, David, *British Strategy and War Aims 1914–1916* (London: Allen & Unwin, 1986).

French, David, *The Strategy of the Lloyd George Coalition* (Oxford: Clarendon Press, 1995).

Frey, M., R. Pruessen, and Tan Tai Yong, eds., *The Transformation of Southeast Asia: International Perspectives on Decolonization* (New York: Sharpe, 2003).

Fromkin, David, *A Peace To End All Peace: Creating the Modern Middle East 1914–1922* (London: Penguin, 1989).

Frostad, Magne, *Jus in bello after September 11, 2001* (Baden-Baden: Nomos, 2005).

Fry, Michael G., Erik Goldstein, and Richard Langhorne, eds., *Guide to International Relations and Diplomacy* (London and New York: Continuum, 2002).

Fukuyama, Francis, *The End of History and the Last Man* (London: Hamish Hamilton, 1992).

Fursenko, Aleksandr, ed., *Prezidium TsK KPSS: 1954–1964* (Moscow: Rosspen, 2003).

Gaddis, John Lewis, *The Long Peace: Inquiries into the History of the Cold War* (New York: Oxford University Press, 1987).

Gaddis, John Lewis, *We Now Know* (New York: Oxford University Press, 1997).

Gaddis, John Lewis, *The Cold War* (London: Allen Lane, 2005).

Gaiduk, I., *The Soviet Union and the Vietnam War* (Chicago: Ivan R. Dee, 1996).

Gaiduk, I., *Confronting Vietnam: Soviet Policy toward the Indochina Conflict, 1954–1963* (Stanford, CA: Stanford University Press, 2003).

Galbraith, John Kenneth, *The Great Crash, 1929* (Harmondsworth: Penguin, 1963).

Gardner, Lloyd C., *Spheres of Influence: The Great Powers Partition Europe from Munich to Yalta* (Chicago: Ivan R. Dee, 1993).

Gardner, Lloyd C., "The Atlantic Charter: Idea and Reality, 1942–1945," in *The Atlantic Charter*, ed. Douglas Brinkley and David Facey-Crowther (New York: St. Martin's, 1994), pp. 45–81.

Gardner, Nikolas, "Sepoys and the Siege of Kut-al-Amara, December 1915–April 1916," *War in History* 11 (2004): 307–26.

Garthoff, Raymond L., *The Great Transition: American–Soviet Relations and the End of the Cold War* (Washington, DC: Brookings Institution, 1994).

Gatrell, Peter, *Government, Industry and Rearmament in Russia, 1900–1914: The Last Argument of Tsarism* (Cambridge: Cambridge University Press, 1994).

Gatzke, Hans, *Stresemann and the Rearmament of Germany* (Baltimore: Johns Hopkins University Press, 1954).

Geary, P. J., *The Myth of Nations: The Medieval Origins of Europe* (Princeton, NJ: Princeton University Press, 2002).

Gellman, Irwin F., *Secret Affairs: Franklin Roosevelt, Cordell Hull, and Sumner Welles* (Baltimore: Johns Hopkins University Press, 1995).

Gellner, Ernst, *Nations and Nationalism* (New York: Cornell University Press, 1983).

Gershoni, Israel, and James P. Jankowski, *Egypt, Islam and the Arabs: The Search for Egyptian Nationhood, 1900–1930* (Oxford: Oxford University Press, 1986).

Giauque, Jeffrey, *Grand Designs and Visions of Unity: The Atlantic Powers and the Reorganization of Western Europe, 1955–63* (Chapel Hill, NC: University of North Carolina Press, 2002).

Gilbert, Martin, and Richard Gott, *The Appeasers* (London: Weidenfeld & Nicolson, 1964).

Gilbert, Martin, *The Roots of Appeasement* (London: Weidenfeld & Nicolson, 1966).

Gilbert, Martin, *Road to Victory* (Boston: Houghton Mifflin, 1986).

Gilbert, Martin, *Never Despair: Winston S. Churchill 1945–1965* (London: Heinemann, 1988).

Girault, René, "Economie et politique internationale: diplomatie et banque pendant l'entre-deux-guerres," *Relations internationales* 21 (1980): 7–22.

Glantz, D., *Stumbling Colossus: The Red Army on the Eve of War* (Lawrence, KS: University Press of Kansas, 1998).

Gleijeses, Piero, *Conflicting Missions: Havana, Washington, and Africa, 1959–1976* (Chapel Hill, NC: University of North Carolina Press, 2002).

Goldberg, Ellis, "Peasants in Revolt – Egypt 1919," *International Journal of Middle East Studies* 24 (1992): 261–80.

Goldman, Merle, and Leo Ou-Fan Lee, eds., *An Intellectual History of Modern China* (Cambridge: Cambridge University Press, 2002).

Goldmann, Kjell, *The Logic of Internationalism: Coercion and Accommodation* (London: Routledge, 1994).

Goldstein, Erik, *Winning the Peace: British Diplomatic Strategy, Peace Planning, and the Paris Peace Conference, 1916–1920* (Oxford: Clarendon Press, 1991).

Goldstein, Erik, and J. Maurer, eds., *The Washington Naval Conference, 1921–1922: Naval Rivalry, East Asian Stability and the Road to Pearl Harbor* (London: Frank Cass, 1994).

Gollin, Alfred, *No Longer an Island* (Palo Alto, CA: Stanford University Press, 1984).

Goncharov, Sergei, and Viktor Usov, "Peregovory A. N. Kosygina i Zhou Enla'ia v Pekinskom Aeroportu," *Problemy Dalnego Vostoka* 5 (1992).

Goncharov, Sergei, John Lewis, and Xue Litai, *Uncertain Partners: Stalin, Mao and the Korean War* (Stanford, CA: Stanford University Press, 1993).

Gooch, John, "Italy before 1915: The Quandary of the Vulnerable," in *Knowing One's Enemies: Intelligence Assessment Before the Two World Wars*, ed. Ernest R. May (Princeton, NJ: Princeton University Press, 1984), pp. 205–33.

Gorbachev, Mikhail, *Zhizn i Reformy*, vol. 2 (Moscow: Novosti, 1995).

Gorodetsky, G., *Grand Delusion: Stalin and the German Invasion of Russia* (New Haven, CT: Yale University Press, 1999).

Gould, Ian, "The Modern Jet Airliner – the Trailblazers," in *Modern Air Transport*, ed. Philip Jarrett (London: Putnam, 2000).

Graebner, Norman A., "Hoover, Roosevelt, and the Japanese," in *Pearl Harbor as History: Japanese–American Relations, 1931–1941*, ed. Dorothy Borg and Shumei Okamoto (New York: Columbia University Press, 1973).

Grenville, J. A. S., *Lord Salisbury and Foreign Policy: The Close of the Nineteenth Century* (London: Athlone Press, 1964).

Gunaratna, Rohan, *Inside Al Qaeda: Global Network of Terror* (New York: Berkeley Books, 2003).

Guoqi, Xu, *China and the Great War: China's Pursuit of a New National Identity and Internationalism* (Cambridge: Cambridge University Press, 2005).

Haggie, Paul, *Britannia at Bay: The Defence of the British Empire Against Japan, 1931–1941* (Oxford: Oxford University Press, 1981).

Hailemariam, Zaude, "La vera data d'inizio della seconda Guerra mondiale," in *Le guerre coloniali del fascismo*, ed. Angelo Del Boca (Rome: Laterza, 1991), pp. 288–313.

Hall, J. A., *The State of the Nation: Ernst Gellner and the Theory of Nationalism* (Cambridge: Cambridge University Press, 1998).

Hallstein, Walter, *Europe in the Making* (New York: W. W. Norton, 1973).

Halpern, Paul, *The Mediterranean Naval Situation, 1908–14* (Cambridge, MA: Harvard University Press, 1971).

Hamilton, Keith, *Bertie of Thame: Edwardian Ambassador* (Woodbridge: Royal Historical Society, 1990).

Hamilton, Keith, and Richard Langhorne, *The Practice of Diplomacy: Its Evolution, Theory and Administration* (London and New York: Routledge, 2000).

Hamilton, Richard F., and Holger H. Herwig, eds., *The Origins of World War I* (Cambridge: Cambridge University Press, 2003).

Hanhimäki, Jussi, "Ironies and Turning Points: Détente in Perspective," in *Reviewing the Cold War: Approaches, Interpretations, Theory*, ed. Odd Arne Westad (London: Frank Cass, 2000), pp. 326–38.

Hanhimäki, Jussi M., and Odd Arne Westad, *The Cold War: A History in Documents and Eyewitness Accounts* (New York: Oxford University Press, 2003).

Hanson, Philip, *The Rise and Fall of the Soviet Economy: An Economic History of the USSR from 1945* (London: Longman, 2003).

Harbutt, Fraser, *The Cold War Era* (Oxford: Blackwell, 2002).

Hardie, Frank, *The Abyssinian Crisis* (London: Batsford, 1974).

Harding, Neil, *Lenin's Political Thought*, 2 vols. (London: Macmillan, 1977, 1981).

Harper, John L., *American Visions of Europe* (New York: Cambridge University Press, 1994).

Harr, John E., *The Professional Diplomat* (Princeton, NJ: Princeton University Press, 1969).

Harris, Jonathan, *Subverting the System: Gorbachev's Reform of the Party Apparat, 1986–1991* (Lanham, MD: Rowman & Littlefield, 2004).

Haslam, Jonathan, *The Soviet Union and the Struggle for Collective Security in Europe, 1933–39* (London: Macmillan, 1984).

Haslam, Jonathan, *The Soviet Union and the Threat from the East, 1933–1941* (London: Palgrave Macmillan, 1992).

Hastings, A., *The Construction of Nationhood: Ethnicity, Religion and Nationalism* (Cambridge: Cambridge University Press, 1997).

Hayes, Bascom Barry, *Bismarck and Mitteleuropa* (Rutherford, NJ: Farleigh Dickinson University Press, 1994).

Headrick, Daniel R., *The Invisible Weapon* (New York: Oxford University Press, 1991).

Headrick, Daniel R., *When Information Came of Age* (New York: Oxford University Press, 2002).

Heckscher, August, ed., *The Politics of Woodrow Wilson: Selections from His Speeches and Writings* (New York: Harper, 1956).

Heideking, J., "Oberster Rat – Botschafterkonferenz – Völkerbund: Drei Formen multilateraler Diplomatie nach dem Ersten Weltkrieg," *Historische Zeitschrift* 91 (1980): 589–630.

Heinrichs, Waldo, *Threshold of War: Franklin D. Roosevelt and American Entry into World War II* (New York: Oxford University Press, 1988).

Heinzig, Dieter, "Stalin, Mao, Kim and Korean War Origins, 1950: A Russian Documentary Discrepancy," *Cold War International History Project Bulletin* 8–9 (1996/7).

Heinzig, Dieter, *The Soviet Union and Communist China, 1945–1950: An Arduous Road to the Alliance* (Armonk, NY, and London: M. E. Sharpe, 2004).

Helmreich, P., *From Paris to Sèvres: The Partition of the Ottoman Empire and the Paris Peace Conference 1919* (Columbus, OH: Ohio State University Press, 1974).

Henig, Ruth, ed., *The League of Nations* (Edinburgh: Oliver & Boyd, 1973).

Henig, Ruth, "New Diplomacy and Old: Reassessment of British Conceptions of a League of Nations, 1918–1920," in *The Paris Peace Conference, 1919: Peace Without Victory?*, ed. M. Dockrill and J. Fisher (Basingstoke: Palgrave Macmillan, 2001), pp. 157–74.

Hennessy, Peter, *The Secret State: Whitehall and the Cold War* (London: Allen Lane, 2002).

Herring, G., *America's Longest War: The United States and Vietnam, 1950–1975* (New York: McGraw-Hill, 1986 edn).

Herrmann, David G., *The Arming of Europe and the Making of the First World War* (Princeton, NJ: Princeton University Press, 1996).

Hershberg, James, "Russian Documents on the Korean War, 1950–1953," *Cold War International History Project Bulletin* 14/15 (2003–4): 369–84.

Herwig, Holger, *"Luxury" Fleet: The Imperial German Navy 1888–1918* (London: Ashfield, rev. edn, 1987).

Heuser, Beatrice, "Victory in a Nuclear War? A Comparison of NATO and WTO War Aims and Strategies," *Contemporary European History* 7 (1998): 315–18.

Hewitson, Mark, *Germany and the Causes of the First World War* (Oxford: Berg, 2004).

Hildebrand, Klaus, *The Foreign Policy of the Third Reich* (London: Batsford, 1973).

Hildebrand, Klaus, *Das vergangene Reich. Deutsche Außenpolitik von Bismarck bis Hitler* (Stuttgart: Deutsche Verlags-Anstalt 1995).

Hill, Alexander, "The Birth of the Soviet Northern Fleet 1937–1942," *Journal of Slavic Military Studies* 16 (2003): 65–82.

Hillgruber, Andreas, *Germany and the Two World Wars* (London: Harvard University Press, 1981).

Hinsley, F. H., *Codebreakers: The Unknown Story of Bletchley Park* (New York: Oxford University Press, 2001).

Hitchcock, William I., *France Restored: Cold War Diplomacy and the Quest for Leadership in Europe, 1944–1954* (Chapel Hill, NC: University of North Carolina Press, 1998).

Hitchcock, William I., *The Struggle for Europe: The Turbulent History of a Divided Continent, 1945–2002* (New York: Random House, 2003).

Hoare, J. E., ed., *Britain and Japan: Biographical Portraits*, vol. 3 (London: Routledge/Curzon, 1999).

Hobsbawm, Eric, *Nations and Nationalism since 1780: Programme, Myth, Reality* (Cambridge: Cambridge University Press, 1990).

Hobsbawm, Eric, and Terence Ranger, eds., *The Invention of Tradition* (Cambridge: Cambridge University Press, 1983).

Hochman, Jiri, *The Soviet Union and the Failure of Collective Security, 1934–1938* (Ithaca, NY: Cornell University Press, 1984).

Hoffman, Bruce, *Inside Terrorism* (New York: Columbia University Press, 1998).

Hoffman, Bruce, "Terrorism Trends and Prospects," in *Countering the New Terrorism*, ed. Ian Lesser et al. (Santa Monica, CA: Rand Project Air Force, 1999), pp. 15–20.

Hoffman, Stanley, "Obstinate or Obsolete? The Fate of the Nation-State and the Case of Western Europe," *Daedalus* 95 (1966): 862–915.

Hoffmann, J., "The Red Army until the Beginning of the German–Soviet War," in *Germany and the Second World War*, vol. 4, *The Attack on the Soviet Union*, ed. H. Boog et al. (Oxford: Clarendon Press, 1998), pp. 72–93.

Hoffmann, J., *Stalin's War of Extermination, 1941–1945: Planning, Realization, and Documentation* (Capshaw, AL: Theses and Dissertations Press, 2001).

Hogan, Michael, *The Marshall Plan: America, Britain, and the Reconstruction of Western Europe, 1947–1952* (Cambridge: Cambridge University Press, 1986).

Holbrooke, Richard, *To End a War* (New York: Random House, 1998).

Holland, R. F., *European Decolonization 1918–1981* (Basingstoke: Penguin, 1985).

Hoover, Herbert, *The Memoirs of Herbert Hoover: The Great Depression, 1929–1941* (New York: Macmillan, 1952).

Hope, Harrison, *Driving the Soviets up the Wall: Soviet–East German Relations, 1953–1961* (Princeton, NJ: Princeton University Press, 2003).

Hourani, Albert, "Ottoman Reform and the Politics of the Notables," in *The Emergence of the Modern Middle East*, ed. Albert Hourani (London: Macmillan, 1981), pp. 36–66.

Howard, C. H. D., *Splendid Isolation* (London: Macmillan, 1967).

Howard, Michael, George J. Andreopoulos, and Mark R. Shulman, eds., *The Laws of War: Constraints on Warfare in the Western World* (New Haven, CT, and London: Yale University Press, 1994).

Hughes, Matthew, *Allenby and British Strategy in the Middle East, 1917–19* (London: Frank Cass, 1999).

Hughes, Matthew, "The French Army at Gallipoli," *Journal of the Royal United Services Institute* 150 (2005): 64–7.

Hugill, Peter, *World Trade since 1431: Geography, Technology, and Capitalism* (Baltimore: Johns Hopkins University Press, 1995).

Hugill, Peter, *Global Communications since 1844* (Baltimore: Johns Hopkins University Press, 1999).

Hull, Isabel V., *Absolute Destruction: Military Culture and the Practices of War in Imperial Germany* (Ithaca, NY: Cornell University Press, 2005).

Hunt, Barry, and Adrian Preston, eds., *War Aims and Strategic Policy in the Great War* (London: Croom Helm, 1977).

Hunt, Michael, *Ideology and US Foreign Policy* (New Haven, CT: Yale University Press, 1987).

Hunter, J. E., and S. Sugiyama, eds., *The History of Anglo-Japanese Relations, 1600–2000*, vol. 4, *Economic and Business Relations* (Basingstoke and New York: Palgrave Macmillan, 2000).

Hurst, Michael, ed., *Key Treaties for the Great Powers 1814–1914*, vol. 2, *1871–1914* (London: David & Charles, 1974).

Hutchinson, J., and A. D. Smith, eds., *Nationalism* (Oxford: Oxford University Press, 1994).

Hynes, Samuel, *A War Imagined: The First World War and English Culture* (London: Bodley Head, 1990).

Ikenberry, G. John, ed., *America Unrivaled: The Future of the Balance of Power* (Ithaca, NY: Cornell University Press, 2002).

Imlay, Talbot, *Facing the Second World War: Strategy, Politics and Economics in Britain and France, 1938–1940* (Oxford: Oxford University Press, 2003).

Iriye, Akira, *The Origins of the Second World War in Asia and the Pacific* (London and New York: Longman, 1987).

Jäckel, Eberhard, *Hitler's Weltanschauung: A Blueprint for Power* (Middletown, CT: Wesleyan University Press, 1972).

Jackson, Kenneth, *Crabgrass Frontier* (New York: Oxford University Press, 1985).

Jackson, Peter, *France and the Nazi Menace: Intelligence and Policy Making, 1933–39* (Oxford: Oxford University Press, 2000).

Jackson, Peter, "France," in *The Origins of World War Two: The Debate Continues*, ed. Robert Boyce and Joseph A. Maiolo (Basingstoke: Palgrave Macmillan, 2003), pp. 86–110.

Jackson, Richard, *The Non-Aligned, the UN and the Superpowers* (Westport, CT: Greenwood Press, 1987).

Jaffe, Lorna, *The Decision to Disarm Germany: British Policy towards Post-War German Disarmament, 1914–1919* (London: Allen & Unwin, 1985).

Jakobsen, M., *The Diplomacy of the Winter War: An Account of the Russo-Finnish War, 1939–1940* (Cambridge, MA: Harvard University Press, 1961).

James, Harold, *The Reichsbank and Public Finance in Germany, 1924–1933: A Study of the Politics of Economics in the Great Depression* (Frankfurt am Main: F. Knapp, 1985).

James, Harold, *The German Slump: Politics and Economics, 1924–1936* (Oxford: Clarendon Press, 1986).

Jankowski, James, and Israel Gershoni, eds., *Rethinking Arab Nationalism in the Arab Middle East* (New York: Columbia University Press, 1997).

Jay, Peter, *The Wealth of Man* (New York: Public Affairs, 2000).

Johnson, Chalmers, *The Sorrows of Empire: Militarism, Secrecy, and the End of the Republic* (New York: Henry Holt, 2004).

Johnston, Tom, *Financiers and the Nation* (London: Methuen, 1939).

Joll, James, "The Decline of Europe 1920–1970," *International Affairs* 49 (1970): 1–18.

Joll, James, and Gordon Martel, *The Origins of the First World War* (London: Longman, 3rd edn, 2006).

Josephson, Matthew, *Empire of the Air* (New York: Arno Press, 1972).

Joyner, C. C., ed., *The United Nations and International Law* (Cambridge: Cambridge University Press, 1997).

Judd, D., *Empire: The British Imperial Experience from 1765 to the Present* (London: Fontana, 1997).

Jun, Tsunoda, "On the So-Called Hull–Nomura Negotiations," in *Pearl Harbor Reexamined: Prologue to the Pacific War*, ed. Hilary Conroy and Harry Wray (Honolulu, HI: University of Hawaii Press, 1990).

Junusov, M. S., et al., *The Theory and Practice of Proletarian Internationalism* (Moscow: Progress Publishers, 1976).

Kagan, Robert, et al., "One Year After: A Grand Strategy for the West?" *Survival* 44 (2002–3): 135–56.

Kahler, Miles, and Werner Link, *Europe and America: A Return to History* (New York: Council on Foreign Relations, 1996).

Kahn, David, *The Codebreakers: The Comprehensive History of Secret Communications from Ancient Times to the Internet* (New York: Scribner's, 1996).

Kaiser, David E., *Economic Diplomacy and the Origins of the Second World War* (Princeton, NJ: Princeton University Press, 1980).

Kaplan, Lawrence, "Alliance," in *Palgrave Advances in Cold War History*, ed. Saki Ruth Dockrill and Geraint Hughes (Basingstoke: Palgrave Macmillan, 2006).

Kash, Douglas, "An International Legislative Approach to 21st-Century Terrorism," in *The Future of Terrorism: Violence in the New Millennium*, ed. Harvey Kushner (Thousand Oaks, CA: Sage, 1998), pp. 163–72.

Kedourie, Elie, *Nationalism* (London: Hutchinson, 1960).

Kedourie, Elie, *In the Anglo-Arab Labyrinth: The McMahon–Husayn Correspondence and its Interpretations, 1914–1939* (Cambridge: Cambridge University Press, 1976).

Keeton, Edward P., *Briand's Locarno Policy: French Economics, Politics and Diplomacy, 1925–1929* (New York: Garland, 1987).

Keiger, J. F. V., *France and the Origins of the First World War* (London: Macmillan, 1983).

Keiger, J. F. V., *Raymond Poincaré* (Cambridge: Cambridge University Press, 1997).

Ken, O. N., *Moblilizatsionnoe planirovanie i politicheskie resheniia (konets 1920–seredina 1930-x godov)* (St. Petersburg: Izdatel'stvo Evropeiskogo universiteta v Sankt-Peterburge, 2002).

Kennan, George F., *The Fateful Alliance: France, Russia and the Coming of the First World War* (Princeton, NJ: Princeton University Press, 1979).

Kennedy, Greg, "1935: A Snapshot of British Imperial Defence in the Far East," in *Far Flung Lines: Studies in Imperial Defence in Honour of Donald Mackenzie Schurman*, ed. Greg Kennedy and Keith Neilson (Portland, OR, and London: Frank Cass, 1997), pp. 190–216.

Kennedy, Greg, *Anglo-American Strategic Relations and the Far East, 1933–1939* (London: Frank Cass, 2002).

Kennedy, M. D., *Estrangement of Great Britain and Japan, 1917–1935* (Manchester: Manchester University Press, 1969).

Kennedy, Paul M., *The Rise of the Anglo-German Antagonism, 1860–1914* (London: Allen & Unwin, 1980).

Kennedy, Paul M., *The Realities behind Diplomacy: Background Influences on British External Policy, 1865–1980* (London: Allen & Unwin, 1981).

Kennedy, Paul M., ed., *The War Plans of the Great Powers 1880–1914* (Boston: Allen & Unwin, 1985).

Kennedy, Paul M., *The Rise and Fall of the Great Powers: Economic Change and Military Conflict from 1500 to 2000* (London: Unwin Hyman, 1988).

Kent, B., *The Spoils of War: The Politics, Economics and Diplomacy of Reparations, 1918–1932* (Oxford: Clarendon Press, 1989).

Kent, John, "British Postwar Planning for Europe, 1942–45," in *The Failure of Peace in Europe, 1943–48*, ed. Antonio Varsori and Elena Calandri (Basingstoke: Palgrave Macmillan, 2002), pp. 40–58.

Keohane, Robert O., and Joseph S. Nye, *Power and Interdependence: World Politics in Transition* (Boston and Toronto: Little, Brown, 1977).

Kershaw, Ian, *Hitler*, vol. 1, *1889–1936: Hubris*; vol. 2, *1936–1945: Nemesis* (London: Allen Lane, 1998, 2000).

Khalidi, Rashid, *Resurrecting Empire: Western Footprints and America's Perilous Path in the Middle East* (Boston: Beacon Press, 2004).

Khlevniuk, O., "The Objectives of the Great Terror, 1937–38," in *Stalinism: The Essential Readings*, ed. D. L. Hoffmann (Malden, MA: Blackwell, 2003).

Khoury, Philip, *Syria and the French Mandate: The Politics of Arab Nationalism, 1920–1945* (Princeton, NJ: Princeton University Press, 1987).

Kiernan, V. G., *European Empires from Conquest to Collapse* (Leicester: Leicester University Press, 1982).

Killingray, David, "The War in Africa," in *The Oxford Illustrated History of the First World War*, ed. Hew Strachan (Oxford: Oxford University Press, 1998), pp. 92–103.

Kimball, Warren F., *The Juggler: Franklin Roosevelt as Wartime Statesman* (Princeton, NJ: Princeton University Press, 1991).

Kimball, Warren F., *Forged in War* (New York: Morrow, 1997).

Kimball, Warren F., "The Incredible Shrinking War: The Second World War – Not (Just) the Origins of the Cold War," *Diplomatic History* 25 (2001): 347–65.

Kimmich, C. M., *Germany and the League of Nations* (Chicago: University of Chicago Press, 1976).

Kindleberger, Charles P., *The World in Depression, 1929–1939* (London: Penguin, 1973).

Kiselev, A. F., et al., eds., *Khrestomatiia po otechestvennoi istorii (1914–1945 gg.): Uchebnoe posobie dlia studentov vuzov* (Moscow: Gumanitarnii izdatel'skii tsentr VLADOS, 1996).

Kitchen, Martin, *Europe Between the Wars* (London: Longman, 1988).

Knipping, Franz, *Deutschland, Frankreich und das Ende der Locarno-Ära: Studien zur internationalen Politik in der Anfangsphase der Weltwirtschaftskrise* (Munich: R. Oldenbourg, 1987).

Knipping, Franz, Hans von Mangolt, and Volker Rittenberger, eds., *The United Nations System and Its Predecessors*, 2 vols. (Oxford: Oxford University Press, 1997).

Knock, Thomas J., *To End All Wars: Woodrow Wilson and the Quest for a New World Order* (Princeton, NJ: Princeton University Press, 1992).

Knox, MacGregor, *Mussolini Unleashed, 1939–1941* (Cambridge: Cambridge University Press, 1982).

Knox, MacGregor, *Common Destiny: Dictatorship, Foreign Policy and War in Fascist Italy and Nazi Germany* (Cambridge: Cambridge University Press, 2000).

Koch, H. W., "The Anglo-German Alliance Negotiations, Missed Opportunity or Myth?" *History* 54 (1969): 378–98.

Koch, H. W., ed., *The Origins of the First World War* (London: Macmillan, 1972).

Kohn, Hans, *A History of Nationalism in the East* (New York: Harcourt, Brace, and Company, 1929).

Kooker, Judith, "French Financial Diplomacy: The Interwar Years," in *Balance of Power or Hegemony: The Interwar Monetary System*, ed. Benjamin M. Rowland (New York: New York University Press, 1976), pp. 83–145.

Kramer, Mark, "Ideology and the Cold War," *Review of International Studies* 25 (1999): 539–87.

Kratoska, P., "Dimensions of Decolonization," in *The Transformation of Southeast Asia: International*

*Perspectives on Decolonization*, ed. M. Frey, R. Pruessen, and Tan Tai Yong (New York: Sharpe, 2003).

Krauthammer, Charles, "The Unipolar Moment Revisited," *National Interest* 70 (2003): 5–17.

Kryuchkov, Vladimir, *Lichnoe Delo*, vol. 2 (Moscow: Olimp, 1996).

Kuitenbrouwer, M., *The Netherlands and the Rise of Modern Imperialism: Colonies and Foreign Policy* (Oxford and New York: Berg, 1991).

Kulik, Boris, *Sovetsko-Kitaiskii Raskol: Prichiny i Posledstvi'ia* (Moscow: IDV RAN, 2000).

Kyle, Keith, *The Suez Crisis: Britain's End of Empire* (London: I. B. Tauris, 2002).

Labanca, Nicola, *Il colonialismo italiano* (Milan: Fenice 2000, 1994).

LaFeber, Walter, *The Clash: US–Japanese Relations throughout History* (London and New York: W. W. Norton, 1997).

Lafore, Laurence, *The Long Fuse: An Interpretation of the Origins of World War I* (London, 1966).

Lamb, Richard, *Mussolini and the British* (London: John Murray, 1997).

Lambert, Nicholas A., *Sir John Fisher's Naval Revolution* (Columbia, SC: University of South Carolina Press, 1999).

Lambi, Ivo N., *The Navy and German Power Politics, 1862–1914* (Boston: Allen & Unwin, 1984).

Landes, David, *The Wealth and Poverty of Nations* (New York: W. W. Norton, 1999).

Langdon, John W., *July 1914: The Long Debate, 1918–1990* (New York: Berg, 1991).

Langer, William L., *The Diplomacy of Imperialism 1890–1902* (New York: Knopf, 1935).

Laqueur, Walter, *The New Terrorism: Fanatics Armed with the Arms of Mass Destruction* (Oxford: Oxford University Press, 1999).

Lauren, Paul Gordon, *Diplomats and Bureaucrats: The First Institutional Response to Twentieth-Century Diplomacy in France and Germany* (Stanford, CA: Hoover Institution Press, 1976).

Lawrence, P., *Nationalism: History and Theory* (London: Pearson, 2005).

Leffler, Melvin P., *The Elusive Quest: America's Pursuit of European Stability and French Security, 1919–1933* (Chapel Hill, NC: University of North Carolina Press, 1979).

Legge, John D., *Sukarno: A Political Biography* (London: Butterworth-Heinemann, 2003).

Leitz, Christian, "Nazi Germany," in *The Origins of World War Two: The Debate Continues*, ed. Robert Boyce and Joseph A. Maiolo (Basingstoke: Palgrave Macmillan, 2003), pp. 11–31.

Lenin, V. I., *Collected Works* (London: Lawrence & Wishart, 1974).

Lentin, Antony, "'*Une Aberration inexplicable*'? Clemenceau and the Abortive Anglo-French Guarantee Treaty of 1919," *Diplomacy and Statecraft* 8 (1997): 31–49.

Leslie, John, "The Antecedents of Austria-Hungary's War Aims," *Wiener Beiträge zur Geschichte der Neuzeit* 20 (1993): 307–94.

Levin, N. Gordon, Jr., *Woodrow Wilson and World Politics: America's Response to War and Revolution* (New York: Oxford University Press, 1968).

Lewis, Cleona, *America's Stake in International Investments* (Washington, DC: Brookings Institution, 1938).

Lewis, Tom, *Empire of the Air: The Men Who Made Radio* (New York: HarperCollins, 1991).

Lie, Trygve, *In the Cause of Peace: Seven Years with the United Nations* (New York: Macmillan, 1954).

Lieven, Dominic C. B., "Pro-Germans and Russian Foreign Policy 1890–1914," *International History Review* 2 (1980): 34–54.

Lieven, Dominic C. B., *Russia and the Origins of the First World War* (London: Macmillan, 1983).

Lieven, Dominic C. B., *Empire: The Russian Empire and its Rivals from the Sixteenth Century to the Present* (London: Pimlico, 2000).

Limberg, Wayne P., "Soviet Military Support for Third-World Marxist Regimes," in *The USSR and Marxist Revolutions in the Third World*, ed. Mark N. Katz (New York: Woodrow Wilson International Center for Scholars, 1990), pp. 51–118.

Lindberg, Leon, *Political Dynamics of European Economic Integration* (Stanford, CA: Stanford University Press, 1963).

Link, Arthur S., *Woodrow Wilson: Revolution, War, and Peace* (Wheeling, IL: Harlan Davidson, 1979).

Lloyd, L., *Peace Through Law: Britain and the International Court in the 1920s* (London: Royal Historical Society, 1997).

Lloyd George, David, *War Memoirs of David Lloyd George*, 6 vols. (London: Odhams Press, 1938).

Logevall, F., "Bringing in the 'Other Side': New Scholarship on the Vietnam Wars," *Journal of Cold War Studies* 3 (2001): 77–93.

Loth, Wilfried, ed., *Crises and Compromises: The European Project 1963–1969* (Baden-Baden: Nomos, 2001).

Loth, Wilfried, *Overcoming the Cold War* (Basingstoke: Palgrave Macmillan, 2001).

Louis, W. R., *Imperialism at Bay* (New York: Oxford University Press, 1977).

Louis, W. R., and R. Robinson, "The Imperialism of Decolonization," *Journal of Imperial and Commonwealth History* 22 (1995): 462–511.

Lowe, Cedric J., *Salisbury and the Mediterranean* (London: Routledge & Kegan Paul, 1965).

Lowe, Peter, *Great Britain and the Origins of the Pacific War, 1937–1941* (Oxford: Oxford University Press, 1977).

Luard, Evan, *A History of the United Nations*, 2 vols. (London: Macmillan, 1982, 1989).

Ludlow, N. Piers, *Dealing With Britain: The Six and the First UK Application to the EEC* (Cambridge: Cambridge University Press, 1997).

Ludlow, N. Piers, *The European Community and the Crises of the 1960s: Negotiating the Gaullist Challenge* (London: Routledge, 2006).

Lukacs, John, *Five Days in London: May 1940* (New Haven, CT: Yale University Press, 1999).

Lukin, Alexander, *The Bear Watches the Dragon: Russia's Perceptions of China and the Evolution of Russian–Chinese Relations since the 18th Century* (Armonk, NY: M. E. Sharpe, 2003).

Lukyanov, A. I., *Perevorot mnimy i nastoyashchii* (Voronezh, 1993).

Lundestad, Geir, *The United States and Western Europe since 1945* (Oxford: Oxford University Press, 2003).

Lynch, Frances, *France and the International Economy: From Vichy to the Treaty of Rome* (London: Routledge, 1997).

Macartney, C. A., et al., eds., *Survey of International Affairs, 1925*, vol. 2 (Oxford: Oxford University Press, 1928).

McCauley, Martin, *Gorbachev* (London: Longman, 1998).

McCormick, Thomas, *America's Half-Century* (Baltimore: Johns Hopkins University Press, 1995).

McDonald, David M., *United Government and Foreign Policy in Russia, 1900–1914* (Cambridge, MA: Harvard University Press, 1992).

MacDougall, Walter, *France's Rhineland Diplomacy, 1914–1924: The Last Bid for a Balance of Power in Europe* (Princeton, NJ: Princeton University Press, 1978).

McJimsey, George, *The Presidency of Franklin Delano Roosevelt* (Lawrence, KS: University Press of Kansas, 2000).

MacKenzie, David, *Apis: The Congenial Conspirator. The Life of Dragutin T. Dimitrijević* (New York: Columbia University Press, 1989).

Mackie, Jamie, *Bandung 1955: Non-Alignment and Afro-Asian Solidarity* (Singapore: Archipelago Press, 2005).

McKillen, Elizabeth, "Ethnicity, Class, and Wilsonian Internationalism Reconsidered: The Mexican-American and Irish-American Immigrant Left and US Foreign Relations, 1914–1922," *Diplomatic History* 25 (2001): 553–87.

Mackinder, H. J., "The Geographical Pivot in History," *Geographical Journal* 23 (1904): 421–37.

McMahon, R., *The Limits of Empire: The United States and Southeast Asia since World War II* (New York: Columbia University Press, 1999).

Macmillan, Margaret, *Peacemakers: The Paris Peace Conference of 1919 and its Attempt to End War* (London: John Murray, 2001).

Maier, Charles S., *Dissolution: The Crisis of Communism and the End of East Germany* (Princeton, NJ: Princeton University Press, 1997).

Mallett, Robert, *Mussolini and the Origins of the Second World War, 1933–1940* (Basingstoke: Palgrave, 2003).

Maney, Patrick J., *The Roosevelt Presence: A Biography of Franklin Delano Roosevelt* (New York: Twayne, 1992).

Marder, Arthur, *Old Friends, New Enemies: The Royal Navy and the Imperial Japanese Navy* (Oxford: Oxford University Press, 1981).

Marguerat, Philippe, *Le IIIᵉ Reich et le pétrole roumain, 1938–1940* (Leiden: Sijthoff, 1977).

Marjolin, Robert, *Le Travail d'une vie. Mémoires 1911–1986* (Paris: Robert Laffond, 1986).

Marks, Sally, "Smoke and Mirrors," in *The Treaty of Versailles: A Reassessment after 75 Years*, ed. M. F. Boemeke, G. D. Feldman, and E. Glaser (Cambridge: Cambridge University Press, 1998).

Marks, Sally, *The Ebbing of European Ascendancy: An International History of the World, 1914–1945* (London: Arnold, 2002).

Marquand, D., *Ramsay MacDonald* (London: Jonathan Cape, 1977).

Marr, David G., *Vietnamese Tradition on Trial, 1920–1945* (Los Angeles: University of California Press, 1981).

Marr, Phebe, "The Development of a Nationalist Ideology in Iraq, 1920–1941," *The Muslim World* 75 (1985): 85–101.

Marshall, P. J., ed., *The Cambridge Illustrated History of the British Empire* (Cambridge: Cambridge University Press, 1996).

Martel, Gordon, "The Limits of Commitment: Rosebery and the Definition of the Anglo-German Understanding," *Historical Journal* 26 (1983): 387–404.

Martel, Gordon, *Imperial Diplomacy: Rosebery and the Failure of Foreign Policy* (Montreal and Kingston: McGill-Queen's University Press, 1986).

Martel, Gordon, *Modern Germany Reconsidered* (London and New York: Routledge, 1992).

Martel, Gordon, ed., *The Origins of the Second World War Reconsidered: A. J. P. Taylor and the Historians* (London: Routledge, 1999).

Martel, Gordon, *The Times and Appeasement: The Journals of A. L. Kennedy* (Cambridge: Cambridge University Press, 2000).

Mason, Mike, *Development and Disorder: A History of the Third World since 1945* (Lebanon, NH: University Press of New England, 1997).

Mastny, Vojtech, *Helsinki, Human Rights, and European Security: Analysis and Documentation* (Durham, NC: Duke University Press, 1986).

Mastny, Vojtech, *The Cold War and Soviet Insecurity: The Stalin Years* (New York: Oxford University Press, 1996).

Matlock, Jack F., *Autopsy of an Empire: The American Ambassador's Account of the Collapse of the Soviet Union* (New York: Random House, 1995).

Matlock, Jack F., *Reagan and Gorbachev* (New York: Random House, 2004).

Mawdsley, Evan, "Crossing the Rubicon: Soviet Plans for Offensive War in 1940–1941," *International History Review* 25 (2003): 818–65.

May, Ernest R., *Strange Victory: Hitler's Conquest of France* (London: Hill & Wang, 2000).

Mead, Walter Russell, *Special Providence: American Foreign Policy and How It Changed the World* (New York: Routledge, 2002).

Mearsheimer, John J., *The Tragedy of Great Power Politics* (New York: W. W. Norton, 2001).

Mélandri, Pierre, *Les États-unis face à l'unification de l'Europe, 1945–1954* (Paris: Pedone, 1980).

Melvin Laird, "Iraq: Learning the Lessons of Vietnam," *Foreign Affairs,* November–December (2005): 22–43.

Méouchy, Nadine, and Peter Sluglett, eds., *The British and French Mandates in Comparative Perspectives* (Leiden: Brill, 2004).

Messerschmidt, Manfred, in *Germany and the Second World War*, vol. 1, *The Build-up of German Aggression* (Oxford: Clarendon Press, 1990).

Michalka, W., *Das Dritte Reich*, vol. 1 (Munich: Deutscher Taschenbuch Verlag, 1985).

Mignemi, Adolfo, ed., *Immagine coordinata per un impero Etiopia 1935–1936* (Turin: Forma, 1984).

Millar, E. S., *War Plan Orange: The US Strategy to Defeat Japan, 1897–1945* (Annapolis, MD: Naval Institute Press, 1991).

Milward, Alan, *The Reconstruction of Western Europe 1945–51* (London: Methuen, 1984).

Milward, Alan, *The European Rescue of the Nation-State* (London: Routledge, 1992).

Milward, Alan, *The Rise and Fall of a National Strategy 1945–1963* (London: Frank Cass, 2002).

Mockler, A., *Haile Selassie's War* (London: Grafton, 1987).

Mombauer, Annika, *Helmuth von Moltke and the Origins of the First World War* (New York: Cambridge University Press, 2001).

Mombauer, Annika, *The Origins of the First World War: Controversies and Consensus* (London: Longman, 2002).

Mommsen, Wolfgang J., and Jurgen Osterhammel, eds., *Imperialism and After: Continuities and Discontinuities* (London: Allen & Unwin, 1986).

Mommsen, Wolfgang J., *Grossmachtstellung und Weltpolitik. Die Aussenpolitik des deutschen Reiches 1870–1914* (Frankfurt am Main: Propyläen, 1993).

Monger, G. W., *The End of Isolation: British Foreign Policy, 1900–1907* (London: Nelson, 1963).

Monnet, Jean, *Memoirs* (London: Collins, 1978).

Moorhead, Caroline, *Dunant's Dream: War, Switzerland and the History of the Red Cross* (London: HarperCollins, 1998).

Moravcsik, Andrew, *The Choice for Europe: Social Purpose and State Power from Messina to Maastricht* (Ithaca, NY: Cornell University Press, 1998).

Morgan, J. H., *Assize of Arms: The Disarmament of Germany and Her Rearmament, 1919–1939* (New York: Oxford University Press, 1946).

Morgenthau, Hans J., *Politics Among Nations: The Struggle for Power and Peace* (New York: Alfred A. Knopf, 1948).

Morrell, Gordon W., "Redefining Intelligence and Intelligence Gathering: The Industrial Intelligence Centre and the Metro-Vickers Affair, Moscow 1933," *Intelligence and National Security* 9 (1994): 518–33.

Morris, A. J. A., *Radicalism Against War 1906–1914: The Advocacy of Peace and Retrenchment* (Totowa, NJ: Rowman & Littlefield, 1972).

Morris, A. J. A., *The Scaremongers: The Advocacy of War and Rearmament 1896–1914* (London: Routledge & Kegan Paul, 1984).

Moses, John, and Christopher Pugsley, eds., *The German Empire and Britain's Pacific Dominions: Essays on the Role of Australia and New Zealand in World Politics in the Age of Imperialism* (Claremont, CA: Regina, 2000).

Mosse, George, *The Nationalization of the Masses* (New York: Fertig, 1975).

Mouré, Kenneth, *The Gold Standard Illusion: France, the Bank of France, and the International Gold Standard, 1914–1939* (Oxford: Oxford University Press, 2002).

Mueller, John, *The Remnants of War* (Ithaca, NY: Cornell University Press, 2004).

Munholland, J. Kim, "The French Response to the Vietnamese Nationalist Movement, 1905–14," *Journal of Modern History* 47 (1975): 655–75.

Münkler, Herfried, *Gewalt und Ordnung. Das Bild des Krieges im politischen Denken* (Frankfurt am Main: Fischer, 1992).

Nader, Ralph, *Unsafe at Any Speed* (New York: Grossman, 1965).

Narinskii, Mikhail M., "The Soviet Union and the Marshall Plan," in *The Failure of Peace in Europe, 1943–48*, ed. Antonio Varsori and Elena Calandri (Basingstoke: Palgrave Macmillan, 2002), pp. 275–86.

Neff, Stephen C., *War and the Law of Nations: A General History* (Cambridge: Cambridge University Press, 2005).

Nehru, Jawaharlal, *The Discovery of India*, ed. Robert I. Crane (New York: Anchor Books, 1960).

Neilson, Keith, "Kitchener: A Reputation Refurbished?" *Canadian Journal of History* 15 (1980): 207–27.

Neilson, Keith, *Strategy and Supply: The Anglo-Russian Alliance 1914–17* (London: Allen & Unwin, 1984).

Neilson, Keith, "Watching the 'Steamroller': British Observers and the Russian Army before 1914," *Journal of Strategic Studies* 8 (1985): 199–217.

Neilson, Keith, "'My Beloved Russians': Sir Arthur Nicolson and Russia, 1906–1916," *International History Review* 9 (1987): 521–54.

Neilson, Keith, "'Greatly Exaggerated': The Myth of the Decline of Great Britain before 1914," *International History Review* 13 (1991): 695–725.

Neilson, Keith, *Britain and the Last Tsar: British Policy and Russia, 1894–1917* (Oxford: Oxford University Press, 1995).

Neilson, Keith, "'Control the Whirlwind': Sir Edward Grey as Foreign Secretary, 1905–1916," in *The Makers of British Foreign Policy*, ed. T. G. Otte (London: Palgrave, 2002), pp. 128–50.

Neilson, Keith, "The Anglo-Japanese Alliance and British Strategic Foreign Policy 1902–1914," in *The Anglo-Japanese Alliance*, ed. P. P. O'Brien (London and New York: Routledge, 2004), pp. 48–63.

Neilson, Keith, *Britain, Soviet Russia and the Collapse of the Versailles Order, 1919–1939* (Cambridge: Cambridge University Press, 2005).

Neilson, Keith, "Unbroken Thread: Japan and Britain and Imperial Defence, 1920–1932," in *British Naval Strategy East of Suez, 1900–2000: Influences and Actions*, ed. Greg Kennedy (London: Taylor & Francis, 2005), pp. 62–89.

Nekrich, A. M., *Pariahs, Partners, Predators: German Soviet Relations, 1922–1941* (New York: Columbia University Press, 1997).

Nelson, Harold, *Land and Power: British and Allied Policy on Germany's Frontiers, 1916–19* (London: Routledge & Kegan Paul, 1963).

Nevezhin, V. A., "The Pact with Germany and the Idea of an 'Offensive War,'" *Journal of Slavic Military Studies* 8 (1995): 809–43.

Nevezhin, V. A., *Sindrom nastupatel'noi voini. Sovetskaia propaganda v predverii 'sviashchennikh boev,' 1939–1941 gg.* (Moscow: AIRO-XX', 1997).

Neville, Peter, *Appeasing Hitler: The Diplomacy of Sir Nevile Henderson* (Basingstoke: Palgrave Macmillan, 2000).

Neville, Peter, "Sir Alexander Cadogan and Lord Halifax's 'Damascus Road' Conversion over the Godesberg Terms 1938," *Diplomacy and Statecraft* 11 (2000): 81–90.

Newton, Scott, *Profits of Peace: The Political Economiy of Anglo-German Appeasement* (Oxford: Clarendon Press, 1996).

Nickles, David Paul, *Under the Wire: How the Telegraph Changed Diplomacy* (Cambridge, MA: Harvard University Press, 2003).

Nicolson, Harold, *Peacemaking 1919* (Boston: Houghton Mifflin, 1933).

Nish, Ian, *The Anglo-Japanese Alliance: The Diplomacy of Two Island Empires, 1894–1907* (London: Athlone Press, 1966).

Nish, Ian, *Alliance in Decline* (London: Athlone Press, 1972).

Nish, Ian, *Japanese Foreign Policy, 1869–1942* (London: Routledge, 1977).

Nish, Ian, *Japan's Struggle with Internationalism: Japan, China and the League of Nations, 1931–1933* (London and New York: Kegan Paul, 1993).

Nish, Ian, *Japanese Foreign Policy in the Interwar Period* (Westport, CT: Praeger, 2002).

Northedge, F. S., *The League of Nations: Its Life and Times, 1920–1946* (Leicester: Leicester University Press, 1988).

Novick, Peter, *That Noble Dream* (Cambridge: Cambridge University Press, 1988).

Nugent, Paul, *Africa since Independence: A Comparative History* (London: Palgrave Macmillan, 2004).

O'Neill, E. F., *A History of Engineering and Science in the Bell System* (New York: The Laboratories, 1975).

Oberdorfer, Don, *The Two Koreas: A Contemporary History* (New York: Basic Books, new edn, 2001).

Offer, Avner, "Going to War in 1914: A Matter of Honor?" *Politics and Society* 23 (1995): 213–41.

Öjendal, J., "Back to the Future? Regionalism in South-East Asia under Unilateral Pressure," *International Affairs* 80 (2004): 532–3.

Osborne, M., *Southeast Asia: An Introductory History* (London: Allen & Unwin, 1998).

Otte, T. G., "Great Britain, Germany and the Far-Eastern Crisis of 1897–8," *English Historical Review* 90 (1995): 1157–79.

Otte, T. G., "The Elusive Balance: British Foreign Policy and the French Entente before the First World War," in *Anglo-French Relations in the Twentieth Century: Rivalry and Cooperation*, ed. Alan Sharp and Glyn Stone (London and New York: Routledge, 2000), pp. 11–35.

Otte, T. G., "'Heaven Knows where we shall finally drift': Lord Salisbury, the Cabinet, Isolation and the Boxer Rebellion," in *Incidents in International Relations*, ed. G. Kennedy and K. Neilson (Westport, CT: Greenwood, 2002), pp. 25–46.

Ovendale, Ritchie, *"Appeasement" and the English-Speaking World: Britain, the United States, the Dominions and the Policy of Appeasement, 1937–1939* (Cardiff: University of Wales Press, 1975).

Overy, Richard, "Strategic Intelligence and the Outbreak of the Second World War," *War in History* 5 (1998): 451–80.

Overy, Richard, *The Dictators: Hitler's Germany, Stalin's Russia* (London: Allen Lane, 2004).

Owen, Norman G., *The Emergence of Modern Southeast Asia: A New History* (Honolulu, HI: University of Hawaii Press, 2004).

Page, Melvin, ed., *Africa and the First World War* (London: Macmillan, 1987).

Paine, Sarah, *Imperial Rivals: China, Russia, and their Disputed Frontier* (Armonk, NY: M. E. Sharpe, 1996).

Palumbo, Michael, "Italian-Austro-Hungarian Military Relations before World War I," in *Essays on World War I: Origins and Prisoners of War*, ed. Samuel R. Williamson and Peter Pastor (New York: Brooklyn College Press, 1983), pp. 37–53.

Parker, R. A. C., *Chamberlain and Appeasement: British Policy and the Coming of the Second World War* (Basingstoke: Macmillan, 1993).

Parsons, Craig, *A Certain Idea of Europe* (Ithaca, NY: Cornell University Press, 2003).

Parsons, F. V., *The Origins of the Morocco Question 1880–1900* (London: Duckworth, 1976).

Peffer, N., "Regional Security in Southeast Asia," *International Organization* 8 (1954): 312–13.

Philbin III, T. R., *The Lure of Neptune: German–Soviet Naval Collaboration and Ambitions, 1919–1941* (Columbia, SC: University of South Carolina Press, 1994).

Pikhoya, P. G., *Sovetsky Soyuz: Istoriya Vlasti 1945–1991* (Moscow: Izdatelstvo RAGS, 1998).

Pineau, Christian, *1956: Suez* (Paris: Robert Laffond, 1976).

Pitteloud, Jean-François, ed., *Procès-verbaux des Séances du Comité international de la Croix-Rouge, 17 février 1863–28 août 1914* (Geneva: Société Henri Dunant/ International Committee of the Red Cross, 1999).

Poidevin, Raymond, *Robert Schuman: homme d'état, 1886–1963* (Paris: Imprimerie Nationale, 1986).

Pollack, Kenneth M., *The Persian Puzzle: The Conflict Between Iran and America* (New York: Random House, 2004).

Pons, Silvio, *Stalin and the Inevitable War 1936–1941* (London: Frank Cass, 2002).

Pons, Silvio, ed., *Reinterpreting the End of the Cold War* (New York: Frank Cass, 2005).

Power, Samantha, *"A Problem from Hell": America and the Age of Genocide* (New York: HarperCollins, 2002).

Prakash, Gyan, "*AHR Forum*: Subaltern Studies as Postcolonial Criticism," *American Historical Review* 99 (1994): 1475–515.

Prazmowska, Anita, *Eastern Europe and the Origins of the Second World War* (Basingstoke: Palgrave, 2000).

Provence, Michael, *The Great Syrian Revolt and the Rise of Arab Nationalism* (Austin, TX: University of Texas Press, 2005).

Rae, John, *The American Automobile Industry* (Boston: G. K. Hall, 1984).

Ragsdale, Hugh, *The Soviets, the Munich Crisis, and the Coming of World War II* (New York: Cambridge University Press, 2004).

Read, Christopher, *Lenin* (London: Routledge, 2005).

Reagan, Ronald, *An American Life* (New York: Simon & Schuster, 1990).

Record, Jeffrey, "Threat Confusion and Its Penalties," *Survival* 46 (2004): 51–71.

Rees, Tim, and Andrew Thorpe, eds., *International Communism and the Communist International, 1919–1943* (Manchester and New York: Manchester University Press, 1998).

Remnick, David, *Lenin's Tomb: The Last Days of the Soviet Empire* (London: Penguin, 1994).

Renzi, William A., *In the Shadow of the Sword: Italy's Neutrality and Entrance into the Great War, 1914–1915* (New York: Peter Lang, 1987).

Resis, Albert, "The Fall of Litvinov: Harbinger of the German–Soviet Non-Aggression Pact," *Europe-Asia Studies* 52 (2000): 33–56.

Reynolds, David, *The Creation of the Anglo-American Alliance 1937–1941: A Study in Competitive Co-*

*operation* (Chapel Hill, NC: University of North Carolina Press, 1982).

Reynolds, David, *From Munich to Pearl Harbor: Roosevelt's America and the Origins of the Second World War* (Chicago: Ivan R. Dee, 2001).

Reynolds, David, *In Command of History* (London: Allen Lane/Penguin, 2004).

Rieber, A. J., "Stalin, Man of the Borderlands," *American Historical Review* 106 (2001): 1651–91.

Robbins, Keith, *Munich 1938* (London: Cassell, 1968).

Robbins, Keith, *Appeasement* (Oxford: Blackwell, 1988).

Roberts, Adam, and Benedict Kingsbury, eds., *United Nations, Divided World: The UN's Roles in International Relations* (Oxford: Oxford University Press, 2nd edn, 1993).

Roberts, Andrew, *A Cambridge History of Africa*, vol. 7, *1905–1940* (Cambridge: Cambridge University Press, 1986).

Roberts, C., "Planning for War: The Red Army and the Catastrophe of 1941," *Europe-Asia Studies* 47 (1995): 1293–326.

Roberts, G., *The Soviet Union and the Origins of the Second World War: Russo-German Relations and the Road to War, 1933–1941* (London: Macmillan, 1995).

Rohwer, J., and M. S. Monakov, *Stalin's Ocean Going Fleet: Soviet Naval Strategy and Shipbuilding Programmes, 1935–1953* (London: Frank Cass, 2001).

Ross, Dennis, *The Missing Peace: The Inside Story of the Fight for Middle East Peace* (New York: Farrar, Straus, & Giroux, 2004).

Ross, Sir Frederick Leith, *Money Talks: Fifty Years of International Finance* (London: Hutchinson, 1969).

Rossos, Andrew, *Russia and the Balkans: Inter-Balkan Rivalries and Russian Foreign Policy, 1908–1914* (Toronto: Toronto University Press, 1981).

Rothwell, V. H., *British War Aims and Peace Diplomacy 1914–1918* (Oxford: Clarendon Press, 1971).

Rowland, Benjamin M., ed., *Balance of Power or Hegemony: The Interwar Monetary System* (New York: New York University Press, 1976).

Roxborough, Ian, *Theories of Underdevelopment* (London: Macmillan, 1979).

Ruane, K., ed., *The Vietnam Wars* (Manchester: Manchester University Press, 2000).

Ruane, K., "Putting America in its Place? Recent Writing on the Vietnam Wars," *Journal of Contemporary History* 37 (2002): 115–27.

Rubenson, Sven, *The Survival of Ethiopian Independence* (London: Heinemann, 1976).

Rubenstein, Alvin Z., *Yugoslavia and the Nonaligned World* (Princeton, NJ: Princeton University Press, 1970).

Ryzhkov, Nikolai, *Desyat let velikikh notryaseni* (Moscow: Proveshchenie, 1995).

Rzheshevsky, Oleg A., ed., *War and Diplomacy: The Making of the Grand Alliance* (Amsterdam: Hardwood Academic, 1996).

Said, Edward, *Orientalism* (New York: Random House, 1978).

Salmon, Patrick, *Scandinavia and the Great Powers, 1890–1940* (Cambridge: Cambridge University Press, 1997).

Samson, Jane, ed., *The British Empire* (Oxford: Oxford University Press, 2001).

Samuelson, Lennart, *Plans for Stalin's War Machine: Tukhachevskii and Military-Economic Planning, 1925–1941* (Basingstoke: Palgrave, 2000).

Sarkar, Sumit, *Modern India 1885–1947* (New York: St. Martin's, 1989).

Sasse, Heinz, *100 Jahre Auswärtiges Amt 1870–1970* (Bonn: Auswärtiges Amt, 1970).

Savel'yev, Aleksandr' G., and Nikolay N. Detinov, *The Big Five: Arms Control Decision-Making in the Soviet Union* (Westport, CT: Praeger, 1995).

Sayre, Francis Bowes, *Experiments in International Administration* (New York and London: Harper, 1919).

Sbacchi, Alberto, *Fascism and the Colonial Experience* (London: Zed Books, 1985).

Sbacchi, Alberto, "Marcus Garvey, the United Negro Improvement Association and Ethiopia, 1920–1940," in *Legacy of Bitterness, Ethiopia and Fascist Italy*, ed. Alberto Sbacchi (Asmara: Red Sea Press, 1997), pp. 1–34.

Schaefer, Ludwig, ed., *The Ethiopian Crisis: Touchstone of Appeasement?* (Boston: D. C. Heath, 1961).

Schild, Georg, *Bretton Woods and Dumbarton Oaks* (New York: St. Martin's, 1995).

Schmidt, Gustav, ed., *Konstellationen internationaler Politik 1924–1932* (Bochum: N. Brockmeyer, 1983).

Schorske, Carl, *Fin-de-siècle Vienna* (London: Weidenfeld & Nicolson, 1980).

Schroeder, Paul W., "Alliances 1815–1945: Weapons of Power and Tools of Management," in *Historical Dimensions of National Security Problems*, ed. Klaus Knorr (Lawrence, KS: University Press of Kansas, 1976).

Schuker, Stephen A., *The End of French Predominance in Europe: The Financial Crisis of 1924 and the Adoption of the Dawes Plan* (Chapel Hill, NC: University of North Carolina Press, 1976).

Schulzinger, R., *US Diplomacy since 1900* (Oxford: Oxford University Press, 1998).

Schwarz, Hans-Peter, *Konrad Adenauer: A German Politician and Statesman in a Period of War, Revolution, and Reconstruction*, vol. 1 (Providence, RI: Berghahn Books, 1995).

Scott, James Brown, ed., *The Reports to the Hague Conferences of 1899 and 1907* (Oxford: Carnegie Endowment for International Peace, 1917).

Scott, William R., *The Sons of Sheba's Race: African-Americans and the Italo-Ethiopian War, 1935–1941* (Bloomington, IN: Indiana University Press, 1993).

Selassie I, Haile, *My Life and Ethiopia's Progress 1892–1937* (Oxford: Oxford University Press, 1976).

Serra, Enrico, ed., *The Relaunching of Europe and the Treaties of Rome* (Brussels: Bruylant, 1989).

Service, Robert, *Lenin: A Political Life*, 3 vols. (London: Macmillan, 1985, 1991, 1995).

Service, Robert, *A History of Modern Russia from Nicholas II to Putin* (London: Penguin, 2003).

Shai, Aaron, *Origins of the War in the East: Britain, China and Japan, 1937–1939* (London: Croom Helm, 1976).

Sharp, Alan, *The Versailles Settlement: Peacemaking in Paris, 1919* (Basingstoke: Macmillan, 1991).

Shay, Jr., R. P., *British Rearmament in the Thirties: Politics and Profits* (Princeton, NJ: Princeton University Press, 1977).

Shepilov, Dmitrii, *Neprimknuvshii* (Moscow: Vagrius, 2001).

Sherry, Michael, *The Rise of American Airpower* (New Haven, CT: Yale University Press, 1987).

Sherwood, Robert E., *Roosevelt and Hopkins: An Intimate History* (New York: Harper, rev. edn, 1950).

Shogan, Robert, *Hard Bargain: How FDR Twisted Churchill's Arm, Evaded the Law, and Changed the Role of the Presidency* (New York: Scribner, 1995).

Siegel, Jennifer, *Endgame: Britain, Russia and the Final Struggle for Central Asia* (London and New York: I. B. Tauris, 2002).

Silberstein, G. E., "Germany, France and the Casablanca Incident 1908–9: An Investigation of a Forgotten Crisis," *Canadian Journal of History* 11 (1976): 331–4.

Simon, Reeva Spector, and Eleanor H. Tejirian, eds., *The Creation of Iraq 1914–1921* (New York: Columbia University Press, 2004).

Simonov, N. S., "'Strengthen the Defence of the Land of the Soviets': The 1927 'War Alarm' and its Consequences," *Europe-Asia Studies* 48 (1996): 1355–64.

Sipols, V., *Taini diplomaticheskie: Kanun Velikoi Otechestvennoi. 1939–1941* (Moscow: TOO "Novina," 1997).

Slezkine, Y., *The Jewish Century* (Princeton, NJ: Princeton University Press, 2004).

Smith, A. D., *Theories of Nationalism* (London: Duckworth, 1971).

Smith, A. D., *The Ethnic Origin of Nations* (Oxford: Blackwell, 1986).

Smith, A. D., *Nations and Nationalism in a Global Era* (Cambridge: Polity Press, 1995).

Smith, Denis Mack, *Mussolini* (London: Weidenfeld & Nicolson, 1981).

Smith, Gaddis, *The Last Days of the Monroe Doctrine, 1945–1993* (New York: Hill & Wang, 1994).

Smith, Tony, *The Pattern of Imperialism: The United States, Great Britain and the Late-Industrializing World since 1815* (Cambridge: Cambridge University Press, 1981).

Smith, Tony, *America's Mission: The United States and the Worldwide Struggle for Democracy in the Twentieth Century* (Princeton, NJ: Princeton University Press, 1994).

Smith, Woodruff D., *The German Colonial Empire* (Chapel Hill, NC: University of North Carolina Press, 1978).

Smulyan, Susan, *Selling Radio: The Commercialization of American Broadcasting* (Washington, DC: Smithsonian Books, 1994).

Soutou, Georges-Henri, *La Guerre de Cinquante Ans: Les relations Est–Ouest 1943–1990* (Paris: Fayard, 2001).

Spaak, Paul-Henri, *Combats inachevés* (Paris: Fayard, 1969).

Springhall, John, *Decolonization since 1945: The Collapse of the European Overseas Empires* (London: Palgrave Macmillan, 2001).

Stein, Burton, *A History of India* (Oxford: Blackwell, 1998).

Stein, L., *The Balfour Declaration* (London: Vallentine, 1961).

Steinberg, Jonathan, *Yesterday's Deterrent: Tirpitz and the Birth of the German Battle Fleet* (London: Macdonald, 1965).

Steiner, Zara, *The Foreign Office and Foreign Policy, 1898–1914* (Cambridge: Cambridge University Press, 1969).

Steiner, Zara, ed., *The Times Survey of Foreign Ministries of the World* (London: Times Books; Westport, CT: Meckler, 1982).

Steiner, Zara, "The Peace Settlement," in *The Oxford Illustrated History of the First World War*, ed. Hew Strachan (Oxford: Oxford University Press, 1998), pp. 291–304.

Steiner, Zara, "The Soviet Commissariat of Foreign Affairs and the Czechoslovakian Crisis in 1938: New

Material from the Soviet Archives," *Historical Journal* 42 (1999): 751–79.

Steiner, Zara, *The Lights that Failed: European International History 1919–1933* (Oxford: Oxford University Press, 2005).

Steiner, Zara, and Keith Neilson, *Britain and the Origins of the First World War* (Basingstoke and New York: Macmillan, rev. edn, 2003).

Stevenson, David, *French War Aims against Germany 1914–1919* (Oxford: Clarendon Press, 1982).

Stevenson, David, *The First World War and International Politics* (Oxford: Oxford University Press, 1988).

Stevenson, David, *Armaments and the Coming of the War: Europe, 1904–1914* (Oxford: Oxford University Press, 1996).

Stevenson, David, "War Aims and Peace Negotiations," in *Oxford Illustrated History of the First World War*, ed. Hew Strachan (Oxford: Oxford University Press, 1998), pp. 204–15.

Stevenson, David, *1914–1918: The History of the First World War* (London: Allen Lane, 2004); also published as *Cataclysm: The First World War as Political Tragedy* (New York: Basic Books, 2004).

Stirk, Peter, *A History of European Integration since 1914* (London: Continuum, 2001).

Stockwell, A. J., "Southeast Asia in War and Peace: The End of European Colonial Empires," in *The Cambridge History of Southeast Asia*, vol. 2, part 2, *From World War II to the Present*, ed. N. Tarling (Cambridge: Cambridge University Press, 1999), pp. 1–58.

Stolper, Gustav, et al., eds., *German Economy, 1870 to the Present* (New York: Harcourt, Brace, & World, 1967).

Stone, D., "The August 1924 Raid on Stolpce, Poland, and the Evolution of Soviet Active Intelligence," *Intelligence and National Security* 21 (2006): 331–41.

Stone, Norman, "Moltke–Conrad: Relations between the Austro-Hungarian and German General Staffs, 1909–14," *Historical Journal* 9 (1966): 201–28.

Storry, G. R., *Japan and the Decline of the West in Asia, 1894–1943* (London: Macmillan, 1979).

Strachan, Hew, *The First World War*, vol. 1, *To Arms* (Oxford: Oxford University Press, 2001).

Strachan, Hew, "The British Army, its General Staff and the Continental Commitment," in *The British General Staff: Reform and Innovation, 1890–1939*, ed. David French and Brian Holden Reid (London and Portland, OR: Frank Cass, 2002), pp. 9–25.

Strachan, Hew, *The First World War in Africa* (Oxford: Oxford University Press, 2004).

Stresemann, Gustav, *Essays and Speeches on Various Subjects* (London: Butterworth, 1930).

Suvorov, V. (pseud.), "Who was Planning to Attack Whom in June 1941, Hitler or Stalin?" *Journal of the Royal United Services Institute for Defence Studies* 130 (1985): 50–5.

Suvorov, V., *Icebreaker: Who Started the Second World War?* (London: Hamish Hamilton, 1990).

Swedenburg, Ted, *Memories of Revolt: The 1936–1939 Rebellion and the Palestinian National Past* (Minneapolis, MN: University of Minnesota Press, 1995).

Sweet, D. W., "Great Britain and Germany, 1905–1911," in *British Foreign Policy under Sir Edward Grey*, ed. F. H. Hinsley (Cambridge: Cambridge University Press, 1977), pp. 216–35.

Tarling, Nicholas, ed., *The Cambridge History of Southeast Asia*, vol. 2, *The Nineteenth and Twentieth Centuries* (Cambridge: Cambridge University Press, 1992).

Taylor, A. J. P., *The Struggle for Mastery in Europe, 1848–1916* (Oxford: Oxford University Press, 1954).

Taylor, A. J. P., "The War Aims of the Allies in the First World War," in *Essays Presented to Sir Lewis Namier*, ed. A. J. P. Taylor and R. Pares (London: Macmillan, 1956).

Taylor, A. J. P., *The Origins of the Second World War* (London: Hamish Hamilton, 1961).

Taylor, A. J. P., *English History* (Oxford: Oxford University Press, 1965).

Temperley, H. W. V., ed., *A History of the Peace Conference of Paris*, vol. 3 (London: Hodder & Stoughton, 1920).

Thomas, Martin, *Britain, France and Appeasement: Anglo-French Relations in the Popular Front Era* (Oxford: Berg, 1996).

Thomas, Martin, *The French Empire between the Wars* (Manchester: Manchester University Press, 2005).

Thompson, Neville, *The Anti-Appeasers* (Oxford: Oxford University Press, 1971).

Thorne, Christopher, *The Limits of Foreign Policy: The West, the League and the Far Eastern Crisis of 1931–1933* (London: Putnam, 1972).

Thorne, Christopher, *Allies of a Kind: The United States, Britain, and the War Against Japan, 1941–1945* (Oxford: Oxford University Press, 1978).

Tillman, Seth, *Anglo-American Relations at the Peace Conference* (Princeton, NJ: Princeton University Press, 1961).

Toland, John, *The Rising Sun: The Decline and Fall of the Japanese Empire, 1936–1945* (New York: Random House, 1970).

Tomlinson, Tom, *The Third World in the Twentieth Century* (London: Edward Arnold, 2001).

Trachtenberg, Marc, *Reparation in World Politics: France and European Economic Diplomacy, 1916–1923* (New York: Columbia University Press, 1980).

Trotsky, Leon, *My Life* (Harmondsworth: Penguin, 1984).

Trotter, Ann, *Britain and East Asia, 1933–1937* (Cambridge: Cambridge University Press, 1975).

Trumpener, Ulrich, "Liman von Sanders and the German Ottoman Alliance," *Journal of Contemporary History* 1 (1966): 179–92.

Tunstall, Graydon A., *Planning for War against Russia and Serbia: Austro-Hungarian and German Military Strategies, 1871–1914* (Boulder, CO: Social Science Monographs, 1993).

Uldricks, T. J., "The Icebreaker Controversy: Did Stalin Plan to Attack Hitler?" *Slavic Review* 58 (1999): 626–43.

Urwin, Derek W., *The Community of Europe: A History of European Integration since 1945* (London and New York: Longman, 2nd edn, 1995).

Utley, Jonathan G., *Going to War with Japan, 1937–1941* (Knoxville, TN: University of Tennessee Press, 1985).

Valone, Stephen J., "'There Must Be Some Misunderstanding': Sir Edward Grey's Diplomacy of August 1, 1914," *Journal of British Studies* 27 (1988): 405–24.

Varsori, Antonio, ed., *Inside the European Community: Actors and Policies in the European Integration 1957–1972* (Baden-Baden: Nomos, 2006).

Vinogradov, Amal, "The 1920 Revolt in Iraq Reconsidered: The Role of Tribes in National Politics," *International Journal of Middle East Studies* 3 (1972): 123–39.

Wallerstein, Immanuel, *The Modern World System: Capitalist Agriculture and the Origins of the European World Economy in the 16th Century* (New York: Academic Press, 1974).

Wallerstein, Immanuel, "The Eagle Has Crash Landed," *Foreign Policy* 131 (2002): 60–8.

Wallerstein, Immanuel, *World-Systems Analysis: An Introduction* (Durham, NC: Duke University Press, 2004).

Walters, F. P., *A History of the League of Nations*, 2 vols. (London: Oxford University Press, 1952).

Wasson, Tyler, ed., *Nobel Prize Winners* (New York: H. W. Wilson, 1987).

Watt, D. Cameron, "Appeasement: The Rise of a Revisionist School," *Political Quarterly* 36 (1965): 191–213.

Watt, D. Cameron, *Succeeding John Bull: America in Britain's Place 1900–1975* (Cambridge: Cambridge University Press, 1984).

Weatherford, Jack, *Genghis Khan and the Making of the Modern World* (New York: Three Rivers Press, 2005).

Weathersby, Kathryn, "Soviet Aims in Korea and the Origins of the Korean War, 1945–1950," *Cold War International History Project Working Paper* 8 (1994).

Weathersby, Kathryn, "'Should We Fear This?': Stalin and the Danger of War with America," *Cold War International History Project Working Paper* 39 (2002).

Webster, C. K., *The League of Nations in Theory and Practice* (London: G. Allen & Unwin, 1933).

Wehler, Hans-Ulrich, *The German Empire, 1871–1918* (Leamington Spa: Berg, 1985).

Westad, Arne Odd, Sven Holtsmark, and Iver B. Neumann, eds., *The Soviet Union in Eastern Europe 1945–89* (Basingstoke: Macmillan, 1994).

Westad, Odd Arne, ed., *Brothers in Arms: The Rise and Fall of the Sino-Soviet Alliance, 1945–1963* (Washington, DC: Woodrow Wilson Center Press, 1998).

Westad, Odd Arne, *The Global Cold War: Third World Interventions and the Making of Our Times* (Cambridge: Cambridge University Press, 2005).

Wettig, Gerhard, "Stalin's Note of 10 March 1952: Historical Context," in *L'Europe: de l'Est et de l'Ouest dans la Guerre froide, 1948–1953*, ed. Saki Dockrill et al. (Paris: Presses de l'Université Paris-Sorbonne, 2002).

Wheeler-Bennett, John, *The Nemesis of Power: The German Army in Politics, 1918–1945* (London: Macmillan, 1964).

White, James D., "Theories of Imperialism in Russian Socialist Thought from the First World War to the Stalin Era," *Coexistence* 30 (1993): 87–109.

White, John Albert, *Transition to Global Rivalry: Alliance Diplomacy and the Quadruple Entente, 1895–1907* (Cambridge: Cambridge University Press, 1995).

White, Stephen, *After Gorbachev* (New York: Cambridge University Press, 1993).

Williams, Gwyneth, *Third-World Political Organizations: A Review of Developments* (London: Macmillan, 1981).

Williams, Marc, *Third World Cooperation: The Group of 77 in UNCTAD* (London: St. Martin's, 1991).

Williams, Rhodri, *Defending the Empire: The Conservative Party and British Defence Policy 1899–1915* (New Haven, CT, and London: Yale University Press, 1991).

Williamson, Jr., Samuel R., *The Politics of Grand Strategy: Britain and France Prepare for War, 1904–1914* (London and Atlantic Highlands, NJ: Ashfield Press, pbk edn, 1990).

Williamson, Jr., Samuel R., *Austria-Hungary and the Origins of the First World War* (New York: St. Martin's, 1991).

Williamson, Jr., Samuel R., and Russel Van Wyk, *July 1914: Soldiers, Statesmen, and the Coming of the Great War: A Brief Documentary History* (Boston: Bedford/St. Martin's, 2003).

Willis, J., *Prologue to Nuremberg: The Politics and Diplomacy of Punishing War Criminals of the First World War* (Westport, CT: Greenwood, 1982).

Wilson, Keith, *The Policy of the Entente: Essays on the Determinants of British Foreign Policy, 1904–1914* (Cambridge: Cambridge University Press, 1985).

Wilson, Keith, ed., *Decisions for War, 1914* (New York: St. Martin's, 1995).

Wilson, Theodore A., *The First Summit: Roosevelt and Churchill at Placentia Bay, 1941* (Lawrence, KS: University Press of Kansas, rev. edn, 1991).

Wolff, David, *To the Harbin Station: The Liberal Alternative in Russian Manchuria, 1898–1914* (Stanford, CA: Stanford University Press, 1999).

Woodward, Bob, *Bush at War* (New York: Simon & Schuster, 2002).

Woodward, E. L., ed., *British Foreign Policy in the Second World War*, vol. 3 (London: HMSO, 1971).

Wu Lengxi, *Shinian Lunzhan, 1956–1966: Zhong Su Guanxi Huiyilu* (Beijing: Zhongyang wenxian chubanshe, 1999).

Yang Kuisong, "The Sino-Soviet Border Clash of 1969: From Zhenbao Island to Sino-American Rapprochement," *Cold War History* 1 (2000): 21–52.

Yapp, M. E., *The Making of the Modern Near East* (London: Longman, 1988).

Yearwood, P. J., "'Consistency with Honour': Great Britain, the League of Nations and the Corfu Crisis of 1923," *Journal of Contemporary History* 21 (1986): 559–71.

Yegorova, N. I., ed., *Cold War and the Policy of Détente: Problems and Discussions* (Moscow: Russian Academy of Sciences, 2003).

Yergin, Daniel, *The Prize: The Epic Quest for Oil, Money and Power* (New York: Simon & Schuster, 1991).

Young, R. J., "The Problem of France," in *The Origins of the Second World War Reconsidered: The A. J. P. Taylor Debate after Twenty-Five Years*, ed. Gordon Martel (London: Allen & Unwin, 1986), pp. 97–118.

Young, R. J., *France and the Origins of the Second World War* (Basingstoke: Macmillan, 1996).

Zagoria, Donald, *The Sino-Soviet Conflict, 1956–61* (Princeton, NJ: Princeton University Press, 1962).

Zelikow, Philip, and Condoleezza Rice, *Germany Unified and Europe Transformed: A Study in Statecraft* (Cambridge, MA: Harvard University Press, 1995).

Zewde, Bahru, *A History of Modern Ethiopia* (London: James Currey, 1991).

Zhai, Qiang, *China and the Vietnam Wars, 1950–1975* (Chapel Hill, NC: University of North Carolina Press, 2000).

Zhang Shu Guang and Chen Jian, "The Emerging Disputes Between Beijing and Moscow: Ten Newly Available Chinese Documents, 1956–1958," *Cold War International History Project Bulletin* 6–7 (1995/6).

Zimmern, Alfred, *The League of Nations and the Rule of Law, 1918–1935* (London: Macmillan, 1936; 2nd edn, 1939).

Zubaida, Sami, "The Fragments Imagine the Nation: The Case of Iraq," *International Journal of Middle East Studies* 34 (2002): 205–15.

Zuber, Terence, *Inventing the Schlieffen Plan: German War Planning, 1871–1914* (Oxford: Oxford University Press, 2002).

Zubok, Vladislav M., "The Khrushchev–Mao Conversations, 31 July–3 August 1958," *Cold War International History Project Bulletin* 12–13 (2001).

Zubok, Vladislav M., "The Brezhnev Factor in Détente, 1968–1972," in *Cold War and the Policy of Détente: Problems and Discussions*, ed. N. I. Yegorova (Moscow: Russian Academy of Sciences, 2003).

Zubok, Vladislav M., and Constantine Pleshakov, *Inside the Kremlin's Cold War: From Stalin to Khrushchev* (Cambridge, MA: Harvard University Press, 1996).

# Index